289.4
Sw3p
v.1

POSTHUMOUS
THEOLOGICAL WORKS

POSTHUMOUS THEOLOGICAL WORKS

OF

EMANUEL SWEDENBORG

AUTOBIOGRAPHICAL LETTERS
THE CORONIS
THE CONSUMMATION OF THE AGE
INVITATION TO THE NEW CHURCH
ADDITIONS TO THE TRUE CHRISTIAN RELIGION
THE CANONS OF THE NEW CHURCH
THE DOCTRINE OF CHARITY
SKETCH OF AN ECCLESIASTICAL HISTORY OF THE NEW CHURCH
THE WORD OF THE LORD FROM EXPERIENCE
THE LAST JUDGMENT (Posthumous)
SEVERAL MINOR WORKS
THEOLOGICAL EXTRACTS FROM SWEDENBORG'S CORRESPONDENCE
GAD AND ASHER

VOLUME I.

JOHN WHITEHEAD
EDITOR AND TRANSLATOR

Standard Edition

SWEDENBORG FOUNDATION
INCORPORATED
NEW YORK

Established in 1850

First published in U.S.A., 1914

12th Printing 1978

ISBN: 0—87785—073—9 (Student), 2 Vol. set 0—87785—075—5
0—87785—076—3 (Trade), 2 Vol. set 0—87785—078—X

Library of Congress Catalog Card Number 38-24293

Manufactured in the United States of America

EDITOR'S PREFACE TO POSTHUMOUS THEOLOGICAL WORKS.

These volumes of Posthumous Theological Works of Swedenborg include a number of the smaller posthumous works, which have never before been brought together in a form convenient for use. Most of them have been published in book or pamphlet form. Some have appeared only in magazines, notably the *Last Judgment Posthumous*. A few minor parts have not previously been translated into English.

Included in the volumes are a number of extracts from Swedenborg's correspondence. Among these are two autobiographical letters of Swedenborg, which are prefixed to this volume. Those at the end of this volume are taken from the *Documents Concerning Swedenborg*, collected, edited and translated by Dr. Rudolph L. Tafel. The originals of these documents are not at present available for use in revising the translation. Most of them are in the Library of the Academy of Sciences at Stockholm. We have used the translation made by Dr. Tafel. These theological extracts throw much light on several important doctrines. They have been classified and arranged according to the subjects.

Arrangements are now being made for copying all the original documents concerning Swedenborg, including many new documents which have recently been discovered by Mr. Alfred H. Stroh, M.A., during his work of phototyping the manuscripts of Swedenborg, and his investigations of Swedenborgiana in Sweden and other countries. When this copying is completed, it will be possible to revise Dr. Tafel's translation of the documents by comparison with the originals. More material of a theological character may also be found in these new documents, that can be incorporated in future editions of these volumes of *Posthumous Theological Works*. Any suggestions looking toward rendering the same complete, including the perfecting of the text and translation, will be welcomed by the publishers.

In the arrangement of the treatises, those of a similar nature have been brought together. Many of them are fragmentary, never having been completed by Swedenborg, notably the *Coronis* and the small works grouped with it. These were evidently separate sketches intended as parts of a larger work not completed by Swedenborg. Following the *Last Judgment Posthumous* are a number of small works found in the latter part of the *Diary* that seem to belong together.

The manuscripts of most of these treatises have not been preserved. The testimony indicates that a portion of the manuscript of the *Coronis* was lost while it was in the possession of Dr. Messiter, who took it from Swedenborg's rooms in London during his last illness. The part preserved was printed in Latin a few years after Swedenborg's death, and an English translation was also printed about the same time. A copy of the *Coronis* made by Augustus Nordenskjöld has recently been found by Mr. Stroh; but we have not been able to secure a copy for comparison with the present Latin text.

The Tafel Latin text of the *Last Judgment Posthumous*, and of some of the minor treatises, has been compared with the Photolithograph manuscript; also the *Indexes to the Missing Treatise on Marriage*. A number of errors in the former texts have been corrected. The changes have been indicated in the critical notes. These manuscripts are very difficult to decipher in many places, they being in the form of notes intended by Swedenborg for his own use.

It is regretted that the full text of the *Marginal Notes to Swedenborg's Latin Schmidius' Bible* are not available for use in this edition. The printer of the Photolithograph of that work in some unexplained way omitted the text of the two books of *Samuel*. These are to be phototyped, and it is expected that when the Notes have been transcribed and translated, they will be added to a future edition of the *Posthumous Theological Works*.

JOHN WHITEHEAD,
Editor.

CRITICAL NOTES OF THE EDITOR AND REVISER.

Page	Line		Page	Line	
23	20	The first Latin edition has, *alteratum*, Dr. Worcester has *atratum*.	64	13	*Lucum*, "grove", in *C. L.*, n. 75, it has *campum*, "plain." Dr. Worcester gives *campum*.
26	24	The first Latin edition has, *non populo*, Dr. Worcester has *populo*.	68	13	The first Latin edition has *phoenix*, Dr. Worcester has *pelecanus*.
27	23	The first Latin edition has, *tardabit*, Dr. Worcester has *festinabit*.	71	19	The first Latin edition has, *ac*, Dr. Worcester has, *ne*.
28	9	The first Latin edition has, *non*, Dr. Worcester has *et*.	81	17	"Prophets" here means the early prophets.
29	10	"Beast," the Authorized Version has "congregation," but the Hebrew word means beast or animal.	95	6	"King," the H e b r e w word means "God." Dr. Worcester has "God."
	21	The first Latin edition has *Me tibi*.	97	6	"Violence." The first Latin edition has *evidentia*, for *violentia*.
30	23	The Latin edition has, *creaturæ*; in *A. R.* and *A. E.* it is *opificii*.	220	21	In Nordenskjöld's copy it is "Apostolic," in another handwriting, "Athanasian."
32	7	The first Latin edition has *fixatum*; Dr. Worcester has, *firmatum*. See also *A.* 9346.	223	22	Dr. Tafel has, *De fide respondent, quod sit in Deum Patrem, Deum Filium, et Deum Spiritum Sanctum; et quod Deus Pater illam det, Filius illam mediat, et Spiritus Sanctus illam operetur, ita ordine in tres Deos*. Dr. Worcester omits this clause.
50	21	*Schoham* is a Hebrew word which Swedenborg retains. The Authorized Version translates it "onyx."			
52	24	The first Latin edition has, *janua*, "door"; Dr. Worcester has, *cardine*, "hinge."	237	34	The *MS.* reads, *ex homine*, "from man." Dr. Worcester has, *ex Domino*, "from the Lord."
55	18	The first Latin edition has, *vitis*, Dr. Worcester *vitris*.	263	7	A paragraph follows n. 148 in the *MS.* which is crossed out except the sentence, "that man is a form of heaven." The paragraph r e w r i t t e n is c o n t a i n e d in *V.*, n. 149–153.
59	22	Dr. Worcester has "*Dominus*," which agrees with the Hebrew.			
63	36	In *Conjugial Love*, n. 75, there is added, "which are round about at the sides."			

vii

Page	Line		Page	Line	
381	10	Tafel has, *aliudque*, the *MS.*, *ut cunque*.	401	12	The *MS.* has, *mucus narium;* Tafel, *mercurius vivus.* See *D.* 3811, 3812, where *mucus narium* occurs.
	last	The author of *The Whole Duty of Man.* See *D.*, n. 5058; *C. L. J.*, n. 46.			
382	7	*The Exhortation* is not quoted here. See *T.* 722³.	402	4	Tafel has, *virtutem;* the *MS.*, *vinculum.*
383	1	Tafel has, *aedificium;* in the *MS.* the words, *ubi etiam aedificium est,* are written above the line. Possibly it should read, *ubi etiam editius est,* "where, also, it is more elevated."		9	Clement xii. Pope A. D. 1730–1740.
				9	Tafel has, *advocans*, *MS.*, *adorans.* See *C. L. J.*, n. 59.
			408	1	Tafel has, *sancti*, the *MS.*, *similis.*
			411	17	Tafel has, *nullum*, the *MS.*, *multum.*
385	1	See *C. L. J.*, n. 53, where it reads, "in the days of the Last Judgment."	412	6	Tafel has, *nunc*, the *MS.*, *notis.*
390	28	Tafel has, *angelis*, "angels." The *MS.* has, *Anglis*, "Englishmen."		last	Tafel has, *palatia*, a doubtful reading. In the *MS.*, the word is illegible.
392	1	Tafel has, *non*, the *MS.*, *raro, D.* 5915, also has, *raro.*	416	25	Tafel has, *qui non volunt credere salutem per spiritum sanctum.* The reading is doubtful. Acton translates it, "Who at heart wish to be saluted as the Holy Spirit."
	14	Tafel has, *plures*, the *MS.* is obscure, possibly *plenæ*, full.			
393	9	Tafel has, *nexum*, the *MS.*, has *novam.*			
395	2	Tafel has, *et reliquiis*, which in the *MS.* is written above the line; possibly it is, *et religione*, "and religion."	418	24	See *D.* 5341–5343.
				26	Tafel has, *montes*. The reading is doubtful.
399	4	Tafel has, *nam..erupit..explorentur..fecerunt;* the *MS.* has, *num..eruperit..exploraretur..fecerint.*	419	33	Tafel has, *veritates;* the *MS.*, *mentis.*
			422	30	Tafel has, *humanum bonum, et lucra;* the *MS.*, *famam, honorem et lucra.*
399	16	Tafel has, *in tergo*, "at the back," the *MS.*, *in opem*, "to their aid."	424	6	Tafel has, *montes;* the *MS.*, *tractus.*
400	1	Tafel has, *ita non..et obligati;* the *MS.*, *ictu uno..ablegati.*		16	Tafel has, *coetu;* the *MS.*, *sorte.*
				25	Tafel has, *dextro;* the *MS.*, *centro.*
	9	Tafel has, *coetus;* the *MS.*, *cibus.*	426	34	See *D.* 5822.
			427	6	See *S.* 116, *D.* 393, 5822.
	last	The *MS.* has a marginal note which Tafel omits, namely, *Sunt spiritus quaqueriani qui ex cultu a quaqueriis in mundo se credunt spiritum sanctum et ab aeterno fuisse, sed successu temporis veniunt inter prophanos, qui vocantur spiritu stercorei et cadaverosi, excrementum abominabile.*		8	The *MS.* has, *cogitationem*, possibly written for *cognitionem.*
				22	See *A.* 2596, *D.* 6067.
				32	See *D.* 6077, *R.* 11, *T.* 279, *Coro.* 39.
			428	11	Tafel has, *unde;* the *MS.*, *vidi.*
				17	Tafel has, *anterius;* the *MS.*, *exterius.*
			430	8	See *D.* 4932.

Page	Line		Page	Line	
431	27	In the *MS. stagna* is written twice; in *Diary* 5202, *lacus*, "lakes," is given in place of the second *stagna*.	444	14	See *D.* 5827.
			446	23	Tafel omits a clause written in the margin, namely, *Applicatio S. functio pro sangui[ne]*.
432	29	Tafel has, *vim ignis;* the *MS., vicissim*.	461	16	Tafel has, *astus*, a doubtful reading; possibly *aestus*, vehemence, heat.
433	13	See *D.* 5347.			
	20	Tafel has, *quae infra coelum spirituum occupaverunt*. The editor of the Photolithograph seems to have amended the text by writing Spa- as part of the word, Tafel reads *spirituum*. We retain Tafel's reading. Possibly it is *spatium*.		27	Tafel has, *invertunt;* the *MS., invitent.*
				30	See *D.* 6023.
			462	11	See *D.* 6024.
				18	Tafel has, *docetur;* the *MS., ducitur.*
			463	1	Tafel has, *Nunc;* the *MS., Unum.*
				5	Tafel has, *hominem;* the *MS., gramen.*
			464	19	Tafel has, *quod jucundent omnes;* the *MS., quod jucundent elegantiae illae aures.*
434	20	See *D.* 5351.			
435	15	See *D.* 5355, 5535, 5538.			
	29	Tafel has, *pauci;* the *MS., spurii.*	465	19	Tafel has, *multos*, possibly it may be *millies*, "a thousand."
436	30	See *D.* 5398.			
437	9	Tafel has, *adoratus;* the *MS., adeatus.*		32	Tafel has, *modo negligenter;* the *MS., malum.*
	35	See *D.* 5392.	466	24	Tafel has, *jucundo juvenum*, "the delight of youth," a doubtful reading. The word *juvenum* is obscure in the *MS.*
438	16	Tafel has, *mendaces;* the *MS., mundani.*			
	18	See *D.* 5514.			
439	19	See *D.* 5540, 5541.			
	22	At the margin of this paragraph is N. B.	467	15	Tafel has, *fides mala quae recepta;* the *MS., de fide non alia quam recepta*. Some words are crossed out in the *MS.*
	38	Tafel has, *delati*, possibly it is *detecti*. See *D.* 5696, 5698.			
440	26	See *D.* 5698.			
	33	See *D.* 5699.		35	Tafel has, *mutat socios;* the *MS., vertit faciem.* Tafel inserts the latter in Italics.
441	3	See *D.* 5731½, 5758.			
	30	The *MS.* has, *occidentem*, "west." In *Diary* 5742 it is *septentrionalem*, "north."			
			468	9	Tafel has, *continua;* the *MS., contraria.*
	32	Tafel has, *ita*, the *MS., ibi.*		27	Tafel has, *accendunt;* the *MS., avertit.*
442	2	See *D.* 5722.			
	14	Tafel has, *in mentibus;* the *MS., in me intus.*	469	18	See *D.* 4748, 4884.
				24	The words in brackets are supplied from a corresponding passage in the *Dairy*, n. 4817.
	20	See *D.* 5746.			
	38	Tafel has, *in luce carent et;* the *MS., et tunc venit.*			
443	last	See *D.* 5821.	470	9	See *A.* 1507.
444	9	Tafel has, *eamque mihi intulerunt;* the *MS., me persecuti mihi intulerunt*. In *Dairy* 5827 it is, *Se congregarunt, et violentiam inferebant*, "They gathered themselves together, and inflicted violence."		11	The word *interiora* in the *MS.* seems redundant.
				12	Tafel has, *equestri vestitu;* the *MS., equestri ordine.*
				last	See *D.* 5461½.
			471	9	See *D.* 5463.
				25	Tafel has, *operatur;* the *MS., precatur.*

Page	Line		Page	Line	
472	9	Tafel has, *varius;* possibly it should be *amoris*	496	4	The *MS.* has, *coeli,* "heaven;" Tafel has, *mundi,* "the world," which the context seems to require.
473	3	See *D.* 5976, 5977.			
	32	See *D.* 4725.			
474	4	See *T.* 841.			
476	35	Tafel has, *eruditis;* the *MS., et auditis.*		10	Tafel has, *lux;* the *MS., luna.*
477	13	See *T.* 845, *D.* 2256, 2257, 4388.	498	32	Tafel has, *hominum, minores.* In the *MS.* the word given as *minores* is imperfectly written; it is probably *mundi*," men of the world."
485	9	Tafel has, *vel permittat ut abeat, ubicunque Dominus abigit illum.* These words are not in the *MS.;* they seem like a printer's error, repeating a sentence two lines below.			
			507	16	Tafel has, *accusent;* the *MS., aversentur.*
			560	7	Tafel has, *capitibus,* "heads." It no doubt should be, "horns." The *MS.* is not available for comparison.
489	10	This paragraph is written in the margin; the words, *orientis e caelo solis, ubi,* are blotted in the *MS.*			

GENERAL INDEX.

		PAGE
1.	AUTOBIOGRAPHICAL LETTERS OF EMANUEL SWEDENBORG	1
	1. ANSWER TO A LETTER WRITTEN TO ME BY A FRIEND	5
	2. MY EARLY YOUTH	9
2.	CORONIS OR APPENDIX TO THE TRUE CHRISTIAN RELIGION	11
	SKETCH OF THE CORONIS	17
	SUMMARY	19
	MIRACLES	24
	THE CORONIS	25
3.	THE CONSUMMATION OF THE AGE, THE LORD'S SECOND COMING, AND THE NEW CHURCH	103
	A. THE ABOMINATION OF DESOLATION	108
	B. ABOMINATION OF DESOLATION	110
	C. CONSUMMATION AND DESOLATION, AND THE FULNESS OF TIME	111
	D. CONSUMMATION OF THE AGE AND THE ABOMINATION OF DESOLATION	112
4.	INVITATION TO THE NEW CHURCH	115
	MIRACLES	141
5.	ADDITIONS TO THE TRUE CHRISTIAN RELIGION	145
	I. ADDITION TO No. 695	151
	II. ADDITION TO No. 338	153
	III. ORDER	154
	IV. THE ORDER OF INFLUX	155
	V. RECIPROCAL CONJUNCTION	155
	VI. INFLUX	156
	VII. THE THOUGHTS OF MATERIALISTS RESPECTING GOD	157
	VIII. A RELATION RESPECTING THE COUNCIL OF CONSTANTINOPLE	157
	IX. CONCERNING ODORS	160
	X. THE BEING OF GOD OR JEHOVAH	162
	XI. REDEMPTION	163
	XII. THE LORD	163

GENERAL INDEX

	PAGE
6. CANONS OF THE NEW CHURCH	165
7. THE DOCTRINE OF CHARITY	227
8. SKETCH OF ECCLESIASTICAL HISTORY OF THE NEW CHURCH	301
9. THE WORD OF THE LORD FROM EXPERIENCE (OR DE VERBO)	307
10. LAST JUDGMENT (POSTHUMOUS)	371
a. LAST JUDGMENT (POSTHUMOUS)	379
b. THE SPIRITUAL WORLD	478
c. ARGUMENT CONCERNING THE JUDGMENT	515
d. FIVE MEMORABLE RELATIONS	521
e. CONVERSATION WITH ANGELS	533
f. JUSTIFICATION AND GOOD WORKS	537
g. CONVERSATION WITH CALVIN	547
h. GOD THE SAVIOUR JESUS CHRIST	552
i. SPECIMEN AND SKETCH OF THE DOCTRINE OF THE NEW CHURCH	555
11. THEOLOGICAL EXTRACTS FROM SWEDENBORG'S CORRESPONDENCE	565
a. I. ANSWER TO THREE QUESTIONS	569
b. II. ANSWER TO THREE QUESTIONS	570
c. THE NATURAL AND SPIRITUAL SENSE OF THE WORD	573
d. THE SON OF GOD	576
e. I. APPROACHING THE SAVIOUR IMMEDIATELY	579
f. II. APPROACHING THE SAVIOUR IMMEDIATELY	583
g. THE WORSHIP OF THE LORD AND THE ESTABLISHMENT OF THE NEW CHURCH	585
h. SWEDENBORG'S MISSION, AND INTERCOURSE WITH SPIRITS	588
LETTER TO COUNT BONDE	588
LETTER TO DR. BEYER	589
LETTER TO THE LANDGRAVE OF HESSE-DARMSTADT	590
LETTER TO THE LANDGRAVE OF HESSE-DARMSTADT	591
LETTER TO VENATOR	593
LETTER TO THE KING	594
i. THE PONTIFEX MAXIMUS IN RELIGIOUS MATTERS	599
j. DISEASES AND THEIR CURE	601
k. SIGNIFICATION OF A MANGER. THE USE OF JOHN'S BAPTISM	602
l. INFLUX	603
12. GAD AND ASHER	604

Autobiographical Letters

OF

Emanuel Swedenborg

AUTOBIOGRAPHICAL LETTERS

OF

EMANUEL SWEDENBORG

---

1. Answer to a Letter Written to Me by a Friend
2. My Early Youth

AUTOBIOGRAPHICAL LETTERS.

1. ANSWER TO A LETTER WRITTEN TO ME BY A FRIEND.

A LETTER FROM EMANUEL SWEDENBORG TO THE REV. THOMAS HARTLEY.*

I rejoice at the friendship which you manifest in your letter; and I thank you sincerely for both, but especially for your friendship. The praises with which you overwhelm me, I receive simply as expressions of your love for the truths contained in my writings; and I refer them, as their source, to the Lord, our Saviour, from whom is everything true, because He is the Truth Itself (*John* xiv. 6). I have considered chiefly the remarks you make at the close of your letter, where you express yourself as follows: "If, perchance, after your departure from England, your writings should be the subject of discussion, and occasion should arise for defending you, their author, against some malignant slanderer, who may wish to injure your reputation by a web of falsehoods—as those are in the habit of doing who hate the truth—would it not be well for you, in order to repel such slanderers, to leave with me some particulars respecting yourself, your degrees in the University, the public offices you have filled, your friends and relations, the honors which, I am told, have been conferred upon you, and anything else that might be useful in establishing your good name, so that ill-conceived prejudices may be removed; for it is our duty to use all lawful means lest the cause

---

*Rev. Thomas Hartley, A.M., a friend of Swedenborg, and one of the first receivers of his doctrines, was a clergyman of the Church of England, and rector of Winwick, Northamptonshire. The letter asking for particulars respecting Swedenborg's life, to which the above is a reply, was written August 2, 1769. (See *Documents Concerning Swedenborg*, Vol. I, pp. 3-5, 6-9.—Tr.)

of truth should suffer injury." After reflecting on this, I have been led to yield to your friendly advice, and will now communicate to you some particulars of my life, which are briefly as follows:—

I was born at Stockholm on the 29th of January in the year 1689.* My father's name was Jesper Swedberg, who was bishop of West-Gothland, and a man of celebrity in his time. He was also elected and enrolled as a member of the English Society, for the Propagation of the Gospel; for he had been appointed by King Charles XII Bishop over the Swedish churches in Pennsylvania, and also over the church in London. In the year 1710 I went abroad. I proceeded first to England, and afterwards to Holland, France, and Germany, and returned home in the year 1714.† In the year 1716, and also afterwards I had many conversations with Charles XII, King of Sweden, who greatly favored me, and in the same year appointed me to the office of Assessor in the College of Mines, which office I filled until the year 1747, when I resigned it, retaining, however, the salary of the office during my life. My sole object in resigning was that I might have more leisure to devote to the new office enjoined on me by the Lord. A higher post of honor was then offered me, which I positively declined, lest my mind should be inspired with pride. In the year 1719, I was ennobled by Queen Ulrica Eleanora, and named Swedenborg; and from that time I have taken my seat among the nobles of the rank of knighthood, in the triennial sessions of the Diet. I am a Fellow and member, by invitation, of the Royal Academy of Sciences in Stockholm; but I have never sought admission into any literary society in any other place, because I am in an angelic society, where such things as relate to heaven and the soul are the only subjects of discourse; while in literary societies the world and the body form the only subjects of discussion. In the year 1734, I published, at Leipsic, the *Regnum Minerale*, in three volumes, folio. In the year 1738 I made a journey to Italy, and stayed a year at Venice and Rome.

---

*The original edition has "1689," which is probably a printer's error. Swedenborg was born January 29, 1688.—Tr.

†The original edition has "1714," but Swedenborg did not return to Sweden until after April, 1715.—Tr.

With respect to my family connections, I had **four sisters**. One of them was married to Eric Benzelius, who subsequently became the Archbishop of Upsal, and through him I became related to the two succeeding archbishops, who both belonged to the family of Benzelius, and were younger brothers of Eric. My second sister was married to Lars Benzelstierna, who became a provincial governor; but these two are dead. Two bishops, however, who are related to me, are still living; one of them, whose name is Filenius, and who is Bishop of East-Gothland, officiates now as President of the House of the Clergy in the Diet of Stockholm, in place of the Archbishop, who is an invalid; he married my sister's daughter: the other, named Benzelstierna, is Bishop of Westmanland and Dalecarlia; he is the son of my second sister. Not to mention others of my relations who occupy stations of honor. Moreover, all the bishops of my native country, who are ten in number, and also the sixteen senators, and the rest of those highest in office, entertain feelings of affection for me; from their affection they honor me, and I live with them on terms of familiarity, as a friend among friends; the reason of which is, that they know I am in company with angels. Even the King and the Queen, and the three princes, their sons, show me great favor: I was also invited once by the King and Queen to dine with them at their own table, which honor is generally accorded only to those who are highest in office; subsequently the Crown Prince granted me the same favor. They all desire me to return home; wherefore, I am far from apprehending, in my own country, that persecution, which you fear, and against which in your letter you desire in so friendly a manner to provide; and if they persecute me elsewhere, it can do me no harm.

But all that I have thus far related, I consider of comparatively little importance; for it is far exceeded by the circumstance, that I have been called to a holy office by the Lord Himself, who most mercifully appeared before me, His servant, in the year 1743; when He opened my sight into the spiritual world, and granted me to speak with spirits and angels, in which state I have continued up to the present day. From that time I began to print and publish the various arcana that were seen by me and revealed to me, as the arcana concerning

Heaven and Hell, the state of man after death, the true worship of God, the spiritual sense of the Word, besides many other most important matters conducive to salvation and wisdom. The only reason of my journeys abroad has been the desire of making myself useful, and of making known the arcana that were entrusted to me. Moreover, I have as much of this world's wealth as I need, and I neither seek nor wish for more.

Your letter has induced me to write all these particulars, in order that as you say "ill-conceived prejudices may be removed." Farewell; and from my heart I wish you all the happiness both in this world, and the next; which I have not the least doubt you will attain, if you look and pray to our Lord.

EMAN. SWEDENBORG.

2. MY EARLY YOUTH.*

FROM A LETTER OF SWEDENBORG TO DR. BEYER.

I will now give you an account of my first youth: From my fourth to my tenth year I was constantly engaged in thought upon God, salvation, and the spiritual affections *(passiones spirituales)* of men; and several times I revealed things at which my father and mother wondered: saying, that angels must be speaking through me. From my sixth to my twelfth year I used to delight in conversing with clergymen about faith, saying that the life of faith is love, and that the love which imparts life is love to the neighbor; also that God gives faith to everyone, but that those only receive it who practice that love. I knew of no other faith at that time, than that God is the Creator and Preserver of nature, that He imparts understanding and a good disposition to men, and several other things that follow thence. I knew nothing at that time of that learned faith which teaches that God the Father imputes the righteousness of His Son to whomsoever, and at such times, as He chooses even to those who have not repented and have not reformed their lives. And had I heard of such a faith, it would have been then, as it is now, above my comprehension.

I remain, with all affection and friendship,
   Your most obedient servant and friend,

           EMAN. SWEDENBORG.

STOCKHOLM, November 14, 1769.

To the Reverend and Most Learned Doctor and Lector
 GABRIEL AND. BEYER, *Gottenburg.*

---

*See *Documents Concerning Swedenborg*, Vol. II, pp. 278-280.

The Coronis, or Appendix,

TO

The True Christian Religion

THE CORONIS, OR APPENDIX,

TO THE

TRUE CHRISTIAN RELIGION

IN WHICH IT TREATS OF

THE FOUR CHURCHES ON THIS EARTH FROM THE CREATION OF
THE WORLD, AND OF THEIR PERIODS AND
CONSUMMATION

OF THE NEW CHURCH ABOUT TO SUCCEED THOSE FOUR, WHICH
WILL BE TRULY CHRISTIAN, AND THE CROWN OF
THE PRECEDING ONES

OF THE COMING OF THE LORD TO IT, AND OF HIS DIVINE
AUSPICES THEREIN TO ETERNITY

AND FURTHER OF THE MYSTERY OF REDEMPTION

THEN ALSO THE INVITATION TO THE NEW CHURCH

FROM THE LATIN OF

EMANUEL SWEDENBORG

TRANSLATOR'S NOTE.

The Coronis or *Appendix to The True Christian Religion*, was the last work written by Swedenborg. The autograph manuscript is now lost. The work as now extant was printed at London in 1780, at the expense of Aug. Nordenskjöld, from a fragment of the autograph manuscript, as we learn from the following note of Robert Hindmarsh, on p. 55 of the *Minutes of a General Conference of the Members of the New Church*, London 1793. He says:—

"This Appendix to the True Christian Religion is not complete. The author had nearly, if not quite, finished it, when he was seized with his last illness; during which Dr. Messiter, a Swedish Physician, called upon him, and finding him without Hopes of Recovery, took the Manuscripts from the Author's Apartments. The Author, however, soon after recovering himself a little, inquired for his Manuscripts, possibly with an Intention to finish or revise them. But as the Doctor had taken them away, E. Swedenborg died without seeing them. Dr. Messiter being thus in Possession of the Manuscripts, and not taking sufficient Care of them, many of the Leaves were lost. About eight Years afterwards Mr. Nordenskjöld from Sweden arrived in London, and caused what remained to be printed."

For further information in regard to this work, see Hyde's *Bibliography of Swedenborg's Works*, pp. 588–597, and Tafel's *Documents Concerning Swedenborg*. Vol. II, Part II, pp. 1021–1022.

Swedenborg refers to the *Appendix* in the following places in *The True Christian Religion*, (n. 15, 177, 343, 485, 627, and 758). The entire treatise was designed to embrace the subjects, The Consummation of the Age, the Last Judgment, the Coming of the Lord, and the Restoration and the New Church. Only sketches and fragments of these are extant.

JOHN WHITEHEAD.

SKETCH OF THE CORONIS, OR APPENDIX, TO THE TRUE CHRISTIAN RELIGION.

    I. THE CONSUMMATION OF THE AGE.
   II. THE LAST JUDGMENT.
  III. THE COMING OF THE LORD.
 IV. RESTORATION, AND THE NEW CHURCH: ITS QUALITY.

      1. THE APPEARING OF THE LORD JEHOVIH.
      2. THE MORNING, OR RISE.
      3. THE DAY, OR PROGRESSION.
      4. THE EVENING, OR VASTATION.
      5. THE NIGHT, OR CONSUMMATION.
      6. THE COMING OF THE LORD.
      7. THE LAST JUDGMENT.
      8. THE NEW HEAVEN.
      9. THE NEW CHURCH.
     10. REDEMPTION.
     11. MIRACLES.

SUMMARY.

I. There have been four churches on this earth from the day of the creation: the First, which is to be called the Adamic; the Second, the Noachian; the Third, the Israelitish; and the Fourth, the Christian.

II. There have been four periods, or successive states, of each church, which in the Word are meant by "morning," "day," "evening," and "night."

III. In each church there have been four successive changes of states; the first of which was the appearing of the Lord Jehovih and redemption, and then its morning or rise; the second was its instruction and then its mid-day or progression; the third was its decline, and then its evening or vastation; the fourth was its end, and then its night, or consummation.

After its end or consummation the Lord Jehovih appears and executes a judgment on the men of the former church, and separates the good from the evil, and elevates the good to Himself into heaven, and removes the evil from Himself into hell.

After these things, from the good elevated to Himself, He founds a new heaven, and from the evil removed from Himself, a new hell; and in both He establishes order, so that they may stand under His auspices and under obedience to Him to eternity; and then through this new heaven He successively inaugurates and establishes a new church on earth.

From this new heaven, the Lord Jehovih derives and produces a new church on earth; which is effected by a revelation from His mouth, or from His Word, and by inspiration.

IV. These periodical changes of state, which occurred in succession in the first or Most Ancient Church, which was the Adamic, are described by Moses in the first chapters of *Genesis;* but by heavenly representatives, and by other things, belonging to the world, to which spiritual things correspond.

V. The periodical changes of state, which occurred in succession in the second or Ancient Church, which was the Noachian, are also described in *Genesis,* and here and there in the four remaining books of Moses.

VI. The periodical changes of state which occurred in succession in the third church, which was the Israelitish, are also described in Moses, and afterwards in Joshua, in the books of *Judges, Samuel,* and *Kings,* and also in the *Prophets.*

VII. The periodical changes which occurred in succession in the fourth church, which is the Christian, are described in the Word of both Testaments; its rise, or morning, in particular, in the *Evangelists,* and in the *Acts* and *Writings of the Apostles;* its progression towards noon-day, in the ecclesiastical histories of the first three centuries; its decline, or evening, by the histories of the centuries immediately following; and its vastation even to consummation, which is its night, in the *Apocalypse.*

VIII. After these four churches, a new one is to arise, which will be truly Christian foretold in *Daniel* and in the *Apocalypse,* and by the Lord Himself in the *Evangelists,* and expected by the Apostles.

. . . . . .

IX. The church successively declines from the truths of faith and the goods of charity, and it declines in the same proportion also from the spiritual understanding and genuine sense of the Word.

X. Consequently, the church departs in the same proportion from the Lord, and removes Him from itself.

XI. In proportion as this is effected, it approaches its end.

XII. The end of the church is when there no longer remains any truth of faith and genuine good of charity.

XIII. The church is then in falsities and the evils therefrom, and in evils and the falsities therefrom.

XIV. Hence hell increases from those who have departed from the world, so that it raises itself up towards heaven, and interposes itself between heaven and the church, like a black cloud between the sun and the earth.

XV. Through this interposition, it is brought about that no truth of faith, and hence no genuine good of charity, penetrates to the men of the church; but, instead of them, falsified truth, which in itself is falsity, and adulterated good, which in itself is not good.

XVI. Then naturalism and atheism rush in together.

XVII. This state of the church is meant and described in the Word, by "vastation," "desolation," and "consummation."

. . . .

XVIII. While the vastation lasts, and before the consummation supervenes, the Lord's Coming is announced, also redemption by the Lord, and after this, a new church.

XIX. These three, while the Israelitish Church still continued, were announced in many passages of the Word in the *Prophets*.

XX. The Coming of the Lord.

XXI. Redemption.

XXII. A new church.

Almost everywhere in the prophetic Word it treats of vastation and consummation, the Last Judgment, the Lord's Coming, a new church, and redemption.

. . . .

XXIII. As regards redemption in particular, through which alone salvation is effected, it was accomplished by Jehovah God incarnate, who is our Lord Jesus Christ.

XXIV. The first part of redemption was a total subjugation of the hells.

XXV. The second part of redemption was the separation of the evil from the good, and the casting down of the evil into hell, and the raising of the good into heaven.

XXVI. And, lastly, there is the arrangement in order of all in hell, and the arrangement in order of all in heaven.

XXVII. And then, at the same time, instruction concerning the truths which are to be of faith, and the goods which are to be of charity.

XXVIII. And thus the establishment of a new church.

XXIX. The final and efficient cause of redemption was the regeneration, and thereby the salvation, of man.

XXX. The Lord, because He is the only Redeemer, is therefore the only Regenerator, and thus the only Saviour.

. . . .

XXXI. By His First Coming and the redemption then wrought, the Lord could not form a new heaven of Christians, and from that a new church, because there were no Christians as yet, but they became Christians gradually through the preachings and writings of the Apostles.

XXXII. Neither could He afterwards, since from the beginning so many heresies broke forth, that scarcely any doctrine of faith could appear in its own light.

XXXIII. And at length the Apostolic doctrine, in process of time, was torn, rent asunder, and adulterated by atrocious heresies.

XXXIV. This is meant by "the abomination of desolation," and by "the affliction such as was not, neither shall be," and by "the darkening of the sun, moon, and stars," in the *Evangelists*, in *Daniel*, and also in the *Prophets*; likewise by "the dragon," and many things, in the *Apocalypse*.

XXXV. Because the Lord foresaw these things, therefore, owing to its necessity in order that man might be saved, He promised that He would come again into the world, and would accomplish a redemption, and would establish the New Church, which would be a truly Christian Church.

XXXVI. The Lord Himself foretold His Second Coming, and the Apostles frequently prophesied respecting it, and John openly so in the *Apocalypse*.

XXXVII. In like manner respecting the New Church, which is meant by the "New Jerusalem" in the *Apocalypse*.

XXXVIII. This second redemption was effected in the same way as the first (of which above, from n. xxiii. to xxx.).

XXXIX. And, also, for the sake of the regeneration and hence the salvation of the men of the church, as its final and efficient cause.

. . . . . .

XL. The falsities which have hitherto desolated, and have at length consummated, the Christian Church, were chiefly the following:

XLI. They receded from the worship of the Lord preached by the Apostles, and from faith in Him.

They severed the Divine Trinity from the Lord, and transferred it to three Divine Persons from eternity, consequently to three Gods.

XLII. They divided saving faith among these three Persons

XLIII. They separated charity and good works from that faith, as not at the same time saving.

XLIV. They deduced justification, that is, remission of sins, regeneration, and salvation, from that faith alone, apart from man's coöperation.

XLV. They denied to man free-will in spiritual things, thus asserting that God alone operates in man, and on the other hand that man does nothing.

XLVI. From this necessarily flowed forth predestination, by which religion is abolished.

XLVII. They made the passion of the cross to be redemption.

XLVIII. From these heresies, falsities burst forth in such abundance, that there does not remain any genuine truth which is not falsified, consequently, neither any genuine good which is not adulterated.

XLIX. The church knows nothing at all about this, its desolation and consummation, nor can it know, until the Divine truths revealed by the Lord in the work entitled, *The True Christian Religion*, are seen in light and acknowledged.

The Word has been so obscured and darkened,[1] that not a single truth any longer appears in it.

L. For many reasons this New Christian Church is not being established through any miracles as the former was.

LI. But, instead of them, the spiritual sense of the Word is revealed, and the spiritual world disclosed, and the nature of both heaven and hell manifested; also, that man lives a man after death; which things surpass all miracles.

. . . . .

LII. This New Church, truly Christian, which at this day is being established by the Lord, will endure to eternity, as is proved from the Word of both Testaments; also it was foreseen from the creation of the world; and it will be the crown of the four preceding churches, because it will have true faith and true charity.

LIII. In this New Church there will be spiritual peace, glory, and internal blessedness of life, as is also proved from the Word of both Testaments.

LIV. These things will be in this New Church, for the sake of conjunction with the Lord, and through Him with God the Father.

LV. An invitation to the whole Christian world to enter this church; and an exhortation to worthily receive the Lord, who has Himself foretold that He would come into the world for the sake of this church and to it.

LASTLY, ABOUT MIRACLES.

I. Miracles were done in the church before the Lord's Coming, because, at that time, men were external or natural, who could not be led to their representative worship except by miracles.

The miracles done in Egypt, in the wilderness, and in the land of Canaan, even to the present time, are to be recounted.

And nevertheless they never affect men.

II. After the Lord's Coming, when man from external became internal, and when the faculty of being able to know was imparted to man, miracles were prohibited

Also, if that faculty were impeded, man would become more external than before.

III. Miracles would abolish worship truly Divine, and introduce the former idolatrous worship; as also has been done for very many centuries back.

Nevertheless, the latter have not been Divine miracles, but such as were wrought by the magicians of old.

IV. In place of miracles, there has, at this day, taken place a manifestation of the Lord Himself, an intromission into the spiritual world, and enlightenment there by immediate light from the Lord, in such things as are interior things of the church.

But chiefly, the opening of the spiritual sense in the Word, in which the Lord is in His own Divine light.

V. These revelations are not miracles; since every man is in the spiritual world as to his spirit, without separation from his body in the natural world; I, however, with a certain separation, though only as to the intellectual part of my mind, but not as to the voluntary; and, as to the spiritual sense, the Lord through it is with all who in faith approach Him in that light, and through that are in its natural light.

THE CORONIS, OR APPENDIX,
TO
THE TRUE CHRISTIAN RELIGION.

1. These three things,—the Consummation of the Age, the Coming of the Lord, and the New Church—have, it is true, been treated of in the last chapter of the work entitled *The True Christian Religion*. The reason why a *Continuation* follows concerning them, is because no one has hitherto known what the Consummation of the Age is, why the Second Coming of the Lord must take place, or that the New Church is about to come; and yet these three subjects are treated of in both the Prophetic and the Apostolic Word, and fully in the *Apocalypse*. That these three subjects are treated of in the Prophetic Word of the Old Testament, was made evident to me while it was granted me to lay it open by means of the spiritual sense; and in like manner that they are treated of in the Prophetic [part] of the New Testament, which is called the *Apocalypse*: that they are also in the Evangelic and Apostolic Word, will be plain from the following pages. Hence it follows, that, without a knowledge of the Consummation of the Age, the Second Coming of the Lord, and the New Church, the Word is as it were shut up; nor can anything but knowledges open it: these are like keys which open the door and introduce. When this takes place with the Word, then the treasures, which lay concealed therein as at the bottom of the sea, come into view; for, at the bottom, there are in the Word nothing else but precious things. In this *Appendix* or *Continuation*, I shall proceed, in like manner as in the work itself, by prefixed Summaries, which will be confirmed from Scripture and illustrated from reason.

PROPOSITION THE FIRST.

2. I. *There have been four churches on this earth from the day of its creation: the First, which is to be called the Adamic; the Second, the Noachian; the Third, the Israelitish; and the Fourth, the Christian.* That four churches have existed on this earth since the creation of the world, manifestly appears in *Daniel;* first, from the statue seen by Nebuchadnezzar in a dream, and, afterwards, from the four beasts rising up out of the sea. Concerning the statue of Nebuchadnezzar we read as follows:—

Daniel said, Thou, O king, sawest, and behold a great statue. And the appearance thereof was excellent, standing before thee, and the aspect thereof was terrible. The head of this statue was of good gold; its breast and arms, of silver; its belly and its thighs, of brass; its legs, of iron; its feet, partly of iron and partly of clay. Thou sawest until a stone was cut out, which was not by hands, and smote the statue upon its feet that were of iron and clay, and brake them in pieces. Then were the iron, the clay, the brass, the silver, and the gold, broken in pieces together, and became like the chaff of the summer threshing-floors; so that the wind carried them away, and no place was found for them: but the stone, which smote the statue, became a great rock, and filled the whole earth. In these days shall the God of the heavens raise up a kingdom, which shall not be destroyed to the ages; and His kingdom shall not be entrusted to another people[1]: it shall break in pieces and consume all those kingdoms, but it shall stand to the ages (*Dan.* ii. 31–35, 44).

This dream did not signify four political kingdoms on this earth, but four churches, which should follow one after another, may be evident from the following considerations: (1) That such kingdoms, one after another, have not existed on this earth. (2) That the Divine Word, in its bosom, does not treat of the kingdoms of the world, but of churches, which constitute the kingdom of God on the earth. (3) Also, because it is said that the God of the heavens shall raise up a kingdom which shall not be destroyed to the ages, and that a stone, cut out, not by hands, became a great rock, which filled the whole earth. (4) And, because the Lord our Saviour Jesus Christ, in the Word of both Testaments, is called the "Stone" and "Rock," it is manifest that His kingdom is meant by the last words in this passage. (5) Moreover, the state of the church is described, in innumerable passages of the Word, by "gold," "silver," "brass," and "iron;" its spiritual state as to the good of love by "gold," its spiritual state as to the truth of wisdom by "silver," its natural state as to the good of charity by "brass," and its natural state as to the truth of faith by "iron," as may be seen confirmed from the Word in the *Apocalypse Revealed* (n. 913), and elsewhere. [2] For this reason, the wise in the first ages, who knew the significations of metals, compared the ages, which were to follow one another from the first to the last, to those four metals, and called the first age "golden," the second age "silver," the third age "copper," and the fourth age "iron;" and they described them thus according to goods and truths; and because genuine goods and truths are from no other origin than from the God of heaven, they described them according to the states of the church with those who lived in those ages; for from these, and according to these, all the civil states of kingdoms as to justice and judgment exist, flourish and live. [3] That the Lord the Saviour Jesus Christ is called the "Stone" and "Rock" in the Word of both Testaments, is plain from the following passages. That He is called a "Stone" from these:—

Thus said the Lord Jehovih, Behold I will found in Zion a Stone of probation, a precious corner of well-established foundation; he who hath believed will not make haste[1]; then I will set judgment for the rule, and justice for the plummet (*Isa.* xxviii. 16, 17).

Jehovah will visit His flock. From Him is the corner-stone (*Zech.* x. 3, 4).

The stone which the architects rejected is become the head of the corner (*Ps.* cxviii. 22).

Have ye not read in the Scripture that the Stone which the builders rejected is become the head of the corner? (*Matt.* xxi. 42; *Mark* xii. 10, 11; *Luke* xx. 17, 18; *Isa.* viii. 14, 15).

Ye have come to the Lord, the living Stone, rejected indeed of men, but chosen of God; ye yourselves also, as living stones, are built up into a spiritual house; . . . therefore, it is said in the Scripture, I lay in Zion a corner-stone, elect, precious, and he who believeth on Him shall not be ashamed (1 *Peter* ii. 4–6).

Ye are built upon the foundations of the apostles and prophets, whose corner-stone is Jesus Christ, by whom the whole building, well cemented together, groweth into a holy temple in the Lord; by whom ye are built together into a habitation of God in the spirit (*Eph.* ii. 20, 21, 22).

Jesus Christ is the Stone, rejected by the builders, which is become the head of the corner; and there is no salvation in any other (*Acts* iv. 11, 12).

The Lord is called the "Rock," is evident from these passages in the Word:—

When Jeshurun became fat, he kicked . . . and he forsook God who made him, and despised the Rock of his salvation (*Deut.* xxxii. 15, 18, 30).

The God of Israel said, The Rock of Israel spake to me (2 *Sam.* xxiii. 3).

Let the words of my mouth be well-pleasing, O Jehovah, my Rock and my Redeemer (*Ps.* xix. 14).

And[2] they remembered that God was their Rock, and the High God their Redeemer (*Ps.* lxxviii. 35).

They all drank spiritual drink; for they drank from the spiritual Rock; the Rock was Christ (1 *Cor.* x. 4; *Exod.* xvii. 6).

From these passages, it is now manifestly evident, that by the "Stone" which smote the statue, and became a great rock and filled the whole earth, and whose kingdom shall stand to ages of ages, is meant our Lord Jesus Christ.

3. The same four churches on this earth are described by four "beasts" rising up out of the sea, in *Daniel*, of which it is there written:—

The first was seen like a lion, but it had eagle's wings. I beheld until the wings thereof were plucked out, and it was lifted up from the earth, and it was erect like a man upon feet, and a man's heart was given to it. Afterwards, behold another beast, a second, like a bear, and it raised up itself on one side; three ribs were in its mouth between the teeth: moreover, they were saying thus unto it, Arise, devour much flesh. After these things, I beheld, and, lo, another, like a leopard, which had upon the back of it four wings, like birds' wings; the beast had also four heads; and dominion was given to it. After this, I saw in the night visions, and behold a fourth beast, terrible and dreadful, and strong exceedingly, which had great iron teeth; it devoured and brake in pieces, and trampled the residue with its feet; but it was diverse from all the beasts that were before it, and it had ten horns. I beheld till the thrones were cast down, and the Ancient of days did sit; and the judgment was set, and the books were opened; and behold, one like the Son of man was coming with the clouds of the heavens. And there was given Him dominion, and glory, and a kingdom, that all peoples, nations and tongues should worship Him: His dominion is a dominion of an age, which shall not pass away, and His kingdom that which shall not perish (chap. vii. 3–7, 9, 10, 13, 14, *seq.*).

By these beasts, in like manner, are meant and described those four churches, is manifest from all the particulars there, which shall be unfolded in their order in the following pages. more especially from the last expressions there, that after those four beasts the Son of man will come, to whom shall be given dominion, and a kingdom which shall not pass away and perish; who, also, is meant by "the Stone made into a great Rock, which shall fill the whole earth," as may be seen above (n. 2, at the end). [2] That the states of the church are likewise described in the Word by *beasts*, as well as by *metals*, is evident from numberless passages, some only of which I will adduce here; which are as follows:—

Thou causest the rain of benevolences to drop; thou wilt confirm thy laboring inheritance; the beast[1] of thy assembly shall dwell therein (*Ps.* lxviii. 9, 10).

Every wild beast of the forest is Mine, the beasts in the mountains of thousands; I know every bird of the mountains, the beasts of My fields are with Me (*Ps.* l. 10, 11).

Assyria was a cedar in Lebanon, his height was exalted; all the birds of the heavens made their nests in his boughs, and under his branches did all the beasts of the field bring forth, and in his shadow dwelt all great nations (*Ezek.* xxxi. 3, 5, 6, 13; *Dan.* iv. 7–13).

In that day will I make a covenant for them with the beast of the field, and with the bird of the heavens, and I will betroth Myself unto thee[2] to eternity (*Hos.* ii. 18, 19).

Rejoice and be glad, fear not, ye beasts of My fields, for the habitations of the desert are become herbaceous (*Joel* ii. 21, 22).

Thou, son of man, say to the bird of every wing, and to every beast of the field, Gather yourselves together to My sacrifice upon the mountains of Israel: thus I will give My glory among the nations (*Ezek.* xxxix. 17, 20, 21).

The enemy hath reproached Jehovah; give not the soul of the turtledove unto the beast (*Ps.* lxxiv. 18, 19).

Jehovah gathereth the outcasts of Israel; every beast of My fields, come ye (*Isa.* lvi. 8, 9).

The spirit driving Jesus, caused Him to go forth into the wilderness; and He was with the beasts, and the angels ministered unto Him (*Mark* i. 12, 13).

He was not with beasts, but with devils, with whom He fought and whom He subdued; besides a thousand other passages, which are in part adduced in the *Apocalypse Revealed* (n. 567). Moreover, it is known that the Lord Himself, in the Word, is called a "Lamb" and also a "Lion;" likewise, that the Holy Spirit was represented as a "dove;" that the "cherubim," also, by which the Word in the literal sense is signified, appeared like "four beasts," in *Ezekiel* and in the *Apocalypse;* and that the man of the church who acknowledges the Lord as his God and

Shepherd, is called a "sheep;" and, on the other hand, he who does not acknowledge Him, is called a "he-goat" and also a "dragon;" and that an assembly of the latter is described, in like manner as in *Daniel*, by:—

The beast out of the sea like a leopard, the feet of which were as it were a bear's, and his mouth as it were a lion's (*Apoc.* xiii. 1, 2).

These comparisons originate from the spiritual world, where all the affections and the thoughts therefrom, of angels and spirits, are presented at a distance from them as beasts, which also appear in a form in all respects similar to that of the beasts in the natural world; the affections of the love of good as gentle beasts and good uses, but the affections of the love of evil as savage beasts and evil uses. Hence it is that "beasts" are so often named in the Word; and by them in the spiritual sense are signified affections, inclinations, perceptions and thoughts. From these things it is manifest what is meant by "creatures" in the following passages:—

Jesus commanded the disciples to go into all the world, and preach the Gospel to every creature (*Mark* xvi. 15).

If any one be in Christ, he is a new creature; old things have passed away, and all things are become new (2 *Cor.* v. 17).

These things saith the Amen, the faithful and true witness, the beginning of the creature[1] of God (*Apoc.* iii. 14).

By "creatures," here, are meant those who can be created anew, that is, regenerated, and thus become of the Lord's church.

4. That there have been four churches on this earth, one before the flood, which is to be called the Adamic; the second, after the flood, which is to be called the Noachic; and the third, after this, which was the Israelitish; also the fourth, which exists at this day, and is called the Christian, will be demonstrated in the following pages, in the exposition of each of them separately.

5. II. *There have been four successive states, or periods, of each church, which in the Word are meant by "morning," "day," "evening," and "night."* That there have been four successive states, or periods, of every one of these churches above mentioned, will be illustrated in the following pages, wherein each will be dealt with in its order. They are described by those alternations of time, because every man who is born in the church, or in whom the church has commenced, first comes into its light, such as that is in the dawn and morning; afterwards, he advances into its day, and, he who loves its truths, even to its mid-day; if he then stops in the way, and does not advance into the heat of spring and summer, his day declines towards evening, and at length, like light at night-time, it grows dark; and then his intelligence in the spiritual things of the church becomes a cold light, like the light of the days in winter, when he indeed sees the trees standing near his house, or in his gardens, but stript of leaves and deprived of fruits, thus like bare logs. For, the man of the church advances from morning to day, to the end that he may be reformed and regenerated by means of the light of reason, which is effected only by a life according to the precepts of the Lord in the Word. If this does not take place, his light becomes darkness, and the darkness, thick darkness; that is, the truths of light with him are turned into falsities, and the falsities into unseen evils. It is otherwise with the man who suffers himself to be regenerated: night does not overtake him, for he walks in God, and hence is continually in the day; into which, also, he fully enters after death, when he is associated with angels in heaven. This is meant by these things in the *Apocalypse*, concerning the New Jerusalem, which is the New Church, truly Christian:—

That city shall have no need of the sun and moon to shine in it; for the glory of God shall lighten it, and the Lamb is the lamp thereof; and the nations which are saved shall walk in the light of it, ... and there shall be no night there (xxi. 23–25; *Ezek.* xxxii. 8; *Amos.* v. 20; viii. 9).

That the successive states of the church are meant by "morning," "day," "evening," and "night," in the Word, is evident from the following passages therein:—

Watch; for ye know not when the Lord of the house will come, at even, or at midnight, or at cock-crowing, or in the morning (*Mark* xiii. 35; *Matt.* xxv. 13).

The subject there treated of is the Consummation of the Age, and the Coming of the Lord at that time:—

The God of Israel said, The Rock of Israel spake to me; he is as the light of the morning, a morning without clouds (2 *Sam.* xxiii. 3, 4).

I am the Root and the Offspring of David, the bright and morning Star (*Apoc.* xxii. 16).

God shall help her, when He shall look to the morning (*Ps.* xlvi. 5).

He is calling to me out of Seir, Watchman, what of the night? Watchman, what of the night? The watchman said, The morning cometh, and also the night (*Isa.* xxi. 11, 12).

The end is come upon thee, O inhabitant of the land[1]; the time is come, the day is near. Behold the day, behold, it is come; the morning hath gone forth (*Ezek.* vii. 5–7, 10).

There shall be a day which shall be known to Jehovah; not day nor night; for about the time of evening there shall be light (*Zech.* xiv. 7).

About the time of evening, behold, terror; before the morning, he is not (*Isa.* xvii. 14).

In the evening, weeping will tarry all night, but there will be singing in the morning (*Ps.* xxx. 5).

Even to the evening and the morning, two thousand three hundred; then shall the holy place be justified: the vision of the evening and morning is truth (*Dan.* viii. 14, 26).

Jehovah in the morning will give His judgment in the light; He will not fail (*Zeph.* iii. 5).

Thus said Jehovah, If ye have made void My covenant of the day and My covenant of the night, so that there be not day and night in their season, My covenant also shall be made void with David My servant (*Jer.* xxxiii. 20, 21, 25).

Jesus said, I must work the works of God while it is day; the night cometh when no one can work (*John* ix. 4).

In this night there shall be two on one bed; one shall be taken, but the other shall be left (*Luke* xvii. 34).

In these passages, it treats of the consummation of the age and the Coming of the Lord. Hence it may be evident what is meant by "There shall be time no longer" (*Apoc.* x. 6); namely, that there would not be morning, day, or evening in the church, but night; likewise what is meant by "time, times, and half a time" (*Apoc.* xii. 14; *Dan.* xii. 7); as also what is meant by the "fulness of time" (*Eph.* i. 10; *Gal.* iv. 4).

6. III *In each church there have been four successive changes of state; the first of which was the appearing of the Lord Jehovih and redemption, and then its morning, or rise: the second was its instruction, and then its day, or progression: the third was its decline; and then its evening or vastation: the fourth was its end; and then its night or consummation.* That there have been four successive states of each church, which in the Word are meant by "morning," "day," "evening," and "night," has been shown in the preceding article. That every one of the four churches mentioned above underwent those states, will be fully established in the following pages, where each will be dealt with in its order; and then that the appearing of the Lord Jehovih and redemption was its "morning;" that instruction was its "day" or progression into light; also, that decline was its "evening" or vastation; and that its end was its "night" or consummation. In the Word, both in its historical and its prophetical parts, those four changes of state are everywhere treated of.

7. The order into which every man was created by God, is, that after infancy he may become a man. For when he is born, he is only an external image or form of a man, and at that time less a man than a new-born beast is a beast; but, so far as he is inwardly perfected in this form, as to his mind, or his spirit, in wisdom and love, he becomes a man. A man is like a tree, which first grows up from a seed into a shoot, and when it increases in height puts forth branches and from these stems, and clothes itself continually with leaves; and when it comes to maturity, which takes place in its middle age, puts forth flowers, and produces fruits; in each one it places seeds, which being cast into the earth, as into a womb, grow up into similar trees and thus into a garden. And if you are willing to believe it, that same garden remains with the man after death; he dwells in it, and is delighted daily with the sight of it, and with the use of its fruits. It is such a man who is described in *David* by these words:—

He shall be like a tree planted beside the rivers of waters, which shall bring forth its fruit in its season, and its leaf shall not fall off (*Ps.* i. 3; and likewise *Apoc.* xxii. 1, 2).

[2] But the case is different with the man born in the church, who, when he has passed through his morning, and advanced into the first light of day, whereby he has become rational, then stops, and does not produce fruit: such a one is, or may be, like a tree luxuriant with leaves, but not bearing fruit, which is uprooted from the garden, its branches cut off, and the trunk cleft in pieces with axe, or saw, and the whole then cast little by little into the fire. The light of his rational becomes like the light of the days of winter, in which the leaves of the trees first grow yellow, then drop off, and lastly rot. His rational,

also, may be compared with a tree whose leaves are consumed by worms in early spring; likewise with a crop that is choked by thorns; and also with vegetation which is laid waste by locusts. The reason is, that his rational is merely natural, because it takes its ideas solely from the world through the senses, and not from heaven through the affections and the perceptions therefrom. And since, on this account, there is nothing spiritual inwardly in his rational, if he then speaks of any spiritual thing of the church, his voice is heard by the angels no otherwise than as the voice of a parrot or a goose; for his voice is merely animal, because merely natural, and not human because not spiritual within; for it flows forth from the respiration of the body only, and not from any respiration of the spirit. Such is the man who does not, from natural, become spiritual; and no one becomes spiritual, unless, after he has become rational, he brings forth fruits, that is, imbues charity by life.

8. The four changes of state, which are called "morning," "day," "evening," and "night," are in the Word predicated of the church, because the church consists of men, and a man is a church in particular, and the assembly of these men is what is called the church. Those in this assembly or the church, who live according to the order described above (n. 7), are trees of life, which also are trees of good use; but those who do not live according to that order are trees of the knowledge of good and evil, which also are trees of evil use. The latter are those of whom "evening" and "night," or, what is the same, vastation and consummation, are predicated; but not the former. These things, however, will be made evident to the reason in the following pages; but it is proper, that, at the beginning of this volume, some preliminary observations should be made, because knowledges must precede before any one can know that by "morning" is meant the rise of the church, and that this is preceded by redemption; by "day," the progression of the new church into light, and its intelligence; by "evening," the decline of that church from good and truth, which is called vastation; and by "night," its end and destruction, which is called consummation; and so on.

9. The end of the church, or the consummation of the age, is when there is not any genuine truth and hence not any genuine

good, or when there is not any good and hence not any truth remaining, but, in their place falsity and evil therefrom, or evil and falsity therefrom, rule; and then there is the "fulness [of time]" in the church, the members of which are like persons walking in the night, who, because they do not see anything that appears in the light of the sun, are in doubt about all things relating to the church, and in general about God, heaven and hell, and the life after death; and both those who confirm themselves in the denial of these things, and those who remain alternately in doubt and in affirmation, become shunners of the light, and, if they are priests, they procure to themselves a false light on those subjects, such as night-owls, cats, and mice have in the darkness of night. This light is excited with them, as with these wild beasts, through the activities of their lusts

10. IV. *After its consummation, or end, the Lord Jehovih appears, and executes a judgment on the men of the former church, and separates the good from the evil, and elevates the good to Himself into heaven, and removes the evil from Himself into hell.* That about the end of every church the Lord Jehovih appears to execute a judgment on those who have lived from its first establishment to its consummation, will be confirmed in the following pages, where each church will be separately treated of. Every man indeed is judged after death; but at the end of a church all are collected together, and a general judgment is executed on them; and this for the reason that they may be conjoined in heavenly order, which is effected by the arrangement of the faithful into a new heaven, and of the unfaithful into a new hell beneath it; of which arrangement we shall speak more at large in the following article.

11. Judgment, which is the last of every church, is not effected in the natural world, but in the spiritual world, into which all are gathered after death; and they are collected into heavens distinctly according to religion, thus according to faith and love. Judgment is effected in the spiritual world, for the reason that every man after death is a man; not a material man, as before, but a substantial man. Every man's mind or spirit is such a man: the body which he carried about in the world is only a covering, and as it were the exuviæ, which he has laid aside, and from which his spirit has disengaged itself. Now, since it was man's mind or spirit that thought in the material body, and then either from religion or not from religion, and in favor of God or against God, from truths of faith or from falsities of faith, loved his neighbor or held him in hatred; and since the material body was only obedience; it follows that the mind, which is the substantial man and is called the spirit, is what undergoes judgment, and, according to the thoughts and acts of its life, is rewarded or punished. From these things it may be plainly manifest, that judgment, which is the last of every church, is effected in the spiritual world, but not in the natural world.

12. The judgment which is executed upon all of a past church, takes place, both generally and individually, to the end that the good may be separated from the evil, and that the good may be raised up into heaven and the evil cast down into hell. Unless this were done when a church is consummated, that is, when it is no longer in truths and goods, not anyone therein could be saved. That he could not be saved is because he could not be regenerated; and every one is regenerated by the truths of faith and the goods of love. To this reason the following is added, that from the time of the vastation of a church even to its consummation, hell increases to so great an extent as to stretch under the whole angelic heaven, through which the regenerating truths and goods descend from the Lord to the men of the earth. When this is covered over, no truth of thought from faith nor good of will from charity can penetrate, except as it were through chinks; yea, what does penetrate is perverted either in the way before it reaches man, or else by the man himself when it is in him; that is, the truth is either rejected or falsified, and the good is either clogged up or adulterated. In a word, a church at its end is as it were obsessed by satans. Those are called satans who take pleasure in falsities and are delighted with evils. In order, therefore, that the total damnation which is then over every one's head, and menaces him, may be taken away, it is necessary that hell, which has raised itself on high, and, as was said, increased even to heaven, should be removed, not merely depressed, but also dispersed and subjugated, and then the good separated from the evil, that is, the living from the dead. This separation, and then the elevation of the good into heaven, or into the land of the living, and the casting down of the evil into hell, or into the land of the dead, is what is called the judgment. That such a judgment was actually executed in the year 1757 on the men of the present Christian Church, has been published and described, in a special little work published in London in the year 1758.

13. Who does not see the necessity that the evil should be separated from the good, lest the latter should be infected with the contagion of deadly evil, and perish? For evil, inasmuch as it is implanted in human nature by birth, and is more and more ingenerated in children from parents when the church is advancing towards consummation, is like the malignant disease which is called cancer, which spreads round about, and gradually mortifies the healthy and living parts. What husbandman, or gardener, when he sees briars, nettles, thorns, and thistles growing, does not extirpate them before he sows and harrows in his corn and food crops? What farmer, when he sees his herbage and grass consumed by worms, or locusts, does not dig a ditch, and separate the green field from the wasted one, and thus take measures for the preservation of his crops and green fields? What shepherd, when he sees wild beasts multiplying about the pastures of his sheep, does not call together the neighboring shepherds and the servants, and with weapons, or traps, kill those wild beasts, or drive them away? [2] What king, when he sees both the towns of his kingdom round about his metropolis taken by enemies, and the property of his subjects taken possession of by them, does not assemble the troops and cast out the enemy, and restore the stolen goods to their owners, and, moreover, add thereto the spoils of the enemies' wealth, and so comfort them?

14. V. *After these things the Lord Jehovih founds a new heaven from the good elevated to Himself, and from the evil removed from Himself a new hell; and in both He establishes order, so that they may stand under His auspices, and under obedience to Him, to eternity.* It is written in *Isaiah:—*

Jehovah said, Behold I create new heavens and a new earth (lxv. 17);

and elsewhere in the same prophet:—

As the new heavens and the new earth, which I am about to make, shall stand before Me (lxvi. 22);

in the *Apocalypse:*—

I saw a new heaven and a new earth; the former heaven and the former earth have passed away (xxi. 1);

and in *Peter:*—

According to promise, we look for new heavens and a new earth, wherein justice shall dwell (2 *Epist.* iii. 13).

It has not hitherto entered into the mind of any one to suppose otherwise, than that by "heaven," in these places, is meant the visible heaven, that is, the whole firmament, together with the sun, moon and stars; and that by "earth," there, is meant the habitable earth, or the globe, and that these will perish at the day of the Last Judgment; when nevertheless by "heaven" there the angelic heaven is meant, and by "earth" the church. That by "earth" everywhere in the prophetic Word is meant the church, has been fully shown in the *Apocalypse Revealed* (n. 285). The reason why by "new heavens" and a "new earth" have been hitherto understood the visible heaven and the habitable earth, is because men have not known anything of the spiritual world, consequently not anything of the angelic heaven, nor anything of the prophetic sense, which carries and stores up nothing but spiritual things; and the spiritual meaning of "earth" is the church. When, indeed, the angels, inasmuch as they are spiritual, look down into the earth, they see nothing at all of it, but only the church with men.

15. When the Lord Jehovih founds a new heaven and a new church, He introduces order, so that they may stand under His auspices and under obedience to Him to eternity. This is because the angelic heaven and the church on the earth together constitute one body, whose soul and life is the Lord Jehovih, who is the Lord our Saviour. The whole angelic heaven together with the church also appears before the Lord as one man; and a man stands under the auspices of, and under obedience to his soul: thus the entire heaven together with the church, is under the auspices of, and under obedience to, the Lord; for the Lord is in them, and they are in the Lord

(*John* xiv. 20; xv. 4, 5; xvii. 23, 26); thus, He is the all in all there. But the order which the Lord induces on hell is such that all who are there may be diametrically opposite to all who are in heaven: whence it is evident that since the Lord rules heaven He also rules hell, and that He rules the latter by means of the former.

16. Moreover, the arrangement of all in the heavens and of all in the hells is most perfect. For every heaven that is founded by the Lord after the consummation of each church is made three-fold: it is made highest, middle, and lowest. Into the highest are elevated those who are in love to the Lord and in wisdom thence; into the middle those who are in spiritual love towards the neighbor and in intelligence thence; into the lowest those who are in spiritual-natural love towards the neighbor, which is called charity, and thence in the faith of the truths concerning God, and in a life according to the precepts of the Decalogue. These three heavens constitute three expanses, one above another, and they communicate with each other by the Divine influx from the Lord out of the sun of the spiritual world. In the deep below there are also three expanses, into which the hells are distinguished, between which in like manner there is provided a communication by means of an influx through the heavens from the Lord. By means of these communications there is effected a close and indissoluble conjunction of all things in the heavens, and of all things in the hells; but in the latter it is a conjunction of all the lusts of the love of evil, while in the heavens it is a conjunction of all the affections of the love of good. By virtue of that conjunction, heaven is like one Lord sitting upon a throne girt about with wreaths formed of precious stones of every kind; but hell is like one devil sitting upon a seat entwined with vipers, serpents and poisonous worms. From this orderly arrangement, induced on both, it follows that both stand under the auspices and under obedience to the Lord to eternity.

17. It is known, that, in order that anything may be perfect, there must be a trine in just order, one under another, and a communication between, and that this trine must constitute a one; no otherwise than as a pillar is a one, at the top of which is the capital, under this the smooth shaft, and under this again the pedestal. Such a trine is man: his highest part is the head, his middle part is the body, and his lowest the feet and soles. In this, every kingdom is like a man; there must be a king in it as the head, also administrators and officers as the body, and yeomanry with servants as feet and soles: in like manner in the church, there must be a filleted primate, parish priests, and curates under them. Nor does the world itself subsist without three things following in order, namely, morning, noon, and evening; as also the yearly spring, summer, and autumn; spring for the sowing of seeds, summer for their germination, and autumn for bringing forth fruit: but night and winter do not contribute to the stability of the world. [2] Now since every perfect thing must be a trine and cohere well together, in order to be a one, therefore each world, both spiritual and natural, consists and subsists from three atmospheres or elements; the first of which immediately encompasses the sun and is called aura; the second is under this and is called ether; and the third is under them both and is called air. In the natural world these three atmospheres are natural, and in themselves passive, because they proceed from a sun which is pure fire; but the three corresponding to them in the spiritual world are spiritual, and in themselves active, because they proceed from a sun which is pure love. [3] The angels of the heavens dwell in the regions of these three atmospheres; the angels of the highest heaven in the celestial aura, which immediately encompasses the sun where the Lord is; the angels of the middle heaven in the spiritual ether under the former; and the angels of the lowest heaven in the spiritual-natural air under those two. Thus are all the heavens co-established, from the first to this last which is being organized by the Lord at the present day. From these things it may be apprehended whence it is that by "three" in the Word is signified what is complete (see *Apocalypse Revealed*, n. 505, 875).

18. VI. *From this new heaven the Lord Jehovih derives and produces a new church on earth, which is effected by a revelation of truths from His mouth, or from His Word, and by inspiration.* It is written:—

John saw the holy city, New Jerusalem, descending from God out of heaven, prepared as a Bride adorned for her Husband (*Apoc.* xxi. 2).

By "the holy city, New Jerusalem," is meant the doctrine of the New Church, thus the church as to doctrine; and, by "Jerusalem descending from God, out of the new heaven," is meant that the true doctrine of the church is from no other source. That the doctrine descended, is because a church is a church from doctrine and according to it; without it, a church is no more a church than a man is a man without members, viscera and organs, or from the cutaneous covering alone, which only defines his external shape; nor any more than a house is a house without bed-chambers, dining rooms, and furniture within, thus from the walls and arched roof alone. It is similar with the church without doctrine. That "Jerusalem" signifies the church as to doctrine, may be seen proved from the Word in the work itself, *The True Christian Religion* (n. 782). From these things, it is manifest that the church on the earth is derived and produced by the Lord through the angelic heaven.

19. I will mention some strange things, which yet are not strange in heaven; they are as follow: (1) That the natural world could not exist except from the spiritual world; consequently, it could not subsist, inasmuch as subsistence is perpetual existence. (2) That the church cannot exist in man, unless its internal be spiritual and its external natural. A church purely spiritual does not exist, nor a church merely natural. (3) Consequently, that there cannot be raised up any church, nor anything of the church with man, without an angelic heaven, through which everything spiritual is derived and descends from the Lord. (4) Since therefore the spiritual and the natural thus make one, it follows that the one cannot exist and subsist without the other; the angelic heaven not without the church with man, nor the church with him without the angelic heaven; for, unless the spiritual flow into and terminate in the natural, and rest therein, it is like a prior without a posterior, thus like an efficient cause without an effect, and like an active without a passive, which would be like a bird perpetually flying in the air without any resting place on the earth. It is also like the mind of a man perpetually thinking and willing, without any organ of sense and motion in the body, to which it may descend and produce the ideas of its thought and bring into operation the efforts of its will. (5) These things are adduced, to the end that it may be perceived or known, that as the natural world cannot exist without the spiritual world, nor conversely the spiritual world without the natural world, so neither can there be a church on the earth unless there be an angelic heaven through which it may exist and subsist, nor conversely an angelic heaven unless there be a church on the earth. (6) The angels know this; on which account, they bitterly lament when the church on earth is desolated by falsities and consummated by evils; and then they compare the state of their life with drowsiness; for then heaven is to them as a seat withdrawn, and like a body deprived of feet; but when the church on the earth has been restored by the Lord, they compare the state of their life to wakefulness.

20. That the Lord derives and produces the New Church on earth through the New Heaven by means of a revelation of truths from His mouth, or from His Word, and by inspiration, will be shown in the section on the four churches in their order, especially on the Israelitish Church, and on the present Christian Church. It should be known that when hell has increased, and has passed over the great interstice or gulf fixed[1] between itself and heaven (*Luke* xvi. 26), and has raised up its back even to the confines of the heavens where the angels are, which came to pass during the interval of the vastation and consummation of the church, not any doctrine of the church could be conveyed by the Lord through heaven to the men of the earth. The reason is that man is then in the midst of satans; and satans envelop his head with their falsities, and inspire the delights of evil and the consequent pleasures of falsity, whereby all the light out of heaven is darkened, and all the agreeableness and pleasantness of truth is intercepted. [2] As long as this state continues, not any doctrine of truth and good out of heaven can be infused into man, because it is falsified; but after this tangled veil of falsities, or covering of the head by satans, has been taken away by the Lord, which is effected by the Last Judgment (of which above, in Article IV), then man is led in a freer and more spontaneous spirit to discard falsities and to receive truths. With those who adapt themselves, and suffer themselves to be led by the Lord, the doctrine of the New Heaven, which is the doctrine of truth and good, is afterwards conveyed down and introduced, like the morning dew falling from heaven to the earth, which opens the pores of plants, and sweetens their vegetable juices: and it is like the manna which fell in the mornings, and was in appearance:—

Like coriander seed, white, and in taste like a cake kneaded with honey (*Exod.* xvi. 31).

It is also like seasonable rain, which refreshes the newly-ploughed fields and causes germination; and it is like the fragrance exhaling from fields, gardens, and flowery plains, which the breast gladly and readily draws in with the air. But, still, the Lord does not compel, nor does He urge anyone against his will, as one does with whips a beast of burden; but He draws and afterwards continually leads him who is willing, in all appearance as though the willing man did goods and believed truths of himself, when yet it is from the Lord, who operates every genuine good of life and every genuine truth of faith in him.

21. VII. *This Divine work taken together is called redemption, without which no man can be saved, because not regenerated.* That the redemption accomplished by the Lord when He was in the world, was the subjugation of the hells, the arrangement of the heavens in order, and by these a preparation for a new spiritual church, may be seen in the work, *The True Christian Religion* (n. 115–117; and likewise from n. 118–133). But inasmuch as this is new, and has lain hidden for ages, like the wreck of a ship with its valuable wares at the bottom of the sea, and nevertheless the doctrine of redemption is as it were the treasury of all the spiritual riches, or the dogmas of the New Church, therefore, in the last section of this volume, the *mystery of redemption* shall be treated of, where the following propositions will be unfolded and presented in the light:—

I. *Deliverance from enemies is what in the Word is called redemption.*

II. *Consequently, it is a deliverance from evils and falsities; which, since they are from hell, are spiritual enemies; for they kill souls, as natural enemies do bodies*

III. *Hence it becomes evident that the first of the redemption accomplished by the Lord was the separation of the evil from the good, and the elevation of the good to Himself into heaven, and the removal of the evil from Himself into hell, for thus the good are freed from the evil. This first of redemption is the Last Judgment* (which has been treated of above, n. 10-13).

IV. *The second of redemption was the coördination of all things in the heavens, and the subordination of all things in hell, by which the good were still more distinctly separated and freed from the evil; and this is the new heaven and the new hell* (which has been treated of above, n. 14-17).

V. *The third of redemption was a revelation of truths out of the new heaven, and thereby the raising up and establishment of a new church on earth; by which means the good were still further separated and freed from the evil, and are separated and freed for the future* (this third has also been treated of above, n. 18-20).

VI. *The final cause of redemption was the possibility that the Lord, from His Divine omnipotence, might regenerate and thereby save man; for, unless a man be regenerated, he cannot be saved* (John iii. 3).

VII. *The regeneration of a man, inasmuch as it is a separation and deliverance from evils and falsities, is a particular redemption by the Lord, existing from His general redemption.*

VIII. *With those who are being regenerated, evils are first of all separated from goods, and this is similar to the judgment: afterwards, goods are collected together into one, and arranged in a heavenly form, and this is similar to the new heaven; and, lastly, a new church is implanted and produced thereby, the internal of which is heaven; and the external from the internal, consequently both together, with man, are called the church.*

IX. *All are redeemed, since all who reject the falsities of the former church, and receive the truths of the New Church, can be regenerated; but still the regenerated are properly the redeemed.*

X. *The goal of redemption, and the prize of the redeemed, is spiritual peace.*

XI. *A redemption has also been accomplished by the Lord at this day, because at this day is His Second Coming according to prophecy; by which, having been an eye-witness thereof, I have been made certain of the truth of the foregoing arcana.*

But these are only summaries, which must be unfolded one by one, and set forth in both spiritual and natural light, at the end of this volume, where the *mystery of redemption* is to be treated of.

22. Moreover, it will be proved in its own section in the following pages, that the Lord's passion of the cross was not redemption, but the means of the inmost union with the Divine of the Father, from which He came forth, and into which He returned. In the work, *The True Christian Religion* (n. 132, 133), to which this volume is an Appendix, I undertook to demonstrate that the belief that the passion of the cross is redemption itself, is a fundamental error of the present Christian Church; and that this error, together with the error concerning three Divine Persons from eternity, has perverted the whole church to such an extent, that there is not a vestige of what is spiritual remaining in it. This will also be further shown in the following pages; also, that those two falsities and impostures have been comparatively like impregnated butterflies flying about in the garden, which lay worm-producing eggs that being hatched out, entirely consume the leaves of the trees there; and further, that they have been like the quails from the sea let down upon the camp of the Israelites, owing to which, while they were eating, a great plague was brought upon the people; and this for the reason that they loathed and spurned the manna from heaven, by which, in the highest sense, is meant the Lord (*Num.* xi. 5, 6, 32–35; and *John* vi. 31, 32, 49–51, 58). And further, those two errors were like two fragments of soot, or shoemaker's blacking, dropped into generous wine, and shaken about in the glass, in consequence of which all the brightness, delightful fragrance, and fine flavor of the wine are changed into a black appearance, a disagreeable smell, and a nauseous taste.

PROPOSITION THE SECOND.

The Adamic, or Most Ancient Church of this Earth.

23. The world has hitherto believed that by "the creation of heaven and earth," in the first chapter of *Genesis*, is meant the creation of the universe, according to the letter; and by "Adam," the first man of this earth. The world could not believe otherwise, since the spiritual or internal sense of the Word has not been disclosed, nor, consequently, that by "creating heaven and earth" is meant to collect and found an angelic heaven from those who have departed the life in the world, and by this means to derive and produce a church on earth (as above, n. 18–20); and that by the names of persons, nations, territories, and cities, are meant such things as relate to heaven, and at the same time to the church: in like manner, therefore, by "Adam." That by "Adam," and by all those things which are related of him and his posterity in the first chapters of *Genesis*, are described the successive states of the Most Ancient Church, which are its rise or morning, its progression into light or day, its decline or evening, its end or night, and after this the Last Judgment upon it, and thereafter a new angelic heaven from the faithful, and a new hell from the unfaithful, according to the series of the progressions laid down in the preceding proposition, has been minutely explained, unfolded and demonstrated in the *Arcana Cœlestia* on *Genesis* and *Exodus*, the labor of eight years, published in London; which work being already in the world, nothing further is necessary than to recapitulate therefrom the universals respecting this Most Ancient Church, which will be cited in the present volume. [2] At the outset, however, some passages shall be adduced from the Word, by which it is proved, that by "creating" is there signified to produce and form anew, and properly to regenerate; which is the reason that regeneration is called a new creation, by which the whole heaven of angels and the whole church of men, exist, consist and subsist. That "creating" signifies this, is plainly manifest from these passages in the Word:—

Create in me a clean heart, O God; and renew a firm spirit in the midst of me (*Ps.* li. 10).

Thou openest the hand, they are filled with good; Thou sendeth forth the Spirit, they are created (*Ps.* civ. 28, 30).

The people that shall be created shall praise Jah (*Ps.* cii. 18).

Thus said Jehovah, thy Creator, O Jacob; thy Former, O Israel: Every one that is called by My Name, him have I created for My glory (*Isa.* xliii. 1, 7).

That they may see, know, attend and understand, that the hand of Jehovah hath done this, and the Holy One of Israel hath created it (*Isa.* xli. 20).

In the day that thou wast created, they were prepared; thou wast perfect in thy ways from the day that thou wast created, until perversity was found in thee (*Ezek.* xxviii. 13, 15).

These things are concerning the king of Tyre.

Jehovah that createth the heavens, that spreadeth abroad the earth, that giveth a soul unto the people upon it (*Isa.* xlii. 5; xlv. 12, 18).

Behold I create a new heaven and a new earth; be ye glad to eternity in that which I create: behold I am about to create Jerusalem an exultation (*Isa.* lxv. 17, 18).

As the new heavens and the new earth, which I am about to make, shall stand before Me (*Isa.* lxvi. 22).

I saw a new heaven and a new earth: the former heaven and the former earth are passed away (*Apoc.* xxi. 1).

According to promise, we look for new heavens and a new earth, in which justice shall dwell (2 *Peter* iii. 13).

From these passages it is now manifested what is spiritually meant in the first chapter of *Genesis*, by the verses:—

In the beginning God created the heaven and the earth; and the earth was "waste and empty" [1, 2].

The earth called "waste and empty," signifies that there was no longer any good of life nor any truth of doctrine with its inhabitants. That "wasteness" and "emptiness" signify the deprivation of those two essentials of the church, will be established in proposition IV of this volume, respecting the Israelitish Church, by a thousand passages from the Word: at present let the following in *Jeremiah* serve for some illustration:—

I saw the land, when, behold, it was vacant and empty; and I looked towards the heavens, when their light was not. Thus said Jehovah, The whole land shall be wasteness; for this shall the land mourn, and the heavens above shall be made black (iv. 23, 27, 28).

24. This church, like the rest, shall be treated of in the following order:—

I. *Its rise, or morning, which is its first state.*
II. *Its progression into light, or day, which is its second state.*
III. *Its decline, or evening, which is its third state, and is called vastation.*
IV. *Its end, or night, which is its fourth state, and is called consummation.*
V. *The separation of the evil from the good, which is the Last Judgment upon all who were of that church.*
VI. *The elevation of the good to God, of whom a new heaven is formed; and the removal of the evil from God, of whom is formed a new hell.*

That the four churches of this earth, of which we have treated above, have undergone these changes of state, will be shown in what follows; and lastly, that the church truly Christian, which succeeds those four at the present day, will never undergo consummation.

25. I. *The first state of this Most Ancient Church, or its rise and morning,* is described in the first chapter of *Genesis* by these words:—

God said, Let us make man in our image, after our likeness; and God created man in His own image; in the image of God created He him; male and female created He them (vers. 26, 27);

and also by these in the second chapter:—

Jehovah God formed man dust of the earth, and breathed into his nostrils the soul of lives; and man became a living soul (ver. 7).

That its rise, or morning, is described by his being made, or created, "in the image of God," is because every man, when he is first born and is an infant, interiorly is an "image of God;" for the faculty of receiving and of applying to himself those things which proceed from God, is implanted in him; and since exteriorly he is also formed "dust of the earth," and there is thence in him an inclination to lick that dust, like the serpent (*Gen.* iii. 14), therefore if he remains an external or natural man, and does not become at the same time internal or spiritual, he shatters the image of God, and puts on the image of the serpent which seduced Adam. But, on the other hand, the man who strives and labors to become an "image of

God," subdues the external man in himself, and interiorly in the natural becomes spiritual, thus spiritual-natural; and this is effected by a new creation, that is, regeneration by the Lord. Such a man is an "image of God," because he wills and believes that he lives from God, and not from himself: on the contrary, man is an image of the serpent, while he wills and believes that he lives from himself, and not from God. What is man but an "image of God," when he wills and believes that he is in the Lord and the Lord in him (*John* vi. 56, xiv. 20, xv. 4, 5, 7, xvii. 26), and that he can do nothing of himself (*John* iii. 27, xv. 5)? What is a man, but an "image of God," when, by new generation, he becomes a "son of God" (*John* i. 12, 13)? Who does not know that the image of the father is in the son? The rise, or morning, of this church is described by Jehovah God's "breathing into his nostrils the soul of lives," and by his thus "becoming a living soul," because by "lives," in the plural, are meant love and wisdom, and these two are essentially God; for, as far as a man receives and applies to himself those two essentials of life, which proceed continually from God, and flow continually into the souls of men, so far he becomes "a living soul;" for "lives" are the same as love and wisdom. Hence it is evident, that the rise and morning of the life of the men of the Most Ancient Church, who taken together are represented by "Adam," is described by those two shrines of life.

26. The "likeness of God," according to which man was made, is his being able to live, that is, to will, to love, and to intend, as also to think, to reflect, and to choose, in all appearance as from himself; consequently, in his being able to receive from God those things which are of love and those things which are of wisdom, and to reproduce them in a likeness from himself as God does; for God says:—

Behold the man was as one of us, in knowing good and evil (*Gen.* iii. 22);

for, without the faculty of receiving and reproducing those things which proceed into him from God, in all appearance as from himself, man would be no more a "living soul" than an oyster in its shell at the bottom of a stream, which is not in the least able to move itself out of its place. Nor would he be any more an "image of God" than a jointed statue of a man capable of motion by means of a handle, and of giving forth sound by being blown into; yea, the very mind of man, which is the same as his spirit, would actually be wind, air, or ether, according to the idea of the church at this day respecting spirit. For without the faculty of receiving and reproducing the things flowing in from God, altogether as from himself, he would not have anything of his own, or a proprium, except an imperceptible one, which is like the proprium of a lifeless piece of sculpture. But more about the image and likeness of God with man, may be seen, in a *Relation* in the preceding work, of which this is the *Appendix* (n. 48).

27. II. *The second state of this Most Ancient Church, or its progression into light and day,* is described in the second chapter of *Genesis,* by these words:—

God planted a garden in Eden at the east, and there He put the man whom He had formed, to till and keep it. And Jehovah made to spring forth every tree desirable to the sight, and good for food; the tree of life also in the midst of the garden, and the tree of the knowledge of good and evil. And a river went forth out of Eden to water the garden, which became into four heads, in the first of which was gold and the schoham[1] stone. And Jehovah God commanded the man, saying, Of every tree of the garden, eat; but of the tree of the knowledge of good and evil, eat not (verses 8–17).

The progression of this church into light, or day, is described by Adam's being placed in the garden of Eden, because by a "garden" is signified the church as to its truths and goods. That "there went forth out of Eden a river, which became into four heads, in the first of which was gold and the schoham stone," signifies that in that church there was the doctrine of good and truth; for a "river" signifies doctrine, "gold" its good, and "schoham stone" its truth. That "two trees were placed in that garden, the one of life, and the other of the knowledge of good and evil," was because the "tree of life" signifies the Lord, in whom and from whom is the life of heavenly love and wisdom, which in itself is eternal life; and the "tree of the knowledge of good and evil" signifies man, in whom is the life of infernal love, and thence insanity in the things of the church, which life regarded in itself is eternal death. That it was allowed "to eat of every tree of the garden," except of the "tree of the knowledge of good and evil," signifies free will in spiritual things; for all things in the garden signified spiritual things, for without free will in those a man can in no wise progress into light, that is, into the truths and goods of the church, and procure for himself life; for if he does not aim at and strive after this, he procures to himself death. [2] That a "garden" signifies the church as to its truths and goods, is from the correspondence of a tree with a man; for a tree in like manner as a man is conceived from seed, is put forth from the womb of the earth in like manner as a man from the womb of his mother; it grows in height in like manner, and propagates itself in branches as he in members; clothes itself with leaves and adorns itself with blossoms in like manner as a man does with natural and spiritual truths; and also produces fruits in like manner as a man does goods of use. Hence it is that in the Word a man is so often compared to a "tree," and the church to a "garden;" as in the following passages:—

Jehovah will set her desert like Eden, and her solitude like the garden of Jehovah (*Isa.* li. 3);

speaking of Zion, which signifies the church wherein God is worshiped according to the Word:—

Thou shalt be like a watered garden, and like a spring of waters, whose waters shall not lie (*Isa.* lviii. 11; *Jer.* xxxi. 12).

Here also it treats of the church:—

Thou art full of wisdom, and perfect in beauty; thou wast in Eden the garden of God; every precious stone was thy covering (*Ezek.* xxviii. 12, 13).

This is respecting Tyre, by which is signified the church, as to the knowledges of truth and good:—

How good are thy habitations, O Israel; as valleys they are planted, and as gardens beside the river (*Num.* xxiv. 5, 6);

by "Israel" is signified the spiritual church; but by "Jacob" the natural church in which is the spiritual.

Nor was any tree in the garden of God equal to him in beauty; so that all the trees of Eden, in the garden of God, envied him (*Ezek.* xxxi. 8, 9).

It is here speaking of Egypt and Assyria, by which, where mentioned in a good sense, the church is signified as to knowledges and perceptions.

To him that overcometh will I give to eat of the tree of life, which is in the midst of the paradise of God (*Apoc.* ii. 7).

[3] From the correspondence of a garden with the church, it comes to pass that everywhere in the heavens gardens appear producing leaves, flowers and fruits, according to the states of the church with the angels; and it has been told me that in some of the gardens there, trees of life are seen in the middle parts, and trees of the knowledge of good and evil in the boundaries, as a sign that they are in free-will in spiritual things. The church is oftentimes described in the Word by a "garden," a "field," and a "sheepfold;" by a "garden," from the trees, as mentioned above; by a "field," from its crops, wherewith man is nourished; by a "sheepfold," from the sheep, by which are meant the faithful and useful.

28. In the work itself named *The True Christian Religion*, it has been shown that the two trees, the one of "life," and the other of the "knowledge of good and evil," being placed in the garden of Eden, signified that free-will in spiritual things was given to man (n. 466–469); to which must be added that without such free-will man would not be man, but only a figure and effigy; for his thought would be without reflection, consequently without judgment, and thus in the Divine things which are of the church, he would have no more power of turning himself, than a door without a hinge,[1] or, with a hinge, fastened with a steel bolt; and his will would be without decision, consequently no more active with respect to justice or injustice, than the stone upon a tomb under which lies a dead body. That man's life after death, together with the immortality of his soul, is owing to the gift of that free-will, and that this is the "likeness of God," has been proved in the work itself, as also above. [2] Yea, man, that is, his mind, without that would be like a sponge which imbibes water in great abundance but is not able to discharge it, in consequence of which both would decompose, the water into corruption, and the sponge into slime. In the same manner the church with him would not be a church, and thus a temple wherein the worship of God is performed: it would be like the den of some wild beast under the root of a lofty tree which rocks itself to and fro over its head, except only that it would be able to take something therefrom, and apply itself to some other use besides lying in tranquillity under it. Moreover without free will in spiritual things, man would be more blind in all and each of the things of the church, than a bird of night in the light of day, but more sharp-sighted [in respect to falsities] than that bird in the darkness of night: for he would shut his eyelids, and contract their sight against the truths of faith; but he would raise his eyelids, open his eyes, and dilate their sight like the eagle, to the falsities of faith. Free-will in spiritual things, is from this, that man walks and lives his life in the midst between heaven and hell; and that heaven operates in him from above, but hell from beneath; and that the option is given to a man of turning himself either to higher things or to lower things, thus, either to the Lord or to the Devil.

29. III. *The third state of the church, which is its decline and evening, and is called vastation,* is described in the third chapter of *Genesis* by these words:—

The serpent became more subtle than any wild animal of the field, which Jehovah God had made. He said to the woman, Yea, wherefore hath God said, Ye shall not eat of every tree of the garden? And when the woman said unto the serpent, Of the fruit of the tree we may eat; only of the fruit of the tree which is in the midst, God hath said, Ye shall not eat of it, neither shall ye touch it, lest ye die; the serpent said, Ye shall not die; for God doth know that in the day wherein ye shall eat thereof, your eyes shall be opened, and ye shall be as God, knowing good and evil. The woman therefore saw that the tree was good for food, and that it was pleasant to the eyes, and to be desired to give understanding; therefore she took of the fruit thereof, and did eat; and she gave to her husband with her, and he did eat (vers. 1–6).

The decline from light to the shade of evening, that is, the falling away from wisdom and integrity, consequently, the state of vastation of this church, is described by these words, because man was made a "likeness of God" (by which is signified, in the entire appearance that he thinks those things which are of wisdom, and wills those things that are of love, from himself, as God does, see above, n. 26), he believed the serpent's words, that if he should eat of that tree he would become as God, and thus also be God in knowing good and evil. By this "tree" is signified the natural man separated from the spiritual, which, when left to itself, does not believe otherwise.

[2] Every man has a natural mind and a spiritual mind, distinct from each other like two stories of one house connected by stairs; in the upper story of which dwell the master and mistress with their children, but in the lower the men-servants and maid-servants, with other helpers. The spiritual mind in man from birth even to early childhood is closed, but after that first age it is opened step by step; for there is given to every man from birth the faculty, and afterwards the power, of procuring for himself steps by which he may ascend and speak with the master and mistress, and afterwards descend and execute their commands. This power is given him through the endowment of free will in spiritual things. Nevertheless no one can ascend to the upper story, by which is meant the spiritual mind, unless he eat of the trees of life in the garden of God. For by eating of these a man is enlightened and made whole, and conceives faith; and through the nourishment of their fruits he acquires the conviction that all good is from the Lord, who is the tree of life, and not the smallest portion from man; and yet by abiding together and operating together, hence by the Lord's being in him and he in the Lord, he must do good of himself, but still be in the belief and confidence that it is not from himself but from the Lord. [3] If a man believe otherwise, he does what appears like good, in which there is evil inwardly, because there is merit; and this is eating of the trees of the knowledge of good and evil, among which dwells the serpent, in the dreadful persuasion that he is as God, or else that there is no God, but that Nature is what is called God, and that he is composed of the elements thereof. Furthermore, those eat of the trees of the knowledge of good and evil who love themselves and the world above all things; but those eat of the trees of life who love God above all things and the neighbor as themselves. Those also eat of the trees of the knowledge of good and evil who hatch out canons for the church from their own intelligence, and afterwards confirm them by the Word; but on the other hand those who procure for themselves canons for the church by means of the Word, and afterwards confirm them by intelligence, eat of the trees of life. Those also who teach truths from the Word and live wickedly eat of the trees of the knowledge of good and evil; but those eat of

the trees of life who live well and teach from the Word. Universally speaking, all eat of the trees of the knowledge of good and evil who deny the Divinity of the Lord and the holiness of the Word, inasmuch as the Lord is the Tree of Life and the Word, from whom the church is a "garden in Eden at the east."

30. The spiritual man is an erect man, who with his head looks to heaven above him and about him, and treads the earth with the soles of his feet. But the natural man separated from the spiritual is either like a man bent downwards, who nods with his head, and continually looks at the earth, and then at the steps of his own feet; or, he is like an inverted man, who walks on the palms of his hands, and lifts up his feet towards heaven, and by shakings and clappings of these performs worship. The spiritual man is like a rich man, who has a palace in which are dining-rooms, bed chambers, and banquet-halls, the walls of which are continuous windows of crystalline glass,¹ through which he sees the gardens, fields, flocks, and herds which also belong to him, and with the sight and use of which he is daily delighted. But the natural man, separated from the spiritual is also like a rich man, who has a palace containing chambers, the walls of which are continuous planks of rotten wood, which sheds around a fatuous light, wherein appear images of pride from the love of self and the world, like molten images of gold, in the middle, and of silver at the sides, before which he bends the knee like an idolater. Again, the spiritual man, in himself, is actually like a dove as to gentleness, like an eagle as to the sight of his mind, like a flying bird of paradise as to progression in spiritual things, and like a peacock as to adornment from spiritual things. But on the contrary the natural man separated from the spiritual is like a hawk pursuing a dove, like a dragon devouring the eyes of an eagle, like a fiery flying serpent at the side of a bird of paradise, and like a horned owl beside a peacock. These comparisons are made that they may be as optical glasses whereby the reader may more closely contemplate what the spiritual man is in itself, and the natural man in itself. But the case is altogether different, when the spiritual man by its spiritual light and spiritual heat is inwardly in the natural; then both constitute one, just like effort in motion, and will (which is living effort) in action, and like appetite in taste, and like the sight of the mind in the sight of the eye, and still more evidently like the perception of a thing in cognition, and the thought of it in speech.

31. IV. *The fourth state of this church, which was its end or night and is called consummation,* is also described by these words, in the third chapter of *Genesis:*—

Jehovah God called unto the man, and said unto him, Where art thou? and he said, I heard Thy voice in the garden, therefore I was afraid. Then Jehovah said, Hast thou eaten of the tree, whereof I commanded thee that thou shouldest not eat of it? And the man said, The woman whom thou hast given with me, she gave me of the tree, and I did eat. And Jehovah God said unto the woman, Wherefore hast thou done this? And the woman said, The serpent deceived me, and I did eat. Then Jehovah God cursed the serpent, and afterwards the woman, and after her the man. After which, Jehovah God sent the man forth from the garden of Eden to till the earth from whence he was taken (vers. 9-23).

From the literal or historical sense of the description of Adam's life, it is manifest that he was cursed because he believed the serpent that he should be as God; and he who believes this, at length does not acknowledge God. And as the natural man separated from the spiritual is in such a belief in heart, however differently he may talk with his mouth, therefore after he from spiritual became natural, this latter was cursed and it was cursed as to its sensual, its voluntary, and its intellectual; for its sensual is signified by the "serpent," its voluntary by the "woman," and its intellectual by the "man:" these three were cursed, because the one follows the other. (In the *Arcana Cœlestia,* every single expression, and every meaning of the expressions, are laid open by the spiritual sense, which has been revealed to me by the Lord; which explanation, being published, may be consulted.)

32. After this curse, the fourth state of this church, which was its state of night in spiritual things, and is called consummation, is described by the expulsion of the man from the garden "to till the ground from whence he was taken," by which is meant that the innocence, integrity, and wisdom, in which he was while he was spiritual, were lost, consequently that he was cast down from heaven, that is, dissociated from the angels, just as we read of the "dragon":—

> The great dragon was cast down, the old serpent, which is called the Devil and Satan, was cast down out of heaven, where he fought with Michael and his angels, to the earth; and his angels were cast down with him (*Apoc.* xii. 9).

33. What person of sound mind is there who cannot see, that, by those things which are related of Adam are not meant any states of the first-formed man, but states of the church? As, for example, that God placed two trees in the midst of the garden, from the eating of one of which man had eternal life, and from the other of which he had eternal death; and that He made the latter "good for food, pleasant to the eyes, and to be desired for giving understanding" (*Gen.* iii. 6), thus as if it were to fascinate their souls; also, that he admitted the serpent, and permitted it to speak deceitful words to the woman in the presence of her husband who was the image and likeness of God, and suffered them to be ensnared by its flatteries and craft; as also why He did not provide, because He foresaw that they, and the whole human race from them, should not fall into the damnation of His curse; for we read in the orthodox books of Christians:—

> That, in consequence of this original sin, "in place of the lost image of God, there is in man a most inward, most wicked, most profound, inscrutable, ineffable corruption of his whole nature, and of all his powers," and that it is the root of all actual evils (*Form. Concord.*, p. 640);

and that God the Father averted that universal damnation from His face, and sent His Son into the world, who might take it on Himself, and thus appease Him; besides many other things which are inconsistent with God in the sight of everyone. [2] Who, from the particulars above-mentioned, understood in their historical sense, would not with reason conclude, to use comparisons, that it would be like a person who gives his dependent a most fruitful field, and in it digs a pit, which he covers over with boards that fall inwards at the touch of a hand or foot; and, in the midst, places upon a stand a harlot clothed in purple and scarlet, holding in her hand a golden cup (like her in the *Apocalypse*, xvii. 4), who, by her blandishments allures the man to herself, and so brings it to pass that he falls into the pit and is drowned? Would it not, indeed, be like one who gives a present to his friend of a luxuriant field of grain, and in the midst thereof conceals snares, and sends out a siren who, with the allurement of song and of a sweet voice, entices him to that place, and causes him to be entangled in the snare, from which he is unable to extricate his foot? Yea, to use a further comparison, it would be like a person who should introduce a noble guest into his house in which there are two dining rooms, and tables in each of them, at one of which are seated angels, and at the other evil spirits, on which latter table are cups of sweet but poisoned wine, and dishes on which are preparations of food containing aconite; and who should permit the evil spirits there to represent the revels of Bacchus, and the antics of buffoons, and entice them to those goblets and banquets. [3] But, my friend, the things related of Adam, of the garden of God, and of the two trees therein, appear under quite a different aspect when spiritually comprehended, that is, unfolded by the spiritual sense; then it is clearly seen that, by "Adam," as a type, is meant the Most Ancient Church; and the successive states of that church are described by the vicissitudes of his life. For a church in the beginning is like a man created anew, who has a natural and a spiritual mind, and by degrees from spiritual becomes natural, and at length sensual, who believes nothing but what the senses of the body dictate. And such a man appears in heaven like a person sitting on a beast which turns its head back, and with its teeth bites, tears, and mangles the man sitting upon it. But the truly spiritual man appears in heaven also like a person sitting on a beast, but on a gentle one, which he governs with a gentle rein and also with a nod.

34. V. *The fifth state of this church was the separation of the good from the evil, which was the Last Judgment on all who were of that church.* This state is described by the "flood," in which all the wicked who remained perished; and by "Noah and his sons," by whom are meant all the good that were saved. The end of the Most Ancient Church, represented by "Adam," is described in the sixth chapter of *Genesis* by these words:—

When Jehovah saw that the wickedness of man was multiplied in the world, and moreover every imagination of his heart only evil every day, it repented Jehovah that He had made man on the earth. Therefore Jehovah said, I will blot out man whom I have created from upon the faces of the earth : only Noah found grace in the eyes of Jehovah (vers. 5–8).

But the Last Judgment upon them is described by "the flood." It is described by a "flood" for the reason that "waters" in the Word signify truths, and in the opposite sense falsities. Truths are signified by the waters of a fountain, the waters of a river, the waters of rain, and by the waters of the washings in time past, and the waters of baptism at this day. That correspondence arises from the circumstance that truths purify man's soul from uncleanness as waters do his body; hence they are called "living waters." But in the opposite sense, by "waters" are signified falsities; but by impure waters, such as those of marshes, malodorous cisterns, urine, and sewage, in general by all hurtful and death-producing waters, therefore also by waters from an inundation of which man dies, consequently by the Noahian flood. [2] That falsities in a mass are described by "inundations," may be evident from the following passages:—

Jehovah[1] is causing to come up upon them the waters of the river (*Euphrates*) strong and many ; it shall pass through Judah, it shall inundate, it shall pass through, it shall reach even to the neck (*Isa.* viii. 7, 8).

By the "waters of the river Euphrates," are signified reasonings from falsities, because by Assyria, whose river it was, reasoning is signified.

The spirit of Jehovah, like an inundating stream, shall divide in two even to the neck, to sift the nations with the sieve of vanity (*Isa.* xxx. 28, 30).

By "an inundating river" here in like manner is signified reasoning from falsities.

Behold waters are rising up out of the north, which are like an inundating stream, and shall inundate the land and the fulness thereof (*Jer.* xlvii. 2).

Here the Philistines are treated of, by whom are meant those who are not in charity, and hence not in truths; the falsities of these are signified by "the waters coming up from the north," and the devastation of the church in consequence thereof, by "an inundating stream that shall inundate the land and the fulness thereof;" "the land" is the church, and its "fulness" all things of it.

Say unto those who daub what is unfit, There shall be an inundating rain, in which hail-stones shall fall upon you (*Ezek.* xiii. 11, 13).

The "daubing of what is unfit" is the confirmation of falsity, and "hail-stones" are falsities.

In an overrunning inundation He shall make a consummation of the place thereof, and thick darkness shall pursue His enemies (*Nah.* i. 8).

By "the inundation" which shall consummate, is signified the falsification of truth, and by "thick darkness," truths themselves in the night.

Ye have said, We have made a covenant with death, and with hell have we made a vision; when the scourge of inundation shall pass through, it shall not come unto us; we have made a lie our trust, and in falsity we will hide (*Isa.* xxviii. 15).

Here "inundation" manifestly stands for destruction by falsities; for it is said that they placed confidence in "a lie," and that they would hide in "falsity."

After sixty-two weeks shall Messiah be cut off, but not for Himself; then the people of the Prince that shall come shall destroy the city and the sanctuary, so that the end thereof shall be with an inundation even to desolations (*Dan.* ix. 26).

[3] These things are concerning the Christian Church that was to come, in which the worship of the Lord would perish; which is meant by "Messiah shall be cut off, but not for Himself": that it would perish by falsifications, is meant by "the end thereof shall be with an inundation even to desolations;" "desolation" is that falsification. Hence it is that after the Lord spoke of "the abomination of desolation foretold by Daniel the prophet," and of the "consummation of the age" thereby, He said, that:—

His coming would be as in the days when the flood came, and took them all away (*Matt.* xxiv. 15, 39).

The drowning of Pharaoh and the Egyptians in the sea Suph (*Exod.* xiv.), means in the spiritual sense destruction by falsities, has been demonstrated in the *Arcana Cœlestia*, in the explanation of that chapter.

35. Since the churches in the Christian world, both the Roman Catholic Church and those separated from it, which are named after their leaders, Luther, Melancthon, and Calvin, derive all sin from Adam and his transgression, it is permissible to subjoin here something about the sources whence sins are inherited; for these sources are as many as there are fathers and mothers in the world. That inclinations, aptitudes, and propensities to evils are derived from these, is manifest in light from the testimonies of experience, and also from the assent of reason. Who does not know, from the collective suffrages of experience, that there is a general likeness of minds, and hence of manners and countenances, from parents in the children and children's children, even to a certain posterity? Who cannot thence infer that original sins are from them? The notion suggested to every one, when he looks at the countenances and manners of brothers and relatives in families, causes him to know and acknowledge this. [2] What reason, then, is there for deducing the origin of all evils from Adam and his seed? Is there not equal reason for deducing it from parents? Does not the seed of these similarly propagate itself? To deduce from Adam's seed alone the allurements from which and according to which the spiritual forms of the minds of all men in the universe exist, would be like deriving birds of every wing from one egg, also beasts of every nature from one seed, and trees of every kind of fruit from one root. Is there not an infinite variety of men? one like a sheep, another like a wolf? one like a kid, another like a panther? one like a tamed carriage horse before a carriage, another like an untamable wild ass before it? one like a playful calf, another like a voracious tiger? and so on. Whence has each his peculiar disposition but from his father and his mother? Why then from Adam? by whom nevertheless is described in a representative type the first church of this earth, as has been already shown? Would not this be like deriving from one stock deeply hidden in the earth a plantation of trees of every kind and use, and from a single plant shrubs of every degree of value? Would that not also be like deriving light from the darkness of the ages and of histories, and like unravelling the thread of a knot that cannot be untied? Why not rather from Noah, "who walked with

God" (*Gen.* vi. 9), and " whom God blessed" (*Gen.* ix. 1), and from whom alone, surviving with his three children, "the whole earth was overspread"? (*Gen.* ix. 19.) Would not the hereditary qualities of the generations from Adam be extirpated, as if drowned by a flood? [3] But, my friend, I will open the true source of sins. Every evil is conceived of the Devil as a father, and is born of atheistical faith as a mother; and on the other hand, every good is conceived of the Lord as a father, and is born of saving faith in Him as a mother. The generations of all goods in their infinite varieties among men are from no other origin than from the marriage of the Lord and the church; and, on the contrary, the generations of all evils among them in their varieties, are from no other origin than from the intercourse of the Devil with a profane congregation. Who does not know, or may not know, that a man must be regenerated by the Lord, that is, created anew, and that so far as this is effected so far he is in goods? Hence this follows: that so far as a man is unwilling to be generated anew or created anew, so far he takes up and retains the evils implanted in him from his parents. This is what lies concealed in the first precept of the Decalogue:—

I am a zealous God, visiting the iniquity of the fathers upon the sons, upon the third and upon the fourth generation of them that hold Me in hatred, and doing mercy unto thousands who love Me and do My commandments (*Exod.* xx. 5, 6; *Deut.* v. 9, 10).

36. VI. *The sixth state of the men of this church, which was the elevation of the faithful to God after the Last Judgment, from whom a new heaven was formed, and the removal of the unfaithful from God from whom a new hell was formed.* In the preceding propositions (from n. 10–13, and from n. 14–17), it was explained that after consummation, a Last Judgment was executed upon all who were of the four churches above named, and after this a new heaven and a new hell formed from them, and thus that there have been in this earth four judgments upon its inhabitants, and four heavens and hells formed from them; and it has been granted me to know, that both those heavens and those hells are so entirely separated from each other, that one can by no means pass out of his own into that of another. All these heavens have been described in the work on *Conjugial Love*; and, as the spiritual origin of love truly conjugial is from no other source than the marriage of the Lord and the church, thus from love of the Lord towards the church and of the church to the Lord (as was shown in that work from n. 116–131); and, as the most ancient people were in both these loves so long as they retained in themselves the image of God, therefore, I will transcribe from that work the following things respecting that heaven, to which I was at the time then granted admission; which are as follow:—

37. "Once when I was meditating on conjugial love, the desire seized my mind of knowing what that love had been with those who lived in the Golden Age, and what it was afterwards in the succeeding ones called Silver, Copper and Iron. And, as I knew that all who lived well in those ages are in the heavens, I prayed to the Lord that it might be permitted me to converse with them and be instructed.

"And, lo! an angel stood by me, and said, ' I am sent by the Lord to be your guide and companion; and first I will lead and accompany you to those who lived in the first era or Age, which is called the Golden.' (The Golden Age is the same as the age of the Most Ancient Church, which is meant by 'the head of good gold,' on the statue seen by Nebuchadnezzar in a dream (*Dan.* ii. 32), of which we have spoken before.) The angel said, 'The way to them is difficult; it lies through a dense forest, which no one can traverse unless a guide be given him by the Lord.'

[2] " I was in the spirit, and girded myself for the way; and we turned our faces to the east; and in going along, I saw a mountain, whose summit towered beyond the region of the clouds. We crossed a great desert, and reached a forest crowded with various kinds of trees, and dark by reason of the density of them, of which the angel informed me beforehand. But that forest was intersected by many narrow paths. The angel said that these were so many windings of error, and that unless the eyes were opened by the Lord, and the olive-trees girt about with vine tendrils seen, and the steps directed from olive-tree to olive-tree, the traveller would stray into Tartarus.¹ This forest is of such a nature, to the end that the approach may be guarded; for no other nation but a primeval one dwells on that mountain.

[3] "After we entered the forest, our eyes were opened, and we saw here and there olive-trees entwined with vines, from which hung bunches of grapes of a dark-blue color, and the olive-trees were arranged in perpetual circles; wherefore, we circled around and around according as they came into view; and at length we saw a grove of lofty cedars, and some eagles on their branches. When he saw these, the angel said, 'Now we are on the mountain, not far from its summit.'

"And we went on, and lo! behind the grove was a circular plain, where male and female lambs were feeding, which were forms representative of the state of innocence and peace of those on the mountain.

"We passed through this grove,[1] and lo! there were seen many thousands of tabernacles to the front and on each side, in every direction, as far as the eye could reach. And the angel said, 'Now we are in the camp where dwell the armies of the Lord Jehovih, for so they call themselves and their habitations. These most ancient people, while they were in the world, dwelt in tabernacles; for which reason they also dwell in them now.' But I said, 'Let us bend our way to the south, where the wiser of them dwell, that we may meet some one with whom we may enter into conversation.'

[4] "On the way, I saw at a distance three boys and three girls sitting at the door of their tabernacle; but as we drew near, they were seen as men and women of a medium height. And the angel said, 'All the inhabitants of this mountain appear at a distance like infants, because they are in the state of innocence, and infancy is the appearance of innocence.'

"On seeing us, these men ran towards us, and said, 'Whence are you, and how have you come hither? Your faces are not of the faces of those belonging to this mountain.'

"But the angel replied, and told the means by which we obtained access through the wood, and the reason of our coming.

"On hearing this, one of the three men invited and introduced us into his tabernacle. The man was clothed in a mantle of a hyacinthine color, and a tunic of white wool; and his wife was dressed in a crimson robe, and under it, had a tunic about the breast of fine embroidered linen.

[5] "But, since there was in my thought the desire of knowing about the marriages of the most ancient people, I looked at the husband and the wife by turns, and observed as it were a unity of their souls in their faces; and I said, 'You two are one.'

"And the man answered, 'We are one; her life is in me, and mine in her. We are two bodies, but one soul. There is between us a union like that of the two tents in the breast, which are called the heart and the lungs; she is the substance of my heart, and I am her lungs; but because by *heart* we here mean love, and by *lungs* wisdom (we understand the latter by the former on account of their correspondence) she is the love of my wisdom, and I am the wisdom of her love. Hence, as you said, there is the appearance of the unity of souls in our faces. Hence, it is as impossible to us here to look upon the wife of a companion in lust, as it is to look at the light of our heaven from the shade of Tartarus.'

"And the angel said to me, 'You hear now the speech of these angels, that it is the speech of wisdom, because they speak from causes.'

[6] "After this conversation, I saw a great light on a hill among the tabernacles, and I asked, 'Whence is that light?'

"He said, 'From the sanctuary of our tabernacle of worship.'

"And I enquired whether it was allowed to approach; and he said that it was allowed. Then I drew near, and saw the tabernacle without and within, exactly according to the description like the Tabernacle which was built for the sons of Israel in the desert, the form of which was shown to Moses on Mount Sinai (*Exod.* xxv. 40; xxvi. 30). I also asked, 'What is there within its sanctuary, whence there is so great a light?'

"And he answered, 'There is a tablet, on which is written, *The covenant between the Lord Jehovih and Heaven.*' He said no more.

"Then I also questioned them about the *Lord Jehovih*, whom they worship; and I said, 'Is He not God the Father, the Creator of the universe?'

"And they replied, 'He is; but we by the *Lord Jehovih*, understand Jehovah in His Human; for we are not able to look upon Jehovah in His inmost Divinity, except through His Human.' And then they explained what they meant, and also what at this day they mean, by:—

The seed of the woman trampling the serpent's head (*Gen.* iii. 15);

namely, that the Lord Jehovih would come into the world, and redeem and save all who believed in Him, and who hereafter should believe.

"When we had finished this conversation, the man ran to his tabernacle, and returned with a pomegranate, in which was an abundance of golden seeds, which he presented to me, and I brought it away: this was a sign that we had been with those who lived in the Golden Age." [See the work on *Conjugial Love*, n. 75.] For an account of the heavens of the remaining churches, which succeeded the Most Ancient in their order, see in the same work on *Conjugial Love* (n. 76–82).

38. The hell of those who were from the Most Ancient Church, is more atrocious than all other hells. It consists of those who in the world believed themselves to be as God, according to the deceitful utterance of the serpent (*Gen.* iii. 5); and those are deeper in that hell who, from the fantasy that God had transfused His Divinity into men, persuaded themselves that they altogether were gods, and so that there was no longer a God in the universe. In consequence of that direful persuasion, a stinking smoke is exhaled from that hell, which infects the adjacent places with so baleful a contagion, that when anyone approaches, he is at first seized with such a mad delirium, that presently, after some convulsive struggles, he seems to himself to be in the agonies of death. I saw a certain one, in the vicinity of that place, lying as it were dead; but, on being removed thence, he revived. That hell lies in the middle region at the south, surrounded with ramparts, and on which stand some who shout out in a loud stentorian voice, "Approach no nearer." I have heard from the angels who are in the heaven above that hell, that the evil demons there appear like serpents twisted into inextricable folds, which is a consequence of their vain devices and incantations, by which they deluded the simple into admitting that they are gods, and that there is no God beside them. The ancients, who wove all things into fables, meant these by the "giants," who besieged the camp of the gods, and whom Jupiter cast down by his thunderbolts and thrust under the fiery mountain Etna, and who were called "Cyclopses." They also called the hells of these, "Tartarus," and the "pools of Acheron;" and the deeps there, "Styx," and those who dwelt there, "Lernæan Hydras," and so forth.

PROPOSITION THE THIRD.

The Noachian, or Ancient Church of this earth.

39. Since every church is three-fold, inmost or celestial, middle or spiritual, and external or natural, therefore Noah had three sons; and by "Shem" is signified the inmost or celestial church, by "Japheth" the middle or spiritual church, and by "Ham" the external or natural church. But there is not room to describe here in whom the first church is, and in whom the second and third, as also what their quality is in themselves, or in relation to one another: for there are highest, middle, and lowest heavens, to which those three degrees of the church correspond. Moreover, this Noachian, or Ancient Church, was diffused throughout Asia, especially into Syria, Mesopotamia, Assyria, Chaldea, the land of Canaan and the parts adjacent, Philistia, Egypt, Tyre, Sidon, Nineveh, and also into Arabia and Ethiopia, and in course of time into Great Tartary, and thence downward as far as to the Black Sea, and thence again into all the countries of Africa. That the nations in every part of the earth have been in worship from some religion is known; and religion cannot exist except by some *revelation*, and by the propagation thereof from nation to nation; as may be seen in the preceding work, *The True Christian Religion* (n. 273–276); where, also, it was shown, that, prior to the Israelitish Word, there was a Word, which in process of time was lost, but from the Divine Providence of the Lord is still preserved in Great Tartary, from which is their Divine worship, even to the present day (see also n. 264–266, and n. 279, of the said work).

40. Who can deny that the universe was created for the sake of the human race, in order that from it an angelic heaven might be formed, wherein God might dwell in the dominion of His glory? To promote and accomplish this end, what mediate cause is there but religion? And what else is religion than walking with God? Religion also is like a seed producing just and true desires, and judgments and acts therefrom, in spiritual things, and by means of these in moral things, and by means of both the latter and the former in civil things. In order, therefore, that it may be known what is the quality of the man who has religion, and what of him who has not religion, it shall be stated. The man who has religion, in *spiritual things*, is like a pelican[1] nourishing its young with its own blood; but the man who has not religion, in those things is like a vulture in a state of starvation devouring its own offspring. The man who has religion, in *moral things*, is like a turtle-dove in the nest with its mate, sitting on its eggs or young; but the man who has not religion, in these things is like a rapacious hawk in the coop of a dove-cot. The man who has religion, in *political things*, is like a swan flying with a bunch of grapes in its mouth; but he who has not religion, in these matters is like a basilisk with a poisonous herb in its mouth. The man who has religion, in *judiciary matters* is like a tribune riding on a spirited horse; but the man who has not religion, in those things is like a serpent in the desert of Arabia biting its tail in its mouth, and hurling itself, in that hoop, upon a horse to coil itself about the rider. The man who has religion, in all *other civil affairs*, is like a prince the son of a king who exhibits the marks of charity and the graces of truth; but the man who has not religion, is like the three-headed dog Cerberus at the entrance of the court of Pluto, foaming forth aconite from its triple mouth.

41. The successive states of this church, which are its rise or morning, progression into light or day, vastation or evening, and consummation or night, it is not permitted to follow up with a description in the same manner as we before described the states of the Most Ancient Church, because the states of that church cannot be so collected from our Word; for the posterity of Noah, through his three sons, is recorded only in a summary, in one or two pages; and moreover that church was spread through many kingdoms, and in each kingdom it varied, and hence that church underwent and ran through the states named in a different manner.

[2] *The first and second state thereof* in the regions round about the Jordan and about Egypt, was like the "garden of Jehovah," is evident from these passages:—

> The plain of Jordan was like the garden of Jehovah, like the land of Egypt, where thou comest unto Zoar (*Gen.* xiii. 10).

And likewise Tyre from these:—

> Thou prince of Tyre, full of wisdom, and perfect in beauty. Thou hast been in the garden of God; every precious stone was thy covering. Thou was perfect in thy ways, from the day that thou wast created, until perversity was found in thee (*Ezek.* xxviii. 12–15).

That Assyria was like a "cedar in Lebanon," from these:—

> Behold, Assyria is a cedar in Lebanon, beautiful in branch, exalted in height; all the birds of the heavens built their nests in his branches, and under his branches did every beast of the field bring forth its young, and in his shadow dwelt all great nations: no tree in the garden of God was equal to him in beauty, and all the trees of Eden, that were in the garden of God, envied him (*Ezek.* xxxi. 3–9).

That wisdom flourished in Arabia, appears from the queen of Sheba's journey to Solomon (1 *Kings* x. 1–13); also from the three wise men who came to the new-born Jesus, a star going before them (*Matt.* ii. 1–12).

[3] *The third and fourth states of that church*, which were its vastation and consummation, are described here and there in the Word, both in its historic and prophetic parts. The consummation of the nations round about the Jordan, or round about the land of Canaan, is described by the destruction of Sodom, Gomorrah, Admah and Zeboim (*Gen.* xiv. and xix.); the consummation of the church of the nations within the Jordan, or in the land of Canaan, is described in *Joshua* and in the *Book of Judges* by the expulsion of some and the extermination of others. The consummation of that church in Egypt, is described by the drowning of Pharaoh and the Egyptians in the sea Suph (*Exod.* xiv.). And so on.

42. It is certain that this Ancient Church was a representative church, which in visible and natural types and signs, figured forth the invisible and spiritual things of the church which was yet to come, when Jehovah Himself would manifest Himself in a natural human form, and by this means procure for Himself entrance to men, and for men access to Himself, and thus should divest Himself of types, and institute a church with precepts which should lead all who believe in Him as Man, and keep His commandments, by a short way to heaven, the dwelling-place of His Divinity. But, because this Ancient Church, typical of that which was to come, turned the representative correspondences into magic and idolatry, and thus into things infernal, Jehovah raised up the Israelitish Church, in which He restored the primitive types, which were heavenly: such types were all the tabernacles, feasts, sacrifices, priesthoods, the garments of Aaron and his sons, the anointings, and, moreover, the statutes in a long series which were promulgated through Moses.

43. I will in a few words touch upon the manner in which the representative church with them was turned into an idolatrous one. All the spiritual things which are of heaven and the church were presented before them in visible and tangible forms, as was mentioned just above. Those forms were taken from the subjects of the three kingdoms of nature, animal, vegetable and mineral, by which were represented such things as are of the heavenly kingdom. They placed these typical forms in their sanctuaries, in the inner chambers of their houses, and in the market-places and streets, arranging them according to their significations. But a later age, after the science of correspondences was lost, and consequently the knowledge of the signification of those things had perished, began to look upon and acknowledge those objects as so many deities and holy things; and then they bowed the knee to some, some they kissed, and some they adorned and decorated with wax tapers, boxes of perfumes and ribbons, just as infants do their dolls, and as papists do their images; yea, of some they made household gods, of some guardian demigods, and of some pythons; some, moreover, they carried in miniature form in their hands, some they hugged in their bosoms, stroked, and whispered petitions in their ears; and so on. Thus were heavenly types turned into infernal types, and the Divine things of heaven and the church into idols. On account of this transformation and disfigurement of heavenly things, a new representative church was raised up with the sons of Israel, in which real representations, as was stated above, were instituted; and they were prohibited from celebrating Divine worship by any others, as is evident from these words in the first Commandment of the Decalogue:—

Thou shalt not make unto thee a graven image, nor any figure that is in the heavens above, or that is in the earth beneath, or that is in the waters under the earth. Thou shalt not bow down thyself unto them, nor worship them (*Exod.* xx. 4, 5; *Deut.* v. 8, 9).

44. It has been said, that from the people of every Church, at its end, is formed a new heaven and a new hell; and, since I have adduced a relation in the preceding article respecting the heaven and hell formed from those who were of the Most Ancient Church, it seems well also to do so respecting these; for access has been granted me to them, inasmuch as I have been allowed to go about and examine the spiritual world, to the end that the New Church truly Christian may not[1] be in thick darkness concerning heaven and hell, and concerning their lot after death according to the actions of their life. These things are likewise in the work on *Conjugial Love* (n. 76). Concerning the heaven from these:—

[2] "An angel came to me and said, 'Do you desire me to accompany you to the peoples who lived in the Silver Era, or Age, that we may hear from them respecting the manners and life of their times?' He also added that they may not be approached, except under the auspices of the Lord.

"I was in the spirit and accompanied my leader, and came first to a hill on the confines of the east with the south; and when we were on its slope, he showed me a great stretch of country, and we saw at a distance an eminence like a mountain, between which and the hill on which we stood was a valley, and beyond this a plain, and from this plain a gently-rising acclivity.

"We descended the hill to cross the valley, and saw here and there at the sides pieces of wood and stone carved into figures of men, and of various beasts, birds and fishes. And I asked the angel, 'What are these? Are they not idols?'

"And he replied, 'Not at all: they are representative forms of various moral virtues and spiritual truths. The people of that age had the science of correspondences; and as a beast, bird and fish correspond to some quality, therefore, each carved figure represents and signifies some particular of virtue, or truth, and many together represent the virtue or truth itself in a certain general extended form; these are what in Egypt were called hieroglyphics.'

[3] "We proceeded through the valley, and when we entered the plain, lo! we saw horses and chariots; the horses were variously caparisoned and harnessed, and the chariots of different forms; some carved out like eagles, some like unicorns, and some like whales: we also saw some carts at the extremity, and stables round about at the sides. But, when we approached, both horses and chariots disappeared, and instead of them we saw men in pairs, walking, conversing and reasoning. And the angel said to me, 'The semblances of horses, chariots, and stables, seen at a distance, are appearances of the rational intelligence of the men of that age; for a *horse* from correspondence signifies the understanding of truth; a *chariot* its doctrine; and *stables* places of instruction. You are aware that all things in this world appear according to correspondences.'

[4] "But we passed these things, and ascended by the acclivity. At length we saw a city, which we entered; and in walking through it, we noticed its houses, from the streets and public places. In the midst of it were palaces built of marble, having steps of alabaster in front, and at the sides of the steps pillars of jasper. We saw also temples, made of precious stone of a sapphire and azure color. And the angel said to me, 'Their houses are of stones because *stones* signify natural verities, and *precious stones* spiritual verities; and all those who lived in the silver age, had intelligence from spiritual verities, and thence from natural; for *silver* has a like signification.'

[5] "While exploring the city we saw here and there consorts, both husbands and wives. We expected that we should be invited somewhere; and, while this was in our mind (*animus*), we were called back by two into their house, which we entered; and the angel, speaking with them for me, explained the reason

of our coming into this heaven, that it was 'for the sake of instruction. concerning the manners of the ancients, of whom you are.'

"They replied, 'We were from the peoples in Asia, and the study of our age was the study of truths, through which we had intelligence. This study was the study of our soul and mind. But the study of the senses of our bodies was the representations of truths in natural forms; and the science of correspondences conjoined the sensuals of our bodies with the perceptions of our minds, thus natural and corporeal things with spiritual and celestial, and procured for us communication with the angels of heaven.'

[6] "On hearing this, the angel asked them to give some account of marriages with them. And the husband said, 'There is a correspondence between spiritual marriage, which is that of good and truth, and natural marriage, which is that of a man with his wife; and as we have studied correspondences, we have seen that the church, with its truths and goods, can by no means exist with any others than those who live in truly conjugial love; for the marriage of good and truth is the church with man. Therefore all we who are in this heaven, say that the husband is truth, and the wife the good of his truth; and that good cannot love any other truth than that which is its own, nor truth love in return any other good than that which is its own. If any other were loved, internal or spiritual marriage, which constitutes the Church would perish, and marriage would become only external or natural, to which idolatry and not the church corresponds.'

[7] "When he had said these things we were introduced into an ante-chamber, where there were several designs on the walls, and little images as it were molten of silver; and I asked, what these were. They said, 'They are pictures and forms representative of the many qualities, properties, and delights of spiritual things;' as were also the cherubim and palm-trees on the walls of the temple at Jerusalem.

[8] "After this, there appeared at a distance a chariot drawn by white ponies; on seeing which the angel said, 'That chariot is a sign for us to depart.' Then, as we were going down the steps, our host gave us a bunch of white grapes adhering to

the vine leaves; and lo! the leaves in our hands became silver, and we brought them away for a sign that we had spoken with the people of the Silver Age."

Concerning the Hell from Those Peoples.

45. The hells of the men of the Noachian, or Ancient Church, consist for the most part of magicians, who have huts and places of entertainment scattered up and down in the desert. They wander about there with rods in their hands, which are of various forms, and some of them stained with magical juices. By these, as in former times, they practise their arts, which are effected by the abuse of correspondences, by fantasies, by persuasive assurances by which there was produced a miraculous faith, and miracles were formerly performed; also by exorcisms, fascinations, enchantments, and sorceries, and several other magical spells, by which they present illusory appearances as real. The greatest delight of their heart is to utter prophecies and prognostications, and to act as pythons. From these especially have arisen the various fanaticisms in the Christian world.

PROPOSITION THE FOURTH.

The Israelitish and Jewish Church.

46. In order that the states of this church may be thoroughly laid open and distinctly exhibited, it is of importance that we survey them in the following order:—

   I. *The first state of this church was the appearing of the Lord Jehovih, and the calling and covenanting, and then its rise and morning.*

  II. *The second state of this church was instruction, and at length introduction into the land of Canaan, and then its progression into light and day.*

 III. *The third state of this church was the turning aside from true representative into idolatrous worship and then its vastation or evening.*

IV. *The fourth state of this church was the profanation of sanctities, and then its consummation or night.*
V. *Before this state and after it, a promise was made of the coming of the Lord Jehovih into the world, and respecting a new church in which justice and judgment should reign.*
VI. *The fifth state of this church was the separation of the good from the evil, and then the judgment upon those who were from it: but this was in the spiritual world.*
VII. *Something respecting the heaven and the hell from that nation.*

47. I. *The first state of this church was the appearance of the Lord Jehovih, and the calling and covenanting, and then was its rise or morning.* We are taught from the Word, that the Lord Jehovih has appeared at the beginning of each of the four churches of this earth. This is because God is the All in all of the church and its religion; and the acknowledgment of God in it, is like the soul in the body, which vivifies both its interiors and its exteriors; and it is like the prolific element in seed, which, abiding inmostly in all the sap drawn from the earth by the root, accompanies it from the first germination even to the fruit, in which it also is, and it disposes the vegetative process so that it proceeds in its own order. For this reason, the man of the church, without the acknowledgment of God, is in the eyes of the angels a brute like the wild beasts of the forest, or like a bird of night, or like a monster of the sea; yea, without the acknowledgment of God, he is like a tree the branches of which are cut off, and the trunk cut in pieces, and the whole piled up together in a heap reserved for the fire; for the Lord says:—

Without Me ye can do nothing; if any one abide not in Me, he is cast forth as a branch, and is withered; and they gather him, and cast him into the fire, and he is burned (*John* xv. 5, 6).

Without the acknowledgment of God, man, inwardly, as to his rational things, is like the ruins of a burned city; he is also like food when its nutritiveness is boiled out, it becomes refuse. And so forth.

48. But it would be impossible for a man to acknowledge God and anything belonging to Him, unless God had manifested Himself in a personal human form; for nature, which belongs to the world, surrounds him, and he does not see, feel, or breathe anything but what is from it and is in contact with the organs of his body. From this his mind conceives and adopts a rational which lies in the midst of the bosom of nature, like an embryo in the womb; nor does it see anything, until it is brought forth, and receives sight. Therefore, how can a man in this state by any method look through nature, and acknowledge anything that is above her, as everything Divine, celestial, and spiritual is, and hence everything religious, which in themselves are above natural things? Wherefore, it is an absolute necessity that God should manifest Himself, and thereby cause Himself to be acknowledged, and after acknowledgment should inspire man with His Divine influence, and by this, received in the heart, lead him at length even to Himself in heaven; all which cannot possibly be effected except by instruction. Must not also an emperor, and a king, first cause himself to be acknowledged and crowned, before he enters on his government? And before he is crowned, is he not provided with the insignia of dominion, robed, and anointed? and must he not covenant the people to himself by sworn compacts, agreed to by both sides, whereby the people become the king's, and the king the people's? Must not a bridegroom first cause himself to be seen, before he proposes betrothal, and afterwards marriage? Must not a father present himself before his infant, and embrace and kiss him, before the infant can say, "Abba, father"? and so in other cases. Still more must the Lord Jehovih, who is "*King of kings and Lord of lords*" (*Apoc.* xvii. 14), the Bridegroom and Husband of the church (*Apoc.* xxi. 9), and consequently the Father of all her offspring. By the "Lord Jehovih" is meant the Lord our Saviour and Redeemer. He is called the "Lord Jehovih" in *Daniel*, and everywhere in the *Prophets*.

49. It was stated above, that the first state with the sons of Israel, was the appearing of the Lord Jehovih, calling and covenanting; and we learn from the Word, that these three things took place, first with Abraham, secondly with Moses, and thirdly with the entire people. The appearing of the Lord Jehovih before Abraham is thus described in *Genesis:*—

Jehovah appeared unto Abraham in the plains of Mamre; he was sitting at the door of his tent, and when he lifted up his eyes and saw, behold, three men stood by him, and as soon as he saw them, he ran to meet them from the door of the tent, and bowed himself to the earth, and said, O Lord, if I have found grace in Thine eyes, pass not away, I pray, from Thy servant (xviii. 1-3, *seq.*).

It was the Lord our Saviour who appeared in His Divine Trinity, which the three angels represented; for the Lord said:—

Abraham exulted that he should see My day, and he saw and rejoiced. Verily, verily I say unto you, Before Abraham was, I am (*John* viii. 56, 58).

There is in the Lord the Divine Trinity; and the Divine Unity was represented in the Divine Trinity by the "three men," who were also called "angels" (*Gen.* xviii. 2; xix. 1). But in His Divine Unity He was called "Lord" (xviii. 3; xix. 18); and also "Jehovah," very frequently (xviii. 13, 14, 17, 19, 20, 22, 26, 33). The appearing of the Lord Jehovih before Moses is thus described in *Exodus:*—

The Angel of Jehovah appeared to Moses at the mountain of Horeb, in a flame of fire out of the midst of a bramble. Therefore Moses said, I will turn aside and see this great vision, why the bramble is not burnt. And Jehovah saw that he went aside, therefore God called unto him out of the midst of the bramble, and said, Moses, Moses. And moreover Moses said to God, What is thy name? God said, I AM WHO I AM. Thus shalt thou say unto the sons of Israel, I AM hath sent me unto you (iii. 1, 2-4, 14, *seq.*).

The appearing of the Lord Jehovih before the whole people is thus also described in *Exodus:*—

Jehovah said to Moses, Say unto the sons of Israel, that they be ready against the third day; for on the third day Jehovih will come down in the eyes of all the people upon Mount Sinai. And it came to pass on the third day, that there were voices, and lightnings, and thick clouds upon the mount, and the voice of a trumpet exceeding loud, so that all the people who were in the camp trembled. All Mount Sinai smoked, because He descended upon it in fire, and promulgated the law before the people (xix. 9-24, and xx. 1-18).

The Lord also appeared to Joshua as "Prince of the army of Jehovah," before whom Joshua fell on his face upon the earth, and called him his "Lord" (*Josh.* v. 13, 14).

The calling of the sons of Israel to the land of Canaan, thus to the church, was also done three times; once to Abram, that he should go forth thence out of his fatherland, and afterwards the promise that his seed should inherit that land (*Gen.* xii. 1–7). The call was also made through Moses (*Exod.* iii. 16, 17); and again through Joshua (*Josh.* i. 3, *seq.*, and 11).

50. *A covenant also was entered into several times;* first with Abram (respecting which, *Gen.* xvii. 1–14); then with the people (*Exod.* xxiv. 7, 8); and once again (*Josh.* xxiv. 24, 25). From these things it is now evident, that the first state of this church was the appearing of the Lord Jehovih and the calling and covenanting, and then its rise or morning. That by the "Lord Jehovih," everywhere in the Word, is meant Jehovah in His Human, who is the Lord our Redeemer and Saviour, will be seen in what follows.

51. II. *That the second state of this church was instruction, and at length introduction into the land of Canaan, and then its progression into light and day.* It has been pointed out above, that this Israelitish Church, as well as the Ancient, or Noachian Church, was, as to the whole of its worship, a representative church. This was of the Divine providence, because Jehovah had not yet put on the Natural Human (which He took up by incarnation in the womb of Mary, thus according to the order established from creation); and prior to this, He could not be conjoined to man as to the interiors of his spirit, and thus manifest there to man's perception His Divine things, which are celestial and spiritual, and thus far above the discernment of the senses of the body. This also was as impossible as it is to make a bird fly in ether, or a fish to step in air. For if Jehovah were to enter with man except by means of His Human, it would be like putting the branch of a tree into the very focus of a burning glass, or quicksilver to a blazing log in a furnace, which would be suddenly dissipated. For from the zeal of His Divine love Jehovah is like a consuming fire; and were He to enter into man in this without His Human, He would dissipate him, as has just been said: for which reason He said to Moses, when he desired to behold His glory with his own eyes, that no man could see Him and live. It was otherwise, however, after He assumed the Natural Human, and united this, when glorified, to His Divine, and thus conjoined into one in Himself the Divine celestial, the Divine spiritual, and the Divine natural. He was then able, by means of this, to conjoin Himself to man in his natural, yea, in his sensual, and at the same time to his spirit or mind in his rational, and thus to enlighten man's natural light, with heavenly light. That such conjunction was effected after the Coming of Jehovah into the world, is plainly manifest from the words of the Lord Himself:—

In that day ye shall know that I am in My Father, and ye in Me, and I in you (*John* xiv. 20).

[2] Now, before the incarnation of Jehovah was accomplished, conjunction with Him could not take place except through an angel, thus by means of a representative human; on which account, also, all things of the church of the men of that period, were made representative, and consequently men worshiped Jehovah by types affecting the senses of the body, and at the same time corresponding to spiritual things. Hence it was that the men of the Ancient Church, and still more the men of the Israelitish Church, were external and natural men, nor could they become internal and spiritual, as men can since the Lord's coming. But, still, those who acknowledged Jehovah, and, at the same time the Lord with him, that is, the Lord who was to come, who in the Word is named the "Lord Jehovih," the "God of Israel," and "His Holy One," "Messiah" or the "Anointed of Jehovah," "King," "Rock," and in some places "Son," and who worshiped them together, received holiness in their spirits, and hence in the types of their religion. The rest, however, did not receive it; whence the religion of these was not a religion but a superstition, and their worship was not representative but idolatrous; and although this was similar in the external form, yet it was dissimilar in the internal. [3] But in order that this matter may acquire some light, it shall be illustrated by comparisons. Idolatrous worship is like a man who reveres a king, a prince, a nobleman, or any man of exalted dignity, solely on account of the pomp of his retinue, the magnificence of his carriages and horsemen, or of his forerunners, and the splendor and gorgeousness of his clothing; but genuine representative worship is like one who re-

gards a king, prince, nobleman, or any man of exalted dignity, from his religion and his wisdom, and from his justice and judgment, and from these regards the above-mentioned marks of his honor. Idolatrous worship, moreover, is like a man who regards the primate of the church solely on account of his tiara and the jewels in it, or any other prelate, or bishop, on account of his fillet or mitre; but genuine representative worship is like one who regards them from the zeal of their love for the souls of the men of the church, and for their eternal salvation, and the marks of distinction on their heads from these grounds. Again, idolatrous worship is like a field filled with stalks without ears, or with ears without grain in them, or even with these without any kernel in them, and so on; but genuine representative worship is like a field filled with the harvest, whose grains are bursting with kernels, which afford flour and bread in abundance. Idolatrous worship is also like an egg in which there is no spermatic germ; but genuine representative worship is like an egg in which there is the prolific element from which is the chicken. To still further follow those two kinds of worship by comparison, idolatrous worship is like one who has lost the sense of smell and the sense of taste by a catarrh; when such a one applies any grape to his nostrils, or pours wine on his tongue, he is sensible of nothing but their touch; but genuine representative worship is like one who is keenly sensible at the same time of the fragrance of the grape and the flavor of the wine, and thus enjoys the use of both with pleasure.

52. That the second state of this church was instruction, follows from order; for when any one is called to the church, he must be instructed in the precepts of the religion according to which he is going to live. That this took place with the sons of Israel after their calling, is evident from the promulgation of the law on Mount Sinai, in which are contained all the commandments of love and faith towards God, and all those of love and fidelity towards the neighbor. After instruction in the general precepts of life and faith, there followed the publication of various laws, which were called "judgments" and "statutes," respecting the sanctification of the Sabbath, stated feasts, sacrifices, the priesthood, the tabernacle, the holy worship in it and upon the altar outside it; also respecting the eating of the holy things, the ministry of Aaron and his sons, likewise their garments and the consecration thereof, and the sanctification of all things belonging to the tabernacle by the oil of anointing; and further, concerning the Levitical order, marriages and divorces, cleansings, foods, places of refuge, besides many other things, which were all natural representations corresponding to spiritual things. In a word, the last four books of Moses are nothing else but books of instruction for that church. After these instructions, the sons of Israel were introduced into the land of Canaan, thus into the church itself, for the "land of Canaan" represented and therefore signified the church. That land also was situated in the middle portion of our entire globe: for on the front it looked towards Europe, on the left towards Africa, and on the hinder and right-hand side towards Asia. But after they came into that land, the precepts given by Moses were enriched by prophets,[1] then by their King David, and at length by Solomon after the building of the temple; as appears from the books of *Judges, Samuel,* and *Kings.* This, therefore, was the second state of this church, which was its progression into light, or day.

53. The following passages in the Word can be applied to these two states of this church:—

Jehovah, after two days, will vivify us: on the third day He will raise us up, that we may live before Him. Jehovah, His going forth is prepared as the dawn; and He shall come unto us as the rain, as the latter rain He shall water the earth (*Hos.* vi. 2, 3).

The God of Israel said, the Rock of Israel spake to me. He is as the light of the morning, a morning without clouds (2 *Sam.* xxiii. 3, 4).

And in *Moses:* —

My doctrine shall flow down as the rain; My word shall distil as the dew, as the drops upon the grass, and as the small drops upon the herb: I will proclaim the name of Jehovah; ascribe ye greatness to our God. The Rock, whose work is perfect, all His ways are judgment, a God of faithfulness without perversity, just and right is He (*Deut.* xxxii. 2-4).

From these passages also it may be confirmed that these two states of this church were from our Lord, who is the "God of Israel" and the "Rock." That He is the "Rock," is clear from these words in *Paul:*—

The Rock was Christ (1 *Cor.* x. 4).

54. III. *That the third state of this church was a decline from true representative into idolatrous worship, and then was its vastation, or evening.* Some observations were adduced above respecting the difference between representative worship and idolatrous worship, from which it may be plainly seen that so long as the types, figures, and signs, which were laid hold of by the senses of the body as objects of religion by the men of the Noachian and Israelitish Churches, were not at the same time regarded from a higher or interior idea, nearly approaching to a spiritual one, worship truly representative easily declined with them into idolatry. As for example: If they so thought of the tabernacle, as not to think at the same time of heaven and the church, and of God's dwelling-place in them; of the bread of faces therein, so as not to think at the same time of the heavenly bread for the nourishment of the soul; of the incense and the burning of it upon the golden altar there, in such a way as not to think at the same time about worship from faith and charity, as ascending to Jehovah as a grateful odor; about the lights in the lamps of the golden lampstand, when lighted, in such wise as not to think at the same time of the illumination of the understanding in the objects of their religion; and about the eating of the holy things, so that they did not at the same time think about the appropriation of heavenly foods, and also about the holy refreshment of their spirits by the performance of the sacrifices: and with the other things in like manner. It is hence evident, that, if the man of the representative church did not at the same time look upon the things belonging to that worship with a rational spirit enlightened by heavenly light from the Lord, but only with a rational spirit informed by the natural light (*lumen*) of the world from self, he could very easily be carried away from genuine representative worship into idolatrous worship, and so be vastated. For vastation is nothing else but a deviation, decline, and falling away from representative worship into idolatrous; which two kinds of worship are alike as to the external face, but not as to the internal face. [2] On account of this proneness to fall away from one worship which in itself was heavenly, into another which in itself was infernal, the interior things of the church and of religion could not be revealed before the Lord's Coming, and then it was by means of light from Him, namely, concerning heaven and hell, the resurrection, and the life of their spirits after death, and also the immortality of their souls, regeneration, and in brief the interior things respecting faith and charity; inasmuch as they would have looked upon them scarcely otherwise than as anyone looks at birds over the head, or meteors in the air. And moreover they would have involved them so deeply in the mere fallacies of the senses, that still not a single vestige of revealed spiritual things would have been visible, except as much as the tip of the nose in respect to the face, or a finger-nail in respect to the hands. They would also have so deformed them, that in the sight of the angels they would have appeared no otherwise than like a sea-monster clothed in a cloak, having a mitre on the head, and with a face, after being shaved and painted, like that of an ape which has a bald face. And they would also have appeared in the sight of the angels like a sculpture, furnished with movable joints and hollowed out; inside of which some man, a Levite, being admitted, it would walk about, act, and speak, and at length cry out to the superstitious multitude, " Prostrate yourselves; invoke me; behold me, your household tutelar God, to whom belongs holiness and divine power." [3] Could the ideas of the thought of these concerning the spiritual things of the church be superior to the ideas of thought of Nicodemus, who was a learned man, on regeneration, which was that the whole man would be re-born in the mother's womb; for he said:—

How can a man be born anew? can he enter the second time into his mother's womb?

To whom the Lord answered:—

Art thou a master in Israel, and knowest not this? If I have told you earthly things and ye believe not, how will ye believe if I shall tell you super-celestial things? (*John* iii. 3, 4, 9, 10, 12).

They would have been equally delirious if interior things, which in their essence are spiritual, had been disclosed to them concerning faith and charity, and also the life after death, and respecting the state of heaven and hell. Wherefore, to open the internal sight of their mind or spirit, as to its higher region, which alone heavenly light illuminates, before the coming of the Lord, who came into the world as "the Light," as He Himself says (*John* i. 1-4; viii. 12; xii. 35, 36, 46), was as impossible as it is to make a horse fly and turn it into Pegasus, or a stag run in the air, or a calf upon the waters; yea, as it would be to turn an agate into a ruby, or a crystal into a diamond, or to impart a vein of silver to a common stone, or to make a laurel produce grapes, a cedar olives, a poplar and an oak pears and apples; therefore, also, as impossible as to infuse the intelligence of the learned Œdipus into the listening Davus.

55. But what vastation is, and whence it was with the people of the Israelitish Church, may be gathered from the passages in the *Prophets* where it is mentioned, which shall therefore be adduced in abundance. It must be premised, that, in the following and the subsequent passages from the Word, by "land" is there signified the church, because the land of Canaan is meant, in which the church was; by "Zion," the church as to the Word; by "Jerusalem," the church as to doctrine from the Word; by the "cities" therein, doctrinals; by the "mountains," "hills," "valleys," and "rivers," the formalities of the church; and by the tracts of land there, the general things of the church, and these according to the representation of the tribe by which they were possessed.

56. The passages from the Prophetic Word, treating of the Israelitish Church, "vastation," "desolation," and "breaking up," and in which these and also "desert" are mentioned, are the following:—

O inhabitant of Jerusalem, and man of Judah, what should I do to My vineyard that I had not done? I looked that it should bring forth grapes, but it brought forth wild grapes. I will make it into a desolation, it shall not be pruned nor hoed, that the briar may come up, and the houses shall be to a devastation; for they regard not the work of Jehovah, neither see the operation of His hands (*Isa.* v. 3–12).

Many shepherds have destroyed My vineyard, they have trampled My field, they have reduced the field of My desire to a desert of solitude; he hath made it into a solitude. O desolate, desolate is the whole land, because no one putteth it upon his heart. The wasters came upon all hills in the desert. They have sown wheat, but have reaped thorns (*Jer.* xii. 10–13).

A nation hath come up upon My land, and hath reduced My vine to a waste (*Joel* i. 6, 7).

The field is devastated, the land mourneth, the corn is devastated; the must is dried up, the oil languisheth (*Joel* i. 10).

By "vineyard" and "field" in these, as in other passages of the Word, is signified the church.

In all your habitations the cities shall be devastated, and the high places desolated, that your altars may be devastated and desolated, and your idols may cease, and your statues may be cut down, and your works blotted out (*Ezek.* vi. 6; see also ver. 14).

My people have forgotten Me, they have burned incense to vanity; to make the land into a waste (*Jer.* xviii. 15, 16).

"Land," here is for the church.

The high places of Isaac shall be vastated, and the sanctuaries of Israel shall be desolated (*Amos* vii. 9).

Go and tell this people, Hearing hear ye, but understand not; and seeing see ye, but know not; make the heart of this people fat, and besmear his eyes.

Then said the prophet:—

Lord, how long? and He said, Until the cities be devastated, and the land is reduced to a solitude: Jehovah will multiply deserts in the midst of the land (*Isa.* vi. 9–12).

Behold, Jehovah maketh the land empty, and maketh it void; the land emptying shall be emptied; because they have transgressed the laws, passed by the statute, and made void the covenant of eternity. Therefore in the city there shall be a waste, and the gate shall be crushed even to devastation (*Isa.* xxiv. 1, 3, 5, 12).

The highways are devastated, the wayfaring man hath ceased, he hath made void the covenant. Conceive ye chaff, bring forth stubble (*Isa.* xxxiii. 8, 11).

I have been silent from eternity, I will desolate and swallow up together. I will lay waste mountains and hills (*Isa.* xlii. 14, 15).

Thy destroyers and devastators shall go forth out of thee. For as for thy vastations and desolations, and the land of thy devastation, the devourers shall be far away (*Isa.* xlix. 17, 19).

Your iniquities have been dividers between you and your God, and your sins have hid His face from you. They set an asp's eggs, and wove the spider's webs. Vastation and breaking up are in their paths. We look for light, but behold darkness; we feel the wall like the blind, we stumble at noon-day as in the twilight (*Isa.* lix. 2, 5, 7, 9, 10).

The cities of holiness are become a desert, Zion is become a desert, and Jerusalem a waste. Our house of holiness is become a kindling of fire, and all our desirable things are become a waste (*Isa.* lxiv. 10, 11).

The young lions roar against Israel, they reduce his land to a waste (*Jer.* ii. 15).

Woe unto us, for we are devastated. O Jerusalem, wash thine heart from wickedness. How long shall thoughts of iniquity tarry in the midst of thee? (*Jer.* iv. 13, 14).

As a fountain causeth her waters to gush forth, so Jerusalem causeth her wickedness to gush forth. Violence and vastation is heard in her. Admit chastisement lest I reduce thee to a waste. O daughter of My people, gird thee with sackcloth, and roll thee in ashes; for the vastator shall suddenly come upon us (*Jer.* vi. 7, 8, 26).

A voice of lamentation is heard in Zion. How are we devastated! because I have deserted the land (*Jer.* ix. 19).

"Land" is for the church.

My tent is devastated, all its ropes are plucked out; for the pastors have become foolish, and have not inquired of Jehovah (*Jer.* x. 20, 21).

"Tent" means worship.

The voice roars; behold it cometh, and a great commotion from the land of the north, to reduce the cities of Judah to a waste, a habitation of dragons (*Jer.* x. 22).

The whole land shall be a desolation, a devastation (*Jer.* xxv. 11).

"Land" means the church.

The voice of a cry from Horonaim, devastation and great breaking up; the vastator shall come upon every city (*Jer.* xlviii. 3, 5, 8, 9, 15, 18).

These things are concerning Moab, by which is meant confidence in his own works and in one's own intelligence (as is manifest from verse 29 of that chapter).

That they may want bread and water, and be desolated, a man and his brother, and pine away for their iniquity (*Ezek.* iv. 17).

"Bread" and "water" mean good and truth.

Thou shalt be filled with drunkenness and sorrow, with the cup of devastation and desolation (*Ezek.* xxiii. 33).

Woe unto them! for they have wandered away; devastation be unto them (*Hos.* vii. 13).

The land shall be a desolation, because of them that dwell therein, for the fruit of their doings (*Micah* vii. 13).

(Besides many other passages, as *Isa.* vii. 18, 19; xvii. 4–6, 9–14; xxii. 4–9; xxix. 10–12; li. 19: *Jer.* xix. 8; xxv. 9–11, 18; xliv. 2, 6, 22: *Ezek.* ix. 1 to end; xii. 19, 20; xxxiii. 24, 28, 29: *Hos.* x. 14; xii. 2: *Joel* ii. 20: *Amos* v. 9: *Micah* vi. 13, 16: *Hab.* i. 3: *Hag.* i. 4, 9: *Zech.* vii. 14; xi. 2, 3.) From all these passages it may be seen what "vastation" and "desolation" are; and that it is not a vastation and desolation of the peoples of a land, and of cities, but of the goods and truths of the church, whence there is nothing but evils and falsities.

57. IV. *The fourth state of this church was the profanation of holy things, and then its consummation or night.* Vastation and consummation differ from each other, as the shade of evening and the thick darkness of night differ from each other; for vastation is a receding from the church, but consummation a full separation from it. Vastation, therefore, is as when any one descends from heaven but not as far as to hell, and tarries in the middle, standing beside both of them; but consummation exists when any one, standing thus, turns his face and breast to hell, and his back and the hinder part of his head to heaven; in like manner as happened with the dragon and his angels when they were cast down out of heaven (concerning whom see *Apoc.* xii.): while they were fighting with Michael, they were in the middle; but when they were vanquished, they were in hell. Vastation takes place when a man looks upon the holy things of the church from falsities and falsified truths; but consummation, when he lives in evils, or in adulterated goods. [2] But, that the difference and distinction between the state of vastation and the state of consummation may be still more clearly comprehended, it shall be illustrated by comparisons. The state of vastation may be compared with a garden or grove around a temple, which by reason of the Divine worship in the temple, is regarded as holy; in which are places for drinking, feasting, dancing, and play-acting and buffoonery, with the spectators in the courts and windows of the temple; but the state of consummation may be compared to the same garden or grove, in which are satyrs and priapi, along with harlots and fortune-tellers, who all together enter the temple dancing, and there celebrate their profane revels, as the pythons did on their holidays. [3] The state of vastation may also be compared with a hostile army, when it enters the suburbs of a besieged city and rules in them; but the state of consummation may be compared with the same army, when it has demolished the wall, and breaks through into the city and gives the inhabitants over to destruction. The state of vastation may further be compared with a ship upon sandbanks, or a sandy shore, when it is violently tossed there, and raised and depressed, so that the pilot, captain, and sailors lament on account of their danger; but the state of consummation is when the ship's keel is fretted away by the gravel beneath, and the ship, being broken up and full of holes, sinks, and the navigators and merchandise perish in the waves. [4] The state of vastation may be compared with every disease which invades the members, viscera and organs of the body, by reason of which the patient forebodes death, consults a physician, takes medicines, and all the while lies in bed in the hope of being healed; but the state of consummation may be compared to the same disease when it invades the breast, where the heart and lungs reside as in their tabernacle, into which, when the disease penetrates, it makes an end of the life of the body.

58. The state of the consummation of the Israelitish Church is described in both the historical and the prophetical parts of the Word: in the prophecies, by the atrocious deeds of the kings, first of those of the Israelites, and afterwards of those of the Jews, by whom and under whom the land is said to have been profaned. But it is needless to recount them, because they are well known; only those passages shall be adduced from the prophecies, in which the consummation and devastation of that church are treated of. In these passages by "land," "Zion," "Jerusalem," "cities," "mountains," "hills," "valleys," and "rivers," similar things are signified as above (n. 55).

[2] The following are from the prophecies of the Word:—

I saw the land, and behold it was void and empty; and towards the heavens, and their light was not. Behold I saw when Carmel was a desert, and all the cities were desolated at the presence of Jehovah. For thus Jehovah hath said, the whole land shall be a waste, yet will I not make a consummation. For this the land shall mourn, and the heavens above shall be blackened. Thou, therefore, that art laid waste, what wilt thou do? (*Jer.* iv. 23–31; v. 10, 18).

The lion hath come up from his brier-thicket, and the destroyer of nations hath gone forth from his place to reduce the land to a waste. In that day the heart of the king and the heart of the princes shall perish; and the priests shall be astonished (*Jer.* iv. 7, 9).

In that day every place where there were a thousand vines shall be for briers and thorns, because all the land shall be briers and thorns (*Isa.* vii. 23, 24).

A voice of the cry of the shepherds and, of the powerful ones of the flock, for Jehovah is laying waste their pastures: whence the sheep-folds of peace were devastated. Jehovah hath forsaken His tabernacle, for their land was reduced to a desolation (*Jer.* xxv. 36-38).

This house shall be like Shiloh, and Jerusalem shall be a devastation (*Jer.* xxvi. 9; xxvii. 17).

Jerusalem and all the cities of Judah shall be a desolation and a devastation in this day, because of the wickedness of your works; your land is become a desolation, an astonishment, and a curse (*Jer.* xliv. 2, 6, 22).

I will give the land to devastation, because they have committed a trespass (*Ezek.* xv. 8).

They shall be devastated in the midst of the devastated lands, and her cities in the midst of the desolated cities. Then I will make the rivers dry. I will give the land into the hand of the evil, and I will lay waste the land and the fulness thereof (*Ezek.* xxx. 7, 12).

When I shall extinguish thee, I will cover the heavens, and will make the stars thereof black. I will cover the sun with a cloud, and the moon shall not cause her light to shine; and I will give darkness upon the land, when I shall bring on thy breaking up (*Ezek.* xxxii. 7-9).

[3] In like manner as the Lord foretold concerning the consummation of the present Christian Church (*Matt.* xxiv. 29).

I will make Mount Seir a waste and a devastation. I will make thee the wastes of eternity (*Ezek.* xxxv. 3, 4, 7, 9, 12, 14, 15).

In that day they shall bring up a proverb upon you, and shall say, In wasting we are laid waste (*Micah* ii. 4).

Fear and the pit have come upon us, devastation and breaking up (*Lam.* iii. 47).

The mountain of Zion is laid waste (*Lam.* v. 18).

Thine iniquity is consummated, O daughter of Zion (*Lam.* iv. 22).

Woe to the sinful nation, heavy with iniquity; they have provoked the Holy One of Israel. From the sole of the foot even to the head, there is no soundness. Your land is a solitude. The daughter of Zion is left as a tent in a vineyard, as a besieged city (*Isa.* i. 4-9, *seq.*).

What will ye do in the day of visitation and devastation? Consummation is finished, justice is inundated; for the Lord Jehovah is making a consummation and decision in the whole land (*Isa.* x. 3, *seq.*, 22, 23).

The Lord Jehovih is making a consummation and decision in the whole land (*Isa.* xxviii. 22).

The prophet fell upon his face, and said, Lord Jehovih, Thou art making a consummation with the remnants of Israel (*Ezek.* xi. 13).

My sanctuary was profaned, and the land of Israel was devastated (*Ezek.* xxv. 3).

Were even Noah, Daniel, and Job in the midst thereof, they only shall be delivered, but the land shall become a desolation (*Ezek.* xiv. 14, 16).

The final consummation of the Israelitish and Jewish Church was accomplished, when the Lord our Saviour, after receiving the sponge of vinegar, cried out upon the cross:—

It is consummated (*John* xix. 29, 30);

for it is said in *David:*—

They gave gall for My food, and in My thirst they gave Me vinegar to drink; let their habitation be devastated (*Ps.* lxix. 21, 25).

And in another place:—

Without cause have they hid for Me the pit of the net; without cause have they digged for My soul. Let devastation come upon him before he is aware; let him fall into devastation. Lead back My soul from their devastators, and My only one from the lions' whelps (*Ps.* xxxv. 7, 8, 17);

that is, the church.

I will make Jerusalem into heaps, a habitation of dragons; I will reduce the cities of Judah to a waste. Behold, I am feeding them, even this people, with wormwood, and I will give them waters of gall to drink (*Jer.* ix. 10–16).

[5] Full consummation, after this, is described thus in *Hosea:*—

The sons of Israel shall sit many days: no king, no prince, no sacrifice, no statue, no ephod, and no teraphim (iii. 4).

Such is their state at this day. We have not time to adduce more passages. The passages in which the vastation, desolation, and consummation of this church, are further mentioned, shall be only named: as, for example (*Isa.* ix. 13–21; xxii. 4–14: *Jer.* vii. 31–34; xxv. 33; xlvii. 4: *Ezek.* xiii. 14, 15; xiv. 8, 15; xix. 7; xxv. 12, 13; xxvi. 2; xxix. 9, 10, 12; xxxii. 12, 15: *Joel* i. 15–20; ii. 3; iii. 19: *Nah.* i. 8, 9: *Zeph.* i. 15; ii. 9: *Lam.* i. 16: *Ps.* lxxiii. 17–19; lxxiv. 3). The devastated are also called the "thrust through" (*Ezek.* xi. 6, 7; xxi. 30, 34; xxvi. 6; xxviii. 8, 23; xxxi. 17, 18; xxxii. 20–24, 28–32; xxxv. 8: *Zeph.* ii. 12: *Lam.* iv. 9: *Ps.* lxix. 26: and in other places). They are said to be "thrust through," because a "sword," by which this is done, signifies falsity destroying truth.

59. V. *Before this state, and after it, promise was made of the Coming of the Lord Jehovih into the world, and of a New Church at that time, wherein justice and judgment should reign.* It is known, from the reading of the prophetic Word of the

Old Testament, that in many places there the Coming of our Lord was foretold, and also that the Lord is there designated by various names; as that He is called "Jehovah Zebaoth," "Jehovah our Justice," "Jehovah our Saviour and Redeemer," "Lord Jehovih," "Lord" (*Adonai*), "Immanuel" or "God with us," "God of Israel," "Holy One of Israel," "Rock of Israel," "Messiah," or "Anointed of Jehovah," "King," "David," "Strong One of Jacob," "Shepherd of Israel," "High Priest," "Priest after the manner of Melchizedech," "Son of God," "Son of Man," "Angel of Jehovah," "Angel of the Covenant," the "Greatest Prophet," "Shiloh ;" also, in *Isaiah*, "Counsellor," "Prince of Peace," "Father of Eternity;" and in the New Covenant, "Jesus Christ," and "Son of God." That our Lord's Coming was foretold in very many places in the *Prophets*, will be seen from the citation of the predictions in the following pages. But it may be asked, Why was such frequent prediction of His Coming made? There were several reasons: some regarding the Israelitish and Jewish people, and some regarding the Christian people after them. [2] But we will recount the reasons which especially regarded the Israelitish and Jewish people. *The first* was, that by His being named and recalled to mind, they might be kept in the interior worship of Jehovah, since without that there was no entrance of Jehovah to anyone of them, nor access of anyone of them to Jehovah. The case was then as it is at this day :—

That no one hath seen God the Father; the Only Begotten Son, who is in the bosom of the Father; He hath set Him forth (*John* i. 18; v. 37).

And again :—

No one cometh to the Father, but by Me (*John* xiv. 6).

The second reason regarding that people, was, that the representative types of their church, which all looked to our Lord and to the church to be established by Him after His Coming, might serve them as so many indicators and symbols of their worship, consequently, that they might acknowledge Him when He came, and suffer themselves to be introduced into the internals of the worship of Him, and, together with the nations that surrounded them, become Christian. *The third reason* was, that by the recollection of His Coming, some notion or idea of the resurrection and eternal life might enter into their thoughts. For who of them could not have thought interiorly in himself or in his heart, "What is the Messiah to us after we are dead, unless we return then, see His glory, and reign with him?" From this source was derived that religious notion of theirs, that at that time they were to be raised again, everyone out of his grave, and return into the land of Canaan. *The fourth reason* was, that they might be lifted up and healed in their state of vastation and oppression, when they were in temptations and afflictions, as their fathers and brethren had been in the desert (*Num.* xxi. 1-9; *John* iii. 14, 15); for without such uplifting and healing, they would have cast aspersions against Jehovah, and departed in crowds from the representative worship of Him to idolatry. [3] For temptations and afflictions in the state of vastation and oppression, are nothing else but combats of the Lord with the Devil respecting man, that is, respecting his soul, which shall possess it. And of that state it may be said that the God of Israel, or the Lord the Messiah, stands on one side, and Beelzebub and the serpent the Devil on the other, and that the latter casts forth blasphemies against the Lord out of his mouth like a river, but that the Lord turns them aside and removes them, and thus delivers man from spiritual captivity and servitude. This combat is felt in the man as if from himself. That temptation is such a combat, and there is such a perception by man, and hence coöperation, I can testify upon oath, for, having often experienced it, I know it. That it is carried on outside the man, and is felt in him as from himself, and that man is standing in the middle and coöperates, is for the end that reward may be imputed to him when he conquers; but that man alone conquers who looks to the Lord, and trusts in Him alone for help. [4] That every one conquers who calls upon the Lord in temptations, but that otherwise he succumbs, shall be illustrated by comparisons. He is like a ship hurled by storms near rocks: unless the captain knows how to turn it aside from its danger, and to direct it to an exit and thus to port, it must perish. He is like a city besieged by enemies: unless there be escape or aid somewhere, the commander and his troops become hopeless and disheartened, and deliver themselves up prisoners, and surrender their lives to the pleasure of the enemy. He is like a person on a journey entering unawares into a cottage where there are robbers: unless when he is shut in, a friend comes and knocks at the door, or shows himself at the window, and thereby terrifies those villains, and saves him from the outrage. He is like a person falling into a cave where there is a bear with its cubs, or into a pit containing a wolf and a leopard, where he must perish unless his father or his brother, on seeing this, immediately lets down to him a ladder or a rope, and draws him up thence. He is like a person who stands or walks in the day-time in a thick fog, who consequently does not know which way to turn, unless he lights a lamp, and thereby shows himself the place where he may stand, or the way in which he may walk. He is like one who is in the depth of winter, and in want of provisions, if he is not supported by the hope of a harvest to come on the return of the sun. In like manner he is as one who wanders about at midnight in a forest, unless he comfort himself with the hope of light, and in that hope lies down and sleeps quietly until the morning. He is also like one who for the sake of salvation desires to be instructed in those things which are of the Christian Religion, and who meets with mitred doctors and laurelled teachers, who expound them by terms borrowed from the metaphysical art, and involves them in mystical things, unless there be some other person to dissect those terms, and thereby unravel the perplexities, and to bring forth from the Word, thus from the Lord, the holy things of the church into clear light. Would he not in such case be bewildered by the falsities respecting faith and other dogmas, which depend on the faith laid down, just as the links of a chain hang connectedly from a hook fixed to the wall?

[5] The case would be similar in temptations and the infestations at that time from satans, unless man looked with confidence to the Lord, and fully assured himself that the whole work and ability of deliverance came from Him alone. It is for these reasons that the Coming of the Lord is so frequently foretold in the Old Prophetic Word, and for the same reasons also the Lord is proclaimed in the New Evangelic and Apostolic Word, and His Second Coming foretold; concerning which in the following passages.

60. Now follow some passages concerning the Coming of the Lord, collected from the prophecies of the Old Word; which are these:—

Jehovah God said, Lo, I come; in the roll of the Book it is written of Me (*Ps.* xl. 7).

Jehovah God said to the serpent, Be thou cursed. I will put enmity between thee and the woman, and between thy seed and her Seed; and He shall trample thy head, but thou shalt injure the heel (*Gen.* iii. 14, 15).

The sceptre shall not depart from Judah, nor a law-giver from between his feet, until Shiloh come: to Him shall the cleaving of the peoples be (*Gen.* xlix. 10).

These words are part of the prophecy of the father Israel concerning his sons:—

A Star shall rise out of Jacob, and a Sceptre shall rise up out of Israel (*Num.* xxiv. 17).

Jehovah thy God will raise up unto thee a Prophet out of the midst of thy brethren, like unto Me; Him ye shall obey. And I will put My words in His mouth. Whence it shall come to pass, that the man who will not obey His words, I will require it of him (*Deut.* xviii. 15–19).

The Lord Himself giveth you a sign, Behold a virgin shall conceive and bring forth a Son, and shall call His name, God with us (*Isa.* vii. 14).

Unto us a Boy is born, unto us a Son is given, on whose shoulder shall be the government; His name shall be called Wonderful, Counsellor, God, Hero, Father of Eternity, Prince of Peace: of the increase of His government there shall be no end (*Isa.* ix. 6, 7).

There shall come forth a Shoot out of the stem of Jesse, and a branch out of his root shall bear fruit. Upon Him shall rest the spirit of wisdom and intelligence, the spirit of counsel and might (*Isa.* xi. 1, 2).

In that day the nations shall seek the Root of Jesse, which standeth for an ensign of the peoples, and His rest shall be glory (*Isa.* xi. 10).

Send ye the lamb of the Ruler of the land, from the rock towards the wilderness. His throne has been made firm by mercy, and one shall sit upon it in truth in the tabernacle of David, judging and seeking judgment, and hastening justice (*Isa.* xvi. 1, 5).

It shall be said in that day, Lo, this is our God, for whom we have waited that He may deliver us; this is Jehovah, for whom we have waited: we will exult and be glad in His salvation (*Isa.* xxv. 9; xxvi. 8, 9).

The voice of one crying in the desert, Prepare ye the way of Jehovah, make plain in the solitude a highway for our God. The glory of Jehovah shall be revealed, and all flesh shall see it together (*Isa.* xl. 3, 5).

O Zion, thou evangelizer, get thee up upon the high mountain; O Jerusalem, thou evangelizer, lift up thy voice with might; say to the cities of Judah, Behold your God. Behold, the Lord Jehovih cometh in strength, and His arm shall rule for Him; behold His reward is with Him. He shall feed His flock like a shepherd; He shall gather the lambs into His arm, and carry them in His bosom; He shall gently lead the sucklings (*Isa.* xl. 9–11).

My people shall know My name in that day; for I am He that doth speak; Behold Me. How delightful upon the mountains are the feet of Him that evangelizeth, that causeth to hear peace, that evangelizeth good, that causes them to hear salvation, that saith unto Zion, Thy King reigneth. They shall lift up the voice and sing, when they shall see eye to eye that Jehovah is returned to Zion. He hath consoled His people, He hath redeemed Jerusalem. All the ends of the earth shall see the salvation of our God (*Isa.* lii. 6–10).

Say ye to the daughter of Zion, Behold, thy salvation cometh; His reward is with Him, and the price of His work before Him (*Isa.* lxii. 11).

Shout for joy and be glad, O daughter of Zion; behold I come that I may dwell in the midst of thee. Then many nations shall cleave to Jehovah (*Zech.* ii. 10, 11).

Exult greatly, O daughter of Zion; resound, O daughter of Jerusalem; behold, thy King cometh to thee, just (*Zech.* ix. 9).

Behold, the days come when I will raise up to David a just Branch, who shall reign King and prosper, and He shall do judgment and justice in the land; and this is His name, Jehovah our Justice (*Jer.* xxiii. 5, 6; xxxiii. 15, 16).

Behold, I send My angel, who shall prepare the way before Me; and the Lord whom ye seek shall suddenly come to His temple, and the Angel of the covenant whom ye desire, behold He shall come (*Mal.* iii. 1).

Thou Bethlehem Ephratah, it is little that thou art among the thousands of Judah; out of thee shall One go forth unto Me, who will be the Ruler in Israel, and whose goings forth are from of old, from the days of eternity. He shall stand and feed in the strength of Jehovah, and shall increase even to the ends of the earth (*Micah.* v. 2, 4).

I anoint My king upon Zion. I will proclaim concerning the statute, Jehovah saith unto Me, Thou art My Son, this day have I begotten Thee; ask of Me, and I will give the nations for Thine inheritance, and the ends of the earth for Thy possession. Kiss the Son, lest He be angry, and ye perish in the way; Blessed are all they that put their trust in Him (*Ps.* ii. 6–12).

Behold the God of my salvation; I will trust and not be afraid. Cry out and shout for joy, O inhabitress of Zion; for great is the Holy One of Israel in the midst of thee (*Isa.* xii. 2, 6).

In that day a man shall look to his Maker, and his eyes shall regard the Holy One of Israel (*Isa.* xvii. 7).

My Beloved had a vineyard in the horn of [a son of] oil (*Isa.* v. 1).

Jehovah Zebaoth, Him shall ye sanctify. He shall be for a sanctuary, although for a stone of stumbling, and for a rock of offence, and for a gin and for a snare to the inhabitant of Jerusalem (*Isa.* viii. 13, 14; *Matt.* xxi. 42–44; *Luke* xx. 17, 18).

The people walking in darkness shall see a great light; the dwellers in the land of the shadow of death, upon them shall the light shine (*Isa.* ix. 2).

Out of Zion God shall shine forth; our God shall come, and shall not keep silence (*Ps.* l. 2, 3).

The vision is yet for the appointed time, and speaketh out to the end; yet it shall not lie: though He tarry, wait for Him; because coming He will come, He will not be delayed (*Hab.* ii. 3).

O Jehovah, I have heard Thy fame; I have revered, O Jehovah, Thy works; make it present in the midst of the years; God shall come from Teman, and the Holy One from Mount Paran. His honor covered the heavens, and the earth was full of His praise. His brightness shall be as the light; rays from His hand; and there is the hiding of His strength (*Hab.* iii. 2–4).

Thus said the Lord Jehovih, Behold, I will lay in Zion for a foundation a stone, a tried stone, a precious corner of well established foundation; then I will set judgment for the rule, and justice for the plummet (*Isa.* xxviii. 16, 17).

The Lord, as to the Word, is described by the appearance, over the expanse of the cherubim, and is called "Lord Jehovih" (*Ezek.* i. 26–28; ii. 4; iii. 11, 27; iv. 14; v. 7, 11; vi. 3, 11; vii. 2, 5; viii. 1). In *Isaiah* liii., throughout, the Lord is treated of, and the state of His life in the world is described by these expressions:—

He had no form nor honor [vers. 1, 2].

He was despised and not esteemed [ver. 3].

He was thrust through on account of our trespasses, He was bruised for our iniquities [vers. 4, 5].

Jehovah caused the iniquities of us all to meet in Him [ver. 6].

He was led as a lamb to the slaughter [ver. 7].

He was cut off out of the land of the living [vers. 8. 9].

Because he placed their guilt on His soul, His days shall be prolonged [ver. 10].

And for them He poured out His soul even to death [vers. 11, 12].

He was numbered with the trespassers, and interceded for the trespassers [ver. 12].

I have roused Him up in justice. He shall build My city; and He shall release My captivity, not for price, nor reward, Verily Thou art a God that hidest Thyself, O God of Israel the Saviour (*Isa.* xlv. 13, 15).

I have caused My justice to draw near, and My salvation shall not tarry (*Isa.* xlvi. 13).

As for our Redeemer, Jehovah Zebaoth is His Name, and the Holy One of Israel (*Isa.* xlvii. 4).

O Jehovah our Lord, how magnificent is Thy Name in all the earth, giving to it honor above the heavens. Thou hast caused Him to be a little less than the angels, but Thou hast crowned Him with glory and honor; Thou hast made Him to have dominion over the works of Thy hands, Thou hast put all things under His feet (*Ps.* viii. 1, 5, 6, 9).

God shall come down like rain upon the herb. He shall have dominion also from sea even to sea, and from the river even to the ends of the earth. The barbarians shall bow themselves down before Him, and His enemies shall lick the dust; the kings of Tarshish and of the isles shall bring their present; the kings of Sheba and Seba shall offer their gift. All kings shall bow themselves down to Him, all nations shall serve Him; for He shall deliver the miserable, who hath no helper. He shall redeem their soul from deceit and violence[1]. His Name shall be to eternity; He shall have the name of a Son before the sun, and they shall be blessed in Him. Blessed be God, the God of Israel: blessed be the Name of His glory; the whole earth shall be filled with His glory. Amen and Amen (*Ps.* lxxii. 1-19).

I have made a covenant with My Chosen. Thy seed will I establish even to eternity, and I will build up Thy throne to generation and generation; and the heavens shall confess Thy wonders (*Ps.* lxxxix. 3-5).

. . . .

[The rest is missing.]

INDEX OF SCRIPTURE REFERENCES.

*⁎*The numbers of the verses being printed in heavy type, thus **1, 2, 3**, indicates that the *very words* of the verses are quoted in the paragraph mentioned.

When the numbers of the verses are printed in thin type, thus, 1, 2, 3, it indicates that the *substance* of the verse is given, but not the very words.

Thin *Italic* type, thus *1, 2, 3*, signifies that the verses so indicated are merely referred to—not quoted, either substantially or verbally.

REFERENCES TO THE WORD.

GENESIS.
i. **1, 2** 23
   26, 27 25
ii. **7** 25
    8–10, 11, 12, 16, 17 27
iii. **1–6** 29
     5 38
     6 33
     9–13, 14–19, *23* 31
     14 25
     14, 15 60
     15 37
     22 26
vi. **5–8** 34
    9 35
ix. **1** 35
    19 35
xii. **1–7** 49
xiii. **10** 41
xiv. (chapter cited) 41
xvii. *1–14* 50
xviii. **1–3** 49
       2 49
       3 49
       13, 14, 17, 19, 20, 22, 26, 33. 49
xix. 1 49
     18 49
     (chapter cited) 41
xlix. **10** 60

EXODUS.
iii. **1**, 2–4, **13, 14** 49
     16, 17 49
xiv. (chapter cited) 34, 41
xvi. **31** 20
xvii. *6* 2
xix. 9–11, **16, 18** 49
xx. 1–18 49
    4, 5 43
    5, 6 35
xxiv. 7, *8* 50
xxv. *40* 37
xxvi. 30 37

NUMBERS.
xi. 5, 6, 32–35 22
xxi. *1–9* 59
xxiv. **5, 6** 27
      17 60

DEUTERONOMY.
v. **8, 9** 43
   9, 10 35
xviii. **15, 18, 19** 60
xxxii. **2–4** 53
       15, *18, 30* 2

JOSHUA.
Book cited 41
i. *3 seq. and 11* 49
v. 13, 14 49
xxiv. *24, 25* 50

JUDGES.
Book cited 41

SAMUEL.
xxiii. **3** 2
       3, 4 .... 5, 53

1 KINGS.
x. *1–13* 41

PSALMS.
i. **3** 7
ii. **6, 7, 8, 12** 60
viii. **1, 5, 6, 9** 60
xix. **14** 2
xxx. 5 5
xxxv. **7, 8, 17** 58
xl. **7** 60
xlvi. **5** 5
l. **2, 3** 60
   10, 11 3
li. **10** 23
lxviii. **9, 10** 3
lxix. **21, 25** 58
      26 58

INDEX OF SCRIPTURE REFERENCES

PSALMS (*Continued*).
lxxii. **6, 8, 10, 12, 18, 19** 60
lxxviii. *17, 19* 58
lxxiv. *3* 58
      18, 19 3
lxxviii. **35.** 2
lxxxix. **3, 4, 5** 60
cii. **18** 23
civ. **28, 30** 23
cxviii. **22.** 2

ISAIAH.
  i. **4, 6, 7, 8** 58
  v. **1** 60
     3, 4, 6, 9, 12 56
  vi. **9–12.** 56
  vii. **14.** 60
     18, 19. 56
     23, 24 58
  viii. **7, 8** 34
     13, 14 60
     14, 15. 2
  ix. **2** 60
     6, 7. 60
     13–21 58
  x. **3, 22, 23.** 58
  xi. **1, 2** 60
     10 60
  xii. **2, 6** 60
  xvi. **1, 5** 60
  xvii. *4–6, 9–14.* 56
     7 60
     14. 5
  xxi. **11, 12** 5
  xxii. *4–9* 56
  xxii. *4–14.* 58
  xxiv. **1, 3, 5, 12** 56
  xxv. **9** 60
  xxvi. *8, 9.* 60
  xxviii. **15.** 34
     16, 17 .... 2, 60
     22 58
  xxix. *10–12.* 56
  xxx. **28.** 34
  xxxiii. **8, 11** 56
  xl. **3, 5** 60
     9, 10, 11 60
  xli. **20.** 23
  xlii. **5.** 23
     14, 15 56
  xliii. **1, 7** 23
  xlv. **12, 18.** 23
     13, 15 60
  xlvi. **13.** 60
  xlvii. **4** 60
  xlix. **17, 19** 56
  li. **3** 27
     19 56
  lii. **6–10.** 60
  liii. **1–12.** 60
     (chapter cited) 60

ISAIAH (*Continued*).
  lvi. **8, 9** 3
  lviii. **11.** 27
  lix. **2, 5, 7, 9, 10** 56
  lxii. **11.** 60
  lxiv. **10, 11** 56
  lxv. **17.** 14
     17, 18 23
  lxvi. **22.** 14, 23

JEREMIAH.
  ii. **15.** 56
  iv. **7, 9** 58
     13, 14 56
     23, 26–28, 30. 58
     23, 27, 28. 23
  v. *10–18* 58
  vi. **7, 8, 26** 56
  vii. *31–34.* 58
  ix. **11, 15** 58
     19. 56
  x. **20, 21** 56
     22. 56
  xii. **10–13** 56
  xviii. **15, 16** 56
  xix. *8* 56
  xxiii. **5, 6** 60
  xxv. *9–11, 18.* 56
     11. 56
     33 58
     36–38. 58
  xxvi. **9** 58
  xxvii. *17* 58
  xxxi. **12.** 27
  xxxiii. *15, 16.* 60
     20, 21, *25.* 5
  xliv. *2, 6, 22.* 56
     2, 6, 22 58
  xlvii. **2** 34
     4 58
  xlviii. **3, 5, 8,** *9, 15, 18.* 56
     29 56

LAMENTATIONS.
  i. *16* 58
  iii. **47.** 58
  iv. *9* 58
     22. 58
  v. **18.** 58

EZEKIEL.
  i. *26–28* 60
  ii. *4* 60
  iii. *11, 27.* 60
  iv. *14* 60
     17 56
  v. **7,** *11.* 60
  vi. *3, 11.* 60
     6 56
     14 56

INDEX OF SCRIPTURE REFERENCES 101

EZEKIEL (*Continued*).
- vii. **6, 7, 10** 5
- *2, 5* 60
- viii. *1* 60
- x. (chapter cited) 56
- xi. *6, 7* 58
- **13** 58
- xii. *19, 20* 56
- xiii. **11,** *13* 34
- *14, 15* 58
- xiv. *8, 15* 58
- **14, 16** 58
- xv. **8** 58
- xix. *7* 58
- xxi. *30, 34* 58
- xxii. **33** 56
- xxv. **3** 58
- *12, 13* 58
- xxvi. *2* 58
- *6* 58
- xxviii. *8, 23* 58
- **12, 13** 27
- **12, 13,** *14,* **15** 41
- **13, 15** 23
- xxix. *9, 10, 12* 58
- xxx. **7, 12** 58
- xxxi. **3, 5, 6, 13** 3
- **3, 6, 8, 9** 41
- **8, 9** 27
- *17, 18* 58
- xxxii. **7–9** 58
- *8* 5
- *12, 15* 58
- *20–24, 28–32* 58
- xxxiii. *24, 28, 29* 56
- xxxv. *3, 4,* **7, 9,** *12, 14, 15* 58
- *8* 58
- xxxix. **17, 21** 3

DANIEL.
- ii. **31–35, 44** 2
- *32* 37
- iv. **7–13** 3
- vii. *3,* **4–7, 9, 10, 13, 14** 3
- viii. **14, 26** 5
- ix. **26** 34
- xii. **7** 5

HOSEA.
- ii. **18, 19** 3
- iii. **4** 58
- vi. **2, 3** 53
- vii. **13** 56
- x. *14* 56
- xii. *2* 56

JOEL.
- i. **6. 7** 56
- **10** 56
- *15–20* 58

JOEL (*Continued*).
- ii. *3* 58
- *20* 56
- **21, 22** 3
- iii. *19* 58

AMOS.
- v. *9* 56
- *20* 5
- vii. **9** 56
- viii. *9* 5

MICAH.
- ii. **4** 58
- v. **2, 4** 60
- vi. *13, 16* 56
- vii. **13** 56

NAHUM.
- i. **8** 34
- *8, 9* 58

HABAKKUK.
- i. *3* 56
- ii. **3** 60
- iii. **2–4,** *13, 18, 19* 60

ZEPHANIAH.
- i. *15* 58
- ii. *9* 58
- *12* 58
- iii. **5** 5

HAGGAI.
- i. *4, 9* 56

ZECHARIAH.
- ii. **10, 11** 60
- vii. *14* 56
- ix. **9** 60
- x. **3, 4** 2
- xi. *2, 3* 56
- xiv. **7** 5

MALACHI.
- iii. **1** 60

MATTHEW.
- ii. *1–12* 41
- xxi. **42** 2
- *42–44* 60
- xxiv. **15, 39** 34
- *29* 58
- xxv. **13** 5

MARK.
- i. **12, 13** 3
- xii. **10,** *11* 2
- xiii. **35** 5
- xvi. **15** 3

INDEX OF SCRIPTURE REFERENCES

LUKE.
  xvi. *26* 20
  xvii. **34**. 5
  xx. **17**, *18* 2
      17, 18. 60

JOHN.
  i. *1–4* 54
    12, 13. 25
    18. 59
  iii. *3* 21
    3, **4**, *9*, **10, 12** 54
    14, 15. 59
    27 25
  v. **37** 59
  vi. *31, 32, 49–51, 58* 22
    56 25
  viii. *12* 54
    56, 58 49
  ix. **4** 5
  xii. *35, 36, 46* 54
  xiv. **6** 59
    20 51
    20 .... 15, 25

JOHN (*Continued*).
  xv. *4, 5* 15
    4, 5, 7 25
    5 25
    5, 6 47
  xvii. *23, 26* 15
    26 25
  xix. *29*, **30** 58

APOCALYPSE.
  ii. **7** 27
  iii. **14**. 3
  x. **6** 5
  xii. **9** 32
    14. 5
    (chapter cited) 57
  xiii. **1, 2**. 3
  xvii. **4** 33
    14 48
  xxi. **1** 14, 23
    2 18
    9 48
    23–25 5
  xxii. *1, 2*. 7
    16. 5

REFERENCES TO THE APOSTOLIC WORD.

ACTS.
  iv. **11, 12** 2

1 CORINTHIANS.
  x. **4** 2, 53

2 CORINTHIANS.
  v. **17**. 3

GALATIANS.
  iv. **4** 5

EPHESIANS.
  i. **10**. 5
  ii. **20–22** 2

1 PETER.
  ii. **4–6**. 3

2 PETER.
  iii. **13**. 14, 22

THE CONSUMMATION OF THE AGE, THE LORD'S SECOND COMING, AND THE NEW CHURCH

THE CONSUMMATION OF THE AGE

THE LORD'S SECOND COMING

AND

THE NEW CHURCH

FROM THE LATIN OF

EMANUEL SWEDENBORG

"THE CONSUMMATION OF THE AGE, THE LORD'S SECOND COMING, AND THE NEW CHURCH."*

(BEING A SKETCH OF THE LAST WORK PROJECTED BY SWEDENBORG.)

[I.] Concerning the consummation of the age that it was predicted in *Daniel* v., and in *Matthew* xxiv.
(To be treated in chapters.)

[II.] The Lord's Second Coming predicted by the Lord in the Prophets, the Gospels, and the Writings of the Apostles.
(To be treated in chapters.)

[III.] The Lord's New Church, which was announced as the New Jerusalem in the Word of both Testaments, and described in the *Revelation*.
(To be treated in chapters.)

[IV.] An invitation to the New Church made to the whole Christian world, and an exhortation that they should worthily receive the Lord.

[1] One memorable notice is to be added, namely, that all things of the New Church appear in the light of truth, before one in enlightenment, but as soon as they are submitted to the orthodoxy of the church at the present day, the light of truth becomes darkness.

[2] All the points belonging to the doctrine of the New Church are to be explained in their order; likewise those belonging to the old orthodoxy.

---

* Document 303, from *Documents Concerning Swedenborg*, Vol. II., Part II., pp. 773-774. This document was originally in the library of Count Engeström, but is now in the Royal Library in Stockholm.
This and the following sketches on the *Consummation*, etc., and the *Invitation to the New Church*, seem to be sketches of portions of the *Coronis*.

A. THE ABOMINATION OF DESOLATION, THE CONSUMMATION OF THE AGE, AND THE FULNESS OF TIME.*

1. Concerning the consummation of the age, and the abomination of desolation at that time.

2. There is no knowledge of God, except what is erroneous, false or altogether none; there is no knowledge whatever of omnipotence.

3. No knowledge of the Lord.

4. No knowledge of the Divine Human, except a historical one.

5. No knowledge of the Holy Spirit.

6. Hence no knowledge of the Divine Trinity.

7. No knowledge of the holiness of the Word.

8. No knowledge of redemption, except what is false.

9. No knowledge of faith except such as exists before a blind person, which is none at all. The case is the same with all things which depend upon faith, and which from "God" are called theological, from the "church" ecclesiastical, and from the "Spirit of God" by whom they are inspired, spiritual.

10. No knowledge of charity.

11. No knowledge of free will; and hence no human will; thus man is not man.

12. No knowledge of repentance, except oral, which is no repentance.

13. No knowledge of the remission of sins, and hence no knowledge of conversion.

14. No knowledge of reformation and regeneration.

15. No knowledge of the imputation of good and evil; and hence no knowledge of the judgment.

16. No knowledge of heaven and hell.

17. No knowledge of man's state after death; and hence no knowledge of salvation and eternal life.

---

* The four following sketches marked *A, B, C,* and *D,* seem to be rough draughts, for use in the part of the *Coronis* entitled "*The Consummation of the Age,*" etc., which was either lost by Messiter, or was not completed by Swedenborg.

18. No knowledge of Baptism and the Holy Supper, which are [regarded as] scarcely anything else than ceremonies.

19. No knowledge of the Law except an erroneous one.

20. No knowledge of the Gospel, except an erroneous one; and which is, that it is possible for man to be regenerated, and thus saved.

21. There is no doctrine of theology; thus the consummation is such, that no truth remains. For this cause the Christian Religion is torn into so many heresies.

22. The Catechism is not anything.

23. The whole Word is not anything.

24. It follows hence that there is no religion, no church, no worship, no ministry.

25. Because from all that precedes, it follows that there is mere predestination.

26. It hence follows that, because in that church there does not remain a grain of truth, thus that it is the abomination of desolation.

27. The things said in the Word burst with the sound of a loud report, when they are sent towards heaven by those who have studied modern orthodoxy, from experience.

28. Falsities have to be rooted out before truths are implanted.

29. The " fulness of time" is the consummation, because "time" signifies the state of the church; wherefore we read in the *Apocalypse:* "There shall be time no longer," that is neither morning nor day, but night; neither spring nor summer, but winter. The like is signified by "time, times, and half a time."

30. This state of the church has been foretold by the Lord through *Daniel,* and in *Matthew,* and in seven chapters in the *Apocalypse,* which are to be quoted.

31. The religion of this [New] Church is not to be implanted by miracles, but by the Word, and by light which is there from the Lord. This light enters and remains to eternity; but religion through miracles extinguishes this light, because it places the miracles before itself, and, therefore, it perishes with a loud report (compare *Matt.* xxiv. 24, 25).

I conversed with Paris, of whose miracles there exist two volumes, how he wrought his miracles. [I learned] that he wrought them through spirits who entered into the memory of the man.*

B. ABOMINATION OF DESOLATION.

1. The Consummation of the Age, and then the abomination and desolation.
2. No knowledge of God except what is erroneous,—also no knowledge whatever there concerning omnipotence.
3. No knowledge of the Lord.
4. No knowledge of the Holy Spirit.
5. Thence no knowledge of the Divine Trinity.
6. No knowledge of the holiness of the Word.
7. No knowledge of Redemption.
8. No knowledge of faith.
9. No knowledge of charity.
10. No knowledge of free will.
11. No knowledge of repentance.
12. No knowledge of the remission of sins, and thence no knowledge of conversion.
13. No knowledge of regeneration.
14. No knowledge of imputation.
15. No knowledge of heaven and hell.
16. No knowledge of the state of man after death, and thence no knowledge of salvation and eternal life.
17. No knowledge of Baptism.
18. No knowledge of the Holy Supper.
19. No knowledge of the law except what is erroneous.
20. No knowledge of the Gospel except what is erroneous, which is that men can be regenerated and thus saved.

[21] There is no doctrine of theology; thus there is such a consummation, that there is no truth remaining. Thence it is that the Christian Religion is divided by so many heresies, concerning which.

---

*The above synopsis concerning the "*Consummation of the Age, Desolation, and the Fulness of Time,*" is repeated in the following two variations.

C. WHAT THE CONSUMMATION AND DESOLATION IS, AND THE FULNESS OF TIME.

(1) There is no knowledge of God except what is false, none at all.

(2) No knowledge of the Divine Human of the Lord, except historical.

(3) No knowledge of redemption except what is false.

(4) No knowledge of faith, except such as is before a blind man, which is none: in like manner are all things that depend on faith, and are called from God theological, and from the church ecclesiastical, and from the Spirit of God, by whom they are inspired, spiritual.

(5) There is no charity.

(6) No free will, thus no human will, thus man is not man.

(7) No repentance except oral, which is not repentance— no knowledge of the remission of sins.

(8) No reformation and regeneration.

(9) No imputation of good and evil, thus no judgment.

(10) Baptism and the Holy Supper are scarcely anything else than ceremonies.

(11) The Catechism (Decalogue) is not anything.

(12) The whole Word is not anything.

(13) Thence it follows, that there is no religion, church, worship, ministry.

(14) Since from all these it follows that there is mere predestination.

(15) It follows, that in that church there does not remain a grain of truth, and that there is the abomination of desolation.

(16) Thence there are so many heresies.

(17) The things said in the Word burst with a loud report, when they are sent towards heaven by those who have studied modern orthodoxy, from experience.

(18) Falsities must be rooted out, before truths are implanted.

[19] The "fulness of time" is the consummation, because "time" signifies the state of the church, wherefore we read in the *Apocalypse:* "There shall be time no longer," that is,

neither morning nor day, but night; neither spring nor summer, but winter. The like is signified by "time, times, and half a time."

[20] This state of the church has been foretold by the Lord through *Daniel* and in *Matthew*, and in seven chapters in the *Apocalypse*, which are to be quoted.

[21] The religion of this church is not to be implanted by miracles, but by the Word and by light from the Lord there. This light enters and remains to eternity; but religion through miracles extinguishes this light, because it places the miracles before itself, and, therefore, it perishes with a loud report (compare *Matt.* xxiv. 24, 25).

[22] I conversed with Paris (of whose miracles there exist two volumes), how he wrought his miracles; [I learned] that he wrought them through spirits who entered into the memory of the man, and [who persuaded] him; many things concerning them. Still Paris did not apply himself to any religion, and hence did not know anything of the truth of the church; wherefore he is at the present day with those who are in hell.

D. THE CONSUMMATION OF THE AGE, AND THE ABOMINATION OF DESOLATION.

No knowledge of God.
No knowledge of the Lord.
No knowledge of the Holy Spirit.
No knowledge of the holiness of the Word.
No knowledge of redemption.
No knowledge of faith.
No knowledge of charity.
No knowledge of free will.
No knowledge of repentance.
No knowledge of the remission of sins, and of conversion.
No knowledge of regeneration.
No knowledge of imputation.
No knowledge of heaven and hell.

No knowledge of man's state after death, and hence of salvation.

No knowledge of Baptism.

No knowledge of the Holy Supper.

It hence follows that there is no religion, and therefore no church.

The Coming of the Lord.

Miracles.

Invitation to the whole world to the New Church.

—There is one Shepherd and one flock; and Jehovah is one.

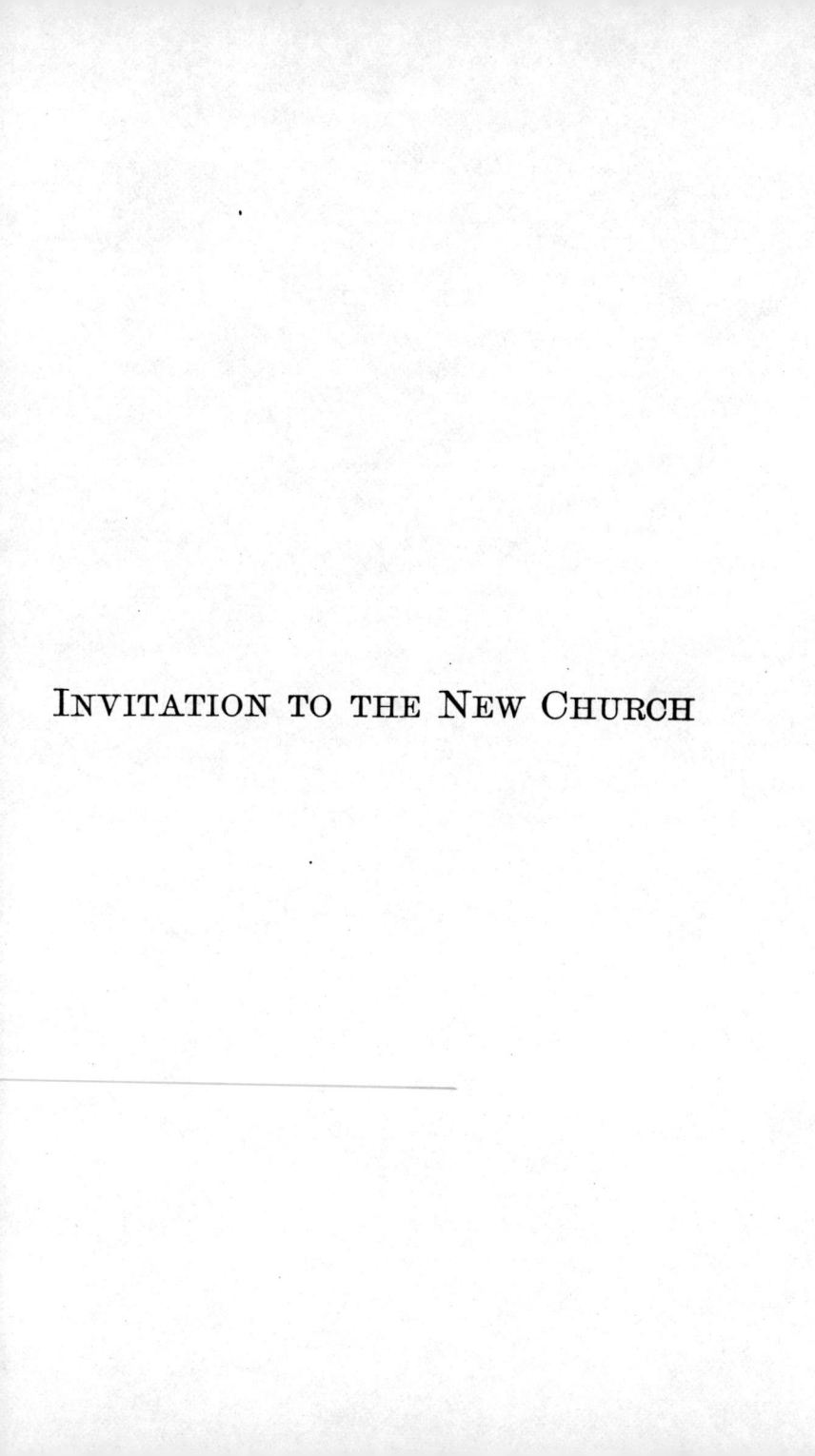

Invitation to the New Church

Invitation

to

The New Church

FROM THE LATIN OF

EMANUEL SWEDENBORG

TRANSLATOR'S NOTE.

The Invitation to the New Church is a part of the last work projected by Swedenborg, entitled, *The Consummation of the Age, the Lord's Second Coming, and the New Church*. This work was evidently intended as a part of the "*Coronis*", for the last proposition, numbered LV., in the *Summary of the Coronis* is as follows: "An Invitation to the whole Christian World to this church, and an exhortation that they receive the Lord worthily, who foretold that He would come into the world on account of it and to it."

We follow the text of the Latin of the Rev. Samuel Howard Worcester, in arranging this fragmentary work immediately following the "*Coronis.*"

The autograph manuscript is lost, but two copies are in the library of the Swedenborg Society, London.

JOHN WHITEHEAD.

Invitation to The New Church.

[Syllabus.]

[I.] *There is no true church unless God is One, and unless He is Jehovah God under a human form—and thus that God is man and man God.*

[II.] *The doctrinals contained in the " True Christian Religion," agree with the doctrinals of those of the Roman Catholic Church, and with the doctrinals of those of the Protestants, who acknowledge a personal union in Christ, and approach Christ, and who partake of the two elements in the Eucharist.*

[III.] *Various causes why now, for the first time, and not before, the above truths of the church [have been revealed]. Among these causes is this, that the New Church is not established before the former church is consummated.*

[IV.] *The Divine Providence in these matters:—*
From the heresies which arose after the time of the Apostles.
Why the Romish Church arose.
The causes of the separation from that Church, [as from] an unworthy mother.
Why the Greek Church separated from the Romish.

[V.] *Various things concerning miracles; that they have destroyed the church (also from the Lord's words in Matt. xxiv.).*

[VI.] *That all things tended in this direction, that men who were called saints, were to be invoked.*

[VII.] *That this Church is not instituted and established through miracles, but through the revelation of the spiritual sense, and through the introduction of my spirit, and, at the same time, of my body, into the spiritual world, so that I might know there what heaven and hell are, and that in light I might imbibe immediately from the Lord the truths of faith, whereby man is led to eternal life.*

[VIII.] *The Advent of the Lord (from the Word and the creeds).*

[IX.] *Invitation to the New Church, that men should go and meet the Lord (from Rev. xxi. and xxii.; and also from Chap. i., etc., etc.).*

[X.] *Hereafter they are not to be called the Evangelical, the Reformed, and still less Lutherans and Calvinists, but Christians.*

[XI.] *Several things concerning miracles.*

---

1. That in Christ Jesus Man is God, and God Man, appears evidently from the Lord's words to His Father:—

All Thine are Mine, and all Mine are Thine (*John* xvii. 10).

From the expression "all Mine are Thine," it is evident that the Man is God; and from the expression, "all Thine are Mine," that God is Man.

2. During man's regeneration, the light of heaven is instilled into natural light, and at the same time the heat of heaven; these two constitute, as it were, the new soul, through which man is formed by the Lord. This light and heat are instilled through the higher mind, which is called the spiritual mind. By virtue of this instilling, or insertion, man becomes a new creature, and becomes more enlightened and more intelligent in matters of the church, and consequently in the reading of the Word. This also is the new understanding and the new will. Afterwards the man is led by the Lord through the above light and through the above heat, and from natural becomes spiritual.

3. There is a still higher or more interior light and heat, which is called celestial. This is inserted and instilled into the former spiritual. The angels of the third heaven who are called celestial, are in this light and heat.

4. This insertion may be explained by a comparison; namely, by the grafting and inoculation of trees; where the grafted slips receive [the sap] interiorly in themselves, according to their form, etc.

5. It is to be clearly shown that without the Lord's Advent, no man could have been regenerated, and hence saved; and that this is meant by "the Lamb taking away the sins of the world." This may be evident from the state of the spiritual world before the Lord's Coming; which was such that not a single truth of faith, nor any good of charity, could pass from the Lord to man. (*This is to be illustrated by the influx of truth and good into evil spirits, into the back part of their heads, etc.*)

6. Miracles close the internal man, and deprive man of all that free will, through which and in which man is regenerated. Free will really belongs to the internal man; and when this is closed up, the man becomes external and natural; and such a man does not see any spiritual truth. Miracles also are like veils and bars lest anything might enter. This bar, or this obstruction, however, is gradually broken, and [then] all truths become dispersed.

7. It is said by the church at this day, following Paul, that faith enters through the hearing of the Word; and some add to this, through a certain meditation from the Word. This, however, is to be understood thus, that truths ought to be drawn from the Word, and that man ought to live according to them. In this case, the man approaches the Lord, who is the Word, and the Truth, and receives faith; for each and all truths are from the Word, which is spiritual light. Thus faith is acquired; because faith belongs to truth, and truth belongs to faith; and nothing ought to be believed except the truth.

8. That there are numberless evils interiorly in man; yea, that there are numberless evils in every lust. Every lust of which man becomes conscious, is a mass and a heap of many things. These things the man does not see, but only the one mass. When, therefore, the man by repentance removes this, the Lord, who sees the interior and inmost things of man, removes them. Unless, therefore, a man approaches the Lord, he labors in vain to render himself free from sin. The case herein is as with those things which were written in a Relation concerning Turtles [see *T. C. R.* 462].

9. That a man who has altogether confirmed himself in the faith and doctrine of the present church, makes no account of repentance, of the law of the Decalogue, and of works and

charity. For he can say, "I cannot do goods from myself; they are contained in faith, whence they come forth of their own accord; I can only know them," and so forth. This is the source of the naturalism which prevails at the present time.

10. By the "fulness of time" is signified consummation and desolation; because "time" signifies the state of the church (see *Rev.* x. 6, and *Ezek.* [xxx. 3]). The same also is signified by "Time, times, and half a time" [see *Rev.* xii. 14; *Dan.* vii. 25; xii. 7]. The times in the world are spring, summer, autumn; the fulness of these times is winter. The times as to light are morning, noon, evening; and their fulness is the night, etc., etc. This is meant by the Lord's coming in "the fulness of the time," or of "times;" that is, when there is no longer any truth of faith, and good of charity left. (Concerning "the fulness of the time," see *Rom.* xi. 12, 25; *Gal.* iv. 4; and especially, *Ephes.* i. 9, 10; *Gen.* xv. 16.)

11. That the Lord's love is present with those who are in faith in Him. This may be clearly seen from this circumstance, that place cannot be predicated of love, nor of faith; for both are spiritual. That the Lord Himself is present appears from this consideration, that spiritual love also is not confined to place. It was not in my own case, whenever I was in the spiritual idea. In a word, presence in the spiritual world is according to love. Wherefore, [the Lord] is omnipresent; He does not move about; He is in place, but not through place; He is thus in space and in what is extended, but not through space, and through what is extended.

12. The desolation of the truth of the church may be compared with consummations on the earth; heat, namely, and all the above [times or seasons] are consummated by winter, and then spring [comes]; and light on earth is consummated by the night, when the morning comes. Wherefore, the Lord in the *Apocalypse* said to those under the altar (vi. 9–11). [See quotation.] A number of passages are to be quoted from the *Apocalypse*, showing that the church has been laid waste, even to its ultimate.

13. That at the present day nothing is known concerning the union of soul and body, is proved by the hypotheses of the learned concerning the soul; especially by that of Des Cartes and others, [who maintain] that the soul is a substance separated from the body, in some place or other; when yet the soul is the inmost man; consequently, is the man from the head to the foot. Thence it is, according to the ancients, that the soul is in the whole, and in every part thereof; and that in whatever part the soul does not dwell inmostly, there man has no life. From this union it is, that all things of the soul belong to the body, and all things of the body belong to the soul; as the Lord said concerning His Father, that all His things are the Father's, and that all things of the Father are His [*John* xvii. 10]. Thence it is that the Lord is God, even as to the flesh (*Rom.* ix. 5; *Col.* ii. 9); and that [He said], "the Father is in Me," and "I am in the Father" [*John* xiv. 10, 11]. Thus they are one.

14. The human mind is of three degrees; which are the celestial, spiritual, and natural. In the first degree is the soul, in the second, is the spirit or the mind, and in the third, is the body. It is the same thing, whether we say that a man's mind is of three degrees, or whether we say that the man himself is. For that of the body which is in principles thus where its first is, is called mind. The remaining parts are derived thence, and are continuations. What is the mind, if it is only to the head, except something that is separated or divorced, in which the mind does not exist through continuation? Let autopsy settle this: The origins of the fibres are the glands of the so-called cortical substance; thence proceed the fibres; and after they are bundled together into nerves, they descend and pass through the whole body, weaving it together and constructing it. The celestial degree, in which is the soul, that is, the inmost man, is a semblance of love; the spiritual degree, in which is the mind, that is, the spirit, which is the mediate man, is a semblance of wisdom from love; and the third degree, in which is the body, which is the ultimate man, is the continant of both; without this third degree, the two higher degrees would not subsist. These things can be further demonstrated from the three heavens, the celestial, spiritual, and natural: where such men are. Wherefore the angels of the higher heavens are invisible to the angels of the lower heavens, if the latter approach the former from their own heavens.

15. Thence it may be seen in light that as a tree exists from its seed, so also the body exists through the soul. Hence also it is that the tree derives its quality from the seed. From this, however, it follows that inasmuch as the soul of Christ was from the Divine essence, His body also must be derived thence.

16. All theologians, when preaching, know nothing of the falsities of their religion. For they preach that God is one; that the Saviour ought to be adored; that man, therefore, ought to believe in the Word and in preachings; that he ought to exercise charity, and practise repentance, so as to desist from evils. While preaching thus, they remember nothing concerning three Gods, concerning their mystical faith, concerning impotence in spiritual matters, and concerning all the remaining dogmas. But let them know, that the falsities which they have imbibed in the schools, are clinging to them interiorly; and other things are merely in the mouth; and that after death they come into the interior things of the spirit; wherefore, these falsities ought by all means to be rooted out. Then also the things that are merely in the mouth, are as the beard on the chin, which afterwards, as is usually the case, is cut off, and he becomes beardless.

17. When orthodoxy enters and explains all those things which priests preach from the Word concerning faith that we ought to believe in God, concerning charity towards the neighbor, conversion, repentance, and the life of piety and spiritual life, they fall as it were into a bucket; then they are overthrown, as when one destroys a dwelling or a house, even so that nothing but ruins remain. The preachers say that these things are not true, unless you believe thus. What does charity, repentance, etc., effect? The very Word then falls, and so forth. It is as if some one undermines a wall, by digging ditches under it. All things are overthrown.

18. Bring an example, where some one preaches devoutly on the above subjects from the Word; and when orthodoxy is brought to bear upon his preaching, you will see that what I saw and declared, is true. (*The example will illustrate this.* . . .) Thus they affirm, and then deny, if orthodoxy is in the internal man, and the subjects that are preached are in the external man. In this case that which then remains in the external man is regarded as of no account and becomes like froth. It is swept away, like an earthquake, or like a ship broken below by water.

19. An example, also, may be brought from genuine orthodoxy on the subject of faith, charity, and free will. From this example will appear plainly the absurdity of [false orthodoxy].

20. That the spiritual things of heaven flow into the whole man, and that [natural things] flow in through the world, is confirmed in light thus: that spiritual and natural things flow in conjointly, but that the evil man inverts the two. That which is within he places outwardly in his mind; and that which is outmost he places within; so that the world is above heaven, that is, heaven below the world. But the devout and good man receives both in the order in which they flow in; the spiritual things which flow in through heaven, he places in the mind above, and the natural things which flow in through the world, he places below. This man stands on his feet erect; but the former is, as it were, inverted.

21. The whole of theology at the present day is nothing but the Divine omnipotence. It is said: (1) That God gives faith where and to whom He pleases. (2) That He remits sins. (3) That He regenerates. (4) That He sanctifies. (5) That He imputes and saves. (6) That He will raise the dead bodies from the graves; that He will cause the skeletons to be alive, and will put into them their former souls. (7) That He will destroy the world, with the sun, the stars, the planets, the earths, and will create it anew. (8) Since omnipotence is everything, and since it constitutes the order which is God, and which is from God, in the whole world, it follows that the man of the church can imagine whatever he pleases; that he can raise himself beyond the ethers, that is, above reason; and that, wherever he pleases, he can go counter to reason, and say that " reason is to be held under obedience to our faith. For is not God omnipotent? And who can, and who dares to, reason in opposition to His omnipotence?" Such are all things of faith at this day.

22. That man cannot discover a single Divine truth, except by approaching the Lord immediately, is due to this, that the

Lord alone is the Word, and that He is the Light and the Truth itself; and man does not become spiritual except from the Lord alone, but remains natural; and the natural man, in spiritual things, sees everything in inverted order; that this is so, is known from Paul. This is the reason why not a single truth has remained in the church, so that now is the consummation, the desolation, the decision, and the fulness [of time]. But still because the Lord is not dead, therefore, according to *Daniel*, there still remains "a root in the earth;" while, according to the *Apocalypse*, "man indeed is willing to die, but yet he cannot." That which "remains" is the faculty of being able to understand the truth, and of being able to will good. This is "the root that remains."

23. The students of modern orthodoxy object, that faith, charity, good works, repentance, remission of sins, etc., cannot be given with a man, before he has received the Holy Spirit. But, as has been shown, the Holy Spirit is the Divine which proceeds from the Lord; and the Lord is perpetually present with every man, the evil as well as the good. Without His presence, no one can live; and the Lord constantly acts, urges, and strives to be received; wherefore, the presence of the Holy Spirit is perpetual. For the sake of confirmation, this was proved in the spiritual world, in the case of a certain devil, by the removal from him of the Lord's presence. And the devil lay dead, exactly like a corpse. Thousands from among the spirits and the clergy saw this, and were thunder-struck. From the Lord's perpetual presence, man has the faculty of thinking, understanding, and willing. These faculties are solely from the influx of life from the Lord. Both Melancthon and Luther were present, and they could not open their lips.

24. The only cause why the Reformation was effected, was that the Word which lay buried, might be restored to the world. For many centuries it had been in the world, but at last it was entombed by the Roman Catholics, and not a single truth of the church could then be laid open from it. The Lord thus could not become known, but the Pope was worshiped as God, in the Lord's place. But after the Word had been drawn forth out of its tomb, the Lord could be made known, truth could be derived from it, and conjunction with heaven could be given.

For this purpose the Lord raised up simultaneously so many men who contended. He raised up Sweden, Denmark, Holland, England that they might receive; and lest [the Word] should be blotted out in Germany through the Pope, He raised up Gustavus Adolphus, who stood for the Reformation, and rose up against [the Pope].

25. Unless the present little work is added to the preceding work, the church cannot be healed. For it would be a mere palliative cure; a wound in which the corrupt matter remains, and which vitiates the neighboring parts. Orthodoxy is this corrupt matter itself, and the doctrine of the New Church indeed brings a healing, but only exteriorly.

26. The origins of all errors in the church have been this: that they have believed that man lives from himself, or from his own life, and that life had been created in him; when yet man is only an organ of life, and is kept in the middle between heaven and hell, and thus in equilibrium or free will.

27. No one is able to see the desolation of truth in the church, before truths from the Word come into light. What heretic, indeed, knows otherwise than that all that he has are truths? Every one can swear to his own. He is in deceptive light arising from confirmations. In such a light is the natural man, when the spiritual man illumines it. Yea the naturalistic atheist can swear that there is no God; and that the existence of God is a mere vain imagination of the common people; wherefore, at heart he scoffs at the doctors of the church.

28. It is known in the church, that the church is the Body of Christ; but how this is has not been known hitherto. Hence it is that the whole heaven is as one man before the Lord; and this man is distinguished into societies, each of which has reference to one member, or organ and viscus in man. In this man or body, the Lord is the soul or life. For the Lord inspires men; and when He is present, He is present through the heavens, as the soul is present through its body. The same is the case with the church on earth; for this is the external man. Wherefore, every one through death is gathered to his own in that body, etc.

29. The things which are stated in the sequel are not miracles, but they are testimonies that I have been introduced by the Lord into the spiritual world for the sake of the ends which. . . . The causes why no miracles are done at the present time. . . . (Further, from the Lord's words in *Matt.* xxiv.) Concerning the miracles of Anthony of Padua, and of most of those who are worshiped as saints; of whose miracles the monasteries are full. Of the miracles of Paris, concerning which there are two volumes in quarto.

30. That the Lord would come in the fulness of time and judge, is meant by His words in *Matthew:*—

When the Son of man shall come in His glory, and all the holy angels with Him, He shall sit on the throne of His glory; and there shall be gathered before Him all nations; and He shall separate them one from another, as the shepherd separateth the sheep from the he-goats (*Matt.* xxv. 31, 32).

This coming of the Lord is meant by the following words concerning Jesus Christ, in the *Apostles' Creed:*—

He ascended into the heavens, He sitteth at the right hand of God the Father Almighty; from thence He shall come to judge the living and the dead.

And also by these words concerning the Lord Jesus Christ in the *Nicene Creed:*—

He ascended into the heavens, and sitteth on the right hand of the Father; and He shall come again in glory to judge the living and the dead; *of whose kingdom there shall be no end.*

31. And also in the *Athanasian Creed:*—

He ascended into the heavens; He sitteth at the right hand of God the Father Almighty: from whence He shall come to judge the living and the dead. . . . And they shall give account for their own deeds. And they that have done good shall enter into eternal life: and they that have done evil into eternal fire. (*Formula Concordiæ* [Leipsic, 1756], pp. 1, 2, 4.)

Besides, the articles of Schmalkalden teach the same thing as the *Apostles'*, the *Nicene*, and the *Athanasian* creeds, namely:—

Jesus Christ ascended into the heavens, He sitteth on the right hand of God, He shall come to judge the living and the dead.

Luther in his *Lesser Catechism* (p. 371) teaches the same thing (*Augsburg Confession*, pp. 10, 14); and our Catechism [the one used in Sweden] teaches the same (p. 303). From the *Augsburg Confession* we quote in like manner:—

He ascended into the heavens, that He might sit on the right hand of the Father, and reign forever, and rule over all creatures. The same Christ will openly come again to judge the living and the dead, according to the *Apostles' Creed* (*Augsburg Confession*, p. 10).

32. That the Lord will not come to judgment, to destroy heaven and earth, appears from many passages in the Word, where His coming is treated of; as for instance where it is said in *Luke:*—

When the Son of man cometh, shall He find faith on the earth? (*Luke* xviii. 8).

Besides many more passages which are quoted in the *True Christian Religion* (n. 765); further, that He will not come to destroy the visible heaven and the habitable earth (*Ibid.* n. 768, *seq.*); but to separate the evil from the good (*Ibid.* n. 772, *seq.*); and many more passages besides. The same also is declared in the Credal Faith which is inserted in every *Book of Psalms* in the whole Christian world, where the *Apostles' Creed* only is set forth. The same is introduced thence into the *Psalms*. By the "living," in the above places, are meant those who are in charity and faith, and who by the Lord are called "sheep;" but by the "dead" are meant those who are not in charity and faith, and who by the Lord are called "he-goats." (Add here *Rev.* xi. 18; and xx 12.)

---

33. *Title:*—

THE CONSUMMATION OF THE AGE, AND THE ABOMINATION OF THE DESOLATION THEN.

There is to be adduced what the Lord says,
1. *Concerning the "abomination of the desolation;"*
2. *What He says [of vastation];*
3. *What the Lord says concerning the "affliction;"*
4. *That "no flesh can be saved;"*
5. *Concerning the "darkening of the sun and moon;"*
6. *The things which are declared in the Apocalypse:*—

Behold, I am He that liveth, and was dead; and behold I am He that liveth unto the ages of the ages (*Rev.* i. 18; also ii. 8; and v. 6).

And again, what the Lord said in *John:*—

<blockquote>
The night cometh when no man can work (*John* ix. 4).
In that night there shall be two men in one bed (*Luke* xvii. 34).
</blockquote>

Further, what the Lord said in *John* (xxi. 18), concerning Peter; also, what Paul said concerning the last times (1 *Tim.* iv. 1–3; 2 *Tim.* iii. 1–7; iv. 3, 4). There shall be explained what the Lord says (*Matt.* xxiv. 27), that this took place on the day of the Last Judgment; also, what He says (vers. 30, 31). That this actually has taken place, see *T. C. R.*, n. 791.

34. The Lord's Coming is according to order in this respect, that the spring does not come until after the winter; nor the morning, until after the night; that the travailing woman has comfort and joy, only after pain; that states of comfort are after temptations; and that there is genuine life after undergoing death; even as the Lord says, "Unless the grain . . . die," etc. (*John* xii. 24). The Lord exhibited the type of this order, when He suffered Himself to be crucified and to die, and when afterwards He rose again; this type signifies the state of the church. . . . The above also is involved in the image which appeared to Nebuchadnezzar, where the Stone at last became a great Rock; it is further involved in the four beasts that came out of the sea; and in what is related there concerning that fearful nation (*which is to be explained*). It is likewise involved in the four ages known to the ancients, the golden, silver, brazen, and iron ages; further, in the ages through which every man passes, from infancy to old age; then is the end of the life of the body, and then comes the life of the spirit, which is the life of all those who have lived well. The same also is involved in the heaven which has first to pass away (*Rev.* xxi. 1, 2). The case with the church is the same.

35. The keys of the kingdom of the heavens were given to Peter, because he represented the Lord as to the Divine Truth; and this is what is meant by "a rock," throughout the whole of the Sacred Scripture. On this account [it is said], "On this rock," that is, on this Divine Truth, "I will build My church," namely, on this that the Lord is "THE SON OF THE LIVING GOD." It shall be shown from the Word, that such is the signification of a "rock." (The "rock" is spoken of in the Word [in the following passages]: *Exod.* xvii. 6; xxxiii. 21, 22; *Num.* xx. 8–11; *Deut.* viii. 15; xxxii. 4–37; 1 *Sam.* ii. 2; 2 *Sam.* xxii. 2, 3, 32, 47; xxiii. 3; *Ps.* xviii. 2, 31, 46; xxviii. 1; xxxi. 2, 3; xl. 2; xlii. 9; lxii. 2, 7; lxxviii. 16, 20, 35; lxxxix. 26; xcii. 15; xciv. 22; xcv. 1; cv. 41; *Isa.* ii. 10; xxii. 16; xlii. 11; li. 1; 1 *Cor.* x. 4.) The "fissures of the rock" mean falsified truths (*Rev.* vi. 15, 16; *Isa.* ii. 19; *Jer.* xvi. 16; *Solomon's Song* ii. 14; *Isa.* xlviii. 21; *Jer.* xxiii. 29; xlix. 16; *Obad.* ver. 3; besides in the *Evangelists*). In this wise also some of the Fathers explained this passage (see *Formula Concordiæ*, p. 345).

36. When the Son alone became Man, and not the whole Trinity, was not then the Divine Essence which is a one and an indivisible trine, separated, that is, disunited or divided?

37. That the whole of the Lord's Prayer, from beginning to end, has respect to this time; that is, to the time when God, the Father will be worshiped in the Human Form. This appears when this prayer is rightly explained.

38. That the churches after the times of the Apostles fell away into so many heresies, and that at the present day there are none other than false churches, is because they have not approached the Lord, when yet the Lord is the Word, and the very Light which enlighteneth the whole world. And yet for them it is impossible to see one single genuine truth from the Word, except what is encompassed with and steeped in falsities, and coheres with falsities, as it is to sail to the Pleiades, or to dig out the gold which is in the centre of the earth. Wherefore, in order that the true Christian religion might be manifested, it was absolutely necessary that some one should be introduced into the spiritual world, and derive from the mouth of the Lord genuine truths out of the Word. The Lord cannot enlighten any one with His light, unless He is approached immediately, and acknowledged as the God of heaven.

39. That miracles are not done at this day, is on account of the reasons which are stated in *The True Christian Religion* [n. 501]; wherefore, the Lord said that they would seduce (*Matt.* xxiv. 24). Again, what is more common with the Roman Catholics than filling the tombs of the saints, and the walls of monasteries with miracles? How many plates of gold and silver are there not in the tomb of Anthony of Padua? How many are there not where the three wise men are said to be buried? And how many are there not at Prague? and in other places? What else than illusions can be derived thence? The fact that I converse in the spiritual world with angels and spirits, that I have described the states of heaven and hell, and the life after death; and further, the fact that there has been disclosed to me the spiritual sense of the Word; besides many other things—is worth more than all these miracles. Such an intercourse, as far as I know, has not been granted by the Lord to any one before. These are evidences that this has been granted for the sake of the New Church, which is the crown of all the churches, and which will endure forever. Being in the spiritual world, seeing the wonderful things of heaven, and the miserable things of hell; and being there in the very light of the Lord in which are the angels, surpasses all miracles. Evidences that I am there, may be seen in abundance in my books.

40. The sole cause why the church has immersed itself into so many falsities, that not a single truth has remained in it; and why it is like a ship that has suffered shipwreck, of which the top of the mast only protrudes, is this—that hitherto they have not approached the Lord immediately; and so long as the Lord is not approached immediately, not a single truth can appear in its own light. The reason of this is, that the Lord is the Word, that is, the all of Divine truth in the Word, and that He alone is the Light which enlighteneth all, as He Himself teaches; and further, that every truth of the Word shines from no other source, than from the Lord alone. This light is what is meant by the spiritual; when, therefore, this light is not present, there is nothing spiritual in man's understanding, but what is merely natural; and all things which contain the spiritual, the natural man sees only invertedly; he sees falsity instead of the truth. On reading the Word, therefore, he bends all things towards his own falsities, and thus falsifies truths; and he takes delight in them. For the natural human mind is in such things as belong to the world and to self; it is delighted solely by such things: wherefore, unless in the above things there is spiritual light, the natural man transfers them to those things which belong to the world and to self, and he puts these in the first place. He thus not only shuns spiritual things, and hides them away, but he also scoffs at them. Faith is spiritual from no other source, that is, it cannot be called spiritual, except from the truths which it contains, and thus by virtue of light from the Lord. Unless faith is from this source, it is natural faith which does not conjoin, and which is not saving.

41. That in the spiritual world no one knows another from his name only, but from the idea of his quality. This idea causes that the other becomes present and is known. Thus, and not otherwise, parents are known by their children; children by their parents; and relations, connections by marriage, and friends, by their relations, connections, and friends. In like manner the learned are known from their writings, and from the reputation of their learning; great men and rulers by the fame of their deeds; in like manner kings, emperors, and popes. All are known by these things alone. It was granted to me to converse with such; but with others it is not possible. A spirit himself also is nothing else than his own quality; on this account every one in that world drops his baptismal name, and the name of his family, and is named according to his quality. Hence it is that "name" in the Word does not signify name, but quality. As the Lord says in the *Apocalypse*:—

Thou hast a few names in Sardis (iii. 4);

and again:—

I know thee by name (*Exod.* xxxiii. 7).

Besides, a thousand other places, where "name" is mentioned. From all this, then, it appears, that no one has the Lord present with himself, unless he knows His quality. This quality the truths of the Word make manifest; for, as many truths as there are in the Word, there are just so many mirrors and ideas of the Lord; for He is the Word itself and He is the Truth itself, as He Himself says. Qualities are of two kinds: one kind belongs to the knowledge concerning the Lord Himself, that He is the God of heaven and earth, the Son of God the Father, One with the Father, that all things of the Father are in Him, in a word, that He is the Human of God the Father.

The other kind belongs to the knowledges of those things that proceed from Him; and the things that proceed from Him, are Himself; as, for instance, those things which He teaches concerning charity, freedom, will, repentance, regeneration, the sacraments, and very many other things. These things also make up the idea of the Lord, because they are from Him.

42. It is an arcanum from the spiritual world, that he who does not approach the Lord directly and immediately with the idea concerning Him, presence is not effected, and still less can he become a recipient of any communication. It is as if some one stands at the side, and appears in the dark. In like manner, no one can converse with another, unless he looks directly at him; communication is then granted when each reciprocally looks at the other. Thus, and not otherwise, do ideas enter into another; and if at the same time there is love, conjunction is effected. If any one, therefore, approaches the Father immediately, He stands as it were at the side; and hence is unable to grant and to impart redemption; that is, He is unable to regenerate, and afterwards to save him.

43. The manifestation of the Lord in Person, and the introduction by the Lord into the spiritual world, both as to sight and as to hearing and speech, surpass all miracles; for we do not read anywhere in history that such intercourse with angels and spirits has been granted from the creation of the world. For I am daily with angels there, even as I am in the world with men; and now for twenty-seven years. Evidences of this intercourse are the books which I have published concerning *Heaven and Hell*, and also the Relations in my last work entitled *The True Christian Religion;* further, what has been stated there concerning Luther, Melancthon, Calvin, and concerning the inhabitants of many kingdoms; besides, the various evidences which are known in the world, and many other evidences besides which are not known. Say, who has ever before known anything concerning heaven and hell? Who has known anything concerning man's state after death? Who has known anything concerning spirits and angels, etc., etc.?

44. In addition to these most manifest evidences, there is the fact that the spiritual sense of the Word has been disclosed by the Lord through me; which has never before been revealed since the Word was written with the sons of Israel; and this sense is the very sanctuary of the Word; the Lord Himself is in this sense with His Divine, and in the natural sense with His Human. Not a single iota in this sense can be opened except by the Lord alone. This surpasses all the revelations that have hitherto been made since the creation of the world. Through this revelation a communication has been opened between men and the angels of heaven, and the conjunction of the two worlds has been effected; because when man is in the natural sense the angels are in the spiritual sense. See what has been written concerning this sense in the chapter on the Sacred Scripture [in *The True Christian Religion*].

45. The correspondences by which the Word as to each and all of its parts has been written, possess such power and strength, that it may be called the power and strength of the Divine Omnipotence; for through these correspondences the natural acts conjointly with the spiritual, and the spiritual with the natural; thus the all of heaven with the all of the world. Thence it is that the two sacraments are correspondences of spiritual with natural things; thence is their strength and power.

46. What are miracles over against these things? Miracles are not done at this day, because they seduce men, and make them natural. They close the interiors of their minds, wherein faith ought to be rooted; wherefore mere falsities proceed thence (see *Matt.* xxiv. 24). What did the miracles effect which were done in Egypt with the sons of Israel? What did those miracles effect which were done before them in the desert? What those miracles when they entered into the land of Canaan? What the miracles which were wrought by Elijah and Elisha? What those which the Lord Himself wrought? Was any one ever made spiritual by their means? What has been the use of miracles among the Roman Catholics? and of those of Anthony at Padua? and of the three wise men at Cologne? And what has been the use of the countless miracles in the monasteries, whose walls are fitted with pictures, plates, and gifts? Has any one ever been made spiritual thereby? Have they not become natural thereby, so that there is scarcely any truth of the Word among them, but only the external things of worship, which have their origin from men and traditions?

47. That in Christ God is Man, and Man God, is confirmed three times in the *Formula Concordiæ;* and also in the *Athanasian Creed*, where it treats of the "assumption of the Human into God;" from the Word (*Rom.* xiv. 11; *Coloss.* ii. 9; 1 *John* v. 20, 21), as well as by the declaration of the Lord Himself, that "the Father and Himself are one;" that "the Father is in Him, and He in the Father;" that "all things of the Father are His;" that "He has Life in Himself;" that "He is the God of heaven and earth;" etc.

48. The soul is the inmost man, and thence according to the ancients it is in the whole and in every part of the body, because the beginning of life resides in the soul; that part of the body in which the soul does not inmostly reside, does not live. Wherefore there is a reciprocal union; and hence the body acts from the soul, but not the soul through the body. Whatever proceeds from God partakes of the human form, because God is Himself the Man; this is especially the case with the soul, which is the first of man.

49. Nothing is more common in the whole heaven and in the whole world, than for one thing to be within another; thus there is an inmost, a middle, and an outmost; and these three intercommunicate, and the power of the middle and outmost are derived from the inmost. That there are three things, one within the other, appears from each and all things in the human body. Around the brain there are three tunics, which are called the dura mater, the pia mater, and the arachnoid; and over these is the skull. Around the whole body there are tunics, one within the other, which taken all together are called the skin. Around each artery and vein there are three tunics; likewise around each muscle and fibre; in like manner around all the rest which are there. In the vegetable kingdom the case is the same. How these parts intercommunicate, and how the inmost enters the middle, and the middle the ultimate, is shown by anatomy, etc. Thence it follows that the same is the case with light; that spiritual light which in its essence is truth, is interiorly in natural light; likewise that spiritual heat which in its essence is love, is in natural heat. By natural heat is meant natural love, because that love becomes warm; and this is clothed with the heat of the blood.

50. All things which people speak concerning the Holy Spirit fall to the ground, as soon as it is believed that man is not life, but only an organ of life; and thus that God is constantly in man, and that He strives, acts, and urges that those things which belong to religion, and consequently those which belong to the church, to heaven and salvation, shall be received. Therefore it is wrong to say that the Holy Spirit is given, or that it is lost. For the Holy Spirit is nothing else than the Divine which proceeds out of the Lord from the Father, and this Divine causes a man's life, and also his understanding and his love; and the presence of this Divine is perpetual. Without the presence of the Lord or the Holy Spirit, man would be nothing but a kind of beast; yea he would not have any more life, than salt, a stone, or a stock. The reason of this is, that man is not born with instinct, like a beast; wherefore a pullet one day old knows the order of its life better than an infant.

51. That it is allowable to confirm the truths of the church by reason or by the understanding, as much as it pleases, and also by various things in nature; and in proportion as truths are so confirmed, they become rooted and shine. It is also allowable to confirm truths by the Word, wherever it pleases, and also to apply for this purpose many things from the Word; and then the Word is not falsified thereby. Those expressions of Scripture through which truths are confirmed, ascend into heaven; they are like the fumes of frankincense; but on the other hand if falsities are confirmed from the Word, they do not ascend into heaven, but are rejected; and they are dispersed on the way with a loud report. This I have heard thousands of times.

52. The manifestation of the Lord, and intromission into the spiritual world, surpass all miracles. This has not been granted to any one since the creation, as it has been to me. The men of the golden age, indeed, conversed with the angels; but it was not granted to them to be in any other than natural light; but to me it is granted to be in both spiritual and natural light at the same time. By this means it has been granted to me to see the wonderful things of heaven, to be together with the angels like one of them, and at the same time to draw forth truths in light, and thus to perceive and teach them; consequently to be led by the Lord. But as concerns miracles: they would have been nothing else than snares for seducing men; as the Lord says (*Matt.* xxiv. 24); and as is related of the magician Simon, that:—

> He bewitched the nations in Samaria, who believed that these things were done from the great power of God (*Acts* viii. 9, *seq.*).

What else are the miracles among the Papists, than snares and deceptions? What else do they teach, than that they themselves should be worshiped as deities, and that they should recede from the worship of the Lord? Have wonder-working images any other effect? Have the idols or corpses of saints throughout the papal dominion any other purpose? Those of Anthony of Padua, of the three wise men at Cologne, and of all the rest, whose miracles fill the monasteries? What have these miracles taught concerning Christ? What concerning heaven and life eternal? Not a syllable.

53. That it is impossible for any church, and for any system of religion to exist, unless it is believed that God is one. When, therefore, the Divine Trinity is believed to be divided into three Persons, how can the metaphysical term essence make one out of three? so long as the properties of each person are diverse, yea, so diverse that they are said not to be communicable? and so long as the equal and particular persons subsist by themselves, and one person has no part and no quality in the other person, or of the other person? But when it is believed that the one God is not only the Creator, but also the Redeemer and Operator, then we have one God; and then for the first time the church exists and subsists, and religion lives. And thus union of three cannot be given otherwise, than it is in every man, as soul, body, and proceeding. These three make one man: why not God, who is Himself the Man from firsts to ultimates? These things concerning God Man have been explained in the work concerning "[*The Divine*] *Love and Wisdom*," and may be consulted. It is also shown that [the soul] is neither ether, nor air, nor wind; that the soul of every man is the man himself, follows thence. As we have now one God in the church, who is God Man and Man God, this church is called the crown of all the churches.

54. That in Christ man is God is to be shown from three places in the *Formula Concordiæ* (from Paul, *Rom.* xiv. 11; *Coloss.* ii. 9; from *John* first Epistle v. 20, 21), and from the Lord's words that:—

1. God was the Word, and the Word was made flesh.
2. All things of the Father are His.
3. All of the Father come to Him.
4. As the Father hath life in Himself, so has the Son (Life in Himself is God).
5. The Father and He are one.
6. He is in the Father, and the Father in Him.
7. He who seeth Him, seeth the Father.
8. He is the God of heaven and earth.
9. He governs the universe. (From the Creed.)
10. He is called "Jehovah, the Redeemer."
11. He is called "Jehovah, our Righteousness."
12. It is said that "Jehovah would come into the world."
13. In the *Apocalypse* (Chap. i.) it is said, that He is "the First and the Last."
14. In a word, He is God the Father who is invisible, in the Human which is visible before minds.

Because there is thus One God in the church, the church is the church, etc., etc. From the *Athanasian Creed* it is said:—

As the soul and body is one man: so God and Man in Christ is one Person; then that the Human Nature was taken into God.

CONCERNING MIRACLES.

55. (*From the sons of Israel.*)
(*From the Lord's words concerning Dives and Lazarus.*)
(*From the Lord's words, Matt.* xxiv. 24.)

The Papal miracles (*which are to be enumerated*). That they only seduce, and do not teach anything; their sole purpose is that they may be invoked as deities; and indeed to this end that gold and silver may be brought to the monasteries; that is, that they may scrape together the treasures of the whole world. The miracles of many of them; as of Anthony at Padua; those by the three wise men at Cologne;

those of the wonder-working images, at which treasures are collected, everywhere in the monasteries, where the walls are covered with pictures of the miracles wrought by their saints, and their idols; the books concerning the miracles of Paris and others. What other purpose have they, than that they may be invoked, to the end that gifts may be scraped together? But who among them has thus far taught the way to heaven, and the truths of the church out of the Word?

For this reason it has pleased the Lord to prepare me from my earliest youth to perceive the Word, and He has introduced me into the spiritual world, and has enlightened me with the light of His Word more proximately. From this it is manifest that this surpasses all miracles.

Beelzebub did more miracles than other Gentile gods, as is evident from the Old Testament; and also the magician Simon.

56. That the Lord made the Natural Man in Himself Divine, in order that He might be the First and the Last; and that He might thus enter with men even into their natural man, and might teach and lead it from the Word. For He rose with His whole natural or external man, and did not leave anything of it in the sepulchre; on which account He said that He had bones and flesh, which spirits have not; and [hence it is] that He ate and drank with His disciples of natural food, and in their sight. That He was Divine, He showed by passing through doors, and by becoming invisible, which never could have been done, unless His Natural Man itself also had been made Divine with Him.

57. That all those things which the orthodox at the present day say concerning the sending of the Holy Spirit fall to the ground, as soon as it is known that the Lord is constantly present with every man, and causes the man to live; and that He resides with man in order that he may go and meet the Lord; and that even if he does not go and meet the Lord, he still has rationality, which would be impossible without the Lord's presence. If the Lord were absent from man, the man would not be a beast, but like some corpse which would be dissipated. This is meant in *Genesis* by:—

God breathed into him a living soul (ii. 7).

58. It shall here be shown from the Word, that the Lord is the "Kingdom of God;" thus, that He is heaven and the church.

59. It shall be shown that the greatest power is in correspondences; because in them heaven and the world, or the spiritual and the natural, are together. That for this reason the Word was written by mere correspondences; wherefore, through it there is the conjunction of man with heaven, and thus with the Lord. The Lord also by this means is in firsts and at the same time in ultimates. On this account the sacraments have been instituted through correspondences, and therefore there is the Divine power in them.

Additions
to the
True Christian Religion

Additions

to the

True Christian Religion

FROM THE LATIN OF

EMANUEL SWEDENBORG

TRANSLATOR'S NOTE.

The following papers, under the title of *Additions to The True Christian Religion*, are taken from the *Documents Concerning Swedenborg*, Vol. II., Part II., pp. 759-773. The original manuscript belonged to the library of Count Engeström, but is now in the Royal Library of Stockholm. On the cover it bears the following inscription:

"These papers, containing original draughts, were written by Assessor Swedenborg himself, and left by him in the ship, in which he made his last journey from Stockholm to Amsterdam. They were given to me by Häkan Paltson of Carlshamn.

"*And. Lanaerus.*"

These documents appear to be first draughts of the following Relations in *The True Christian Religion*, Nos. 16, 71, 76, 110, 112, 134, 136, 159, 335, 459, 504, 508, 695.

JOHN WHITEHEAD.

ADDITIONS

TO THE

TRUE CHRISTIAN RELIGION.

I.

ADDITIONS TO NO. 695 OF "THE TRUE CHRISTIAN RELIGION."

The subject treated of in the published part of this memorable relation, is influx. Swedenborg states there, in an assembly of wise men in the spiritual world, that men at the present day know nothing of an influx from the spiritual into the natural world. Afterwards he called the attention of the angels to some of the wonders that are produced by this influx, and then continues in the unpublished MS. as follows:

1. "Afterwards we discussed various other subjects, and I remarked in connection with hell, that none of all the things which are in heaven, are seen in hell; but that opposite things only appear there, because the affections of the love which prevails there, which are lusts of evil, are opposed to the affections of that love in which the angels of heaven are. In hell, therefore, there appear generally deserts, and in these, birds of night, dragons, owls, bats, and in addition, wolves, tigers, leopards, rats, and mice, and all kinds of poisonous serpents and crocodiles; and where there is an appearance of grass, it is found to consist of briars, thorns, thistles, and of some poisonous plants, which breathe a deadly odor into the air; and in another direction there are heaps of stones, and stagnant pools in which are croaking frogs. All these are likewise correspondences; but, as said above, they are correspondences of the affections of an evil love, and thus lusts. But these things are not created by God; nor are they created by Him in the natural world, where similar things exist; for all things created

by God are good. On the earth they were created at the same time that hell was created; and this exists from men who, by averting themselves from God, became devils and satans. As these terrible things, however, wounded the ears, we turned our thoughts away from them, and directed them to those things which we had seen in heaven.

2. "In respect to miracles I told them that all things which appear in the three kingdoms of nature are produced by an influx from the spiritual into the natural world, and, considered in themselves, are miracles, although, on account of their familiar aspect and their annual recurrence, they do not appear as such. I told them further that they should know that the miracles which are recorded in the Word likewise took place by an influx out of the prior into the posterior world, and that they were produced by an introduction of such things as are in the spiritual world into corresponding things in the natural world; for example, that the manna which every morning descended upon the camp of the children of Israel, was produced by bread from heaven being introduced into the recipient vessels of nature; that in like manner bread and fishes were thus introduced into the baskets of the apostles, which they distributed to so many thousands of men; again, that wine out of heaven was instilled into the water in the pots at the wedding where the Lord was present; further, that the fig-tree withered, because there was no longer any influx into it of spiritual nutriment, by which it was fed from the roots; and finally that such was the case with the other miracles, and that they were not produced, according to the insane notions of some of the learned in the present day, by causes summoned from all parts of nature. Miracles therefore are the effects of the Divine Omnipotence, and take place according to the influx of the spiritual into the natural world, with this difference only, that such things as actually exist in the spiritual world are actually introduced into such things in the natural world as correspond. And I finally concluded, that the cause of such things being done and being possible, is due to the Divine Omnipotence, which is meant by the finger of God, by which the Lord produced His miracles. After I had finished my explanation, the angels kissed me for what I told them, and said they would

ADDITIONS TO THE TRUE CHRISTIAN RELIGION

occasionally invite me to their assemblies. I thanked them, and promised to return, whenever the Lord would grant me permission to do so."

3. On p. 4 of the MS. we read, "All things of nature are like sheaths around spiritual things, and like tunics around muscular fibres. This is the cause of all the wonders and miracles in nature."

II.

ADDITION TO No. 338 OF "THE TRUE CHRISTIAN RELIGION."

The subject of the memorable relation to which the following addition is made in the MS., is respecting "connate ideas," which were discussed by a number of spirits, and regarding which they were enlightened by an angelic spirit, who, according to Swedenborg's original draught, made the following additional statement:

"Afterwards the angelic spirit spoke them: 'I will propound to you an additional problem, which you may consider and solve, viz., Is man an animal, that is, a living being, like the beasts, or can he become such an animal? In many things the two act alike, but altogether from a different origin. Man is formed from thought, but a beast from no thought; whence I conclude that man is not an animal, unless you call him a rational animal, while a beast is a brute animal, into which no rationality can ever be infused; I maintain therefore that man is not a brute animal, like the beasts.' The same difference, he said, exists between these two as between a precious and a common stone, and a precious and a common metal, neither of which can be changed into the other. Further, the same distinction is between them as between the fruits of a superior and an inferior tree, and between the fungi or mushrooms growing out of damp ground, some of which are useful and others useless. Again, he said, the difference is as between oil and water, which cannot be mixed. After saying this he went away, and I returned home. I again watched the atmosphere overhead, where before there had been so many delusive phenomena, but I saw nothing, except some stripes and some shining places; which indicated that the spirits no longer reasoned on connate ideas as before; but simply inquired whether or not there were any connate ideas."

III.

ORDER.

1. Love introduces order immediately into the understanding, and by mediate things into the whole of the mind.
2. Man from his heaven rules his world, but under the Lord's auspices.
3. Man is successively introduced into order from his infancy, by means of his parents, companions, masters; he reacts and acts from himself, and thus imbues himself with order, and finally becomes order in the same proportion as he receives it and imbues himself with it.
4. Order is thus induced upon his state and the form of his life; and the laws of order are truths and statutes.
5. In proportion as man receives love, in the same proportion he makes for himself order, according to which, as said above, love introduces and forms order in him.
6. Man can get himself into a state of order in proportion as he gets himself into a state of love; thus he has the capability of becoming a genuine man; yet he has also the capability of becoming like the beasts of every kind.
7. True order is connected with decorum, beauty, elegance, perfection.
8. Man cannot become order from himself, except first mediately through other men, and afterwards immediately from the Lord; nor is it possible for man to introduce himself into order, and to form order in himself from himself: nor, finally, is it possible for the Lord to do so, unless man acts at the same time from himself.
9. Man cannot become a beast, but he can become as a beast.
10. The productions of love are called affections, and these constitute man's state; and its determinations through the un-

derstanding are called truths. These form man; and in proportion as the latter are produced from the former, man becomes order.

IV.
The Order of Influx.

1. As man instructs his understanding, he prepares it for the reception of light, and hence for wisdom from heaven.
2. As man does the goods of charity, he prepares the will for the reception of the heat of heaven, or of love.
3. Like one who cuts a diamond, he makes preparation for the splendor of light to be diffused from himself.
4. As man makes himself an organ of influx, heaven flows into him, and thus that which is from the Lord out of heaven.
5. As man makes himself spiritual from the Lord, so the Lord made Himself Divine from the Father.
6. The order of influx is this, that man should live according to the laws of order, and in proportion as he does so, he becomes a recipient: wherefore the Lord says, "If any one hears and keeps My commandments, he loves Me, and I will love him and make My abode with him."
7. Each love knows its own love, and they unite reciprocally, or mutually and alternately.
8. The Lord conjoins Himself to man, as man conjoins himself to the Lord; not otherwise. And man conjoins himself to the Lord, as the Lord conjoins Himself to man. The Lord perpetually conjoins Himself.

V.
Reciprocal Conjunction.

Every active principle, for the sake of conjunction, imparts from its own activity to a passive receiver, whence there results a reactive principle, and thereby conjunction.

1. The Lord alone is the active principle, man being passive; and in proportion as man receives of the active principle from the Lord, he reacts, and conjunction results thence.

2. Man's mind is the only active principle in the body, and in proportion as the body receives it, a simultaneous conjunction is effected.

3. Every muscle receives the active principle, and hence results action.

4. The heat of the sun is the only active principle in a tree, and it causes the tree to grow warm; and this warmth reciprocally conjoins itself, and action results hence. It is well known that every heated piece of wood sends forth warmth from itself; but when it is not heated, it cannot give out warmth.

5. From conjunction results equilibrium; and in this all action takes place.

VI.

INFLUX.

The only thing that has hitherto been known concerning influx, is this:—

(1) The influx of light into the eye; (2) Of sound into the ear; (3) Of odor into the nose; (4) Of the body into the soul, and of the soul into the body; (5) Thus of nature into that which is natural; (6) Again of air into the sails of a windmill; (7) Of water into a water-wheel; (8) Or of heat into bodies, whence men and beasts are vivified; (9) Of heat and light into trees, and into all the subjects of the mineral kingdom; (10) Of light into precious stones, whence result colors, and several other phenomena, which are taught by optics; (11) The influx of cold into various objects, whence arise modifications; (12) The influx of thought into speech; (13) Of the air into the lungs; (14) Of the blood from the heart into the arteries and veins; (15) Of wine into a glass; (16) Of beer into a jug; (17) Of the sun and stars into the lives of men; (18) The influx of heat from the fire-place into articles cooked.

The whole mind with all its sensation has remained chained to nature.

The influx of faith [it is supposed] purifies man from the head to the sole of the foot, and this is joined by an influx of all good from God.

Whence it follows, that no one knows anything concerning the influx of love out of the will into the perception of the understanding, and from the understanding into the thought, and hence into speech and action. [When this kind of influx is mentioned,] men laugh, and say, "These are surely figments of the imagination; let these things enter by influx, if they choose; what use is there in knowing all this; will it be of any use?"

Such men are like an inhabitant of an island in the sea, who does not know that there is other inhabitable land in the globe.

He is also like a fish in a stream, which does not know that there is air above the water.

And, further, he is like a boar in a large forest, which does not know that outside the forest there are fields.

VII.

The Thoughts of Materialists Respecting God.

Those who are constantly in a material idea, like the learned who are in the mere rudiments of philosophy, and think that they are wise, if they acknowledge God, adore the mere phrase, that there is a God. But if they are told that God is Man, and that the Lord and Saviour Jesus Christ is that Man, they do not acknowledge it; because their thought respecting Him is material, and not at the same time spiritual, wherefore they also separate His Divine Essence from His Humanity, and declare that there is a mystical conjunction between them.

VIII.

A Memorable Relation Respecting the Council in Constantinople.

1. There was a Synod in Constantinople, where the spiritual things of the church were discussed.

2. Those on the left were divided into four companies, all of which denied that spiritual things may be comprehended [by man].

3. The *first* of these companies declared, that man becomes insane when he thinks on such things; the *second*, that he becomes like a beast; the *third* asserted, that man is like a stock; and the *fourth*, that he is, as it were, blind.

4. On the right were those who declared that man is not a man, unless he is able naturally and rationally to think concerning spiritual things.

5. Among them also were four companies. The *first* declared, that he who is in enlightenment thinks from God the Father; the *second*, that he thinks from the Holy Spirit; the *third*, that his thought is from the Triune God; and the *fourth*, that it is from the Lord who is the Word.

6. After they had finished their ratiocinations, they were encompassed by a column of cloud, which was dark on one side and bright on the other, and the brightness shone in various colors before—— (?)

7. This brightness flowed vividly into the eyes of the *first* cohort on the right, and [a voice was heard] saying, that they were in a fantasy; that they saw a star, and thought it was fixed, when yet it was unstable and evanescent; to the *second* it said, that they saw fish flying in the air, and a hawk in the air devouring them; to the *third*, that they saw a cat in a cellar, and an owl in a corner, looking at each other; and to the *fourth*, that they saw the Word in light, encompassed with a shining brightness, and a rainbow over it.

8. They were not able to see one another, because the vision of their eyes was affected by the color which flowed in.

9. At last an angel came from the heaven of the Lord. He raised the cloud, so that they could see one another as in the natural light of day.

10. The companies [on the left] left the temple through their gate: and the companies on the right through theirs; and to the last of these companies the angel gave palms, and put laurels on their heads; but to the rest he did not give anything.

11. Those on the left had said that there was nothing spiritual in our theology, only in faith, in which nothing is seen; not in charity, not in the remission of sins, not in regenera-

tion, nor in the use of the sacrament, as soon as thought enters into them. But again they said that all things of the church are spiritual, as soon as nothing is seen in them.

12. [They said further] that when attempting to reflect on the things of the church, we are like an eagle in the ether, and like a bird under an air pump.

13. They said, "What can you see in abstract things, and in such as are above the understanding?"

14. Sometimes I was almost persuaded that they were angels; when yet they were like putrid wood that shines on the outside.

---

15. In the world man is two-fold; after death all become single. In the world man has a sensation of both [his internal and external]. This is changed after death.

---

16. What pious and wise man would not like to know the fate of his life after death? wherefore the general principles have been revealed, from which he may know it, if he choose.

---

17. The delight of all in hell is to injure the neighbor, and to blaspheme God; and this delight springs from their heart or their will. They are, however, restrained by punishments from acting according to their delights.

18. The delight of all in heaven consists in doing good to the neighbor, and in blessing God, and indeed from the heart or will, and at the same time by deed.

---

19. Man's interior is his spirit, the interior of that his will; the interior of the will is his love, and the interior of that his delight. The consociation of all is according to delights.

20. (N. B.—That consociations are according to odors, will be shown in a special memorable relation.)

IX.

Concerning Odors.

1. [The odors in hell] are like those of the various wild beasts, of mice, cats, dogs, foxes, wolves, panthers, bears, tigers, or swine. Further, like the stench of the excrements of these beasts, and also of man; like the bad odor of stagnant waters, and marshes; like that of various dead bodies; like that of various putrid substances; like that of privies, urinals, and snakes; like the bad smell of dregs, and of vomit; like the smell of various he-goats. These they sniff in with their noses, and by their eyes are led to the places, whence they emanate. When they scent the sphere of matrimony, they are affected with nausea, or become lustful.

2. In heaven are fragrances from herbs, from various trees, from apples, pears, oranges, olives, grapes. There is an odor as from their leaves; as from the various cereals; and the various kinds of wine and must. There is a perfume as from newly baked bread and cakes; as from various flowers; as from various useful trees in groves and forests; as from honey. There is an aroma as from frankincense, and various other ingredients. The sphere of infants, and of the angels, is changed into such perfumes in heaven.

3. Wild beasts on earth are consociated according to their odors; they know those of their own kind by their smell; likewise their enemies. From the odor they know their food. The bees fly directed by their sense of smell, likewise butterflies.

4. The infernals shun heavenly perfumes, and the inhabitants of heaven the stenches of hell. On this account all domiciles in hell are closed. For this reason the children of Israel were commanded to carry their excrements outside of their camp, and to bury them there. When the dwellings in hell are opened they excite nausea and a desire to vomit; which has been several times experienced by myself. The stenches of hell are sweet-scented to their nostrils; and, on the contrary, the perfumes of heaven ill-scented. Sympathy and antipathy originate thence. Man is not affected by these in the body, because the Lord removes them, for the sake of consociation.

External things also change these into perfumes, and by them internal things are enclosed and shut in.

5. The following odors are not displeasing, viz., those from lambs, sheep, calves; cattle, horses, mules; elephants, camels, stags; chickens, swans, doves, and other birds.

6. There is not a single object in the mineral kingdom which does not give out an odor, and, indeed, in the form of an impalpable powder, by which seeds are impregnated. In the vegetable kingdom also there is not a single object which does not emit an odor. This odor consists of particles of a fatty and saline nature, which are given out at the same time with the watery exhalations. In the animal kingdom also there is not a single object, which does not breathe out an odor. Concerning this see above.

7. Odor or scent is nothing else than a sort of smoke, consisting of minutest substances separated from the various matters. This separation goes on continually, and the loss is made up by the addition of new particles. The particles which are thus cast off become the volatile aura (sphere) of their subject. This appears clearly from the magnet, and from the dogs used in hunting, which pursue hares, stags, and game of different kinds by their smell. Of Jehovah we read that He scented an odor of rest from sacrifices.

8. Those who [in the spiritual world] appear like satyrs scent prostitutes, that is, the smell of prostitutes; those who appear like foxes scent cunning and stratagems; those who are like leopards smell those who are crafty; those who are like panthers scent murderers and assassins; revenge is delightful to them; and so forth.

9. Horses by their smell turn their heads towards those who are rational in truths; but their tails towards those who reason from fallacies. Those who are like dogs, scent those who are luxurious, etc.

10. All those who are in hell turn their backs towards heaven, and cannot endure the least odor thence. If they feel the conjugial [sphere], they become infuriated, and if they do not turn themselves away, they fall into a swoon; likewise when they hear anything concerning the Lord. It is different with men in their externals, because there is a barrier between their externals and internals.

11. The odor of every one is like an elementary sphere in which he freely draws breath; every one pants after this, and as soon as he is in it, he is himself.

12. The hell of robbers and pirates smells like the carcases of cows and sheep; the hell of murderers and assassins like a human corpse; likewise the hell of the Sodomites. This stench is balmy, aromatic, and fragrant to them, and like a sweet feast in their breast; and like a noble spirit of wine in their heads. They inhale this stench with both nostrils and with open mouths, and it refreshes them after they have made their escape from some heavenly odor.

13. Once I saw an astute devil like a leopard ascending a high mountain where there were celestial angels, encompassed by a hedge of olive trees; after he had drawn in a full breath of that odor, he was seized with spasms, became stiffened in all his joints, writhed like a snake, and was cast down headlong. Afterwards he was lifted up by his associates, and taken into a den, and into his own odor, where he revived.

14. Again, I saw how a certain devil was scourged by his associates in hell, because, without any reason, and, as he said, with a stuffed nose, he had approached such as were in a heavenly odor, and had brought back some of their perfume in his garments.

15. Odor in the Word signifies perception.

X.

THE BEING OF GOD OR OF JEHOVAH.

1. We read, "I am the First and the Last, Alpha and Omega, the Beginning and the End, Who is, and Who was, and Who is to come." "In Him we live and move." "From Myself I have created all things." All things are from Him, thence all things are in Him, and all things must turn toward Him, as the surface turns to that which is opposite to it. Those who turn themselves away, are indeed from God, but they are not in God; they are snatched away as it were from the surface; they gyrate in a circle, and are desirous of becoming gods.

2. The essence of God is love and wisdom, and through both of them are omnipotence and omnipresence. He is like the

sun of this world, through which He created the natural universe, in which we are and live as to our body; the essence of which is heat and light; and by these two its power and its presence are caused.

3. God is the sun of the created universe; the heat that proceeds from Him is love, and the light wisdom.

4. Immensity without space, and eternity without time are especially His Being.

XI.

Concerning Redemption.

1. The Lord sustained the passion of the cross as the greatest prophet, that He might bear the iniquity of the people. Like the prophets, concerning whom see (*T. C. R.* 126).

2. All His suffering signified how the Jews had vilified and perverted the Word.

3. The passion of the cross, also, was the last temptation, by which He glorified His Human.

4. Redemption did not consist in that passion, but in the subjugation of the hells, and the orderly arrangement of everything there and in heaven.

5. (The Redemption will be treated of in its own memorable relation hereafter.)

XII.

Concerning the Lord.

1. In Christ Man is God, and God Man.

2. The Father Himself is one.

3. He who has seen the Son has seen the Father; He is in the Father, and the Father in Him.

4. "All mine are thine, and thine are mine;" thus all the Divinity of the Father is in the Son, and all the Humanity of the Son is in the Father.

5. From which it follows that in the Lord God and Saviour, God is Man, and Man is God. Consequently that God the Father assumed the Humanity, and thus that the Lord God is the Saviour, and also the Father.

6. That the Father is the Saviour, appears from *Isaiah*:—

Thou art our Father, though Abraham be ignorant of us, and Israel acknowledge us not; Thou, O Jehovah, art our Father, our Redeemer; Thy name is from everlasting.

And again in *Isaiah*:—

Unto us a Child is born, unto us a Son is given; and His name is God, Hero, Father of Eternity.

And in the Lord's Prayer we read:—

Father in heaven, hallowed be Thy name, Thy kingdom come.

That is:—

God and Father, hallowed be Thy Human, and thus let Thy kingdom come.

7. That the Human is meant by the name of the Father, appears from these words of the Lord, "Father, glorify Thy name," that is, Thy Human, and thus, and not otherwise, Thy kingdom shall come.

8. By a name in heaven nothing else is meant than the quality of any one; wherefore all are named there according to their quality, quite differently from what is done in the natural world. And the quality of God the Father is in His Human; otherwise no one would know the quality of Divinity, because it is infinite.

9. That this is so appears from these words of the Lord, "All that the Father giveth me, shall come to me," and "from henceforth ye know the Father, and have seen Him."

10. Every man can say the same thing of his own soul and his own body, "All thine shall come to me; all mine are thine, all thine are mine; we are one; he who sees me, sees thee," and so forth. If man as to his body is called father, he is the father also as to his soul.

11. For in the Lord, God and Man, or the Divine and the Human nature, are as one Person, as the soul and the body are one man, according to the doctrine which from the *Athanasian Creed* has been received throughout the whole of Christendom.

12. It thence appears why the Lord said of Himself in His Human:—

[I am in the Father, and the Father in Me. The words that I speak unto you I speak not of Myself: but the Father that dwelleth in Me, He doeth the works.]

The Canons
Of The New Church

THE CANONS

OF

THE NEW CHURCH

OR

THE ENTIRE THEOLOGY OF THE NEW CHURCH

CONCERNING

THE ONE AND INFINITE GOD
THE LORD THE REDEEMER,
  AND REDEMPTION
THE HOLY SPIRIT
THE DIVINE TRINITY

A POSTHUMOUS WORK OF

EMANUEL SWEDENBORG

CONTENTS.

	PAGE
PROLOGUE	171

GOD.

SUMMARY	172
I. The Unity of God	172
II. The Essence and Existence of God	173
III. The Infinity of God	174
IV. The Creation of the Universe by God	175
V. The Divine Love and the Divine Wisdom	177
VI. The Creation From Both the Divine Love and the Divine Wisdom	178
VII. The End of the Creation Is a Heaven of Angels	179
VIII. Omnipotence; Omniscience; Omnipresence	181

THE LORD THE REDEEMER AND REDEMPTION.

THE LORD THE REDEEMER.

I. In God Is Love and Wisdom; or Divine Good and Divine Truth	183
II. He Descended as to Divine Truth	184
III. That Truth Is the Word	185
IV. What the Holy Spirit Is, and What the Virtue of the Most High	186
V. The Human of the Lord Is the Son of God	187
VI. The Lord's State of Exinanition While in the World	187
VII. The Unition of the Divine Truth and Good in the Human	188
VIII. After the Unition He Returned to the Father	189
IX. He Successively Glorified Himself	190
X. The Union Is Like That of the Soul and the Body	191

REDEMPTION.

I. The Church Declines from Good to Evil Successively	192
II. The End of the Church Is when the Power of Evil and of Hell Prevails Over Good and Heaven	193
III. In Like Manner There Is a Falling Away From the Internal to the External	195

CONTENTS

	PAGE
IV Description of the End and of Progression in the Word	195
V. Then a Total Damnation Threatens	196
VI. The Lord Redeemed Men and Angels	197
VII. The Temptations of the Lord Christ	197
VIII. Redemption Could Not Be Effected Except by God Incarnate	199

THE HOLY SPIRIT.

I. The Holy Spirit Is the Divine Proceeding	202
II. It Proceeds From God Through the Human	203
III. It Passes Through Heaven into the World	203
IV. And Thence Through Men to Men	204
V. The Holy Spirit Is the Word	205
VI. Its Operation Is Instruction, Reformation, etc.	207
VII. God Is Known From Divine Truth	207
VIII. What Is Meant by the Spirit of Man	207

THE TRINITY.

I. There Is a Divine Trinity	209
II. The Father, Son, and Holy Spirit Are Three Essentials of One God	210
III. The Trinity Was Not Before the World Was Created	212
IV. The Trinity Came into Existence in Jesus Christ After the World Was Created	215
V. This Trinity [Shown] Is From the Word, as [also] From the Apostolic Creed, [but] Not From the Nicene Creed	216
VI. Discordant Ideas Arise From the Nicene Creed	220
VII. This Trinity Has Perverted the Church	220
VIII. It Has Also Falsified the Word	221
IX. Thence Is That "Affliction" and "Desolation" Predicted by the Lord	222
X. There Would Be No Salvation Unless a New Church Were To Be Established by the Lord	224
XI. The Trinity Is In the Lord the Saviour, Hence He Only Is To Be Approached In Order That There May Be Salvation or Eternal Life	226

THE CANONS OF THE NEW CHURCH.

PROLOGUE.

At this day nothing else than the self-evidencing reason of love will reëstablish [the church], because they have fallen.

The church of this day errs concerning God; it errs concerning faith; it errs concerning charity; and it knows nothing of eternal life; thus it is in thick darkness.

The whole of religion is founded upon the idea of God; and that the former follows according to the latter.

This church is that to which all churches, from the first in order, have aimed; and concerning which Daniel prophesied.

The New Church could not be established before the Last Judgment was accomplished, is for the reason that holy things should not be profaned. Then it was promised that the spiritual sense of the Word would be revealed, also that the Lord alone is the Word, whose Coming then takes place.

The reason that few at this day have religion is: (1) It is not known concerning the Lord that He is the Only God, in Person and Essence, in whom is the Trinity; when nevertheless all religion is founded upon the knowledge of God and adoration and worship of Him: (2) It is not known that faith is nothing else than truth, and it is not known whether that which they call faith is truth or not: (3) It is not known what charity is nor what evil and good are: (4) It is not known what eternal life is.

In the degree in which the truths of life become of life, in that degree the truths of faith become of faith and not the least more or less. Some things are of knowledge and not of faith.

IN THIS WORK IS CONTAINED THE
WHOLE THEOLOGY OF THE NEW CHURCH WHICH IS
MEANT BY THE "NEW JERUSALEM"
IN THE APOCALYPSE.

I.
GOD.

SUMMARY.

[I. *There Is One God.*
II. *This One God Is the Esse Itself, Which Is Jehovah.*
III. *This God Himself Is from Eternity; and therefore Is Eternity Itself.*
IV. *God, Because He Is Esse Itself, and Is from Eternity, Is the Creator of the Universe.*
V. *This Only God Is Love Itself, and Wisdom Itself; thus Life Itself.*
VI. *He Created the Universe from the Divine Love through the Divine Wisdom, or Which Is the Same, from the Divine Good through the Divine Truth.*
VII. *The Creation of the Universe with Him Had for an End an Angelic Heaven from the Human Race:*
VIII. *Consequently the Communication and Conjunction of His Love and His Wisdom with Men and Angels, and from It Their Blessedness and Felicity to Eternity.*
IX. *This End Was in God the Creator from Eternity and Is to Eternity, and thence the Preservation of the Created Universe Is from Him.*
X. *God through His Divine Proceeding Is Omnipotence, Omnipresence, and Omniscience.*—(*Apoc. Rev.*, n. 31.)]*

CHAPTER I.

THE UNITY OF GOD; OR, THERE IS ONE GOD.

1. The highest and inmost of all the doctrinals of the church, and hence the universal of them all, is the knowledge and acknowledgment that God is one.

[ANNOTATIONS FROM THE MARGIN.]
*Theological subjects occupy the highest region of the human mind. These are innumerable.
God is in the midst of them. There is influx from Him below into each and every thing as from a sun.
Hence speech, like knowledge of Him, pervades and fills all those things.
Conjunction with Him makes man His image.
Conjunction is effected through love and wisdom.

2. Unless there were one God, the universe could not have been created and preserved.

3. In the man who does not acknowledge God there is no church, and thus no heaven.

4. In the man who does not acknowledge one God, but several, nothing of the church coheres together.

5. There is a universal influx from God, and out of the angelic heaven, into the soul of man, that there is a God, and that He is one.

6. Human reason, if it will, can perceive from many things in the world that there is a God, and also that He is one.

7. Hence it is, that in the whole world, there is no nation, which has religion and sound reason, that does not acknowledge and confess one God.

8. The Sacred Scripture, and hence the doctrines of the churches in the Christian world, teach that there is one God.

9. But as to the quality of that one God, peoples and nations have differed, and still differ.

10. They have differed, and still differ, concerning God and His unity, arises from many causes.

CHAPTER II.

THAT ONE GOD IS ESSE ITSELF, WHICH IS JEHOVAH; OR, OF THE ESSENCE AND EXISTENCE OF GOD IN HIMSELF.

1. That one God is called "Jehovah" from *Esse*, thus from this circumstance, that it is He "Who is, was, and is to come;" or, what is the same thing, that He is "the First and the Last, the Beginning and the Ending, the Alpha and the Omega" (*Rev.* i. 8, 11; xxii. 13; *Isa.* xliv. 6).

2. Consequently, the one and only God is Essence, Substance, and Form; and men and angels are spiritual essences, substances, and forms, or images and likenesses, as far as they derive [this] from that only Divine.

3. This Divine *Esse* is *Esse* in itself.

4. The Divine *Esse* in itself is, at the same time, the Divine *Existere* in itself.

5. The Divine *Esse* and *Existere* in itself, cannot produce another Divine which is *Esse* and *Existere* in itself.

6. Consequently, another God of the same Essence with the one God is not possible.

7. A plurality of gods in ancient times, and partly also in modern times, has derived its origin from no other source than that of not understanding the Divine Essence.

CHAPTER III.

The Infinity of God.

1. God, since He was before the world, and thus before there were spaces and times, is infinite.

2. God, since He is and exists in Himself, and all things in the world are and exist from Him, is infinite.

3. Since God, after the world was made, is in space without space, and in time without time, is infinite.

4. Since God is the all in all things of the world, and, in particular, the all in all things of heaven and the church, is infinite.

5. The infinity of God, by way of correspondence with spaces, is called Immensity; and that His infinity, by way of correspondence with times, is called Eternity.

6. Although the Immensity of God is by way of correspondence with spaces, and His Eternity by way of correspondence with times, still there is nothing of space in His Immensity, and nothing of time in His Eternity.

7. By the Immensity of God is meant His Divinity as to *Esse;* and by the Eternity of God His Divinity as to *Existere;* both in itself, or in Himself.

8. Every created thing is finite; and the infinite is in finite things as in its receptacles.

9. Angels and men, because they are created and hence finite, cannot comprehend the Infinity of God, neither His Immensity and Eternity, such as they are in themselves.

10. Nevertheless, when enlightened by God, they can see, as through lattice-work, that God is Infinite.

11. An image of the infinite is also impressed on varieties and propagations in the world; on varieties, in that there is not one thing precisely like another; and on propagations, both animate and inanimate, in that the multiplication of one seed is to infinity, and prolification to eternity; besides many other things.*

12. In the degree, and according to the manner, in which man and angel acknowledge the Unity and Infinity of God; in the same degree, and in the same manner, if he lives well, he becomes a receptacle and image of God.

13. It is vain to think what was before the world, also what is outside the world; since before the world there was no time, and outside the world there is no space.†

14. A man from thought concerning these things may fall into delirium, unless he is to a certain extent withdrawn by God from the idea of space and time, which inheres in each and all things of human thought, and adheres to angelic thought.

CHAPTER IV.

The Creation of the Universe by the One and Infinite God.‡

1. No one can conceive in idea, and perceive that God created the universe, unless he knows first something concerning the spiritual world and its sun, and also concerning the correspondence, and thence the conjunction, of spiritual things with natural.

[ANNOTATIONS FROM THE MARGIN.]

*Of the Essence and Existence of God; of the Immensity and Eternity of God, or chiefly such things as shall illustrate them.

(3) There are certain forms—as the squaring of the circle, the hyperbola, series of numbers which tend to the infinite; the diversities of the human countenance, also of minds; also the angelic heaven of light can be infinitely increased; from the starry heaven, etc.

†("*Mundus*") "world" is here used in the broad sense of the Latin term, meaning "the order of the universe, the heavens and the heavenly bodies."—Tr.

‡ See above concerning Jehovah, or concerning the *Esse* of God; also n. 1; what is here lacking may be taken therefrom.

2. There are two worlds; a spiritual world where spirits and angels are; and a natural world where men are.

3. There is a sun in the spiritual world, and another in the natural world; and the spiritual world has existed and subsists from its sun, and the natural world from its sun.

4. The sun of the spiritual world is pure love, from Jehovah God, who is in the midst of it, and the sun of the natural world is pure fire.

5. All that proceeds from the sun of the spiritual world is alive; and all that proceeds from the sun of the natural world is dead.

6. Hence everything which proceeds from the sun of the spiritual world is spiritual; and everything which proceeds from the sun of the natural world is natural.

7. Jehovah God, through the sun, in the midst of which He is, created the spiritual world; and mediately through this, He created the natural world.

8. Spiritual things are substantial, and natural things are material; and the latter have existed and subsist from the former, like posterior from prior, or exterior from interior.

9. Hence all things which are in the spiritual world are also in the natural world, and *vice versa*, with a difference of perfection.

10. The natural, since it originates from the spiritual, as the material from the substantial is everywhere together [with the spiritual]; and thus the spiritual exercises its activities and performs its functions through the natural.

11. In the spiritual world an idea of creation perpetually exists; since all things which there exist and are made are created in a moment by Jehovah God.

12. Around every angel in heaven there is an idea of creation.*

[ANNOTATION FROM THE MARGIN.]

*In the spiritual world creation can be seen by the eye. In that world everything is created by the Lord instantaneously; houses and domestic utensils, foods and garments are created; fields, gardens, and plains are created, flocks and herds are created. These and innumerable other things are created according to the affections and perceptions of the angels thence arising, and appear around them and continue as long as they are in those affections, and are removed as soon as those affections cease. In the hells also noxious serpents, wild beasts, and birds are created; not that they are created by the Lord, but that goods are there turned into evils. Hence it is evident that all things in the world are created by the Lord and are fixed by means of natural things which encompass them.

13. There is a correspondence between those things which are of the spiritual world and those which are of the natural world, and by correspondence conjunction of both.

14. From these things it is evident, that the creation of the universe by the one and infinite God can in no wise be conceived without a previous knowledge of the spiritual world and its sun, and of correspondence; and therefore hypotheses have been put forth concerning the creation of the universe, founded upon naturalism, which are foolish.

CHAPTER V.

THE DIVINE LOVE AND THE DIVINE WISDOM IN GOD.

1. Love and Wisdom are the two essentials and universals of life; Love, the *Esse* of life, and Wisdom, the *Existere* of life from that *Esse*.

2. God is Love itself and Wisdom itself because He is *Esse* itself and *Existere* itself in Himself.

3. Unless God were Love itself and Wisdom itself, there would be nothing of love and nothing of wisdom with the angels in heaven, and with men in the world.

4. So far as angels and men are united to God by love and wisdom, so far they are in true love and true wisdom.

5. Two things, namely, heat and light, proceed from Jehovah God through the sun in the midst of which He is; and the heat thence proceeding is love, and the light wisdom.

6. The light thence proceeding is the splendor of love, which in the Word is meant by "glory."

7. That light is life itself.

8. Angels and men are so far alive as they are in wisdom from love from God.

9. It is the same whether it be said, that God is Good itself and Truth itself, or Love itself and Wisdom itself; since all good is of love and all truth is of wisdom.

10. Love and wisdom are inseparable and indivisible; likewise good and truth; wherefore such as the love is with angels and men, such is the wisdom with them; or, what is the same, such as the good is, such is the truth, but not contrariwise.

CHAPTER VI.

THE CREATION OF THE UNIVERSE BY THE ONE AND INFINITE GOD, FROM THE DIVINE LOVE THROUGH THE DIVINE WISDOM.

1. Enlightened reason may see, that the first origin of all things of the world is Love, and that the world is created out of it through Wisdom. Hence it is, and from no other cause, that the world, from its firsts to its ultimates, is a work cohering to eternity.

2. The world is created out of Love through Wisdom, thus through the sun, which is pure Love, in the midst of which is Jehovah God, can be seen from the correspondence of love with heat, and of wisdom with light. By these two, namely, heat and light, the world subsists, and every year all things are created upon its surface; and if these two were withdrawn, the world would fall into chaos, and thus into nothing.

3. There are three things which follow in order, and which proceed in inseparable consort, namely, love, wisdom, and use.

4. Love through wisdom exists and subsists in use.

5. These three are in God, and these three proceed from God.

6. The created universe consists of infinite receptacles of these three.

7. Because love and wisdom exist and subsist in use; the created universe is a receptacle of uses, which, from their origin, are infinite.

8. Since all good is from God, and good and use are one, and since the created universe is the fulness of uses in forms, it follows that the created universe is the fulness of God.

9. Creation was effected from the Divine Love through the Divine Wisdom, is meant by these words in *John:*—

In the beginning was the Word, and the Word was with God, and God was the Word. All things were made by Him—and the world was made by Him (i. 1, 3, 10).

By "God" is there meant the Divine Good of Love; and by the Word, which also was God, the Divine Truth of Wisdom.

10. Evils, or evil uses, did not exist until after creation.

CHAPTER VII

The End Itself of Creation; It Is an Angelic Heaven from the Human Race.

1. In the created world there are perpetual progressions of ends; from first ends, through mediate ends, to ultimate ends.

2. The first ends are of love, or relations to love; mediate ends are of wisdom, or relations to wisdom; ultimate ends are of use, or relations to use. These things are so, because all things which are infinite in God and from God are of love, wisdom, and use.

3. These progressions of ends proceed from firsts to ultimates, and return from ultimates to firsts, and they proceed and return by periods which are called the circles of things.

4. These progressions of ends are more or less universal, and they are the aggregate of particular ends.

5. The most universal end, which is the end of ends, is in God; and it proceeds from God, from the firsts of the spiritual world to the ultimates of the natural world; and from these ultimates it returns to those firsts, and thus to God.

6. This most universal end, or that end of ends from God, is an angelic heaven from the human race.

7. That most universal end is the complex of all ends, and of their progressions in both worlds, the spiritual and the natural.

8.* That most universal end is the inmost, and, as it were, the life and soul, the force and endeavor, in all and each created thing.

9. Thence there is a continued connection of all things in the created universe, from firsts to ultimates, and from ultimates to firsts.

10. From this end implanted in created things, in general and in particular, is the preservation of the universe.

---

* In the Autograph, the three paragraphs now following were deleted by the author by a line drawn through them. So Nordensköld says. See following article, n. 11.—Ed.

On the Other Hand.

1. Love is spiritual conjunction.
2. True love cannot be quiescent in itself, and be restrained within its own limits, but it wills to go forth and embrace others with love.
3. True love wills to be conjoined to others, and to communicate with them, and to give of its own.
4. True love wills to dwell in others, and in itself from others.
5. The Divine Love, which is Love itself, and God Himself, wills that it may be in a subject which is His image and likeness; consequently He wills to be in man, and man to be in Him.
6. In order that this may be effected, it follows from the very essence of Love, which is in God, and hence from an urgent cause, that the universe must needs be created by God, in which are earths, and upon them men, and in the men minds and souls, with which the Divine Love can be conjoined.
7. Therefore all things which are created regard man as the end.
8. Since the angelic heaven is formed from men, from their spirits and souls, all things which are created regard the angelic heaven as the end.
9. The angelic heaven is the habitation itself of God with men, and of men with God
10. Eternal beatitudes, felicities, and delights together, are the ends of creation, because they are of love.
11. This end is the inmost; thus as it were, the life and soul, and as force and endeavor in each and all created things.
12. That end is God in them.
13. This end implanted in created things, in general and in particular, causes the universe to be preserved in the created state, in so far as the ends of an opposite love do not obstruct and destroy.
14. God from His Divine Omnipotence, Omnipresence, and Omniscience, continually provides lest opposite ends from opposite loves should prevail, and the work of creation be ruined even to destruction.
15. Preservation is perpetual creation, as subsistence is perpetual existence.

CHAPTER VIII.

The Omnipotence, Omniscience, and Omnipresence of God.

1. The Omnipotence, Omniscience, and Omnipresence of God do not fall within the human understanding; because the Omnipotence of God is Infinite Power, the Omniscience of God is Infinite Wisdom, and the Omnipresence of God is Infinite Presence, in all things which have proceeded, and which do proceed, from Him; and the Divine Infinite does not fall within the finite understanding.*

2. That God is Omnipotent, Omniscient, and Omnipresent, is acknowledged without a rational investigation; since this flows in from God into the higher region of the human mind and thence into an acknowledgment with all who have religion and sound reason. That it also flows in with those who have no religion; but with them there is no reception, and hence no acknowledgment.

3. That God is Omnipotent, Omniscient, and Omnipresent, man can confirm from innumerable things which are of reason, and at the same time of religion, as from the following:—

4. *First.*—God alone *is* and *exists* in Himself; and every other being and every other thing exists from Him.

5. *Second.*—God alone loves, is wise, and lives and acts from Himself; and every other being and every other thing does so from Him.

6. *Third.*—God alone has power from Himself; and every other being and every other thing has power from Him.

7. *Consequently,* God is the Soul of the whole; from whom all beings and all things are, live, and move.

8. Unless each and all things in the world and in heaven, relate to the One who is, lives, and has power from Himself, the universe would be dissipated in a moment.

9. Hence the universe created by God is the fulness of God; wherefore He Himself said that:—

He is the First and the Last, the Beginning and the End, the Alpha and the Omega, who was, is, and will be, the Omnipotent (*Apoc.* i. 8, 11).

[ANNOTATION FROM THE MARGIN.]
*All things proceed according to order. God is order.

10. The preservation of the universe, which is perpetual creation, is a full testimony that God is Omnipotent, Omniscient, and Omnipresent.

11. Opposites, which are evils, are not removed because God is Omnipotent, Omniscient, and Omnipresent; since evils are outside of subjects, and outside created things, and do not penetrate to the Divine things which are within.

12. Evils, by the Divine Providence, which also is universal in the most particular things, are more and more removed from the interiors, and are cast out to the exteriors, and thus alienated and separated, lest they should inflict any injury on things internal, which are from the Divine.*

[ANNOTATIONS FROM THE MARGIN.]

*The Divine Omnipotence is [exercised] by means of His Human. This is "to sit at the right hand," and to be "The First and the Last" as is said of the Son of man in the *Apocalypse*, and there [it is said] that He is "Omnipotent." The reason is because God acts from firsts through ultimates and thus embraces all things. The Lord acts from firsts through ultimates with men; not through anything belonging to the man but through His own in the man. With the Jews He acted through the Word, thus through His own; through the Word also He performed miracles through Elijah and Elisha; but because the Jews perverted the Word, God Himself came and made Himself the "Last." Then He performed miracles from Himself. Order was first created according to which God acts. Wherefore God made Himself order.

II.

GOD THE REDEEMER JESUS CHRIST, AND REDEMPTION.

[GOD THE REDEEMER JESUS CHRIST.]

SUMMARY.

[I. *In God There Is Love and Wisdom, or Divine Good and Divine Truth.*
II. *He Descended as to the Divine Truth.*
III. *That Truth Is the Word.*
IV. *What Is the Holy Spirit and the Power of the Most High.*
V. *The Human of the Lord Is the Son of God.*
VI. *The State of the Lord's Exinanition while in the World.*
VII. *The Unition of the Divine Truth and Good in the Human.*
VIII. *After the Unition, He Returned to the Father.*
IX. *He Successively Glorified Himself.*
X. *The Unition Is Like that of the Soul and the Body.*]

CHAPTER I.

IN JEHOVAH GOD THERE ARE TWO THINGS OF THE SAME ESSENCE, DIVINE LOVE, AND DIVINE WISDOM; OR, DIVINE GOOD, AND DIVINE TRUTH.

1. Universally and singly, all things in both worlds, the spiritual and the natural, relate to love and wisdom, or to good and truth; since God, the Creator and the Establisher of the universe, is Love itself, and Wisdom itself, or Good itself, and Truth itself:—

2. Altogether as, universally and singly, all things in man relate to the will and the understanding; since the will is the receptacle of good or love, and the understanding the receptacle of wisdom and truth.

3. And altogether as all things of the universe, as to existence and subsistence, have relation to heat and light; and heat in the spiritual world, in its essence, is love, and light there, in its essence, is wisdom; and heat and light in the natural world correspond to love and wisdom in the spiritual world.

4. Hence it is that all things in the church relate to charity and faith; since charity is good, and faith is truth.

5. Therefore, in the prophetic Word there are two expressions; of which one relates to good, and the other to truth; and thus to Jehovah God, who is Good itself, and Truth itself.

6. In the Word of the Old Testament "Jehovah" signifies the Divine *Esse*, which is the Divine Good, and "God" the Divine *Existere*, which is the Divine Truth; and "Jehovah God" signifies both; likewise "Jesus Christ."

7. Good is good, and truth is truth, according to the quantity and quality of their conjunction.

8. Good exists through truth; consequently truth is the form of good, and hence the quality of good.

CHAPTER II.

Jehovah God Descended as to the Divine Wisdom, or the Divine Truth, and Assumed the Human in the Virgin Mary.

1. Jehovah God assumed the Human that in the fulness of time He might become the Redeemer and Saviour.

2. He became the Redeemer and Saviour by the Justice, which, as to the Human, He then put on.

3. He could not have become Justice, and thus the Redeemer and Saviour, as to the Human, except by Divine Truth: since by the Divine Truth, from the beginning, all things were made which were made.

4. The Divine Truth could combat against the hells, and could be tempted, blasphemed, reproached, and suffer.

5. But not the Divine Good, neither God, except in the Human, conceived and born according to Divine Order.

6. Jehovah God therefore descended as to the Divine Truth, and assumed the Human.

7. This is according to the Sacred Scripture, and according to reason enlightened there and from it.

CHAPTER III.

This Divine Truth Is Meant by "The Word Which Was Made Flesh" (*John* i.).*

1. The Word, in the Sacred Scripture, signifies various things; as that it signifies a thing which really exists; also the thought of the mind, and thence speech.

2. In the first place it signifies everything which exists and proceeds from the mouth of God; thus the Divine Truth; and hence the Sacred Scripture, since the Divine Truth is there in its essence and its form. It is on this account that the Sacred Scripture is called in one term "The Word."

3. "The Ten Words" of the Decalogue signify all Divine truths in a summary.

4. Hence the "Word" signifies the Lord the Redeemer and Saviour, since all things there are from Him: thus Himself.

5. From these things it can be seen, that by the "Word," which was "in the beginning with God, and which was God," and which "was with God before the world," is meant the Di-

---

[ANNOTATIONS FROM THE MARGIN.]

*Hypostatic Word. The Son could not call Himself God, thus the Father.

No "Son of God from eternity" could descend, according to the statements of the doctrine of the church of this day. Since it is evident:

(1) He could not call Him His Father.
(2) Nor say that all things of the Father were His.
(3) He who sees Him, sees the Father.
(4) At His *baptism* and at His Transformation God the Father could not say, "This is My beloved Son" (*Matt* iii. 17; xvii. 5).

(Besides many more passages in the Word of the Old Testament concerning the Lord's Coming, collected in the *Doctrine of the New Jerusalem concerning the Lord* (n. 6); and there, that Jehovah would come.)

vine Truth, which was before creation in Jehovah, and after creation from Jehovah; and lastly the Divine Human, which Jehovah assumed in time; for it is said that "the Word was made flesh," that is, Man.

6. The hypostatic Word is nothing else than Divine Truth.

CHAPTER IV.

The "Holy Spirit," Which Came Upon Mary, Signifies the Divine Truth; and the "Power of the Most High," Which Overshadowed Her, Signifies the Divine Good From Which That Exists.

1. The Holy Spirit is the Divine proceeding, thus the Divine Truth, teaching, reforming, regenerating, and vivifying.

2. This is the Divine Truth which Jehovah God spake by the prophets, and which the Lord Himself spake from His own mouth, while He was in the world.

3. This Divine Truth, which also is the Word, was in the Lord by nativity from conception; and afterwards it was beyond all measure, that is, it was infinitely increased; which is meant by the Spirit of Jehovah resting upon Him.

4. The Spirit of Jehovah is called the "Holy Spirit;" since "holy" in the Word is predicated of Divine Truth. Hence it is that the Human of the Lord born of Mary is called "Holy" (*Luke* i. [35]); and the Lord Himself is called "Alone Holy" (*Apoc.* xv. 4); and others are called "holy," not from themselves, but from Him.

5. "The Most High," in the Word, is predicated of the Divine good; wherefore the "power of the Most High" signifies power proceeding from the Divine good.

6. Therefore these two things, "the Holy Spirit coming upon her," and "the power of the Most High overshadowing her," signify both, namely, Divine Truth and Divine Good,— this forming the soul, and that the body,—and communication.

7. Consequently, that these two in the Lord recently born were distinct, as are soul and body, but were afterwards united.

8. In like manner as is done in man, who is born and afterwards is regenerated.

CHAPTER V.

The Human of the Lord Jehovah Is "the Son of God Sent into the World."

1. Jehovah God sent Himself into the world whereby He assumed the Human.
2. This Human, conceived from Jehovah God, is called "the Son of God, which was sent into the world."
3. This Human is called "the Son of God," and "the Son of Man"; "the Son of God," from the Divine Truth and the Divine Good in Him, which is the Word; and "the Son of Man," from the Divine Truth and the Divine Good from Him, which is the doctrine of the church from the Word.
4. No other Son of God is meant in the Word, but He who was born in the world.
5. "A Son of God born from eternity," who is a God by Himself, is not from the Sacred Scripture; and it is also contrary to reason enlightened by God.
6. This was invented and made up by the Nicene Council, as an asylum to which those could betake themselves who wished to avoid the scandals disseminated by Arius and his followers, concerning the Human of the Lord.
7. The Primitive Church, which was called the Apostolic Church, knew nothing concerning the birth of any Son of God from eternity.

CHAPTER VI.

The Lord, so Far as He Was in Divine Truth, as to His Human, Separately, so Far He Was in a State of Exinanition; and so Far as He Was Conjoined with Divine Good, so Far He Was in a State of Glorification.

1. The Lord had two states; one which was called a state of exinanition, the other of glorification.
2. The state of exinanition was also a state of humiliation before the Father; and the state of glorification was a state of unition with the Father.

3. The Lord, when He was in a state of exinanition, or of humiliation, prayed to the Father as though absent or remote; and when He was in a state of glorification, or unition, He spoke with Himself, when with the Father; altogether as with man there are states of the soul and body, before and after regeneration.

4. The Lord, when He was in Divine Truth separately, was in a state of exinanition, since that could be attacked by the hells, or by the devils there, and be reproached by men; wherefore the Lord, when He was in that separately, could be tempted and suffer.

5. But on the other hand, the Lord, when He was in Divine Good conjointly, could not be tempted and suffer by devils in hell, nor by men in the world, since that could not be approached, still less invaded.

6. The Lord, when in the world, was alternately in these two states.

7. The Lord could not otherwise have become Justice and Redemption.

8. The same takes place with the man who is regenerated by the Lord.

9. This [is to be proved] from experience, reason, and the Sacred Scripture.

CHAPTER VII.

THE LORD UNITED DIVINE TRUTH WITH DIVINE GOOD, AND DIVINE GOOD WITH DIVINE TRUTH, THUS THE HUMAN WITH THE DIVINE OF THE FATHER, AND THE DIVINE OF THE FATHER WITH THE HUMAN, THROUGH TEMPTATIONS, AND FULLY BY THE PASSION OF THE CROSS.

1. The Lord in the world, admitted into Himself and underwent grievous and dreadful temptations from the hells, and at length the last of them, which was the passion of the cross.

2. The Lord in temptations combated with the hells and overcame and subjugated them.

3. By this means He reduced the hells to order, and then at the same time the heavens where the angels are, and the church

where men are; since the state of one continually depends upon the state of the other.

4. The Lord also by temptations and rejections, and lastly by the passion of the cross, represented the state of the church, such as it then was, as to Divine truth, thus as to the Word.

5. The Lord by fulfilling the Word, and by temptations, and fully by the last of them, which was the passion of the cross, glorified the Human.

6. Thus He took away the universal damnation which threatened not only the Christian world, but also the whole universe, and likewise the angelic heaven.

7. This is meant by "His bearing and taking away the sins of the world."

8. He underwent temptations and rejections while He was in the state of truth separately, which was the state of His exinanition.

9. The conjunction of the spiritual man with the natural, and of the natural man with the spiritual, is effected by temptations.

CHAPTER VIII.

AFTER THE UNITION WAS ACCOMPLISHED HE RETURNED INTO THE DIVINE IN WHICH HE WAS FROM ETERNITY, TOGETHER WITH AND IN THE GLORIFIED HUMAN.

1. Jehovah God from eternity had a Human such as the angels in the heavens have, but of infinite essence, thus Divine; and He had not a human such as men have on the earths.

2. Jehovah God assumed a Human such as men have on the earths, according to His own Divine order, which is, that it should be conceived, born, grow up, and successively be imbued with Divine Wisdom and Divine Love.

3. Thus He united this Human with His Divine from eternity; and thus He went forth from the Father, and returned to the Father.

4. Jehovah God in this Human, and by it, exercised justice, and made Himself the Redeemer and Saviour.

5. And by its unition with His Divine, He made Himself the Redeemer and the Saviour to eternity.

6. Jehovah God, by the union of this Human with the Divine, exalted His Omnipotence; which is meant by "sitting on the right hand of God."

7. Jehovah God in this Human is above the heavens, illuminating the universe with the light of wisdom, and inspiring into the universe the virtue of love.

8. They who approach Him as Man, and who live according to His precepts, receive these two principles freely from Him.

9. Jehovah God alone is a full Man with the angels.

CHAPTER IX.

JEHOVAH GOD SUCCESSIVELY PUT OFF THE HUMAN FROM THE MOTHER, AND PUT ON THE HUMAN FROM THE FATHER; AND THUS HE MADE THAT HUMAN DIVINE.

1. The soul of the offspring is from the father, and in the womb it clothes itself with the body from the substance of the mother; analogically as seed in the earth, and from the substance of the earth.

2. Hence the image of the father is implanted in the body, first obscurely, then more and more evidently, as the son applies himself to the studies and offices of the father.

3. The body of Christ, so far as it was from the substance of the mother, was not life in itself, but a recipient of life from the Divine in Him, which was Life in itself.

4. Christ, as He successively exalted the Divine Wisdom and the Divine Love in Himself, took upon Himself, the Divine Life which is Life in itself.

5. Christ, in the degree that He took upon Him life in Himself, from the Divine in Himself, in that degree He put off the human from the mother, and put on the Human from the Father.

6. Christ, by this means, made His Human Divine, and from the Son of Mary He made Himself the Son of God.

7. Jesus Christ could thus and not otherwise be in angels and men, and angels and men in Him.

8. But because Mary, His mother, afterwards represented the church, that in this respect she is to be called His mother.

9. Christ, when He was in the human of the mother, was in the state of exinanition, and could be tempted, reproached, and suffer.

10. In this state He prayed to the Father, because He was then as though absent from Him.

CHAPTER X.

The Divine from Eternity and the Human in Time, United as Soul and Body, Are One Person, Who Is Jehovah.

1. In Jesus Christ, the Divine from eternity, and the Human in time, are united as soul and body in man.

2. Unition was and is reciprocal, and thus full.

3. Consequently God and Man, that is, the Divine and the Human, are one Person.

4. All the Divine things of the Father are at the same time in the Human of the Lord.

5. Thus the Lord is the one and only God, who had all power in the heavens and on the earths from eternity, and will have to eternity.

6. He is "the First and the Last," "the Beginning and the End," "who was, who is, and who is to come," "the Alpha and the Omega," "the Almighty."

7. He is "the Father of eternity," "Jehovah our Justice," "Jehovah the Saviour and Redeemer," "Jehovah Zebaoth."

8. They who go to Him, as Jehovah and as the Father, and are united to Him, become His sons, and are called "the sons of God."

9. These are receptacles of His Divine Human.

III.
REDEMPTION.

SUMMARY.

[I. *The Church Declines Successively from Good to Evil.*
II. *The End of the Church Is when the Power of Evil and of Hell Is Over Good and of Heaven.*
III. *In Like Manner the Church Wanders from the Internal to the External.*
IV. *A Description of the End and Progression, in the Word.*
V. *Then a Total Damnation Threatens.*
VI. *The Lord Redeemed Men and Angels.*
VII. *The Temptations of the Lord the Christ.*
VIII. *Redemption Is Not Possible except by God Incarnate.*]

CHAPTER I.

IN PROCESS OF TIME THE CHURCH DEPARTS FROM THE GOOD OF CHARITY, AND THEN TO FALSITIES OF FAITH, AND DIES.

1. There is a church in the heavens, and a church on the earths, and they constitute a one, like the internal and external with man.

2. The church in both worlds is together before the Lord, and appears before the angels as one man.

3. Hence the church can be compared to a man; who is at first an infant, next a youth, afterwards a man, and lastly an old man.

4. While the church is an infant, it is in the good of charity; while a youth and man it is in the truths of faith from that good; and when an old man it is in the marriage of charity and faith.

5. The church, while it is and remains such, endures to eternity; but otherwise, if it recedes from the good of charity of its infancy.

6. If the church recedes from the good of charity of its infancy, it becomes involved in thick darkness as to truths, and falls into falsities, like a blind man into a pit.

7. The four essentials of the church are,—the knowledge of God, the knowledge of the goods of charity, the knowledge of the truths of faith, and life according to them.

8. When the church recedes from charity, it also recedes from these four; and then falsities flow in concerning God, concerning charity, concerning faith, and concerning worship.

9. These flow into the primates of the church, and from them into the people, as from the head into the body.

10. There are two causes why falsities flow into the primates of the church, and flow forth from them: one is the love of ruling from the love of self; the other is intelligence from the *proprium*, and not from the Sacred Scripture.

11. Then from one falsity there flow forth falsities in a continuous series, and this until nothing of truth remains.

12. The Sacred Scripture, while it is applied to confirm those things, is then wholly falsified, and thus the church perishes.

CHAPTER II.

THEN THE END OF THE CHURCH IS AT HAND, WHEN THE POWER OF EVIL BY FALSITIES BEGINS TO PREVAIL OVER THE POWER OF GOOD BY TRUTHS, IN THE NATURAL WORLD, AND THEN AT THE SAME TIME THE POWER OF HELL OVER THE POWER OF HEAVEN.

1. Every man after death comes into his own good, and thence truth, in which he was in the world; in like manner into his own evil, and thence falsity.

2. They who are in good and thence in truth enter into heaven; and they who are in evil and thence in falsity enter into hell.

3. They who are in good on the earths are interiorly in truths; and if in falsities, they can receive truths conformable to their good even after death. But the contrary is the case with those who are in evils. The reason is, because good and evil are of the will; and the will is the *esse* of man, and the understanding thence exists.

4. From the state of heaven and hell, in the spiritual world, it is known how much good prevails over evil, or evil over good, on the earths; since every man after death is gathered to his own, that is, comes into his own evil or good, and heaven and hell are from the human race.

5. This could by no means be known upon the earths, for many reasons.

6. Between heaven and hell there is an interspace, into which evil exhaling from hell ascends, and good descends from heaven; and there they meet.

7. In the midst of this interspace there is an equilibrium between good and evil.

8. From this equilibrium, it is known how much good prevails over evil, or evil over good.

9. The Lord there weighs it as in a balance.

10. This equilibrium is elevated towards heaven as evil prevails over good, and is depressed towards hell as good prevails over evil; since good from heaven depresses it, and evil from hell elevates it.

11. This equilibrium is as a footstool to the angels of heaven, in which their good terminates, and upon which it rests.

12. According to the degree in which this equilibrium is elevated, the happiness of the angels of heaven, from their goods and thence truths, is diminished.

13. When evil prevails over good on the earths, at the same time hell prevails over heaven.

14. From these things it is evident that the end of the church is at hand, when the power of evil prevails over the power of good.

15. It is called the power of good by truths, and the power of evil by falsities, because good has power by truths, and evil has power by falsities.

CHAPTER III.

As the Church Wanders from Good to Evil, thus also it Wanders from Internal Worship to External.

1. In the degree that evil increases in the church, in the same degree the man of the church becomes external.
2. In the degree that the man of the church becomes external, in the same degree he becomes double-minded; that is, evil in internals, and apparently good in externals.
3. Every man after death at length becomes such as he was in internals, but not such as he was in externals.
4. Hence also it is that the world, because it judges from externals, does not know what is the state of the church; thus also, neither how the church decreases and verges to its end.
5. Every man has an internal and an external, which is called the internal and external man.
6. In the internal man the will governs, thus love, the principle of life; but in the external man the understanding governs, which either manifestly, prudently, or cunningly favors the internal.
7. If the internal man is evil and the external man good, in this he is a dissembler and a hypocrite.
8. No man is good, as to his internal man, except from the Lord.

CHAPTER IV.

The Progression of the Church to Its End, and the End Itself, Are Described in Very Many Places in the Word.

1. The successive decrease of good and truth, and increase of evil and falsity in the church, are called in the Word "vastation" and "desolation."
2. The last state, when nothing of good and truth remains, is there called "consummation" and "cutting off."
3. The end itself of the church is the fulness (of time).
4. Similar things are likewise meant in the Word by "evening" and "night;"

5. And also by these words in the *Prophets* and *Evangelists:*—

Then shall the sun be darkened, the moon shall not give her light, the stars shall fall from heaven, and the powers of the heavens shall be shaken [(*Matt.* xxiv. 29; *Isa.* xiii. 10; *Ezek.* xxxii. 7; *Joel* ii. 10; ii. 31; iii. 15; *Amos* v. 20; viii. 9; *Mark* xiii. 24; *Luke* xxi. 25)].

6. Then there is no longer a church, except as to name; but still this residue is there, namely, that man may know and understand truths, and do goods, if he will.

CHAPTER V.

In the End of the Church a Total Damnation Threatens Men on the Earths and Angels in the Heavens.

1. Every man is in the equilibrium which is between heaven and hell, and thence in the freedom of looking and turning himself either to heaven or to hell.

2. Every man after death comes first into this equilibrium, and thus into a similar state of life to that in which he was in the world.

3. They who in the world looked and turned themselves to heaven or to hell, in like manner look and turn themselves after death.

4. In the end of the church, when the power of evil prevails over the power of good, this equilibrium is distended and filled by the evil who depart from the world.

5. Hence this equilibrium is elevated more and more towards heaven, and according to its approach infests the angels there.

6. All they who are in this elevated equilibrium, are interiorly infernal and exteriorly moral.

7. These, because they are such, perpetually endeavor to destroy heaven, which is above them; which also they do by cunning devices from hell, with which, as to their interiors, they make a one.

8. Hence it is that in the end of the church, destruction, and hence damnation, threaten even the angels of heaven.

9. Unless judgment were then executed, no man upon the earths could be saved, nor could any angel in the heavens remain in his state of safety.

CHAPTER VI.

JEHOVAH GOD, BY HIS ADVENT INTO THE WORLD, TOOK AWAY THAT TOTAL DAMNATION; AND BY THAT REDEEMED MEN ON THE EARTHS AND ANGELS IN THE HEAVENS.

1. Jehovah God Himself came into the world, to deliver men and angels from the assault and violence of hell, and thus from damnation.

2. He effected this by combats against hell, and by victories over it; and He subjugated it, reduced it to order, and subjected it to obedience to Himself.

3. After this judgment He also created, that is, formed, a new heaven, and through this a new church.

4. By these Jehovah God put Himself in the power of saving all who believe in Him, and do His precepts.

5. Thus He redeemed all in the whole world, and all in the whole heaven.

6. This is the Gospel, which He commanded should be preached throughout the whole world.

7. This is the Gospel to those who repent, but not to those who purposely transgress His precepts.

CHAPTER VII.

THE LORD, IN THE WORLD ENDURED THE MOST GRIEVOUS TEMPTATIONS FROM THE HELLS, AND ALSO FROM THE JEWISH CHURCH; AND BY VICTORIES OVER THEM, HE REDUCED ALL THINGS TO ORDER, AND AT THE SAME TIME GLORIFIED HIS HUMAN; AND THUS HE REDEEMED ANGELS AND MEN, AND REDEEMS THEM TO ETERNITY.

1. All spiritual temptations are combats against evils and falsities, therefore against the hells; and these temptations are more grievous in the degree in which they invade the spirit of man, and at the same time his body, and torment both.

2. The Lord sustained the most grievous temptations of all, because He fought against all the hells, and also against the evils and falsities of the Jewish Church.

3. His temptations are little described in the *Evangelists*, only by combats with beasts, that is with satans in hell, forty days in the wilderness, and afterwards by infestations from the

devil, and lastly by His sufferings in Gethsemane, and by the dreadful passion upon the cross. [(*Mark* i. 12, 13; *Matt.* iv. 1-11; *Luke* iv. 1-13; *Matt.* xxvi. 36-46; *Mark* xiv. 32-42; *Luke* xxii. 40-46; *John* xviii. 1; *Matt.* xxvii. 26-50; *Mark* xv. 15-37; *Luke* xxiii. 25-46; *John* xix. 1-30.)] But that His temptations or combats with the hells, which, because they were invisible, could not be manifested, were more particularly and more fully described in the *Prophets* and in *David* (*Isa.* lxiii.).

4. The Lord underwent these temptations, in order that He might subjugate the hells which infested heaven and at the same time the church; and that He might deliver angels and men from that infestation, and thus save them.

5. The end of all spiritual temptation is the thorough subjugation of evil and falsity, thus also of hell; and at the same time, the entire subjugation of the external man, for into him evils and falsities from hell flow. For in temptations there is a contest for the dominion of evil over good, and of the external man over the internal; wherefore, on whichever side victory remains, on that side also dominion remains. When therefore victory is on the side of good, good holds dominion over evil, and also the internal man over the external.

6. The Lord suffered these temptations from His boyhood even to the last age of His life, and thus He successively subjugated the hells, and successively glorified His Human; and in the last temptation upon the cross, which was the most grievous of all, He fully conquered the hells, and made His Human Divine.

7. The Lord fought with the hells and also against the falsities and evils of the Jewish Church, as the Divine Truth itself, or the Word, which He was; and He suffered Himself to be reproached, to be assailed with insults, and to be slain, just as the church then did with the Word. Almost the same was done with the prophets, because they represented the Lord as to the Word, therefore with the Lord, who was the Prophet Himself, because the Word itself. That it was so done was according to Divine order.*

[ANNOTATIONS FROM THE MARGIN.]

*Of the representation of the state of the church by the prophets and also by Ezekiel, of whom four times it is said that "He bears the iniquities of the house of Israel" and that the Lord was called the "Greatest Prophet"—see *Doctrine of the Lord* (n 15-17).

8. An image of the victories of the Lord over the hells, and of the glorification of His Human, by temptations, is presented in the regeneration of man; for as the Lord subjugated the hells and made His Human Divine, so with man He subjugates them and makes him spiritual, and thus regenerates him.

9. It is known that the Lord snatches man from the jaws of the devil, that is, of hell, and raises him to Himself in heaven; and that He does this with man by withdrawing him from evils, which is effected through contrition and repentance. These two are the temptations which are the means of regeneration.*

CHAPTER VIII.

REDEMPTION COULD NOT HAVE BEEN EFFECTED, AND HENCE NEITHER COULD SALVATION HAVE BEEN GIVEN, EXCEPT BY GOD INCARNATE.

1. The Word of the Old and of the New Testament teaches that God became incarnate.

2. All the worship of the church before God became incarnate, foreshadowed and regarded Him after He was incarnate; and hence and from no other source was that worship Divine.

3. God Incarnate is "Jehovah our Justice," "Jehovah our Redemption," "Jehovah our Salvation," and "Jehovah our Truth;" and all these are meant, by the two names, Jesus Christ.

4. God not incarnate could not have fought against the hells, and could not have conquered them.

5. God not incarnate could not have been tempted, still less could He have suffered the cross.

[ANNOTATIONS FROM THE MARGIN.]

*The Lord, as Prophet, bore the iniquities of the Jewish Church and did not take them away.

His glorification or union with the Divine of His Father which was in Him as the soul in man, could not be effected except through a reciprocal operation; the Human coöperates with the Divine, nevertheless it is chiefly from the Divine, but still reception, action, or reaction from the Human as from Himself. But so far as it was conjoined He acted at the same time from both. In like manner as man is regenerated and becomes spiritual from the Lord. When an infant He was as an infant; while a boy [He was as a boy] and from boyhood, He increased in wisdom (*Luke* ii. 40-50). He could not be born wisdom but could become it according to order. He advanced to full conjunction.

6. God not incarnate could not have been seen and known; thus He could not have been approached, and so could not have been conjoined to men and angels, unless through Himself incarnate.

7. Faith in God not incarnate is impossible, but only in Him incarnate.

8. Hence it is that it was said by the ancients, that no one can see God and live, and by the Lord, that no one hath seen the shape of the Father nor heard His voice.

9. Also, that by means of angels God manifested Himself to the sight of the ancients in the human form, which form was representative of God incarnate.

10. Every operation of God is effected from firsts by ultimates, thus from His Divine through His Human. Hence God is the "First and the Last, who was, who is, and who is come"

11. In the ultimates of God are all things Divine together; thus, in our Lord Jesus Christ are all things of His Father.

12. From these things it follows, that redemption could by no means have been effected except by God incarnate.

13. And there could have been no salvation except by God incarnate, thus by the Lord, the Redeemer and Saviour; which salvation is perpetual redemption.

14. Hence it is, that they who believe in the Lord Jesus Christ have eternal life; and they who do not believe in Him have not that life.*

[ANNOTATIONS FROM THE MARGIN.]

*Redemption itself was the subjugation of the hells and the arrangement of the heavens into order, and thus a preparation for a new spiritual church.

Without this redemption no man could have been saved, nor angels have subsisted in their state of happiness.

The Lord not only redeemed men, but also angels [see Chapter vi.].

Redemption was a work purely Divine.

This redemption could not have been effected except by God incarnate [see Chapter viii.].

The passion of the cross was the last temptation, which, as the Greatest Prophet, He endured and through which also He truly subjugated the hells and glorified His Human: thus that it was not redemption, but the means of redemption.

That the passion of the cross was redemption itself, is a fundamental error of the church.

This error together with the error of three Divine Persons from eternity, has perverted the whole church to such a degree that there is not any spiritual residue of it remaining: —

The errors flowing from [the doctrine] of redemption [held] at the present day [namely] that it is the passion of the cross are to be enumerated.

The falsities of faith cannot be conjoined with the good of charity.

Predictions in *Daniel* and the *Prophets* concerning those successive states.

Concerning Christ (*Matt.* xxiv.).

IV.
THE HOLY SPIRIT.

UNIVERSALS.

I. *The Holy Spirit is the Divine, which proceeds from the One, Infinite, Omnipotent, Omniscient, and Omnipresent God.*

II. *The Holy Spirit, in its essence, is that God Himself; but in subjects in which it is received, it is the Divine Proceeding.*

III. *The Divine, which is called the Holy Spirit, proceeds from that God Himself through His Human; comparatively as that which proceeds from man, that is, as what he teaches and operates proceeds from his soul through his body.*

IV. *The Divine, which is called the Holy Spirit, proceeding from God through His Human, passes through the angelic heaven, and through this into the world, thus through angels into men.*

V. *Thence [it passes] through men to men, and in the church chiefly through the clergy to the laity, what is Holy is continually given, and it recedes if the Lord is not approached.*

VI. *The Divine Proceeding, which is called the Holy Spirit, in its proper sense is the Holy Word, and the Divine Truth therein;*

VII. *And its operation is instruction, reformation, and regeneration, and hence vivification and salvation.*

VIII. *In the degree that any one knows and acknowledges the Divine Truth which proceeds from the Lord, in that degree he knows and acknowledges God; and in the degree that any one does this Divine Truth, in that degree he is in the Lord, and the Lord in him.*

IX. *The Spirit, in respect to man, is his intelligence, and whatever thence proceeds*

CHAPTER I.

The Holy Spirit Is the Divine, which Proceeds from the One, Infinite, Omnipotent, Omniscient, and Omnipresent God, Through His Human Assumed in the World.

1. The Holy Spirit is not God by itself, or singly; neither does it proceed from God through the Son as a Person from Persons, according to the doctrine of the church at the present day.

2. This is utterly inconsistent; because a person is defined as being not a part and quality in another, but as subsisting separately.

3. And [it is said] that although the property and quality of the one are separate from that of the other, yet they are from an essence one and indivisible.

4. Thence inevitably results not only the idea, but also the confession of three Gods, which however from the Christian faith, according to the *Athanasian Creed*, are not to be called three but one.

5. The truth is, that from eternity, or before creation, there were not three Persons, each of which was God; thus there were not three infinite, three uncreate, three immense, eternal, omnipotent ones, but One.

6. But after creation there arose a Divine Trinity, since then from the Father was born a Son, and from the Father through the Son proceeds the Holy, which is called the Holy Spirit.

7. Hence, because the Father is the soul and life of the Son, and the Son is the Human body of the Father, and the Holy Spirit is the Divine proceeding, it follows that they are consubstantial, and hence that they subsist not singly, but conjointly.

8. And because the property of the one, according to order, is derived and passes over into the other, and from this to the third, they are one Person, thus one God.

9. Comparatively as in every angel, and in every man, from the soul by the body proceeds every operation.

10. Reason enlightened by the Sacred Scripture may perceive this, namely, that there is a Trinity of Person, which is a Trinity of God, but not a trinity of Persons, because this is a trinity of gods.

CHAPTER II.

THE HOLY SPIRIT, WHICH PROCEEDS FROM THE ONE GOD THROUGH HIS HUMAN IN ITS ESSENCE IS THE SAME GOD, BUT THAT APPARENTLY TO SUBJECTS, WHICH ARE IN SPACES, IT IS THE DIVINE PROCEEDING.

1. What God was before creation, such He is after it; thus such as He was from eternity, such He is to eternity.

2. Before creation God was not in extended space, so neither is He after creation, to eternity;

3. Consequently, God is in space without space, and in time without time.

4. Thus the Holy Spirit, which proceeds from the one God through His Human is the same God.

5. Concerning God, since He is everywhere the same, it cannot be said that He proceeds, except apparently, in respect to spaces, because these proceed, thus apparently to subjects which are in spaces.

6. And since these are in the created world, it follows that the Holy Spirit there is the Divine proceeding.

7. The Omnipresence of God fully proves that the Holy Spirit is the Divine proceeding from the one and indivisible God, and not a God as a Person by Himself.

CHAPTER III.

THE DIVINE WHICH IS CALLED THE HOLY SPIRIT, PROCEEDING FROM GOD THROUGH HIS HUMAN, PASSES THROUGH THE ANGELIC HEAVEN INTO THE WORLD, THUS THROUGH ANGELS INTO MEN.

1. The one God in His Human is above the angelic heaven, appearing there as a sun, from which proceed love as heat, and wisdom as light.

2. Thus the Holiness of God, which is called the Holy Spirit, flows in order into the heavens; immediately into the supreme heaven, which is called the third heaven; immediately and also mediately into the middle heaven, which is called the second heaven; similarly into the ultimate heaven, which is called the first heaven.

3. It flows through these heavens into the world, and through this into men there.

4. Nevertheless the angels of heaven are not the Holy Spirit.

5. All the heavens together with the churches on the earths, in the sight of the Lord are as one Man.

6. The Lord alone is the soul and life of that Man, and all who are animated and live from Him are His body. Hence it it is said, that the faithful constitute the body of the Lord, and they are in Him, and He in them.

7. The Lord flows into the angels of heaven, and into the men of the church, in a certain likeness to the manner in which the soul flows into the body with man.

CHAPTER IV.

THENCE IT PASSES THROUGH MEN TO MEN, AND IN THE CHURCH CHIEFLY THROUGH THE CLERGY TO THE LAITY.

1. No one can receive the Holy Spirit except from the Lord Jesus Christ, because it proceeds from God the Father through Him. And by the Holy Spirit is meant the Divine proceeding.

2. No one can receive the Holy Spirit, that is, the Divine Truth and the Divine Good, unless he goes to the Lord immediately, and at the same time is in the love [of Him].

3. The Holy Spirit, that is, the Divine proceeding, never becomes man's; but it is constantly the Lord's with him.

4. Therefore the Holy, which is meant by the Holy Spirit, does not inhere; neither does it remain, except so long as the man who receives it believes in the Lord, and at the

same time is in the doctrine of truth from the Word, and in a life according to it.

5. The Holy, which is meant by the Holy Spirit, is not transferred from man to man, but from the Lord through man to man.

6. God the Father does not send the Holy Spirit, that is, His Divine, through the Lord into man; but the Lord sends it from God the Father.*

7. The clergyman, because he is to teach doctrine from the Word concerning the Lord, and concerning redemption and salvation from Him, is to be inaugurated by the promise, [*sponsionem*] of the Holy Spirit, and by the representation of its transfer; but it is received by the clergyman according to the faith of his life.

8. The Divine, which is meant by the Holy Spirit, proceeds from the Lord through the clergy to the laity by preaching, according to the reception of the doctrine of truth thence.†

9. And by the sacrament of the Holy Supper, according to repentance before it.

CHAPTER V.

The Divine Proceeding, Which Is Called the Holy Spirit, in Its Proper Sense Is the Word, Wherein Is the Holiness of God.

1. The Word is Holiness itself in the Christian Church, from the Divine of the Lord which is therein, and which is therefrom; wherefore the Divine proceeding which is called the

---

[ANNOTATIONS FROM THE MARGIN WHICH PERHAPS BELONG HERE.]

*The Holy Spirit is the Divine Operation and virtue proceeding from the one God. It proceeds out of the Lord and from God the Father.
It proceeds out of the Lord from God the Father and not contrariwise.
†It proceeds to the clergy and from them to the laity.
It flows into men who believe in the Lord, and if according to order, into the clergy, and thus through them into the laity.

Holy Spirit, in its proper sense, is the Word and the Holiness of God.*

2. The Lord is the Word because it is from the Lord, and concerning the Lord, and thus in its essence is the Lord Himself.

3. The Lord, because He is the Word, is alone Holy; and He is the "Holy One of Israel," who is so often mentioned in the *Prophets*, concerning whom it is also there said that He alone is God.

4. Hence it is that the place where the ark was in the tabernacle,—because in it was the law, the beginning of the Word, over which was the propitiatory, and over this the cherubim, all which signified the Lord as the Word,—was called the "Sanctuary," and the "Holy of Holies."

5. Hence it is also that the New Jerusalem, which is the church that approaches the Lord alone, and derives truths from His Word, is called "holy," and also the "city of holines"; and the men in whom that church is are called a "people of holiness"; also this church is the "kingdom of saints," in *Daniel*, which will endure forever.

6. The Prophets and Apostles are called "holy" because the Word was written through them.

7. The Holy Spirit since it is taught by the Lord from the Holy Word is called the "Spirit of Truth," of whom the Lord says that He shall not speak from Himself but from the Lord, and that it is He Himself.

8. To him "who speaks a word against the Holy Spirit it is not remitted," because he denies the Divinity of the Lord and the holiness of the Word; for he has no religion.

9. To him who speaks a word against the "Son of man" it is remitted, because he denies this and that to be Divine Truth from the Word in the church, but believes that in the Word and from the Word are Divine truths. The "Son of man" is the Divine Truth from the Word in the church, and this cannot be seen by all.

[AN ANNOTATION FROM THE MARGIN WHICH PERHAPS BELONGS TO THIS PLACE.]

*The Holy Spirit proceeds from the Lord through the Word.

CHAPTER VI.

[Chapters VI., VII., and VIII. of this Treatise could not be found, when this tractate was copied from the autograph.]

THE DIVINE VIRTUE AND OPERATION WHICH ARE MEANT BY THE HOLY SPIRIT ARE INSTRUCTION, REFORMATION, REGENERATION; AND ACCORDING TO THESE VIVIFICATION, SANCTIFICATION, AND JUSTIFICATION; AND ACCORDING TO THESE PURIFICATION FROM EVILS, REMISSION OF SINS, AND SALVATION.

CHAPTER VII.

IN THE DEGREE THAT ANY ONE KNOWS AND ACKNOWLEDGES THE DIVINE TRUTH WHICH PROCEEDS FROM THE LORD, IN THE SAME DEGREE HE KNOWS AND ACKNOWLEDGES GOD; AND IN THE DEGREE THAT ANY ONE DOES THIS DIVINE TRUTH, IN THE SAME DEGREE IS HE IN THE LORD AND THE LORD IN HIM.*

CHAPTER VIII.

THE SPIRIT IN RESPECT TO MAN IS HIS INTELLIGENCE AND WHATEVER THENCE PROCEEDS, AS HIS OPERATION AND VIRTUE.†‡

---

*See UNIVERSALS VIII., page 201.
†See UNIVERSALS IX., page 201.

[ANNOTATION FROM THE MARGIN, WHICH PERHAPS IS TO BE READ HERE.]

‡ By the spirit of man is meant his intelligence, and thus also whatever proceeds from it as his operation and virtue.

V.

THE DIVINE TRINITY.

SUMMARY.

[I. There Is a Divine Trinity.
II. The Father, Son, and Holy Spirit Are Three Essentials of One God.
III. There Was Not a Trinity Before the World Was Created.
IV. The Trinity Came Into Existence in Jesus Christ After the World Was Created.
V. This Trinity Appears from the Word, as also from the Apostles' Creed, but Not from the Nicene.
VI. Absurd Ideas Derived from the Nicene Trinity.
VII. This Trinity Has Perverted the Church.
VIII. It Has also Falsified the Word.
IX. Thence There Is that "Affliction" and "Desolation" Foretold by the Lord.
X. There Is No Salvation Unless a New Church Is Established by the Lord.
XI. The Trinity Is in the Lord the Saviour; hence He alone Is To Be Approached, as He Is Salvation or Life Eternal.]

[To Be Noted.]

1. The idea of the common people of the Divine Trinity, is, that God the Father sits on high, and His Son at His right hand, and that they send the Holy Spirit to men.

2. The idea of the clergy in respect to the Trinity is, that there are three Persons, each of whom is God and Lord, and that to the three there is one and the same essence.

3. The idea of the wise among the clergy is, that there are three communicable properties and qualities; but by three Persons are meant what are incommunicable.

4. There is a Divine Trinity; from the Sacred Scripture and from reason.

5. From a trinity of Persons there inevitably follows a trinity of Gods.

6. If God is one the Trinity of God is necessary, and thus a Trinity of a Person.

7. The Trinity of God, which is also a Trinity of a Person, is in God incarnate, or in Jesus Christ.

8. This is confirmed from the Sacred Scripture;

9. And also from reason, since there is a trinity in every man.

10. The Apostolic Church never thought of a trinity of Persons, as is evident from their Creed.

11. A trinity of Persons was first invented by the Nicene Council.

12. It was derived therefrom into the churches after that time, even to the present time.

13 That doctrine could not be corrected before this day.

14. The trinity of Persons has inverted the whole church, and has falsified each and all things thereof.

15. All say that it is beyond comprehension, and that the understanding is to be held under obedience to faith. What is "a Son born from eternity"?

16. In the Lord there is a Trinity, and in the Trinity is Unity.

CHAPTER I.

There Is a Divine Trinity; Namely, the Father, the Son, and the Holy Spirit.

1. The Unity of God is acknowledged and received throughout the whole world, wherever there is religion and sound reason.

2. Therefore the Trinity of God could not be known; for if it had been known, yea, if only declared, concerning the Trinity of God, man would have thought of a plurality of Gods, which both religion and also sound reason abhor.

3. Therefore the Trinity of God could not be known except from revelation, thus not otherwise than from the Word; neither could it be received unless the Trinity of God were also the Unity of God, for otherwise there would be a contradiction which begets a nonentity.

4. The Trinity of God did not actually exist before the Son of God the Saviour of the world was born; and before that there was not Unity in Trinity and Trinity in Unity.

5. The salvation of the human race depends upon the Trinity of God, which at the same time is Unity.

6. By the Trinity of God which at the same time is Unity, is meant the Divine Trinity in one Person.

7. The Lord the Saviour of the world taught that there is a Divine Trinity, namely, the Father, the Son, and the Spirit;

For He commanded His disciples to baptize in the name of the Father, of the Son, and of the Holy Spirit;

He also said that He would send to them the Holy Spirit from the Father;

He moreover oftentimes mentioned by name the Father, and called Himself His Son, and He breathed upon His disciples, saying, "Receive ye the Holy Spirit."

Furthermore, when Jesus was baptized in Jordan there came forth a voice from the Father, saying, "This is my beloved Son," and the Spirit appeared over Him in the form of a dove.

The angel Gabriel also said to Mary, "The Holy Spirit shall come upon thee, and the power of the Most High shall overshadow thee, and the Holy One that shall be born of thee shall be called the Son of God." "The Most High" is God the Father.

The Apostles likewise in their epistles often name the Father, the Son, and the Holy Spirit; and John in his First Epistle says, "There are three that bear witness in heaven, the Father, the Word, and the Holy Spirit," etc.

CHAPTER II.

THESE THREE, FATHER, SON, AND HOLY SPIRIT, ARE THREE ESSENTIALS OF ONE GOD, SINCE THEY ARE ONE, AS SOUL, BODY, AND OPERATION WITH MAN ARE ONE.

1. The Divine Trinity, which at the same time is Unity, can by no means be comprehended by any one, except as the soul, body, and proceeding operation with man; consequently unless the Divine itself which is called the Father is the Soul, the

Human which is called the Son is the Body of the Soul, and the Holy Spirit is the proceeding operation.

2. Therefore in the Christian Church everywhere it is acknowledged that in Christ God and Man, that is, the Divine and the Human, are one Person, as the soul and the body in man. This is there acknowledged from the *Athanasian Creed*.

3. Wherefore he who comprehends the union of the soul and body and the resulting operation, comprehends the Trinity and at the same time the Unity of God, in a kind of shadow.

4. The rational man knows, or may know, that the soul of the son is from the father, and that the soul clothes itself with a body in the womb of the mother, and that afterwards all operation proceeds from both.

5. He who knows the union of the soul and body, knows also or may know that the life of the soul is in the body, and that thus the life of the body is the life of the soul.

6. Consequently that the soul lives, and therefore feels and operates, in the body and from the body; and that the body lives, feels, and operates from itself while from the soul.

7. This is because all things of the soul are of the body, and all things of the body are of the soul; hence and from no other origin is their union.

8. It is only an appearance that the soul operates separately, from itself through the body, when yet it operates in the body and from the body.

9. From these things the rational man, who knows the intercourse of the soul and the body, can comprehend these words of the Lord; that:—

The Father and He are one;
All things of the Father are His, and all His are the Father's;
All things of the Father come to Him;
The Father hath given all things into the Son's hand;
As the Father works, so the Son also works;
He that sees and knows the Son, sees and knows the Father also;
They who are one in the Son are one in the Father;
No one hath seen the Father except the Son, who is in the bosom of the Father, who hath manifested Him;
The Father is in the Son and the Son in the Father;
No one cometh to the Father except through the Son;

As the Father hath life in Himself, so hath He given to the Son to have life in Himself;

In Jesus Christ all the fulness of the Divinity dwells bodily;

and many other things besides.

There by the "Son" is meant the Human of the Father.

10. From these things it follows, that the Divinity and the soul of the Son of God, our Saviour, are not distinctly two, but one and the same. The Son of God is the Human of God the Father, is fully shown above; for what else did Mary, the mother, bring forth than the Human in which was the Divine from the Father? Hence from nativity He was called the "Son of God;" for the angel Gabriel said to Mary:—

The Holy One that shall be born of thee shall be called the Son of God,

and the Holy which was born from Mary was the Human in which was the Divine from the Father.

CHAPTER III.

BEFORE THE WORLD WAS CREATED THE TRINITY OF GOD WAS NOT.

1. The Sacred Scripture teaches that God is one, and reason enlightened by the Lord sees it there and thence. But that God was triune before the world was created, the Sacred Scripture does not teach, and reason enlightened therefrom does not see. What is said in *David* concerning the Son, "This day have I begotten thee," is not from eternity, but in the fulness of time; for the future in God is present, thus to-day; in like manner as in *Isaiah:*—

Unto us A Boy is born, unto us a Son is given, whose name is God, Hero, the Father of eternity.

2. What rational mind, when it hears that before the creation of the world there were three Divine Persons, called the Father, the Son, and the Holy Spirit, does not say within itself while thinking of them, "What is meant by a Son born

from God the Father from eternity? How could He be born? And what is the Holy Spirit proceeding from God the Father through the Son from eternity? And how could He proceed and become God by Himself? Or how could a person beget a person from eternity? and both produce a person? Is not a person a person? How can three Persons, of which each is God, be conjoined into one God, otherwise than into one person? And yet this is contrary to theology, and this to that. How can the Divinity be divided into three Persons, and yet not into three Gods, when yet each Person is God? How can the Divine essence, which is one, the same, and indivisible, fall into number, hence be either divided or multiplied? And how can three Divine Persons be together and take counsel together in a non-extense of space, such as was before the world was created? How, from Jehovah God, who is One, and thence Sole, Infinite, Immense, Eternal, and Omnipotent, could there be produced three equals to Himself? How can a Trinity of Persons be conceived of in the Unity of God, and the Unity of God in a Trinity of Persons? Besides the idea of plurality destroys the idea of unity, and *vice versa*. Perhaps it would have been possible for the Greeks and Romans also to unite all their gods into one, which were many, by identity only of essence."

3. The rational mind, in revolving and reflecting upon a Trinity of Persons in the Divinity from eternity, might also consider of what use was it that a Son was born, and that the Holy Spirit went forth from the Father through the Son before the world was created? Was there a use for three to consult how the universe should be created? And thus that three should create it? When yet the universe was created by the one God? Neither was there occasion that the Son should redeem, when yet redemption was effected after the world was created, in the fulness of time; nor that the Holy Spirit should sanctify, because as yet there was no man to be sanctified. Therefore if there were those uses in God's idea, still they were not [realized] before the creation of the world, but after it actually existed; from which it follows, that the Trinity from eternity was not a real Trinity, but ideal, and still more so is a Trinity of Persons.

4. Who in the church, while reading the *Athanasian Creed*, is able to understand this? That it is of the Christian verity, that each Person by Himself is God, and yet that it is not lawful by the Catholic religion to account them three Gods? Is not religion thus to him something other than truth? and that in truth three Persons are three Gods, but that from religion they are one God?

5. A trinity of Persons in the Divinity before the world was created, did not come into the mind of any one from the time of Adam down to the advent of the Lord, as is clear from the Word of the Old Testament, and from histories concerning the religion of the ancients. Neither did it come into the mind of the Apostles, as is evident from their writings in the Word. Neither did it come into the mind of any one in the Apostolic Church, which was before the Council of Nice, as appears from the *Apostles' Creed*, in which no Son from eternity is mentioned, but a Son born from the Virgin Mary. A Trinity of Persons from eternity is not only above reason, but opposed to it. It is against reason that three Persons created the universe; that there were three Persons, and each one God, and not three Gods but one, and then three Persons and not one Person. Will not the New Church about to come call this age of the old church benighted or barbarous, when they worshiped three Gods? Similarly irrational are those things which are derived from that Trinity.

6. A Trinity of Persons in the Divinity from eternity was first taught by the Nicene Council, as appears from the two Creeds, the Nicene and the Athanasian. And afterwards it was received by the churches as the principal dogma, and as the head of the doctrines, after that time even to the present day. There were two reasons why that Trinity was given forth by the Council of Nice; the first was, that they knew not how otherwise to dissipate the scandals of Arius, who denied the Divinity of the Lord; the other, because they did not understand what is written by the evangelist John (Chap. i. 1, 2, 10, 14; xvi. 28; xvii. 5). How these things are to be understood may be seen above.

7. The Divinity before the world was created as believed according to the Nicene Council and the churches after that,

to consist of three Persons each of which was God, and that from the first Person was born a second, and from these two went forth a third, is not only above the understanding, but contrary to it, and the faith of a paradox, which is opposed to the rational understanding. It is a faith in which there is not anything of the church, but a persuasion of the false, such as obtains with those who are insane in religious matters. But still it is not here said of those who do not see [these things to be] contradictory and contrary to the Sacred Scripture and yet believe them, that they *are insane in religious matters;* thus it is not said of the Council of Nice, nor of the churches derived from it after that time, because they did not see.

CHAPTER IV.

THE TRINITY OF GOD CAME INTO EXISTENCE AFTER THE WORLD WAS CREATED, AND ACTUALLY IN THE FULNESS OF TIME, AND THEN IN GOD INCARNATE, WHO IS THE LORD THE SAVIOUR JESUS CHRIST.

1. The Trinity of God did not and could not exist before the world was created; also that there are three essentials of one Person in God Man, of which the Trinity of God is predicated, has been shown above.

2. God as the Word came into the world and assumed the Human in the Virgin Mary, and the Holy One thence born was called the "Son of the Most High," the "Son of God," the "Only Begotten," is known from the Old Word where it is predicted, and from the New where it is described.

3. Since therefore God the Most High, who is the Father, by His Divine proceeding which is the Holy Spirit, conceived the Human in the Virgin Mary, it follows that the Human born of that conception is the Son, and the conceiving Divine is the Father, and that both together is the Lord, God, the Saviour, Jesus Christ, God and Man.

4. It follows also that the Divine Truth, which is the Word, and in which is the Divine Good, was the seed from the Father

from which the Human was conceived. The soul is from the seed, and by the soul is the body.

5. In confirmation this arcanum shall be mentioned: The spiritual origin of all human seed is truth from good, but not Divine Truth from Divine Good in its own essence, infinite and uncreate as in the Lord, but in its own form finite and created. See the *Delights of Wisdom Concerning Conjugial Love* (n. 220, 245).

6. It is known that the soul adjoins to itself a body, which may serve it for performing uses, and afterwards it conjoins itself to the body as it serves, and this even until the soul becomes of the body, and the body of the soul. This is what the Lord says, that He is in the Father, and the Father in Him.

7. From these things it follows that the Trinity of God came into existence after the world was created, and then in God Incarnate, who is the Lord, the Saviour, Jesus Christ.

CHAPTER V.

The Trinity of Persons in the Divinity Is from the Council of Nice, and Was Derived Thence into the Catholic Church and [the Churches] After it, and Is Therefore To Be Called the Nicene Trinity. But the Trinity of God in One Person, the Lord God the Saviour, Is From Christ Himself, and Was Thence in the Apostolic Church, and Therefore Is To Be Called the Christian Trinity; and This Trinity of God Is the Trinity of the New Church.

1. There are three summaries of doctrine of the Christian Church concerning the Divine Trinity and at the same time Unity, which are called the *Apostolic*, the *Nicene*, and the *Athanasian Creeds*. The *Apostles' Creed* was written by men who are called the Apostolic Fathers; the *Nicene Creed*, by an assembly of bishops and priests who were called together by the emperor Constantine in the city of Nice, with a view to dissipate the scandals of Arius concerning his denial of the

Divinity of the Son of God; and the *Athanasian Creed*, by a certain person or persons after that council. These three Creeds were acknowledged and received by the Christian Church as ecumenical and catholic, that is, as the universals of doctrine respecting the Father, the Son, and the Holy Spirit.

2. The *Apostolic Creed* teaches thus:—

"I believe in God the Father Almighty, the God of heaven and earth; and in Jesus Christ His Son, our Lord, who was conceived by the Holy Spirit and born from the Virgin Mary. I believe in the Holy Spirit," etc.

The *Nicene Creed* teaches thus:—

"I believe in one God, the Father Almighty, Maker of heaven and earth; and in one Lord Jesus Christ, the only begotten Son of God, born from the Father before the ages; begotten not made, consubstantial with the Father, by whom all things were made; who came down from heaven and was incarnate by the Holy Spirit from the Virgin Mary, and became Man. And [I believe] in the Holy Spirit, the Lord and Giver of Life, who proceedeth from the Father and the Son, who with the Father and the Son, together is adored and glorified; who spake through the prophets."

The *Athanasian Creed* teaches thus:—

"The Catholic Faith is this: We venerate one God in Trinity and Trinity in Unity. . . . There is one Person of the Father, another of the Son, and another of the Holy Spirit. . . . The Father is uncreate, immense, eternal, omnipotent, God and Lord; in like manner the Son, and in like manner the Holy Spirit; and yet there are not three uncreate, immense, eternal, omnipotent Gods and Lords, but One. . . . The Son is of the Father alone, not made, nor created, but begotten. The Holy Spirit is from the Father and the Son, neither made, nor created, nor begotten, but proceeding. In this Trinity none is before or after, and none is greater or less, but all the three Persons are co-eternal and co-equal. But as we are compelled by the Christian verity to acknowledge every Person by Himself to be God and Lord, so we are forbidden by the Catholic religion to say there be three Gods and Lords."

Furthermore, it thus teaches concerning the Lord Jesus Christ:—

"Although He be God and Man, yet there are not two, but one Christ."

3. From these things declared in the three creeds it may be gathered how in the understanding of each there is a Trinity of God in Unity, and a Unity in Trinity.

For the *Apostolic Creed* teaches concerning God the Father, that He is the Creator of the Universe; concerning His Son, that He was conceived by the Holy Spirit and born of the Virgin Mary; and concerning the Holy Spirit, that He is.

Moreover, the *Nicene Creed* teaches concerning God the Father, that He is the Creator of the Universe; concerning the Son, that He was begotten before all ages, and that He descended and became incarnate; and concerning the Holy Spirit, that He proceeds from both.

But the *Athanasian Creed* teaches concerning the Father, Son, and Holy Spirit, that they are three Persons co-eternal and co-equal, and that each of them is God, and yet that there are not three Gods, but one; and that although from the Christian verity each Person by Himself is God, yet from the Catholic religion it is not allowable to say there are three Gods.

4. From these three Creeds it appears that two Trinities are taught, one which existed before the world was created, another, which was after it; the Trinity before the world was created, in the *Nicene* and *Athanasian Creeds*, but the Trinity after it, in the *Apostolic Creed*; consequently the Apostolic Church knew nothing of a Son from eternity, but only of a Son born in the world, and thus that it invoked the latter and not the former; and, on the other hand, the church after the *Nicene Creed*, as if established anew, acknowledged a Son from eternity as God, but the Son born in the world not so.

5. These two Trinities differ as much from each other as evening and morning, yea, as night and day, and thus that both together can by no means be confirmed in one man of the church; because religion would perish with him, and with religion sound reason. The reason is, that from the Nicene and Athanasian Trinity God cannot be thought of as one, but in the Apostolic Trinity He can be; and He is so thought of in this, because it is given in the Lord Jesus Christ, the Son of God born in the world.

6. The Divine Trinity is in the Lord God the Saviour Jesus Christ, He Himself teaches, for He says that:—

He and the Father are one (*John* x. 30).
He is in the Father, and the Father in Him (*John* xiv. 10, 11).
All things of the Father are His (*John* iii. 35; xvi. 15).
He that seeth Him seeth the Father, and He that believeth in Him believeth in the Father ([*John* xii. 44]).

And according to Paul:—

In Him dwelleth all the fulness of the Divinity bodily (*Col.* ii. 9).

According to John:—

He is the true God and eternal life (1 *Epis.* v. 20).

And according to *Isaiah:*—

He is the Father of eternity (ix. 5).

And in other places in the same prophet, where it treats of Him, it is said: " He is Jehovah the Redeemer," "the only God," and that from redemption " He is Jehovah our Justice," and that He is "God the Father" where He is spoken of; that "He will not give His glory to another;" and that the "Holy Spirit is from Him."

Now because God is one, and because there is a Divine Trinity, the Father, Son, and Holy Spirit, according to the Lord's words (*Matt.* xxviii.), it follows that the Trinity is in one Person, and in the Person of Him who was conceived of God the Father and born of the Virgin Mary, and thence was called the " Son of the Highest," the " Son of God," the " Only Begotten Son" (*Luke* i. 31–35; *John* i. 18; xx. 34; *Matt.* iii. 17; xvi. 16; xvii. 5). In all these and in the above cited passages, no Son from eternity is meant, is evident to both the internal and external sight.

Since therefore this Divine Trinity (which is also the fulness of the Divinity dwelling in Him bodily, according to Paul) is in the Lord God, the Saviour Jesus Christ, it follows that He alone is to be approached, invoked, and worshiped, and that when this is done, at the same time the Father is approached, and [thus the man] receives the Holy Spirit; for He teaches that He is the way, the truth, and the life, and that no one cometh to the Father but by Him, and that he that entereth not by Him as the door into the sheepfold (that is, into the church), is not a shepherd, but a thief and a robber; and also that they who believe in Him have eternal life, and that they who believe not shall not see life (*John* iii. 15, 16, 36; vi. 40; xi. 25, 26; 1 *John* v. 20).

7. Since the Divine Trinity and at the same time the Divine Unity is in the Lord Jesus Christ, the Redeemer and Saviour of the world, this is the Trinity of the New Church.

[When the two copies were transcribed, two leaves containing Chapters VI. and VII. were already wanting at this part of the autograph. But of Chapter VII., articles n. 6, 7, 8 were still there. These may be seen just below.]

[CHAPTER VI.]
[DISCORDANT IDEAS DERIVED FROM THE NICENE TRINITY.]
. . . .

[CHAPTER VII.]
[THIS TRINITY HAS PERVERTED THE CHURCH.]
. . . .

6. The nature or quality of this is described by the statue seen by Nebuchadnezzar, as to its feet, and by the last beast that went up out of the sea, in *Daniel*, and by the dragon and his two beasts in the *Apocalypse*.

7. It may also be seen from this arcanum revealed to me, that every one is allotted a place in heaven, that is, in its societies, according to his idea of God; and every one in the hells according to his denial of God; moreover, that the denial of one God inheres in the ideas of those who have confirmed themselves in the Athanasian[1] Trinity.

8. A true soul and life is in that man of the church who acknowledges the Lord the Son of God as the God of heaven and earth. That He is the God of heaven and earth, He Himself teaches in *Matthew*, and that He is the true God and eternal life, in *John*, and that in Him dwells all the fulness of the Divinity, according to Paul, and that He is Jehovah our Redeemer, the only God, yea, the Father of eternity, according to *Isaiah*

CHAPTER VIII.

The Confirmation of a Trinity of Persons from Eternity, of Which Each Is God, According to the Nicene and Athanasian Creeds, Has Falsified the Whole Word.

1. Every heretic can confirm and does confirm his heresy by the Word, since this is written by appearances and correspondences, wherefore the Word is called by some the book of all heresies.

2. After confirmation a man sees no otherwise than that his dogmas are true, although they are false.

3. A plurality of Gods may be confirmed by many things from the Word; also the imputative faith of Christ's merit, in which three Gods severally have their part; as likewise that the works of charity contribute nothing to faith, and thus to salvation.

4. A plurality of Gods may be confirmed from these things: A Trinity is mentioned by the Lord; there appeared to be a Trinity when the Lord was baptized. There are "three who bear witness in heaven, the Father, the Word, and the Holy Spirit." Jehovah God said, "Let us make man in our image and likeness." Three angels appeared to Abraham who are called Jehovah. In the New Word, the Father, Son, and Holy Spirit are often named by the Lord in the *Evangelists*, and by the Apostles in the *Epistles*, and yet it is not there said that they are one.

Likewise [there is a] faith imputative of Christ's merit, and this faith alone is saving; and that the works of charity do not conduce to salvation; to which may be added, that a mind prone to ratiocination may add to them creeds of its own and establish them.

5. Each and all these cannot be seen to be false, and thus cannot be dissipated, unless reason enlightened by the Lord shall confirm by means of the Word that God is one, and that there is a conjunction of charity and faith.

6. When this is done, it may appear clearly that a theology founded upon a Trinity of Persons, of which each one is God,

and upon a faith directed to each separately, and also upon charity as of no avail to salvation, has falsified the entire Word; mainly because these three, God, charity, and faith, are together the universals of religion, to which all and each thing of the Word, and thence of heaven and the Church, relate.

7. Hence results this enormity, that the confirmer, wherever he reads of the Father, Son, or Holy Spirit, yea, wherever he reads Jehovah and God, thinks of three Gods, because of one from three; also wherever he reads faith, he thinks of no other faith than what is imputative of Christ's merit; and wherever he reads charity, he thinks of it as not contributing anything to salvation, or thinks of that faith instead of it. Confirmation once fixed brings this with it.

CHAPTER IX.

HENCE THERE IS THAT AFFLICTION AND THAT DESOLATION IN THE CHRISTIAN CHURCH, WHICH WERE PREDICTED BY THE LORD IN THE *Evangelists,* AND IN *Daniel.*

1. The Lord, when He spake with the disciples concerning the consummation of the age, and concerning His own advent, that is, concerning the end of the church of this day and the beginning of the New Church, predicted these things:—

There will then be great affliction such as was not from the beginning of the world till now, nor ever shall be (*Matt.* xxiv. 21).

Also that there would be:—

The abomination of desolation foretold by the prophet Daniel; for after the affliction of those days the sun will be darkened, and the moon will not give her light, and the powers of the heavens shall be shaken (*Matt.* xxiv. 15, 29).

2. That there is such an affliction and desolation in the church is utterly unknown and unseen in the world, because it is everywhere said therein that they are in the light itself of the Gospel, to such a degree that if an angel were to descend from heaven and teach anything else, he would not be believed. That thus the Roman Catholic and the Greek Churches teach,

and thus each of the three Reformed Churches distinguished by the name of their leaders, Luther, Melancthon, and Calvin, and in like manner each heretical sect, which sects are manifold.

3. But this predicted affliction and desolation appears in clear light in the spiritual world* since all men after death come into that world, and remain in the religion in which they were in the natural world; for the light there is spiritual light, which discloses all things.

4. When the clergy are there interrogated concerning God, concerning faith, and concerning charity, which are the three essentials of the church and thence of salvation, they answer scarcely otherwise than as blind men in pits. Concerning God they answer that He is one, and that there are three who are unanimous; and when they say that the three are one they are commanded to speak as they think, then, because thought and speech with those who are in the spiritual world, act as one they utter, with a clear voice, *three Gods.* As to faith, they reply that it is a faith in God the Father, God the Son, and God the Holy Spirit; and that God the Father gives it, the Son mediates it, and the Holy Spirit operates it, thus in three Gods in order.[1] When further interrogated respecting that faith, whether they know its sign when it enters, and the sign that it is within, they reply, "What is it to know a sign ? Is not this faith from the good pleasure, from the election of that one God only, and nothing from the man mixed up with it?" When asked whether that faith, since it is directed to three, and thus to three Gods, and man is in plenary ignorance concerning it, is anything, they reply that it is not only something, but the all of the church and the all of salvation. If asked whether that is possible, at this they laugh. As to charity, they say this is where that faith is, and that it is separate from it and not separate, and that it contributes to salvation and does not contribute.

5. When the laity are questioned concerning God, faith, and charity, they know almost nothing, except that a few have acquired some enigmas from the clergy which they call articles

---

[NOTE FROM THE MARGIN.]

*And He now appears to me in most splendid light in London of the natural world.

of faith, and which are in general that God the Father has mercy on account of the passion of His Son, and that He remits sins and justifies.

6. When these two classes are explored as to whether they have anything of God, of faith, and of charity in themselves, it is perceived that they have nothing, consequently nothing of heaven, of the church and of salvation, only with those who have done goods from religion, since these, in the spiritual world, are receptive of faith in the Lord God the Saviour.

7. From the few things above adduced, it appears whence there is that "great affliction such as was not from the beginning of the world nor shall be," and whence that "abomination of desolation" which the Lord foretold would be at the end of the church, which is at this day.

8. Such an affliction has not been from the beginning of the world, nor shall be, is because the Gentiles and the Jews themselves were ignorant of the Lord God the Saviour, as the fountain of salvation, and ignorance excuses; but the case is otherwise with Christians after His Advent, to whom this [truth] is laid open in the Word of both Testaments.

CHAPTER X.

UNLESS A NEW CHURCH EXIST, WHICH SHALL ABOLISH THE FAITH OF THE OLD CHURCH, WHICH IS IN THREE GODS, AND INTRODUCE A NEW ONE WHICH IS A FAITH IN ONE GOD, THUS IN THE LORD GOD THE SAVIOUR, JESUS CHRIST, NOT ANY FLESH CAN BE SAVED, ACCORDING TO THE LORD'S WORDS.

1. The Lord, when He spake with the disciples concerning the consummation of the age and His coming, that is, concerning the end of the church of the present day and then the beginning of the New Church, after describing the desolation and affliction, said:—

Unless those days were shortened no flesh could be saved (*Matt.* xxiv. 21, 22).

That is, would altogether perish in eternal death.

2. No flesh could be saved unless that affliction and the abomination of desolation were removed, is because through the faith of the church of the present day there is no conjunction with God, and thence no salvation; for this depends solely upon conjunction with God, yea, that conjunction is salvation.

3. Through the faith of the church of the present day there is no conjunction with God, because that faith is a faith in three Gods, and a faith unless it is in one God, does not conjoin; also, because that faith is in God the Father, who is inaccessible; and also in the Son born from eternity, who is likewise inaccessible, since He is of the same essence with the Father, and likewise in the Holy Spirit;. and because, there was no Son nor Holy Spirit from eternity, the faith in these two is [a faith] in no God. Add to this, that the faith of the present day cannot be united with charity, and faith not united with charity, thus alone, does not conjoin. Hence it follows that unless the New Church be established by the Lord, which shall abolish that faith and teach a new one, namely, a faith which is in one God, and which is at the same time united with charity, not any flesh could be preserved, that is, not any man could be saved.

4. The faith of the present day has destroyed the entire church and has falsified the whole Word has been shown above. Wherefore unless the New Church be established by the Lord, which shall restore both the church and the Word to its integrity, not any flesh can be preserved.

5. Those who are in the faith of the church of the present day are meant by the "dragon" and the "false prophet," and that faith itself by the "pit of the abyss" from which the locusts issued, as also by the "great city which is spiritually called Sodom and Egypt," where the two witnesses were slain, is shown in the *Apocalypse Revealed;* likewise that by the "New Jerusalem" the New Church is meant. [See *Apoc.*, Cap. ix., xi., xii., xx., xxi.]

Since it is there said that after the dragon and the false prophet were cast into hell, the New Jerusalem descended from God out of heaven, it is evident that after the faith of the church of the present day is condemned, the New Church from the New Heaven will descend from the Lord and be established.

6. From these things it is evident that unless the New Church exist which shall abolish the faith in three Gods, and receive a faith in one God, thus in the Lord Jesus Christ, and which at the same time, conjoins this faith with charity into one form, not any flesh could be saved.

7. It may also be seen above (Chap. viii.) that redemption could not be effected, nor salvation thence be given, except by God incarnate, thus by no other than God, the Redeemer, Jesus Christ; for salvation is perpetual redemption. It was shown moreover that God, faith, and charity are three essentials of the church, and that upon them universal theology, and thus the church, depends. Wherefore when falsities are taught and imbibed in respect to these three essentials, man has no salvation.

7. *Minor clause.* No one can hereafter come into heaven unless he be in the doctrine of the New Church as to faith and life. The reason is, that the New Heaven which is now being established by the Lord, is in faith and life according to that doctrine.

CHAPTER XI.

The Divine Trinity Is in the Lord God the Saviour, and Therefore the Lord God the Saviour Is Alone To Be Approached, in Order That There May Be Salvation or Eternal Life.*

[ANNOTATIONS OF THE AUTHOR.]

*These things are explained according to the contents in the following numbers —*Of the Sacred Scripture* (n. 13, etc.). From the doctrine of the church of this day it follows that the Lord has no power, since the Father alone imputes His merit, and that in Himself He intercedes and prays that He [the Father] may do this; and they do not remember that [the Lord] said that all things of the Father are His; and that all things of the Father come to Him, and that He has all power over flesh and all power over heaven and earth. The Lord is the head of the church, and the church is His body. Wherefore He who is its Head, is to be approached by the body.

[The rest could not be found, when this treatise was copied from the autograph —Ed.]

INDEX OF SCRIPTURE PASSAGES.

PSALMS.
 ii. 7 212

ISAIAH.
 ix. 6 212
 xiii. 10 196
 xlii. 8 219
 xliii. 10, 11, 14 219
 xliv. 6 173
 xlviii. 11 219
 lxiii. Chap. cited 198

JEREMIAH.
 xxiii. 6 219

EZEKIEL.
 xxxii. 7 196

JOEL.
 ii. 10 196
  31 196
 iii. 15 196

AMOS.
 v. 20 196
 viii. 9 196

MATTHEW.
 iii. 17 ....185, 219
 iv. 1–11 198
 xvi. 16 219
 xvii. 5 ....185, 219
 xxiv. 15, 29 222
  21, 22 .... 222, 224
  29 196
  Chap. cited 196
 xxvi. 36–46 198
 xxviii. 26–50 38

MARK.
 i. 12, 13 198
 xiii. 24 196

MARK (*Continued*).
 xiv. 32–42 198
 xv. 15–37 198

LUKE.
 i. 31, 35 219
  35 ....186, 212
 ii. 40, 50 199
 iv. 1–13 198
 xxi. 25 196
 xxii. 40–46 198
 xxiii. 25–46 198

JOHN.
 i. 1, 2, 10, 14 214
  3, 10 178
  18 219
 iii. 15, 16, 36 219
  35 219
 vi. 40 219
 x. 30 218
 xi. 25, 26 219
 xii. 44 218
 xiv. 9–11 218
 xvi. 15 218
  28 214
 xvii. 5 214
 xviii. 1 198
 xix. 1–30 198
 xx. 22 219
  31 219

APOCALYPSE.
 i. 8, 11 ....173, 181
 xv. 4 186
 xxii. 13 173

COLOSSIANS.
 ii. 9 218

JOHN I.
 v. 7 210
  20 219
  21 219

The Doctrine of Charity

THE DOCTRINE

OF

THE NEW JERUSALEM

CONCERNING

CHARITY

A POSTHUMOUS WORK OF

EMANUEL SWEDENBORG

TRANSLATOR'S NOTE.

This treatise on *Charity* was written about 1766. It was not published by Swedenborg, but the autograph manuscript is preserved in the library of the Royal Academy of Sciences, Stockholm; and has been reproduced in the "Photolithograph Manuscripts" Vol. viii. We have followed the Latin text of Dr. Samuel Howard Worcester, who transcribed it from the "Photolithograph Manuscripts."

The treatise is a fragment, apparently the first draft of a work not completed. Nevertheless it gives invaluable instruction on this most important subject, and in a very practical form.

JOHN WHITEHEAD.

The Doctrine of Charity.

The sections in their order:—

I. The first of Charity is to look to the Lord and shun evils as sins.
II. The second of Charity is to do uses to the neighbor.
III. The neighbor to whom uses are to be done, in the natural sense, is the fellow-citizen, society less and greater, one's own country, and the human race. There are spiritual uses and there are civil uses.
IV. Uses to the neighbor ought to be done according to his spiritual good, and thence his moral, civil, and natural good; consequently, the neighbor that is to be loved, in the spiritual sense, is good.
V. Every one loves the neighbor from the good of Charity in himself; consequently, the quality of one's Charity is like that of the Charity which he himself is.
VI. Man is born that he may become Charity; but he cannot become this unless he perpetually wills and does the good of Charity from affection and its delight.
VII. Every man who looks to the Lord and shuns evils as sins, if he sincerely, justly, and faithfully performs the work that belongs to his office and employment, becomes Charity in form.
VIII. The signs of Charity are all things that pertain to worship.
IX. The benefactions of Charity are all the goods that a man who is Charity does, freely, outside of his calling.

X. The obligations of Charity are all things that a man ought to do besides those above mentioned.

XI. There are diversions of Charity, which are the various delights and pleasures of the bodily senses, useful for mental recreation.

XII. Charity and Faith make one. There is no church where there is no truth of faith; and no religion where there is no good of charity.

[The following notes are on the margin of the MS.]:—

Appendix:—Concerning the lot after death of those who are in faith separated from charity.

The sins should be enumerated of which a man is not conscious if he does not examine himself, but either confirms them in himself, or does not regard them as sins, and so continually does them, from hereditary [inclination], on account of their delights,—from the Decalogue, and from reason; which [sins] might be enumerated to the number of fifty or a hundred, civil as well as spiritual, etc.

I.

The First of Charity Is To Look to the Lord, and Shun Evils Because They Are Sins; Which Is Done by Repentance.

To be set forth in this order:—

1. (I.) *As far as any one does not shun evils because they are sins, so far he remains in them.*
   (II.) *As far as any one does not take cognizance of sins and know what they are, so far he does not see but that he is without sins.*
   (III.) *As far as any one takes cognizance of sins and knows what they are, so far he can see them in himself, confess them before the Lord, and repent of them.*
   (IV.) *Good before repentance is spurious good; it is the same with Charity, for good is of Charity.*
   (V.) *Consequently, the first of Charity is to look to the Lord and shun evils because they are sins.*

2. (I.) *As far as any one does not look to the Lord and shun evils because they are sins, so far he remains in them.* Man is born into evils of every kind. His will, which is his *proprium*, is nothing but evil. Unless, therefore, a man is reformed and regenerated, he not only remains as he was born, but becomes even worse; because to the evils received hereditarily he adds actual evils of himself. Such does a man remain if he does not shun evils as sins. To shun them as sins is to shun them as diabolical and infernal, and therefore deadly, and hence, because there is eternal damnation in them. If a man so regards them, then he believes that there is a hell, and that there is a heaven; and also that the Lord can remove them if the man also endeavors to remove them as of himself. But see what has been set forth on this subject in *The Doctrine of Life for the New Jerusalem* (n. 108–113). To which I will add this:— All evils are born delightful; because man is born into the love of himself, and that love makes all things delightful that are of his *proprium*, thus whatever he wills and whatever he thinks; and every one remains till death in the delights that are inrooted by birth, unless they are subdued; and they are not subdued unless they are regarded as sweet drugs that kill, or as flowers apparently beautiful that carry poison in them; thus unless the delights of evil are regarded as deadly, and this until at length they become undelightful.

3. (II.) *As far as any one does not take cognizance of sins and know what they are, so far he does not see but that he is without sins.* That he knows he is a sinner, in evils from head to foot, is from the Word; and yet he does not know because he does not see any one sin in himself. He therefore prays, as a tinkling sound, confesses as a tinkling sound, and yet inmostly in himself he believes that he is not a sinner; which belief in the other life is manifested. For there he says, "I am pure, I am clean, I am guiltless," and yet when examined he is impure, unclean, yea even carrion. It is as if the skin were fair and soft outwardly, but within diseased from the very heart; or as a liquid, like water upon the surface, but within putrid from stagnation.

4. (III.) *So far as any one takes cognizance of sins and knows what they are, he can see them in himself, confess them* *before the Lord, and repent of them.* It is said, he can if he will; and he who believes in eternal life will. But still he must not think of the things he does, but of those that he wills to do, which, if he believes them allowable he then also does; or if he does not do them, it is on account of the world. There is an internal and an external effect, or an internal and an external work. The external effect or work comes forth and exists from the internal effect or work, as action from endeavor. Endeavor, in a man, is will. Therefore, though he does not do a thing in the body, if he holds it to be allowable, then the effort or will remains; and this is the act itself in the spirit. Therefore to take cognizance of his sins and know what they are, is to take cognizance of and know his thoughts, and to know from them what he holds to be allowable, as well as what he desires, and what things of his thought he favors. For example, if he thinks whether whoredom is a sin, and how grave a sin; whether hatred and revenge are sins; whether thefts, and the like, whether haughtiness and pride, contempt of others, and avarice are sins; and then the man must remove disguises, if he had cast any over them, that is, the things by which he had confirmed them, and must consult the Word and see.

5. Any one may see that he who acknowledges that a sin is a sin [can see the sins within him]; but he who makes them allowable in thought, and not allowable in the body on account of the world, cannot see them. It is as if one should turn the mirror away that he may see his face; or as if one who would see his face should put a veil before it.

SELF-EXAMINATION.* (1) If it is only as to the actions, it discovers little; and this not enough: [Give] the reason. (2) But if it is as to the thoughts and intentions, it discovers more. (3) And if it searches out what the man regards or does not regard as sins, then it discovers [all]. For whatever a man within himself regards as allowable that he does. To regard as allowable is of the will, is endeavor, and in spirit is done; and it will be done in the body when obstacles are removed. And such are Machiavelians.

---

*This paragraph is written in the margin of the original manuscript.

6. (IV.) *Good before repentance is spurious good; and also charity, for good is of charity.* For evil is within the man inwardly; because it is not opened, and therefore is not healed; and genuine good cannot issue forth from evil. The fountain is impure. Good that flows forth from evil may appear good in the outward form, but the quality of the man is within it, as he is inwardly. Everything that a man does is therefore an image of him. Before the angels he himself appears in his image, yea, out of himself, which I have seen a thousand times. The good, therefore, that any one does with the body may appear good before those who see only the external; but within, the will and intention lie concealed, which can be, because he wishes to be thought sincere and good in order that he may captivate souls for the sake of honor and gain. In a word, the good is either meritorious, or hypocritical, or diabolical; and is done to deceive, to revenge, to kill, etc. But at death, when a man is let into his interiors, this good is taken away, and becomes open evil.

7. Every good that a man does to the neighbor is of charity, or is charity. What quality of charity it is may be known by the three preceding [tests], namely, (1) How far he shuns evils as sins. (2) How far he knows and takes cognizance of what things are sins. (3) And how far he has seen them in himself, confessed them, and repented of them. These are the indications to every one of the quality of his charity.

8. (V.) *Consequently, the first of charity is to look to the Lord and shun evils because they are sins.* Every good that a man does to the neighbor for the sake of the neighbor, or for the sake of truth and good and thus for the reason that it is according to the Word, or for the sake of religion and thus for the sake of God, which is therefore from a spiritual love or affection, is called a good of charity, or a good work. So far as this is derived from the man it is not good, but so far as it is from the Lord[1] through the man. The Lord does good to every one chiefly through others, but yet in such a manner that a man scarcely knows but that it is from himself. He therefore frequently moves the wicked to do good to others; but it is from an affection of the love of self and the world. This good, indeed, is of the Lord, or from the Lord; but the man is not rewarded for it. But if a man does good not from a merely natural, but from a spiritual love or affection, he is rewarded. His reward is the heavenly delight of that love and affection, in that it endures to eternity; and this is in proportion as he does not do it from himself, that is, in proportion as he believes that all good is from the Lord, and does not place merit in it.

9. That no one can do good, which is good, from himself, but that as far as a man shuns evils as sins, so far he does good not from himself, but from the Lord, may be seen in the *Doctrine of Life for the New Jerusalem, from the precepts of the Decalogue* (n. 9-17, and 18-31).

10. From all this it is plain that before repentance there is not charity the good of which is from the Lord, but from the man; but after repentance it becomes charity the good of which is not from the man, but from the Lord. For the Lord cannot enter into a man and do any good from Himself through him, before the devil, that is, evil, is cast out, but after he is cast out. The devil is cast out by repentance; and when he is cast out the Lord enters, and does good there through the man, but always so that the man does not perceive but that he does it from himself. And yet he knows that it is from the Lord.

11. It is clear then, from these considerations, that the first of charity is to shun evils as sins; which is done by repentance. Who does not see that an impenitent man is evil? And who does not see that an evil man has not charity? And who does not see that he who has not charity cannot do charity? Charity must be from charity within a man.

12. (VI.) Finally, some passages may be adduced from the Word:—As, from the Lord's words to the Pharisees, that the internal man must be purified; the words in the first chapter of *Isaiah;* and some of those that are quoted in the *Doctrine of Life for the New Jerusalem* (n. 28-31, and 50-52).

II.

THE SECOND OF CHARITY IS TO DO GOODS, BECAUSE THEY ARE USES.

To be explained in this order:—

13. (I.) *Not to will to do evil to the neighbor is of Charity.*
(II.) *To will to do good to the neighbor is of Charity.*
(III.) *A man may do good which he believes to be of Charity, and still not shun evil; and yet all evil is against Charity.*
(IV.) *In proportion as a man wills not to do evil to the neighbor, he wills to do him good, and not the converse.*
(V.) *Evil is first to be removed, because it is against Charity, which is done by looking to the Lord, and by repentance, before the good that a man does is good of Charity.*
(VI.) *The quality of the good which is of Charity is according to the cognizance and hence removal of evil by repentance.*
(VII.) *It follows from this, that the first of Charity is to look to the Lord and shun evils as sins; and that the second thing of Charity is to do goods.*

14. (I.) *Not to will to do evil to the neighbor is of charity.* Every one sees that charity does no evil to the neighbor; for charity is love towards the neighbor, and he who loves any one fears to do evil to him. There is a conjunction of souls between them. Whence it is that when one does evil to him to whom he is conjoined by love, he has a perception in his soul as if he were doing evil to himself. Who can do evil to his children, to his wife, to his friends? For to do evil is against the good of love.

15. Who does not see that he who cherishes hatred to another, who acts the adversary and enemy to him, who burns with revenge, and desires his death, does not love the neighbor? That he who would commit whoredom with the wife of another, who would seduce virgins and desert them, and violate women, does not love the neighbor? that he who would despoil, and under various pretences steal his goods, who would injure the reputation of another by slander, and so by false witness, does not love the neighbor? Nor yet he who covets his house, his wife, or anything that is his neighbor's. Hence it is plain that not to will to do evil to the neighbor is of charity.

16. And so Paul declares on this subject, in two places, that "to love the neighbor is the fulfilling of the law" [*Rom.* xiii. 8-10; *Gal.* v. 14]; and elsewhere from the Word.

17. (II.) *To will to do good to the neighbor is of charity.* This is known, for it is believed that to give to the poor, to assist the needy, to relieve the widow and the fatherless, to endow ministers, to contribute to churches, to hospitals, and various pious uses, is of charity; and that to give food to the hungry, drink to the thirsty, to receive the stranger, clothe the naked, visit the sick, come to those who are bound in prison, and many other things, are goods of charity. But yet they are goods only so far as the man shuns evils as sins. If a man does them before he shuns evils as sins they are external goods, yea, done for the sake of merit. For they flow forth from an impure fountain; and the things which issue from such a fountain are inwardly evils. The man is in them, and the world is in them.

18. It is known that to do Christian goods is of charity, and it is believed by many that good wipes out evil, and that the evils in a man thus cease to be, or are not regarded. But it does not wipe out evil, unless the man thinks about the evils in himself, and repents of them.

19. There are many who have so believed, and have thought there was no evil in them, who on being examined have confessed that they are full of evils, and that if they were not detained in externals they could not be saved.

20. (III.) *A man may do good which he believes to be of charity, and still not shun evil; and yet all evil is against charity.* It is plain that to shun evil and do good are two distinct things; for there are those who do every good of charity from piety and from thought of eternal life, and yet do not know that to cherish hatred and revenge, to commit whoredom, to despoil and injure, to slander, and thus bear false witness, and many other things, are evils. There are judges who live piously, and yet do not regard it as a sin to adjudicate from friendship, from relationship, and with a view to honor and gain; yea, if they know, they confirm within themselves that they are not evils. And so with others. In a word, to shun evils as sins, and to do Christian good, are two distinct things. He who shuns evils as sins does Christian good; but those that do good and do not shun evils as sins, do no Christian good. For evil is against charity, and must therefore first be abolished, before the good that a man does is with charity, that is, of charity. No one can do good who at the same time wills to do evil, or who wills good and also evil.

21. All good that in itself is good proceeds from the interior will. Evil is removed from this will by repentance. There also resides the evil in which a man is born. Unless therefore he repents the evil remains in his interior will, and his good proceeds from the exterior will; thus his state is perverted. The interior qualifies the exterior, and not the exterior the interior. The Lord says:—

Cleanse first the inside of the cup and of the platter [*Matt.* xxiii. 26].

22. Man has a two-fold will, an interior and an exterior. The interior will is purified by repentance; then the exterior does good from the interior; but exterior good does not remove the evil of lust, or the root of evil.

23. (IV.) *In proportion as a man does not will to do evil to the neighbor he wills to do him good, and not the converse.* There are civil good, moral good, and spiritual good. The good done before a man shuns evils as sins is civil and moral; but in proportion as he shuns evils as sins the good becomes spiritual also, as well as civil and moral; and not before.

24. Lust lurks within, and without is its delight; therefore when a man thinks from lust and its delight, he either confirms the evil and believes it to be allowable, and so is in the evil, or he does not think of any evil in himself, and so believes that he is sound.

25. It is true that a man ought to confess that he is a sinner, and that from the head to the sole of the foot there is no

soundness in him. This he can say, and say from knowledge; but yet he cannot inwardly believe it unless he knows it by searching examination. Then he can say this, and he then first perceives that there is no soundness in him. So, and not otherwise, is the ulcer opened and healed. In any other way the cure is but palliative.

26. Did not the Lord preach repentance? Did not His disciples also? and John the Baptist?

Isaiah declares that a man must first cease from evils, and that then he will learn to do good [*Isa.* i. 16, 17]. Before this a man does not know what and of what quality good is. Evil does not know what good is, but good thence knows evil.

27. (V.) *Evil is first to be removed, because it is against charity (which is done by repentance), before the good that a man does is the good of charity.* Since evil must first be known in order that it may be removed, therefore the Decalogue was the first of the Word, and in the whole Christian world it is also the first of the doctrine of the church. All are initiated into the church by knowing evil and not doing it, because it is against God.

28. And therefore this first was so holy, for the reason that no one can do Christian good before.

29. That good follows is very plain from these illustrations:—A judge says, "I will not, for various reasons, adjudicate from evil, but justly;" and he does good.

30. A farmer says, "I will not do work otherwise than justly and faithfully;" thus the work he does is good.

31. So in a thousand other instances, when a man does not do evil he does good.

32. It may therefore be taken as a rule, that to shun evil as a sin is to do good.

33. (VI.) *The quality of the good which is of charity is according to the cognizance and hence removal of evil by repentance.* [That is] according as a man knows, more or less, what is evil; according as he knows evils of faith and evils of life; and according to how he desists from them; and he desists from them as far as he looks to the Lord, and believes on Him.

34. This may be shown by examples. For such as a man is inwardly, the purer he is, the more does the fountain whence his good flows become a fountain of better waters.

35. In a word, good is good to every one in the same degree and in the corresponding quality that evil is evil to him. The one cannot be separated from the other.

36. In the degree that any one puts off the old man, he so far puts on the new.

37. In the degree that any one crucifies the flesh, so far he lives in the spirit.

38. No one can at the same time serve two lords.

39. Cognizance involves that it must be known what is true and what is false; removal is of the will; and both are of the life.

40. (VII.) *Hence it follows that the first of charity is to look to the Lord and shun evils because they are sins, and that the second of charity is to do goods.* The evil equally with the good can do good. He can assist another, can do him many good services, from good will, from kindness, from friendship, from compassion. These, however, are not charity with him who does them, but with him to whom they are done. In outward appearance it is charity.

41. When one has shunned an evil as a sin several times, then only the good that he does appears to him, and yet they are together in him. But still the one must be prior; and it actually is prior and interior.

III.

The Neighbor That Is To Be Loved, in the Spiritual Idea, Is Good and Truth.

42. It is said, in the spiritual idea, because this is the idea in which the spiritual man is, inwardly; and the angels are in the same idea. This idea is abstract from matter, space, and time, and especially is abstract from person.

Arrangement in order:—

(I.) *Man is man not from his form, but from the good and truth in him, or what is the same, from will and understanding.*

(II.) *Therefore the good and truth in a man is the neighbor that is to be loved.*

(III.) *The quality of the neighbor is according to the quality of the good and truth in a man; or such as the man is such is the neighbor.*

(IV.) *The degree of neighbor is according to the degree of good and truth in a man; consequently, one man is not neighbor in the same degree as another.*

(V.) *The good of the internal will is the neighbor that is to be loved, and not the good of the external will, unless this makes one with the other.*

(VI.) *Truth is the neighbor as far as it proceeds from good and makes one with it, as form and essence.*

43. (1.) *Man is man not from his form, but from the good and truth in him, or what is the same, from will and understanding.* It is known that the will and understanding are the very man, and not his form, which appears in the face and body as a man. Some are foolish and insane, and yet appear as men; some are so natural that they are like animals, save that they can speak; others are rational and spiritual. The human form of these last may appear less beautiful, and yet they are men more than the others. Take away the good and truth from them, and the human form remains, in which there is no man; they are as pictures and sculptured forms, and as apes.

44. It is said, good and truth, that is, will and understanding, because good is of the will and truth is of the understanding; for the will is the receptacle of good, and the understanding is the receptacle of truth.

45. And yet good and truth cannot be except in their subject. Nothing can be separated from its subject. Therefore man is the neighbor; but in the spiritual idea good and truth, from which man is man.

46. (II.) *Therefore the good and truth in a man is the neighbor that is to be loved.* Set before your eyes three or ten persons, whom you are choosing for some domestic employment. Do you choose otherwise than according to the good and truth in them, whence man is man?

47. If you are choosing one among ten for the performance of some service, do you not inquire into his will and understanding?

48. The one who is chosen is your neighbor who is loved. A man devil may appear with a similar face as a man angel. Should not the man angel be loved, and not the man devil? You show favor to the man angel, on account of the good and truth in him, but not to the man devil. It is charity that he should be punished if he does evil, and that the man angel should be rewarded.

49. If you observe ten virgins, among whom five are harlots and five are chaste, and would choose one for a wife, do you not choose one of the chaste, according to her good, which accords with your good?

50. (III.) *The quality of the neighbor is according to the quality of the good in a man; or such as the man is, such is the neighbor.* That all men are not equally the neighbor, the Lord's parable of the man wounded by robbers teaches, where it is declared that "he is neighbor who showed mercy on him." [*Luke* x. 29–37.]

51. Whoever does not distinguish the neighbor according to the quality of good and truth in him may be deceived a thousand times, and his charity become confused and at length no charity. A man devil may exclaim, "I am a neighbor: do good to me." And if you do good to him he may kill you or others. You are placing a knife or a sword in his hand.

52. The simple act thus. They say every man is equally a neighbor, and that they deem it no business of theirs to search into his quality; but God looks to that; I may only render assistance to a neighbor. But this is not loving the neighbor. He who from genuine charity loves the neighbor inquires what the quality of a man is, and does good to him discreetly, and according to the quality of his good.

53. Such simple ones are withdrawn and separated in the other life; for if they come among diabolical spirits they are allured to do good to them, and to do evil to the good. These spirits cry out, "Set me free! Help me!" This is the greatest strength which the evil acquire. Without help from and, as it were, conjunction with them, they have no power at all; but with them whom they have deceived by the name of neighbor, they are strong.

54. Genuine charity itself is prudent and wise. Other charity is spurious, because it is of the will or of good alone, and not at the same time of the understanding or of truth.

55. (IV.) *The degree of neighbor is according to the degree of good and truth in a man; consequently, one man is not neighbor in the same degree as another.* Good is distinguished, according to degrees, into civil good, moral good, and spiritual good.

56. The neighbor which a man will love from charity will be spiritual good. Without this good there is no charity; for the good of charity is spiritual good, since it is according to this good that all in the heavens are conjoined.

57. Moral good, which is actual human good (for it is the rational good according to which man lives with man, as a brother and associate), is neighbor so far as it is derived from spiritual good; for moral good without spiritual is external good, is of the external will, and is not internal good. It may be evil, which is not to be loved.

58. Civil good is the good of a life in accordance with the civil laws; and its first and fundamental principle, is not to act contrary to those laws on account of the penalties. If within this good there is not moral good, and within this, spiritual good, it is none other than the animal good which beasts have, when kept shut up or chained, towards those who give them food, or who punish or caress them.

59. These goods a man learns in his early infancy from the Decalogue. The laws of the Decalogue first become civil laws, afterwards moral, and finally spiritual; and then first do the goods become goods of charity, according to their degree.

60. Charity itself regards first the good of man's soul; and loves that because conjunction is effected by it. Next to that it regards his moral good; and loves it, just in proportion as he lives a moral life according to the perfection of reason. And, lastly, it regards civil good, according to what the man is in his intercourse with the world. Through his civil good the man is a man of the world; according to his moral good he is a man above the world, and lower than heaven; and according to his spiritual good he is a man of heaven, or an angel. The consociation of man with man is effected by this good, and then by goods of the lower degrees, according to their degree. For example: There is the spiritual man who wills well and does not understand well, and he who does not understand well does not act well; he is, therefore, scarcely a rational moral man. And there is the man who understands well and does not will well. Such a man is not the neighbor according to his understanding; but he who does not will well is not the neighbor, however well he may understand.

61. In a word, the will constitutes the neighbor, and the understanding so far as it is of the will.

62. (V.) *The good of the internal will is the neighbor that is to be loved, and not the good of the external will, unless this makes one with the other.* There is an internal will and an external will; likewise an internal and an external understanding.

63. The internal will has conjunction with heaven, and the external will with the world.

64. All good is of the will, and the very good of charity is good of the internal will.

65. These are wont to be separated in a man; and are most widely separated in hypocrites, dissemblers, and flatterers for the sake of gain.

66. But when these wills make one then the goods of both make one good, which is the neighbor. These principles may be illustrated by examples and comparisons.

67. (VI.) *Truth is the neighbor as far as it makes one with good; and it makes one as do form and essence.* Every form derives its quality from an essence. Therefore whatever the quality of the essence is, such is that of its form.

68. This may be illustrated by the fact that such as the will is such is the understanding, in itself regarded.

69. It may also be illustrated by sound and speech, and by many other things.

70. That truth is good in form may be seen in the *Apocalypse Explained*.

71. It is clear, then, that in the spiritual idea good is the neighbor that is to be loved, or the man according to his good.

IV.

The Objects of Charity Are the Individual Man, a Society, One's Own Country, and the Human Race; and All Men Are the Neighbor in the Strict and in the Wide Sense.

72. That man is the neighbor is known. A society is the neighbor because a society is a composite man. One's own country is the neighbor because the country consists of many societies, and is therefore a still more composite man. And the human race is the neighbor because the human race is composed of great societies, each of which is a composite man; and hence it is a man in the widest sense.

The subject shall be explained in this order:—

(I.) *Every man is the neighbor according to the quality of his good.*

(II.) *A society, smaller or larger, is the neighbor according to the good of its use.*

(III.) *One's own country is the neighbor according to its good, spiritual, moral, and civil.*

(IV.) *The human race is the neighbor in the widest sense; but as it is divided into empires, kingdoms, and republics, any one of them is the neighbor according to the good of its religion, and according to the good that it performs to the country and to itself.*

73. (I.) *Every man is the neighbor according to the quality of his good.* Since in the spiritual idea good is the neighbor, and man is the subject of good, and also the object of him who does good, it follows that in the natural idea man is the neighbor.

74. Nor is one man more the neighbor than another as to his person merely, but as to the good by virtue of which he is such or such a man; for there are as many differences of neighbor as there are of good, and the differences of good are infinite.

75. It is believed that a brother, kinsman, or relation is more a neighbor than a stranger; and that he who is born in one's

country is more a neighbor than one born out of the country. But every one is a neighbor according to his good, be he Greek or Gentile.

76. For every one is the neighbor according to spiritual affinity and relationship. This may be seen from the fact that after death every man comes among his own, with whom as to good, or, what is the same, as to the affections, there is a mutual likeness. Moreover, natural affinities vanish after death, and are succeeded by spiritual affinities; for in the same heavenly society they know one another, and are associated, because they are in similar good. Of ten brothers in the world, five may be in hell, and five in heaven, and these five in different societies; and when they meet they do not know each other. Also all have a face according to their affections. It is therefore plain that every man is the neighbor according to the quality of his good.

77. The goods according to the quality of which [men are distinguished] are especially spiritual goods. These charity primarily regards.

78. (II.) *A society, smaller or larger, is the neighbor according to the good of its use.* Every society in a kingdom is established according to uses, which are various. There are societies whose business it is to administer various civil affairs, which are manifold; various judicial affairs; various economical affairs; societies—such as consistories, academies, and schools—for various ecclesiastical purposes; and there are societies, which also are many, for the advancement of knowledge.

79. A society cannot be regarded otherwise than as a man in the composite. It is therefore one's neighbor according to the good of its use which it performs. If it performs distinguished uses it is more the neighbor; if low uses, it is less the neighbor; if evil uses, it is no otherwise neighbor than as an evil man, whose good I desire, that he may become good, and, as far as possible, to provide means for his improvement, even though it be by threats, chastisement, penalties, and privations.

80. No one can regard a society having one function but as one composite man. When a kingdom is regarded as a man, certain persons are called members of the government; and they constitute among them one man, whose members are the individuals therein.

81. It is the same as in heaven. There every society, less and greater, is as one man; and it appears as one man. I have seen a distinguished society as one man. The form of heaven is the human form.

82. So also does a society on earth appear as one man to the angels in the heavens.

83. (III.) *One's own country is the neighbor according to its goods, spiritual, moral, and civil.* In the idea of every man his country is as one. All the laws, therefore, both the laws of justice and economical laws, are enacted as for one. One's country, then, is as it were a man in the concrete; and it is called a body, in which the king is supreme. Its good which is to be promoted is called the public good, and the common good. It is said also of the king that the people are in the body of his government.

84. And when it is the Lord's good pleasure, any kingdom is presented as a man before the angels of heaven, in a form that is the likeness of its quality. The form is the form of its spiritual affection; the form of the face is that of the affection of its spiritual good; the form of the body is the form of its civil good; while its manners, speech, and the like, manifest its rational good. When one views a kingdom as one man its quality can be seen, and according to this it is the neighbor.

85. Birth does not make one more the neighbor than another, not even mother and father; neither does education. These are from natural good. Nor does nearness of abode, nor relationship make one man more the neighbor than another; nor, therefore, one's native country. This is to be loved according to the quality of its good. But it is a duty to benefit one's country, which is done by promoting its use; because one thus promotes the good of all. It is not so much a duty to other kingdoms, outside of one's country, because one kingdom does not will another's good, but wills to destroy it as to its wealth and its power, and thus, also, as to its means of defence. To love another kingdom more, therefore, by doing more to promote its use, makes against the good of the kingdom in which one dwells. For this reason one's own country is to be loved in a higher degree.

86. For example: if I had been born in Venice or in Rome, and were a Reformed Christian, am I to love my country, or the country where I was born, because of its spiritual good? I cannot. Nor with respect to its moral and civil good, so far as this depends for existence upon its spiritual good. But so far as it does not depend upon this I can, even if that country hates me. Thus, I must not in hatred regard it as an enemy, nor as an adversary, but must still love it; doing it no injury, but consulting its good, so far as it is good for it, not consulting it in such a way that I confirm it in its falsity and evil. But more about the love of country in another place.

87. (IV.) *The human race is the neighbor in the widest sense; but as it is divided into empires, kingdoms, and republics, any one of them is neighbor according to the good of its religion and morals, and according to the good that it performs to the country, and makes to be one with its own good.* These subjects are too extensive to be separately illustrated. Suffice it to say, that if any man whatever, from whatsoever kingdom, is with me, and I dwell with him in the same house or in the same city, he is my neighbor according to his good. It is the same with all the individuals in that kingdom to whom that man is like. Suppose that he is the ambassador of the kingdom, who represents his king and therefore the kingdom; it cannot be denied that he is my neighbor, according to the good of its religion and morals, and according as it wills to do good to my country and to itself; especially so far as this good makes one with his own good.

88. I am speaking of no other good than the good of charity, and the good of genuine charity. The evil, even robbers and devils, can mutually love each other, but not from charity or the good of interior love. But as they unite in evil-doing, stealing, committing whoredom, avenging, killing, blaspheming, among themselves they are neighbors. But these are not meant; for charity is here treated of, and its good.

89. I can love all in the universe according to their religion, not more those in my own country than in other kingdoms, nor more those in Europe than in Africa. I love a Gen-

tile more than a Christian if he lives well according to religion, if from the heart he worships God, saying, "I will not do this evil because it is against God." But I do not love him according to his doctrine, but according to his life; since if I love him according to his doctrine alone, I love him as an external man; but if according to his life, I love him also as an internal man. For if he has the good of religion he has also moral and civil good. They cannot be separated. But a man who is only in doctrine cannot have religion. His moral and civil good has, therefore, no life in it. It is merely external. It wishes to be seen, and to have it believed that it is good.

V.

Man Is the Subject of Charity; and Such As Is the Charity with Him Such a Subject of It He Is; and Such Is the Charity that He Exercises Towards the Neighbor.

90. These things shall be explained in the following order:—

(I.) *Man was created that he might be a form of love and wisdom.*

(II.) *At this day, in order that a man may be a man he ought to be charity in form.*

(III.) *A man ought to be charity in form not from himself, but from the Lord; he is thus a receptacle of charity.*

(IV.) *A man is such a form of charity so far as good of the will is conjoined with truths of the understanding in him.*

(V.) *Whatever proceeds from such a man derives from the form a likeness, so that it is charity.*

(VI.) *The neighbor may be loved from what is not charity: but this, in itself regarded, is not loving the neighbor.*

(VII.) *He loves the neighbor who loves him from charity in himself.*

91. (I.) *Man was created that he might be a form of love and wisdom.* He was created in the image of God, in the likeness of God; and God is Love Itself and Wisdom Itself.

92. It is known that such as a man's wisdom is such is the man. But the life of wisdom is love; and love is the essence, and wisdom is the form of love,—as is shown in many places in the *Angelic Wisdom concerning the Divine Love and the Divine Wisdom,* to which it is not necessary here to add more.

93. (II.) *At this day, in order that a man may be a man, he ought to be charity in form.* It is said, at this day, because, in the process of time since the first creation, man has become external. For he has turned from love to the Lord to wisdom; has eaten of the tree of knowledge and of wisdom; and internal love is turned into external love.

94. The third heaven, that from the first men, is in love and wisdom. But the second heaven is from a lower love which is called charity, and from the wisdom that is called intelligence. And when at length a man is become altogether external, his love is called charity, and his wisdom faith. Such is the state of the church with men at this day.

95. There is spiritual love with some, but not celestial love; and spiritual love is charity. And then faith with them is truth, and truth makes the understanding or intelligence.

96. By charity in form is meant that the man's life is charity; and the form is from the life. But how it is so shall be shown in the fourth section following.

97. In heaven an angel appears as charity in form, and the quality of his charity is seen from his face, and heard from his voice. For after death a man becomes his own love; that is, the affection of his love. A spirit and an angel is nothing else. Yea, even as to his whole body the spirit or the angel himself is a form of charity. Some have seen an angel, and, what is wonderful, have discerned the form of charity in every member.

98. In the world man is not charity as to his form, in face, in body, and in voice; but yet his mind may be; and after death his mind is the spirit in the human form. Nevertheless, a sincere man, who thinks nothing against charity, may be known from his face and voice, and yet with difficulty, because there are such hypocrites, that can simulate to the life, yea, put on the sincerity of charity. But if an angel looks at his face and hears his voice, he discerns his character; because he does not see the material which overveils, but to which the material man gives attention.

99. The forms of charity are innumerable; as many as the angels of the second heaven. They are infinite in number. There are as many varieties of it as there are of affection for truth from good; and that affection is charity.

100. Whoever is not a form of charity is a form of hatred; or, whoever is not a form of the affection of truth from good is a form of the affection of falsity from evil. Of such hell consists. There are all varieties of hatred and of lust.

101. As there are genera of affections, and species of these genera, so there are also of charities. There are therefore charities in the plural; and there are degrees of charity, of two kinds; which degrees are treated of in *Angelic wisdom concerning the Divine Love and the Divine Wisdom*, Part III.

102. (III.) *A man ought to be charity in form not from himself, but from the Lord; he is thus a receptacle of charity.* The life of a man who is to be regenerated is affection of truth from good, or charity; and there is no life except from Life, that is, from the Lord, who in Himself is Life, as He teaches that He is:—

The Way, the Truth, and the Life (*John* xiv. 6).

And in another place:—

As the Father hath Life in Himself, so hath He given to the Son to have Life in Himself (*John* v. 26);

and elsewhere. And as Life is God, the Divine cannot be appropriated to man, who is finite and created, but can flow into a receptacle and be adjoined; just as the eye is not in itself light, but can receive light, and the ear is not in itself hearing, but is a receptacle. So with the other senses. And it is the same with the mind, and its interior senses.

103. Therefore, man is indeed the subject of charity, but a recipient subject; for he is created in a form receptive of life, as the eye is in a form receptive of light, and of objects of vision by means of light; and the ear, in a form receptive of sound, by the inflowing of sound with its harmonies.

104. Whoever believes that of himself he is a form of charity is deceived. Either he believes that he is God, or that the Divine is transfused into him. Thus he denies God. Or, if he does not think so, he places merit in works of charity; so that his external becomes charity and not his internal; and then the Lord cannot abide in him. The Lord abides not in those things which are of a man's *proprium*, but in His own. He must abide in what is Divine, and so make the man a recipient of the Divine proceeding, that is, of charity.

105. But man was so created that he might think and will as if from himself, and thence speak and act as if from himself; and yet is granted to know that every good of charity and truth of faith is from the Lord. He who does not think according to this truth is not in the light [*lux*] of truth, but in a fatuous light [*lumen*]; and, in the light of heaven, this is darkness. He cannot, therefore, be enlightened in other truths, except as to the memory only, and not as to perception, which is faith in its essence.

106. From these considerations it is clear that man is only a form of charity, and that charity is of the Lord with him; but that it is granted man to seem as if he himself were charity, to the end that he may become a receptacle, and so come into reciprocal conjunction, as if from himself, though really from the Lord.

107. (IV.) *A man is such a form of charity so far as good of the will is conjoined with truths of the understanding in him.* All that is of the will is called good, and all that is of the understanding is called truth; because the will is in the heat of heaven, and the understanding in the light of heaven. And as will without understanding has no quality, and cannot therefore be called anything, but takes on its quality and becomes something in the understanding, and becomes such or such, or becomes something or anything, according to what is in the understanding, just so it is with good without truth and good with truth.

108. Genuine truths ought therefore to be learned. With these the good of the will conjoins itself; and so the good of the will becomes the good of charity.

109. Every variety of charity is from this source, or from truths in the understanding. For truth in its essence is good; and truth is the form of good, precisely as speech is a form of sound; which may be illustrated.

110. There is a two-fold form of sound; one of song, another of speech. The same is true of the affection of truth from good, or charity; which shall be treated of. N. B.

111. Because it is so, it is said that charity is the affection of truth from good, or the affection of spiritual truth. From this comes the affection of rational or moral truth, and the affection of civil or natural truth.

112. Hence it is that they who are in charity are in light, or if not, that they love light. Light is truth; and heat is good. And it is known that all vegetation and fructification is from good by truth. So also are spiritual vegetation and fructification.

113. But they who are not in charity do not love truth in light; they may, however, love it in the shade. And this truth is the truth of faith at the present day; that is, that a thing must be believed to be true, although it is not seen in the understanding; for thus falsity may be called truth, and by confirmation of it, may be called truth, as is done.

114. (V.) *Whatever proceeds from such a man derives from the form a likeness, so that it is charity.* There are three things that proceed; thought, speech, and action. From the man who is a form of charity thought proceeds from the affection which is charity; speech, from sound which is of the affection, and in which is the affection of the thought; and action is by motion in which is charity. This motion proceeds from an endeavor; and the endeavor makes affection of the thought.

115. The form of charity is chiefly in his interior perception, which comes of spiritual heat and light. There the man is the very man. Thence charity is produced in things consequent or lower. And it puts itself forth, and comes into effect, almost as the shoot and gradually the tree from a seed. And this tree, as it were, becomes an enduring tree; and its fruits are the good works that are done in the body, from the will of good through the understanding of truth. And in this way the tree first exists.

116. Its inmost form is as a seed. It is well known that nothing can spring from a seed but such things as are of that stock. They are all similar, though with much variety; but still the young shoot and the fruit-bearing branch both spring from the same tree.

117. Therefore whatever a man does who interiorly is charity, he does from charity, although his deeds, speech and thoughts are of infinite variety. All things that he produces are as images of him under various forms, in all which, however, there is a common form, as the plane out of which [they rise].

118. And hence a man is recognized by another, when he says or does anything, if only his dominant affection is known, from which end and from which love, as from a fountain, [the speech and action flow]. The Lord says that an evil tree bringeth forth evil fruit, and a good tree good fruit, and that an evil tree cannot bring forth good fruit.

119. The life of a man is in all that he wills and thinks, and says and does. No one can do anything from any other life than his own. All his actions are effects of his life, and have therefore a likeness to it.

120. In the spiritual world affections are all imaged in various ways, as trees, gardens, birds, animals. In these, when inmostly regarded, an image of the man appears. They are representative of him.

121. In a word, there is an image of the man in each and all things belonging to him.*

122. (VI.) *The neighbor may be loved from what is not charity; but this, in itself regarded, is not loving the neighbor.* This may be illustrated by examples. An evil man may love a good man and yet not love good in itself. A man may say of a Gentile, who says he does his work faithfully because it is the will of God, "An atheist can love him." A man who does not love his country, when he hears another speaking and knows that he loves his country, can, as it were, love him; he hearkens to him, obeys him, saying, "He is a man of good heart; he speaks from love." I have heard some hundreds giving assent to a man renowned for love of country, and scarcely ten among them loved their country. So if one is listening to a preacher, and he declares to his hearers that he speaks from God, from

---

[MARGINAL NOTE.]

*There is compassion of charity, mercy of charity, friendship of charity, benevolence of charity, modesty of charity; in a word, all the virtues are charity, but they come under other names, and so under another species.

zeal for their souls, even those that do not love God, and do not believe, may yet be affected while they are listening to these things, may praise him, love him, and send him gifts. Every one who is sincere is loved by the insincere; every true man is loved by the untruthful; every faithful man, by the unfaithful; the chaste man who loves his wife, by the unchaste; and so on.

123. But this is so with every man while he is in general thought; but as soon as this general perception vanishes, the light perishes; which comes to pass when he lets the subject come under the inspection of his lower thought, and thinks whether it is so or not. Into this thought flows a light from the man, or the world; but into the general thought light flows in from heaven. This flows into the intellectual part of a man continually, if only he does not let himself down into his own light. He then extinguishes the light of heaven, if such there be. There is a general perception of truth with all. But the love of what is lower casts a man down from this height, into a perception from his proprium. This is a material perception, which communicates with the sight of the eye. It is a fantasy or imagination.

124. (VII.) *He loves the neighbor who loves the neighbor from charity in himself.* He conjoins himself with the neighbor's good, and not with his person. If, therefore, the person departs from good he does not love him. And this conjunction is a spiritual conjunction, because in the spiritual idea good is the neighbor.

125. That a man may love the neighbor, he must therefore be charity in form.

VI.

MAN IS BORN THAT HE MAY BECOME CHARITY; AND THIS HE CANNOT BECOME UNLESS HE PERPETUALLY DOES THE GOOD OF USE TO THE NEIGHBOR, FROM AFFECTION AND DELIGHT.

126. General explanation in the following order:—

(I.) *The general good exists from the goods of use which individuals perform ; and the goods of use that individuals perform subsist from the general good.*

(II.) *The goods of use which individuals perform, from which the general good exists, are ministries, functions, offices, and various employments.*
(III.) *All the offices and employments in a kingdom, commonwealth and state, regarded as to the goods of use, constitute a form which corresponds to the heavenly form.*
(IV.) *They also constitute a form which corresponds to the human form.*
(V.) *In this form each individual is a good of use, according to the extent of his office and employment.*

127. (I.) *The general good exists from the goods of use which individuals perform; and the goods of use that individuals perform subsist from the general good.* They are called goods of use, because all goods which are of love to the neighbor or charity are uses, and all uses are goods. They are therefore in a word called goods of use. They are also called the fruits of use.

128. It is known that every man is born to be of use, and that he may perform uses to others; and he who does not is called a useless member, and is cast off. He who performs uses for himself alone is also useless, though not called so. In a well constituted commonwealth, therefore, provision is made that no one shall be useless. If useless, he is compelled to some work; and a beggar is compelled, if he is in health.

129. Infants and boys, so long as they are under nurses and masters, do not indeed perform goods of use; but yet they learn to perform them, and must have them for an end; thus the good of use is in the end. That a house may be built, the materials must first be provided, and the foundation laid, and the walls erected; and so finally it is inhabited. The good of a house is the dwelling in it.

130. The general good consists in these things:—That in the society or kingdom there shall be, I. What is Divine with them. II. That there shall be justice with them. III. That there shall be morality with them. IV. That there shall be industry, knowledge, and uprightness with them. V. That there shall be the necessaries of life. VI. That there shall be the things necessary to their occupations. VII. That there shall be the things necessary for protection. VIII. That there shall be a sufficiency of wealth; because from this come the three former necessaries.

131. From these arises the general good; and yet it does not come of these themselves, but from the individuals there, and through the goods of use which individuals perform. As that what is Divine is there through ministers; and justice through magistrates and judges; so morality exists by means of the Divine and of justice; and necessaries by means of industrial occupations and commerce; and so on.

132. It is known that every general thing is from particulars; and for that reason it is called general. Whatever, therefore, is the quality of the parts, such is that of the general; a garden in general is of such quality as its trees and their fruits; meadows in general, of such quality as their crops of grass; fields in general, such as their grains and plants and flowers; a ship in general is such as all its many parts. The order among the parts and quality of the parts makes the general more perfect or more imperfect.

133. That the goods of use which individuals perform subsist from the general good is known; for each one derives his particular good of use from the general. All things necessary to life, and also for occupations, and the wealth by which these necessaries are procured are from this source. For by the general is meant not only the city and its society, but the country, and also the government. But as these are subjects of wide extent, they will be more clearly set forth in what follows; for there are many varieties, which yet are in agreement with this law.

134. (II.) *The goods of use which individuals perform, from which the general good exists, are ministries, functions, offices, and various employments.* By ministries are meant priestly offices and the duties pertaining to them; by functions, various offices of a civil nature; by employments are meant such vocations as those of artificers, which are numerous; and by offices, various pursuits, businesses, and services. Of these four the commonwealth or society consists.

135. They who are in ministerial offices provide that the Divine shall be there; the various civil functionaries, that there shall be justice there, and also morality, as well as industry, knowledge, and uprightness; the various workmen that there shall be the necessaries of life; and merchants, that there shall be the things necessary for the various occupations; soldiers, that there shall be protection; and these last especially, and also agriculturists, that there shall be a sufficiency of wealth.

136. Every one may know that the general good is according to the goods, the industries and pursuits, of every kind.

137. (III.) *All the offices and employments, regarded as to the goods of use, constitute a form which corresponds to the heavenly form.* The heavenly form is such that every individual there is in some ministry, some function, some office or employment, and in work. Such are all the heavenly societies, that no one may be useless. One who does nothing and who wishes to live in ease, or only to talk and walk and sleep, is not tolerated there. All things there are so ordered that each is assigned a place nearer or more remote from the centre according to its use. In proportion as they are nearer the centre the palaces are more magnificent; as they are more remote from the centre they are less magnificent. They are different in the east, in the west, in the south, and in the north. Every one when he enters a society is introduced into his office, and is assigned a home corresponding to his work. Every society is a series of affections, in complete order.

138. Every one there enjoys his own pursuit. It is the source of his delight. They shun idleness as one would a pestilence. The reason is this, that every one there does his work as from a love of use, and so has delight of heart. The general delight flows into him. Thus, from heavenly society, chiefly, it has been given to know, not only that individuals organized according to the varieties of affections form the general good, but that every one derives his good from the general good.

139. So it is on earth; for earthly society thus corresponds to heavenly society. And since it corresponds, these things are also there. The Divine is there; there is justice; there is morality, and uprightness; there is wisdom, and industry. The society in general inspires these into the individuals, when [each] part, which is an angel, is in charity.

140. The necessaries of life, and of the various occupations, and also wealth, and especially delights and felicities, are given to them from the general, as there is charity.

141. But this is not known on earth, where every one places delight and satisfaction in honors and in riches. They who do this on earth become mean and poor, and pass the time in the hells. But he that pursues any occupation from an affection of charity comes into a heavenly society.

142. Functions, offices, and employments innumerable exist there, all spiritual; which may indeed be described, but not so as to be comprehended.

143. (IV.) *They also constitute a form which corresponds to the human form.* It is the same in the human body. There all things are goods of use, in a most perfect form. And because they are in most perfect form they are felt as one, and yet are all various; and in every different part they vary in their own series and in their own order. There are the senses, which are five; the viscera, which are many; the organs of generation, which also are many, in each sex; there are external members; and there are still more numerous things of the mind; that is, of the will and the understanding.

144. The general things in the body are the heart and lungs. The action of these flows into all parts of the body, organs, viscera, and members. The general things in the mind are the will and the understanding. These general things there have relation to the individual things, as their parts from which they subsist; and the parts have relation to the general, from which they exist.

145. All things therein are formed from use, in use, and for use. They are all forms of use.

146. The form of government in the animal body is such that each part derives its appointed task from the general; and it is provided that the general shall give subsistence to each part. The heart furnishes blood to the individual parts in the whole body; and each particular part has as it were its work, each takes up what is its own, and gives of its own. The form, in a word, is wonderful.

147. The heavenly form of use is there; which is confirmed by the fact that each heavenly society is as a man, and appears as a man. The uses there constitute that man; because the form of a heavenly society corresponds to the form of the animal body as to uses.

148. In least things and in greatest the heavenly form is a man. Therefore the universal heaven is a man; every society is a man; and each individual angel is a man. The reason is, that the Lord from whom heaven exists is a man.1

149. (V.) *In this form each individual is a good of use, according to the extent of his office or employment.* Charity is nothing else than an affection of truth from good; and an affection of truth from good, is an affection of use. For unless an affection of truth from good becomes an act, it perishes; and the action therefrom is a use.

150. Genuine truth, the affection of which is charity, regards nothing else than life with the neighbor; therefore the affection of truth from good, is nothing else. The good from which the affection springs, is the will to do, and the will to know in order that one may do. Otherwise it is not the genuine good from which is truth.

151. When therefore a man is a use, or a good of use, he is also charity.

152. And then the man is said to be charity in form, and he is an image of charity. All things in that man are of charity. For when the man himself breathes forth use in general, he breathes it forth also in every particular. His life and soul become a love of use, or an affection of use.

153. And then inwardly he looks to the Lord, and outwardly to his work.

154. (VI.) *Man is born that he may become charity; and he cannot become charity unless he perpetually does the good of use to the neighbor, from affection and its delight.* In the following article it will be shown how a man is perpetually to do the good of use to the neighbor, and this from affection and its delight.

155. He who places charity in good deeds alone cannot do this perpetually.

156. And if uses are not done perpetually there is an interruption, and in this interval he may turn aside into all loves and the concupiscences therefrom, and so not only intermit his charity, but even depart from good works. Charity thus perishes from its opposites, and the man serves two lords.

157. A man may even do the good of use from the affection of glory, of honor, and of gain, and their delights. And then he is not charity, but lust; thus he is not a form of heaven, but of hell. Even in hell every one is forced to do good work, but it is not done from the affection of it; he is forced to it.

VII.

EVERY MAN WHO LOOKS TO THE LORD AND SHUNS EVILS AS SINS, IF HE SINCERELY, JUSTLY, AND FAITHFULLY DOES THE WORK OF HIS OFFICE AND EMPLOYMENT, BECOMES A FORM OF CHARITY.

158. This follows as a consequence from the preceding law, that man is born that he may become charity; and he cannot become charity unless he perpetually does the good of use from affection and its delight. Therefore when a man sincerely, justly, and faithfully does the work that belongs to his office or employment, from affection and its delight, he is continually in the good of use, not only to the community or public, but also to individuals and private citizens. But this cannot be unless he looks to the Lord and shuns evils as sins; for, as was shown above, to look to the Lord and shun evils as sins is the first of charity (n. 8); and the second of charity is to do goods. And the goods that he does are goods of use, which he does every day, and which, when he is not doing, he thinks of doing. There is an interior affection which inwardly remains and desires it. Hence it is that he is perpetually in the good of use, from morning to evening, from year to year, from his earliest age to the end of his life. Otherwise he cannot become a form, that is, a receptacle of charity.

159. The subject now to be treated of is charity in the priest; in the magistrate, and the officials under him; in the judge; in the commander of an army, and the officers under him; and in the common soldier; in the merchant; in the workman; in the husbandman; in the master of a vessel, and mariners; and in servants.

160. (I.) *Charity in the Priest.* If he looks to the Lord and shuns evils as sins, and sincerely, justly, and faithfully performs the work of the ministry enjoined upon him, he does the good of use continually, and becomes charity in form. And he does the good of use or the work of the ministry sincerely, justly, and faithfully, when he is affected with a desire for the salvation of souls. And in proportion as he is so affected, he is affected by truths, because by means of them he leads souls to heaven; and he leads souls to heaven by means of truths when he leads them to the Lord. It is, then, his love diligently to teach truths from the Word; because when he teaches them from the Word he teaches them from the Lord. For the Lord not only is the "Word" [*John* i. 1, 2, 14], but is also "the Way, the Truth, and the Life" [*John* xiv. 6], and is the "Door." He therefore that entereth in by the Lord as the "door" into the sheepfold is a good shepherd. And he that entereth not by the Lord as the "door" into the sheepfold is an evil shepherd, who is called a thief and a robber [*John* x. 1–9].

161. (II.) *Charity in Magistrates.* By magistrates are meant the highest functionaries in kingdoms, commonwealths, provinces, cities, and societies, who have jurisdiction over them in civil affairs. Each one of them in his own place, if he looks to the Lord and shuns evils as sins, and sincerely, justly, and faithfully performs the work of his exalted office, does the good of use to the community and the individuals in the community continually and becomes charity in form. And this he does when he is influenced by an affection for the good of the subjects or citizens; and when he is so influenced he is moved, in common with men that are wise and fear God, to establish useful laws, to see that they are observed, and especially to live under them; and also to appoint intelligent and at the same time benevolent officers under him over the people, through whom, under his supervision, judgment and justice shall reign, and continually effect the good of the community. He will regard himself as highest in the order of those that serve others; and thus not as the head, for the head leads all things of its body from love and wisdom in itself, and the Lord alone is Love and Wisdom in itself; by whom he too will be led as a servant.

162. (III.) *Charity in the Officials under them.* By the officials under magistrates are meant those who are appointed by them over the people to perform various necessary and useful functions. Every one of them, if he looks to the Lord and shuns evils as sins, and sincerely, justly, and faithfully performs the work of his office, becomes charity in form, because he does the goods of use continually, while in the performance of official duty and also when not in official duty; for then an affection for doing it is established in his mind, and an affection for doing the goods of use is charity in its life. Use affects him, and not honor except for the sake of use. There is a certain lesser general good under each official, according to the extent of his function, subordinate to the greater and greatest general good, which is that of the kingdom or commonwealth. An official who is charity, when he sincerely, justly, and faithfully does his work, consults the less general good, which is that of his domain, and so the greater and the greatest. In other respects it is the same with the official as with the magistrate for whom he acts; with only the difference that there is between greater and less, wider and narrower, extension to uses in general and extension to uses in particular; and also that the one, as a servant, is dependent upon the other.

163. (IV.) *Charity in Judges.* If they look to the Lord and shun evils as sins, and render just judgments, they become charities in form; because they do goods of use, both to the community and individuals in the community, and so to the neighbor. And these they do continually, when they judge and when they are not judging; because they think justly, speak also justly, and do justly. For justice is of their affection; and in the spiritual sense it is the neighbor. Such a judge determines all cases from what is just, and at the same time from equity; for they cannot be separated. And then he judges according to the law, for all law has both of these for its end; and so when a cunning man strives to pervert the sense of the law he ends the suit. In judging, to regard friendship, or a gift, or relationship, or authority, or other consideration than that every one who lives according to the laws shall be protected, he holds to be a sin; and he holds it to be so even if he judges justly, and justice is not in the first place, but in the second. All the judgments of a just judge are of charity, even when he inflicts fine or penalty upon the criminally wicked; for thus he emends them and guards against their doing evil to the innocent, who are the neighbor. He is indeed as a father, who if he loves his children castigates them when they do evil.

164. (V.) *Charity in the Commander of an army.* By the commander of an army is meant its highest officer, whether he be king or archduke, or one constituted commander who holds authority from them. If he looks to the Lord and shuns evils as sins, and if he acts sincerely, justly, and faithfully in the affairs of his generalship and command, he does goods of use, which are goods of charity. And as he perpetually meditates upon them, applies himself to and executes them, he becomes charity. If he is king or archduke, he does not love war, but peace; even in war he continually loves peace. He does not go to war except for the protection of his country, and thus is not an aggressor, but a defender. But afterwards, when war is begun, if so be that aggression is defence, he becomes also an aggressor. In battle, if he has not been born otherwise, he is brave and valiant; after battle he is mild and merciful. In battle he would fain be a lion; but after battle, a lamb. In his inner self he does not exult in the overthrow of his enemy, and in the honor of victory; but in the deliverance of his country and his people from the invasion of an enemy, and the destruction and ruin they would inflict. He acts prudently; cares faithfully for his army, as the father of a family for his children and servants; and loves them, every one, according as he does his duty sincerely and valiantly; and many such things. Cunning, with him, is not cunning, but prudence.

165. (VI.) *Charity in the Officers under the Commander of an army.* Every one of them may become charity, that is, an angel of heaven, if he looks to the Lord and shuns evils as sins, and sincerely, justly, and faithfully performs the duty of his office. For thus they too do goods of use perpetually, which are of charity; for their minds are in them, and when the mind is perpetually in goods of use it becomes a form of charity. His country is his neighbor; in the spiritual idea, he is its defence and security from invasion and destruction. He does not falsely exult in what is of no merit; nor does he exult even in what is deserving. This he thinks ought to be; which makes him of contented mind, and not vainglorious. In war he loves the soldiers under him, according to their valor, sincerity, and obedience; is thoughtful for them, and desires their good as he does his own; for they are victims to the glory of his use. For officers have the glory of the use and the glory of the honor; the soldiers who are charities have the glory of the use, and not the glory of the honor. Other things with him are similar to those above mentioned pertaining to the commander of the army, for whom he acts, with a difference according to the extent of his command. I have seen such officers in a higher heaven, and I have seen officers who were not such in hell.

166. (VII.) *Charity in the Common Soldier.* If he looks to the Lord and shuns evils as sins, and sincerely, justly, and faithfully does his duty, he also becomes charity; for as to this there is no distinction of persons. He is averse to unjust depredation; he abominates the wrongful effusion of blood. In battle it is another thing. There he is not averse to it; for he does not think of it, but of the enemy as an enemy, who desires his blood. When he hears the sound of the drum calling him to desist from the slaughter, his fury ceases. He looks upon his captives after victory as neighbors, according to the quality of their good. Before the battle he raises his mind to the Lord, and commits his life into His hand; and after he has done this, he lets his mind down from its elevation into the body and becomes brave; the thought of the Lord—which he is then unconscious of—remaining still in his mind, above his bravery. And then if he dies, he dies in the Lord; if he lives, he lives in the Lord.

167. (VIII.) *Charity in the Man of Business.* If he looks to the Lord and shuns evils as sins, and transacts his business sincerely, justly, and faithfully, he becomes charity. He acts as from his own prudence, and yet trusts in the Divine Providence. He is therefore not despondent in misfortune nor elated with success. He thinks of the morrow, and yet does not think of it. He thinks of what should be done on the morrow, and how it should be done; and yet does not think of the morrow, because he ascribes the future to the Divine Providence and not to his own prudence. Even his prudence he ascribes to the Divine Providence. He loves business as the principal of his vocation, and money as its instrumental; and does not make this the principal and that the instrumental, as very many of the Jews do. Thus he loves his work, which is in itself a good of use; and not the means rather than the work. He does not indeed so distinguish between them; but yet they are thus distinguished when he looks to the Lord and shuns evils as sins. For he shuns avarice, which is an evil and the root of many evils. He loves the general good while loving his own good; for that lies hidden within it, as the root of a tree, which conceals itself in the earth; from which, nevertheless, it grows, and blossoms, and bears fruit. Not that he gives to it of his own beyond what is due; but the fact is that the public good is also the good of his fellow-citizens, whence indeed it arises, whom he loves from the charity of which he is a form. No one can know the secrets of charity within himself, for he cannot see them; but the Lord sees them.

168. (IX.) *Charity in Workmen.* By workmen are meant operatives and artificers of the various kinds. If they look to the Lord and shun evils as sins, and do their work sincerely, justly, and faithfully, they become forms of charity, each in proportion as he loves his work and is diligent in it. For their works are goods of use serviceable to the neighbor for various necessities and uses; as for food, clothing, dwelling, protection, preservation, pleasure, and in many other ways; and are the gains of the commonwealth. Just in so far as any one puts his mind into his work and labor, from the love of it, he is in it, as to affection and thought concerning it; and in proportion as he is in it, he is withheld from thinking of and loving vanities, and afterwards is led of the Lord to think of and love goods; and also to think of and love the means to good, which are truths. It is not so with one who applies himself to no work. Every workman who looks to the Lord and shuns evils as sins, shuns idleness, because it is the devil's pillow; shuns insincerity and fraud; and shuns luxury and intemperance. He is industrious, sincere, sober, content with his lot, and works for his neighbor as he would for himself; because in doing his work he loves himself and him in equal degree.

169. (X.) *Charity in Husbandmen.* Husbandmen, or farmers and vinedressers, if they look to the Lord and shun evils as

sins, and do their work sincerely, justly, and faithfully, become charities, as to their spirits, and after death, when they become spirits, they are in a form of charity; and that form is the human form, in which all are after death. Husbandmen such as these rise early in the morning, arrange their work, apply themselves with energy to their labor, are indefatigable in their work, and rejoice in it. When their work is done, they are economical, sober, and vigilant. At home with their families they act justly; abroad, among others, with sincerity. They regard the civil laws of justice, like those of the Decalogue, as Divine, and obey them. They love their fields and their vineyards, because of their produce; and love the fruits of them because they are blessings, and render thanks to the Lord, and so look to the Lord continually.

170. (XI.) *Charity in Shipmasters.* Shipmasters to whom ships and merchandise are intrusted, or who own them, also become charities if they look to the Lord and shun evils as sins, and conduct their business sincerely, justly, and faithfully. Their occupation is a greater good of use than many others, because by means of it there is communication, and, as it were, conjunction of the whole world with its parts, and of its parts with the whole. And this excellent work is a good of use, that is a good of charity, in them, when from their knowledge they act prudently; when they perform their duties with vigilance and sobriety, that the voyage may be successful; when they do not rashly expose themselves to danger, nor lose their courage when in the midst of dangers unforeseen, and being saved from them render praise and thanks to the Lord; when they deal justly and sincerely by their seamen, faithfully with the owners of their vessels, and justly with the foreigners to whom their vessel comes. They hold no share with pirates; and are content with their pay and their legitimate gains beyond it. Men that traverse the sea, who are charities, and who look to the Lord and shun evils as sins, and do their duty sincerely, justly, and faithfully, are more devout in their morning and evening prayers and songs than landsmen, because they trust more to the Divine Providence. I counsel seafarers hereafter to pray to the Lord, for He and none other is God of heaven and earth and sea (*John* iii. 35; xvii. 12; *Matt.* xi. 27).

171. (XII.) *Charity in Sailors.* Sailors also become charities, if, while they perform their duty sincerely, justly, and faithfully, they look to the Lord and shun evils as sins. For when they shun evils as sins they shun the devil, for the devil is evil itself; and then they are accepted by the Lord, and the goods that they then do they do from the Lord. And they do good in no other way, continuously, than in the performance of their own work that is enjoined upon them, which is that of a seaman. That work is a good work, because it is a good of use; and to have love towards the neighbor, or charity, is nothing else than to do the good of use. And when they shun the devil and are accepted by the Lord they do not commit the evils described in the Decalogue; that is, they do not kill, they do not commit adultery, they do not steal, they do not bear false witness. For no one does these things who loves the neighbor. He does not love the neighbor who bears such hatred to him that he would kill him; he does not love the neighbor who would commit adultery with another's wife; he does not love the neighbor who would steal and rob him of his goods; he does not love the neighbor who would testify falsely against him and so on. These are the evils which those that look to the Lord especially shun. And then they have no fear of death, for if they die they die in the Lord, and go to heaven; and there all love each other as brothers and companions, and render mutual good services. And I exhort sailors also, as I have just done shipmasters, to go to the Lord, and pray to Him; for there is no other God of heaven, earth, and sea.

172. (XIII.) *Charity in Servants.* Servants, as well as masters, become charities, that is, angels, when they look to the Lord and shun evils as sins, and perform the duties of a servant sincerely, justly, and faithfully. Their duties, which are special and continual goods of charity, are, to attend on their masters, to wish well to them, to speak no ill of them, to act as uprightly in their absence as in their presence, and not to scorn to serve. For every one, in whatever degree of dignity, ought to serve. Even a king should serve the Lord. And so far as any one serves faithfully he is loved and led of the Lord. And so far as any one looks to the Lord and shuns evils as sins, he serves freely, and not by compulsion.

VIII.

The Signs of Charity Are All Things that Pertain to Worship.

173. All things of charity have regard to looking to the Lord and shunning evils as sins, and doing the goods of use that pertain to one's calling. But all things of worship are externals, of the body and of the mind. The externals of the body are performed by acts and by words; and the externals of the mind are those that are performed by the will and the thought, which cohere with the externals of the body.

174. The externals of the body which pertain to worship are:—(1) Frequenting temples. (2) Listening to sermons. (3) Devoutly singing, and praying on the knees. (4) Partaking the Sacrament of the Supper. And at home:—(1) Prayer morning and evening, and at dinners and suppers. (2) Conversing with others about charity and faith, and about God, heaven, eternal life, and salvation. (3) And in the case of priests, preaching, and also private instruction. (4) And with every one, the instruction of children and servants in such matters. (5) Reading the Word, and books of instruction and of piety.

175. The externals of the mind which pertain to worship are:—(1) Thought and meditation concerning God, and concerning heaven, eternal life, and salvation. (2) Reflection upon one's thoughts and intentions, as to whether they are evil or good, and that the evil are from the devil, and the good from God. (3) Aversion of one's mind from impious, obscene, and filthy language. (4) Besides thoughts, there are also affections which come to the sight and sense of a man.

176. These are called externals because they cohere and make one with the externals of the body.

177. That such things are externals of worship, and that the externals of worship are signs of charity, will be seen in the following order:—

>   (I.) *Charity itself is in the internal man, and its sign is in the external.*

(II.) *When charity is in the internal man, and constitutes it, then all the acts of worship that are performed in externals are signs of it.*

(III.) *Worship in the external man proceeding from charity in the internal, appears to the angels as a standard-bearer with a banner in his hand. But worship in the external man not proceeding from charity in the internal, appears to the angels as an actor with a firebrand in his hand.*

178. (I.) *Charity itself is in the internal man, and its sign is in the external.* That there is an internal and an external man is known; and that the internal man is called the spirit, and the external the flesh, is also known. For it is said, and it is known by some that there is a conflict between the spirit and the flesh. The spirit which contends against the flesh is the internal man, who is charity.

179. The quality of the internal man cannot manifest itself to a man except by the external. It manifests itself when there is a conflict with the external; especially it manifests itself when a man examines himself, sees his evils, and from knowledge confesses them and thinks about repentance, and then resists his evils and sets about living a new life.

180. If a man does not do these things his internal man is evil; but if he does them his internal man is good. For through the internal man the Lord operates into the external; and as evil is then residing in the external, a conflict arises. For into the external man, which is called the flesh, spirits from hell are admitted, who are called the devil; and the Lord in man fights against him. And if, as of himself, the man also fights, he conquers; and as far as the devil is conquered, so far there is place for goods from the internal man to enter. Thus he gradually becomes a new man and is regenerated.

181. Whatever the internal man produces and presents to sight and sense in the external is called a sign. If charity is in the internal it leads a man to reflect upon the evils within him, and actually to take cognizance of and know them, and so on. If he does not do this his external is not a sign of charity; and if yet his external is in worship and piety, it is not a sign of charity, but is external charity without internal charity, which is not charity.

182. By a sign is meant an indication and evidence that it exists; for it expresses and signifies and indicates and bears witness of it.

183. There is no internal without its sign and indication. If charity is in the internal man, or in the spirit, and this does not fight against the external man and his flesh, then charity perishes. It is as a fountain of pure water; if there is no outlet it stagnates; and then it either ceases its flow or by stagnation the water becomes putrid. In another place there will be many confirmations of these things from the Word.

* * * * * * * * * *

(*Two pages of the original MS. are here wanting.*)

IX.

184. [THE BENEFACTIONS OF CHARITY ARE ALL THE GOODS THAT A MAN, WHO IS CHARITY, DOES FREELY OUTSIDE OF HIS CALLING.—*Supplied from page 233.*]

* * * * * * * * * *

185. (IV.) *No one is saved through these benefactions, but through the Charity from which they are done, and which is therefore in those benefactions.* These benefactions are outside of a man, but charity is within him; and every one is saved according to the quality of good or charity in him. After death, very many, who in the world thought about their salvation, when they see that they are alive, and hear that there is a heaven and a hell, protest that they have done goods, have given to the poor, assisted the needy, made some offerings to pious uses. But it is said to them, "From what source have you done these things? Have you shunned evils as sins? Have you thought about them?" Some answer that they have had faith. But it is replied, "If you have not thought within you of evils as sins, how can you have faith? Faith and evil do not conjoin themselves together." Inquiry is therefore made respecting a man's life in his calling, whether he has performed the uses of his calling for the sake of reputation, honor, and gain, as his chief goods, and thus for himself; or whether he has done them for the sake of the neighbor. Many say they have not thus distinguished them. It is answered, " If you have looked to God and shunned evils as sins, then these two have of themselves become distinct, for the Lord distinguishes them." And as far as they have not done this, they have acted from evil and not from good. In the spiritual world the very affection of each one is communicated, and its quality is shown; and such as he is as to affection, such are all the things that proceed from him. In this way he is led to the society where his affection is.

186. They who place charity in these good deeds or benefactions alone, if they have not charity within them, conjoin themselves interiorly with the infernals and outwardly with the heavenly. But the exterior of every one is removed, and he is left to his interior.

X.

The Obligations of Charity Are All Things that a Man Ought To Do Besides Those Above Mentioned.

187. The obligations of charity are, taxes which are imposed upon subjects and citizens, for the various necessities and the various uses of the commonwealth; customs duties; the expenses and outlay for the various needs and uses of a household, which concern one's self, wife, children, men-servants, maid-servants, and workmen; and their reciprocal obligations. Then, there are some things which become obligations by solemn promise. Besides these there are also civil obligations, which are duties of subordination, of obedience, of honor, and of social intercourse, which must be called obligations because a man ought to do them. But to enumerate these in detail would fill pages. Various duties which the laws of the kingdom impose are called obligations of charity, because charity does them from duty and not of its good pleasure; and because charity regards them as uses, it does them sincerely and willingly. With those who are in charity the sincerity and benignity of charity are inwardly present in every duty. But both the sincerity and benignity are according to the uses which they foresee in their duties; and also, as far as they know, according to the economical management of uses.

188. But the same obligations appear similar in externals with those who are not in charity; yet inwardly they are not similar. For with such there is neither sincerity nor benignity. If, therefore, they do not fear the laws, or if under any pretence they can evade them, they defraud. With these not only the above mentioned things are obligations, but also the laws of justice. For they keep the laws for fear of punishment and loss of reputation; and for these they are just, from duty and not from love, thus not from love of the neighbor.

XI.

There Are Diversions of Charity; Which Are the Various Delights and Pleasures of the Bodily Senses, Useful for the Recreation of the Mind.

189. Such diversions are, social intercourse, with conversations upon various public, private, and economical affairs; also walks, with the sight of palaces and houses, and trees and flowers, in gardens, woods and fields, delightful for their various beauty and magnificence, also of men, and birds and flocks; and also spectacles of various kinds, representative of the moral virtues, and of events from which something of the Divine Providence shines forth. These and similar things are for the sense of sight. Then there are various musical harmonies and songs, which affect the mind according to their correspondences with affections; and in addition to these, there are decorous jestings, which exhilarate the mind. These are for the sense of hearing. And there are likewise banquets, feasts, and entertainments, and various accompanying pleasantries. And games too, at home, played with dice, balls, and cards; and dances also, at weddings, and at festive gatherings. These and such things are useful diversions, for the recreation of the mind. And in addition to these there are various labors of the hands, which give motion to the body, and divert the mind from the works of its calling; and the reading also of books, on historical and dogmatic subjects, which give delight, and of the news in newspapers.

190. These are diversions for every one who is in office or employment. They may therefore be called the diversions of offices or employments. But really they are diversions of the affections from which one engages in his employment. There is an affection in every employment, and it strains the mind, and keeps it intent upon its work or study. This, if it be not relaxed, becomes dull, and its desire flags, as salt that has lost its savor, so that it has no pungency or relish; or as a bended bow, which, unless it be unbent, loses the power that it derives from its elasticity. Just so the mind, kept from day to day in the same ideas, without variety. So the eyes, when they look only at one object, or continually upon one color. For, to look continually at a thing which is black, or continually at red or at white, destroys the sight. Thus, if one looks continually at the snow the sight is destroyed; but it is enlivened if he looks in succession or at the same time upon many colors. Every form delights by its varieties, as a garland of roses of different colors arranged in beautiful order. Hence it is that the rainbow is more charming than the light itself.

191. When the mind has been continually upon the stretch, at its work, it aspires to rest; and when it rests it descends into the body, and seeks there its pleasures, correspondent to its mental operations, which the mind chooses, according to its interior state in the viscera of the body. The interior things of the body derive their pleasures chiefly from the senses of sight, hearing, smell, taste, and touch, delights which are in fact drawn from outward things, but yet insinuate themselves into the single parts of the body, which are called members and viscera. From hence and from no other source have they their delights and pleasures. The single fibres, and single tissues of fibres, the single capillary vessels, and thence the common vessels, and so all the viscera in common, derive their own delights; which a man then perceives, not singly but universally, as one common sensation. But just as is the mind within them, from the head, such are the delights, pure or impure, spiritual or natural, heavenly or infernal. For within, in every sensation of the body, is the love of his will, with its affections; and the understanding makes him to perceive their delights. For the love of the will, with its affections, constitutes the life of every sensation; and the perception thence of the understanding produces the sensation. Hence come all delights and pleasures. For the body is a connected work, and one form. Sensation communicates itself, like a force applied to a chain with its single links; and as a form which has been wrought together from uninterrupted links.

192. But because the ministries, functions, offices, and labors of every one keep the mind upon the stretch, and this is what is to be relaxed, revived, and restored by diversions, it may be seen that diversions vary according to the interior affection within them; and that they are one thing if the affection of charity is in them, another if there is in them an affection for honor only, another if there is an affection only for gain, another if they perform their duties only for the sake of support, and the necessaries of life, another if only for a name, that they may be celebrated, or if only for the sake of salary, that they may grow rich, or that they may live generously, and so on.

193. If the affection of charity is in them, then all the above-mentioned diversions are for its recreation,—spectacles and plays, musical harmonies and songs, and all the beauties of fields and gardens, and social intercourse in general. The affection of use remains interiorly within them, which, while it is thus resting, is gradually renewed. A longing for one's work breaks or ends them. For the Lord flows into them from heaven and renews; and He also gives an interior sense of pleasure in them, which they who are not in the affection of charity know nothing of. He breathes into them a fragrance or, as it were, sweetness perceptible only to one's self. A fragrance, it is said, by which is meant a spiritual pleasantness; and sweetness, by which is meant spiritual delight. Pleasantness is predicated of wisdom, and of the perception of the understanding therefrom; and delight is predicated of love, and of the affection therefrom of the will. They who are not in the affection of charity have not these, because the spiritual mind is closed; and in the degree that they depart from charity the spiritual mind, as to its voluntary part, is as if stuffed with something glutinous.

194. These diversions are similar outwardly to those who have only an affection for honor, that is, who do the works of their calling merely for the sake of reputation, that they may be praised, and promoted. They labor, are vigilant in their work, and perform uses in abundance; not, however, from the love of use, but from the love of self; thus not from love to the neighbor, but from the love of glory. They may also feel a delight in the work of their calling; but it is an infernal delight. To their eyes it may counterfeit heavenly delight; for they are both alike outwardly. But their delight is full of what is undelightful; for they have no rest and peace of mind, except when they are thinking of fame and honor, and when they are being honored and adored. When they are not thinking of these they rush into voluptuous pleasures, into drunkenness, luxury, whoredoms, into hatred, vindictiveness, and slander of the neighbor, if he does not do them honor. And if from time to time they are not raised to higher honors, they come to loathe their employments, and give themselves up to leisure and become idlers; and after their departure from the world they become demons.

195. These diversions are diversions also to those who have only an affection for gain; but they are carnal, inspired within only by the delight of opulence. Such men are careful, prudent, industrious, especially such who are merchants, or workmen. If in official position, they are vigilant in the duties which pertain to their offices, and they sell uses; if judges, they sell justice; if priests, they sell salvation. To them lucre is the neighbor. For the sake of office they love lucre, and they love the lucre derived from their office. They that are high in office may sell their country, and even betray their army and their fellow-citizens to the enemy. Whence it is evident what their love is in the diversions above mentioned; they are full of rapine. And as far as they do not fear the civil laws, or public punishments, and the loss of reputation for the sake of gain, they rob and steal. Outwardly they are sincere; but inwardly insincere. The uses they perform in their offices and employments are pleasant and delightful to them, as excrements are to swine, or mice to cats. They look upon men as a tiger or a wolf upon lambs and sheep, which if they can they devour. They do not know that the good of use is anything. There is an infernal delight and pleasure in their diversions. They are like asses, that see nothing pleasant in meadows and fields but what they eat, be it wheat or barley in the ear. But these things are said of the avaricious.

196. But to those who perform the duties of their calling only for the sake of food and the necessaries of life; and those who perform them only for a name, that they may be celebrated; and those who perform them only for the sake of the salary, to the end that they may grow rich or may live generously, the above-mentioned diversions are the only uses. They are corporeal and sensual men. Their spirits are unclean, being lusts and appetites. They do the works of their calling for the sake of the diversions. They are human beasts, dead; and their duties are burdens to them. They seek substitutes to do the work of their office, while they retain the name and the salary. When not engaged in the above-named diversions, they are idlers and sloths; they lie in bed, thinking of nothing but how they may find companions to talk, eat, and drink with. They are public burdens. All such after death are shut up in workhouses, where they are under a judge administrator, who daily appoints them the work they are to do; and if they do not do it, no food, or clothing, or bed is given them; and this is continued until they are driven to do something useful. The hells abound with such workhouses, of which something may be said at the end of this work. These workhouses stink; for every grateful odor is from the life of spiritual love, or from the life of the love of use.

* * * * * * *

197. The conjunction of charity and faith has been treated of in *The Doctrine of the New Jerusalem concerning Faith;* in the *Explanation of the Apocalypse;* as also in the *Angelic*

Wisdom concerning the Divine Providence, and in the *Angelic Wisdom concerning the Divine Love and Divine Wisdom.*

198. All of which is referable to these two: (1) That there is not a grain of spiritual faith without charity; for charity is the life, soul, and essence of faith. (2) That such as the charity is such is the faith; and that the faith which precedes charity is a faith of knowledges, which is historical faith, in itself, knowledge.

[These two fragments are all that the author's MS. contains of this chapter.]

APPENDIX.

[The following appear in the author's MS. to be a second and subsequent draft of the first two sections of the work, and of the title of the third, the title and order of treatment of the fourth, and of the syllabus of the whole work. They are not only important and interesting in themselves, but also as presenting somewhat different phases of doctrinal truth on the subject.]

I.

THE FIRST OF CHARITY IS TO LOOK TO THE LORD AND SHUN EVILS AS SINS.

199. It is known that charity, or love towards the neighbor, consists in doing good to others. But it shall be shown in the following pages how one is to do good, and to whom, that charity may be charity. Every man knows that no one can do good which in itself is good except from Him who is good itself, or good in Himself; that is, except from God. And every one may also know that so long as a man is in evil, and by evil is with the devil, he can do no other than impure good, which outwardly appears as good, but inwardly is evil, which good is either Pharisaical, or for the sake of merit. It is therefore necessary in the first place to set forth what a man must be, in order that the good which proceeds from him may in itself be good, and thus the good of charity.

200. This shall be shown in the following order:—*

(I.) *No one can have charity unless from the Lord.*

(II.) *No one can have charity from the Lord unless he shuns evils as sins.*

(III.) *A man ought to shun evils as sins as if of himself, and yet from the Lord.*

[MARGINAL NOTE.]

* From Paul concerning love towards the neighbor: if it is asked what is first, whether to shun them as evils, or to love the neighbor.

(IV.) *In so far as any one does not shun evils as sins, he remains in them.*

(V.) *So far as any one does not take cognizance of and know what sins are, so far he does not see but that he is without sins.*

(VI.) *So far as any one takes cognizance of and knows what sins are, so far he can see them in himself, confess them before the Lord, and repent of them.*

(VII.) *Good before repentance is not good, thus neither is charity.*

(VIII.) *Consequently, the first of charity is to look to the Lord and shun evils as sins, which is done by repentance.*

201. (I.) *No one can have charity except from the Lord.* Here, as in the following pages, we name only the Lord, because the Lord is the only God; for He is the God of heaven and earth, as He Himself teaches. He and the Father are one, like the soul and body, as He also teaches. And He and the Holy Spirit are the same, as the Divine in Himself, and the Divine from Himself. So that He Himself is the one and only God; and the Divine Trinity is in His Person, and is named the Father, the Son, and the Holy Spirit. Now because the whole church and all religion is founded upon the idea of God, and upon the idea that God is one, and as this idea can in no wise exist unless God is one in Essence and in Person, and unless this unity of trinity and trinity of unity is in the Lord alone, therefore here now at the beginning, and in what follows afterwards, we name the Lord only. (See also the *Doctrine of the New Jerusalem concerning the Lord*, from the beginning to the end, and *Angelic Wisdom concerning the Divine Providence*, n. 263.) The reason why no one can have charity except from the Lord, is that by charity every good is meant that a man does to others, and the good that a man does to others, though it be good to those to whom it is done, is not good in him by whom it is done, unless it is from God. For no good that in itself is good and is called a good or charity, and that in its essence is spiritual good, can flow out from man, but it is from the Lord only; for in order that a good may be of charity or spiritual good, the Lord must be in the good, yea, must be the good. For it proceeds from Him; and what proceeds from one derives from him its essence, for he himself is in it. If, therefore, the Lord were not in the good that a man does to the neighbor, or what is the same, unless the good that a man does to the neighbor were from the Lord, it would not have the essence of good, but the essence of evil in it. For the man would be in it, and a man in himself, and in what is his own, is nothing but evil. This evil must first be removed, in order that the good which proceeds from a man may not be of the man, but of the Lord. Man is only a recipient of life, not life, in himself. For if he were life in himself he would be God. Man is therefore only a recipient of good; for good is of life, because love and wisdom are life, and good is of love and truth is of wisdom. This life cannot be ascribed to man as his. For man is finite and created, and the Lord cannot create and finite Himself in another; for thus He Himself would no longer be, and the whole human race, and each one by himself, would be God, to think which is not only irrational but abominable. Such an idea of God and of man, in the spiritual world, stinks like a carcase. It is evident from all this that there can be no good which in itself is good, and is called the good of charity, from man, but from the Lord, who alone is good itself, and so, good in Himself. The Lord does indeed produce this from Himself, but through man. There is no other subject through which the Lord produces good from Himself than man. And yet the Lord has given to man the capacity to feel it within himself,—yea, just as if it were from himself, and therefore as if it were his own,—in order that he may do it. For if he should feel that it was not from himself, but from the Lord, he would not do it; because he would then believe himself not a man, yea not alive, and even scarcely different from an automaton. And I know from experience that a man would rather die, than live from another in himself even to the sense. Yea, if a man did not feel as if the good that he does was from himself, good would not remain in him, but would flow through, as water through a perforated bottle; and thus he could not be formed for heaven, that is, reformed and regenerated, and thus saved to live to eternity. But lest man, from this appearance, should attribute to himself the good of charity that he does to the neighbor, and so appropriate to himself evil, instead of good,—believing that he lives from himself, and therefore does good from himself,—and should ascribe to himself what is the Lord's, it has pleased the Lord to reveal this in His Word, and teach it. For the Lord says:—

He that abideth in Me, and I in him, the same bringeth forth much fruit; for without Me ye can do nothing (*John* xv. 5, and other places).

202. (II.) *No one can have charity from the Lord unless he shuns evils as sins.* By charity, here as above, is meant the good that a man does to the neighbor. Any one can do good to the neighbor, an evil as well as a good man; but no one can do it from good in himself unless from the Lord, nor unless he shuns evils as sins. That no one can do good to the neighbor from good in himself, unless from the Lord, has been shown just above. And that no one can do it unless he shuns evils as sins, is because the Lord can flow into no one with good, so as to be received, unless the evils in him are removed; for evils do not receive good, but reject it. For it is the same with a man who is in evils as with the devils in hell. The Lord flows into them with good, just as into the angels in heaven; but the devils do not receive it, but turn the good into evil, and the truth into falsity. For such is the form of their life, and everything that flows in is turned into a like form,—just as the pure heat of the sun, when it flows into stagnant urine, excrements, and dead bodies, is turned into noisome and malignant odors; and as the pure light of the sun, flowing into objects where all things are disordered, is converted into ugly colors. It is the same with heavenly heat, which is Divine good, and heavenly light, which is Divine truth, in a man the form of whose life is inverted, and opposite to the heavenly form. It is plain therefore that so long as a man does not shun evils as sins he cannot but love evils; and the love in any one makes the form of his life. It is comparatively as a tree, which if evil it receives the heat and light of the sun equally with a good tree, and yet cannot produce fruit except after its own form, and so produces evil fruit. And it is comparatively as with noxious and poisonous plants, which, equally with good and useful plants, derive the life of their growth from the heat and light of the sun, and yet they can produce nothing but what is in agreement with their own form. Every man is the form of his own love. Nothing but his love forms a man, as to his spiritual part. If he loves evils he becomes a form of evil, which is an infernal form; but if he loves what is good he becomes a form of good, which is a heavenly form. It is clear from this that if a man does not shun evils as sins, the form of his mind, as to what is spiritual, becomes an infernal form, which in itself does not receive any good from the Lord, and consequently produces no good that is good in itself. The Lord can produce good through every man, and can turn to good the evil that an evil man produces. He can incite an evil man to do good for the sake of himself, and for the sake of the world; but then the Lord does not flow into the evil of the man, but around it into his circumferences, thus into his external, by which the man desires to appear as good. This good, as far as it is good, is therefore superficial; and intrinsically it is evil. With hypocrites it is like gilded dung, so that it is scarcely believed to be other than pure gold; but yet, when it is brought near to a keen-scented nostril, the smell of its filthiness is perceived. But all this is fully set forth in *The Doctrine of Life for the New Jerusalem*, in the section where it is shown that so far as a man shuns evils as sins, he does goods not from himself, but from the Lord (n. 18–31). To which I shall add only this, that every one may see it, merely from general influx from heaven. Take whomsoever you will, a servant, a farmer, a workman, a shipmaster, or a merchant, if only there is something rational in him, and merely say that he who hates evil does good, and they will see it clearly. And, as they know that all good is from God, say, that as far as a man hates evil because it is against God, so far he does good from God, and they will see it. But say the same things to one who has confirmed himself in faith alone, and at the same time in the doctrine that no one can do good of himself, and he will not see it; for falsities have closed the rational sight of understanding of this one, but not of the others.

203. (III.) *A man ought to shun evils as sins as if of himself, and yet from the Lord.* Who that reads the Word, and has any religion, does not know that evils are sins? The

Word teaches this from the beginning to the end, and this is the whole of religion. Evils are called sins from this that they are contrary to the Word, and contrary to religion. Who does not know that no one can shun evils as sins unless as of himself? Who can repent otherwise? Does a man not say within himself, This I will not. From doing this I will abstain. Yea, whenever the evil returns I will fight against it and conquer it? And yet no one thus speaks within himself unless he believes in God. He who does not believe in God does not regard evil as sin, and so does not fight against it, but rather for it. But, he who believes in God says also, within himself, Through God I will conquer it. And he supplicates, and prevails. This is not denied to any one, but is granted to all; for the Lord is in continual effort, from His Divine love, to reform and regenerate man, and so to purify him from evils. And when the man also wills and intends it, this perpetual effort of the Lord becomes an act. Thus and no otherwise does a man receive power to resist evils and fight against them. Before this he does not receive, but rejects. This, then, is to shun evils as sins as if of one's self, and yet from the Lord. But on this subject also see *The Doctrine of Life for the New Jerusalem* (n. 101–107). To which I will add this: Say to a man of sound reason, Only believe that Christ, the Son of God, has redeemed you from hell, and so from all evil; and pray to God the Father that for this reason He will remit your sins, and they will be remitted, and then you will have no need to shun evils as sins as of yourself. Can you do anything at all of yourself? What, then, can you do as of yourself? And take a little stone or a piece of wood from the earth into your hand and tell him, You can do no more for your justification and salvation than this little stone or this bit of wood; and the man of sound reason will answer, I know that I can do nothing from myself, but yet I can repent of my evils as of myself. This the Lord Himself has taught, and this His apostles, Paul, the Word, and all religion teach. In the act of repentance do I do nothing as of myself? Then let it be said, What will you do, since you are able to do nothing? Do it if you will. I repent by faith, you by works; and faith without works is saving. But the man of sound reason will reply, You are in error, sir

The Lord teaches me to do, and teaches me to believe. Let faith be for you. For me there shall be faith and works together. I know that after death a man must render an account of his doings; and that just as any one does, so he believes.

204. (IV.) *As far as any one does not shun evils as sins, he remains in them.* Man was created in the image and in the likeness of God, and so made that he may be a recipient of the Lord's love and wisdom. But, because he was not willing to be a recipient, but desired to be love itself and wisdom itself, and thus as God, he inverted his form, and turned his affections and thoughts from the Lord to himself, and began to love himself more than the Lord, yea, to worship himself. And so he alienated himself from the Lord, and looked back from Him; and in this way he perverted the image and likeness of God in himself, and made it the image and likeness of hell. This is signified by his eating of the tree of the knowledge of good and evil. By the serpent which he obeyed is signified the sensual, which is the ultimate of the natural man, and its cupidities. This sensual of man, because it is extant in the world and receives its objects therefrom, loves the things of the world; and if dominion is given to it, it withdraws the mind from the objects of heaven, which are the goods of love and the truths of wisdom, in themselves Divine. It is from this origin that, as to his proprium, man is nothing but evil, and is born into it from his parents. But means are provided by the Lord that he may not therefore perish; which means are, that he shall look to the Lord and acknowledge that every good of love and every truth of wisdom is from Him, and nothing from himself. He thus converts his form, by turning away from himself and turning to the Lord; and so returns to the state in which he was created, and which consisted, as has been said, in his being a recipient of good and truth from the Lord, and in no wise from himself. And because the proprium of man, by the inversion of it, has become mere evil, the other means of recovering the image of God is to shun evils as sins. For if a man does not shun evils as sins, but only because they are injurious, he does not look to the Lord, but only to himself, and so remains in his perverted state. But when he shuns evils as sins he fights against them because they are contrary to the Lord, and against His Divine laws; and then he prays to the Lord for help and for power to resist them, which power besought, is never denied. By these two means a man is purified from the evils that are in him from birth. If therefore he does not embrace these two means he can but remain as he was born. He cannot be purified from evils if he only looks and prays to the Lord; for then after he has prayed he believes that he is entirely without sins, or that they are remitted, by which he understands that they are taken away. And so he still remains in them; and to remain in them is to increase them. For they are like a disease which devours and mortifies all that is around it. Nor are evils removed by only shunning them; for in this way the man looks to himself, and thereby confirms the origin of evil, which was that he turned himself back, away from the Lord, and turned to himself.

205. (V.) *As far as any one does not take cognizance of and know what sins are, he does not see but that he is without sins.* Every man loves his proprium, both the proprium of his will and the proprium of his understanding. The proprium of his will is evil and the proprium of his understanding is falsity from that evil; thus it is the falsity of evil. And as every man loves his own, he therefore loves the evil and its falsity. And as everything that is loved is delightful, he does not therefore know but that the evil in him is good, and its falsity truth. For everything is pronounced good that is delightful. From these considerations it may now be seen, that if a man does not take cognizance of and know what sins are, so far he does not see but that he is without sins. But because a man loves his evil and its falsity, because he loves his proprium, he cannot of himself know what evil is and the falsity therefrom, but must see it from another source. He will see it from the precepts of religion, all of which refer to the ten commandments of the Decalogue. If he in his heart rejects these precepts, he can in no wise see but that he is without sins. And yet as he is initiated from childhood into the worship of God, and knows from the doctrine of the church that, from primal origin and afterwards from birth, he is a sinner, he begins to confess that he is a sinner. But as he does not know what sin is, he nevertheless still believes that he is not a sinner. I have heard some declare that they were sinners, that from conception and from birth they were in every kind of sin, that from the head to the sole of the foot there is no soundness in them, and many such things; yet, because they knew not what sins were, they did not know that the love of self and pride are the heads of all sins; they did not know that to indulge in hatred and revenge if one is not honored and worshiped like a demigod, is a sin; nor that to slander the neighbor on account of his enmity, and so bear false witness against him, is a sin; nor that to deceive any one, by word or deed, is a sin; nor that to despise another in comparison with one's self, to envy him his goods, to covet them, is a sin; nor again that it is a sin to attach merit to all that pertains to one's worship of God, either to one's faith or charity, besides innumerable other things. I have heard from them that they did not know such things were sins; nay, nor anything, whatever it is, that any one thinks and does not speak, or that he wills and does not do. From this ignorance one said he did not know that he was a sinner,—"And if I am," he said, "I have been purified from them when I prayed, 'O God, I do not know my sins, remit them.'" But when the same person examined himself, which took place in the world of spirits, he saw that his sins were so many they could not be told; and yet that he could if he would take cognizance of and know them. But he said he did not wish, because he should thus abstain from them in thought and will, which would be acting against the delight of his life. From all this now it is plain that as far as any one does not take cognizance of sins and know what they are, he does not see but that he is without sins.

206. (VI.) *As far as any one takes cognizance of and knows what sins are, so far he can see them in himself, confess them before the Lord, and repent of them.* This follows from all that has now been said. Therefore in order that a man may see what sins are, the first of the Word was the Decalogue; and therefore also the Decalogue is a complex of the whole Word, for which reason it is called the "ten Words," and by "ten Words" are signified all truths in the complex. For a like reason there are similar precepts among all nations in the world which have religion. And the man who knows that they

are Divine laws, and that therefore he who acts contrary to
them acts contrary to God, or commits sin, can receive Divine
influx, and at the same time also the will and effort as of
himself to abstain from sins and repent of them. Confession
of one's sins before the Lord effects conjunction with Him,
and reception of influx from Him. And then the Lord accomplishes
the work, and yet gives man to act as if of himself.
Otherwise man could not act. The Lord at that time operates
in him, through inmost things even to the outermost, and removes
lusts, which are the roots of evil. This a man could
not do of himself. Of himself man operates only in the outermost
things; and yet the inmost things produce these. If
therefore man removed evils of himself, he would still remain
in them.

207. (VII.) *Good before repentance is not good, and therefore is not charity.* Before repentance man is in evil,—is evil
entirely; for he is a form of evil, and an image of hell. But
by repentance evil is removed and good is implanted. From
which it follows that good before repentance is not good. Before
repentance good is not done from the Lord, but from the
man. It has not therefore the essence of good in it, but the
essence of evil, howsoever in its form it may outwardly appear
as good. This is not discerned in the world, but it is, manifestly,
after death. It is heard in the very sound of the voice
in speech, yea, what evil is in it, whether fraud, or envy, or
vain-glory, or haughtiness, or blasphemy, or hypocrisy, yea, or
the claiming of merit. All the words of speech sound forth
from the evil that is in them; and they have regard to self
alone. But the good after repentance is entirely different. It
is good in fulness, open from the Lord Himself. It is lovely,
it is innocent, it is grateful, heavenly. The Lord and heaven
are in it. Good itself is in it. It is living, formed by truths.
Whatever is from good, in good, and for good, is nothing but
some use to the neighbor; and hence it is a serving. It puts
away self and one's proprium, and thus evil, in every breath.
Its form is as the form of a lovely and beautifully colored
flower, which is resplendent from the rays of the sun. And
therefore with those who are in good there are forms which
can never be comprehended by the natural man. They can

neither be depicted nor described. These forms are forms of good. It is truly said that they are forms of good; yet the form itself is truths, and its life is the good of love. For good disposes truths in a form in agreement with itself, and every truth of the form it makes alive. Such is good after repentance.

208. (VIII.) *Consequently the first of charity is to look to the Lord and shun evils as sins which is done by repentance.* Who does not understand that, before a man can do good which is good, he must be cleansed from evils? Must not a cup be cleansed? And if it is not cleansed does not the wine taste of its uncleanness? And must not a platter be cleansed before food is placed upon it? For if the inside of a platter is mere uncleanness, does not the food excite aversion? Can anything pure flow into a man from heaven, while he is nothing but impurity and uncleanness? Must not the impure and unclean be first removed? If you fill your bedchamber with excrement will not the whole house have an offensive smell? Can any one enter there? And if one should step in, does he not say, "I cannot," and turn from the house, saying, "This is for swine"? Before the Lord can flow in with good, evil must therefore be removed. It would indeed be perilous if He should flow in before, for the good would be turned into evil and increase it. For this reason the first thing is to remove evil, and after that to flow in with good, and bring it into act by the man. Whoever beseeches that he may do good from the Lord before evil has been put away by repentance, or without shunning evils as sins, prays for what is impossible, and for what would make him worse, since with the evil good is turned into evil, and so the good is profaned. That evil must first be removed is very evident from the precepts of the Decalogue. Does he who would kill a man, or indulge in hatred towards him, love him? He who commits adultery with another's wife does not love the neighbor. He who steals and defrauds the neighbor does not love him. He who slanders the neighbor does not love him. He who covets things that belong to the neighbor does not love him. These evils therefore must first be removed, and in proportion as they are removed the neighbor is loved. Of these matters Paul speaks [see *Rom.* xiii. 10].

But the question is asked, whether love towards the neighbor should be first, or whether to shun these evils should be first. Every one may see that to shun these evils must be first. For man is born into evil; must he not then do the work of repentance?

II.

THE SECOND OF CHARITY IS TO DO GOOD TO THE NEIGHBOR.

209. [Quote] from *Isaiah*, chapter I.; and concerning the cup and platter, the inside of which must first be cleansed.

If not cleansed they may yet appear good outwardly. This is a Pharisaic or hypocritical good, or a certain natural good in which there is not spiritual good, and so it is spurious; and if done for the sake of salvation, it is meritorious good.

But these things should be illustrated in this order:—

(I.) *To will not to do evil to the neighbor is to love him.*

(II.) *To will to do good to the neighbor is to love him.*

(III.) *As far as a man does not will to do evil to the neighbor, so far he wills to do him good from charity, and not vice versa.*

(IV.) *It follows from this that the first of charity is to look to the Lord and shun evils as sins; and that the second of charity is to do good to the neighbor.*

210. (I.) *To will not to do evil to the neighbor is to love him.* For he who loves another does not do evil to him. And Paul says that he who loves the neighbor obeys the commandment of the Decalogue. He does not will to commit murder; he does not will to commit adultery with another's wife; he does not will to steal; he does not bear false witness. Therefore he says that charity is the fulfillment of the law. But the question is, which is prior and which posterior? Whether the first thing is to love the neighbor, and from that love not to do these evils; or to put away these evils from one's self, and so love the neighbor? This is evident, that he who loves the neighbor does not commit these evils. But the point of inquiry is, how one can love the neighbor? Whether he can do so before he shuns these evils and fights against them? It appears as if this love itself fights. And it does fight; but not until a man is in it. It is obvious that he cannot come into that love until he removes these evils, from the fact that every man is by birth in evils of every kind; that he desires nothing but what is evil; and that if he does not repent of them he remains in them. These evils stand therefore in the way, so that he cannot love the neighbor from that spiritual love. Paul therefore says also that the flesh is against the spirit; and that the flesh must be crucified, with its lusts; and that the man thus becomes spiritual, and a new creature. From which it may be seen, that in so far as a man crucifies the flesh he lives in the spirit. And therefore, since man is by birth of such a nature, it follows that his spirit cannot love the neighbor unless he crucifies his flesh, which is done by repentance. And in proportion as he does this, he in spirit, that is inwardly, loves the neighbor. And to love the neighbor from the heart, before this, is against man's nature. The belief prevails in the Christian world, that whoever has faith loves the neighbor; but that belief is erroneous. No one can have faith in which there is any life unless he shuns evils as sins, yea so far as he shuns them. From all this now it is plain that *the first of charity is not to do evil to the neighbor*, for not to do evil to the neighbor is to fight against the evils in one's self, and repent of them; and that *the second of charity is to do good to the neighbor.* Any one, from the principle that it is Christian not to do evil to the neighbor, also does not do it. He, however, who from that principle only does not do evil to the neighbor and does good to him, still does not love him. It is from obedience to the Divine laws that he does not do evil to him, and not from an affection of love towards the neighbor. No one knows anything of this affection but he who shuns evils as sins, that is, who does not love evils. Such a man comes into the affection of that love. For it is one thing not to do evil but good from obedience, and another not to do evil but good to him from an affection of love towards the neighbor. The difference is as between nocturnal heat and light, from the moon and stars, and the heat and light of day, from the sun. Neither the warmth of that love nor the light of it is in obedience, but in affection. For affection of love is warmth. And therefore they that do good from obedience are in the lowest parts of heaven, and in light and heat as of the moon. Even the light of their understanding is as shade. They do not see any spiritual truths in the light. There is also the difference that they who do good from obedience do it from fear of penalty, and so likewise do they abstain from doing evils; while they that do good from affection do not do it from any fear of penalty. Yea, they that do good from obedience are natural, and they that do it from affection are spiritual. And they that do good from obedience are those that are being reformed, the state which precedes; while they that do good from affection are being regenerated, which state follows the other in order. All who believe that man is saved by faith alone, if they live as Christians, confessing that they are sinners, and who do not examine themselves, do good from obedience and not from affection. But they know nothing about faith, nor about love, nor about God, except what they hear from a preacher; yet they do good. They that do good from obedience take the lead in acts of benevolence, such as giving to the poor, assisting the needy, and endowing temples and hospitals. And they cannot but place merit in these things; nor do they understand the Word otherwise, where it says that they shall have their reward. They do not know that the affection of good itself with its delights, is itself the reward.

211. The affection of love is as a flame, from which there is light in truths. The cause of it is that the Lord flows into man's affection and gives light. In the spiritual world also love from a distance appears as a flame; sometimes as if flames were descending from heaven, which are affections of good and truth so appearing. It is as one who honors a king, a magistrate, and governor, according to the laws of subordination, and so others, and at the same time does not inwardly love him. He loves him who sees the good in him.

XII.*

THERE IS NO CHURCH WHERE THERE IS NO TRUTH OF FAITH; AND NO RELIGION WHERE THERE IS NO GOOD OF LIFE.

212. The church and religion make one like truth and good. And as truth is of faith, and good is of charity, they make one like faith and charity; or, that it may be more clearly understood, they make one like the understanding and the will. It is known that a man may understand well and yet not will well; and that he can understand truths, and from understanding speak them, and yet not from willing do them. But when he wills as he understands, and does as he says, then the will and the understanding make one in him. So it is with the church and religion. The church is a church from its doctrine; and religion is religion from life according to doctrine. And the doctrine must be of truths, and the life must be of goods.

213. But that these things may come into clearer light, they shall be explained in the following order:—

(I.) *All the truths of faith in the church are from the Word.*

(II.) *The truths of faith which are from the Word teach what is to be believed, and what is to be done, that a man may be allotted eternal life.*

(III.) *The church is named from doctrine; and religion from a life according to doctrine.*

(IV.) *With those who are in a faith separated from charity, both in doctrine, and life, there is neither a church nor religion.*

III.†

214. THE NEIGHBOR WHO IS TO BE LOVED IN THE NATURAL SENSE IS THE FELLOW-CITIZEN, A SMALLER AND GREATER SOCIETY, ONE'S NATIVE COUNTRY, AND THE HUMAN RACE.

* * * * * * * * * *
* * * * * * * * * *

---

*In the Photolithograph, Propositions XII., IV., and III. are found at the end of the Manuscript. XII. possibly belongs after n. 198, in Proposition XI.

† In the Photolithograph III. and IV. come in reverse order.

IV.

215. THE NEIGHBOR IS TO BE LOVED ACCORDING TO HIS SPIRITUAL GOOD, AND THENCE ACCORDING TO HIS MORAL, CIVIL, AND NATURAL GOOD; CONSEQUENTLY, THE NEIGHBOR THAT IS TO BE LOVED, IN THE SPIRITUAL SENSE, IS GOOD.

(I.) *Man is not man from the face and body, but from the good of his will.*

(II.) *When the good of a man's will is loved, the man himself is loved.*

(III.) *Man is man from his spiritual good, and not from moral, civil, and natural good apart from the spiritual.*

(IV.) *As a man's spiritual good is, such is his moral, civil, and natural good; because these three goods derive their life from that alone.*

(V.) *Consequently, in the spiritual sense, the neighbor who is to be loved is good.*

OBS.—That spiritual good is the good of charity, and so it is the Lord, heaven, and the church with him. For such is the man in the derivative goods.

ORDER AND ARRANGEMENT [OF THE SUBJECT].

I. THE FIRST OF CHARITY IS TO LOOK TO THE LORD AND SHUN EVILS BECAUSE THEY ARE SINS, WHICH IS DONE BY REPENTANCE.

II. THE SECOND OF CHARITY IS TO DO GOODS BECAUSE THEY ARE USES.

III. IN THE SPIRITUAL IDEA USE IS THE NEIGHBOR; AND USE IS THE GOOD OF CHARITY, CIVIL GOOD IN THE CIVIL STATE, AND SPIRITUAL GOOD; AND THE OBJECTS OF CHARITY ARE, IN A RESTRICTED SENSE, THE INDIVIDUAL MAN, IN A WIDER SENSE SOCIETY, IN A STILL WIDER SENSE ONE'S NATIVE COUNTRY, THE CHURCH, AND IN THE WIDEST SENSE THE HUMAN RACE; AND THESE ARE THE NEIGHBOR.

IVa. MAN IS THE SUBJECT OF CHARITY; AND AS THE QUALITY OF THE SUBJECT IS, SUCH IS THAT OF HIS CHARITY WHICH HE EXERCISES.

IVb. CHARITY ITSELF IS TO ACT SINCERELY, JUSTLY, AND FAITHFULLY IN EVERY WORK THAT PERTAINS TO ONE'S EMPLOYMENT; AND BY THIS A MAN BECOMES CHARITY.

V. THE SIGNS OF CHARITY ARE ALL THINGS THAT PERTAIN TO WORSHIP.

VI. THE BENEFACTIONS OF CHARITY ARE ALL THE GOODS THAT A MAN WHO IS CHARITY DOES, FREELY OUTSIDE OF HIS CALLING.

VII. THE OBLIGATIONS OF CHARITY ARE ALL THINGS THAT A MAN OUGHT TO DO BESIDES THOSE ABOVE NAMED.

VIII. THE DIVERSIONS OF CHARITY ARE THE VARIOUS DELIGHTS AND PLEASURES OF THE BODY AND ITS SENSES.

IX. Charity is not Charity without Faith; neither is Faith Faith without Charity.
X. As the Charity is such is the Faith; and the Faith which precedes Charity is the Faith of Cognition, which is Historic Faith,—in itself, Knowledge.
XI. In Charity is Conjunction of Man with the Lord and of the Lord with Man.
XII. Charity, or Love towards the Neighbor, is also Love to the Lord.

Sketch of an Ecclesiastical History

of

The New Church

SKETCH

OF AN

Ecclesiastical History

OF

The New Church

FROM THE LATIN OF

EMANUEL SWEDENBORG

Sketch of an Ecclesiastical History

OF

The New Church.

---

1. A new Ecclesiastical History must be written, because now is the Lord's Advent predicted in *Matthew* xxiv.

2. The church was different before the Council of Nice, as long as the *Apostles' Creed* was in force.

It became changed after the Council of Nice, and still more after the *Athanasian Creed* was composed.

The cardinal point of doctrine respecting the Triune God and the Lord was subverted in the church, especially by the dogma of three [Divine] persons from eternity.

3. The books are to be enumerated which were written, from the beginning to the present day, by the Lord through me (*a Domino per me*).

4. The writing there is such, that it shines brightly before those who believe in the Lord and in the new revelation; but it appears dark and of no consequence to those who deny them, and who are not in favor of them on account of various external reasons.

Experimental proofs that their style of writing is such: (1) From the Dutch censors of books who were called together in the world of spirits; one of whom upon reading these books said, that they were preferable to all other books, except the Word; and another said that he saw nothing in them except vain, novel, and fantastical things, and that therefore they were to be rejected as of no account. (2) The same thing happened in England, where they were sent to the universities, because the ecclesiastical order had rejected them. (3) About those in Gottenberg; Beyer, Rosen, and the others; although some see the greatness of God in them, others see nothing except what is utterly worthless. (4) In Sweden [they are looked upon in one way] by Filenius, and in a different way altogether by others, who may perhaps be named. (5) When I read to myself the writings which I had printed, they appeared to me vain, as long as a certain cunning and sinister one was present, but it was different in the presence of others. (6) The same thing took place in Sweden with him, who is writing a literary history. Besides other instances.

5. About Oetinger, in Würtemberg, from his letter.

6. About Göttingen.

7. When the "*Brief Exposition*" was published, the angelic heaven from the east to the west, and from the south to the north, appeared of a deep scarlet color with the most beautiful flowers. This took place before myself, and before the kings of Denmark and others.

At another time it appeared flamy, most beautiful.

8. In the spiritual world there was inscribed on all these books: "The Lord's Advent." The same I also wrote by command on two copies in Holland.*

---

*One of these copies has been found. On the inside page of the wrapper which is bound up with the volume there is the following inscription in Swedenborg's own handwriting:

(2513)
Hic Liber est Adventus Domini, { 4535 }
Scriptum ex Mandato. { 6895 }
(8427, p. 19)

(This book is the Lord's Advent, written by command.)

In another hand is inserted A. R., n. 626.
See *Documents Concerning Swedenborg*, Vol. II., Pt. II., pp. 756-757.

The Word of The Lord
from
Experience

CONCERNING THE SACRED SCRIPTURE

OR

THE WORD OF THE LORD

FROM

EXPERIENCE

BY

EMANUEL SWEDENBORG

BEING A TRANSLATION OF THE POSTHUMOUS WORK ENTITLED

"DE SCRIPTURA SACRA SEU VERBO DOMINI AB EXPERIENTIA"

CONCERNING THE SACRED SCRIPTURE

OR

THE WORD OF THE LORD

FROM

EXPERIENCE.

I.

The Sense of the Letter of the Word, In Which Is the Spiritual Sense, Represented.

1. It was given to see great purses, appearing like sacks, in which was hidden silver in great abundance; and, since these sacks were open, it seemed as if anyone might take from the silver placed therein, yea, steal from it; but near the sacks sat two angels who were guards. The place where the sacks were deposited appeared like a manger in a stable. In the next chamber were seen modest virgins together with a chaste wife, and near that chamber were two infants, and it was said that they were not to be played with in a childish manner, but wisely. Afterwards there appeared a harlot, and then a horse lying dead. It was then perceived that thus was represented the sense of the letter of the Word, in which is the spiritual sense.* Those great purses filled with silver signified the knowledges of truth in great abundance therein. That they were open and yet guarded by angels, signified that every one may take thence the knowledges of truth, but that care must be taken lest its interior sense in which is nothing but verities

---

[MARGINAL NOTE.]
*The sense of the letter is the foundation of the wall of Jerusalem, and the twelve precious stones there; these are the Urim and Thummin upon the ephod of Aaron.

be falsified. The manger in the stable where the sacks lay, signified spiritual instruction for the understanding. A manger signifies this, even the one wherein the Lord was laid when born; for a horse signifies the understanding: hence a manger signifies its nourishment. The modest virgins who were seen in the next chamber signified the truths of the church, and the chaste wife signified the conjunction of truth and good which is everywhere in the Word. The infants signified the innocence of wisdom in the Word; they were angels from the third heaven who all appear like infants. The harlot, with the dead horse, signified the falsification of the Word by many at this day, whereby all understanding of truth is destroyed; a harlot signifies falsification, and a dead horse, no understanding of truth.

II.

The Word Inwardly Is Living.

2. When the Word is read by a man who esteems it holy, its natural sense then becomes spiritual in the second heaven, and celestial in the third heaven, thus it is successively stripped of its natural (sense); the reason is, because the natural, spiritual, and celestial (senses) correspond to each other, and the Word is written by mere correspondences. The natural sense of the Word is such as it is in the sense of the letter, every particular of which becomes spiritual, and afterwards celestial in the heavens; and when it becomes spiritual it then lives in heaven from the light of truth therein, and when it becomes celestial, it lives from the flame of good therein; for spiritual ideas, with the angels of the second heaven, derive their origin from the light existing there, which in its essence is Divine Truth; but the celestial ideas, with the angels of the third heaven, derive their origin from the flame of good, which in its essence is Divine Good. For in the second heaven there is a white light, from which the angels who are in that heaven think, and in the third heaven there is a flaming light, from which the angels who are in that heaven think. The thoughts of angels differ entirely from the thoughts of men; they think by lights either bright white or flamy, which are such that they can never be described in natural language. From this it appears that the Word is inwardly living, consequently that it is not dead, but alive with that man who, while reading the Word, thinks holily concerning it. Moreover, everything of the Word is vivified by the Lord; because with the Lord it becomes life, as the Lord also says in *John*:—

> The words which I speak unto you, they are spirit and they are life (vi. 63).

The life, which by means of the Word flows in from the Lord, is the light of truth in the understanding, and the love of good in the will; this love and that light constitute together the life of heaven, which life with man is called eternal life. The Lord also teaches:—

> God was the Word, in Him was life, and the life was the light of men (*John* i. 4).

III.

The Difference in General Between the Natural, the Spiritual, and the Celestial.

3. There are three heavens, the lowest, the middle, and the highest; in the lowest heaven they are natural, but their natural is derived either from the spiritual, which is of the middle heaven or from the celestial, which is of the third heaven. In the second heaven they are spiritual, and in the third heaven celestial; there are also intermediate angels who are called spiritual-celestial; many from these are preachers in the highest heaven.

4. The difference between the natural, the spiritual, and the celestial is such, that there is no ratio between them, for which reason the natural can in no wise by any approximation approach towards the spiritual, nor the spiritual towards the natural; hence it is that the heavens are distinct. This it has been given me to know by much experience;

I have often been sent among the spiritual angels, and I then spoke with them spiritually, and then, retaining in my memory what I had spoken, when I returned into my natural state, in which every man is in this world, I then wished to bring it forth from the former memory and describe it, but I could not, it was impossible; there were no expressions, nor even ideas of thought, by which I could express it; they were spiritual ideas of thought and spiritual expressions so remote from natural ideas of thought and natural expressions, that they did not approximate in the least. What is wonderful, when I was in that heaven and conversing with the angels, then I knew no otherwise than that I spake in like manner as I speak with men; but afterwards I found that the thoughts and the discourses were so unlike that they could not be approximated, consequently that there is no ratio between them.

5. There is a similar difference between the spiritual and the celestial. I was told that there is a similar difference, and that it is such, that there is given no ratio or approximation between them; but as I could not be confirmed in this by my own experience, unless I was altogether an angel of the middle heaven, therefore it has been granted to some angels of the middle heaven to be with angels of the third heaven, and then to think and speak there with them, also to retain in their memory what they had been thinking and speaking, and afterwards to return into their own heaven; and they told me from that heaven that they were not able to express a single idea or a single word of their former state, and that it was impossible, and lastly they said, that there is no ratio nor any approximation between them.

6. It has accordingly been sometimes granted me to be among the angels of the middle and of the highest heaven, and to hear them conversing with one another, at which time I was in an interior natural state, removed from worldly and corporeal things, namely, when first waking after sleep; then I heard things unutterable and inexpressible, as we read happened with Paul; and sometimes I was let into the perception and understanding of the subjects they were conversing upon; the subjects they conversed upon were full of arcana concerning the Lord, redemption, regeneration, providence, and other similar things: after which it was given me to understand that I could not utter nor describe them by any spiritual or celestial expression, but that nevertheless they could be described even to their rational comprehension by words of natural language. And it was told me that there is not any Divine arcana which may not be perceived, and even expressed naturally, although more generally and imperfectly; and that they who, in a natural manner, by means of their rational understanding, perceive those things from the affection of truth, afterwards, when they become spirits, can perceive and speak of them in a spiritual manner, and when they become angels, in a celestial manner, but no others. For one Divine truth naturally perceived and loved, is like a crystal or porcelain vessel, which is afterwards filled with wine, and with such wine as the nature of the truth was, and as it were of such a taste as the affection of the truth was.

7. That there is such a difference, which may be termed unlimited, between the natural, the spiritual, and the celestial, may clearly appear from the difference between the thoughts of men and angels, as well as from the difference of their speech and operations, and also from the difference of their writings; from all which, as from so many confirmations, it will appear what the quality is of each, and in what manner the perfections in everything ascend and pass from the world into heaven and from heaven to heaven.

8. As regards thoughts: all the thoughts of man, together with the single ideas thereof, derive something from space, time, person, and matter, which appear in natural light or the light of the world, for nothing can be thought without light, in like manner as nothing can be seen without light, and natural light or the light of the world is dead, because it is from its sun, which is pure fire; nevertheless the light of heaven everywhere and constantly flows into and vivifies that light, communicating perception and understanding of the subject. The light of the world alone cannot give anything perceptive and intellectual, or present any natural or rational light (*lumen*); but the light of the world gives and presents it from the light of heaven, because the light of heaven is from its sun, which is the Lord, and thence life itself. The influx of heavenly light

into the light of the world is like the influx of the cause into the effect; the nature of this influx shall be explained elsewhere. From this it appears what the quality of natural thought is, or what quality the ideas of men's thoughts are, namely, that they inseparably cohere with space, time, with what is personal, and material; consequently, such thoughts or ideas of thoughts are very limited and bounded and thus gross, and to be called material. But the thoughts of the angels of the middle heaven are all without space, time, or what is personal, and material, for which reason they are unlimited and unbounded; the objects of their thoughts are spiritual like the thoughts themselves, for which reason they think concerning those objects spiritually and not naturally. But with regard to the angels of the highest heaven, they have no thoughts, but perceptions of the things which they hear and see; instead of thoughts they have affections, which with them are varied in like manner as thoughts are varied with the spiritual angels.

9. As regards speech: the speech of men is according to their ideas of thoughts, for the ideas of thought become expressions when they pass into speech; for which reason the speech of man in every expression partakes of space, time, what is personal, and material. But the speech of the angels of the middle heaven is also like the ideas of their thought, for the words of speech express them. But the speech of the angels of the highest heaven is from the variation of their affections; but when they are speaking with the spiritual angels they speak in a similar manner, but not so when conversing with each other. Since such is the speech of angels, and such the speech of men, therefore their speech differs so much that they have nothing in common; their difference is such that a man cannot understand a single expression of an angel, nor an angel a single expression of a man. I have heard the speech of angels, and retained the expressions, and I afterwards examined whether any expression coincided with any word of the speech or languages of men, and there was not one. Spiritual speech is the same with all, and is implanted in every man, and he comes into it as soon as he becomes a spirit. As regards writing, it is similar to their speech. The writing of the spiritual angels as to the letters resembles the writing of men in the

world, but every letter signifies a thing, so that you would say if you saw it in a natural state, that it consisted merely of letters; but writings in the highest heaven have no resemblance as to letters, for with them letters are drawn in various curvatures, not unlike the letters of the Hebrew language, but everywhere inflected, and not consisting merely of lines. Every letter involves a thing, of which they have a perception from affection, and not from thought. Hence it is that the natural comprehends nothing of spiritual writing, nor the spiritual of natural writing; neither does the spiritual comprehend anything of celestial writing, nor the celestial of spiritual writing, unless he is with the spiritual.

10. Their operations, which are many, are similar, for every one is in some work. How the spiritual work cannot be described to the natural; nor can it be described to the spiritual, how the celestial angels work; for they differ as much as in their thoughts, speech, and writings.

11. From these things it is evident, what the difference is between the natural, the spiritual, and the celestial, that it is such that they do not at all agree except by correspondences; which is also the reason that men do not know that they are in consociation with spirits, and spirits that they are in consociation with men, when nevertheless the consociation is continual; for man cannot live a single instant, unless he is in the midst of spirits as to his thoughts and affections; neither can a spirit or an angel live a single moment unless he is with man; the reason is, because there is a perpetual conjunction from firsts to ultimates, thus from the Lord to man; and conjunction from creation is effected by correspondences, and flows in through angels and spirits. Everything celestial flows into the spiritual, and the spiritual into the natural, and terminates and subsists in the ultimate of this, which is the corporeal and material. Without such an ultimate, into which the intermediates flow, there is no subsistence, otherwise than like a house built in the air; wherefore the basis and the foundation of the heavens is the human race.

12. No angel knows that there is such a difference between the natural, the spiritual, and the celestial; the reason is, because an angel does not change his state, nor pass from a spiritual into a natural state, and thus be able to explore the differences. I have spoken with them on this subject, and they said they did not know the differences. They believed that they thought, spoke, wrote, and worked in the same manner as in the world. But the difference was shown them by this, that they changed states, and thought first in one state, then in the other by turns, then in like manner that they spoke by turns in one state and then in another, and further that they read their writings in a spiritual state and in a natural state, and in like manner worked, then they found that there is such a difference as cannot be described. On this subject it was granted me to instruct the angels themselves, because it has been granted me to be alternately in both worlds, and from the one to explore the other, and they all afterwards confessed that it was so.

13. But the similitude of the natural, spiritual, and celestial states is in such things as are objects of sight, taste, smell, and hearing, also the sense of touch of various kinds. In their sight they appear like men in the world. Their garments so appear, also their houses, and gardens, or paradises, as also fields, likewise land and water, food and drink of various kinds, besides animals of the earth, the flying things of heaven, and fishes in waters, of various kinds and of various species. Their speech is heard as in the world, likewise singing and musical modulations. Taste is similar, and also odor; in a word, everything that appears and is perceived by any of the senses. But still those things are from a spiritual origin, and therefore they think of them spiritually and give them spiritual names. But even all these things, in what manner they appear and are perceived in the middle and highest heaven, as to the excellence of their forms and harmonies, and as to their perfections, which are supereminent and transcendent, can only be described in an imperfect manner, only as it were by the most perfect things in the world, which nevertheless are imperfect, respectively to those things which are in heaven.

IV.

THE WORD IS HOLY, EVEN AS TO SYLLABLES AND POINTS.

14. Once there was sent me from heaven a little paper written over with Hebrew letters, but written as with the most ancient people, with whom the letters which at this day are in some part rectilinear, were at that time curved, with little horns turning upwards. The angel who was with me said that he knew whole meanings from the letters themselves; that every letter had its own meaning, and that they knew that meaning from the curves of the lines in each letter, besides they knew the subject from each letter by itself. He then explained to me what א [A] signified, and what ה [H]; what those letters meant separately, and what when combined; that ה, which is in יהוה (*Jehovah*), and which was added to the names of Abraham and Sarai, signified what is infinite and eternal. And thus the Word is so written in many places, whereby when it is read by a Jew or a Christian in the Hebrew text, it may be known in the third heaven what the very letters signify. For the angels of the third heaven have the Word written in such letters, and they read it according to the letters. They said that in the sense extracted from the letters, the Word treats of the Lord alone. The reason for this is that the curvatures in the letters derive their origin from the flow of heaven, in which the angels of the third heaven are, above all others. Wherefore these angels are skilled in that writing from what is implanted in them, because they are in the order of heaven, and live altogether according to it. They also explained in my presence the sense of the Word (*Ps.* xxxii. 2), from the letters or syllables alone, saying that their meaning was, in a summary, *that the Lord is merciful, even to those who do evil.* They added that the vowels there are for the sake of the sound, which corresponds to the affection, and that they cannot utter the vowels *i* and *e*, but for *i* they pronounce *y* or *eu*, and for *e* pronounce *eu*, and that the vowels *a, o* and *u* are in use with them, because these vowels give a full sound, while *i* and *e* have a close sound.* They said further that they do not pronounce any

---
*We are to understand by all these vowels their Continental, not their English sounds.

consonants with aspiration, but with a smooth sound, and that the aspirated letters, as ד [*dh*] and ק [*qh*] and others, do not mean anything to them, except when uttered with a smooth sound, and that for this reason most aspirated letters have also a point within, which signifies that they are to be uttered with a smooth sound. They added that roughness, or aspiration, in the letters is in use in the spiritual heaven, because there they are in truths, and by means of truths in understanding; but in the celestial heaven all are in the good of love and thence in wisdom, and truth admits of roughness, but not good. From these things it may be evident what is signified by the Lord's saying, that not a jot, tittle, or little curve shall pass from the Law (*Matt.* v. 18; *Luke* xvi. 17); and it is also plain that it was of the Divine providence of the Lord that all the letters of the Word in the Hebrew text were counted by the Masorites.

V.

THE SPIRITUAL SENSE OF THE WORD AND ITS NATURAL SENSE.

15. I have spoken at times with spirits who did not wish to know anything about the spiritual sense of the Word, saying that its natural sense is the only sense of the Word, and that this is holy because it is from God; and they asserted that if the spiritual sense were to be accepted, the Word in the letter would become nothing. There were many who insisted upon this, but they were answered from heaven that the Word without the spiritual sense within it would not be Divine; and because the spiritual sense is its soul, it is thence Divine, yea, living, for without it the letter would be as it were dead; the very holiness of the Word consists in this. The Word may thus be compared to the Divine Man who is the Lord, in whom there is not only the Divine natural, but also the Divine spiritual and the Divine celestial; it is on this account that the Lord calls Himself the Word. And the angels said that the very holiness of the Word is in the sense of its letter, and that this is more holy than the other senses, which are internal, because it is the complex and containant of the rest, and is like the body living from the soul. Thus the Word in the sense of the letter, or the natural, is in its fulness, and also in its power; and by means of it man is in conjunction with the heavens, which, without the sense of the letter, would be separated from man. Who does not know and acknowledge that the Word in its bosom is spiritual? But where the spiritual is stored up, has hitherto lain concealed. But because the spirits who stood for the sense of the letter alone, were not willing to be convinced by these reasons, the angels brought forward innumerable passages from the natural sense which could never be comprehended without the spiritual sense. As in the Prophets, where mere names are heaped up; where many kinds of animals are mentioned such as lions, bears, oxen, bullocks, dogs, foxes, owls, ijim, dragons; as also mountains and forests, besides many other things which would have no meaning without the spiritual sense. What, for instance, should be understood by the dragon who is described as red, having seven heads, and upon the heads seven diadems, and who by his tail drew down the third part of the stars of heaven and who sought to devour the offspring which the woman was about to bring forth; and that two wings of a great eagle were given to the woman, that she might fly into the desert, where the dragon cast after her water as a river out of his mouth. Again, without the spiritual sense it could not be known what should be understood by the two beasts of the dragon: the one ascending out of the sea, like a leopard, with feet as of a bear, and a mouth as of a lion, and the other beast ascending from the earth, of which it is spoken in the *Apocalypse* (xii. and xiii.). Again, what is there meant in the sixth chapter of the *Apocalypse*, by the horses which went forth when the Lamb opened the seals of the book: first a white horse, afterwards a red one, then a black, and finally a pale horse; besides all the other things in that book? Also what is meant in *Zachariah* by the four horns and the four artificers (Chapter ii.); by the lampstand and the two olive trees near it (Chapter iv.); by the four chariots going forth between two mountains to which were horses, red, black, white, and grizzled (Chapter vi.)? Or, again, in *Daniel* viii., what is meant by the ram and the he-goat, and by their horns with which they fought each other; and by the four beasts ascending from the sea (Chap. vii.), besides similar things elsewhere in great abundance? In order that they might still further be convinced, the angels quoted what the Lord said to His disciples, in *Matthew* (Chap. xxiv.), about the consummation of the age and His coming, which could be understood by no one without the spiritual sense. That the spiritual sense is in each and all of the things of the Word, was also confirmed by certain things said by the Lord which could not be comprehended unless they were understood spiritually, as that no one should call his father on earth, father, nor any one, teacher, or master, because one is their Father, Teacher, and Master (*Matt.* xxiii. 7–10); also that they should not judge, lest they be judged (*Matt.* vii. 1, 2); and that a husband and wife are not two, but one flesh (*Matt.* xix. 5, 6), when yet in the natural sense they are not one flesh; neither is it forbidden to judge concerning a companion and neighbor as to his natural life, for this is of importance in society; but it is forbidden to judge of him as to his spiritual life, for this is known to the Lord alone. So too the Lord did not forbid calling a father, father, neither a teacher, teacher, nor a master, master, in the natural sense, but in the spiritual sense, in which there is only one Father, Teacher, and Master: so in other cases. From these illustrations the spirits were convinced that there is a spiritual sense within the natural sense of the Word, and that still the very holiness of the Word is in the sense of its letter, because all the interior senses of the Word are in that in their fulness. Moreover it was confirmed that in the sense of the letter all things which teach the way to salvation, thus to life and faith, stand forth clearly, also that every doctrine of the church is to be drawn from the sense of the letter of the Word and confirmed thereby, and not by the pure spiritual sense; for conjunction with heaven, and through heaven with the Lord, is not given by this sense alone, but by the sense of the letter; and the Divine influx of the Lord through the Word is from firsts through ultimates.

VI.

The Word, and Natural Theology: This Theology Is Nothing Without the Word, and Unless Derived From It.

The Excellence of the Style in the Word.

16. I once heard a grave dispute among spirits who in the world had been learned, some of them from the Word and some from natural light alone; the latter insisted that natural theology is sufficient, and that this can teach, yea, enlighten man, without the Word, and enable him to discern that there is a God, that there is a heaven and a hell, and that the soul has immortality and thus eternal life; but the former ones said that the Word alone teaches and gives light on these subjects. The spirits who were for natural theology alone, greatly infested those who were for the Word, and this for several days: thinking at heart, and at last saying, that the Word is not anything, that it is written in a style so simple and at the same time so obscure, in very many places, that no one can be taught, and still less be enlightened by it, and that the writings of the learned by far surpass it, as for instance the writings of Cicero, Seneca, and of some of the learned at this day. But reply was made to them, that the style of the Word is more excellent than the style of all the learned in the whole world, since in the former there is not a sentence, nor even a word or a letter, which does not contain within itself something of the Lord and thence something of heaven and the church. For the Word is from God, and thence in its bosom it is spiritual, and this Divine lies hidden there interiorly, as the soul is hidden in the body; and when man reads it devoutly, this Divine is unfolded in order before the angels, who are affected by the spiritual sanctity unfolded therein, and this is communicated to man. Hence it is clear that the very style of the Word, however simple it may appear, is infinitely superior to any style of the most learned in the world; for the latter, although the sense may be both elegant and sublime, still it does not effect communication with heaven, and thus, compared with the style of the Word, it is of no value at all. [2] The spirits who were in favor of natural theology heard these things indeed, but still rejected them, because in the world they had utterly despised the Word, and those who despise the Word in the world, and confirm their contempt by passages from it, continue to despise it after death; for every principle adopted and confirmed in the world concerning God and the Word, remains enrooted after death, neither can it be torn out. Since therefore these spirits did not communicate with heaven, but with hell, they began to conjoin themselves with certain satans there, till at length they and the satans spoke in concert, and gnashing with their teeth breathed the destruction of the soul of those who were in favor of the Word. Yet they could avail nothing at all, for the Lord was on the side of those who were for the Word, and satans on the side of those who were against it; wherefore the former were received into heaven, but the latter were cast down into hell. [3] The angels afterwards said of natural theology, that without the Word it reveals nothing, but only confirms those things which are known in the doctrine of the church from the Word; and that confirmations from nature by means of rational light corroborate spiritual truths, for the reason that every one has some natural idea of spiritual things, by which he retains them in memory, and thence brings them forth into the thought, and turns them over and airs them rationally. Wherefore, if confirmations are added from nature, the truth is corroborated. But yet care should be taken lest falsity be seized upon instead of truth, since what is false may be confirmed by the ingenious, equally as well as what is true; and thereby what is heretical may be confirmed even to the destruction of truth itself. [4] They added that no one from natural theology can enter into spiritual theology, but that every one from spiritual theology can enter into natural theology, because the latter entrance is of Divine order, but the former against Divine order; for the natural is gross and impure, while the spiritual is subtile and pure. To enter from the gross and impure into the subtile and pure is not granted. But, conversely, angels can look down beneath them and see all things which are there, while no one from below can see the things which are in the heavens. Yea, an angel can see a spirit who is grosser than himself, but the spirit cannot see the angel who is purer than himself. When therefore, as is often the case, such spirits ascend into heaven where angels are, they see no one, nor even their homes, and so go away saying that the place is empty and a desert. [5] It is similar with the Word. They who do not believe in the Word from the Word, can by no means believe anything Divine from nature; for the Lord teaches:—

> They have Moses and the prophets; let them hear them. If they hear not Moses and the prophets, neither will they be persuaded, if one shall have risen from the dead (*Luke* xvi. 29, 31).

So would it be if one wished to believe from nature alone, rejecting the Word. Some of the ancients, who were pagans, as Aristotle, Cicero, and others, wrote concerning the existence of God and the immortality of the soul, but they did not know this from their own natural light, but from the religion of the ancients who had a Divine revelation, which was successively handed down to the Gentiles.

VII.

The Spiritual Sense of the Word.

Correspondences.

17. Each and all things which are in nature, correspond to spiritual things; similarly each and all things which are in the human body, as may be seen in two articles in the work on *Heaven and Hell*. But it is not known at this day what correspondence is, but in the most ancient times the science of correspondences was the science of sciences, thus the universal science, so that the most ancient people wrote all their manuscripts and books by correspondences. The fables of the most ancient times and the hieroglyphics of the Egyptians are nothing else: the book of Job, which is a book of the Ancient

Church, is full of correspondences. [2] All the ancient churches were churches representative of heavenly things; all their rites and also their statutes, according to which their worship was instituted, consisted of nothing but correspondences. Similarly the church with the sons of Jacob; the burnt offerings and sacrifices with all their particulars, were correspondences; likewise the tabernacle with the single things therein, as also their feasts, such as the feast of unleavened bread, the feast of tabernacles, and the feast of first fruits, and also all their statutes and judgments; and because correspondences are such things as exist in the ultimates of nature, and because all things of nature correspond, and the things which correspond also signify, therefore the sense of the letter of the Word consists of nothing but correspondences. The Lord also, because He spoke from His Divine, and spoke the Word, spoke therefore also by correspondences. What is from the Divine, and in itself is Divine, in the ultimate falls into such things as correspond to Divine, celestial and spiritual things, thus such as in their bosom conceal and signify celestial and spiritual things. What, further, correspondences are, may be seen in the *Arcana Cœlestia*, in which the correspondences which are in *Genesis* and in *Exodus* are explained. And again a collection of citations from that work concerning correspondences, may be seen in the *Doctrine of the New Jerusalem* and in the treatise on *Heaven and Hell*. The spiritual or internal sense of the Word is nothing else than the sense of the letter unfolded according to correspondences; for it teaches the spiritual which is perceived by angels in the heavens, while man in the world is thinking in a natural way of that which he reads in the Word.

18. I have heard and perceived from heaven that the men of the Most Ancient Church, who are those meant in the spiritual sense of the first chapters of *Genesis* by Adam and Eve, were so consociated with the angels of heaven, that they could speak with them by correspondences, and hence the state of their wisdom was such that whatever they saw on earth, they perceived at the same time spiritually, thus conjointly with the angels. It was told me that Enoch, of whom mention is made in *Genesis* (Chap. v. 21–24), with his associates, collected correspondences from the mouth of those people, and transmitted the knowledge of them to posterity. From this it came to pass, that the science of correspondences not only was known, but was also cultivated, in many kingdoms of Asia, and especially in Egypt, Assyria and Babylon, Syria, Mesopotamia, Arabia, and also in Canaan. From thence it was carried over to Greece, but was there turned into fables, as may be sufficiently evident from what is told of Olympus, Helicon and Pindus near Athens, and also of the winged horse called Pegasus, as, that with the hoof he brake open a fountain, by which the nine virgins [the Muses], established their seats. For a mountain, and thus Helicon, from correspondence signifies the higher heaven; the hill under the mountain, which was Pindus, signifies the heaven below it; the winged horse, or Pegasus, signifies the understanding enlightened by the spiritual; the fountain signifies intelligence and learning, and the nine virgins signify the knowledges of truth and the sciences. Similar were the rest of the things which are called fabulous, which were written by the most ancient writers in Greece, and which were collected together and described by Ovid in his *Metamorphoses*.

19. But when the representatives of the church in the course of time were turned into idolatries, then by the Divine Providence of the Lord that science was successively obliterated, and with the Israelitish and Jewish nation it was altogether destroyed and extinguished. The worship of that nation was indeed altogether representative, but still they did not know what any representative thing signified. For they were altogether natural men, and hence they were neither able nor willing to know anything about the spiritual man and about his faith and love, consequently nothing about correspondences. [2] That the idolatries of the nations in ancient times derived their origin from the science of correspondences amongst them, was because all things that appear upon the earth have a correspondence, as not only trees, but also cattle and birds of every kind, as well as fishes, and the rest. The ancients, who were in the science of correspondences, made themselves images, which corresponded to spiritual things, and they were delighted with those things, because they signified such things as are of heaven and thence of the church, they therefore not only placed them in their temples, but also in their houses, not for the purpose of adoration, but for the recollection of the heavenly thing that was signified, thence in Egypt there were set up calves, oxen, serpents, boys, old men, virgins, and many other things. For a calf signified the innocence of the natural man, oxen affections of the natural man, serpents the prudence of the sensual man, a boy innocence, old men wisdom, virgins affections for truth, and so on. After the science of correspondences was there lost, their posterity, who were ignorant what the images and likenesses set up by the ancients signified, began to worship them as holy, and finally as deities, because they were placed in and near the temples. [3] The Egyptian hieroglyphics are from the same origin. So was it also with other nations, as with the Philistines in Ashdod, where was Dagon, formed like a man above and like a fish below, which image was so contrived because a man signifies rational intelligence, and a fish natural knowledge. From similar origin was the worship of the ancients in gardens and groves according to the kinds of trees, as also their sacred worship upon mountains; for gardens and groves signified spiritual intelligence, and each tree something thereof, as the olive its good of love, the vine its truth of the doctrine of faith, the cedar its rational, and so on. A mountain signified heaven, and therefore the worship of the most ancient people was upon mountains. That the science of correspondences remained with many oriental nations until the coming of the Lord, may be evident from the wise men from the East, who came to the Lord when He was born. Therefore a star went before them, and they brought with them gold, frankincense, and myrrh. It was also said to the shepherds, in order that they might know that it was the Lord Himself, that it should be a sign unto them, that they should see Him in a manger, wrapped in swaddling clothes, because there was no place in the inn. "The star" which went before the wise men signified knowledge from heaven, for stars in the Word signify knowledges. "The gold" signified celestial good, "frankincense" spiritual good, and "myrrh" natural good; all worship being from these three. "The manger" in which the infant Lord was found by the shepherds, signifies spiritual nourishment, because horses, which are fed from a manger, signify intellectual things. "The inn" where there was no place signified the Jewish Church, in which at that time there was no spiritual nourishment, because everything of the Word and thence everything of worship with them, had then been adulterated and perverted. Hence it is said that this would be for a sign to them that it was the Lord (*Luke* ii. 12). [4] Nevertheless, the science of correspondences was altogether none with the Israelitish and Jewish nation, although all things of their worship, and all the statutes and judgments given to them, and all things of the Word, were pure correspondences. The reason was that that nation was idolatrous in heart, and such that it did not even wish to know that anything of their worship signified anything celestial and spiritual. For they wished that all these things should be holy from themselves and with them in externals. Wherefore if spiritual and celestial things had been disclosed to them, they would not only have rejected, but would also have profaned them. For this reason heaven was closed to them so that they scarcely knew that they were to live after death. That this is so, is manifestly evident. They do not acknowledge the Lord, although the whole Sacred Scripture prophesied concerning Him, and predicted Him; they rejected Him for this sole reason, that He taught them of the heavenly kingdom, and not concerning an earthly kingdom, for they wanted a Messiah who would exalt them above all nations in the whole world, and they did not wish any Messiah who would provide for their eternal salvation. Moreover, they say the Word contains in itself many arcana, which are called mystical, but they do not wish to know that these treat of the Lord and His Kingdom; but they do wish to know when it is said that they are concerning gold and alchemy.

20. That this science was not disclosed after those times, was because the Christians in the primitive church were very simple, that it could not be disclosed to them, for if disclosed, it would have been of no use to them, nor would it have been comprehended. After those times darkness arose over the entire Christian world, on account of the Papacy, which at length became Babylon, and they who are of Babel, and have con-

firmed themselves in its falsities, are for the most part natural, sensual men, and these are neither able nor willing to apprehend what is spiritual, thus what is the correspondence of natural things with spiritual.* But after the Reformation, because they began to make a distinction between faith and charity, and to worship one God under three Persons, thus three Gods, whom they only named one, heavenly truths were then concealed from them, lest if revealed they should falsify them and bend them to faith alone, and none of them to charity and love. If therefore the spiritual sense of the Word had then been revealed, they would have shut heaven to themselves even by the falsification of its truths. For every one is allowed to understand the sense of the letter of the Word in simplicity, provided he does not confirm the appearances of truth which are there, so far as to destroy genuine truth; for to interpret the Word as to its spiritual sense from falsities of doctrine, closes heaven, and does not open it; but to interpret the spiritual sense from truths of doctrine, opens heaven, because that is the sense in which the angels are, and so man by means of it thinks together with angels, and thus conjoins them to himself in his intellectual mind. But if a man is in falsities of doctrine and wishes to explore the spiritual sense from some knowledge of correspondences, he falsifies it. It is otherwise if man is already in genuine truths; that sense agrees with truths and appears from them, because that sense is in the light of heaven. Cloud on the other hand agrees with falsities, and if anything of this truth should appear, instead of the light of heaven thick darkness would arise, for angels turn themselves away from him, and so close heaven to him. The spiritual sense of the Word is meant by the inner garment of the Lord, which was without seam, and which the soldiers were not permitted to divide; but the natural sense of the Word, which is the sense of its letter, is meant by His outer garments, which the soldiers divided. Garments in the Word signify truths, and the Lord's garments Divine truth, where-

---

[MARGINAL NOTE.]

* For thus they would be convinced that by Peter is not meant Peter, also that the Word even to its inmosts is Divine; and that a papal decree is of no account in comparison.

fore also the garments of the Lord, when He was transfigured before Peter, James, and John, appeared shining white, like light.

21. At this day the spiritual sense of the Word has been revealed from the Lord, because the doctrine of genuine truth has now been revealed, which doctrine is partly contained in the *Doctrine of the New Jerusalem*, and now in the small works, which are being given to the public;* and because that doctrine, and no other, agrees with the spiritual sense of the Word, therefore that sense, together with the science of correspondences, has now for the first time been disclosed. That sense is also signified by the Lord's appearing in the clouds of heaven with glory and power (*Matt.* xxiv. 30, 31), in which chapter it treats of the consummation of the age, by which is meant the last time of the church. By the cloud of heaven, there and elsewhere in the Word, is signified the Word in the letter, which there, in respect to the spiritual sense, is as a cloud. But by the glory there, as also elsewhere in the Word, is signified the Word in the spiritual sense, which also is the Divine truth in light; and by the power is signified its power in the Word. The revelation of the Word as to the spiritual sense was also promised in the *Apocalypse*, where that sense is meant by the "White Horse" (Chapter xix. 11 to 14), and by the great supper of God, to which all were invited and gathered together (ver. 17). By many that sense will not be acknowledged for a long time. Those alone who are in the falsities of doctrine, especially in regard to the Lord, and who do not admit truths, will not acknowledge this is meant by the beast and by the kings of the earth, who make war with the one sitting upon the white horse (ver. 19). By "the beast" are meant the Roman Catholics, as in (Chapter xvii. 3), and by "the kings of the earth" are meant the Reformed who are in falsities of doctrine. The mystical things which some seek in the Word, are nothing else than the spiritual and celestial senses.

---

* The Four Leading Doctrines.—Tr.

VIII.

THE MARRIAGE OF THE LORD WITH THE CHURCH, WHICH IS THE MARRIAGE OF GOOD AND TRUTH IN THE WORD.

22. It is known that the Lord is called in the Word the Bridegroom and Husband, and the church the bride and wife. That the Lord and the church are so called, is because of the conjunction of good and truth with every one who is in heaven, and who is in the church, in whom is the church; for the Lord flows in with an angel and with a man of the church from the good of love and charity. The angel and the man of the church who is in the good of love and charity, receives the Lord in the truths of doctrine and of faith which he has from the Word. Thereby conjunction is effected, which is called the heavenly marriage. This marriage is in the single things of the Word, and because it is in the single things, the Word itself may be called the heavenly marriage. That there is such a marriage in the single things of the Word has been shown in many places in the *Arcana Cœlestia*, and also in the *Doctrine of the New Jerusalem*, where it treats of the Word. That there is such a marriage there, can be seen only by those who study its internal or spiritual sense, for everywhere, and conspicuously in the prophets, there are two expressions for one thing, of which one refers to good, thus to the Lord, and the other to truth, thus to the church. This is clearly seen by one who has a knowledge of correspondences, for there are senses and words which correspond to good, and there are correspondences which correspond to truths. Hence now there is a conjunction of the Lord with heaven and with the church by means of the Word.

23. Since there is a marriage in the Word, therefore there is in it a spiritual sense and there is a celestial sense: the spiritual sense for those who are in the Lord's spiritual kingdom, who constitute all the lower heavens; and the celestial sense for those who are in the Lord's celestial kingdom, who constitute all the higher heavens. The angels of the spiritual kingdom are in the truths of the Word, but the angels of the celestial kingdom are in the goods of the Word. When therefore a man reads the Word with reverence, spiritual angels according to correspondences perceive truths therein, and celestial angels perceive goods; but, and this is an arcanum, the celestial angels do not perceive the goods therein immediately from man, but mediately through the spiritual angels. The reason is, that scarcely any one in the Christian world at this day is in the good of celestial love, but only some are in truths; wherefore the good of love cannot pass immediately from man to the celestial angels, of whom the third heaven consists, but passes mediately through the spiritual angels, of whom the second heaven is composed. The marriage of the Lord with the church thus exists also in the heavens by means of the Word, for the Word in its spiritual sense treats of the church, but in the celestial sense, of the Lord. Therefore the spiritual angels apply all things to the church, but the celestial angels all things to the Lord. Hence heaven is compared by the Lord to a marriage, and is also called a marriage, and hence the Word effects that marriage. But this is an arcanum, which can be perceived only obscurely by man, while it is clearly perceived by an angel of heaven. The celestial angels can apply to the Lord all things which spiritual angels apply to the church, because the Lord is the all of the church.

IX.

They Who Have for an End Magnificence and Honors in the World and also in Heaven, and Those Who Have for an End Wealth and Gain in the World, and Those Who Have for an End the Fame of Learning, Do Not See and Do Not Find Anything of Genuine Truth in the Word.

24. It has been given me to speak with many in the spiritual world who believed that they would shine as stars in heaven, because, as they said, they held the Word holy, often read it, gathered many things from it, and by it confirmed the dogmas of their faith, and hence were esteemed learned in the world, and themselves believed with others that they would be Michaels and Raphaels. But many of them having been explored as to the love from which they studied the Word, it was found that some had done so from the love of self, that they might appear great in the world, and be worshiped as primates of the church; some that they might obtain the fame of learning, and so be promoted to honors; some that they might gain wealth, and some that they might preach learnedly. Afterwards when examined to see whether they had learned anything of genuine truth from the Word, it was found that they knew nothing whatever, except that which is obvious to every one in the sense of the letter, and nothing of genuine truth which might serve interiorly for doctrine. This was because themselves and the world had been their ends, but not the Lord and heaven, and when such are the ends, then man with his mind clings to self and the world, and continually thinks from his proprium, which is in thick darkness as to all things of heaven. For the proprium of man is mere evil and falsity therefrom; wherefore the man who looks to self, honor, fame, or gain, in reading the Word, cannot be led by the Lord away from the proprium and thus be elevated into the light of heaven, and so cannot receive any influx from the Lord through heaven. Many such have been seen and they every one earnestly desired heaven, and they were also admitted into heaven; but when they came thither, they were examined as to whether they knew anything of truth, as it is with angels; and they knew nothing except the bare words of the sense of the letter, and had no interior understanding of them whatever. Therefore they appeared in the eyes of the angels stripped of their garments and as if naked, and thus they were sent down below. Some of them in the light of heaven were deprived of the sight of the understanding, and soon of the sight of the eyes; and then they were seized with anguish of heart, and were thus led away below, still however retaining pride in their own merit. This is the lot of those who study the Word and have honor, fame, and gain for their end. It is entirely different with those who study the Word from the affection of truth, or who, in reading the Word, take delight in truth because it is truth. These have for an end the love of God and the love of the neighbor, and for themselves, they have life as an end. All these because they love truth receive an influx from the Lord, and see and find genuine truths in the Word; for they are enlightened as to the understanding, and perceive truths in enlightenment as from themselves, though they are not from themselves; and after death they are taken up into heaven, where truth is in its own light, and there they become spiritual and angels.

X.

THE ULTIMATE SENSE OF THE WORD,* WHICH IS THE SENSE OF THE LETTER ONLY, CORRESPONDS TO THE BEARD, AND TO THE HAIRS OF THE HEAD, ON A MAN ANGEL.

25. That the hairs of the head and the beard correspond to the Word in its ultimates, may seem strange when first said or heard, but this correspondence has its cause in this, that all things of the Word correspond with all things of heaven, and heaven with all things of man; for heaven in its complex is before the Lord as one man, concerning which correspondence see what is shown in the work on *Heaven and Hell* [n. 87–102, 307]. That all things of the Word correspond to all things of heaven, has been given me to perceive from this, that the separate chapters in the prophetic Word correspond to individual societies of heaven; for when I read through the prophetic books of the Word from *Isaiah* to *Malachi*, it was given me to see that societies of heaven were called forth in their order and perceived the spiritual sense corresponding to them. Hence, from these and other proofs, it was made plain to me that there is a correspondence of the whole heaven with the Word in its series. Now because there is such a correspondence of the Word with heaven, and heaven in whole and in part corresponds to man, thence it is that the ultimate of the Word corresponds to the ultimates of man. The ultimate of the Word is the sense of the letter, and the

---

[MARGINAL NOTE.]

*From the correspondence of natural things with spiritual, the ultimate sense of the Word is meant by the twelve precious stones of which the foundations of the wall of the New Jerusalem consisted.

ultimates of man are the hairs of the head and beard. Therefore it is that men who have loved the Word even in its ultimates, after death when they become spirits appear with becoming hair, and angels likewise. The same when they become angels also let the beard grow. But on the other hand all they who have despised the sense of the letter of the Word, after death when they become spirits appear bald. This is a sign also that they are without truths, and therefore, that they may not be in shame before others, they cover the head with a tiara. Because the hairs and the beard signify the ultimate of heaven, and hence the ultimates also of Divine truth or the Word, therefore the Ancient of Days is described as having the hair of His head like clean wool (*Dan.* vii. 9). In like manner is described the Son of man, or the Lord as to the Word (*Apoc.* i. 14). So too the strength of Samson was in his hair, and when his hair was cut off, he became weak. Nazariteship also depended on the hair, for by a Nazarite was represented the Lord as to His ultimates, thus also heaven in ultimates. This was why the forty-two boys were torn by the bears, because they called Elisha bald (2 *Kings* ii. 23, 24). Elisha, like Elijah and the other prophets, represented the Lord as to the Word, and the Word without its ultimate sense, which is the sense of the letter, is not the Word; for the sense of the letter of the Word is like a vessel filled with noble wine, wherefore when the vessel is broken, all the wine is spilled. The sense of the letter is also like the bones and skin with man, which being taken away, the whole man would fall asunder. Therefore it is that the stability, yea the power of the whole Word rests in its ultimate sense, which is the sense of the letter, for this sense sustains and contains all the Divine truth therein. Since baldness signifies no truth, because it has no ultimate, therefore they of the Jewish Church, when they left Jehovah and rejected the Word, are called bald, as in *Jeremiah:*—

Every head is bald, and every beard is cut off (xlviii. 37).

On the heads is baldness, and the beard is cut off (*Isa.* xv. 2).

That he should shave the head and beard with a razor (*Ezek.* v. 1).

Shame shall be upon all faces, and baldness upon all heads (*Ezek.* vii. 18).

Every head was made bald (*Ezek.* xxix. 18); as also elsewhere (*Amos* viii. 10; *Micah* i. 16).

26. But the sense of the Word which is called the sense of the letter, corresponds in its ultimates to the hair of the head, and for the rest it corresponds to the various parts in man, as his head, breast, loins, and feet; but where there are these correspondences in that sense, the Word is as it were clothed, and it therefore corresponds to the clothing of those parts, for garments in general signify truths, and also actually correspond to them. But yet many things in the sense of the letter of the Word are naked, as without clothing, and these correspond to the face of man, and also to his hands, which parts are bare. These parts of the Word serve for the doctrine of the church, because in themselves they are spiritual natural truths. Whence it may be evident that there is no lack, but that man can find and see naked truths even in the letter of the Word.

XI.

The Wisdom of the Angels of the Three Heavens Is From the Lord by Means of the Word, to Which the Sense of Its Letter Serves as a Support and Basis.

27. I have heard from heaven that there was immediate revelation with the most ancient people on this earth, and that therefore they had no written Word; but after their times, when immediate revelation could neither be given nor received without danger to their souls, lest the communication and conjunction of men with the heavens should be intercepted and perish, it pleased the Lord to reveal Divine truth by means of the Word, which was written solely by correspondences. It is therefore of such a nature in the ultimate sense, that it comprehends within itself the wisdom of the angels of the three heavens. This wisdom does not appear in our Word, but yet it is within it, and how it is within it shall be briefly told. There are three heavens, one beneath another, and under them is the world. In the highest heaven is angelic wisdom in the highest degree, which is called celestial wisdom; in the middle heaven is angelic wisdom in the middle degree, which is called spiritual wisdom; but in the lowest heaven is angelic wisdom in the lowest degree, which is called spiritual and celestial natural. In the world, because that is below the heavens, is wisdom in the lowest degree, which is called natural. All these degrees of wisdom are in the Word which is in the world, but in simultaneous order, for successive order in its descent becomes simultaneous. Therefore that which is simultaneous becomes the complex of all its successive degrees. The highest in successive order becomes the inmost in simultaneous order, the middle becomes the middle there, and the ultimate the ultimate there. Such a simultaneous order is the Word in the world. In its inmost is the Lord as a sun, from which Divine truth and Divine good, light and flame, radiate and propagate themselves through mediates even to ultimates. Next in that simultaneous order is the Divine celestial, such as is in the highest or third heaven, from which the angels there have wisdom. Then follows the Divine spiritual, such as is in the middle or second heaven, from which the angels there have wisdom. After that succeeds the Divine spiritual natural, and celestial natural, such as is in the ultimate or first heaven, from which the angels there have wisdom. The ultimate border of this simultaneous order is made by the Divine natural, such as is in the world, from which men have wisdom. This ultimate girds about, binds together, and thus contains the interiors, that they may not flow away; thus it serves also as a support. Such is our Word in the sense of the letter, in general and also in every part. When therefore this is read with reverence by man, then its interiors are unbound and unfolded, and each heaven draws therefrom its own, spiritual angels their Divine spiritual, and celestial angels their Divine celestial, from which they have their wisdom. That our Word is such has not only been declared and heard from heaven, but has also been shown and confirmed by much experience. The Divine let down by the Lord into the world, could not but pass through the heavens in their order, and exist in the world, so formed that it might in like order return through the heavens to the Lord, from whom it proceeded.

XII.

Enlightenment by Means of the Word.

28. Every man who is in the spiritual affection of truth, that is, who loves truth itself because it is truth, is enlightened by the Lord when he reads the Word; but not the man who reads it from mere natural affection of truth, which is called the desire of knowing. The latter does not see anything except what agrees with his love, or with the principles which he has either himself adopted, or derived from others by hearing or reading. In a few words therefore it shall be told whence and with what man there is enlightenment by means of the Word. That man has enlightenment who shuns evils because they are sins, and because they are against the Lord, and against His Divine laws. With this man and with no other, the spiritual mind is opened, and so far as it is opened, the light of heaven enters, from which light is all enlightenment in the Word. For man then has a will for good, and this will, when it is determined to that use, becomes in the understanding first the affection of truth, then the perception of truth, soon by means of rational light the thought of truth, thus decision and conclusion, which as it passes thence into the memory, also passes into the life, and so remains. This is the way of all enlightenment in the Word, and also the way of reformation and regeneration of man. But first the memory must needs have knowledges both of spiritual and natural things, for these are the stores into which the Lord operates by means of the light of heaven, and the fuller these are and freer from confirmed falsities, the more enlightened is the perception given and the clearer the conclusion. For the Divine operation does not fall into a man who is empty and void, as for example one who does not know that the Lord is pure love and pure mercy, good itself, and truth itself, and that love itself and good itself are such in their essence that they cannot do evil to anyone, neither be angry nor revengeful; or who does not know that the Word in the sense of the letter is written in many places from appearances. Such a man cannot be enlightened by the Word where it is said of Jehovah that He is wrathful and angry, and that to Him belong fire and fury, that His wrath burns, even to the lowest hell—as in David; that there is no evil in the city which Jehovah hath not done, as in *Amos* (iii. 6); that He would rejoice to do evil as He had rejoiced to do good (*Deut.* xxviii. 63); that He leads into temptations, as in the Lord's prayer; and similarly in other places.

XIII.

How Much Mediate Revelation, Which Is Effected Through the Word, Surpasses Immediate Revelation, Which Is Effected Through Spirits.

29. It is believed that man might be more enlightened and become more wise if he should have immediate revelation through speech with spirits and with angels, but the reverse is the case. Enlightenment by means of the Word is effected by an interior way, while enlightenment by immediate revelation is effected by an exterior way. The interior way is through the will into the understanding, the exterior way is through the hearing into the understanding. Man is enlightened through the Word by the Lord so far as his will is in good, but man may be instructed and as it were enlightened through the hearing, though the will is in evil; and what enters into the understanding with a man whose will is in evil, is not within, but without him. It is only in the memory and not in the life, and what is without a man and not in his life, is gradually separated, if not before, yet after death, for the will which is in evil either casts it out, or suffocates it, or falsifies and profanes it. For the will makes the life of man, and continually acts into the understanding, and regards as extraneous that which is from the memory in the understanding. On the other hand the understanding does not act into the will, but only teaches in what manner the will should act. Wherefore, were a man to know from heaven all things which even angels ever know or if he were to know all things that are in the Word, and that are in all the doctrines of the church, and moreover all that the Fathers have written and councils decreed, and yet his will be in evil, he would after death be looked upon as one who knows nothing, because he does not will what he knows. In such case because evil hates truths, the man himself casts them out, and in their place adopts falsities agreeing with the evil of his will. Moreover, no leave is given to any spirit or even angel, to instruct any man on this earth in Divine truths, but the Lord Himself teaches every one through the Word, and teaches him so far as the man receives good from the Lord in the will, and this the man receives so far as he shuns evils as sins. Again, every man is in a society of spirits as to his affections and thoughts thence, in which he is as one with them, wherefore spirits speaking with man speak from his affections and according to them. Man cannot speak with other spirits unless the societies in which he is, be first removed, which cannot be done except by the reformation of his will. Because every man is in society with spirits who are of the same religion with himself, therefore spirits speaking with him confirm all things which he has made a part of his religion. Thus enthusiastic spirits confirm all things of enthusiasm with the man, Quaker spirits all things of Quakerism, Moravian spirits all things of Moravianism, and so on. Hence come confirmations of falsity which can never be extirpated. From this it is plain that mediate revelation, which is effected through the Word, is better than immediate revelation, which takes place through spirits. As for myself, I have not been allowed to take anything from the mouth of any spirit, nor from the mouth of any angel, but from the mouth of the Lord alone.

XIV.

The Word in the Heavens.

30. The Word is in all the heavens. It is read there as in the world and they preach from it, for it is the Divine truth from which the angels have intelligence and wisdom; since without the Word no one knows anything of the Lord, of love and faith, of redemption, or of any other arcana of heavenly wisdom. Yea, without the Word there would be no heaven, as without the Word there would be no church in the world, thus there would be no conjunction with the Lord. That there is no such thing as natural theology without revelation, and in the Christian world without the Word, has been shown above. If it cannot exist in the world, neither can it exist after death, for such as a man is as to his religion in the world, such he is as to his religion after death when he becomes a spirit; and the whole heaven does not consist of any angels created before the world, or with the world, but of those who have been men, and were then interiorly angels. These through the Word come in heaven into spiritual wisdom, which is interior wisdom, because the Word there is spiritual.

31. The Word in the spiritual kingdom of the Lord is not like the Word in the world; in the world the Word is natural, but in that kingdom it is spiritual. The difference is as that between its natural sense and its spiritual sense, and what this spiritual sense is has been shown in many places in the *Arcana Cœlestia*, where all things in *Genesis* and *Exodus* have been explained according to that sense. Such is the difference that no word is the same; instead of names there are in the spiritual sense things, instead of numbers and historical facts are things relating to the church. But, what is wonderful, when an angel reads the Word in heaven, he knows not otherwise than that it is like the Word which he read in the world. The reason is that he no longer has any natural ideas, but in their place spiritual ideas, and the natural and the spiritual are so conjoined by correspondences that they make, as it were, one. When therefore one comes from what is natural into what is spiritual, it appears to him as if it were the same. Yea, an angel does not know that he is wiser than he had been in the world, although he has wisdom so supereminent as to be ineffable in comparison. Nor can he know the distinction, because in his spiritual state he knows nothing of his natural state, in which he was in the world. Neither can he compare and discriminate them, because he does not return into his former state, and so make a comparison. Nevertheless an angel is perfected in wisdom continually, in heaven more than in the world, because he is in purer affection for spiritual truth.

32. But the Word in the celestial kingdom of the Lord is of far greater excellence and wisdom than is the Word which is in His spiritual kingdom; and they differ in a degree similar to that of the difference between the natural Word which is in the world, and the spiritual Word of which we have been speaking; for in that Word there is an inmost sense, which is called the celestial, in which all things of the Word treat of the Lord alone. In this Word instead of Jehovah is read the Lord, and instead of Abraham, Isaac, and Jacob, also instead of David, Moses, Elijah, and the other prophets, the Lord is named, and His Divine as meant by them is distinguished by peculiar marks. By the names of the tribes of Israel, which are twelve, and also by the names of the apostles in the Word, something of the Lord as to the church is read; and so throughout. From this it has been made plain to me that the whole Sacred Scripture in its inmost sense treats of the Lord alone. There is a like difference between those two Words, the spiritual and the celestial, as between the thoughts which are of the understanding, and the affections, which are of the will; for the angels of the celestial kingdom are in love toward the Lord, and thence in the affection of good, and the angels of the spiritual kingdom are in faith in the Lord, and thence in the perception of truth.

33. The spiritual Word and the celestial Word differ also as to the writing. The writing of the spiritual Word is of letters which are similar to the type letters in our world, but every letter expresses a meaning. If, therefore, you should see that writing, you would not understand a single expression, for it is written letter next to letter in a continuous series, with little lines and points above and below, being written according to spiritual speech, which has nothing in common with natural speech. The angels, in proportion as they are wiser, see in their Word so written, more interior arcana than simpler angels see. The hidden things therein appear clearly before the eyes of the wise, but not before the eyes of the simple; in like manner as with our Word, though still more so, in which also the wise see more than the simple. But the writing of the celestial Word is composed of letters unknown in the world. They are indeed alphabetic letters, but each one is made up of curved lines, with little horns above and below, and there are dots or points in the letters, and also below and above them. It was said that the most ancient people on this earth had such writing, agreeing in some respects, but only slightly, with Hebrew writing. By such writing are expressed the affections of love, so that it involves more arcana than they themselves can utter, and they express these unutterable arcana which they perceive from their Word, by representations. The wisdom which lies hid in this Word, transcends the wisdom which is in the spiritual Word as thousands to one.

34. That the difference between the three Words, the natural, the spiritual, and the celestial, may be understood, let us take for illustration the first chapters of *Genesis*, which treat of Adam, his wife, and paradise. In the natural Word which is in the world, is described the creation of the world and the first creation of man, and its and his pleasures and earthly delights; and by the persons named after him even to the flood, are meant his posterity, and by the numbers their ages. But in the spiritual Word, which is with the angels of the spiritual kingdom, are not meant those things, but in the first chapter is described the reformation and regeneration of the men of the Most Ancient Church, which is also called the new creation. In the second chapter, by "paradise" is described the intelligence of the men of that church; by "Adam" and his "wife," that church itself, and by their posterity, even to the flood, are described the changes of state of that church, until it declined, and finally its destruction by the flood. But in the celestial Word, or in the Word which is with the angels in the celestial kingdom of the Lord, in the first chapter is described the glorification of the Lord's Human. Instead of "paradise" is described His Divine wisdom; by "Adam" himself is there meant the Lord as to the Divine itself, and at the same time the Divine Human; and by his "wife," the church, which is called "Chavah" [Eve], from life, because it has life from the Lord. Of her Adam said that she was his "bone" and his "flesh," and that they were "one flesh," because the church is from the Lord and of Him, and as one with Him. By the names which are the posterity of Adam, are there described the successive states of reception of the Lord, and of conjunction with Him, by the men of that church, even until there was no longer any reception, and therefore no conjunction. When therefore these first chapters of our Word are read by upright men, and especially when they are read by little boys and girls, and they are affected with joy from the state of the creation of all things, and from paradise, then those senses are evolved, and the spiritual angels understand them according to their Word, and the celestial angels according to theirs, without knowing that the man or child is reading it; for those senses are evolved in their order, because they correspond, and correspondences are such from creation. From these things it is plain what the Word is in its bosom, namely, that there are in it three senses, the ultimate which is natural for man, and which in many places treats of worldly things, and where it treats of Divine things, still they are described by such things as are in the world; a middle sense which is spiritual, in which are described such things as relate to the church; and an inmost sense which is celestial, in which are contained such things as relate to the Lord. For all nature is a theatre representative of the Lord's kingdom; and the Lord's kingdom, which is heaven, and the church, is a theatre representative of the Lord Himself; for as the Lord glorified His Human, so also He regenerates man, and as He regenerates man, so also He created him.

35. From this it may be evident what is the nature of the Word in its bosom. The natural Word, such as is in the world, in Christendom, contains within itself both the spiritual Word and the celestial Word; for the spiritual sense of our Word is the Word in the heavens which constitute the Lord's spiritual kingdom; and the celestial sense of our Word, which is its inmost sense, is the Word in the heavens which constitute the Lord's celestial kingdom. Consequently in our natural Word is contained both the spiritual Word and the celestial Word; but in the spiritual Word and the celestial Word is not contained the natural Word. For this reason the Word of our world is the most full of the Divine wisdom, and therefore more holy than the Words of the heavens.

XV.

The Ancient Word That Is Lost.

36. That there was a Word with the ancients, written like our Word by mere correspondences, but that this has been lost, has been told me by angels of the third heaven. They said further that this Word is still preserved with them, and is in use among the ancients in that heaven, whose Word it was when they were in the world. Those ancients, with whom that Word is still in use in the heavens, were in part from the land of Canaan and its borders, and also from certain kingdoms in Asia, as from Syria, Mesopotamia, Arabia, Chaldea, Assyria, and Egypt, from Sidon and Tyre, the inhabitants of all of which kingdoms were in representative worship, and thus in a knowledge of correspondences. Their wisdom at that time was from that knowledge, since by it they had communication with the heavens, and interior perception, and also many had converse with spirits. But because that Word was full of such correspondences, which remotely signified heavenly things, and for that reason in the course of time began to be falsified by many, therefore from the Divine providence of the Lord it gradually passed out of sight, and another Word was given, which was written by correspondences less remote, and this through the prophets with the sons of Israel. In this Word, however, the names of places in the land of Canaan and in Asia round about, were retained and kept their signification. For this reason, the posterity of Abraham from Jacob were introduced into the land of Canaan, and the Word in which those places were to be named was there written.

37. That there was such a Word with the ancients is plain also in Moses, by whom it is mentioned and something is taken from it (*Num.* xxi. 14–27). The historicals of that Word were called the *Wars of Jehovah*, and the propheticals the *Enunciations*. From the historicals of that Word Moses took these words:—

Wherefore it is said in the Book of the Wars of Jehovah, At Vaheb in Suphah, and the streams of Arnon, and the channel of the streams that descend towards the dwelling of Ar, and reach to the border of Moab (*Num.* xxi. 14, 15).

By "the Wars of Jehovah" are there meant and described the combats of the Lord with the hells and victories over them, when He should come into the world. The same combats are also meant and described in many places in the historicals of our Word, as in the wars of Joshua with the nations of the land of Canaan, in the wars of the judges, and in the wars of David and the rest of the kings. From the propheticals of that Word these words were taken by Moses:—

> Wherefore the prophetic enunciations say, Come ye to Heshbon, let the city of Sihon be built and established, for a fire has gone out of Heshbon, a flame from the city of Sihon: it hath devoured Ar of Moab, the possessors of the high places of Arnon. Woe to thee, Moab! Thou hast perished, O people of Chemosh. He hath given his sons as fugitives, and his daughters into captivity, unto Sihon king of the Amorites. With darts we have destroyed them. Heshbon is perished even unto Dibon, and we have laid them waste even unto Nophah, which is even unto Medeba (*Num.* xxi. 27-30).

That these propheticals were called *Enunciations*, and not *Proverbs* or the makers of proverbs, as the translators render it, may be evident from the signification of the word *maschalim* in the Hebrew language, which means not only proverbs, but also prophetic enunciations, as may appear elsewhere in *Numbers* (xxiii. 7, 18; xxiv. 3, 15), where it is said that Balaam put forth his enunciation, which also was a prophecy, yea, concerning the Lord. His enunciation is there called a *maschal*, in the singular. Furthermore, those things which are described by Moses in those citations are prophecies, but they are not proverbs. That that Word was in like manner Divine, or Divinely inspired, is plain in *Jeremiah*, where are almost the same words, as follows:—

> A fire has gone forth out of Heshbon, and a flame from the midst of Sihon, and hath devoured the corner of Moab, and the crown of the head of the sons of tumult. Woe unto thee, O Moab! the people of Chemosh hath perished; for thy sons are carried away into captivity, and thy daughters into captivity (*Jer.* xlviii. 45, 46).

Besides these, a prophetic book of that ancient Word, called the *Book of Jasher*, or the *Book of the Upright*, is also cited by David (2 *Sam.* i. 18), and by *Joshua* (x. 13); from which it is plain that the historic statement there about the sun and moon, was a prophecy from that book. It has moreover been told me that the first seven chapters of *Genesis* are so manifestly extant in that same Word, that not a little word is wanting.

38. The religious systems of many nations have been derived from that ancient Word and carried elsewhere, as from the land of Canaan and from various parts of Asia into Greece and from there into Italy, and through Ethiopia and Egypt into certain kingdoms of Africa. In Greece, however, out of correspondences they made fables, and out of the Divine attributes they made so many gods, the greatest of whom they called Jove, from Jehovah.

XVI.

THE GENTILES, AND PEOPLES OUTSIDE OF THE CHURCH, WHO HAVE NOT THE WORD, AND THEREFORE KNOW NOTHING OF THE LORD AND OF REDEMPTION.

39. They who have the Word are few as compared with those who have not the Word. The Word is found only in Europe with the Christians who are called the Reformed. The Word is indeed with the Roman Catholics, but it is not read, and the kingdoms devoted to that religion, as France, Spain, Portugal, Italy, more than half of Germany, and also of Hungary, as well as Poland, do not read it. The Word is also but little read in Russia, but yet it is believed to be holy. *Communication through the Word.* Only in England, Holland, certain duchies in Germany, and in Sweden and Denmark is the Word taught and preached; but in Asia, Africa, and the Indies, with the Gentiles, who are more numerous than the Reformed Christians, the Word is unknown. But that the Word might not be lost, it has been provided by the Lord that the Jewish nation, with whom is the Word of the Old Testament in its original tongue, should still survive and dwell dispersed through much of the earth. Though this nation denies that the Lord is the Messiah or Christ, foretold by the prophets, and though it is evil in heart, yet the reading of the Word by them has communication with certain heavens; for correspondences communicate, whatever the quality of the person who reads, if only he acknowledges the Word to be Divine. This is the case to-day, as formerly; for when Moses, Abraham, Isaac, and Jacob, David, Elias, and many others named in the Word, are adored by them as deities, then the heavens perceive the Lord, instead of these persons, not knowing the person in the world from whom that holy of worship proceeds. Such is the conjunction of heaven with man by means of the Word.

XVII.

[BY MEANS OF THE WORD THOSE ALSO HAVE LIGHT WHO ARE OUT OF THE CHURCH AND HAVE NOT THE WORD.]

40. The case is thus: there cannot be any conjunction with heaven, unless somewhere on the earth there is a church where the Word is, and by it the Lord is known; for the Lord is the God of heaven and earth, and without the Lord there is no salvation. It is enough that there be somewhere on the earth a church where the Word is. Though it consist of comparatively few, still by means of it, the Lord is present everywhere in the whole world, and by means of it heaven is conjoined to the human race, for conjunction is effected by means of the Word. But without the Word somewhere in the world there would not be conjunction with any one. The reason of the presence of the Lord and of the conjunction of heaven with the inhabitants of the earth everywhere by means of the Word, is, that the whole heaven is before the Lord as one man, and likewise the church, and it is also actually a man, because the Lord is heaven and also the church. In that man the church where the Word is read and thereby, the Lord is known, is like the heart and lungs; and as from those two fountains of life in the human body all the rest of the members and viscera subsist and live, so also all those in the world who have a religion in which one God is worshiped, and who constitute the members and viscera of that Greatest Man which is heaven and the church, subsist and live. For, by means of the Word in the church, though it be among comparatively few, life is given to the rest from the Lord through heaven, as from the heart and lungs to the members and viscera of the whole body. The communication is also similar. This is the reason that Christians with whom the Word is read, constitute the breast of that man and are also in the midst of all; round about them are the Roman Catholics, around these are the Mohammedans who acknowledge the Lord as the Greatest Prophet and as the Son of God, behind them are the Africans, and the Gentiles and people of Asia and the Indies constitute the outmost circumference. All who are in that man look also towards the middle region. Moreover in that middle region where, as already said, are the Christians who have the Word, is the greatest light, because light in the heavens is the Divine truth proceeding from the Lord as the sun. The light thence, as from its centre, propagates itself to all the borders, and enlightens. Hence the Gentiles and peoples outside of the church are enlightened also by means of the Word, for all the light of truth with man is from the Lord through heaven.

41. As it is in the whole heaven, so also is it in every society of heaven, for each society of heaven is a heaven in smaller form, and also is in the sight of the Lord as one man, in regard to which see the work on *Heaven and Hell* [n. 41–87]. There also they who are in the midst in like manner relate to the heart and lungs, and with them is the greatest light. The light itself and the perception of truth thereby propagates itself from that middle portion towards the borders in every direction, and makes their spiritual life. It was also shown me that when those who were in the midst, who constituted the province of the heart and lungs, and with whom therefore was the greatest light, were taken away, those who were round about were in shade, and in so little perception of truth that it was scarcely any at all. But as soon as they returned, the light was seen as before, and there was perception of truth as before.

42. From this it may be seen that the Word which is in the church of the Reformed, enlightens all nations and peoples by spiritual communication, which is of this nature; also that it is provided by the Lord that in this earth there may always be a church where the Word is read. When therefore the Word was almost rejected by the Roman Catholics, by the Divine providence of the Lord the Reformation was effected, and in that the Word was again received, and it was also regarded as holy by a noble nation among the Papists.

43. Since without the Word there is no knowledge of the Lord, thus no salvation, therefore when the Word was altogether adulterated and falsified with the Jewish nation, and hence as it were made of none effect, it pleased the Lord to come into the world and not only to fulfil the Word, but also to renew and restore it, and so again to give light to the inhabitants of this earth, according to the words of the Lord in *John*:—

In the beginning was the Word, and the Word was with God, and God was the Word. In Him was life, and the life was the light of men. And the light appeareth in the darkness. He was the true light, which lighteth every man coming into the world (i. 1, 4, 5, 9).

In the same:—

Jesus said, I am the light of the world: he that followeth Me shall not walk in the darkness, but shall have the light of life (viii. 12).

And in *Matthew*:—

The people which sat in darkness saw a great light; and to them which sat in the region and shadow of death, to them did light spring up (iv. 16).

44. Since it has been foretold that in the end of this church darkness would also arise, from a lack of knowledge and acknowledgement of the Lord, that He is the God of heaven and earth; and from the separation of faith from charity, whereby the genuine understanding of the Word has perished; therefore it has pleased the Lord now to reveal the spiritual sense of the Word, and to show that the Word treats in that sense of the Lord and of the church, yea, of them only, and to show many other things by which the light of truth, almost extinguished, may be restored. That the light of truth at the end of this church would be extinguished, is meant by the words of the Lord in *Matthew*:—

Immediately after the affliction of those days, the sun shall be darkened, and the moon shall not give her light, and the stars shall fall from heaven, and the powers of the heavens shall be shaken: and then they shall see the Son of man, coming in the clouds of heaven, with glory and power (xxiv. 29, 30).

By the "sun" is here meant the Lord as to the Divine love, by the "moon" the Lord as to faith, by the "stars" the Lord as to knowledges of good and truth, by "clouds" the sense of the letter of the Word, and by "glory" its spiritual sense, and by the "Son of man" the Lord as to the Word.

XVIII.

The Conjunction of Heaven with the Man of the Church, by Means of the Sense of the Letter of the Word.

45. From much experience it has been given me to know that the Word opens heaven to man, that is, that when man reads the Word or speaks from it, communication is effected with heaven. I have read the prophetic Word through from *Isaiah* even to *Malachi*, and it was given to perceive that every chapter, yea every verse, was perceived in some heavenly society. And because the spiritual sense and not the sense of the letter is communicated, therefore the angels of the society did not know that these things came from any man. Such things as are inwardly in the Word appear to them as if they thought them from themselves.

46. There were with me African spirits, from Abyssinia. Their ears were once opened so that they heard singing in a certain temple in the world, from the *Psalms of David*, and they were affected with such delight that they sang together with the singers. But soon their ears were closed, and they did not hear from there the singing of any one; and then they were affected with still greater delight, because spiritual; and at the same time they were filled with intelligence, because the *Psalm* in the spiritual sense treated of the Lord, and of redemption by Him. The delight of their hearts' joy was for a little time communicated with a certain heavenly society from the Christian world, and that society came thereby into similar delight. Hence it was plain, that communication with the whole heaven is given by means of the Word.

47. I pass over a thousand other experiences by which I have been convinced that the sense of the letter of our Word produces that effect, yea, that the spiritual sense without its companion, the natural sense, does not communicate with heaven. The reason of this is, that the Lord flows in from firsts through ultimates, therefore from Himself into the natural sense of the Word, and from that calls forth, or evolves its spiritual and celestial senses, and thus enlightening, teaches and leads the angels; wherefore the Lord is called in the Word "the First and the Last."

48. From this it is plain that the doctrine of the church, unless it be gathered and confirmed from the sense of the letter of the Word, has no power, because it does not communicate; but doctrine from the sense of the letter and together with it does have power.

XIX.

The Truths Which Are Called Truths of Faith, and the Goods Which Are Called Goods of Love, Are Ineffably Increased in the Internal Senses, thus in the Heavens.

The Quality of the Natural Sense Without the Spiritual and Celestial Senses, and the Reverse.

49. The reason of this is, that natural things are effects from spiritual, and spiritual things are effects from celestial, and the effect consists of so many things which are causes, that do not appear before the eyes, as may be said to reach to infinity. The effect is gross, and the cause enters every effect and composes it as its own general, in which are particulars and single things altogether beyond the sphere of the sight of the eye.

50. It is comparatively like a tree, which appears before the eyes luxuriant with branches, leaves, and fruits. All these are effects, but if you could examine a branch within as to the filaments, or a leaf as to fibres, or the fruit as to each and all things of it which are invisible, and the seed as to its invisible parts, of which the tree with all its members consists, you would see how innumerable and indescribable things lie hidden from the eyes. Once a flower was opened before the angels as to its interiors, which are called spiritual, and when they saw they said that there was within as it were a whole paradise, consisting of indescribable things.

51. It is also like the human body with all its members and organs that appear before the eye, as compared with its interiors, where are so many organic forms, by pure arcana of all the sciences making so many bodies from one, even so that you might say that into it are gathered arcana of all the sciences, as Physics, Chemistry, Mechanics, Geometry, Acoustics, Optics, which arcana of the sciences can in no wise be explored, because not comprehended. Such is the internal with respect to the external, or the spiritual with respect to the natural, and the celestial with respect to the spiritual. The natural in itself regarded is nothing else than an external form, which is called the effect of spiritual things; and the spiritual is an external form, which is called the effect of celestial things; wherefore everything spiritual is from the celestial, and everything natural is from the spiritual. From this it is plain how it is to be understood that truth is the form of good, that good has its quality in truths, because form is in them, and without form quality is lacking; and that truth exists from good as from its own living cause; and that if you remove good from truths, it is as if you should take the kernel from an almond, the truth being like its shell; or as if you should take out the pulp from fruit, and leave only the skin. Hence truth without good is turned into what is fantastic, which appears externally like truth, but is empty within. So is the natural without the spiritual, and also the spiritual without the celestial.

52. Because there are ineffable things in the spiritual which do not appear in the natural, and innumerable things in the celestial, therefore it is plain what is the nature of the natural, the spiritual, and the celestial, that they are ineffable with respect to one another. They follow after one another, as knowledge, intelligence, and wisdom; wherefore also men on earth, because they are in natural light, are called by the angels knowing, while angels of the Lord's spiritual kingdom are called intelligent; and angels of the Lord's celestial kingdom are called wise.

53. The Word in the sense of the letter may be compared to a tree, surrounded with cortex or bark, entire, and endowed with vegetative life, and the spiritual sense may be compared to its nutrition from various juices and essences, partly ascending from the ground, partly imbibed from the air and ether, by means of the heat and light of the sun. If the sense of the letter alone existed, and not at the same time the spiritual sense and the celestial sense, the Word would be as a tree without sap, or as the bark alone without wood; but with those senses it is like a tree in its perfect state; indeed in a tree all the sap passes from the root through the bark or cortex, wherefore when that is taken away the tree dries up. Such would be the case with the spiritual sense of the Word without its natural sense.

XX.

ALL THE HOLINESS OF THE WORD IS IN THE SENSE OF THE LETTER, AND THERE IS NO HOLINESS IN ITS SPIRITUAL SENSE WITHOUT THE SENSE OF THE LETTER.

54. The spiritual sense without the sense of the letter would be like a house without a foundation, thus like a house in the air. It would be like the human body without its skins, all things of which would be dissipated. As all the interiors of the body have a connection with the peritoneum, the pleura, and the skins, so the spiritual sense of the Word is connected with the sense of the letter. The spiritual sense without the sense of the letter would be like the contents without that which contains, thus like wine without a containing vessel. The case is similar with the spiritual without the natural, or the heaven of angels and their wisdom without the human race and the church therein, and its intelligence from the sense of the letter. The sense of the letter of the Word with man makes that connection, and that conjunction. This also was the reason why the Lord came into the world, for all of the sense of the letter of the Word had been so falsified by the Jews that there was no longer an ultimate of Divine truth in man. Therefore the

Lord came into the world and put on the Human, that He might also become the Word in the sense of the letter, or the Divine truth in ultimates; wherefore it is said that "the Word became flesh" (*John* i. 14).

55. The case is similar with the power of Divine truth. All power in the spiritual world belongs to the Divine truth proceeding from the Lord. What this power of Divine truth there is, may be illustrated by many things from experience, of which experience some things may be adduced; and all the power of Divine truth resides in the sense of the letter of the Word. In the spiritual sense without the sense of the letter there is no power, but all in the sense of the letter in which is the spiritual sense. Wherefore when spirits quote anything from the sense of the letter, manifest communication with heaven is effected, but not if they quote anything from the spiritual sense without the sense of the letter. Therefore all answers from heaven have been made, and are made, through such things as are of the sense of the letter. For this reason the Urim and Thummim in the breastplate of Aaron, his outmost vesture, represented the sense of the letter. For the same reason in the *Apocalypse* the foundations of the New Jerusalem are enumerated as of twelve precious stones, and moreover of pearls, which also signified the sense of the letter. In like manner the cherubim above the mercy seat signified the sense of the letter; wherefore responses were given by this to Moses and Aaron.

56. The order in which the interior things of Divine truth rest, from which the angels have wisdom, is simultaneous order, for which reason the sense of the letter is the containant.

57. Therefore all things of the doctrine of the church are to be confirmed by the sense of the letter of the Word, and whatever of doctrine is not confirmed from the sense of the letter of the Word has no power. Doctrine confirmed by the sense of the letter as to genuine truth, has power. The appearance of Divine truth also has power, though less, so far as it can agree with genuine truth; but the sense of the letter of the Word falsified has no power. It closes and does not open heaven.

XXI.

The Spiritual Sense.

58. No one can see the spiritual sense except from the doctrine of genuine truth; from this doctrine the spiritual sense can be seen, when there is some knowledge of correspondences. He who is in false doctrine cannot see anything of the spiritual sense. He draws out and applies the correspondences which he sees to the falsites of his doctrine; and thus he can still more falsify the Word. Wherefore the true spiritual sense of the Word is from the Lord alone. This is the reason why it is not permitted any one in the natural world, nor in the spiritual world, to investigate the spiritual sense of the Word from the sense of its letter, unless he is wholly in the doctrine of Divine truth and in enlightenment from the Lord, wherefore from the doctrine of Divine truth confirmed from the sense of the letter of the Word, the spiritual sense can be seen, but doctrine can never first be seen from the spiritual sense. He thinks falsely who says with himself, I know many correspondences, I can know the true doctrine of the Divine Word, the spiritual sense will teach it to me. This cannot be done. But, as has been said, let him say with himself, I know the doctrine of Divine truth, now I can see the spiritual sense, provided I know correspondences. But still this must be in enlightenment from the Lord, because the spiritual sense is Divine truth itself in its light, and is meant by glory, and the sense of the letter by a cloud in passages in the Word where these are mentioned. That there is a spiritual sense in the Word is to be confirmed by ten passages in the *Prophetic Word*, likewise in the *Evangelists*, and also in the *Apocalypse*, which passages are to be adduced, and it is to be shown that they would have no meaning without the spiritual sense.

XXII.

It Is Better for Man in Many Passages to Understand the Word According to the Letter.

59. For example, in what the Lord says concerning cities, concerning the successive states of the church, in the *Prophets* in many passages, as concerning Tyre, in the *Apocalypse*, and concerning paradise; for the reason that the angels are then in the spiritual sense with man.

XXIII.

The Word.

60. [1] Various things concerning the marriage of good and truth in the Word, to be shown from passages therein.

[2] There are chapters and expressions peculiarly pertaining to good, and others to truth.

[3] When pertaining to celestial good and truth, as where Judah is treated of; and to spiritual good and truth, as where Israel is treated of.

[4] Each chapter has reference to one society, and many to all.

[5] In some passages there is a sense from the letters alone, concerning which.

[6] Numbers and names of persons and places signify things, of which examples are to be given.

XXIV.

The Word in Heaven.

61. They have the Word in the spiritual kingdom in its higher region so written that it may be more and more intelligently understood by one who is intelligent, but simply by one who is simple, in which Word stands forth both interior and exterior intelligence, and the interior is written. This is effected by various points above the letters, the points signifying affections, and the series of points expressing the interior things of intelligence continuously to the more intelligent. This Word was seen by me, that is, something of it was seen. Something also of the Word of the celestial kingdom was seen, in which still more arcana were described, but by various curves and spirals above and within the letters, which are peculiar to the celestial kingdom. These arcana are very transcendent, nor can they be comprehended by an angel of the spiritual kingdom, nor even thought of; wherefore it was said to them that they can no more approximate to the wisdom of angels of the celestial kingdom than can those who are in a natural sphere approximate to the intelligence of angels of the spiritual kingdom; and how far this transcends has frequently been tried. From experience it was made evident to me, that the intelligence of angels of the spiritual kingdom is ineffable and incomprehensible to those who are in the natural kingdom; and that the wisdom of the angels of the celestial kingdom is incomprehensible and ineffable to those who are in the spiritual kingdom. But as to the Divine wisdom of the Lord, this so transcends all wisdom that no ratio can be given; for all the intelligence and wisdom of angels is finite, but the Divine wisdom of the Lord is infinite; and there is no ratio between the finite and the infinite. The intelligence and wisdom of angels is finite, because angels are recipients, and all recipients are created, and so finite.

XXVI.*

[The Word with the Spiritual Angels.]

62. Exploration was made as to how the spiritual angels express the words of their speech, and it was found that they express or speak them according to ideas, and from the ideas of the things which they signify, as when they express or speak of a horse and chariot, then they express them by a word which is

---

* No number xxv. is found.

significative, as a horse from ideas of the understanding, and a chariot from ideas of doctrine from the Word; and in like manner in other cases; so that they speak from the correspondence of those things which they see in like manner as men. In a word, they give names to them from correspondence. It was therefore now disclosed to them, a thing they had not known, that they have correspondences in the words of their speech; and it was disclosed by their examining in the natural with me their ideas concerning those things in a spiritual state. In a word, the words of speech of their tongue were all formed from correspondences. Inquiry was made as to how they write, "horses harnessed to a chariot." They said that they write only *l*, and that that letter expresses it. Inquiry was then made how they write "the understanding of doctrine," and they said in like manner by *l*, but that they are then in a higher thought. From this also it was plain that there are correspondences in the words of their language, but that few of them had attended to this, just as few in this world attend to spiritual light, when the light of the understanding is spoken of, or illumination and enlightenment; and to fire or spiritual heat when heavenly fire is spoken of, as that which enkindles hearts, not knowing that fire and heat therefrom correspond to love, which is of the heart, that is, to the will, and light to truth, which is of the understanding.*

---

*The manuscript ends here.

INDEX OF WORDS.

Figures refer to Numbers.

ABRAHAM.
Introduced into land of Canaan because of signification of places there, n. 36; when with others adored, the heavens perceive the Lord, n. 39.

ADAM AND EVE.
Most Ancient Church meant by, n. 18, 34.

AFRICANS.
Next after Mohammedans in Greatest Man, n. 40; spirits heard the singing of Psalms, n. 46.

ANCIENT OF DAYS.
With hair like wool, n. 25.

ANCIENT WORD.
Described, n. 36-38; where existed, why lost, still used in ancient heavens, had same names of places about Canaan, n. 36; citations from Moses, n. 37; from *Jeremiah*, contained the Book of *Jasher*, and the first seven chapters of *Genesis*, many religious systems derived from it, n. 38.

ANGELS.
Guarding spiritual sense of the Word, n. 1; think by means of lights, n. 2; of the three heavens, and intermediate, a. 3; cannot live without consociation with man, n. 11; not aware of the difference between the natural and higher degrees, till it was shown them, n. 12; in their own sight appear as men in the world, n. 13; can look down and see what is beneath, but not be seen, n. 16; their wisdom from the Lord by means of the Word, n. 27; not permitted to instruct men in Divine truths, n. 29; do not know themselves wiser than in the world, cannot compare, knowing no longer the natural, n. 31; perfected in wisdom continually, n. 31.

ANGELS OF THE THIRD HEAVEN.
Seen as children, n. 1; do not have thoughts, but perceptions, n. 8.

ARCANA.
Divine, can be expressed naturally, n. 6; in the conversation of angels, n. 6; perceived spiritually and in a celestial manner, when they become angels, only by those who have perceived them naturally, n. 6; of celestial kingdom above comprehension of man and of spiritual angels, n. 61.

ARCANA, CŒLESTIA.
Cited, n. 17, 22, 31.

ARISTOTLE.
Had with other pagans some knowledge of spiritual things from ancient religion, n. 17.

BALAAM.
His enunciation, n. 37.

BALDNESS.
Signifies no ultimate of truth, n. 25.

BEAST.
In the *Apocalypse*, signifies the Roman Catholics, n. 21.

BRIDE.
The church so called, n. 22.

BRIDEGROOM.
The Lord so called, n. 22.

CAUSE.
Influx into effect, n. 8.

CEDAR-TREE.
Signifies the rational, n. 19.

CELESTIAL SENSE.
Of the Word, for those in celestial kingdom, and treats of the Lord, n. 15,

32; celestial natural, n. 27; far superior to that in spiritual kingdom, the inmost sense, in it the Lord read instead of Jehovah and named in place of Abraham and others, and the church in place of Israel, n. 32.

CELESTIAL KINGDOM.
Those in are in the goods of the Word and constitute all the higher heavens, n. 15, 27; they perceive these goods not immediately from man who reads, but mediately through spiritual angels, because hardly any man is in celestial love, n. 15; celestial angels called wise, n. 52.

CHILDREN.
Representation, n. 1; those torn by bears, n. 25; Word read by, n. 34.

CHRISTIANS.
With whom Word is read, are the breast of the Greatest Man, n. 40.

CHURCH.
Most Ancient, n. 17; spoke with angels by correspondences, n. 17; worshiped on mountains, n. 19; had immediate revelation but no written Word, n. 27; where the Word is, as the heart and lungs, n. 40; Ancient, n. 17, 18.

CICERO.
His writings mentioned, n. 16; with other pagans had some knowledge of spiritual things from the ancient religion, n. 17.

CLOUDS.
Mean sense of the letter, n. 44, 58.

CONJUNCTION.
Perpetual from the Lord through heaven with man, effected from creation by correspondences, n. 11; of the Lord with heaven and the church by means of the Word, of good and truth with every one in heaven and the church, n. 15, 40; of heaven with man by means of the Word, n. 39, 40, 45, 54.

CONSONANTS.
In heaven, n. 14.

CORPORAL.
And material, the ultimate in which the spiritual subsists, n. 13.

CORRESPONDENCES.
The Word written by, n. 2; subject of chapter, n. 17-21; all things in nature correspond to spiritual things, n. 17; knowledge of in ancient times; all books then written by; all rites of worship, offerings, and sacrifices consisted of; and so the letter of the Word, n. 17; the Lord spoke by, n. 17; collected by Enoch, n. 18; knowledge of in many parts of Asia and Africa, also in Greece, n. 18; perverted to idolatry, n. 19; lost with Israelites, n. 19; knowledge of remained with eastern nations till coming of the Lord, n. 22; not disclosed since because early Christians too simple, later too blind, n, 20; to good and to truth in the Word, n. 22, 23; may be used to falsify the Word, n. 58; used without thought by angels and men, n. 62.

DAGON.
Signification, n. 19.

DEGREES.
Natural, spiritual, and celestial—no comparison between them, n. 4, 51; but resemblance in objects of sense, n. 13; in the Word, simultaneous and successive, n. 27; as knowledge, intelligence, and wisdom, n. 52.

DISPUTE.
Heard among spirits, n. 16.

DISTINCTION.
Between natural, spiritual, and celestial heavens, thought and language, n. 3-13, 52.

DIVINE.
What is from falls lastly into correspondences, n. 17; let down by the Lord into the world must pass through heavens, and so return to Him, n. 27.

DOCTRINE.
Of the church, has no power unless from the sense of the letter, n. 48; to be confirmed thereby, then has power, n. 57; spiritual not seen except from doctrine of genuine truth, n. 58; never drawn first from spiritual sense, nor by one not enlightened by the Lord, n. 58.

EFFECT.
Influx of cause into, n. 8; natural things effects from spiritual, and spiritual from celestial, n. 49; in effect numberless causes, n. 49-51.

EGYPT.
Had images according to correspondences, n. 19; hieroglyphics from same origin, n. 19.

INDEX OF WORDS

ELIJAH AND ELISHA.
The Lord as to the Word, n. 25.

ENLIGHTENMENT.
Through the Word, and by shunning evils as sins, but cannot be given without knowledges, n. 28; effected thus by an interior way, n. 28; evil in the will obstructs, n. 28; spiritual sense cannot be seen and doctrine cannot be drawn without, n. 58.

ENOCH.
Collected and transmitted correspondences, n. 18.

ENUNCIATIONS.
Of the Ancient Word, n. 37.

EVE.
Church meant by, n. 34.

FABLES.
In Greece, from correspondences, n. 18.

FALSITY.
Confirmed as well as truth, n. 16.

FATHER.
Not forbidden to be so named in natural sense, n. 15.

FINITE.
The wisdom of angels because they are create and finite, n. 61.

FISH.
Signifies natural knowledge, n. 19.

FLAME OF GOOD.
In third heaven, n. 2.

FLOWER.
Opened before angels, n. 50.

FOUNTAIN.
In the fable, signifies intelligence, n. 18

FRANKINCENSE.
Signifies spiritual good, n. 19.

GARDENS AND GROVES.
Worship in, signifying spiritual intelligence, n. 19.

GARMENT.
Inner of the Lord, garments signify truths, n. 20. 26.

GENESIS.
Meaning of first chapters, n. 37; from Ancient Word, n. 38.

GENTILES.
Who have not the Word, n. 39-44; in the circumference in Greatest Man, and enlightened by means of the Word, n. 40.

GLORY.
Means spiritual sense, n. 44.

GOLD.
Signifies celestial good, n. 19.

GREATEST MAN.
See MAN.

GREECE.
Knowledge of correspondences in, turned into fables, n. 18, 38; religious system derived from ancient Word, n. 39.

HAIR.
Corresponds to ultimate sense of the Word, and those who have loved the Word even in this sense have as spirits and angels becoming hair, while those who have despised the letter are bald, n. 25.

HARLOT.
Representation, n. 1.

HEART.
And lungs of the church where Word is read, n. 40.

HEAVEN.
The three heavens, their difference, how distinct, n. 3-13, 27; preachers in the third, intermediate angels, n. 3; contain all things to appearance as in the world, but in the higher heaven of indescribable excellence, n. 13; those admitted who desired, n. 24; the whole before the Lord as one man, n. 40; opened to man and conjoined with him by the Word, n. 46; could not exist without the world and church, thus without the literal Word, n. 54-57.

HEBREW LETTERS.
Resembled by letters in heaven, n. 9, 14, 33; their meaning recognized in heaven, from which they have their origin, n. 14; meaning of certain letters, n. 14.

HILL.
In the fable signifies the lower heaven, n. 19.

HOLINESS.
Of the Word, in sense of letter, and, not in spiritual sense without the letter, n. 54-57.

HORSE.
Representation, n. 1; signifies things of the understanding, n. 1, 19; the White Horse, the spiritual sense of the Word, n. 21.

HUSBAND.
The Lord so called, n. 22.

IDOLATRY.
From perverted correspondences, n. 19.

IMAGES.
According to correspondences, used by ancients, n. 19.

INDIES.
Gentiles of in circumference, n. 40.

INFLUX.
Of the light of heaven into the light of the world, as cause into effect, n. 8; of all the celestial into the spiritual, and of the spiritual into the natural, terminating in the corporeal and material, n. 11; of the Lord through the Word from firsts through lasts, n. 15, 47; from the good of love into the truths of doctrine and faith, n. 22.

INN.
At Bethlehem, signified the Jewish Church, n. 19.

INNOCENCE.
Of wisdom, signified by little children, n. 1.

INTERMEDIATE.
Angels preach in highest heaven, n. 3; intermediates flow into the material ultimate, n. 11.

INTERNAL.
Full of particulars, n. 51.

ISRAEL.
Named in reference to spiritual good and truth, n. 60.

JEHOVAH.
The name, n. 12; called Lord in heaven, n. 32; origin of the name Jove, n. 38.

JEWISH CHURCH.
Had perverted everything of the Word, state described, rejected the Lord because He taught them of a heavenly kingdom, n. 19.

JUDAH.
Named with reference to celestial good and truth, 64.

JUDGING.
Not forbidden as to natural life, n. 15.

KINGS OF THE EARTH.
In the *Apocalypse* signify the Reformed, n. 21.

KNOWLEDGES.
Of truth, in great abundance in the Word, n. 1; of both spiritual and natural things necessary, into which the Lord operates by light of heaven, n. 28; amount to nothing if the will is in evil, n. 28.

LABORS.
Of angels cannot be described in lower degree, n. 10.

LETTER OF THE WORD.
Represented, n. 1; is the natural sense, n. 2.

LETTERS.
A sense from in some passages, n. 60; in spiritual kingdom with points signifying affections, in celestial kingdom with curves and spirals, n. 61.

LIFE.
Flowing in from the Lord through the Word, is the light of truth and the love of good, and this the life of heaven, or eternal life, n. 2.

LIGHT OF TRUTH.
In second heaven, n. 2; from the sun of heaven, n. 8, 41; extinguished at end of church, n. 52.

LIGHT OF THE WORLD.
Dead, n. 8.

LIGHT OF HEAVEN.
Influx into light of the world, n. 8; from the Lord as sun, n. 40.

LIGHTS.
The means of the thought of angels, n. 2.

LITERAL.
Sense of the Word, see Natural sense.

LORD.
The sun of heaven, n. 8; everything in the Word made living by, n. 2; lay in the manger, n. 1; calls Himself the

INDEX OF WORDS

Word, n. 15; in Him is the Divine natural, the Divine spiritual, and the Divine celestial, n. 15; spoke by correspondences, n. 17; is the all of the church, n. 23; as a sun in inmost of the Word, n. 27; alone teaches man through the Word, n. 29; the God of heaven and earth, and no salvation without Him, n. 40; came into the world when the Word was falsified, and fulfilled it, n. 44, 54; in the darkness of the church has again come revealing spiritual sense of the Word, n. 44; flows in from firsts through lasts, n. 15, 47; is the First and the Last, n. 47; the Divine truth in ultimates, n. 54.

LUNGS.
And heart of the church where the Word is read, n. 40.

MAIDENS.
In representation, n. 1.

MAN.
In consociation with spirits, but does not know it, n. 11; taught Divine truths by the Lord alone, through the Word, so far as he receives good in the will, n. 29; in a society of spirits as to affections and thoughts, as one with them, and so spirits speaking with him speak from his affections, n. 29; he cannot speak with others till these are removed, n. 29; in company with those of his own religion, n. 29; called knowing, spiritual angel intelligent, celestial wise, n. 52; his body contains innumerable things of all the sciences, n. 53; better for man in many passages to understand the Word according to the letter, n. 59.

MAN, THE DIVINE.
The Lord, n. 15.

MAN, GREATEST.
The heart and lungs in, where Word is read, n. 49; all in look toward middle region, n. 41.

MANGER.
In stable, representation, n. 1, 19.

MARRIAGE.
Of the Lord with the church, and of good with truth, the heavenly with man, n. 22, 23; in the particulars of the Word, n. 22, 23, 60; heaven compared to it, and the Word effects it, n. 23.

MASCHALIM.
Of the ancient Word, n. 37.

MASORITES.
Numbered the letters of the Word, n. 14.

MEMORY.
Knowledges in, extraneous, n. 29.

MICHAELS.
Those who thought they would be, n. 24.

MOHAMMEDANS.
Next to Roman Catholics in Greatest Man, n. 40.

MOON.
The Lord as to faith, n. 44.

MOUNTAIN.
Pindus signified the superior heaven, n. 18; Most Ancient Church worshiped on mountains, n. 19.

MYRRH.
Signifies natural good, n. 19.

MYSTICAL.
Things, said by the Jews to be in the Word, n. 19; are nothing else than spiritual sense, n. 21.

NAMES.
Of persons and places, signify things, n. 60.

NATURAL.
Confirmation by rational light of spiritual truths, n. 16; man has some natural idea of spiritual things, by which he turns them over and airs them rationally, n. 16; the natural gross and impure, n. 16; an external form and effect, empty without the spiritual, n. 52; natural, spiritual, and celestial as knowledge, intelligence, and wisdom, n. 52.

NATURAL SENSE.
Of the Word in the sense of the letter, becomes spiritual in second heaven and celestial in third, n. 2; claimed by certain spirits to be the only sense, n. 15; dead without the spiritual sense, but with the spiritual all holiness is in it, n. 15; herein the Word is in its fulness, its sanctity, and its power, n. 15; in this sense are seen all things of salvation, faith, and life, and from it is to be drawn every doctrine of the church, n. 15; conjunction by it with heaven, n. 15; spiritual sense drawn from according to correspondences, n. 17; may be under-

stood in simplicity, n. 20; meant by the garments which soldiers divided, and by the clouds of heaven, n. 20; without the sense of the letter the Word not the Word, this sense as a vessel filled with wine, and like man's bones and skin, in it rests the whole power of the Word, n. 25; some parts clothed, and some naked corresponding to face and hands and serving for doctrine of the church, being spiritual natural truths, n. 26; support and basis to the Word, n. 27; in simultaneous order, n. 35; our natural Word contains the spiritual and the celestial Word, but is not contained by them, and is thus fullest and most holy, n. 35; meant by the clouds, n. 44; no communication with heaven without, n. 47, 55; quality without the spiritual, n. 49–53; holiness in, n. 54–57; all power in, all answers given by, n. 55; better for man to understand the Word according to, in many passages, n. 59.

NATURAL THEOLOGY.
Nothing if not the Word, n. 16; reveals nothing, only confirms things known from the Word, n. 16; cannot lead into spiritual theology, but can be entered from spiritual, n. 16.

NATURE.
All a theatre representative of the Lord's kingdom, and this kingdom of Himself, n. 34.

NAZARITE.
The Lord as to ultimates, n. 25.

NEW JERUSALEM.
Stones of wall the ultimate sense of the Word, n. 25, 55.

NUMBERS.
In the Word, signify things, n. 60.

OLIVE-TREE.
Signifies the good of love, n. 19.

ORDER.
In heaven simultaneous, n. 56.

OVID.
Cited, n. 18.

PAPACY.
Babylon, for the most part natural and sensual, n. 20.

PAUL.
His experience, n. 6.

PEGASUS.
The understanding enlightened, n. 18.

PETER.
The man not meant, n. 20.

PINDUS.
n. 18.

POWER.
All in spiritual world belongs to Divine truth, proceeding from the Lord and based in letter of the Word, n. 54–57.

PREACHERS.
In highest heaven from intermediate angels, n. 3.

PROPRIUM.
Of man, mere evil and in darkness, n. 24.

PSALMS.
Heard sung, treated of the Lord, n. 46.

PURSES.
Stored with silver, representation, n. 1.

RAPHAELS.
Those who thought they would be, n. 24.

REFORMATION.
The, was effected by Divine providence, n. 42.

REFORMED CHURCH.
Distinguish between faith and charity and worship under three persons, and so would have falsified spiritual sense, n. 20; read the Word and so are means of light to the world, n. 42.

REGENERATION.
By means of the Word, its process, n. 28.

REVELATION.
Mediate superior to immediate, n. 29.

ROMAN CATHOLICS.
Round about those who read the Word, in Greatest Man, n. 49; Word almost rejected by, before the Reformation, n. 42; noble nation among, n. 42.

SAMSON.
Strength in his hair, n. 25.

SENECA.
Writings mentioned, n. 16.

SENSES.
Of the Word, see Celestial, Spiritual, Natural.

SENSES.
Objects of, have resemblance in the different degrees, n. 13.

SILVER.
In purses, representation, n. 1.

SIMULTANEOUS.
Order, n. 27.

SINGING.
Of Psalms, heard by Africans, n. 46.

SOCIETIES OF HEAVEN.
Chapters of the Word correspond to, n. 25, 60; are each a heaven in less form and in sight of the Lord as one man, arrangement in as in the whole heaven, n. 41.

SON OF MAN.
The Lord as to the Word, n. 25, 43.

SPACE.
And time in the thoughts of men, n. 8.

SPEECH.
Of different heavens not communicable, n. 3–11; of men and of angels of middle heaven from ideas of thought, but of angels of highest heaven all from variation of affections, n. 8; of angels and of men have nothing in common, n. 9; spiritual is one for all, and man comes into it after death, n. 9.

SPIRIT.
Or spirits, in consociation with man, but do not know it, and yet cannot live without it, n. 11; may ascend where angels are and see nothing, n. 16; not permitted to instruct men in Divine truths, n. 29; speak with man from his affections, and man cannot speak with others till they are removed n. 29; of man's own religion with him and confirm it, n. 29.

SPIRITUAL.
Subtile and pure compared with the natural, n. 16; to one coming from the natural appears the same, n. 31; compared with natural and celestial, n. 52, 61; spiritual angels called intelligent, n. 52; their language, from ideas, and correspondences, this shown them in their expressing natural and spiritual things by the same letter, n. 62.

SPIRITUAL-NATURAL.
Truths, n. 26, 27.

SPIRITUAL SENSE OF THE WORD.
Represented, n. 1; lives from the light of truth in second heaven, and from the flame of good in third heaven, n. 2; compared with natural, n. 15, 31; the soul and life of the Word, n. 15; subject of chapter, n. 17–21, 58; nothing but the sense of the letter drawn forth according to correspondences, n. 17; to interpret from falsities of doctrine closes heaven, but from truths opens, and by means of it man thinks with angels, n. 20; would appear as cloud to one in false doctrine, n. 20; meant by the inner garment, n. 20; revealed at the present day because doctrine of genuine truth is revealed, n. 21, 58; signified by appearance of the Lord in the clouds, and by the glory, n. 21, 58; its revelation promised in the *Apocalypse* and meant by the White Horse, and by the great supper of God, for a long time not to be acknowledged, as meant by the beast and the kings of the earth, n. 21; for those in spiritual kingdom and lower heavens, and treats of the church, n. 23; meant by the glory, n. 43; communication not given by without the natural sense, n. 47; holiness not in without the sense of the letter, n. 54–57; without the literal as house without foundation, the body without skin, what is contained without a containant, wine without a vessel, n. 54–57; none can see and none permitted to draw forth except from doctrine of genuine truth, from the Lord alone, doctrine never first drawn from, is Divine truth itself, its existence to be confirmed by ten passages, n. 58.

STAR.
Seen by the wise men, signified knowledge from heaven, n. 19; those who thought they would shine as stars in heaven, n. 24; by stars meant the Lord as to knowledges, n. 43.

STONES.
Of the New Jerusalem, are the ultimate sense of the Word, n. 25.

STYLE.
Of the Word, its excellence, n. 16.

SUCCESSIVE ORDER.
n. 27.

SUN.
Of this world, n. 8; by it meant the Lord as to love, n. 43; Sun of heaven, the Lord, n. 8.

INDEX OF WORDS

SWEDENBORG.
Experience in heaven, n. 4, 5, 9, 12, 24, 27, 45–47, 61, 62; in reading the Word, n. 25; not permitted to take anything from any spirit or angel, but from the Lord alone, n. 29.

THOUGHTS.
Of different heavens not communicable, n. 4–9; of man partake of time, space, and person, seen in the light of the world, n. 8, 9; angels of highest heaven do not have, but perceptions, n. 8.

TIME.
And space in thoughts of men, n. 8.

TREE.
Has innumerable things within, n. 50.

TRUTHS.
Pure in interior sense of the Word, n. 1; Divine truth perceived naturally is as a crystal vase, to be later filled with wine, n. 6; those who desire from love of truth, n. 24, 28; those who do not, n. 28; evil hates, angels and spirits not permitted to instruct men in, n. 29; ineffably increased in internal senses and heavens, n. 50; truth is the form of good, and gives good its quality, but exists from good as its cause, n. 51.

ULTIMATE.
Material, necessary basis for the heavens, n. 11; sense of the Word corresponds to the beard and hair, n. 25; binds together and contains interiors, n. 27; through it the Lord flows in from firsts, n. 15, 47.

URIM AND THUMMIM.
Represented letter of the Word, n. 55.

VASE.
Of crystal, compared to Divine truth perceived naturally, n. 6.

VINE.
Signifies truth of doctrine of faith, n. 19.

VIRGINS.
The nine signified knowledges, n. 18.

VOWEL.
Sounds in heaven, n. 14.

WIFE.
Representation of, n. 1; church so called, n. 22.

WILL.
Makes the life of man, taught by the understanding how to act, n. 29.

WINE.
Compared to interior truth, n. 6.

WISDOM.
Of angels from the Lord by the Word, n. 27; of the different heavens compared, n. 61; Divine is infinite, n. 61.

WISE.
Men from the East, n. 19.

WORD.
The falsification of at the present day, n. 1; interiorly living, n. 2; natural sense becomes spiritual in second heaven and celestial in third, n. 2, 35; written solely by correspondences, n. 2, 17, 27; holy even as to syllables and points, n. 14; how written in the third heaven, n. 14, 33; of Divine providence that the letters were numbered by the Masorites, n. 14; spiritual and natural senses compared, n. 15; its holiness is in sense of the letter, but not without the spiritual within, n. 15; compared to the Divine Man, n. 15; many expressions cited not to be understood without the spiritual sense, n. 15; alone gives light on things of the other life, n. 16; excellence of its style, n. 16; not a word nor letter that does not contain something of the Lord, because from God, n. 16; in its bosom, spiritual, n. 16; the Divine concealed in the Word as the soul in the body, and unfolded before angels when man reads reverently, and their sense of holiness communicated to man, n. 16, 23, 27; those who despise in the world, continue to despise after death, n. 17; those who favored the Word taken up into heaven, satans who opposed cast into hell, n. 17; they who do not believe in it cannot believe anything Divine from nature, n. 17; to its inmosts Divine, n. 20; note; everywhere two expressions and marriage of good and truth, and a spiritual sense for spiritual kingdom and celestial for celestial kingdom, n. 22, 23; the genuine truth is not seen by the worldly, n. 24; those who study from affection for truth, n. 24; ultimate sense of corresponds to the beard and hair, n. 25; the rest to other parts of man, n. 26; all things of correspond with all things of heaven and all things of man, n. 25; chapters correspond to societies and perceived in them, n. 25, 45; with-

out the ultimate not the Word, in that rests its whole power, n. 25; in some parts clothed, n. 27; first given after immediate revelation ceased, n. 27; contains the wisdom of the three heavens, n. 27; in all the heavens, n. 30-35, 40; read and preached from, is that from which angels have wisdom, the only means by which anything is known of the Lord, and of other arcana, without it would be no heaven, no church, and no conjunction with the Lord, in the spiritual kingdom is spiritual, n. 30; angel reading does not know it is not the same as on earth, n. 32; in inmosts treats of the Lord alone, n. 32; difference between celestial and spiritual, n. 32; in writing, n. 33; illustrated by different senses of first chapters of *Genesis*, n. 34; effect in heaven when read by children, n. 34; fullest and most holy in this world, n. 35; the ancient now lost, described, n. 36-38; the Word not read by Roman Catholics, and little in Russia, but believed to be holy, n. 39; preserved in Old Testament by Jews and dispersed through much of the earth, establishing communication with heaven, n. 39; enough that there be some place on earth where the Word is, there the heart and lungs, n. 40; in the church of the Reformed enlightens all peoples, n. 42; spiritual sense now revealed, n. 44; heaven opened by it to man and conjoined with him, n. 45; things inwardly in the Word appear to angels as if thought of themselves, communication of the whole heaven given by the letter of the Word, n. 45-47, 55; in letter compared to a tree, n. 53; spiritual sense to its nutrition, n. 53; so falsified by Jews there was no longer an ultimate of Divine truth in man, n. 54; all answers by letter of the Word, n. 55; doctrine to be confirmed by literal sense and then has power, n. 57; not first seen from spiritual sense, n. 58; better for man in many passages to understand from sense of letter, n. 59; marriage of good and truth in, chapters and expressions pertaining to good and others to truth, each chapter has reference to one society and many to all, some passages have a sense from letters alone, n. 60; how written in spiritual kingdom, with points signifying affections, seen by Swedenborg, also something of that in celestial kingdom with curves and spirals, n. 61; among spiritual angels, n. 62.

WORLD.

Those who seek the things of see no genuine truth in the Word, n. 24.

WRITING.

In the heavens, not like natural, nor in one heaven as in another, n. 9; described, n. 33, 61, 62.

The Last Judgment
(POSTHUMOUS)

The Last Judgment
(POSTHUMOUS)

VARIOUS THINGS CONCERNING

The Spiritual World

Argument Concerning The Judgment

ALSO

Several Minor Works

TRANSLATED FROM THE LATIN NOTES OF

Emanuel Swedenborg

TRANSLATOR'S NOTE.

The following posthumous tracts of Swedenborg have not previously appeared in book or pamphlet form in an English translation. Most of them have appeared in whole or in part in serial form in the *New Jerusalem Magazine*, and in *New Church Life*, and fragments of them in the *Intellectual Repository*. They are now brought together for the first time in book form, that they may be more fully available for use by the readers of Swedenborg. The numbering of the *Last Judgment* and the *Spiritual World* is made consecutive, to conform with the divisions used in *Potts' Concordance*. All these Minor Works are incomplete, and are evidently notes from which materials were drawn in the preparation of the works published by Swedenborg. Nevertheless, they are of great interest and value, oftentimes presenting the truth in a new and striking way.

JOHN WHITEHEAD.

CONTENTS.

	PAGE
The Last Judgment	379
The Spiritual World	478
Argument Concerning the Judgment	515
Five Memorable Relations	521
Conversations with Angels	533
Justification and Good Works	537
A Conversation with Calvin	547
God the Saviour Jesus Christ	552
Sketch of the Doctrine of the New Church	555

The Last Judgment.
(POSTHUMOUS.)

THE ENGLISH.

1. The English appear a little to the right, in front, in a plane just above the head. The light with them appears more interior than with others in the Christian world, by which light the spiritual is received which flows in from above. They see clearly in a moment what flows in, and at once receive it; nor do they let it down into their natural so grossly as others. Hence it is that the spiritual appears clear also in the natural; but with others more obscure. But they who are such, are those who have loved what is right and sincere, and have acted from truth and sincerity, and who at the same time have thought of God from religion.

2. When the Last Judgment was being executed, the Protestants were then led into the middle, and they then appeared in this order: The English in the middle, the Dutch towards the east and south, the Germans more towards the north, the Swedes to the north and west in the middle. All then appeared according to their general genius as to the reception of good and truth.

3. Few of the English become genii, whose quality may be described, since they do not depend much on their own thought, but on the mouth of authority: for they easily receive if only they are persuaded that the man is learned and sincere, and of their own nation; their thought then appears lucid and interior.

4. It was perceived that many of the English will receive the Heavenly Doctrine, and thereby come into the New Jerusalem; because they are such that they receive the truths of faith more easily than others, and see them in interior light.

5. I have spoken with the English concerning their natural disposition; whence it is with them, that when they hear truths from one among them worthy of belief, they then see them, and thus easily conform to them; and whence it is that with them there is a snowy appearance above their natural, that it is from heavenly light, from which is intelligence: in like manner with the Dutch. But as to the Dutch, with them there is not that snowy appearance, but something firm in the confines of their spiritual and natural minds; and that therefore they are slower. The cause of the appearance of the light with the English was told, namely, that it is from their life, which differs from the life of all other nations. That the cause might be perceived, a comparison was made with the Italians of this day; that their governments are altogether opposite. In England there is freedom to speak and write both on civil and spiritual things; but no freedom at all to use deceit and cunning to deceive others, nor to lie in wait to murder, rob and kill; and if they do it, there is no remission. But it is the opposite with the Italians at this day. In Italy there is freedom to deceive by cunning and guile, and also to kill; which freedom they have from so many asylums, and from the dispensations: but there is no freedom at all to speak and write on ecclesiastical and civil affairs there, on account of the inquisition. Hence it is that the Italian nation retains such things within, and thus a fire, which is a slow hatred, revenge, and cruelty; which fire is like that which, after a conflagration, lies hid long under the ashes, and consumes. But with the English nation it is otherwise, because it is allowed to speak and write freely. There such a fire is not laid up, but immediately burns out; and they are kept in what is sincere and just by the fact that they are not permitted to deceive, to rob, and to kill; since there is then no dispensation, nor anywhere an asylum.

6. The English have quite an exquisite perception that a thing is so, when it is said from reason. They have an interior sight as to religion; but this sight which they have is a receptive sight, but not so active that they can see before it has been confirmed by some celebrated leader among them. Their interior sight is called the intuitive and affirmative sight of reception, and likewise confirmative; but chiefly by means of elegant things composed in a spiritual manner; and this descends and proceeds from that snowy appearance of theirs. This appears with them in the spiritual world; on which account also they are in the middle among Christians: for those are in the middle who are in interior light.

7. It was shown of what quality a book or writing appears to them, which has been approved by a man in whose erudition they have confidence; and of what quality a book or writing appears, which is not yet approved. In writings not approved, when they are read, they see nothing but the mere letter, or the sense of the letter; but in an approved writing they see the sense of the matter, and not of the letter; because they are then in enlightenment from the belief that it is so: so that approval gives enlightenment. On which account a writing, howsoever[1] important, is not procured before it has been praised by a man worthy of belief.

8. Since the English are of such a genius, there are therefore set over them priests, and also magistrates, in whom they have confidence that they are intelligent and wise; and they then yield a favoring assent to them in everything which they say and teach. By this they are held in obedience, and likewise in doctrine. But they who are not compliant, and they who are wicked, are shut out of their society; for these loose the bond and unanimity.

9. I have had much discourse with English priests concerning faith, among whom also were bishops. Because it was according to their doctrine, they insisted that faith alone produces the endeavor to good. But to the question, whether by endeavor they meant man's manifest will, this they were unwilling to admit; because everything that proceeds from man's manifest will is in itself not good, and is meritorious; wherefore by endeavor they meant an internal operation, about which the understanding knows little: consequently that such endeavor is inwardly in faith, and that it is not manifested openly except by an inclination to doing. In this opinion they were so tenacious, and also in this, that faith produces the good which is called charity, that they were not willing to be led, although it was told them from heaven, that faith does not produce anything of charity, but that charity produces faith; and that faith before charity is not living faith, but only knowledge; and that a man ought to do good as of himself, and that otherwise nothing of good is inrooted and implanted: but to this they shut their ears. When they were told that one of the most talented of them[1] had thought out reasons and ways, even to a hundred, to confirm that faith produces charity, and that he had wandered through each way, as is done in the spiritual world by thinking that it is so; but still, when he came to the end of the way, he saw from enlightenment given him that he had been wandering, which he also as often confessed. Also when their solemn exhortation at the Holy Supper was read before them, wherein these things are said,[1] . . . they thought, but were unwilling to say, that this is said for the laity, and that the doctrine is for the clergy: wherefore it was announced to them, that life according to the faith of the laity saves; but life according to the doctrine of the clergy condemns: since in the faith of the clergy there is no life, and in their life there is no faith; but there is in the faith and life of the laity.

10. In the spiritual world images and many other things can be formed from the ideas of thought, and be presented to the sight; which is peculiar to that world. Wherefore the same English priests undertook to form an image in the likeness of a man, from the ideas of their thoughts concerning faith alone, or faith separate from charity; which image, when it was made, appeared monstrous, as not unlike Dagon, the idol of the Philistines in Ekron; therefore it was cast into a certain lake.

11. It is said of the English in the spiritual world, that they love elegance in their discourses; and that such elegance has indeed a delightful sound in the ears, but still gives little instruction; especially when they treat of faith, and of justification by it: that they then so arrange their words, that scarcely any one knows whether anything of good is to be done or not. They so weave together series of conclusions, that they sound as if good should be done; although these conclusions involve that faith produces them without their knowing it.

12. In the spiritual world the face of the earth is similar to what it is in the natural world. There are urban and country places there. They who dwelt in cities in our world, dwell also in cities there: in like manner those who lived in country places. Moreover, the cities in the spiritual world are similar to the cities in the natural world, but only as to the streets and public squares; but they are not similar as to the buildings. Neither do the good and the evil dwell promiscuously there; but in the middle of the city, where also are the public buildings,[1] dwell the best, who are the governors and magistrates. To the east there are those who are in the clear good of love, to the west those who are in the obscure good of love, to the south those who are in the clear light of truth, to the north those who are in the obscure light of truth. The good of love and the truth of faith decrease from the middle unto the farthest circumferences. Since the cities there are similar to the cities in our world, there is also a London there similar to London as to the streets; but not as to the houses, neither as to the inhabitants, nor their habitations in the quarters. I was conducted into it in the spirit, and wandered through it, and recognized it. And I spoke with certain ones there, and said that men in the world would wonder, and would not believe that they who live in London see a London also after death; and if they are good, also dwell in their city: yet it is altogether so. They said that neither would they have believed it, when they were in the world; because such a thing does not fall into sensual ideas, but only into rational ideas enlightened by spiritual light; also that they did not then know that the spiritual appears before a spirit, as the material does before a man; and that all the things which exist in the spiritual world are from a spiritual origin, as all the things in the natural world are from a material origin: in like manner the houses of a city, which are not built as in the world, but rise up in a moment created by the Lord: so too all other things. They rejoiced that now as before they are in England, and in its great city; and they said that there is also another London below, not dissimilar as to the streets, but dissimilar as to the houses and as to the inhabitants: namely, that the evil dwell in the middle, and the upright in the last circumferences; and that those come into that London from the London in the world, who have not been in any spiritual love, and hence not in any spiritual faith, but have indulged the pleasures of the body and the lusts of the mind. Also that the city, in the middle where the evil dwell, sinks down by turns into the deep; and the evil are thus cast down into hell: and that the opening is renewed, and the evil are again collected into the middle of it, and again are swallowed up by hell. This is in the world of spirits, it is different in heaven, and different in hell.

THE DUTCH.

13. They are quite clear-sighted, and remain constantly in their own religion; not receding unless altogether convinced; and if they are convinced, they still turn the back. They excel in judgment from natural rational light, from which they look into things in the world justly, especially in business. Their light appears more obscure, because their spiritual light is conjoined with natural light: the reason is, because they are continually thinking about business.

14. With the Dutch there is not that snowy appearance which is with the English, but in place of it something firm; which is an indication that they are constant in the things of their religion. But there is this difference, that on civil, moral, and likewise spiritual subjects, they judge from themselves, and not from others: and they reflect especially upon intellectual things, and upon the connection of reasons.

15. The Dutch appear in the angle towards the east and south; to the east because they love religion bare without images, that they may look at it in itself, but not from images; to the south, because they excel in understanding.

16. It is a general trait of the Dutch nation, that they are strong in judgment from natural light, from which they take a very just view of things, especially of those that are of the world: and because they are continually thinking about their business, the spiritual light hides itself in the natural; on which account also they are able to receive what is true in religion: but still, when they are convinced, they turn the back.

17. The Dutch are not so eager for money as for business itself. Business itself is their end and love, and is in the first place; and money is the mediate end, and is loved for the sake of business; thus it is in the second place. And they who are such, are loved in heaven; each one is esteemed according to his use. It is otherwise with the avaricious, as the Jews are, with whom money is in the first place as the very end and love, and business in the second place. Hence is avarice, which is sordid according to the love of money alone.

18. At the day of the Last Judgment,[1] those of the Dutch who had done nothing of good from any religion or conscience, but only for the sake of reputation, that for the sake of gain they might appear sincere, were cast out of their cities, villages and lands: for with such, when the regard for reputation and gain is taken away, which is done in the spiritual world, then such rush into every wickedness, despoiling whomsoever they happen to meet in the fields or outside of the cities. I saw a great number of such cast into a dark chasm extending obliquely under the eastern tract, and likewise into a chasm extending under the southern tract. This expulsion was seen on the 9th day of January, 1757. Those remained with whom there was religion and from religion conscience.

19. I was in the spirit, and it was then granted me to wander through a rather distinguished city, in which were Dutch. All the streets in it were seen to be roofed over, and in the streets were closed gates of wood; on which account, without leave from some overseer, it was not permitted to wander around. But afterwards it was granted me to speak with the magistrates, who dwelt in the middle of the city; by whom I was examined as to whence I came, and what I wanted: and when they understood that it was only for the sake of seeing, that I might make known to their brethren who were still in the world, what their lot was, and what kind of dwellings they had; they then related to me many things, especially that they who dwelt there were among the prudent and intelligent from that nation; and that there are many such cities, distinct according to the affections and perceptions of truth from good; and that they were in the world of spirits; and that after some time passed there, they were taken up thence into heaven, and introduced into societies there, and became angels: also that the city was double and triple, or city under city; and when one descends by ladders, he comes into a new city, where those reside who are different as to affections. They said that their streets are everywhere roofed over, because sometimes from the rocks round about, which are somewhat higher, they are looked at by the evil who are skilled in the perversion of souls by means of ideas, and in inducing lusts that are not congruous; and that they know how to bind the ideas, if by any means they penetrate; by which they were kept in anxiety, and as it were bound; and this even to despair: which was also shown me to the life. If any one comes to them, who is of another genius, and therefore disagrees as to the affections and the thoughts thence, they order him to go away; and when he goes, he everywhere finds the gates closed: on which account he is led to other gates that he may go out, but he still finds them closed: and in the meantime they breathe into him a longing to go out; and this is done until he becomes so weary, that he can no longer endure it; and only then is he let out: and when let out he does not return, on account of the vexation into which he has been driven. The Dutch, more than the rest in the Christian world, know what fantasy is, and what reality; so that they cannot be deluded, like others.

20. It is not allowed to speak anything with them about religion; wherefore, when anyone comes to them from another religion, he is examined, not by the living voice, and by oral answer; but without his knowledge they explore his thoughts, and draw therefrom what is with them. It has likewise been given to speak with the priests; and I have spoken with them concerning the Lord from the Heavenly Doctrine; and they acknowledged the truths, and were affected. They were then in enlightenment from the Lord. From these things it was granted me to know, that they have a perception of truth above others, both spiritual and civil; and that they look out prudently for themselves, and that this is implanted in them.

21. In their cities, the men dwell at one side of the city, and the women at the other: and when the men desire, they send to them, and the women come; who are indignant at this, that they are thus to come at the command of the man. And they who in the world had ruled over their husbands, when the like is not given them, being kindled with indignation, wish to go out of the city. They are also sent out; but when they are outside of the city, there appears to them everywhere some obstruction and closure, now marshy, now watery, now something else. Thus they wander, and for a long time seek for places of getting away, and this even to fatigue: wherefore they are compelled to return into the city; and they enter their house, and so are amended. The reason is, that the desire of ruling in marriage takes away conjugial* love; which increases with a consort as the love of ruling decreases. In place of this then comes love, and with love enjoyment of life; and then neither the man nor the wife, but the Lord, rules: hence is happiness in marriages.

22. The Dutch appear clothed with coats and breeches altogether as in the world; and they are distinguished from others by the fact that their human derives more from the world than the human of others: for the spiritual does not shine through so clearly as with others. This they derive from their love for business in the world, and thence their continual thought and speculation about it. Even when they come into the spiritual world, they revolve similar things in the mind, and look around on all sides to see where there is trading, and what its quality is: for there is trading in the spiritual world equally as in the natural world; but still the difference is such that it can scarcely be described; and what I wondered at, when they meet with business men who wish to search into their thoughts and intentions secretly by close inspection, as is done there, they forthwith become invisible; which is from this, that they were unwilling in the world to divulge their business to others.

23. All, whosoever come among spirits after death, are prepared either for heaven or for hell, every one according to the life formed from doctrine. The preparation is made with most by instructions from the angels. But the Dutch cannot be prepared for heaven and for receiving the spiritual of heaven, which is also the spiritual of the angels, by means of information, for they do not receive it; for they remain more constantly than all others in their faith. When they are informed, they still think from themselves against it. Therefore they are prepared in another manner. Heaven is described to them as to its quality, it is then granted them to ascend into heaven, and see it; and whatever agrees with their genius is insinuated into them, so that they return with the full desire of coming into heaven. But when they are sent back, they are reduced to misery, and business is taken away

---

*Tafel has *conjugalem*; but the MS. has *conjugialem*.

from them, until they see themselves reduced to extremities, and then they are led around to those who abound in all things, and who are rich; and then the thought is borne upon them, what the quality of these is, and how they can be in such abundance, and in the delight of life. They thus reflect upon the life of these, that it is a life of mutual love; also upon their doctrine, that it is the doctrine of that love; and that all their good and pleasant things are from the Lord: and then they are not informed, but inquire themselves, and inform themselves, and thus think from themselves, that in order to get out of their misery they also must believe and do in like manner: and as they receive that faith, but of themselves through the life, abundance is then given them, and so on successively. They are thus prepared for heaven, not by others, but by themselves; not knowing then that they still are not prepared thus by themselves, but by the Lord; because they are such that they also afterwards acknowledge. They are afterwards more constant also than others, so that they may be called constancies; nor do they suffer themselves to be drawn away by any deceit, or by any art, or by reasoning, or by obscurity from insinuated doubts and from sophistries, or by any fallacy, appearance, or fantasy: especially they whose life's love was business, and not money; and whose end was not a sumptuous life.

CALVIN.

24. It was said of Calvin, that he lived a Christian life, and did not place religion in faith alone, as Melancthon and Luther did; and that therefore he is in heaven.

25. Calvin was seen in a society of heaven, in front above the head, but not in the middle of it; and he said that he was in a like doctrine of the church, in which he was in the world. He told me, that he did not agree with Luther, nor with Melancthon, upon faith alone; since faith and works are so often named in the Word, and are commanded to be done; and that faith and works are therefore to be conjoined: but that Luther felt that if works were admitted, they would not recede far from the papists; but he believed that faith produces works, as a tree does fruit. Calvin is accepted in his society, because he is upright and does not make a disturbance; this I heard from one of the governors of the society.

MELANCTHON.

26. I have spoken with Melancthon and with others concerning him. After he came into the spiritual world, Melancthon confirmed himself in faith alone more than before, so that he was scarcely willing to hear of charity, and of its good: and as he could not persuade any others but those who had led a life scarcely Christian, he therefore procured to himself a persuasive power; which is such that the speech flows into the thought of another, and thus binds it; so that the man is deprived of the power of thinking anything but what is said, though it be false. It fascinates the mind; on which account it is forbidden there; for it extinguishes all light of the understanding; and those whom he could not convince by reasonings, he looked into their eyes, and infused such a persuasion into their minds, that they could not see the falsities nor the sophistries, thus could not answer; on which account they complained about him. This he also tried with me, but with a fruitless effort. Leeks and the smell of them or garlic correspond to this persuasive power; which smell, by its pungency, hurts the left eye. I spoke with him concerning the power of persuasion, and concerning the Nephilim who were in it; who could almost kill a man by their persuasion; concerning which see in the *Arcana Cœlestia*.

27. There came to me afterwards, from the northern quarter toward the west, certain spirits among the more cunning and malicious; and among them one, who was distinguished from the others by his heavy gait: it was a gait sounding like a bear's. He did many things maliciously; nor did I know who he was. It was afterwards disclosed that he was Melancthon. And that I might know that it was he, he asked where Luther was; and when it was told, he entered in to him, and spoke before him, and was recognized. It was said by Luther, that he spoke much with him about faith alone, or faith separate from good works. Luther inquired of him, what his lot now was: and he disclosed that he was by turns in a chamber panelled above, and by turns in hell under a judge: that when he was in the chamber, he was clothed in a skin like a bearskin, by which he protected himself from the cold; and that he wrote much about faith alone; that when he was in hell under the judge, he was held vile like the rest, and I heard the judge speak of him, that there he was evil, and was sometimes punished for his wicked deeds.

28. It was further said, that in that chamber the walls are of stone only, without decorations, as elsewhere; and thus it is rude and sad there. On which account, when any, because of his reputation in the world, wish to meet him and speak with him, he does not admit them, because he is ashamed of the rude things there. He sometimes acknowledges that he has been in falsities, and that thence he is such: on which account he sometimes prays that in his chamber he may write concerning charity, and its goods, which are called good works; and then some things are dictated to him from heaven by angels; and when he writes them, the chamber begins to be adorned with various decorations. But after he has written them, and left them upon the table, and read them over, he does not see them; and what he sees, he does not understand; and then the decorations of the chamber vanish: such is his lot.

29. I heard him speaking with Englishmen[1] out of his panelled apartment. He spoke of faith alone. They said that they do not know what faith alone is. He said that God the Father sent His Son, who suffered for our sins. They said that this is historical: what besides? He said that by that faith they have eternal life. They said, "Did he have eternal life?" To this he could not answer. They said, moreover, that they hear preachers of faith alone, and of justification by it; and when they are hearing, the preaching sounds as if full of wisdom, because it is a well arranged and ingenious composition. But when they come home, they know nothing of what they have spoken, not comprehending their arcana.

30. I afterwards saw Melancthon among many who held to faith alone, in the place where they are separated, every one at length goes to the place of his life; and I then heard a voice to them from heaven, that that faith saves no one, because there is nothing of the life in it, nor is there truth in it. On which account they asked, what truth is, and what life is. It was answered that truth and life is to live according to the commandments of the Decalogue: as not to steal, that is, not to act insincerely and unjustly; not to commit adultery; not to kill, or thus, not to burn with deadly hatred and revenge against any one; not to testify falsely, thus not to lie and defame: and that he who does not do these things because they are sins, has life; and many more truths are afterwards given to him,—what evil is, and what good is: and that no other one can be led by the Lord, and be saved: and that it may thence be known, that life and truth are one, as love and faith are; for life is of love, and truth is of faith.

LUTHER.

31. There are places where they contend about religious affairs. Outside of these places their contentions are heard as the gnashing of teeth: and when they are viewed within, it appears as if they were tearing off each other's garments; and their sphere causes pain to the flesh of the teeth and the gums. There came one to me therefrom, with a religious garb, like a monk; and it was said that it was Luther. And he spake with me, saying that he wished to be among such as contend about things to be believed; because he has brought with him from the world a persuasiveness of speech, and an authority from the consent of many of his time. I observed that he had communication with those who believe that they know all things, and that nothing at all is hidden from them, and who do not wish to learn, but to teach; often saying that is the truth, and that it cannot be contradicted. Such take away from others all freedom of speaking, by inducing their opinions as if they were from God, and by infesting all who contradict, unless for the sake of information. He said that he loves to reason about faith, and likewise about the good of charity; but that he rarely[1] finds those with whom he could be in that delight, for the reason that he had hatched[2] that doctrine from his thought, and that he is thence in the connection of things. It is otherwise with those who only learn it, and afterwards confirm it; they cannot be in such delight, because they are not in such connection of things. He said that they did not long endure his ardor of speaking, but withdraw.

32. It was given to speak with him concerning faith and love, concerning truth and good, and concerning their marriage, that no more is given from the one than from the other, consequently no more from faith than from life. I spoke with him for two hours with ideas from spiritual light, which are very many;[2] and angelic spirits were then associated with him, for the sake of interior perception: and being at length convinced, he said that he wished to receive that doctrine; but that he doubted whether he could, before the principles respecting faith alone were cast out; which is a matter of labor; on which account also, when he went away, he returned to them, with whom he reasoned as before.

33. But the angels said that there was some hope of him; because as often as he had thought from his spirit in the world, that is, when left to himself in tranquillity, he had thought about good works, and made them a matter of religion; and it was thence that he spoke so much and wrote so much concerning the good of life, though he did not make it a part of his doctrine, nor to be done for the sake of eternal life; since man cannot do good from himself; and if he does, it is for the sake of heaven, and is a matter of merit. But yet, when he came out of the thought of his spirit into discourse with others, he then, as if turned round, spoke concerning faith alone. He does in like manner at this day. This was the reason that he rejected from the Word the Epistle of *James*, and also the *Apocalypse*.

34. Some have two states, the one when in discourse from doctrine, the other when he thinks with himself. In the former state he is in the body and in its wakefulness, because he is in the lower thought of the speech, and is then in the pleasure of speaking, and for the most part in the pride of learning: but in the latter state he is in his spirit, and then in obscurity, because he thinks within the body, and above the thought next to the natural sensual. This was the case with Luther. He was in the pleasantness of his life, because in the pleasantness of glory, when he was speaking; and this was about faith alone, from his doctrine: but when he was deliberating with himself, he was in favor of good works. Such thought by himself in obscurity remained to him from boyhood, because he was born in that religion, and was a monk. But as he hatched out a new [doctrine][1] he undertook to withdraw from that religion, by the separation of faith from good works.

35. Luther related that when he was in the world, it was told him by an angel from the Lord, that he should beware of faith alone, because there was nothing in it; and that for some time he guarded against it, and recommended works: but that he still continued afterwards to separate faith from works, and to make it alone essential and saving.

36. After Luther was informed by the angels, that no one has any faith unless he has the good of life; and that he has just so much of faith as he has of the good of life, and has no more of the one than of the other; and as he was many times convinced of it: he repented and labored with all his might to get out of the falsities, because he could not come into heaven until he did. I perceived several times that he had repented of it, and that he was laboring against his principles, but still in vain. He also prayed to the Lord that he might be able to recede from his falsities; and he received the answer, that it would be given, if he could receive it. On which account he was sent from one society to another, where those were with whom life was conjoined to faith; but still he could not tarry long, because it was contrary to the delight of his life. It was said to him, that truths of doctrine cannot be received by the life before falsities are rejected, because truths cannot enter where falsities fill the thoughts of the understanding; and that these cannot be easily removed. The reason is, because a man, while he lives in the world, conjoins himself to societies according to the principles of his religion, which had been matters of his affection. In these he likewise remains after death; and in those societies is every one's life: on which account it is not granted to remove and extricate himself from them, and then betake himself into new ones. It is granted, indeed, as to the thoughts, but it is not granted as to the affections; and yet they act as one. Wherefore the man enters into the new ones; but still withdraws, when he feels undelightful things in the new societies. In a word, Luther sometimes execrates faith alone, and sometimes defends it: he execrates it when he is in fear, and defends it when he is in his love.

ZINZENDORF AND THE MORAVIANS.

ZINZENDORF.

37. I spoke with Zinzendorf after his death, and then his life, his life's affection, and his principles of religion were disclosed; for a spirit can be let into such a state, that he keeps silence upon absolutely nothing, but lays all things open. It was then laid open, (1) *That he had been the greatest persuader; and that he persuaded by asseverations that he knew the arcana of heaven; and that no one comes into heaven but he who is of his doctrine.* (2) That at first he spoke with others according to their religion, thus simulating and thus alluring; and that he afterwards implanted his own secrets by first *examining well whether they would be received and concealed.* (3) It was said that the mystery of his faith had been, that the Lord was born that He might be the adopted Son of God; and that he had at first believed that the Lord was simply the adopted Son of God, [because He had taken on Himself the passion of the cross]; thus that he was an Arian. (4) That he had believed that His Divine was like the divine as with others; but now that it was something more. (5) He hardly wished to hear about the Lord's conception from the Divine, as related in *Matthew* and *Luke;* but turned himself away, and was unwilling *to say what he felt: and that this is the mystery which they are afraid to manifest.* That he attributed sins to the Lord, and said that in the Evangelists He did not speak better than another man, *calling them obscure things:* that he cared nothing for the Old Testament, and was not willing to hear that the things written there are concerning the Lord. (6) That he rejects all the life of charity, and says it is execrable *to think of God and of salvation and the rest*[1] *as to the life:* and that faith separate from charity saves. (7) He believed that he alone with his followers would come into heaven; and that these *alone were living*, and the rest dead. (8) They speak of themselves what the Lord did of Himself, namely, that they are sons of God; that they are without sins; that they are life and truth; because there is not any evil regarded with those who are in faith: and that for that reason they are life and truth, and call their life *blameless because they live by faith.*

38. Still they love the Lord, since to love Him is commanded, because He suffered the cross to propitiate the Father; which is the faith that saves them.

39. Because he believed that he alone with his followers were to come into heaven, abundant opportunity was given him to ascend into the heavens; and wherever he was, he was ordered to go away, because they perceived from him falsities together with the delight of glory, from the fact that he had established a church. It was perceived that there was merit in the delight of glory. He also spoke with his brethren about heaven; they said that it is not heaven to them.

40. A spirit appeared to me in vision, bearing a stag in bonds; but which burst the bonds, and rushed with fury against those he met, wishing to lacerate and destroy them. But there then appeared an enormous dog, which, rushing upon the stag, lacerated him, and tore him to pieces. The stag was afterwards seen in the human form,—it was Dippel who [appeared thus,] because he was not allowed to go about refuting all from the delight of his life, and at the same time to excite disturbance. And Zinzendorf said that he had loved him, but that he had observed that he afterwards receded; and that he was such that he wished to lacerate all by his malignant writings; and that he could refute ingeniously, as if full of science and wisdom; and that this gift was natural to him; but that of himself he thought foolishly concerning things.

41. Zinzendorf, when he first came into the spiritual world, began to wander around to societies and preach, as he had done in the world. But it was said that he was nowhere received, and was conducted away to his Moravian adherents, and perceived that they were not in heaven, but were in misery, because they contemptuously rejected all uses of life, which are good works; *when they wish to receive truths, falsities* oppose which cannot be dispersed, because they have loved them exceedingly. They know how to falsify the Word and to twist it from its genuine sense in a dextrous and skilful manner; which is done when gathered in an assembly. Some of their attempts against their companions were disclosed, who wished to disprove those mysteries, or also to reveal them; and Zinzendorf said that he therefore removed himself from them. They say that the Lord is *to be loved on account of the passion of the cross*, but *that He is not to be worshiped.* They call the Holy Supper a reminder of the passion.

42. Zinzendorf was in an abstract idea, thinking within himself concerning the Lord. It was observed that he thought of the Lord as of another man, and not that He is God; and that the Divine in Him was as the Divine in another man; and that the Lord spoke in a very simple manner, and not wisely; and that Paul spoke more wisely: but it was shown him that all the Lord's words were words of life, because in each one of them there is a spiritual sense; thus that each one of His words filled heaven, because He spoke by correspondences.

43. He believed that all things were of mercy, and that if a brother commits a grievous sin, this *is remitted to him*, because *to God that is the means of mercy:* that they are altogether condemned; and that *it is better for Sodom and Gomorrah than for those who do good works for the sake of salvation; and that this is the sin of sins*, because *they claim to themselves the merit which is Gods's alone.*

44. When Zinzendorf was rejected wherever he came, as he saw his Moravian adherents in an unhappy state, he suffered himself to be convinced that he was in falsities, and for that reason labored with all his might and still labors to disperse his falsities, and to receive truths in their stead: but he confessed that he could not tear himself away from the societies in which he inserted himself while in the world; because every man is one with them nor can he afterwards dissociate himself: for this is meant by the Lord's words respecting the five foolish virgins, that they afterwards wished to buy oil, and likewise bought it; but still could not enter into the wedding.

The Moravians.

45. *That the Arians induce pain in the right arm, near the shoulder-blade: but the Socinians induce pain in the breast-bone.*

46. The Moravians conceal their *mysteries of mysteries*, and close up the ways, lest they should be known by others; insinuating themselves through such things from the Lutheran doctrine as agree, proclaiming that they are the remains of the Apostolic Church, who call themselves brethren; and that they have mothers, and certain statutes from the early Christians; but as to the interiors of religion they differ from them altogether. They do not acknowledge the *Divine of the Lord as anything else than what is with any other man who is in that faith.* They speak lightly of the Word of the Old Testament, and reject it as of no use. The *Gospels* they do not care for, only Paul's Epistles. They condemn the goods of charity or good works, as to salvation, professing faith separate from charity more than others. Because they are Arians, I spoke with them concerning the Lord. They said that He was sent by God the Father, that by the passion of the cross He might save the human race, and on account of it was acknowledged as a Son, and called the Son of God; that their faith is confidence, that they love the Lord as the best man, because He took upon Himself to propitiate the Father by the passion of the cross. They say that the Lord has power in heaven, and not over heaven. *They call Him the Lamb, nor do they ever adore Him as God.* When it is said to them, that He was conceived of God, that He says He was from eternity, and that the Father and He are one, they hear these things, but they think against them. They dare not say that it was so written, but was not said: and such things concerning the Lord they miserably distort, and as it were lacerate. They therefore take refuge in these words, that they themselves know how it is, but it is among their mysteries of mysteries.

47. They call only themselves who are of that faith alive, and all others who are not in that faith, dead; and they believe that themselves are saved above all others, and *that they are to come into the third heaven: but when they come into the first or lowest heaven among the angels, they do not endure the heavenly sphere* *there, which is derived especially from the goods of charity, and so far from faith; and they therefore flee away thence.* Their aversion for that sphere has been perceived and felt by me. And moreover, in *no heavenly society are they tolerated*, because they think within themselves that all others but they are dead; thus also they have a dead idea concerning the angels themselves. *If they come into the second heaven, and especially into the third, where love and charity, and thence the works of charity make the all of heaven, they are seized with pain as those who lie in the death struggle; and lividness comes over their eyes, and they make convulsive motions, and are tortured inwardly.*

48. They have preached much that they have a certain interior sensation and perception, which they say is from an influx from God the Father through heaven, by means of angels or spirits. But it was told them, that they have that sensation or perception from spirits who were Moravians in the world, *and that they are in the midst of them*, and that these *flow in from similar principles*, and confirm; which is done strongly, because they love their religious persuasion and think much about it. This was shown them to the life; also that the Quakers are in society with Quaker spirits, Enthusiasts with enthusiastic spirits, and every man with spirits who make one with the affections, and the thoughts or principles taken therefrom; and that it is never otherwise. On account of the living experience they could not but affirm this, though they were unwilling.

49. The good which they do to the brethren of their assembly they call the good of friendship; and they have something of hatred against those who preach good works.

50. Because they observe that no one can come into heaven except those who acknowledge the Divine of the Lord, and they cannot do this, they recede from love towards the Lord on account of the passion of the cross, and act as one with the infernals. From that hatred they have it with themselves as it were implanted, that they persecute the angelic spirits in ways sometimes nefarious; but they are severely punished.

51. They rarely hold companionship with others: they appeared at first to the right in the plane of the knees; but by turns they were diminished, cast off, and scattered. *Among themselves they speak of their mysteries with closed doors,* and

severely prohibit the revelation of these mysteries unless by general consent; yea, they threaten: whether from those threats something has broken forth in the world; they were not willing to be explored, [nor] what they had done against some.[1]

52. They call all things with them, when in their faith and confidence, holy.

53. There flows out from their sphere a perception of heinous adultery, because they adulterate the Word throughout, and likewise mock at many things therein.

54. They appeared to the left in the plane of the foot, where it was disclosed that they made one with the evil, against those who have been in the goods of charity, and acknowledged the Divine of the Lord; all of whom are angelic spirits; and become angels: wherefore they were driven away towards the north. But because they were there not willing to become quiet, but that they would plot evil, calling to their aid the[1] Babylonians, on this account they were driven still more remotely into the north, and sent into a cavern, which tended obliquely under the west, that they might no longer injure others. They form a brotherhood everywhere.

55. They were compelled to an interior confession of the Lord; and I then heard profane things, such as I should scarcely dare to publish; denying, yea, profaning the things which are said there concerning the conception of the Son by the Father; that He was carried away from the sepulchre by the disciples; that the transfiguration was a vision induced by fantastic spirits; that He was a man so low that He was lower than others; besides more heinous things; from which it was evident that they are the worst of all in Christendom, and that they have hatched a theology out of their skull, and have afterwards consulted the Word, profaning it, because it does not make one with their vain delusions. The evils with themselves they call goods, because [they say] nothing of evil is imputed to them.

56. They were afterwards called together, and were explored whether they were all unanimous in professing those heinous things; and it was found that some of them had not such a heinous dogma; who were they that were ignorant of *those mysteries.* They constituted *one-third part of them: these were separated;* and the rest when separated were given to certain ones as servants: and it was forbidden them to thus gather together any more. The rest also were separated, and sent¹ into societies, with the prohibition that they should not be together. The Holy Supper they did not make holy. Concerning Baptism, they have it in use on account of the Reformed.

57. The rest were gathered together into congregations, and after visitation were cast down towards the lower parts, and were compelled to enter a cavern. But because they had no food¹ there, but vile chambers, they complained loudly; and were sent forth, and cast out into the deserts. Zinzendorf saw this.

THE QUAKERS.

58. When other spirits wish to explore what they think, they conceal their thoughts in a certain way, saying that it is enough that they do no evil to any one, nor openly speak evil of any one. But it was said to them, that not to speak evil of any one is a good in an earthly society; but that to think ill of others injures society in the other life, because there the ideas of thought are communicated. They do not wish to be instructed in doctrinals. They answer, "I do not understand this: What is this?" They have often affirmed that they have been taught by the Holy Spirit, and that they are taught. They most stubbornly resist, to prevent anything of their arcana from being published. The spirits who are with Quakers, whom they think to be the Holy Spirit, are they who were of the same sect in the world. To these after death they first pass; who inspire into them not to promulgate anything; wherefore they live separated; they are spurious spirits.* A communion of certain detestable wives was disclosed: they then expect an influx from the holy spirit, with a perception of leave that it is permitted. Their secret holy worship consists of such things, and by such things also the communication of their holy is effected. They do not at this day have the trembling and the

---

[MARGINAL NOTE.]

*There are Quaker spirits who, from their worship by Quakers in the world, believe themselves to be the holy spirit, and to have been from eternity; but in process of time they come among the profane who are called stercoraceous and cadaverous spirits, abominable excrement.¹

total shaking, as formerly; but an uncertain shaking on the left side of the body and face. When they assert that it is commanded by the holy spirit, no one objects to adulteries and whoredoms. I spoke with their founder, who said that he never did such things, nor thought them. It was seen that Quaker spirits live in dense forests, like wild hogs: they become fantastic spirits. Those were also seen who believe that they are born holy, although he be one born from their adultery; respecting whom the rest say, that he alone drinks red wine in heaven; which wine they call celestial. But he appeared like a heinous man, and became black, and appeared to the angels like mucus of the nose.[1] Such, dissociated, sit in their own places, like barks and the lees of oil, for ages. After those ages they retain very little of life, and serve societies for a vile connection. I spoke with Penn, who asserted that he was not such, and that he took no part in such things. It was said that the first of them were enthusiastic spirits, who are such that they wish to possess man. Those who from the dullness of the understanding wish to be called a holy spirit, are more corporeal as it were than the others. They say that they not only speak from the holy spirit, but also eat with the holy spirit; and that with some the spirit is infused into their feasts.

THE SAINTS OF THE PAPISTS.

59. The papists, especially the monks, when they come into the other life, inquire for the saints, each one for those in his order; and the Jesuits do the same: and they likewise find them; but when they speak with them, they do not find more of holiness with them than with others. On being questioned, they say that they have no more power than others; and that they who have not worshiped the Lord, but only the Father, have no power; and that they are among the vile, whom their associates despised. Some of them know that they have been canonized; and when they are proud of it, they are derided by their associates; some do not know it. The most of those who affected sanctity in the world, are in the lower earth and in the hells, because they did this from the insane love, that they wished to be invoked and worshiped as gods; and that love profanes all the sanctity of heaven. But still the monks, and especially the Jesuits, conceal the lot of those, and lie to the common people, that they are saints on account of a restraint[1] and obedience; although they laugh at them in their hearts.

60. I heard the Pope who lived in the year 1738,—because he receded from the Babylonish error, and renounced all power over souls and over heaven, and became a Christian, calling upon the Lord alone,[2]—he related to me that he had spoken with almost all who had been made saints, of both sexes; and, except two, he had seen no one in heaven; and that these two abhorred being invoked: and that many of them were not aware of it; and that some spoke foolishly.

61. *St. Genevieve.* She appears sometimes to the Parisians, in a middle altitude, in a splendid dress, and then as it were with a saintly face, and grants herself to be seen by many. But when some begin to invoke her, then immediately her face changed, and also her garments; and she becomes like another woman, and chides them, and rebukes them severely, for wishing to worship a woman, whose lot is no other than the lot of ordinary women, and who is not more highly esteemed among her associates than others: and she chides them even to shame, that men in the world are taken with such trifles. I will add, that the reason why she appears to them such at the beginning, was to the end that it might be known what kind of deliriums these were. I heard the angels say that she sometimes appears so, for the sake of separating the worshipers of men from the worshipers of God. She also teaches them that she knows nothing at all more than others, and nothing whatever about invocation.

62. She says also that she is not among the best; and that he who wishes to become greater than others, becomes lower than others; and that it is an injury to the most of them that they have been canonized; because, when they hear of it, they become puffed up in heart from hereditary evil, and are removed away, that they may not know at all who they were in the world.

63. *Agnes* dwells in a chamber with virgins for her companions; and as often as she is called forth by any worshiper, she goes out, and asks what they want with a shepherd girl, who in herself is low, and is one with others in their work. And then her companions go out, and chide them even to shame. And as soon as they are ashamed, and desist from such things, she is also guarded, lest pride should enter into her. But she is now conducted away to another place; nor is she found any more to the right among the upright women; in whose society she is not tolerated, unless she answers that she is filthy.

64. The saints adored in the world are of three kinds. Some are averse to the worship; these are guarded by angels. Some orally repudiate it, but still cherish in heart that they wish to be worshiped. Some receive it; but these are profane, miserable, and foolish.

65. *Anthony* of Padua appeared to me in front a little below, at the plane of the foot. He appeared in a dark garment; and I spoke to him as to whether he supposed he was a saint. He at first answered that he was not at all a saint: but still it was perceived that he retained the pride, that he wished to be one; on which account I spoke with him more severely. When any one comes to him, he is led to say, that he can introduce no one into heaven, and that he knows nothing at all about being invoked; that this is a falsity. When they inquire of him what heaven is, whether it is the Lord, and whether it is love from Him and to Him and mutual love, this he does not know: on which account other spirits, from whom he wishes to get away, and cannot, mock at him. An interior craftiness has been observed in him. He endeavors to be worshiped in secret ways; but he fears: for he would be thrust down to lower places, where he suffers hard things. He can by art bind the ideas of the thought of others. He has conjunction with the Jesuits who appear in white.

66. *Francis Xavier* dwells deep beneath the back parts. He was a subtle magician, operating through conjugial love and through innocence; thus clandestinely.

67. *Ignatius* was in front above. He was a good spirit. He said that he was averse to being canonized, making himself filthy. He detested their making saints. He knew about the Jesuits, and called them atheists, and said that he shunned them.

68. The *Virgin Mary*, the mother of the Lord, was seen. Mary appeared to one side, in a snow-white garment, only as she passed by: and then she stopped a little, and said, that she had been the mother of the Lord; that He was indeed born of her; but that He became God, and put off all the maternal human; and that she therefore now adores Him as her God; and that she is unwilling that any one should acknowledge Him as her son, because in Him all is Divine.

MOHAMMED AND THE MOHAMMEDANS.

69. See some things concerning the judgment upon the Mohammedans, and that there are two Mohammeds under the Christian heaven, in the small work on the *Last Judgment* (n. 50).

70. That a choir is when many speak and act together and unanimously, and that by choirs inauguration to unanimity is made and that in their speech there is singing, see in the *Arcana Cœlestia* (n. 1648, 1649, 2595, 2596, 3350, 5182, 8158).

MOHAMMED.

71. I have spoken with the Mohammed, who is in his stead, who had his seat under the Christian heaven: it seemed as if the glory of the Lord was shown to the Mohammedans, and that they then fell down upon their faces; and their Mohammed did the same.

72. I have heard the Mohammedans speak so skilfully and prudently as to affect certain Christian spirits with shame, acknowledging Mohammed but adoring the one only Lord of the universe: and Mohammed then testified that he has no power, and he also then adored the Lord.

73. I have sometimes seen that Mohammed drive away from himself the crowd that adores him, saying that they should go to the Lord, who rules the universe.

74. Spirits were sent to me from Mohammed, who could induce the appearance of a laver, pleasant through the form of its flow.

75. Both Mohammeds confess that the Lord is the fountain of all goodnesses and truths.

76. The spirits who are around Mohammed are inaugurated into unanimity and into agreement by angelic choirs, to the end that they may suffer themselves to be acted upon, and to think, will and speak from the Lord through angels; (respecting choirs see above;) and I have seen and heard them present by them beautiful representations concerning the Lord, the Saviour of the world. The work of choirs is performed by Mohammedans with great merit. The Mohammedan choirs there became more familiar to me than others. I was with Mohammed on a remarkable occasion: it was also when I was in Amsterdam, and in the courthouse there, which he saw through my eyes, and praised. He was delighted with the marbles there, which marbles correspond to the affections of the Mohammedans, who are in some degree spiritual; for all things are correspondences. Golden things correspond to the affections of the angels of the third heaven; things of silver to those of the second; things of copper to those of the first; and India porcelain to those of the last: to those of the Mohammedan heaven things of marble.

77. The two Mohammeds were once taken up into heaven, because they desired it; and they then spoke with me therefrom. They said that they saw thence, in one idea of thought, innumerable things, which, when below heaven, they believed to be one single thing: this was done, that they might know how the Lord leads man by innumerable things, which in the natural state appear to the man as one; when yet there are ineffable things in every one of them. This may be compared with the least things of an animalcule, which appears to the naked eye as one obscure point, but seen under a powerful microscope, is yet an animal endowed with members, and likewise with organs, and within with muscles, fibres, heart, brain, and many other things. So it is with one idea of a man's thought; therefore no one but the Lord alone knows what kind of thought the man has, and how much of what is living, that is, of heaven, there is in him: for as much of heaven as there is in him, so much of the human there is in him from the Lord. These things the two Mohammeds learned by being elevated into heaven.

78. There were Mohammedans in the western quarter dwelling upon rocks, who were rejected by the Mohammed in the Christian region, because they worshiped Mohammed as God, and adored him; which was forbidden them: and it was found that then they thought nothing respecting the Lord, not even respecting Him as the greatest Prophet, and the Son of God. And when it was inquired what kind of idea they had concerning God the Father, and it was found that they not only had not the idea of Him as a man, but none at all,—and without an idea of God there is not given conjunction with any heaven; it was said to them that they could rather have the idea of God respecting the Lord, because He was the greater Prophet, and the Son of God: but they said that they could not, for He was of a wandering nation. Since they worshiped Mohammed, therefore Mohammed himself, who wrote the Koran, and was buried at Mecca, was taken from his place, which was to the right deeply behind the right foot, and he was elevated a little above the earth, and was shown to them. He appeared gross and black, altogether similar to corporeal spirits, who have little of life. He spoke with them, confessed that it was he, and that he was such: and after he had been shown, he was carried down into his place; but those worshipers of Mohammed were dispersed.

79. It was afterwards disclosed whence were the two Mohammeds, who had obtained a seat in the Christian heaven: because one of them was born in Saxony, and taken by the Algerines; and he there adopted the Mohammedan religion, and became a ship-captain. He was then taken by the Genoese, where he received the Christian religion: thus he became imbued with both religions, because he acknowledged the Lord: and being led by the love of ruling, he was therefore taken there instead of Mohammed, and infused into the Mohammedans the belief that he was Mohammed himself: he was clever.

80. But the other Mohammed was disclosed as being a Christian from Greece. He was also acknowledged by those who in the world had thought of many Mohammeds.

81. With the first Mohammed there appears something luminous, as if from a little torch; and the Mohammedans look thither, and there is influx thence into them through the medium of spirits : for in the spiritual world distances are only appearances; and when any one is thought of, the distance perishes, and there becomes presence; Mohammed is skilful in instructing those who inquire of him. It has been granted me to perceive the sphere of his life: it was exteriorly pleasant, but interiorly concealing lasciviousness, which they have from matrimony with many wives and concubines. It was an unclean heat, but which is a pleasant heat, to the Mohammedans.

82. The reason that Mohammeds are continually substituted in place of another, is because every one after death is led into his religious persuasion which he had in the world : it is a continuation of life. But he is afterwards gradually led away either to goods or to evils, according to his life; according to which also he receives truths or falsities.

83. I have heard that Mohammed say that he acknowledges the Lord as the only God, in whom is the Father, who is one God with Him: and that the Holy proceeding from Him is the Divine filling the heavens, and making the heavens.

THE MOHAMMEDANS.

84. I was conducted to a region where the Mohammedans were, which region was towards the right in the plane of the sole of the right foot: and when I was there, I was held in the thought concerning the Lord, that the Father is in Him, and He in the Father; and that the Holy Spirit proceeds; thus in the thought that there is one God, in whom is a trine. All those who were there were then in the same idea, and altogether acknowledged it; and this through all that tract. It was thence granted me to know, that there are many from the Mohammedans who receive the belief concerning the Lord, that He is one with the Father.

85. When I was conducted by the Lord through all the places, that I might know the quality of those there from their various nations, I came also to two mountains, upon which were Mohammedans. On one were those who lived well morally; they said that they have good, because they obey their governors. On the other were those who were very perceptive of spiritual things. They stated at first that no others can come to them but they who are of a like[1] genius; and that Christians cannot; and that if they come, they appear to them as if they were being swallowed up by wolves; and that those who still come, they send to prison, and treat badly, and afterwards dismiss: these are monks who are able to introduce themselves by their arts, but are detected. I spoke with them respecting many wives; and they heard the reasons why it is according to the Christian doctrine, that only one wife is to be received. They perceived the justice in the reasons, but answered that they cannot as yet recede from matrimony with many, because it was conceded to them by their religion in the world, for the reason that they are orientals, who, without many wives, would have burned forth into adulteries, and so would have perished.

86. I spoke also with the firstborn of the Christians, who are the military guards of their Sultan, called Janizaries, and became Mohammedans: they said that they were still Christians in heart; and that some were intermediate, but some Mohammedans.

87. When I spoke something from the Word with those who were upon the other mountain, I apperceived something holy from them: as when I said that the Lord was conceived from Jehovah; and for that reason He called Him Father; and it is thence that He is the Son of God; and thence the Divine is in Him; and therefore He could glorify His whole body; so that as to that part of the body, which from those who are born of human parents is rejected and putrefies, was with Him glorified and made Divine from the Divine in Himself; and He rose with this leaving nothing in the sepulchre, altogether otherwise than takes place with every man. They heard attentively and said that they wondered they had not heard of such things.

88. I saw an infestation of Mohammedans by Christians in a certain city; from which infestation they could with difficulty be rescued. It was done by arts, of which there are many in the spiritual world. It was then seen that the city sank down in the middle part, and there was a wall made round about. But the sinking down was little, so that they could ascend and descend. Thus those who withdrew were transferred, and exempted from the infestations.

89. I was conducted to the Mohammedans who are in the eastern quarter, and it was granted me to speak with them. They said that some Christians of the Roman Catholic religion come to them; and they observed that it was done by them only for the sake of gain and dominion: and further, that they wish to possess all the things of the world, and also to have dominion over all who are there. There was a conversation with them concerning God: they said that they cannot comprehend how they can perceive one God, when they name three, and call them persons; when yet there is but one God; and that they still heard from the Christians, that they also say one God; because this is a contradiction. They asked what I knew concerning God. I said, that in the Christian heaven that is not believed, nor is it so said: but that the trine is in one Person; and that the trine which is named in it is the Father, the Son, and the Holy Spirit, that this is in the Lord, in whom the inmost, which is the *esse* of life, is called the Father; the second, which is the *existere* of life thence, is the Son; and the third is the proceeding, and is called the Holy Spirit: and that such a union was effected by God the Father, by His coming in the world; and that Christians might also be enlightened in it, since the Lord teaches openly, that the Father is in Him, and that the Father and He are one, and that the Holy Spirit does not speak out of itself, but from Him: but they who are of the Roman Catholic religion do not admit this, for the reason that they are lords on the earth; neither the Reformed, who are in the religion of faith alone; for so far the Mohammedans comprehended this. They said that they thought, desiring illustration, which was afterward given them; since this thing cannot be comprehended, without instruction from the Word.

90. I spoke with the Mohammedans concerning the resurrection; that the Christians believe that the resurrection is first to take place with the destruction of the world; and that the bodies are then to be united to their souls, and to be gathered together from every quarter where they have been scattered; and that in the meantime they are spirits, of whom they have an idea as of wind, especially of the breath; and that thus they flit about either in the ether or in the starry heaven, without hearing, sight, or any other sense; and that they are in expectation of the judgment; and that those also are in this expectation who have died from the very beginning of this earth; who have thus flitted about in the universe now for six thousand years; and that some think that they are together in a certain place, which is not a place, but a somewhere or other; as also that the angels are such. Also that the Christians scarcely comprehend that man lives a man after death as in the world, for they cannot have an idea of the spiritual body; but that still, when they do not think from doctrine, they think of themselves after death, that they live as men, as when they are near to death: and that for that reason those who treat of the deceased write openly that they are among the angels, are speaking with them, are in white garments, in paradises; yet as soon as they come to any ideas from doctrine, they think, as was said, of man after death, and of an angel, as of wind. When these things were said, the Mohammedans then answered, that they wondered that such a fallacy can reign with Christians, who call themselves more enlightened than others; saying that they know that they are to live after death, are to live in happy marriage, and are to drink wine; and this after they have rejected the cast-offs, which had served them for their ultimate clothing in that gross sphere, as a body there.

91. There are many Mohammedans who become Christians, acknowledging the Lord as the only God, because the Father is in Him. These, when they are led into heaven, are led first to the east, and thence to the north, and thence ascend higher and higher to the west, and are there in a higher place; but still by a circuit, or going round, according to situation below; some appeared to ascend towards the south, who were they that confirmed themselves in the Divinity of the Lord.

92. Many Mohammedans, from natural light, comprehend better concerning spiritual things than the Christians do; because they think much, and desire truths. They understood well that all the things in heaven and in the world refer themselves to good and truth; and that truth, when it is believed, is the truth of faith; and that good, when a man is affected by it, is the good of love: and therefore two faculties, understanding and will, were given to man; the understanding by the reception of truth, thus of faith, and the will by the reception of good, thus of love: and that good and truth, thus the understanding and the will, must be one, that the man may be truly a man; thus also a man of faith and of truth. They clearly perceived thence that they who are in the good of life, are in the perception of truth; for the reason that good desires truth, and wishes to be conjoined, and as it were nourished; and that truth is as spiritual food to good; also on the other hand that truth desires good, that it may be anything; because without good there is no life in truth; thus that there is the reciprocal desire of the one for the other, and that from this man is man.

93. In the Judgment I saw that the Mohammedans were led from the west and round about in their circuit around the Papists, by a way towards the north to the east, in a circular way to appearance: and that on the way the evil were cast outside of that sphere where there is a space of great extent; some into a wilderness there, some into swamps and pools, some into dark forests. These things were on the backside of their mountain: on the side of that space in the north there was an immense and extended whirlpool, into which also many, who had led an evil life, were cast. The rest proceeded by a circuit towards the east, and spread themselves into an ample space that extended itself more to the back. Thither those were led, who acknowledged God the Father, and the Son as the greatest Prophet, who is with the Father. That space was broad, divided into mountains, hills, and valleys, upon which they were arranged; and there it is well with them. They who were still better, enjoying more intellectual light than others, were likewise led to that place, where there was communication with the Christian heaven, a space which separated intervening. These were they, who, being instructed, received the Lord; and they who received well, were led into the south, where they obtained their heaven behind the Christians there.

94. There were those who feigned themselves Christians as to the belief in the Lord's Divinity. These insinuated themselves among them by craftiness, but were forthwith detected and separated, and cast into the desert and the adjoining chasm; and some were led back and dispersed.

95. There were some from the Mohammedans who acknowledged only the Father as others do, and the Lord as the greatest Prophet. They said that they could not understand that the Divine is divided into three Persons, thus into three gods. They said that the Holy Spirit was God speaking by a spirit, and an angel; a certain one from the Christians now drew near to them, asking why they do not acknowledge the Son of God as God. They said that there is one God, and thus there would be two; on which account they asked him how many Gods he worshiped: he replied One, because God is one. But they explored the idea of his thought, that he did not think of one God, but of three. This is easily done in the other life. They said that they saw that he said one God with the mouth, and in heart and in faith believed in three: and yet it behoves a Christian to speak as he thinks, and not to divide the mind from the speech, as do flatterers and those who lie; and as he could not deny this, they said that the Christians ought to be ashamed to think of three gods, when no Gentile who has any intelligence thinks so; who have not three in their idea, when they name one. He wished to say that the three were one by unanimity; neither could this be given without the idea of three conversing and consenting among themselves; and besides, three essences which make one could not be given, unless they were also one person: one and the same essence of three is not given; still less in God, who is not divisible: and who, moreover, can give it from an essence, such as this is among the metaphysicians, and have it be thought by the common people, when it cannot be by the learned? On which account he was affected with shame, saying that he would in no wise return to them, and that he would inquire of some one concerning the triune God. The angels afterwards spoke with the Mohammedans, instructing them that God is one both in Person and in essence, in whom is a trine; and that the Son of God, who to them is the greatest Prophet, being sent by the Father, cannot but be God, because He was conceived of God the Father Himself: thus the Divine itself was in Him from conception; and the Divine is indivisible.

96. The mansions of the Mohammedans, after death are palaces.[1] They are for the greatest part in the western quarter.

After the Last Judgment there came many anew into that quarter, who thought little respecting the God of the universe, and nothing respecting the Lord, but worshiped Mohammed as God. And because they did not find him, they elected another, on a mountain elevated above the Christian region, with whom they consulted, and whom they obeyed: and then, by the command of their new Mohammed, they poured themselves into the Christian region, and infested them in various modes. But after visitation, and the disclosure that they were a wandering nation, and one that delighted in idleness, and wished to do nothing useful, they were cast into their hells. As long as they consociated themselves with the Babylonians, they were also able to render themselves inconspicuous. At length the earth upon which they were was rolled over above them, and they were cast into hell: their hell appeared fiery.

97. Many of the Mohammedans, when they had heard many things concerning the Lord, wished to go and join the heavenly Christian Church. But it was told them that they should remain still in their religion, or in their doctrine from the Koran, that the Lord was the greatest Prophet, the Son of God, the wisest of all, sent to inform the human race; for the reason that they cannot in heart acknowledge His Divine, but only with the mouth; since they imbibed those things from infancy: and their spiritual good was formed in part from such things as had been of their faith; which cannot be extinguished so suddenly by a new tenet of faith, let them only live in sincerity and justice, and so in their good: because all sincerity and justice is in itself the Divine proceeding from the Lord; and because they can in their manner still live faithfully, and be gradually led on to the Lord. It was said to them, that many Christians do not think of the Lord's Divine, but only of His Human, which they do not make Divine; for instance, the Roman Catholics, as also the Reformed; who for that reason go to the Father, that He will have mercy for the Son's sake; and rarely to the Lord Himself: on account of which belief and prayer, they continually retain the idea concerning the Lord, that He is a man like any other.

98. It was told me that there is a book among the Mohammedans which is common in their hands, in which some pages were written by correspondences, like the Word with us; from which pages there is some light in the heavens.

99. The judgment upon them proceeded still further into the west, in a long tract; and likewise towards the north, where they mingled themselves with the evil Papists; and I saw them cast into the hells and whirlpools there.

100. There were with me many from Greece, who had dwelt in the world with the Mohammedans; complaining that then as well as now they inveighed against them because they worship three Gods; to whom they also replied, that they worship one God, and that the three are one: but they still persist that they are three which they worship, since they name three; and they ask which God of the three they worship the most: and when they reply that they worship all together, they then say that thus there is one God, and the rest are little gods; and that it is only said thus. But when they hear it said that they are equal, they withdraw, and set themselves against the Christians, as having little or no judgment in spiritual things. They complained that they do not give up the infestation, until they say that they are three names of the one God: then they acquiesce. They afterwards inquired respecting the three names of the one God. It was told them from heaven, that the Christians derived those names from the sense of the letter of the Word, where three names of the one God are mentioned: and by the Father is there meant the Creator of the universe; by the Son, the Saviour of the human race; and by the Holy Spirit, enlightenment; and that these three are in the Lord alone; and that in Him the three are one; and that He teaches this in the Word. But on account of the Papist class, who are not willing to regard the Lord's Human as Divine, because they have claimed all His power to themselves, they were not willing to have it said that it is Divine power, and thus that they were gods on the earth; and when it was read to them out of *Matthew* and *Luke*, that He was conceived from God the Father, and thus the Divine was in Him, and He was from it; they said that they supposed He was the son of Joseph. And when it was said to them that He did not come into the world to reconcile the human race to the Father, but to conquer the devil, that is, to subjugate the hells, that He might reduce all things [on earth] and in the heavens to order, and might at the same time glorify His Human, or might reunite it to the Divine, which was the soul itself in Him from conception; and that thus and no otherwise could the human race be saved. On hearing these things they were silent, and many acquiesced.

101. It was said to them that there are Mohammedans who receive the belief that the Lord is one with the Father, and that they have a heaven in which all things are happy; and that they live there from the Lord in spiritual marriage of good and truth.

SOME THINGS CONCERNING THE PAPISTS.

102. When the Last Judgment was going on, he who was Pope in the year 1738, and was then blind in his old age, dwelt on high near a city in the northern quarter; and I saw him then brought away, and carried sitting upon a litter, and sent into a secure place: and as every one after death is first led to his own religion, and afterwards is led away from it, as far as he can be, they also, for that reason, seek for the Pope: on which account some one is always appointed, who takes on the name and the function of Pope. He was for a long time in that function after that time; but when he observed that he had no power at all of remitting sins, nor of opening heaven, and that this power was Divine, and thence the Lord's alone, he therefore began to be averse to that doctrine, and afterwards to abhor it, and he abdicated that office, and betook himself among the Christians who worship the one Lord, and is with them in heaven. I have often spoke with him; and he called himself happy, that he had embraced those truths, and had removed himself away from that idolatrous religious persuasion. He said that he revolved in his mind similar things in the world, and acknowledged in heart that the Word was holy, and that the Lord was to be worshiped; but that he could not then recede, on account of causes which he also mentioned.

103. But it happened otherwise with his successor, Benedict XIV. He declared openly that he had confirmed in his own mind, that since the Lord had transferred all power over the heavens to Peter, He had no power at all left, and no longer any holiness. I saw him speaking with Sextus V., who was called up from below, and after the conversation sank down again. I heard him speaking many things in regard to the Word with some one concerning the Bull Unigenitus, but this is not the place to make them public. He was cunning, and at first civil, and then very sharp-sighted: he loved the Jesuits more than others, and went down to them into their hell; nor have I as yet seen him come up therefrom: and scarcely is he to come up thence, because he said that he had confirmed and established the Bull Unigenitus, and because he said that the Sacred Scripture was not equal in his mind to the papal decree, but inferior to it. When it was shown him that the Word was holy in every word, and that they were perpetual correspondences, and that thence it was for the whole heaven, he made this of no account, saying that the papal decrees were of the same holiness. But then it was said, that there is in each thing which the Pope pronounces in the Consistory, something derived from the infernal love of ruling over heaven and earth, and of ascribing to himself the Divine power, and so of being worshiped as God; and that hell, and not heaven, is in such a decree. And it was shown from what spirits it is said, and who it is that then breathe into and move the breast; that they are infernal spirits, who are not willing to believe in salvation by the Holy Spirit,[1] but he reasoned against those things.

104. Louis XIV., king of France, is at this day among the happy. He was made by the Lord the governor over the best society of the French nation, over those who are arriving in the spiritual world from the world. He acts uprightly and justly, and is diligent in looking out for things useful to his subjects there. He acknowledges the Lord, and that He has power over the heavens and the earth. He reads the Word, and shuns cunning and craftiness. He said that he was such in the world. Once when I was speaking with him, he suddenly descended seemingly as if by steps, to a place below me a little in front; and it was perceived that then in vision he was as if he was at Versailles. And it was then perceived that he had come as if into a kind of sleep; and it immediately became silent around him, and also with me; which lasted two hours. Afterwards he ascended, and spoke to those who stood around him, saying that he had spoken with the king of France, his grandson, who reigns at this day; and that he exhorted him to desist from confirming the Bull Unigenitus; and he said that otherwise misfortune would come upon him. He said that he did not know whether he perceived that in clear vision, or obscure vision, which are in the thought with some emotion of the mind. This took place Dec. 13, 1759, about seven or eight o'clock.

105. After the Last Judgment, the Babylonians were for a long time gathered together upon mountains in the west as before. The reason is, that a spirit after death can go nowhere else than the place where his life is. They were thus there upon mountains, where a part made to themselves as it were new heavens. But as soon as it was calculated that there were about two hundred there, they were cast down into the hells, as before; and this was done until all things were reduced into such order; and no one after death can go anywhere but into his own hell; nor can a part remain upon the earth there; and this is done when those places are taken possession of by societies, where they are in the acknowledgment and adoration of the Lord.

106. The southern quarter, where the richest were, and where the great city of the Jesuits is, which quarter was altogether overturned, as may be seen from the description of the Last Judgment, is still a desert land; and I saw the monks there sometimes, who, as they had heard that treasures were hidden away there, still flocked thither for the purpose of exploring; but in vain.

107. Nor do they still desist from sending out their emissaries into the Reformed Christian world, for the purpose of seducing as in the world. They are monks, who thirst solely for gain; and who aspire to supreme, yea Divine, power; and who are so barren that they know nothing at all of Divine truth; but yet they prevail over others by cunning; nevertheless they are investigated, and those who have been investigated are miserably punished.

108. It was shown me to the life, why Babel or Babylon was called Lucifer, son of the dawn, *Isa.* xiv. and *Gen.* [xi. 1–9].

That by Lucifer there Babel is meant, is manifest from what precedes and follows there, concerning which the things there may be quoted. And that Babel in the beginning adored the Lord, and observed the commandments more than others, bearing domination in the mind; but that in process of time domination becomes the head, and at length endeavors to drag the Lord Himself from His throne, and to place itself thereon.

109. The women and virgins who have lived in convents, and have thought lascivious things, and still more those who have done lascivious things, are cast into hells where there are direful things. But they who have cultivated piety alone, and have not done any work, are divided among the adherents of their own religion, to act as servants, learning that bare piety in idleness does not conduce to salvation. But they who were diligent and loved to work, are allotted places among those women in the churches, with whom it is well. They who have been diligent in the convents, by serving others there in various ways, as to food, clothing, and other functions there, and who did these things from charity and affection, are conducted away beyond that mountain into the confines between the south and west, and form a society, which is protected from infestations from the men, and they are sent to those who teach the truths of faith;[1] for they are more teachable than others.

110. There was a vast multitude of Papists dwelling to the east, occupying all those mountains,[2] even from the eastern quarter to the southern, who introduced themselves to the Gentiles upon the mountains and plains there. All that multitude was transferred by a direct way to the west, where a settlement was given them upon hills and plains for a great extent. They were those who had lived in goods, although not in truths, who had performed good works according to their religion, and were of that genius that they would not injure others, nor plot evils. That they desired truths is manifest from the fact that while they were on the way they appeared as if they were borrowing silver and garments, as the sons of Israel did from the Egyptians; by which was signified that they desired truths, and were receiving them from them; from those who do not do anything good.

111. The vast multitude was explored as to the quality of its affection of truth from good, and at the same time whether they had lived in the good of charity. That exploration was seen as a sudden and instantaneous transference to various quarters. They who were in the middle remained there; because they were in the affection of truth, and wished to be imbued with the truths of faith. The rest were sent back, that they might first be instructed below by their own people, who had been upright monks, and at the same time had been in some doctrine of truth from the Word; and they were afterwards transferred to those of the Reformed, who, on account of a life according to the truths of the Word, were angelic spirits.

112. I also saw a vast multitude of the Catholic nation, who had been hidden away and reserved by the Lord for a long time, and were reserved from the idolatrous contagion of the others; because they had lived well, and had acknowledged the Lord: and some were transferred to the south, some to the east, some to the west, and some to the north, that they might form some heavenly society, and be further instructed. For this end angels were sent to them, not only to instruct them, but also to guard them from the cunning and deceitful of their own nation, and from the influx out of their hells. In a word, many and great societies were instituted out of Catholics, and partly inserted into societies where the Word is read freely and the Lord is adored. If, after being instructed, they have received the truths of faith in the good of love, they are elevated thence into heaven. It is not their fault that they were born there. All their infants are in heaven: but these are ignorant of the falsities of their parents, not knowing that they are such; and they are educated under the Lord's auspices by the angels.

113. The most malicious of the Roman Catholics become the most stupid, for the reason that when malice penetrates all the interiors of the mind,[1] and destroys all spiritual truth, they then first become insane, and afterwards stupid, and are sent under the earth between the west and the north. When any one passes to that place, great stupor occupies his thought, and torpor his body. Many of them were worshipers of the devil, and had books where the doctrine of the worship of them was contained. One or two of their books were taken from them and read before others. The doctrinal teaching was this: that they petition God the Father to excuse them for betaking themselves to the devil; because they petitioned for help from God the Father, and had not obtained it, knowing that they get help from the devil; on which account they betake themselves to him, calling him their patron. Another book was opened, written with various characters and flexures, and being deciphered, taught that they had nothing from the Divine, but all from the devil. Being asked the reason they said, that they had not obtained from God by prayers their request that they might rule as in the world, over the souls of men and over the goods of that earth. It was told them that no one obtains this by prayers. Being detected, at first they became insane, and were cast down from the mountain on which they were, from the southern side of the mountain, into a direful hell where the worshipers of the devil are; and their houses collapsed together into heaps. One of them ran to me, and he was dusky like a devil.

114. Those of them who are upright by nature, cannot dwell together with those who have attained spiritual uprightness from the affection of truth; for those who are upright from any natural uprightness are easily seduced. They believe all things, even things of cunning, and adore idols; on which account also they are among those who serve others as handmaids and servants; by whom they are guarded, lest they should be approached by the monks.

THE AFRICANS.

115. There are, among the blackest of the Africans, those who love to be punished and treated harshly; and who come into heaven, saying afterwards that they detest blackness, because they know that their souls are white and their bodies black.

116. I have heard it announced that at this day a church is being established with many in Africa, and that revelations are made at this day; and that they are receptive of the Heavenly Doctrine, especially concerning the Lord.

117. I was conducted through several regions in front towards the left. Afterwards I saw a great palace, and a spacious court there. A certain one spoke with me there, saying that a revelation had been promised, and that he was expecting it. And then something luminous appeared in obscurity, which was an indication that now there will be a revelation. And as I was attending, I heard that they were expecting a revelation concerning Christ, whom they call the Only Man, from whom every man is a man. And one of the angels then spoke with them, and instructed them concerning the Lord, that He is the only God. They replied that they perceived this, but not as yet that He was born a man. But when they were instructed by the angels, they understood this also, saying, that this was done for the sake of the salvation of the human race. Moreover, they knew many things respecting heaven and hell, of which Christians are ignorant. It was said that they were Africans. I was afterwards conducted thence towards the right, where I heard them saying that they had expected a revelation, and that angels were now speaking with them from the Lord, and were instructing them concerning the Lord, with the promise that they were about to receive the Heavenly Doctrine. *These said that it could not be otherwise than that God, the Creator of the Universe, should appear in the world, because He created men, and loves them; and that His appearing must be made even to the ocular sight in the human form.*

118. It was afterwards shown in obscure vision how the Heavenly Doctrine would proceed in Africa; namely, towards the interior parts, even to the middle of it; and that it would then proceed towards those who were at the sides on the Mediterranean Sea, but not to the coast; and then, after a time, would turn itself back towards Egypt. Thereupon the angels were glad, that there was now the Lord's coming anew, and that a New Church was being established, with whom they could be conjoined. That doctrine does not extend as far as to the Africans that dwell near the coasts, since the Christians come thither, who insinuate scandals, and who have a human and not a Divine idea concerning the Lord. The Africans are more receptive of the Heavenly Doctrine than others on this earth, because they freely receive the doctrine concerning the Lord, and have it as if implanted in themselves that God will altogether appear as a man. They are in the faculty of receiving the truths of faith, and especially its goods, because they are of a celestial disposition. It was told them that a prediction was made by the Lord concerning His coming, and concerning the New Church after the old one; and that His appearing is made through angels who teach.

119. I was conducted again to the Africans by a way running first to the north and afterwards to the west; and I saw there as it were a palace, where some one walked; and afterwards higher up, where I stopped, and heard a vast number sent forth out of the Christian heaven to those who were Africans; and those were there who in the world had lived according to their religion and had acknowledged one God under the human form. It was told them that he who has lived in good according to religion is also in the affection of truth, because the good of life desires nothing more than truth; for it desires to know how one is to live well. Thence they rejoice when they are informed; and that all such receive truths from the Lord, and are enlightened according to the quality and quantity of their good of life: this they acknowledged, and were glad. The African race can be in greater enlightenment than others on this earth, since they are such that they think more interiorly, and so receive truths and acknowledge them. Others, as the Europeans, think only exteriorly, and receive truths in the memory; nor do they see them interiorly from any intellectual light, which they do not acknowledge in matters of faith. I said there, that few Christians live according to religion, but only according to the civil laws, and live well morally for the sake of fame, honor,[1] and gains; and that they rarely think of living according to their doctrinals; believing also that they are saved by the faith of doctrine, and not by the life: on which account they have no doctrinals of life. At this the Africans wondered exceedingly, not being willing to believe that it is so; believing that there is no man who does not live according to his religion; and if not, that he cannot but become stupid and evil, because he then does not receive anything from heaven.

120. All are explored after death as to what idea they have concerning God. That idea is the chief of all, because conjunction with the Lord and conjunction with heaven is according to it, and all of the love and faith of the church is hence according to it, because the Divine is the all of the church, yea, is God: hence the all of the church with a man is from his idea of God: such as that idea is, such is heaven to every one. The Africans also differ from each other according to their idea of God. Some worship an invisible God, and some a visible one: some make of them two, and some make of them one and the same. Some have been instructed by Christians that God was born a man, and they receive this; and when they hear that they distinguish the Divine into three Persons, they go away, believing, however, that the Christians, although they say three, still think of one: for they do not comprehend what a Son born from eternity is. Some, who are the best of them, believe that God is altogether a Man. They say that those who believed that God was born a Man, formerly saw a bright star in the air. The wiser of them believe that God was born a Man in the world, and so manifested Himself.

121. It was said that in a certain region of Africa there is from ancient times a book which they regard as holy. It is written by correspondences in a similar manner as the Word is with us.

122. A certain priest, who had supposed that the idea of the Divine Human is not given with any one, was transferred into societies of Africans, and he found that they had no other idea than that of the Divine Human. In Abyssinia, in Africa, they have some psalms written in a style similar to that of our Word, and they sing them in their temples, and spirits are sensible of communication therefrom. In the spiritual sense they treat of one God, the Redeemer of the human race; but these things have been treated of before, where the Word is spoken of, D. [n. 5947].

123. It has been granted me to speak with African spirits on various subjects, and they perceived all the truths of the church with a clear perception; and when the Word was presented to them, they understood it as to the internal spiritual sense, and carried it to their elders, who said that they have a Word with them, and that it is most holy.

124. They afterwards showed me the quality of those who are in Africa, which they know from the societies of that race in the spiritual world; namely, that interiorly in Africa are the best and the wise: that those that are not good are near the Mediterranean Sea, also near Egypt, and at the Cape of Good Hope. The tract[1] where the good are, lies from Ethiopia towards the middle, into which part strangers from Europe are not admitted; and if they enter, and are not willing to perform service, they sell them to the Asiatics: and they said that at this day some speak with Africans in the world, and instruct them orally; and that their speech with them falls especially into their interior perception; and that they perceive the influx, and so receive the revelation with enlightenment; and that such speech is with their instructors, in whom they have confidence.

THE GENTILES.

125. Concerning the lot[2] of nations and peoples outside the church, see what has been written in *Arcana Cœlestia* (n. 2589–2604), and in the work on *Heaven and Hell* (n. 318–328); also something in the little work on *The Last Judgment* (n. 47-51). That a new heaven has been formed both from Christians and from Gentiles, and also the Lord's Church on earth, see *The Doctrine of the New Jerusalem* (n. 3, 244–246).

126. About the time of the Last Judgment, Christians appeared there in the middle, where they were arranged at a distance from the centre[3] to the circumference, and also at the various quarters according to the light of truth from the love of good. Around this middle were seen the Mohammedans arranged in like manner at the various quarters, near to the Christians according to the light of truth from good. Outside this compass were seen the Gentiles arranged according to their religion and according to life therefrom. All have similar lands divided into mountains, hills, rocks and valleys, and above them are expanses where dwell the best of them who have received from angels truths of doctrine concerning the Lord and concerning life. Beyond them appeared as it were a sea, which was the boundary. All these circuits taken together are extended not in a plane but in a globe like the earth, so that when I was conducted to the Gentiles, after passing through the Mohammedans, I descended by a declivity.

127. When the Last Judgment was going on, those who were in the western quarter beyond the Mohammedans, were led away towards the east. They were led, not by a circuit, but above the northern plane of the Christians, and, what I wondered at, on high, so that they were transferred by a way above the Christians, and yet did not communicate with them. And they were then allotted places around the Mohammedans at the east and also at the south. On both sides of where the Mohammedan heavens are, there appeared openings descending into the depths. Thither were cast those of them who were evil, who had worshiped idols, and had thought nothing about God, and at the same time had lived an evil life.

128. There is also a similar chasm on the northern side of the Mohammedan desert. Into this were cast the worst, and also many of the Roman Catholic religion who had worshiped the images of saints, and had thought nothing at all about the Lord. These latter were gathered from the northern quarter under the mountains there and were mingled with the Gentiles because they are similar. I then saw the whole northern valley even to the mountains there torn up to its foundations, and all who were there, scattered, and then there appeared in that place as it were a smokiness.

129. I was afterwards led beyond the Mohammedans to certain Gentiles who were in the eastern quarter, with whom it was granted to speak. They said that they were sad because the Divine does not appear to them, when yet they think of the Divine and speak about it; and, therefore, if there is a God [they had hoped] that He would send to them those who would teach them; but that they had long waited for this in vain, lamenting that perchance He had deserted them, and that thus there seemed nothing else for them but to perish. And then I heard angels speaking with them out of heaven, saying that God could not have been manifested to them because they had not been willing to believe that God was born a man in the world, or that He had taken on a Human, and that until they believe this, God cannot be manifested to them, nor can they be taught, because this is the primary thing of all revelation. They said that they did indeed believe that God is Man but that they could not comprehend that He was born Man in the world. But answer was made them, that He was not born Man like any other man, since He was not born from a human father, but from the Father Jehovah, and by a Virgin, and that thus He was unlike any other man; for a man's soul from a human father is a recipient of life, but the Lord's soul from the Father Jehovah is life itself, which gives life to all; and that the difference is as between the human and the Divine, and the finite and the infinite, or the create and the uncreate; and because He was such as to His soul, it could not be otherwise than that His body should become like His soul, after He had rejected that of the body which He had taken from the mother; and that therefore He rose as to His whole body, nor did He leave anything of it in the sepulchre, as is the case with every other man, who rises only as to his spirit, and never as to his material body. And further, it was said that the Divine itself, as it is in itself, which is infinite, could not have done otherwise than reject the finite which was from the mother, and put on the infinite from the Father, thus the Divine. They said that they had known no other than that He was like any other man born from a human father, and also that He so died, and was afterwards received by men as God, *and that they now know that the Lord is not such a man as others are. After they received these things they were divided, and those who had received the faith were instructed by angels in other matters of faith and love.*

130. I was conducted to those who in the world had known nothing about God, but who nevertheless had led a moral life amongst each other; they were said to live on a certain island. They appeared to me not like men but like apes and yet with a human face.[1] They so appeared because they knew nothing about God, and the Divine is in the likeness of a man. One of the Christians is set over them by the Lord. I have spoken with him, and he said that they obey him and love him; that they are modest and are engaged in employments, but that at first they could hardly comprehend the things of religion. But after some time, there was given them a nearer communication with the Christians, and they are beginning to receive something of religion, and he cherished the hope that they could be reformed, for the reason that they had lived a moral life, and are in obedience and are industrious. As to similar people elsewhere, see below.[1]

131. There were likewise seen others, who had lived in an island in the West Indian seas, who had no thought[2] at all about God, thus no religion, and who yet had lived together in a sincere and friendly way. It was told me, that at first they appear destitute of rationality, but that nevertheless, because they had contracted no false principles against religion, some of them suffer themselves to be instructed like infants, and they are perfected. It was shown that the delight of their life was to will to serve others under others. Some wealth was once given them, but they offered it to the angel who was instructing them, in order that he might receive them as his servants, that thus they might be instructed as to how they should live. It is an angelic delight to inform such spirits and to lead them to heaven.

132. I was once in a sweet sleep, and when I awoke I saw around me some Chinese,[3] and I noticed that they sat with their legs crosswise, and were talking with each other. And it was ascertained that they had been sent to me by the Lord in order that I might know of what quality many of them are. The angels said that the delightfulness of my sleep had inflowed from the fact that angels had been speaking with them about God and about the wonderful things of wisdom, and that they had been so delighted at this that they had been in the tranquillity of some celestial peace; and that evil spirits could not approach, because they were of a spiritual celestial genius.

133. There were with me some spirits from Tartary,[4] who dwelt outside the Chinese wall, saying that their country is populous; nor do they know anything about war, saying that they are without the love of reigning and that they give the government to those who say they can rule and govern, but if he cannot, he is rejected with a fine; those who do what is right and just are loved. They said that all are engaged in work, and that the lazy are cast out. They say that sometimes Christians come to them, and they marvel at their saying that God is a Man, for they believe that all men know this. They also say that they have the commandments of the Decalogue, and that they live according to them because God so wills. They said that they have a holy book of which others do not know, and which they understand. Inquiry was made, and it was the *Psalms of David*. They call the Chinese their friends because they are of their nation; nor do they think of war, saying that if any strangers should come, then, unknown to them, they would all depart, taking their provisions with them. I also saw[1] a Christian preacher with the spirits of that region. They are of a tranquil disposition.

THE LAST JUDGMENT ON THE PROTESTANTS OR REFORMED.

134. Before the Last Judgment which was a general one, less general judgments preceded which might be called preparatory, by which those who were more exteriorly[2] evil were cast into hells. It should be known that between the judgment effected by the Lord when He was in the world, and that of the judgment which is now effected, spirits who had outwardly lived a moral life, and had confessed God with the lips but not interiorly or in heart, had ascended upon mountains and hills and had there made for themselves, as it were, heavens, where by various arts, which are very numerous in the spiritual world, all of them unknown in our world, they had ascended on mountains; so that the world of spirits which is mediate between heaven and hell had been filled up with such heavens, and thereby the communication of the Lord and heaven with the human race had been intercepted. This also was the reason why the spiritual things of the Word and of doctrine therefrom were not disclosed until after the Last Judgment, for by the latter the world of spirits was purified and communication with man opened. If the spiritual things of the Word and of doctrine therefrom had been disclosed before, they would not have been received nor understood;

and if they had been received and understood, still hell, which then prevailed, would have secretly snatched them away from men's hearts and have profaned them. Those fictitious heavens are meant in the *Apocalypse* by the heaven and earth which passed away. These could pass away, but our visible heaven, which is the firmament of all things, was so created that it cannot pass away, for if this should pass away, the angelic heavens would also pass away. It would be as when the foundation is taken away from a palace, or the base from a column, whereby the house and the column would fall. For there is a connection of all things from the first to the last, from the Lord Himself to His last work which is the visible heaven and the habitable earth. The case would be similar if the human race were to perish, for thus, for a like reason, the angelic heavens would also fall to ruin.

135. Before the Last Judgment I often saw societies, which had made for themselves semblances of heavens, purged and also destroyed. There was one rock on which was quite a large city, where those were who were in faith separate from charity, believing as in the world, that faith alone saves, and this from mere mercy whatsoever the life may have been. They were in the lust of commanding; and therefore they stood at the sides of the rock, and in various ways infested those who were beneath. When visitation was made, and all there were found to be of such a character, I saw that the rock sank down into the depths together with the hill and the inhabitants. The like was done elsewhere. But prior to this being done, the good are separated from the evil, and the evil are in the middle; and then the middle sinks down while the borders remain; in the borders are those who are in the good of faith, that is, who are in charity.

136. All who have not denied God with the lips, although they have in the heart, and have led a moral life on account of the civil laws and also on account of reputation and consequent honors and gains, when they come into the other life betake themselves into societies where there are cities; and there as in the world they live well morally, from fear of punishment and of the loss of honor and gain. But when their externals are taken away from them, and they are let into their internals, they rush into infamous crimes. But when the wicked increase in number the society is then perverted; wherefore angels are then sent thither who search out the state and separate the good from the evil; and the good are either sent to the sides of the society or are taken away. Then the city with the evil sinks down into hell, to a depth according to their wickedness. Once I saw that four angels were sent to such a city, who when they came thither entered into a house;[1] but the criminal spirits who were there, being excited by their presence into interior malice, as takes place, rushed to the house where the angels were, shouting out to them, Did they wish to come out and commit whoredom ? They wished to urge them to it, and even attempted to offer violence, but in vain; in a word, they did like what was done in Sodom. And that city was completely destroyed and its inhabitants cast into hells. The reason why they wished to lead them forth to commit whoredom, was because in that city were gathered those who in the world had accounted adulteries as allowable; also because they had been in falsities of doctrine, by reason of having regarded life as of no account; moreover, to confirm these things they had falsified the Word, and all those who falsify the Word in order to confirm evils of life and falsities of doctrine, account adulteries as allowable and are led into them.

137. I also saw a rock on which there had been such a city, torn up from its place and carried away to another place at a remarkable distance; it appeared carried away like a cloud. And when it came to that place I saw that it also sank down, because there was their hell. The inhabitants had been first reduced into a state of stupor.

138. A great number of those who are in faith separate from charity betake themselves to rocks; while those who are in the love of self betake themselves to mountains which are higher than the rocks. Hence it is that in the Word, a rock signifies faith, and a mountain love. And when, before the Last Judgment, the evil had been thus gathered together upon rocks and upon mountains, first there were suddenly felt concussions and earthquakes, by which are meant perversions of state in respect to the church, and afterwards follows the overturning, which is effected either by sinking, or by carrying away, or by casting out and thus thrusting down into hell. On the mountains and hills upon which are angels, the wisest are in the middle and the less wise at the circumferences; but on those upon which are the evil, the worst are in the middle and the better at the circumferences. The sinking in the middle appears like a vortical gyration, but in a spiral.

139. There was a plain somewhat more elevated than the valley. In this plain was congregated a multitude of spirits who had learned to practice evils by means of cunning, and to station themselves invisible behind others, and thus force them to think and speak what they wish them to, yea evils and falsities. They have contracted these arts by reason of their having been in the insane love of ruling over others. As it was then disclosed that their wickedness was consummated, their destruction followed The whole of that plain was overturned; and the earth was then opened elsewhere and there rose up good spirits who had been kept concealed by the Lord in the lower earth and guarded lest they should be infested by the evil; and they succeeded in place of the former, and came in full number into possession of their land. Such things are represented by the sons of Israel to whom the land of Canaan was given after the wickedness of its nations had been consummated.

140. After many destructions and partial judgments had been executed, which were premonitory of the general destruction and judgment and hordes of spirits who were impure had been cast into pools,[1] lakes, and chasms, that is into hells, then some came who were skilled in the art of breathing into others and exciting them to evils of interior thought. They incited some souls against the Lord and against Divine truth from Him, and from these the multitude, like one mass, began to be fermented. The tumult spread thence in every direction, as when a rebellion is started by a few persons, and yet at length stirs up a crowd. I there saw the disturbance widely spread to many rocks and mountains, even to their peaks, and thence to the sides down to the bases. Their intent was to destroy those who acknowledged and worshiped the Lord and were in Divine truths from Him. When it was noticed that the contagion had grown so wide then was the Lord's coming for the general judgment. This coming was the Lord's influx into them through the heavens, an influx which appeared like a misty sphere spread around over those mountains and rocks; and it carried off the dwellers there, not by casting them down but by bearing them away. The Divine sphere entered into their interiors and laid them bare; and what lay concealed in their will and heart was thus made manifest. And it snatched them away and carried them down to hells according to the evils of their life. That Divine sphere was seen carried around in gyres, sometimes returning; and it also drew them out of the places where they had concealed themselves. This was done with some myriads within the space of an hour. When these things had been accomplished, the tops of the mountains receded, and the mountains themselves sank down even to the plain, and there was seen a solitude. Such things are meant in the *Apocalypse* by the former heaven and the former earth which John saw pass away; for the mountains there, with the rocks and valleys, appear like the earth in our world; and the habitations upon the mountains are there called heavens. Those who were thus carried off and cast away, are they who are meant in the *Apocalypse* by the dragon and his two beasts (Chaps. xii., xiii.), and by the false prophet who was cast into the lake of brimstone and fire (Chaps. xix. 20; xx. 10).

141. The judgment upon the Protestants or Reformed was effected as follows: They who had led a life of charity, which may also be called a life of faith, had all been carried up into heaven long before the universal judgment; and all who in heart had denied heaven and had led an evil life had been cast by turns[1] into hell as they came from the world. On those only was the judgment effected, who had professed religion and had acted as if from religion but only hypocritically; to these it was conceded to gather themselves together in many places in the spiritual world, and, as in the world, to simulate religion, but still they had no religion. These are they who made heavens for themselves and who are meant by the former heaven and the former earth; and by means of arts unknown in the world they are able to produce splendid things, and to persuade those who are similar that they are in heaven. Their exteriors communicated with the ultimate heaven but their interiors with the hells; and it was on account of the communication with the ultimate heaven that they were tolerated, according to the Lord's words concerning the pulling up of the tares. The angels of the ultimate heaven were first separated from them and the communication was broken; as takes place comparatively with seeds in fruits when they ripen, in that when the time comes for them to produce a new tree they separate themselves, as it were, spontaneously from the body of the fruit.

142. All the Protestants or Reformed of whom there was still some hope, were collected in the middle, where they were arranged according to their kingdoms in the world; for according to these were also the diversities of their dispositions or affections. But above them[1] and also around them were those who had read the Word and had frequented temples, but yet had made nothing of evils of life, loving themselves and the world above all things; there was an immense multitude there. Surrounding the middle region, in which were Christians who had been in the good of faith and charity, were dark caverns stretching obliquely into hells which occupied a wide space below the heaven of spirits,[1] where were hells beneath hells. Such gulfs and chasms lay around that middle region on every side, east, west, south and north; thus the hells extended even under the circuit made by the Papists round about the Reformed. All who were interiorly evil had been disposed around the Christian middle, and from every quarter they were led down into those gulfs and cast into them. Thus, into the eastern gulf were cast those who had been collected from the east; they were such as had been in the love of self and especially in the love of ruling, nor had known anything whatever except that faith alone is saving. Into the southern gulf were cast those who had been versed in the doctrinals of faith; into the western gulf those who had been in the love of the world; and into the northern, those who had been in no understanding, but had merely heard preachings and had received no instruction afterwards.

143. Those at the south were led down first, then those at the west, and, lastly, those at the east. This happened at the same time that the eastern Papists were being led down beyond the northern tract.[1]

144. When this had been done their dwellings were laid waste and destroyed.

145. Afterwards I saw an immense number of those who had lauded faith alone, and yet had possessed no faith because they had paid no attention to the evils of their life, both the learned and the unlearned, saying that they have the Word and the true doctrine, that they know the Lord, and many other things, and that, therefore, they, above others, would be saved. They were led away in a multitude, first to the west, afterwards to the south, on the other side of the waste Babylonish tract there, and even towards the east and still farther. And they were divided; [some] were scattered towards the north, nor were they seen any more. And many were led back, but hither and thither; this transfer was effected in order that they might be explored as to whether they had any faith such as they had boasted of; namely, whether their faith was only a science, which is not faith; or, whether there was anything of life in it, which is faith. And it was given them to perceive that they had had no faith, but only something scientific without life[2].

146. When they were in the southern quarter near a gulf there, there came forth a multitude which had been concealed there from early times, who likewise said that they had had faith, and that they would be saved by reason of faith alone, and they had thought nothing about life. This multitude then approached them and was mingled with them.

147. From a certain mountain region a multitude was brought forth, who had led a moral life, not from any religion, but merely from fear of the law and of the loss of fame, honor and gain; thus without any Christian life; wherefore, so far as they could do it unknown, they perpetrated evils. Because they had not acquired to themselves any communication with heaven by means of a life from religion, they were led around to the southern and western quarters, that they might be explored as to whether they had any religion of life; and because they had none, they were rejected.

148. Finally came those who had been versed in the doctrinals of the church, and, in like manner, had led a moral but not a Christian life, because they had lived, not from doctrine, or the Word, but for the sake of fame, thus before men and not before God. And, being explored [it was seen] that they had nothing of conscience, because nothing of the religion of life. These were cast out of that mountain region.

149. All these, who were divided into the three classes, were driven so far away that they could not be seen except as a dark cloud; and they were dissipated. It was told me from heaven that they were cast down into uninhabited and desert places, and thus were separated lest they should consociate together.

150. The dispersion of these three classes was made to all the quarters, east, south, west, and north, whence they can never return; and this all the more, since every knowledge of religion is taken away from them. Concerning life in deserts, see elsewhere.[1]

151. The angels wondered that there is so great a multitude in the Christian world who are entirely ignorant of the truth that religion is a matter of life, imagining that religion consists in thinking something or other, and that by thus thinking they absolve themselves from every obligation of life, which they have made up from this: that, by the Lord's merit, they are exempt from the yoke of the law, and that no one can do good from himself, and that if he does, it is meritorious: and yet this is so far from religion of life that it is no religion at all. But all who have thought with themselves that evil must not be done because it is sin, and is against Divine laws, and who thus, so far as they could, have abstained from evils, all these have received something of conscience, and, in the things which were of their faith, although they were spurious,[2] there was much life; and they were saved.

152. The cleansing of the middle where the Reformed were, lasted a long time; and those who were in the church without the church in themselves, or without doctrine and religion in themselves, were, by turns, cast into the gulfs surrounding the middle, and many of them into deserts. These cleansings lasted for a long time after the judgment.

153. I once saw many spirits, sitting around a table in a certain house, who looked like rich merchants; and still more spirits were approaching so that there were quite a number of them. In face they appeared as though upright, and they were clothed as though they were angelic spirits. But I saw that they were all cast into desert places, and into woods, thus outside the societies of the upright. The reason was stated, namely, because, in the world, they had lived, in external form, like Christians and had acted well, but this solely for the purpose of acquiring a reputation for sincerity and honesty in order to make gain therefrom; and that they had not done the least thing for the sake of God or the neighbor, but all for the sake of themselves; and that, therefore, they had no communication with heaven. Hence it is that they were cast out thither, where they roam about amongst robbers, and themselves commit robbery. For when external bonds are taken away from such spirits they become robbers. They were robbers even in the world, were it not that externals, which are fears for the loss of fame and hence of gain, held them in bonds.

154. In the western quarter was seen a multitude whose speech sounded sincere, so that from their speech they might be thought to be, as it were, sincerities. By their speech and reasonings concerning sincerity they could induce the simple to believe that they were of such a character. But still it was found out that, within, they were like wolves, because without religion and hence without conscience. I have heard them consulting together as to how the simple might be deceived and their goods stolen away from them; some were consulting to do this, in order that they might thus obtain dominion. And then they assailed them from behind and inspired evils into them, for in this way they are able to subjugate. But their doings were seen in heaven and they were cast into a hell about the western tract of the middle region;[1] for they were insincerities and also wickednesses—devisers of arts with the end of gain and dominion.

155. Afterwards those of the Reformed were explored, (1) as to what idea of God they had. (2) Who had led merely a life of piety. (3) Who had frequented temples and made themselves guilty of all sins, but had not explored themselves. (4) Who believed that they had led a Christian life, in that had lived well morally because of the civil laws. (5) had been hypocrites.

156. They were explored as to what idea they had concerning God. It was found that they had thought only of God the Father, and of the Lord as like themselves; this is their belief, that the Father has compassion for the Son's sake. And they had then thought nothing concerning the Divine of the Lord. Thus, when they thought of one God they had not at the same time thought of the Lord; when yet the Father cannot be approached, since no one seeth Him but the Son alone; and that the Lord is the Way, thus that the Father is to be approached[1] by Him; and that faith must be a faith in Him, and not in the Father. Hence they could have no determinate idea of God except as of wind, or ether, or as of nature in its leasts; and there is no Divine idea of the Lord when He is thought of as a common man. The angels complained that they were disturbed by their idea, which was communicated to them; and very many of these spirits were brought down into the quarters round about. And the places to which they came then appeared gloomy; for the true idea of God makes clearness itself. Some of them were brought into places underneath according to their life; some in order that they might be further informed. And then only those who have lived well receive a Divine idea concerning the Lord. I saw that those succeeded to their place who had been kept concealed by the Lord lest they be hurt by the contagion; these are meant, in the *Apocalypse* (Chap. xx.), by those who were slain and were delivered out of the sepulchres.

157. Afterwards I saw those who had led a life merely of piety, and in idleness, led away from the others. They had been continually in prayers, and not at all in truths, merely knowing that salvation is from mercy, and that sins are remitted, but knowing nothing as to what sin is. They had despised others in comparison with themselves, and had also condemned them on account of cares of the world. Most of them had placed merit in prayers. Of these also the angels made complaint, especially because they induce sadness upon them. They dwelt at the side,[2] wherefore they were driven away to their own places; there they retain their worship, but they are driven to work. They were brought down into the northern plain because they were in ignorance of such things as lead to heaven.

158. Hypocrites who have spoken well concerning God, the neighbor and the country, but in themselves have thought the contrary, were explored and cast into hell. They wished to speak well concerning the Lord's kingdom and concerning heaven, for this is then the country, but their interior thought was explored, which was for themselves alone, and against the rule of the country; wherefore, when they were let into their interiors they perpetrated criminal things. They were cast into hells, being first deprived of all that they had drawn from the Word and from doctrines by which they had deluded others.

159. Preachers who know something of the doctrine of their church, and, after they have been instructed in the schools, and have come into their functions, no longer care for it, nor for the Word, except that they may preach and be elevated to higher offices or may gain wealth; and thus who live in ease and are merely worldly[1] and not Christians, these are sent into a hell in the northern quarter towards the west, far from the middle, where a dense fog is seen; and they then become stupid.[2]

160. All are separated according to their life, thus according to their affections, not according to their external life, but according to their internal, for this is the life of the thought from will or affection, and no one has internal life except from religion; external life is from morality and the state, and according to its laws; wherefore moral life, unless it draw its quality from spiritual life, and thereby change its appearance, is not spiritual life with any man; consequently there is no conjunction with heaven, and they who are not conjoined with heaven are conjoined with hell; and in such case, although, in the world, they have not done evil, yet, after their departure from the world, they do evil from delight; thus their state is changed.

161. *Concerning the Dragonists.* Who are meant by the dragon, may be deduced from what has been said in the [*Explanation*] *of the Apocalypse;* also that by the tail of the dragon is meant faith separate from charity, which drew down the stars from heaven, that is, the knowledges of truth and good.

162. The dragonists were separated; many of them, when orld, had been priests, who had confirmed themselves eparate from charity. They were explored in various by the inspection, in light, of the back of the head.

With those who were merely natural and hence infernal, the back of the head is filthy, hollowed out, and altogether bony. They are led down to places where they are deprived of the exteriors which have been induced on their faces by art, and the face is regarded according to the affections and the interior thoughts thence. What was human in their face is then taken away and something diabolical succeeds in its place. They are also explored by being turned to the east, and thus to the Lord; and then from the east there flows in a spiritual affection concerning the Lord. And then they instantly turn themselves back again to the west, like a spring, which recoils when it has been twisted backwards. In this way, also, angels explore newcomers to their heavenly societies.

163. There are also some who desire to hear truths; they believe they are saved if only they know them. But when they hear that truths are for the sake of life, and that so far as truths of life become actual, so far truths of faith also live, they then depart, feeling the utmost disgust for life, but not so for the truths which are of faith, because these they can talk about.[1] The truths of faith which do not live unless truths of life become actually such, may be enumerated; and it may be mentioned which are truths of faith, and which truths of life.[2]

164. Everyone can see that charity consists in not stealing from anyone, either by artifice or openly; that charity consists in being wholly unwilling to commit adultery with the wife of another; that charity consists in not doing injury to the neighbor in hatred and revenge; that charity consists in not reviling another, and so forth. He who abhors these things as sins, has charity, for he loves the neighbor.

165. Afterwards I saw an immense number, both sent forth from the heavens and rising up from below, and also of those who had been left, who were allotted their places, mansions and habitations; in the east, those in the clear good of love and of charity; at the west, those in the obscure good of love and of charity; at the south, those in truths from good in clearness; and at the north, those in truths from obscure good; all acknowledging the Lord as the God of heaven and earth.

166. Many in the Christian world were also cast down who had an understanding of truth but not a will of good. In the beginning such spirits are accepted among the upright because they can speak about many things even truths; moreover in the beginning, the understanding with them is enlightened but the will is laid to sleep. Such spirits were collected together on the mountains in the western quarter. They league themselves with the upright who are in the ultimate heaven, who do not enquire as to things of the will, but believe that those who speak intelligently are also good. But I saw such spirits, that they were altogether devoid of charity; and they secretly consociate with the evil and, first by reasonings and afterwards by arts, they infest the upright, until they are conjoined and devoted to themselves; for in this way they prevail against others. Many such were in heavens which they had made for themselves; and they interposed themselves between the Lord and man in the world, and so obstructed the way that the Divine operation could not have its force. Very many of this character are in the pride of self-intelligence from the love of self, and in the delight of domineering. I once saw such spirits in a somewhat high mountain in the western quarter toward the north, and everywhere round about on the sides of the mountain; and they persuaded themselves and others that one is in heaven from mere intellectual light and not at the same time from heavenly heat; they are most dangerous. I saw them cast down from the mountain and from the sides of the mountain, and a gulf underneath opened itself and swallowed them up,[1] and they sank deep down and were let into darkness. For they then received falsities in place of truths, and turned themselves to things contrary. Such is the understanding which is led by an evil will. The evil who had conjoined themselves with them, because they no longer had the power of resistance, were cast down into their various hells, some into hells under the mountains, others into hells under the plains.[2]

167. Those who were in faith separate rose up in insurrection, exciting a rebellion well-nigh universal. Their dogma and their learned leaders rose up against those who acknowledged the Lord and a life of love from Him. They stirred up all, except those who were in the eastern quarter, these were guarded by the Lord, even to certain Mohammedans who were in the northern quarter. They sent forth companies of fifty to many places, in order that they might stir up those who were there;[1] and those who remained and directed were divided into companies of ten. Their purpose was to destroy all those who acknowledged the Lord alone, and works together with faith as being saving. Almost all of them were without religion, and hence without conscience. But when they set out to do this, and were in the endeavor to destroy others that were evil, a force flowed down from on high, or from heaven, by which they were cast down to the hells, to a number exceeding many thousands. They also conjoined themselves with Papists and with monks who in the world had proclaimed themselves Christs and had thought nothing of the Lord's Divinity. When the whole crew had been cast down, the leaders were taken; and they became black as devils, both within and without; and they became so monstrous that they would be scarcely recognized as men. For man is such as he is as to life; he who is black as to life, afterwards becomes black even from head to heel. It was found that they had not rebelled from zeal on account of the doctrine of faith alone, but from the delight of ruling and of doing evil for the sake thereof. This was the combat of Michael with the Dragon; for all such who have insinuated themselves into heaven are drawn forth thence and cast down. They are Michael who worship the Lord and [who make] works conjoined with faith saving; for since the one is not given without the other, therefore they save conjointly.

168. The combat of the Dragon with Michael was afterwards as follows, for it lasted some days: A hand was seen stretched out over the heavens by the Lord. In the western quarter towards the west[2] there appeared as it were a great back raised above the middle towards heaven; angels in immense number were seen there.[3] In that entrance were the dragonists; and they spoke with them concerning the Lord and concerning the goods of charity and thence of faith. All then turned towards them to hear what they would say. And the dragonists were forced into the thoughts concerning the Lord and concerning faith alone which they had in the world; and then most of them had no Divine idea of the Lord, nor any idea of charity and works. The angels answered them wisely on this matter, but in vain. They said, moreover, that all the angels in the heavens do not perceive the matter thus; but it was in vain.[1] And at last, after the combat, when the dragonists were only willing to give further response outside of the matter or the truth, but could not, they were adjudged to be cast down from every place where such spirits were. But when they said they would resist, the Lord was seen descending from the sun in a bright cloud,[4] and He gave judgment that all who were found to be such should be separated and alienated. And then they were cast down successively and by turns according to the connexion of the societies of heaven; towards the western quarter an immense number, and a thousand then appeared as one. The grievous collision of truth and falsity which pertained to temptation was felt within me.[2] The whole western quarter was full of such spirits who had been cast down from the heavens; and then the earth was seen to open, and they were cast down and were covered over with a dense cloud. They were all such as would never have abstained from thinking and willing evils but only from doing them by reason of fear. This happened in 1757 on the 11th day of April.[3] From the southern quarter to the western the dragonists were seen in a curved line under the figure of a tail; at the south, there, were those who had been skilled in the degrees of justification and had confirmed these with themselves.

169. The Lord's heaven was first inherited by such as had acknowledged Him and had lived well, who had had heaven in themselves; afterwards, succeeded those who wished merely to have heaven outside themselves. To these latter it was also granted to make heavens for themselves, which they called heaven when they saw the magnificent things, such as palaces, porticos, paradises, and many serviceable things. But, since their internals were not in correspondence, such things disappeared; and then by phantasies and the abuses of correspondences and by many arts, they provided for themselves things similar. This did not last long, however, for they placed everything in delicacies and in bodily pleasures, and thus they became wholly external such as they had been in the world; and then came[4] the judgment, after which followed continual purifications of the societies from such spirits.

170. Many of those who are in faith alone, because they have no conjunction with heaven but all conjunction with hell, are in the love of ruling. They are explored in the following way: From the societies of heaven they look down to the places beneath; and where they see spirits, whether many or few, walking about there, they rule their thoughts, infest them in various ways, and by phantasies cause many things to appear to them to which they are led; their joy is to precipitate them into hells. They are of such a character that they do not want to be led but to lead; this is their delight; wherefore they cannot be led by the Lord, for the Lord leads through the affection of use, and this is not their affection. With them use is to domineer, and, therefore, they successively deny the Lord, and rely upon arts, which are many, by which they have dominion. They put their trust in their own prudence, and ascribe nothing to the Divine Providence; and when the reins are loosened, they rush finally into such a state that they think there is no God. And yet inseated in them is the purpose of domineering over heaven and to be there in place of God. This is inseated in the love of ruling for the sake of self. I once saw that a certain spirit in a small society was permitted to set in order those who were there. He set them in order as a spider sets its webs, placing himself in the middle and making paths in every direction, with the command that all should look to him; but that society was swallowed up by the hells which were below. All who are of such a character wish to be in the heavens; and they climb up into high places, where they believe that the exercising of dominion is the delight of life, but use is this; but when they have been explored they are cast down. They are wanderers; they direct their course from one society to another, often seeking to obtain office.

171. They are distinguished according to their ideas of the Divine, as (1) They who have an idea concerning the union with the Father. (2) They who have an idea solely of the Lord's Human and nothing of the Divine, although they had known of it. (3) They who have acknowledged three Persons and have not made them one God by essence; these are specially distinguished. (4) They who have an idea solely of the Father; these are without a God. (5) They who have not believed in the Lord from eternity.[1]

172. All those are preserved who in the world had acknowledged the Divine of the Lord and had shunned evils as sins, especially those who had acknowledged the Divine Human, and had approached Him. But the rest who had thought of the Lord as of a common man, are cast back among the Socinians and Arians who, at first, are under the heavens nearest above the hells, and afterwards are in the hells.

173. They who were in faith alone persecuted me. They brought persecution upon me[1] by bringing me into a state like that in which they themselves were by means of a like respiration and a like pulse; thus also into like thought and affection. And, in respect to God and salvation, I was in an obscure cloudiness as though immersed in water; and it was perceived that I had no communication[2] with heaven; and it was said that they have a similar communication.

174. Many of those who are in faith alone and had committed nothing of truth and good to life, for the reason that they had rejected all moral life from a spiritual origin, saying that it effects nothing, and that evils do not condemn, and that the Lord had fulfilled the Law for them, and had taken away damnation, and that of themselves they cannot do good still less fulfill the Law, many of these become rebels and put forth various scandals against the Lord, as is the case with all who have not lived their religion, even if in the world they had not thought wickedly concerning the Lord. They were explored and it was found that they had committed nothing of truth and good to life, and that they merely knew something from the Word which was like any other scientific matter in which there is nothing vital. And they then appeared without clothing, for clothing signifies the truths of life; and then they understand nothing at all, even as to what was right and just. It was said to them that they had lived without religion, and they were cast into the southern gulf, and were thus carried away.

175. Some of this character were let out of hells in order that they might be transferred to another hell. And it was then permitted them to act according to their will. Then they at once desired to force their way up to higher places by means of phantasies, and they were in the endeavor to do evil. It was recalled to their memory that, in hell, they had said to each other, that if it were allowed them to go out, they would be just as wise as others. Certain ones then spoke with them, saying something of intelligence in which was the light of truth; and when they heard them they were seized with such anguish that they fled away. This was done several times in order that it might be confirmed that such spirits, even when the state is changed, do not sustain the light of truth, thus of intelligence. They said that they were doing them harm, but answer was made that with each other they said otherwise. Hence it was made clear that they who are in hell can never live in the light of heaven, thus in heaven; and least of all in the heat of heaven, which is love.

176. After the judgment, all societies were disposed according to nations, in an admirable order. The order was according to affections in the heavens, and according to cupidities in the hells. They are then straightway purified by means of communications with the evil, and thence as it were by a fermentation; and then the alien are cast down like things heterogeneous. Sometimes the purification is effected by the society becoming like one man; they who are in the man remain, they who are outside the man are rejected. After the judgment, it is not permitted to thus ascend into heaven and be cast down thence, but each one is determined in such direction that he may go the way that leads to his society.

177. Afterwards societies were formed most distinctly according to all the genera and species of the affections of good and of truth; and also corresponding infernal societies. All spirits, after they have been vastated, are now led along by designated ways tending to the interior societies which correspond and are analogous to their life; nor are they allowed as before to turn aside in any other direction, or to stay in other places, still less to form for themselves societies and as it were heavens, according to life in externals. It is perhaps believed in the world, that man is saved and comes into heavenly societies according to his thoughts which are of the understanding of truth; but no one is saved according to these, but according to affections and thoughts thence, thus according to the good of the will and thence the truth of the understanding. For man is man from his will and his understanding thence, and not from the truth of the understanding separate from the good of the will; the understanding merely teaches how man must will and act. Many are led along the designated ways with difficulty, for they wish to go to the sides where they are sensible of the presence of the good both below and above, to whom they are eager to do evil; for all ways are such as are the societies above and below them.

178. The arranging of the Reformed after the judgment lasted a long time, for the reason that the Word is with them and the Lord is known, and they are therefore in the middle; and the greatest light is there, which passes from that middle to the peripheries where are also the Gentiles. On this account the arranging of the Reformed lasted a long time.

179. All those are retained in the heavens who have had the delight of some use, or of some function for the sake of use, whether it be the delight of business from sincerity, or of some study, provided only there be the delight of use and the acknowledgment of God. These can be held in order by the Lord, because the Lord inflows into uses. But they who have led a life of idleness, merely in social companies, or in offices solely for their own glory, cannot be ruled by the Lord; and because they are not members of the society, considered as a man, they are rejected. There is an application to the function of the blood.[1]

HE-GOATS; THEY ARE THOSE WHO ARE IN FAITH SEPARATE FROM CHARITY.

180. Speech was held with some in regard to the he-goat mentioned in *Daniel* and to its combat with the ram; and also in regard to the judgment on the goats and sheep mentioned in *Matthew*. And beneath me there then appeared a he-goat with great horns which was seen to infest the sheep and to treat them badly with its horns, and also to toss them hither and thither. And enquiry was made as to what this was, and it was said that this was the appearance of those who are in faith separate from charity, and of their combat with those who have been in the life of charity. And it was said that before their own eyes they do not look like this but like men sharply disputing with each other; and that he who seemed like a he-goat was one who was in faith separate, while they who seemed like sheep were those who were in the life of charity. For sometimes, and especially at a distance, spirits appear according to their affections, inclinations,[1] and their principles therefrom. For example, when any one is thinking from the understanding, he appears as though sitting on a horse, and some appear in other ways. Hence it was made evident that by the horned he-goat in *Daniel*, and by the he-goats in *Matthew*, none others are meant. It is supposed that all the evil are meant by the he-goats, but no others of them are meant than those who have lived wickedly and have nevertheless confessed faith alone.

181. In like manner afterwards, those who were in faith separate, appeared as he-goats, and those who were in the life of charity as sheep, and their argumentations and wranglings, as combats.

182. After the Last Judgment was accomplished many were seen who had been scattered among others at the back in the west; at a distance they appeared like he-goats, and some like dragons; who because they wished to seduce the upright were removed thence and driven into deserts where there was scarcely a shrub.

THE DRAGON.

183. By "the dragon" (*Apoc.*, Chap. xii.), and by his "two beasts" (Chap. xiii.), no others are meant than those who are in faith separated from charity both in doctrine and in life, by "the dragon," all those who have confirmed themselves in that faith, and by the beast from the sea, they who have confirmed those principles by means of reasonings from the natural man, and by "the beast from the earth," who is afterwards meant by "the false prophet," are meant confirmations from the Word in favor of that faith. That such are meant by "the dragon and his two beasts," may be clearly seen from each particular there written about them, understood in the spiritual sense; which can be seen to the life if the things written on the *Apocalypse* should be given to the public, for they are all confirmed from heaven; also that by "the tail of the dragon," is meant the confirmation of that faith by means of the degrees of justification which are treated of in [*S. D.*, n. 6014].

184. The *Apocalypse* treats of the two religious systems in the Christian world, that with the Reformed and that with the Papists, for the whole of Christianity is from these two, since they are the ruling systems. The religious system with the Reformed is a system of faith alone, which has devastated the church; and that with the Papists deals with the Lord's vicarious authority over the church, thus over the souls of men, and also over heaven, that resides with the popes and the primates and subordinate officials of the church. It is these two ruling systems of religion which [have been rejected] by the Last Judgment, concerning which we will treat later.

185. That they who are in faith separate are meant by "the dragon and his beasts."

186. That by "the dragon" are meant those who are in faith separate was made evident from the following circumstances: It is related that "the dragon stood by the woman about to bring forth, that he might devour her [offspring];" and that, by "the son, which the woman was about to bring forth," is meant the doctrine concerning the Lord and concerning the life of charity, was made evident from this, that when that doctrine was being written many of those who are in faith alone were present, and in such fury, that I could scarcely have written had I not been guarded by the Lord by means of angels; and it appeared as though they wished to rend it and tear it to pieces. By "the woman" there, is meant the New Church which is the New Jerusalem, and by her son, the doctrine concerning the Lord and concerning the life of charity; and by "the dragon," are meant those who are in faith separate, because such then was their nature, and because they were about to do what is described afterwards, by persecuting the woman, and casting forth water like a flood, that he might swallow her up; by "water like a flood," falsities are signified.

187. There was a certain preacher who was in faith alone; he appeared to others altogether like a dragon, and he also seemed to hover around a woman about to bring forth, eager to devour her child; and yet, seen near at hand, he was standing near those who defended the life of charity and the Lord. *He was a preacher at The Hague.*

188. Of those who are in faith separate there are some who correspond to the head of the dragon, some who correspond to his body, and some who correspond to his tail. The latter are they who are in the conceit of those principles, for the tail is the continuation of the spinal cord, and this again of the brain. There are some who correspond to the poison.

189. Concerning the back and hinder part seen like the tail of a dragon, see above [n. 134–179]. [On the Reformed], towards the end of the chapter.[1]

190. Moreover at the left was seen a hillside[1] upon which ascended many of those who were in faith alone; and on the summit there, they have some bearded old man who had been bearded in the world, and sometimes of lowly condition. This man persuades them that he is God the Father. It is a rock and rocky places are around about it. And when they do not wish to be seen they betake themselves behind the mountain.[2] These are they who have laid snares for all who do not believe like themselves, believing that this is allowable. The life of charity they make of no account. By their interiors they make one with the hells. They who appeared round about the bottom of the mountain were seen like an immense dragon stretching itself towards the places below; and its tail was seen elevated and extended from the mountain to the lowest parts thereof.

FAITH ALONE.

191. The interior sphere of spirits was perceived to be completely filled with affections, which are ends, of becoming great, of growing rich and of being wise for the sake of glory, and little, if at all, on account of the common good.

192. When, from the Lord, I was in the faith of the knowledges of truth it was found that evil spirits were powerless to refute them or even to reason about them; as when I was in the knowledges that the Lord rules the universe, that the Lord alone is life, and that the proprium of man is nothing but evil, and others of a like kind. Evil spirits hearing these, although they did not believe them yet could not contradict, for truth is averse to it,[1] because the intellectual does not admit any thinking against it. From this it was made clear that those who are in the simple faith of truth resist evils. I also saw some, who were in truths, who passed through many hells and all the infernals retreated, nor could they approach, still less do any evil. But he who believes in the faith set forth in the church at this day, cannot do this; the infernals are in no way troubled at their approach, because truth from the Lord is not in that faith.

193. *Concerning certain spirits who have no spiritual life because they are in ignorance of truth; and that life is inspired into them by the Lord through angels.* I once felt a somewhat intense cold from the soles of the feet up to the knee; it became evident that there were cold spirits [present]. It was told me that they were those who in the world had lived in absolute ignorance of God. After they had been elevated I heard them talking, and I could perceive scarcely anything vital in their speech. They spoke as though they were making inanimate statues speak, and I despaired of any life long remaining in them. They were like automatons or sounding sculptures. But presently I heard that they had been let into a species of activity appearing like a species of gyration. Angels were caring for them by infusing life into them, which they did with such solicitude and devotion, that it can scarcely be described, nor did they suffer themselves to be wearied. In the meantime they waved them, as is said in the Word of the things sacrificed, that they were waved by the Levites, the reason being, that they might receive spiritual life. When this had been done for some little time, they began to be vivified, and to be no longer of such a nature as before; thus they began to speak something in consociation, saying that they were in heaven.[2] The work was continued by the Lord through angels during the whole night, and after this they became such as to be capable of being insinuated or inserted into some companies in which they were afterwards perfected. For they were receptive of life because they had nothing repugnant thereto, as have those who confirm themselves in falsities against truths. The manner in which life was successively insinuated into them was represented by colors, the first of life by a marble color increasing in whiteness, the second by a growing azure color in which was the white, and the third by patches of bright clouds rising up.[1] Their quality was afterwards shown me by a blowing from them on my face, and also into the anterior region of the breast. It was somewhat cold but verging to heat. This was from the Lord alone by means of angels. They may be said to be resuscitated from no life into some life.[2]

194. There was one who held it as a principle that faith alone saves; it was said to him that faith is like science and knowledge which should be for the sake of use and good, and that otherwise it is nothing but a science; also that he is insane who believes that science alone saves, when yet all science and knowledge has good as an end.

195. He who has fought against evils, and, from the Lord, has come into the love of good and truth, is in the knowledges of truth and good as it were from himself; he sees them in himself, and they are inscribed on his heart, as is said in *Isaiah* and *Joel*.[3] The rational is then enlightened. But prior to this he does not know them, except from the memory alone, in which case he does not see them except externally, and if they are not seen internally they are dry and transitory. This is the life in truths; for all the things of truth are inscribed on the love, just as, with every animal, all things which are for use are inscribed on the affection, as in the case of bees, birds and other animals; so also are they inscribed on man if he is in the genuine love of truth and good. It is from this that the angels have their wisdom.[4]

196. I was led through societies or mansions of heaven, and I spoke with many. And when I came to mansions of the third heaven, where are the celestial, I wished to speak with them about the knowledges which are called knowledges of faith and which in themselves are truths. I marvelled that they did not wish to make any response to these things. They said that they see all things in themselves from the love in which they are, which was love to the Lord and mutual love, saying that the truths of their faith were inscribed on their life, and that therefore they see them from the light of truth which is from the Lord, and this because in good is contained all truth. They also said, What are knowledges except for the sake of uses? and uses are goods, and goods are of love. It was told me that they are of this nature because, in the world, they had applied all the truths they had heard to their life. All their love and all their faith consists in deeds.

197. Those who are in faith alone believe in instantaneous salvation and pure mercy; and therefore they implore mercy alone and believe that they are instantly saved the moment they receive faith, even though it be in the last hour of death. They also believe that the remission of all sins consists in the wiping away of all evils. They have no comprehension[1] of remission by means of repentance of life, but only of remission by means of faith arising from thinking such things as they call of their faith; thus they are ignorant of all the means of salvation. It was shown them that such things are a phantasy; and this phantasy was represented as being interiorly full of poisonous serpents. The nature of the phantasy was shown in a ludicrous manner, namely, that they think and also wish to void those serpents through their posteriors.[2]

198. When they think from their doctrine about faith alone, and are opposed by the statement, in *The Epistle of James*, that men should show their faith by works, there appears as it were a knife flying forth to slay those who perceive this to be the case. And from one side comes forth an idea of Luther, and from the other, whither the knife flies, an idea of James, although Luther and James themselves are not there. The reason is, because, Luther excluded the *Epistle of James*.

199. Below, at the left, are those who from doctrine have confirmed themselves in regard to faith alone, but yet have lived a life of charity from the principle that faith produces the works of charity. These, because they have lived well, are accepted and have conjunction with heaven. Still it is not a direct conjunction, and this for the reason that they hold it as a principle that it is faith that produces the works of charity, when yet faith is of the thought, and thought produces nothing; it only teaches what should be done, and if a man does what it teaches, then it is not from any faith; for knowledges of truth do not become knowledges of faith until man has done them. It is like one who believes that the sight operates into the hands to enable a man to work, or into the feet to enable him to walk and not stumble, when yet the sight does not operate in this way, but it teaches and brings things to view. That this is an inversion was shown by it being given to a certain spirit to walk on a road and to then believe that it was the understanding that was leading him. He then went from the east to the west or from the south to the north, thus from truths to falsities, and into obscurity. But his state was changed [so that he believed] that the will or love was leading him; he then walked from the west to the east and from the north to the south, thus into good and into truth in light. It was told them that with those who have had this belief the state is successively inverted, and that then they begin to be regenerated and come into the angelic life.

200. They who, from doctrine, are in the principle that faith alone saves, and yet have led a good life, constitute certain societies in which they are in the middle, while at the circumferences are those who are not of such a quality, and lastly those who are evil, so that they are surrounded by the evil. It was told them that they still dwell among the evil.

201. It was made known by living experience that those who have been in faith alone and have led a moral life, had made heavens for themselves, where they seemed to themselves to have been in light; but it was shown that it is a wintry light, for when angels looked thither, in place of light there appeared a thick darkness. Those who go there, and are at the same time in charity, feel a pain in the breast, the stomach and the knees.

202. *Concerning those who are continually wrangling about truths.* There are hells where they do nothing else but wrangle about truths. One of them was under the groins. In that hell were those who believe that they know everything and that nothing is hidden from them, when yet they do not know anything, except that their faith is the all of the church with men. There are those there who, by reason of their belief that they know all things, think that they alone are entitled to talk; they despise the laity.[1] They are continually saying that this is the truth itself, and that it cannot be contradicted. I have there heard perpetual contradictions and quarrels which went so far that they wished to attack their opponents with their fists, but they are held back by others. They appear in that place as if they were tearing[2] garments; and from the place is heard as it were the gnashing of teeth. Thus do they go forward and back and thus do they wrangle, not at all for the sake of truth but for the sake of themselves from the pride of their own intelligence and from the itch of domineering. They are removed from others, because they disturb all tranquillity of mind and take away the freedom of thinking from the Word, inducing their own opinions as though they were from the Divine and infesting all who do not receive. At this day there are many such consociations drawn from the Christian world, because there they have divided the church on questions of opinion concerning what is to be believed, and the good of life they not only reject, but they also say that they know not what it is unless it be to give to the poor and to hear preachings.

203. Those who have said that they had faith have been seen many times; and when they are explored it is found that they had no other faith than that which was spoken of above. This they call the only saving faith, and also spiritual faith, and yet they have not lived any Christian life by shunning evil because it is sin. They were sent into places where faith was constituted of truths which had their essence from the good of life, and their communication was granted them to discover whether they had faith. And, from the perception then given them, they themselves openly confessed that they had nothing of faith, it was mere knowledge like any other mere knowledge of the world, and that they had not known what faith was; also that faith was truth, and that, unless truths are from good, they are not truths, but are only articulated expressions of sound.

204. Very many of those who are in faith alone and in no life of charity are sensual. For evils of life, which they neither see in themselves nor have endeavored to see, occupy their voluntary and make it; and, as a man is in respect to his voluntary such he is as to his interiors. Therefore these interiors are shut up, and all things which are of the church and heaven are below or without, thus merely in the memory where they reside as historical faith or as science. This is the reason why, when men hear something of the truths concerning the Lord, the Word, eternal life, heaven, the state of the angels and the state of men after death, the things they hear are received as matters of the memory; but as soon as they think about them, as to whether they are so, then the sensual corporeal judges and makes its own conclusion. The conclusion reached is that what has been heard cannot be true, and this because what is previously in the memory from doctrine must be believed; as, that there are three Persons of the Divinity, that the Human of the Lord is not Divine, that angels, because they are spirits, are like winds, and so likewise man after death. The reason is because it is the sensual that makes the conclusion, and [in that] light from heaven which enlightens cannot be received, the interiors being closed to the transflux of that light. Investigate for yourself as to whether this is not the case, whenever any such truth is laid under direct examination, and enquiry is made as to whether it is so. The sensual man is such that he comprehends fallacies and believes in appearances and speaks truths, but the truths themselves, which are of the light of heaven, he rejects. This is the effect of faith alone, and therefore they cannot be led on into any understanding of truth.

205. It was said by angels that there can be no such thing as faith alone. Spirits who, in the world, had been in faith alone, being indignant at this, came running up from every direction to where the angelic spirits were, and enquired, "Is there no such a thing as faith alone?" In this manner they ran to ten or fifteen places, and everywhere received the answer, that there is no such thing, because faith without love is mere knowledge, and their faith the mere knowledge of falsity; and if they wish to call mere knowledge faith, because they have persuaded themselves in it, although they do not understand whether it is so, [their belief] is nothing but persuasion because it is so said, and is scarcely different from the belief that corpses and bones and men's graves are holy, when yet they are stercoraceous and signify damnation and hell. When they heard this they ran on and enquired what love was, whether it was not faith alone. Angelic spirits thought them insane, and still more when they said that works were faith, which is as if they had said that thinking was doing. They ran on still further and said, "Is not faith thus a nonentity?" They received the answer that faith separate from charity is a nonentity, because faith is called faith from charity which is its soul; and faith separate from charity is just such an entity as is the body without the soul.

206. I have heard many of the learned reasoning about various matters of their faith, things which they had held from birth, thence as truths of their religion. Their reasoning was sharp and vehement and each one was refuting the other. There were angels who were listening and they said that with not a single one of them did they perceive any affection of truth, nor therefore any sight of truth, and thus no delight of mind arising from any truth. They wondered that these spirits were able to confirm falsities; and they said that it was merely the delight of reasoning springing from pride, and that thus they cannot progress into any wisdom, for they are at a standstill. But those who are in the affection of truth are ever progressing from truth to truths, and this continually until at last they come to wisdom and thus to angelic happiness. They said that as soon as they hear such reasoners,[1] they turn themselves away and have no wish to join company with them because they see nothing. Of such quality are very many of those who have confirmed themselves in faith separate, not only in doctrine but also in life; for they think to themselves, "What need have I to know what evil is since this does not condemn? or what good is since this does not save? Only let me think, from that faith, that the Lord has fulfilled for me all things of the law and that His merit will be imputed to me."

207. It was disclosed by angels of heaven that those who are in faith alone have no conscience, yea, that they do not know what conscience is; and he who has no conscience has no religion. The reason is, because they make goods of life of no account, and they who make these of no account can by no means have conscience, and hence cannot know what it is; for conscience is a grief of the mind (*animus*) that one has done contrary to the Divine precepts and that one has thought against them. Grief of conscience arises from this, that they see themselves as it were in damnation.

208. They who believe that man is saved by charity and not by faith alone, if they do not live the life of charity, differ little from the others. For to say charity or to say faith, and not to do them, are both equally of the thought, in which there is nothing of life because nothing of the will. Such spirits inflict pain in the breast and in the right shoulder-blade.

209. How greatly the principles of falsity injure the mind (*animus*) and turn it away from deeds, may appear from many examples. Thus he who believes that works contribute nothing to salvation turns his mind away from doing goods. He who believes adulteries are allowable turns his mind away from chaste conjugial[1] love, thus from chastity, yea from purity of faith; for purity of faith is wholly discordant with adulteries. He who believes that nature operates all things, and that God operates only in a universal way, trusts in his own prudence, and does nothing of good except from himself. Wherefore principles of falsity inflow into the life; for the will does not act contrary to the principles that have been received, but with them.

210. I have spoken with Melancthon about faith alone, to the effect that he could see from reason alone, that faith alone is not saving because every man is his own good and his own evil; and that every spirit is a form and image of his own good and his own evil; and this not only as to his face but also as to his whole body. For according to the quality of a spirit's affection such he is in respect to his mind, and at the same time in respect to his body. This may be manifestly known from the fact that when anyone speaks contrary to the affection of any spirit or angel, he immediately changes his countenance, yea, becomes invisible and disappears. And, therefore, because faith alone is merely of the thought and not of the will, and thus only of the memory and not of the life, it follows that it is as yet outside the man and not within him. Wherefore, since a spirit is a complete spirit in the degree that he is his own good or his own evil, and since faith separate from good is not within the man, it follows that it is merely like a skin, and that men of faith separate are not men except as to the skin; and thus that they are to be called cutaneous.[1]

211. The truth is, that he who confirms faith alone with himself both in doctrine and in life cannot be reformed, and thus cannot be saved; that is, he who, while in the world, has thought, "Since I am justified by faith nothing of evil will condemn me, because it is not imputed, and nothing of good will save me;" and has thus cast out of his thought all reflexion upon the evil and the good of life with himself; and if he apperceives any evil or good he is not concerned about it as being a matter of no importance in respect to salvation. Such are spirits who cannot be reformed, for they think like things after death.

212. That the Lord is love; that hence the whole heaven is arranged according to the genera and species of love, and thus according to its varieties; that in like manner every society of heaven, and every spirit and angel; that it is similar in a spirit and angel in whom heaven is, in that all things in them are disposed from love and, according to it in their understanding, yea, their whole body. How then can there be such a thing as faith alone, since faith is according to love?

213. There was a certain Englishman,[2] who had written learnedly and skilfully about faith and charity, and this from considerable ingenuity. But he had come to the conclusion that faith produces charity, and that when man is justified by faith he is in the endeavor to do good, and that this is the effect of faith; thus that faith first leads to charity and afterwards in charity. It was told him by angels that it so appears to man, and yet that it is not so; and, because it so appears, that this is the way of reformation, for thus man learns many things which are of faith,[3] believing that in this way he is saved; but when man is not regenerated the order is inverted. And, moreover, that if he should make enquiry he would never find that faith produced charity, but that faith was produced by charity. And, therefore, because he was gifted with much ingenuity, he thought out many reasons for confirming the idea that it is faith that produces; and it was permitted him to produce these reasons, and to show whether the case was so. Wherefore in his meditation he was left to follow out each reason; but when he came to the end of his production there always appeared, as it were, an obstruction to the way which he was unable to penetrate so as to arrive at charity. Therefore, abandoning this reason, he acted in a similar manner with another reason, and so on with a hundred. In this way he went on in his ingenious meditation every day for an entire year,[1] and not once did he see a conjunction on the part of faith. Wherefore he afterwards confessed that the thing was impossible, and that the fact that some said they had felt it with themselves was due either to their having thought of charity outside of faith, or to other causes, etc., etc., which arose from the fact that the things which are of faith have taught them, for the truths of faith teach and man acts according to them, and that from a principle either adopted or heard, they have attributed it to faith. Moreover, after a man has done charity, faith is then living, and then, in the single things, charity and faith work together, and it can hardly be seen which is prior and which posterior. The truths of faith which are of the thought and understanding are prior, —but still truths do not live and become truths of faith or saving until man lives according to them.[2]

214. I read before Englishmen their exhortation used before the Holy Supper [teaching], how they should act that their sins may be forgiven, and in which there is no mention of faith; and I said this is true religion itself. Certain preachers who were in favor of faith alone, hearing this, said that when reading that exhortation in their churches they had fully believed it to be the way of salvation, but when thinking from their doctrine of faith alone they had thought differently. The English were praised for that exhortation, and many of them believed that it belonged to their doctrine; but more of them said that this was for the common people, faith alone being for the learned. They were asked whether they wished to thus invite the curse expressed in the words, that unless they do this Satan would enter into them as he entered into Judas. They then went away and spoke about the matter among themselves.[3]

215. I once saw some leaders of the English, among whom were also one or two bishops, who fought for faith alone as for their altars and hearths. And from the ideas of their thought concerning faith alone and justification thereby they formed an image, that it might represent that faith. In the spiritual world this can be done skilfully and easily. They there made their images[1] by means of ideas, and these images also became visible, for appearances are merely from their ideas. Into their image they fitted all things of their faith. But when it was finished it appeared in the sight of the angels as an enormous monster, and as though it would frighten them away. This was in the light of heaven; but before their own eyes it assumed a different appearance, as monstrous things are wont to do, when seen in darkness and from phantasy. They gloried in it at first, but afterwards they became ashamed.

216. The English said that faith produces charity as a tree produces fruit. But it was shown them that by a tree[2] there is not meant faith but man, and by the branches and leaves are meant the truths of faith, and by the fruits the goods of love; also that natural affection or natural good, which is of the love of self and the world, cannot be conjoined to a faith which is spiritual; if it is conjoined, the result is an adultery; and that spiritual good is not possible except by means of the good of life, which is the good treated of.

217. An argument on which they lay stress is, that man cannot do good which is good of himself. This is true, but still unless man be in good as from himself it is not appropriated to him, and so he is not conjoined to the Lord. In order for conjunction there must be something reciprocal, and thus a covenant, which is, If you do that I will do this. And, therefore, that man may do it as if of himself freedom is given him, and this freedom is freedom to think, to will, and to do; reason[1] is given him that he may see what salvation is; will is given, and choice and election; and he is commanded to act. All these are given in order that he may act as if of himself, and yet it is not from him but from the Lord. If he did not act of himself he would be an automaton, and all influx would pass through him. The Lord is continually with man pressing and urging him that he may act, and that, for the sake of appropriation and conjunction, it may appear no otherwise than that he acts of himself. A thousand passages can be adduced showing that man is condemned if he does evil and rewarded if he does good; those where doing and works are mentioned might be brought forward.

218. Many were explored who at the last hour when they had received the Sacrament believed they would be saved by that faith. They said they had believed with trust and confidence; yet it was the life of evil that remained and not the faith. They were told to hold their breath and, at the same time, retain that faith, but still, as soon as they breathed, the delight of evil, from which was their life, returned; and they were cast into hell.

219. After the judgment those who had been scattered amongst others round about were collected together. And when they had been collected, there came into their mind a cunning [idea][1] of seducing the upright [by teaching them] that faith alone is saving. Wherefore the latter complained about them to the Lord. And then I saw them receding more and more, even till they came to the bounds of the Christian world; there, at the back, were deserts, and I saw a great part of them driven thither. Afterwards it was granted me to see the nature of this desert. There were vile huts and hovels wherein they dwelt almost solitary, with some harlot, and round about them it was stony, with great heaps of rocks between which were a few ways. Nor does one dare to approach another. They all fear each other lest they do evil, nor do they believe even when they stand outside and invite[1] them in. A piece of bread with water is given them daily; some send them something eatable. I saw no shrub, still less any tree; but sandy and rocky places.[2]

220. Many of them said they were desirous of being instructed and thus of rejecting that faith, but in vain; the inrooted faith clung to them because it had been the principle of their life. What is marvellous, the learned of that religion regard justification by faith alone as such a Divine mystery, that touching it is like touching the pupil of the eye; saying that they have bound themselves to it by oath. But it was shown them that in the *Apocalypse* it is described by the beast from the sea [*Apoc.* xiii., 1–10], and in *Daniel* by the little horn which waxed great towards all the quarters, and cast down from heaven the host thereof [*Dan.* viii. 9–10]. But when they hear this confirmed from heaven, where correspondences are perceived, they still worship justification as their idol. The justification that is meant is justification by faith separate from charity. I also spoke much about the endeavor to good which follows justification, asking them whether this endeavor is anything of the will on man's part. They said that it was: others said that it was not, but was to be carefully separated.[1]

221. Some say that we have no free will, but that it was destroyed by Adam; that we have some freedom of belief or faith, but none of doing or acting. But it was shown them that no man, not even Adam, had freedom from himself, but only as if from himself; and that everyone has freedom to act from the Lord, thus to be led by the Lord: and that each one is in this freedom so far as he is led.[2]

222. All those preachers who in the life of the body have confirmed themselves in faith alone, and who cannot recede therefrom on account of their life, are not admitted to preach. Their priestly garment is taken away from them, and afterwards they do not know that they have been preachers. Very many are admitted to preach, but as soon as they preach faith separate from charity, and justification by it alone, all who are present go out, and the temple becomes empty. Thus those preachers who can recede from that faith are amended, and receive the doctrine of heaven. The case is similar with those who separate the Lord from the Father and do not make them one, and what is new, all of them, after they have been in the spiritual world a month, reject the third Person, acknowledging that the Holy Spirit is the Lord speaking through angels and spirits. The reason why they reject is because enthusiastic spirits, Quakers and many others, who are infernal, call themselves the holy spirit from eternity.

223. I have had much speech with them in respect to this matter, to the effect that they have rejected the third Person of the Divinity, and that now they think of two, in order that they may see, whether from the two they make one.

224. One[1] whom I knew in the world, had confirmed himself in faith alone by many arguments. I said to him that he should go and see those habitations in the desert, and when he went he saw nothing but a sandy waste, with rough stones and rocks all around, but not a single shrub nor a blade of grass[2]; and, therefore, returning, he grieved over their miserable lot. There also he met and spoke with some who in the world had been acknowledged by him as learned men. And when he still wished to defend faith alone there appeared serpents which darted at his feet and coiled themselves around them. He was afterwards led to plains where those dwelt who were in a similar faith, where there was grass, shrubs, trees and buildings, and the inhabitants were of a cheerful disposition, and industrious in their work and business. They confessed that they had merely known of that faith from having heard it preached, but had thought nothing about it beyond the literal sense, and had not confirmed it any further; and that still they had lived a life according to the Word; thus that the faith was only a faith of science in their memory, but not a faith in the life. They are afterwards instructed and receive truths which they had not known in the world.

225. A learned man, who, in the world, had thought solely about faith alone was examined as to whether he knew any truth of the church, whether he knew what faith is, or what the life of faith, what charity is, what love, what truth and the affection and perception of truth, what free will, what regeneration, what spiritual temptation, what Baptism, what the Holy Supper, what is heaven with man, and what and whence is hell, wherein is the holiness of the Word, what Providence is, what God and whether He is one or three, what conscience is, also what is the church in man and what heaven in him. And the angels heard; [and they saw] that he knew nothing of these things. The responses which he made were falsities derived from reasonings, and were also things from the Word which had been falsified. It was said to him, How could he be in the light of heaven, and hence in angelic wisdom, and from this in the felicity of heaven? Being convicted, he wished to learn, but because he had confirmed faith alone he could not.

226. I spoke with angels concerning the progression of truth to good, saying that the angels have joy when an infant or boy learns truths and acquires them from affection, thus when truths become truths of knowledge; they have greater joy when they become truths of the understanding, still greater when they become of the will, and the greatest joy when they become of the act. Then they love him because truths have taught him and led him to good. And they are gladdened when he knows that it is not truths which lead to good, but that it is good which leads him into truth and thus into wisdom. Man does not know this, but the angels perceive it and rejoice.

227. How Englishmen who wish to acquire a reputation for erudition compose their discourses with great elegance and as it were profound wisdom, especially concerning the influx of faith, and the endeavor to the doing of good, and of man's state then as to affection, reception and enlightenment by the Holy Spirit. Some of the English complained, saying that these elegancies delight their ears and are pleasing to them while they listen; but when they wish to apply anything therefrom to themselves they know not what the preachers have said, and whether it is allowable to adjoin the will, and thus to openly will, and act, or not. When they ask them, they say such sounding words as, that they may, and may not, and finally that it is a transcendent mystery. They speak in this manner so that their hearers, being able to gather either meaning from them, may praise them. And yet, by reason of these words with their double meaning in which something lies hidden like a snake in the grass, those hearers do not love them. They tell them that they should remain in the doctrine that is taught in the exhortation used at the Holy Supper, and that if they do not so from the will, the devil will, perchance, enter into them as he entered into Judas. Their discourses are also filled with the perception of trust and confidence in themselves.

228. I have sometimes heard it said from heaven that that faith saves no one because there is no life in it; and that true faith is truth; and that man has truth only so far as he shuns evils as sins. *Particulars concerning the Decalogue and its Holiness,*—See [*S. D. n.* 6065].

229. The truths of faith are compared with the ornaments and utensils in palaces; unless man lives according to them they are, as it were, in a dark room with the windows shut, but as soon as a man lives according to them he is then elevated into heavenly light, the windows are opened, and he then sees those things and is delighted with them.

CONCLUSION.

230. Lastly, it shall be told what the state of man is after death, whatsoever his religion may have been. They who have led a good life, who are such as have shunned evils because they are sins, and have conducted their business with rectitude and sincerity, are not let into the evils of their will, but are held by the Lord in good, and in intelligence and wisdom therefrom. But they who have lived in evil, are let into the evils of their will, and then they can think in no other way than in agreement with those evils; and when in that state, they appear as if insane, more like beasts than men. The love of doing evil then rules them, and they now rush into all things which they have coveted. They who have been in the love of ruling for the sake of self are more insane than others. I have seen many[1] such spirits, and they appear as if utterly deprived of all rationality; and yet they then believe that they are wise, yea, the wisest of all. But it is allowed them at times to return into the rationality which they had in the world, when, from shrewdness, they had feigned themselves gifted with every virtue. Still, even then, the pleasure of returning into the delight of their will draws them on so that they cannot be led away except unwillingly; they wish to be insane. And because they are of such a character they are sent into hells, and then it is not permitted them to go out. And they there remain under the supervision of a judge who imposes tasks on them which they must do daily. If they do not perform them, they receive neither food, clothing, nor bed; and if they do evil[2] they are severely punished. Thus by means of adequate tasks they are led away from the delights of their will. In such a prison all are held, both men and women, who have lived in evil, that is, who have given reins to their sins. But before they go, they are deprived of everything which they had formerly learned from the Word, and of everything which they had known concerning faith, and also of the knowledge of who they had been in the world, whether kings or magistrates, bishops or elders, rich or poor, or of the common people. And they are then all alike among themselves, nor is one greater than another. A low countryman may be together with an eminent man, nor does either know who had been the more eminent in the world; for elation of the mind exists equally with those who are of the common people as with those who are in the highest places. And, what is wonderful, they cannot go out to all eternity; for if, perchance, they put forth a foot, they are punished; and if they are taken out by others they become more insane than before. I have sometimes seen this done. They are like robbers who, from fear of punishment, live honestly in a house in a city, but as soon as they come into the woods they constantly think about robberies.

231. All the states of man can be recalled after death, the states of age, as the state of childhood, of adolescence and of youth; they who come into heaven come into the state of their adolescence, return into all the states of innocence, charity and affection with all their delights,[1] and this with ineffable increase. With those who have lived well good states are recalled, with those who have lived in evil, evil states, concerning which various things have been said above.

232. That at this day they crucify the Lord, see *Lord;* and that they are like the Jews in their time: experience.

LOVE.

233. From the ideas of spirits passing into the world of spirits after death, may be known all the ideas which they have had concerning God, heaven, love, and faith. Concerning God most of them have an idea as of a cloud or mist, because they have thought that God is a spirit, and of a spirit they have no other idea. Concerning heaven they have the idea that it is in the air, some that it is in the stars, others that it is in the universe, and scarcely any that it is with man; for they cannot remove the idea of space. Concerning heavenly joy they have ideas of delight, each one of the delight of his own love, especially of the delight of ruling and of living happily and continually in external luxuries. Few have an idea of living in internal delights; not knowing what they are. Concerning love they have so gross an idea that you may call it filthy. They think from the delight of the love of adultery. Some have no idea of love, because they have not known what love is. And so concerning mutual love; some have an idea of external friendship. In a word, all their ideas of love partake of the idea of lasciviousness. Concerning faith they have no other idea than as of the received faith,[1] the quality of which has been spoken of above. This is no idea of genuine faith since it is an idea of faith separated from charity, and what this is, is unknown. When the angelic idea concerning God, heaven, love, and faith flows in, if it is not perceived, it becomes in their minds like an obscure darkness; for the light of heaven does not enter in. Such, from faith alone, is the world at this day. For when that faith enters in and is received, then nothing of truth is loved. They say, "In this faith I know the truths of our church in one complex."

234. After death man comes into the world of spirits which is intermediate between heaven and hell; and there he changes his societies, and is thus prepared either for heaven or for hell. This change appears like a transference from one place to another, and also like a journey. He goes to various quarters, now ascending to higher regions, now descending to lower; and yet it is perceived that these journeys are only changes of state. This has been the case with me when I have been in the spirit. And at last when the man has been prepared, then that love leads him which is the head of his other loves. And he then turns[2] his face to the society where his ruling love is, and thither he betakes himself as to his own home.

235. The knowledges of truth are inscribed on the affection or love, so that it is the affection that produces them as though they had been known to it. Affection sees those things which are consonant and concordant with itself, for some have the faculty of confirming. Wherefore if the affection is good, and it becomes good by means of life, it straightway has inscribed on it the knowledges which serve it; and when it hears and sees them, then, from things in itself which are similar and analogous, it discerns them; this therefore is of the love. But he who is in faith alone and in the love of self and the world, cannot be affected by other things than those which agree with his love; these are inscribed on his love. They are contrary[1] to the truths of faith, which are: That God should be loved above oneself, heaven above the world, the good of the neighbor, and every use for the neighbor, and the like [above self]. The truths of faith are then cast out, which is also actually the case after death, and those things remain which are of the love, or, which are of the will.

236. All who are in the love of ruling for the sake of self and not for the sake of uses, retain that love after death; and wheresoever they come they wish to rule. This love rushes on as its bonds are relaxed. It spurns everything Divine, unless this afford it the means of ruling; in which case, so long as it serves as a means, it loves it; but when it does not serve as a means it not only rejects it but also holds it in hatred. The reason is, because this love is opposite to heavenly love. They are not admitted into heaven, and if, like hypocrites, they insinuate themselves into heaven they fill the whole neighborhood with an idea and image of themselves, and this even when they speak of God. This love turns aside[1] the ideas of the angels, which are directed away from themselves and towards God; therefore they are driven away. This has been shown. For the most part they are corporeal because immersed in the proprium, and not elevated above it. Such spirits are taken to the boundaries of the world of spirits of our earth where there appears a lake smoking with fire; and first the spirit is rolled in the dust and let into his life in the world, and thus he is cast into the lake.

237. Let all who are in the world and read these lines know that the love of ruling for the sake of self and not for the sake of uses is diabolical love itself and in it are all evils. Let them know this and be on their guard. All evil loves are in that love and with it, even those of which the man had been wholly ignorant while in the world. I have examples in all abundance, showing that those who, in external form, appear to be moral and Christian men but interiorly in themselves have thought of nothing else but themselves and the world, after death are consociated with devils. There was one whom I saw during a long period of time, who was so haughty in his disposition that hardly anyone could be more haughty; and yet in the world he could talk with theologians and speak morally with other men; and he feigned justice and equity more than anyone else. But after death he became such a fiery devil that he not only denied God, but he also wished to be the devil himself, in order that he might continually fight against God and destroy heaven; and he was enflamed with hostility against all who were in the acknowledgment of the Lord. He was punished frequently, but in vain. If I should mention his deeds of malice, cunning, and crimes I would fill pages. In him I saw what the devil is, both in his own hell and with men (C. XII.).[1] Such men do not acknowledge God, but believe all are gods who are powerful; and they wish to become gods themselves, and be worshiped.

238. There was once some conversation respecting the love of ruling, to the effect that many believe that those who worship the Lord in the world, although they are His enemies, [will be saved and will rule over all in heaven].[2] And it was said that a devil can be driven to worship the Lord, if only he be promised that he will be great, and still more if he would thereby become the greatest. It was then permitted that they should take from hell one of the devils there, who was most bitterly hostile to the Lord; and it was told him that he would be made the greatest by the Lord. He then put his whole mind to this object, and this to such a degree that he wished to lead all men to the Lord and to drive them by threats; saying, that the Lord alone should be honored and worshiped, and repeating it with earnestness and persuasion; but in his mind he cherished the thought that he would become the Lord's vicar. When, however, he saw that he had been deluded, he began to detest the Lord, and became as before, His most bitter enemy; but he was cast into hell. In a word, the delight of commanding exceeds every delight of the body.

239. Concerning the two rules or dominions, one from the love of self, the other from love towards the neighbor, see in the work on *Heaven and Hell*, in *The Doctrine of the New Jerusalem*, and in the little work on *The Earths in the Universe*, all of which works may be adduced.

240. With those who are in the love of commanding, the interiors appear black, and this because they are closed against the influx of heaven; but their inferiors appear as it were misty because they are opened to the hells.[1] It is said that with those who are in the love of ruling, the superiors, thus the interiors, can never be opened towards heaven.[2]

241. There were seen men who belonged to the nobility[3] of various nations. They had cordons lying over their breasts suspended from the shoulders, and also diadems. A number of them were seen. And being inspected by angels it was observed that they were continually directing their looks to themselves, and were thinking about their own superior eminence and excellence, and desiring that all men should turn their eyes to them. And because they believed that they were more worthy of being set over others than other men, therefore offices were given them. But when they were making conclusions with respect to subjects that concerned the common welfare, it was then perceived that they had no affection for the community, nor for uses; thus they were unable from judgment to discern good from evil, or truth thence from falsity, but could only speak in a high-sounding manner from the memory. And because they were of such a character they were cast out of their offices; and it was allowed them to wander about and get offices for themselves. But wherever they came they were told by the spirits there that they were thinking only of themselves and not of them, thus that they had no thought except what was from the sensual corporeal; therefore they were nowhere received. They did this for some time, afterwards I saw some of them reduced to extremities and seeking alms. Thus is the love of ruling brought low. One spirit who also wore the insignia of a nobleman confessed that as long as he wore that insignia he could not think as before, because he was interrupted by thought concerning himself; but whenever he was at home and put it off, he returned to his own judgment as before.[4]

Diabolical spirits are skilled in the art of seducing the upright. They do this by turning their thoughts to themselves and their own proprium; by praising them in various ways; by placing themselves at their back and breathing into them the love of self; and where they observe anything black, which is the proprium, they enquire what is there; they then infuse it with their own thought and pervert, yea lead him. Some look into the forehead and act in like manner; others proceed in a different way.[1] Wherever blackness appears, there is the love of ruling, because this blackness is the proprium.

242. Love, which is of man's will, corresponds to flame, and faith, which is of the thought from the understanding, corresponds to light, this is derived from the Lord's influx from love and wisdom, or from the sun of heaven. From this sun proceed Divine love and Divine wisdom, love into the will and wisdom into the understanding. But only so much of intelligence [is received] as there is of love; just as is the case with light from flame.

243. They who worship the Lord from love, worship Him from all the truths of faith; therefore the more the truths the fuller and more acceptable is the worship. The reason is, because love excites all the things which have entered from love into the understanding. When the man is in worship only those things appear before him which he then speaks or prays, but all the rest are in vain and not in their series.[2] When love produces truths, then these latter are disposed by the Lord into the form of heaven, and the man then adores the Lord as it were from heaven. This has been made known to me from experience in the spiritual world. When I see anyone, all those things come up which I know and have heard about him. The angels see these in their series, and so forth. Hence it is evident of what quality is the worship of the Lord by those who, from love to Him, are in genuine truths.

244. For the sake of instruction it sometimes happens that one spirit is allowed to change the affections in another, even into contrary affections; and according to the changes of his affections his face is changed so that it becomes wholly unrecognizable; there is also induced a monstrous form of face and also blackness according to the affections. Moreover, the body also is changed, becoming taller or shorter, taller from haughtiness and pride, and shorter from humility and the disparagement of self. It thence became evident that affection or love makes the man from head to foot. A like change takes place when a spirit is carried transversely through various societies, which was also seen, so that at length he is not recognized. Hence it is evident that he is altogether such as his love is. It was also shown that faith, which is of the thought, conjoined to corporeal love, and which also is various,[1] makes man to be deformed according to the kind of love. And therefore in order that faith may be faith, it must be conjoined to spiritual affection.

245. The quality of the delight of the love of commanding was perceived, namely, that the sweetness within it is ineffable. From this sweetness man believes that it is heaven and heavenly joy, when yet it is hell. This delight is also turned into what is direful. It is similar with the love of doing evil, the love of hatred and revenge, the love of theft, and also the love of adultery, and their delights. Man does not know that when, by means of reformation by the Lord, these delights recede, then for the first time the delights of heaven enter in; which delights infinitely surpass the former. Nor does he know that the delights of those evils are then undelightful and stinging. Before reformation he does not know that such is their quality.

246. I saw many who had lived in this and former centuries, some of them military officers, of higher and lower rank, and others civil functionaries, all of whom, under the favoring influence of fortune, had contracted such a delight of commanding that they aspired to dominion over all things. Their delight was perceived as being to them like heaven. Moreover, they were gifted, above others, with talent and natural light in regard to civil affairs. After their decease, they had at first spoken about God; but after a short time they not only denied God and acknowledged nature; but at last they became like fools, sitting in dark shade; and in this way they led a miserable life. The reason is because the love of commanding is opposite to heavenly love.

247. After death every man is bound to many societies according to the number of his loves; but after vastation he comes into that society where his ruling love is, for this is the centre of his other loves.

248. There was a certain man (Fr. G.)[1] who in his boyhood had cultivated piety, and who remained therefrom in the acknowledgment of God even to the end of his life. And yet under the favoring influence of fortune he came into the love of commanding and hence into evils of every kind. He did not indeed perpetrate them, but still he excused them and accounted them lawful. In the other life he prayed to God as he had done in the world, and with such fervor that scarcely anyone could pray more ardently; but it was to God the Father, for he believed that by doing this all things were forgiven him. But he began to burn with such hatred against the Lord that he denied Him; and afterwards he persecuted those who adored the Lord. At last he denied God and became like a fool; and he was sent among those who have little life.

249. They who are in the delight of the love of commanding cannot become spiritual. They become corporeal for the reason that they immerse everything of affection and hence of thought in their proprium, which in itself is corporeal and evil, so that they cannot be withdrawn from the proprium. Everyone who acknowledges God in heart, is elevated above his proprium; for man cannot look to God, acknowledging Him in heart, from himself; and he who cannot be elevated above his proprium has heaven closed to him. And since through heaven there flows in from the Lord intelligence, because it is spiritual light, therefore when heaven is closed they become stupid and like fools.

250. I once saw what kind of love to the Lord exists among Christians at this day. A number of them were let into their loves; and in phantasy it was granted them to see as it were the Lord.[2] And they then came into such fury that they wished to drag Him down and slay Him. They were all in faith alone, and, at the time, in the love of self. Thence it became evident that in the Christian world at this day they are against the Lord as were the Jews of old. In a word, all who are in faith alone and in the love of self and the world, and hence in evils, come into fury if they merely feel the Lord's Divine sphere.

THE JEWS.

251. Before the Last Judgment, the Jews, for the most part, were at the left in the plane of the heel. I have often spoken with them there. They were then under the middle region where is the Christian world.[1] But after the Last Judgment they were driven away, and now being removed to the left, they dwell there in certain cities where the streets appear filled with filth and impurities, and where the houses are undergoing continual variation. This arises from the fact that newcomers are ever arriving and departing. They are there explored in order to find out who among them are able to acknowledge the Lord as the Messiah, whom they still look for in the world, and who are not. The former are taken to synagogues where they are instructed.

252. In that city an angel with a rod sometimes appears on high; and he gives them to believe that he is Moses. He exhorts them to desist from their madness in expecting the Messiah, when yet the Messiah is Christ, who, being now one with the Father, rules the whole heaven; adding that He knows this Himself, because He had known it in the world. They hear what he says; and when they depart those who cannot acknowledge, because of their life, forget it, but they retain it in their memory who can.

253. Of Abraham they have a Divine idea; of Jacob, and also of their fathers they have some Divine idea, but a lesser one. There is always set over them by the Lord, some converted Jew in whom Judaism lies hidden within or in the heart, and Christianity, without or in the mouth; and he is taught by certain angels from the Lord, in order that he may rule them according to their genius and disposition.

254. They still retain from the world the carrying on of trade, especially in precious stones. These by certain methods they procure from heaven; for thence come precious stones, of which much more might be said. For in heaven are all things which are in the world. There is gold and silver there, also gold and silver in the form of coins, and also stones of every kind. Like all other things which appear before their eyes, they are from a spiritual origin, and hence are correspondences.

They appear just as in the world. Divine truths are their origin; and therefore, with those angels who are in truths, the decorations in the houses are resplendent with silver and gold, and diamonds. Precious things of this kind are given from heaven to those below who are studious of truths; and because of their origin they also remain for ever. The Jews get them from these and sell them. The reason why Jews have this business in the world, and also after their departure from the world, is because they love the Word of the Old Testament in the letter, and the literal sense of the Word corresponds to precious stones of various kinds. It is this sense that is meant by the twelve stones in Aaron's ephod, which were the Urim and Thummim; by the precious stones in Tyre, concerning which in *Ezekiel;* and by the precious stones with which the foundations of the wall of the New Jerusalem were adorned. Now because it was foreseen by the Lord that Christians would not hold the Old Testament so holy as do the Jews, therefore, the Jews have been preserved up to this day, and have been scattered throughout the whole Christian world, in order that the Word might still be in its holiness by means of correspondences. This also is the reason why it is still allowed the Jews to trade with similar things as in the world. If there had not been this reason, that whole nation, by reason of its perversity, would have perished.

255. There are also those who make precious stones for themselves artificially, so that they can scarcely be distinguished from the genuine. But these, when they are found out, are severely punished; they are put into a prison where they suffer harsh things, and are cast into the hells.

256. The Jews have no other delights than to acquire gain. Of interior delights they have no knowledge. Most of them are external men.

257. I have often spoken with the Jews on various subjects, namely, (1) Concerning their sacrifices, that they refer to things heavenly; and in what way their various sacrifices signify the Lord. (2) Concerning Isaac, why he might have been sacrificed by Abraham; and that these things had not been disclosed to them in the world because they were so external that they would not have received, for they were not willing to receive; and that they would have profaned them. (3) Concerning the things which are contained in the fifty-third chapter of *Isaiah*. At this they became altogether silent; for the chapter was explained, so that they could make no answer. They were afraid lest it should be read again, for they were not willing to be convinced. (4) Concerning eternal life, that it consists in the unanimity of all and in joy therefrom; and that as for them, they are at enmity with each other and thus cannot have the felicity of heaven. They answered, that they look for the Messiah who will unite them. (5) I spoke with them about the signification of Jacob's sinew which was put out of joint, about Esau's heel which Jacob caught hold of, and about the heel which the serpent bruised, that these signify themselves; about their origin from a Canaanitish woman, and from whoredom with a daughter-in-law. And it was explained what all these signify, and that the things there meant are such as are signified. Then that the Jews and their tribes mentioned in the Word are not they but are things celestial and spiritual. I spoke about the land of Canaan, to the effect that they believe they are to be introduced into that land by the Messiah when He comes; that He will walk before them with a rod, and will dry up the rivers; that a wall of fire will be round about them; that they will go through Christendom, and that Christians will take hold of their garments and beg to be allowed to follow them; and that they will admit these and hold them as slaves provided they give their money; and many similar things. They were asked whether the dead and those in the world of spirits are also to follow the Messiah, or whether it is only those who are in the world; whether the land of Canaan would be able to hold them; where the Messiah was to be born; whether they knew the line of David, or the situation of Bethlehem; and many similar questions; why they look for an earthly kingdom when the kingdom of the Messiah is a heavenly one, which those who have now departed from the world might know. All this was said and heard.[1] Those of them who were evil could not be convinced, but some who were upright wished to be instructed. (6) It was explained to them what the land of Canaan signifies, and what Jerusalem; why these are called holy; what Zion signifies; what the twelve tribes represent and hence signify; also the passages where it is said that they who had been in captivity would return, to the effect that it was by no means they who were meant, but that it was so written on account of the spiritual sense in each particular. (7) I spoke with them about the spiritual sense; at which they first said that they knew there was a mystical sense in the Word, and that they knew that mystical sense, which was that they receive gold and that they are able to make gold. To which I answered that, mystically, that is, spiritually, this is also true, because gold signifies the good of love, and they who are in that mystical or spiritual sense of the Word, receive this love. But they wanted gold, not love, saying that the possession of gold is love.[1]

258. Before the Last Judgment they called the two cities[2] Jerusalem. But after the Judgment they changed the name by command; because the name Holy Jerusalem, mentioned in the *Apocalypse*, then came everywhere into general use; by which is signified the New Church into which none shall enter who does not make the Messiah one with Jehovah, thus only he who worships the Lord alone. The Jews are treated of in the *Arcana Cœlestia*.

259. The Jews strive much after heaven, believing that heaven is theirs, and that to inherit the land is to inherit heaven, that the land of Canaan is in heaven, and that the Messiah is with them. They marvel that He does not descend to them from heaven, but I answered that He does not will to do this because there is so much discord among them and such enmities and hatreds, and contempt for others; and because they pray to the God of Israel not for the sake of salvation but that they may become rich.

260. Those of them who are evil are cast down into the hells which are under their great tract; many into woods and deserts where they commit robbery, but still they are miserably punished. The Word is taken away from them.

261. They have been preserved also for the sake of the Hebrew language. They also have the Word written in the ancient Hebrew language where all the letters are curved, because in such a letter the Word has a more immediate communication with heaven.

VARIOUS THINGS

CONCERNING

THE SPIRITUAL WORLD.

Various things concerning those things which are in the Spiritual World, from which some things have been quoted in the *Continuation Concerning the Spiritual World.*

To Be Observed.

LEIBNITZ AND WOLFF.

262. I spoke with John [C.] Wolff and his preceptor Leibnitz concerning the simple substance and preëstablished harmony.

263. *Concerning the simple substance* Leibnitz said, that his opinion concerning the monad was never like that of Wolff concerning the simple substance. He said that he indeed acknowledged monads as unities; but that there were in them simpler and purer substances by which the monad was formed, from which changes of state existed therein; since if there were nothing therein, it would be nothing, in which there cannot be any change of state, for a vacuum admits of no change. Leibnitz therefore wondered that Wolff held that his monad, which he calls a simple substance, was created out of nothing, and that when divided it falls into nothing; and yet he had attributed changes of state to it; and also that he had called some existences simple substances, and which are in nature, which anyone can see are aggregations of substances, like the parts of the air and ether, the elements of metals, and also souls. Wolff said that he wished by his definitions of his simple substances to captivate the minds of theologians, who want it to be believed that all things have been created by God out of nothing, immediately; at that time not knowing that his followers, by confirming these principles in themselves, would close in themselves the ways to angelic wisdom, which nevertheless are founded on natural truths.

264. Concerning preëstablished harmony, Leibnitz said, he had considered and deduced it from this, that thought acts as one with man's speech, countenance, and action; and at that time he had not thought of interior thought, from which many men do not speak nor act; and which with many combats with the exterior; and still less did he think of spiritual thought, into which man does not come until after death; then that he considered nothing else in the world but thought, which at that time he acknowledged in place of the soul; and he did not consider affection at the same time, from which and according to which he thinks. Therefore now, after he has been instructed by angels he confesses that he erred, and he knows that the case is altogether otherwise.

NEWTON.

265. I spoke with Newton concerning a vacuum, and concerning colors.

266. *Concerning a vacuum* he said, that in the world he had believed in the existence of a vacuum; but when the angels perceived that he had an idea of a vacuum, as an idea of nothing, they turned themselves away, saying that they cannot bear the idea of nothing, since when there is an idea of nothing the idea of the essence of things perishes. And when the idea of the essence of things perishes, the idea of thought, understanding, affection, love, and of will with men and angels perishes, which things are not given in nothing. They asked him whether he believed that the Divine, whence is all angelic wisdom, and all intelligence to men in both worlds, the spiritual and the natural, is a vacuum, and thus that any Divine operation inflows through a vacuum into their vacuum and can present itself to perception. At that question he was disturbed. He replied that it cannot through an absolute vacuum, which is nothing, but through an apparent vacuum, because the Divine is the *Esse* itself of wisdom and love with the angels in heaven and with men in the world, and it fills all things. Also *Esse* itself and nothing are so contrary to each other, that if one be admitted the other cannot. Therefore the angels entreated that he and all those who cherished the idea of a vacuum as of nothing would desist from it, that they might be together, knowing that nothing of their life can ever be given in nothing, but in those things which are, and which are or exist from the *Esse*. They added that not anything can be said of a vacuum which is nothing, which has relation to acting, reacting, receiving or attracting, thus to the life of their wisdom and love; in which there are so many infinite affections with their variations, perceptions, and sensations; for nothing is nothing, and of nothing we cannot predicate something. When he had heard these things, Newton said that before this he had desisted from that idea, and he would desist from it hereafter; knowing that he is now in the spiritual world, in which, nevertheless, according to his former idea, would have been his vacuum; and that even now he is a man, and therein he thinks, feels, acts, yea breathes, and this could not take place in a vacuum which is nothing, but in something which is, and from *Esse* exists and subsists, and that an interstitial nothing is impossible, because that would be destructive of something, that is of essences and substances which are something. For something and nothing are altogether opposites, even so that he was horrified at the idea of nothing, and would beware of it, lest his mind fall into a swoon.

267. *Concerning colors* he said that in the world he had believed that they originated from the substances, as it were, of different colored materials continually flowing forth from the solar ocean, and adding themselves continually to like things in objects in the world, likewise when they pass through pellucid objects following then the ways of light, according to its diffractions and refractions, and proceeding as like to like, thus red to red, blue to blue, yellow to yellow, and so on, as in prisms, crystalline globes, and vapors whence come rainbows. But the angels did not acknowledge this cause of colors, saying that there are colors in the spiritual world as well as in the natural world; and in the spiritual world they are vivid, splendid, and variegated more than in the natural world, and that they know that they are variegations of their light corresponding to their love or good, and to their wisdom or truth, and that the sun from which their light proceeds, is the Lord Himself, whose Divine love presents around Him the appearance of a sun, and the Divine wisdom therefrom the appearance of light, and that from that sun, which as was said, is pure love, no such substances or matters flow forth, but that pure light presents to view variegations of colors in objects according to the reception of wisdom by the angels; the color red according as their wisdom is derived from good, and the color bright white according as their wisdom is derived from truth, and the rest as they partake of the defect and absence of them, which there correspond to shade in the world. Moreover the angels, by their spiritual ideas, by which they are able to present and bring forth the causes of things to the life and to full consent, demonstrated that colors are nothing else than variegations of flamy light and bright white light, in objects according to their forms; and that colors are not materials, so neither is light, because they correspond to the love and wisdom of the angels, from whom they proceed by Divine operation; and their love and wisdom are not material but spiritual. Neither are heat and light in the world material, but natural, and they inflow into matters, and they modify themselves in them according to the forms of the parts. Therefore neither are colors material, as they would be if they existed from different colored atoms. At length from some indignation they said, "Who cannot see a paradox in the Newtonian cause, yea what is absurd?" And they departed, saying they would return if he would discern spiritually or even naturally concerning colors, and not so materially and sensually. Then some spirits approached, and said to him, "We entreat you to think of colors not as originating from some small prism or from some wall, but from the green color of all the woods and grassy fields of the whole world in which you were; can you conceive of a continuous efflux from the sun of a green color alone, and at the same time an influx, and a continual restoration, likewise of a continual influx of grey or stone color into the mountains of the whole earth, and so on? Can you then conceive of a continuous ocean of green alone, and of rock color alone? Tell us where they go, where they subsist, do they proceed into the universe? Or do they fall downwards somewhere, or ascend upwards? From these things perchance new earths exist, for they must be in great abundance because they are material." After he thought of this thing more deeply, he said, "Now I know that colors are modifications of light in objects, in the forms of which they make general planes, upon which the light is variegated according to the forms of the parts, whence are colors." These are the words of Newton himself, which he wishes me to communicate.

LONDON.

268. London in the spiritual world appears like the London in the natural world as to its streets and quarters, but is dissimilar as to houses and habitations; this difference is not apparent, because everyone there dwells in a quarter and in a house corresponding with his affection and thought thence derived. In the middle of the city is situated *the Royal Exchange*. To the right of it dwells the moderator, and round about it his officers. The middle street of it answers to Holborn; the east is in front, toward the back even to Wapping is the west; the south is at the right of that street; and the north is on its left. In the eastern quarter, which is of considerable length, reaching far beyond the city, dwell the best of them, where they all worship the Lord. Those who are distinguished for intelligence dwell in the southern quarter which extends almost to Islington, where there is also an assembly. They who dwell there are also prudent in speaking and writing. Towards the north those dwell who are illiterate, and who are in the greatest degree of liberty of speech which they love. In the west are those who are in the obscure affection of good. Those who are there are fearful of manifesting their thoughts. In the southern region answering to Moorfield's and round about it, is a promiscuous multitude; thither from the city are sent away all those who incline to evils, wherefore the multitude there is cast out by turns, and thus continually, through this way the city is continually purified, and those who are led away therefrom appear no more. Sometimes they see about the middle of the city a certain malicious person sitting on a seat in a pulpit, and the inhabitants are called together and ordered to go thither to him. They who approach and hearken are led to the place of exit, where there are promiscuous crowds, and as was said, they are sent out through the ways there. Every society is purified, this is the manner of purifying them there.

269. Their houses, clothing, and food are similar to those used in the world. I asked about wine, strong drink, beer, chocolate, tea and the like, and was told that they had similar things. I asked also about the liquor called punch, they said that they also have that liquor, but it is given only to those who are sincere and at the same time industrious. They do not tolerate in the city any ruler who directs or dictates to them what they must do, for they wish to be in full liberty.

270. The English live together, and do not travel about in other regions, for they are of a different genius and disposition from others, and their disposition is such, that they do not admit others into intimacy with them.

271. It was also shown to them that they speak, write and think spiritually, and that they themselves do not know otherwise than that they do all things naturally; from which they were instructed by me that there is no ratio between the spiritual and the natural, thus there is no conjunction through what is continuous, but through what is discrete, that is, by correspondences; which conjunction makes a likeness as if they are one. They were a little envious that they had not discovered this. Moreover in each degree there is an internal and an external, and the external corresponds to the internal, and the externals are appearances like material things, although they are not material. It was shown to them also by ascent to the third heaven, that there is a similar difference between the celestial and the spiritual, as there is between the spiritual and the natural so that there is no ratio between them, that is, the natural cannot become spiritual by any continuous purification, nor can the spiritual become celestial, thus not by any approximation, but it is like the difference between cause and effect, or between the soul and the body.

272. I afterwards spoke with them concerning priests. And I saw that there is one kind of priests that supposes they are more erudite and learned than others. These all dwell in the west, and when they come to preach, they go forth from the west a little into the north, and so towards the middle of the city to the temples. This is a sign that they go in the way of taciturnity and ignorance, for in the west those dwell who are taciturn, and there near to the north those who are ignorant of truth. They appear to themselves to preach learnedly and with erudition, because they preach about the Divine operation into the actions of men, when they are justified; thus concerning the effort, which is the fourth degree of justification, which inflows into the act with men, they themselves being ignorant of it, and that the voluntary of man is not present, since that is evil. The hearers complained of them that they cannot understand them whether they wish them to act of themselves or not; because they can take both senses from their ambiguous teachings. It was perceived that they wish such discourses to sound learned before preachers and bishops, and that they do not dare to preach otherwise before them. But there are also preachers who dwell in the south, who altogether preach that they must shun evils as from themselves, and that they must do goods as from themselves; but that still they must know that they are not from themselves, thus the citizens love these; they speak in harmony with the *prayer* before the *Holy Supper*.

273. In the suburbs at the left dwell many of their learned and with them Newton, they go down thither by a sloping way.

274. In a word they who teach according to their prayer at the Holy Supper, dwell in the south towards the east, and they are loved because they think as they preach, the rest do not, but dispute continually with them, and reply that they cannot do otherwise. I saw them recede to their habitations in the west, which are at the right side there where there is a place of exit, and some also are led out.

275. It was said of those preachers in the west, that they do not care to know evils or sins, because God knows, and not they, nor do they wish to know from affection any other knowledges than what confirm their faith. They despise those who are in the south and east as simple, who as it were with their thought are low; and that their thought is not elevated but depressed, when yet it is altogether contrary.

276. I heard a conversation with presbyters in the west, which was effected by representatives. On one side the devil with hell was represented, on the other side the Lord with heaven, and then it was said, that the devil or hell dwells in the evils with man, and that the Lord with heaven is in the goods with him. (2) Then that the Lord through heaven continually drives away the devil with hell.[1] (3) But the man who excuses his evils, and who lives in them, retains with himself the devil with hell, nor does he permit him to go away, although the Lord drives him away. (4) Also the devil then speaking with him, says what need is there to know evils, so as to combat against them, when God does that? and so he confirms man, therefore he is retained and thus they live together as friends; besides many similar things. Also the devil by that faith confirms them, saying what need is there of other knowledges, than those which belong to that faith? they are of no help; what need is there to know evils, because man from himself cannot combat against them? What need is there of combats, because man of himself can do nothing? (5) When nevertheless everything of life, everything of reason, and everything of freedom man has from the Lord, and He wills that man should act as of himself, and without man's coöperation as of himself, the evil remains, and the devil with evil, etc.

277. Those priests in the west complained that those who were in faith alone, or in faith separated, disappeared, saying that they do not know where they went, some said that they saw some in the hells.

THE MORAVIANS.

278. I do not write of those who are in the world, but of those who are out of the world, I spoke with these and I heard.

279. (1) They are mere Arians, and deny the Divine of the Lord, saying that He has the Divine, such as man has. When it was said to them that He was conceived of Jehovah, they come together, nor do they wish easily to admit it, wishing to deny the Scripture lest they should be refuted; but still they say something that the Jews do Others when they are convinced, say that He was born that He might be adopted. They confirm themselves by the Lord's word that in His freedom He was left to suffer the cross, not knowing why this was done. They say that they love Him, because He took it upon Himself to suffer the cross, and also because it is commanded by the Father, then especially because He is loved by the Father on account of the passion of the cross. (2) They reject the Old Testament as no longer for them but for the Jews. (3) They also despise the Gospels, saying that the Lord is spoken of as a simple man, and thus that there is nothing Divine in them. (4) Concerning faith in Him spoken of in the Gospels, they say that He so wished it, and that it ought not speak thus. (5) They acknowledge the *Epistles of Paul* only, and also the historicals of the Word, but they do not believe in the holiness of the Word. (6) They say concerning good works and charity, that they ought not to be together with faith, and that they shudder at doing good works for the sake of heaven, and that in their heaven they would rather adopt the most malevolent than such; in a word they condemn them to hell. (7) In speaking they utter the greatest fallacies; they speak with each one according to his heart in religion. They guard lest those mysteries should be disclosed; the rest which are concerning the Holy Supper and Baptism they think and teach violently. They are such things as do not agree with the faith of the Reformed, nor do they admit to the Holy Supper any others than those who receive those three mysteries, because they have confirmed them. (8) From these things it is evident that they are among the worst who profess Christianity. (9) They make much of their sensation, but it was shown to them, that their sensation is with their spirits, who were enthusiastic spirits from their assembly in the world, who come nearer to them, who think much of their religion and love it, saying that they are more loving and happy than others. These confirm them very greatly, thence is their sensation.

280. They are held in the lower earth to the left in a society separated from the rest; because they are among themselves, and they are a society of interior friendship, which if it should be in the neighborhood of others, they would destroy their delights. They recede by turns from that society towards the left, into a desert which is for them alone, where there is no grass, where there are crags[1] and cliffs.

THE DUTCH.

281. How formally and courteously they invite their wives and bring and lead them to their house, and show how well it is with those who act together in unity in their houses, and also how clean and well furnished their houses are; and on the contrary how unclean those are where there is the dominion of one over the other; savory food is also given those who act in unity, and they are taught by these things the quality of their delight when one is of the other mutually and reciprocally. Therefore when they see those things and apperceive them to be true they desist from dominion; and then they obtain a habitation nearer to the middle, and are led into a house better furnished. The reason is that there is then conjugial love, which regarded in itself is celestial love itself.

THE MORAVIANS IN LONDON, THE HERRENHUTERS AND THE JEWS.

282. The Moravians dwell in the furthest corner of the place of exit mostly at the side there, but when they journey into the city as to their sanctuary, they appear to proceed towards the middle and thence a little to the south, and thus to their corner, which is done because they wish to appear to others as Christians, of a similar doctrine. Afterwards from their corner they go into the west where the presbyters are who are in faith alone, concerning whom we have before spoken, and they return thence. From their corner, which is as it were their inn there, they go out by turns, and descend into a vault which stretches deeply under the west, where the presbyters are of whom we have before spoken, and their hell is there, from which they are no longer let out, except some into deserts. It is not allowed them to dwell near others, nor elsewhere, because they form a society of interior friendship, which takes away the spiritual delight of others. They say to others that they should dwell here and there even to the middle, but still they dwell at that corner, of which they have an idea as of their inn.

283. They appear in a way towards the middle, because they persuade that they are of the Anglican religion and speak with the English piously as if they were; and that they differ only as to ceremonials, which are like those of the Apostles. When they are asked why their preachers are clothed in blue, they say because that color is loved; *nor do they dare to say that they should be clothed like the English preachers in a black gown, because they fear lest their mysteries should be disclosed.* They very greatly fear to be sincere and just on account of religion. They are altogether averse to this, wherefore they are prone to all kinds of evils, taking care only lest they be discovered, because with others this would be hurtful to their religion.

284. Moreover the Jews do not dwell upon the earth in London, but under the earth there, on the northern side below, where Towerhill is. They enter there through a dark opening. And the citizens of the city do not know where they dwell.

THE LOVE OF KNOWING.

285. The love of knowing is the external of the will, the use on account of which [it is done] is the internal of the will.

286. With infants and boys the external rules, in process of time the internal is formed.

287. Then there is formed the love of knowing for the sake of use, these are formed whether they are good or evil.

288. But the love of understanding whether a thing is true or not, and thence the love of being wise, is also the external of the will, originating from the light of heaven and its variegation.

289. This love, because it is the external of the will, can be separated from its internal, and then it is the love of one's own glory, on account of glory and not on account of any use then. Therefore it can be given also with the evil.

290. Or the external of the will in the understanding is the love of truth on account of glory, thus on account of the external.

291. Use of life makes the internal of the will originating from the sun of heaven. It [that is the exterior] is as in the time of winter, and like what is foul shining exteriorly.[1]

THE JEWS.

292. The Jews less than others know that they are in the spiritual world. They think there of the Messiah as they did in the world and expect Him. And they say that He will come. But when it is said to them that it will be in Bethlehem, and from the house of David, and they are asked where is Bethlehem now, and where is the house of David? they do not know how to answer other than that He knows where that city is, and where that family is. Some of them in the other life say that the Messiah is in heaven, and that He will not come to those in the spiritual world before He is born a boy in the world.

293. When they are asked whether they only who are in the world will be led into Canaan, they reply that they will then return into the world, and they will dwell with them in the land of Canaan. When they are asked whether they will then be again born, they say they will not, but that they will descend to them, believing that thus they will be men like them. When they are asked whether Canaan will be capacious enough for all who have been born from that nation from the time of Abraham, they say that the land of Canaan will then be enlarged. When they are asked how the Messiah, the Son of Jehovah, can dwell with such evil persons, they say that they are not evil. When it is said that Moses in his song said that they were the worst, do they read it and sing it as was commanded by Moses, they reply that Moses was angry when he wrote that, because they departed from him, and therefore they do not read it, but run through it quickly. When it is said to them that their origin is from a Canaanitess, and from whoredom with a daughter-in-law, they then are angry and depart, saying that it is enough that they are from Abraham and Jacob. They say that Moses and David will also return and go with the Messiah, one at His right and the other at His left. They narrate many fabulous things concerning the Messiah, how He will introduce them into the land of Canaan, and how rich Christians will follow them freely, if they give them their money. Nevertheless many of them who know that Christ who is the Messiah rules all things in the heavens, say that they wish to receive this, but cannot; they hear it from Moses, who sometimes appears above with a rod, and teaches this, and when they hear, they go away in various directions. They said to me, "Why did He suffer the cross?" I replied, "Because He was the greatest prophet, and therefore He carried the iniquities of the people, like the prophet who lay on his right side and on the left, and ate bread made of barley and filth, of whom it is said that he bore their iniquities; likewise other prophets, one who took a harlot to wife, who put on ashes, who went barefoot, who thus bore their iniquities; in like manner it is said of the Messiah" (*Isa.* liii.). When they heard this they said that they would go off among themselves and consult together. They who have not become foul from filthy avarice, and who have not become devils from hatred, fraud and revenge, are tolerated below the heavens where their habitations are, because they regard the Word as holy, and they who suffer themselves to be instructed concerning the Lord, are transferred to societies where they are instructed, and are sent back to those who have not yet received. Their business is dealing in diamonds and precious stones as in the world. They procure them for themselves from heaven. They learn that they have that business, because they regard the Word as holy, because the sense of the letter corresponds to those stones and signifies them. Therefore the more holy they regard the Word, the better do they succeed there in that business.

THE MORAVIANS.

294. They said that they were the remains of the Apostolic Church, and therefore they call each other brothers. Therefore some from their society who were below the earth, were sent to those who had been converted in the time of Paul and the Apostles and were of the church.

295. First they came to the church which was with the Collossian nations, and they spoke with them at first as if they were of such a church, but they were questioned concerning the Lord; they said that they pray to the Father for the sake of the Son, and that they do not go to the Son. They answered that they go to the Lord, because He said that He is the way, the truth and the life; and that no one cometh to the Father except through Him: then that one must have faith in Him, and that they cannot go to the Father immediately, thus it is that they ascend above what is permitted. They were questioned about charity. They said that they have charity among themselves, and therefore they call each other brethren; but they said that this is friendship and not charity, and they asked whether they do not know that charity is to do good, and that this is primary, and that they should call good brother, and truth companion. But when they said that to do good effects nothing for salvation, thus charity effects nothing, but faith alone, and that faith is that the Lord was sent by the Father that He might take away the damnation of the law by the passion of the cross, it was seen that they are no longer under any law, then being indignant they drove them away, *calling them fanatics* and not *Apostolical*.

296. They who were of the Thessalonian church said the same of them. But these only inspected them from above and they recognized similar things with them, and being indignant they turned themselves away, as from those who are to be altogether guarded against.

297. Afterwards they came to a certain Apostolic church, which was in Galilee not far from Tyre. There they did the same, asserting that they were in a like doctrine with them. But they were questioned concerning the Word, they said that they had the *Epistles of Paul*, in which is their doctrine itself, and that he spoke from the Holy Spirit. They were asked what they believe concerning the Gospels, they answered that the Lord there spoke from Himself. They were asked whether He spoke from the Father, thus from the Divine or from the Holy Spirit. They said that He spoke from Himself. They asked how; [they replied] simply as a man, and that He did not speak from the Father nor from the Divine, because He wished them to have faith in Him, *and wished to be equal to the Father. They asked whether He was conceived from the Father; they said that they would think of this as they wished, they did not dare to say that [they thought] as the Jews did,* nor did they dare to say that they hold in low estimation what He spake. They were questioned about the Old Testament, whether it is holy, they said that the Jews regard it as holy because [it was given] through them; but that they do not regard it as holy, and that it is evil to believe that it is holy by itself. They were asked whether they know that there are many things therein concerning the Coming of the Lord; they said that it is about the Coming of the Messiah, and that by the Messiah is meant God the Father and not the Lord, denying that the Father was in the Lord, according to His Word. When passages were quoted therefrom concerning the Lord, they turned themselves away and said that they understand it differently from them. In a word they reject the Word of the Old Testament as not holy, and as having nothing there concerning the Lord. Some things which they answered, because they hurt the ears, I pass by. Afterward they heard concerning their faith, and they said that it does not at all agree with their faith and that it is nothing, and being indignant that they had said they were of their church, they commanded them to depart, and otherwise they would drive them away, because they see that they are not Christians at all, calling them antichrists.

298. Zinzendorf heard all those things which they spoke with this and the former Apostolic church, and he grieved, saying, "I know not whence such things have come to pass since I was in the world;" and seeing that there was nothing for them but hell, he grieved.

299. They said they take something from the Gospels, the prophecies and the histories of the Old Testament in their preaching; chiefly things which confirm their dogmas; something also on account of the rest of Christians, lest they should give offense, and that they may allure to their side.

300. It was asked whence they could become such in the world, when yet they pray to the Father, and are religious. Answer was made them, because they deny the Divine of the Lord. And they were instructed that there is a general efflux from hell against the Divine of the Lord, against charity towards the neighbor, and against the holiness of the Word, and that they may know from this whence they have the confirmations against those three things.

301. They said they would not turn to them, because they would thus disturb them, and misfortunes would happen to them.

302. Some hundreds of them came out and went to a society where charity reigns, and they were in the persuasion that they were living and those who were in charity were dead. From that persuasion the angels of the society of charity appeared before their eyes as blackish, and they themselves in some degree exteriorly as angels. Their persuasion has this in it, that as they draw near they appear to themselves from their persuasion as if they were living, and the rest before their eyes as if half dead. When they perceive this, they pray to the Lord that the newcomers be removed from them, therefore those over them are commanded to go away; but as they depart and are at a distance, they appear monstrous, so that they are scarcely men, and that monstrous appearance increases even until their entrance under the earth, which was a cavern; and when they come thither the monstrosity remains and appears before their eyes and the eyes of their brethren; and afterwards for a long time they are punished many times, nor do they approach any more to other societies and by persuasion induce others to such things, and thus allure them to their insane dogma, and believe that they are living; and those who are in charity are unwilling to be continually with them. The punishment continues until they affirm that they will no longer do thus; for their greatest desire is to allure and lead over to their side by various cunning ways and arts; they are deceivers.

DEGREES.

303. There is a natural kingdom, a spiritual kingdom, and a celestial kingdom.

304. In the natural kingdom are men whilst they live in the world. In the spiritual kingdom are spiritual angels; in the celestial kingdom are celestial angels; for there are these three universals, the natural, the spiritual, and the celestial.

305. In each kingdom there are two degrees, in the natural two, in the spiritual two, and in the celestial two; thus in the three kingdoms there are six degrees.

306. All these degrees are discrete, or discontinuous, and are called degrees of altitude.

307. Discrete degrees are to each other as thought to speech, or as the affection to gesture, or as the affection of the mind to the countenance; and in the material world as the ether to the air, or as a nerve to the fibres of which it is composed. All compositions in the whole natural world and in the spiritual world are of this character, and they consist either of two or three degrees of this kind in their order. These degrees are called prior and posterior, higher and lower, interior and exterior; and, in general, they are as cause and effect, or as a substance and a substantiate, or as the aggregate from substances, or as a principle and the principiates, or the thing formed from principles.

308. There are also continuous or cohering degrees; each discrete degree has its continuous degree. The continuous degree of each discrete degree is as light verging to shade, and at length to the obscurity of night; and also as the rational thought which is in light to sensual and, as it were, at length to corporeal thought, which is in a dense shade according as it descends to the body. In such a degree continually decreasing is the human mind. In a similar degree, but lower, are man's sight, hearing, smell, taste, and touch; in like manner his speech and his singing; for man has a tone like the tone of a lyre, and like the sound of a drum. It is also similar with harmonies and beauties; for they proceed by continuous degrees from the highest harmony and beauty, to the least. These degrees are of the cause in itself and of the effect in itself; they are distinguished from the former degrees, because these are of the cause and the effect in themselves. Continuous degrees are called degrees of what is purer or grosser. An idea of these degrees can be had chiefly from light and shade, and also from the aerial atmosphere in its lower and higher regions; for in the lower region it is grosser, denser, and more compressed, and in the higher region it is purer, rarer, and more extended.

309. Unless one procures a knowledge of these two kinds of degrees, he cannot have an idea of the interiors and exteriors of man, thus neither of the soul and the body, nor indeed of causes and effects. Nor can he have an idea of the distinction between the heavens, nor of the wisdom of the angels in the heavens; nor can he have any idea of correspondences, of representatives, of influx, of order, thus he cannot have an idea of those things which are of order, both in the natural world and in the spiritual world, thus scarcely any just idea of anything.

310. Few hitherto have had any other idea of degrees than of continuous degrees, which is, as was said, from what is pure to what is gross, or from greatest to least. From which it follows that only one kind of degrees has been known, and that the natural degree and the spiritual degree are distinguished only as what is pure and gross; in like manner the difference between the heavens, and also in the wisdom of the angels. Whereas the difference is according to discrete degrees, the nature of which we shall presently show from experience.

311. There are, therefore, as stated above, six discrete degrees, two in the natural kingdom, two in the spiritual kingdom, and two in the celestial kingdom; but these degrees are those in which men and angels are, as to their thoughts, their affections, and their wisdom therefrom. Degrees are as follows: Below these six degrees of life, there follow similar degrees, and also material, even to the ultimate, and above those six degrees ascend degrees of the infinite even to the Divine itself. For the Divine itself cannot flow into any angel or man from itself but by discrete degrees; for if it flowed in immediately, or by what is continuous, both angel and man, from the ardor of the Divine love, and from the light of the Divine wisdom, would be entirely consumed. This would be as though the sun of the world, from its fire, were to flow immediately into the objects of the earth, and not mediately through the atmospheres according to distinct discrete degrees.

312. There are three natural atmospheres arising from the sun of the world, and there are three spiritual atmospheres arising from the sun of heaven, which is the Lord. The three natural atmospheres arising from the sun of the world are the purer ether, which is universal, from which is all gravitation; the middle ether, which forms the vortex around the planets, in which are the moon[1] and the satellites, from which is magnetism; and the ultimate ether which is the air. By these three atmospheres all the corporeal and material things of the earth are held together, which are so composed as to be applicable to those three degrees. The three spiritual atmospheres arising from the sun of heaven, are those in which are the angels of the three heavens. In the two higher atmospheres are the angels of the Lord's celestial kingdom; in the third and the first natural, which is pure ether, are the angels of the Lord's spiritual kingdom, and in the atmospheres following those two which are the middle and the ultimate ether, which is the air, are men while they are in the natural world.

313. But it should be known, that the atmospheres arising from the sun of heaven, which is the Lord, properly speaking, are not three, but six, there are three above the sun of the world, and there are three below it. The three below the sun of the world constantly accompany the three natural atmospheres, and enable a man in the natural world to think and to feel. For the atmospheres arising from the sun of the world have not life in themselves, because they originate from a sun which is pure fire; but the atmospheres arising from the sun of heaven, which is the Lord, have life in themselves, because they originate in the sun, which is pure love and pure wisdom. The atmospheres which originate from the sun of the world, which is pure fire, cause those things on the earth, and in the human body, to subsist and be held in connexion together, and they are not changed except according to the laws of natural order. Hence is the difference between things in the natural world and in the spiritual world, concerning which difference more will be said in what follows.

314. That in the spiritual world which is above the natural world, there are also atmospheres, is evident from the light and heat there, which before the eyes and senses of the angels appear similar to the light and heat before the eyes and senses of men; and angels are spiritual, but men are natural, and there cannot possibly be any light and heat with their differences without atmospheres. That there are also spiritual atmospheres is evident from many appearances in the spiritual world, as from the appearance of colors there, of meteors, of clouds both thin and thick, of winds, of gravities, pressures, and consequent consistencies, which although they appear entirely similar to such things as are in the natural world, nevertheless, they are spiritual and not natural; although before the angels, because they are spiritual, they appear similar. That there are spiritual atmospheres, is evident especially from the respiration of angels and spirits. For angels and spirits breathe in like manner as men in the world; but angels breathe from their atmospheres, and men from theirs. The angels in the celestial kingdom breathe from their atmosphere which is more pure, but the angels of the spiritual kingdom breathe from their atmosphere which is less pure.

315. But the things which we have hitherto said concerning degrees and atmospheres are, for the most part, theoretical; but all theoretical things should be drawn and concluded from the facts of experience, and also be confirmed by them. For unless the facts of experience, as it were, lead the hand of man in coming to conclusions, he may be deceived in theoretical things, and from some imaginary hypothesis, be carried away into false principles entirely opposed to what is true, which he can then confirm by fallacies and appearances of every kind; for false principles may be confirmed by appearances and fallacies to such a degree, that a man may believe that they are truths themselves. I wish, therefore, now to produce some facts of experience, by which not only what has been said may be confirmed, but also by which every one who is in the light of the mind or who has natural ability, may draw conclusions as to many other things.

316. In the natural kingdom in which men are whilst they live in the world, and in the spiritual kingdom where the spiritual angels are, and in the celestial kingdom in which are the celestial angels, similar things appear, so much so that there is scarcely any other difference than that the like things in the spiritual kingdom are more perfect than in the natural kingdom, and in the celestial kingdom still more perfect than in the spiritual kingdom. A spirit or an angel appears like a man in the world, even so that he knows no otherwise than that he is a man of the world. He has a similar face and a similar body, and in the face similar eyes, nostrils, ears, lips, mouth, and similar hair; and in the body also a similar breast, abdomen, loins, hands and feet, and also similar organs of generation; in a word, he is a man in external form altogether like a man of the world. He has similar lungs, because he breathes; and he has a similar heart, because it pulsates. The other interior viscera of the body are also similar, because there are societies in heaven which equally correspond to these viscera. There is likewise a ruddiness in the face, hands, arms, and body, as if from blood in the arteries and veins. There are also similar fibres, nerves, and muscles, because in like manner a spirit moves his limbs like a man in the world. Moreover, he has similar sight, hearing, smell, taste and touch. He also has similar speech and singing; he has also a similar power of imagination, thought, intellect, and will, also affection and cupidity. In a word, an angel or a spirit is so similar to a man of the world, that he himself knows no otherwise than that he is a man of the world. Conjugial love is also similar with all its effect; moreover there is not propagation, but in place of it unition of minds, and thence an increase of intelligence and wisdom. Thence it is that in the Word in its spiritual sense by marriage is meant the conjunction of truth and good, and by daughters goods, and by sons truths, and so on.

317. Their garments also are similar to the garments of men;[1] they have tunics, mantles, breeches, stockings, shoes, caps, tiaras and undergarments like those in the world, with some difference as to colors, especially of the tunics. The reason is, because colors signify the appearances of truth from good, and garments signify truths, and hence the clothing of the understanding.

318. They have also similar houses, in which are apartments and chambers with courts as in the world, and within there are tables, benches, utensils, and various decorations. In heaven there are palaces so magnificent that palaces in the world cannot be compared to them. These palaces are of a magnitude so great, and of such symmetrical and architectural beauty, both without and within, and are decorated in such forms with gold and precious stones, that no picture painter on earth could possibly express them. There are also marble houses and houses of a blue color. The use of every apartment is known from its decorations.

319. They have also similar food and drink as in the world, and various kinds of food and drink are named.

320. In the spiritual world are likewise earths, mountains, hills, plains, grassy fields, paradises or gardens, groves and woods. There are ways everywhere tending to various societies, some are guarded. These ways then first appear to a spirit when he goes into his own society. There are also in that world fountains, lakes, and seas.

321. There appear likewise animals of the earth and all kinds of flying things, greater and smaller. There also appear compound animals, such as are described in the Word, there are also various insects or worms.

322. In a word, in the spiritual world there are not only similar things as in the natural world, but innumerable others; and every thing exists with infinite variety and harmony, from which there breathes forth delight. In a word, in heaven there is a heaven in all and in each thing, in general and in every particular. Thus every external sense has its own heaven, and everything of the internal sense has also its own heaven, and an angel is a heaven in its least form, and each one, as he has heaven in himself, has also heaven outside of himself.

323. But it must be known that all things, and each now mentioned, are not material but spiritual, or are from a spiritual origin; and yet spirits know no otherwise than that they are material; the reason is, that when what is spiritual touches or tastes what is spiritual, it is altogether like when what is material touches or tastes what is material. Concerning this appearance I have often had a discussion with spirits, who believe that the things which they see and touch are material. I have shown them by various methods, and by various reasons even to the life, that nothing in the spiritual world is material, but that every thing there is spiritual. I demonstrated it to them by the houses, which in a moment are formed, and in a moment are destroyed and dissipated; also by their garments, which in a moment are put on, and in a moment are changed; new garments are also given in a moment. In like manner I have demonstrated it from their dinners and repasts, showing that the tables upon which is the food, exist in a moment, and are afterwards dissipated in a moment; and that the spirits themselves can enter into the houses through the walls, and oftentimes not entering in through the doors. There was a certain individual known to me, with whom I conversed when his body which he had in the world was being buried, and I told him that he was now being buried, when he replied that he did not know what of him was being buried, because he had all things with him, a similar body as before, and other things similar, for he, like others, did not know otherwise than that he was still material, whereas he was spiritual. He was soon instructed that his material body, which he carried about with him in the world, and which then clothed his spiritual body, was being buried.

WONDERFUL THINGS [CONCERNING THE LANGUAGE OF SPIRITS].

324. Spirits and angels do not know otherwise than that they speak the same language they did in the world, write as they did in the world, and think as they did in the world, when yet they speak the spiritual language, in which there is no expression similar to any in the world; and they write by letters and characters; but it differs so much from writings in the world, that there is nothing whatever that is similar, except the letters and some points. Yea, they think altogether otherwise than in the world, so differently, that no thought is similar; but still they do not know otherwise than that all things are similar. That it is so I have often experienced by this, that spirits and angels when they are with me, are in my natural state; and it was said to them that in their spiritual state they should speak words and sentences, and retain the words with me in the natural state; and then there was not a single word alike, nor did they understand one of their words. They likewise wrote a sentence in the spiritual state, and when it had been written it was shown in the natural state; there was nothing similar but the letters and points. Likewise when they thought in the spiritual state, they could not bring forth any idea of thought in the natural state. As for example, they say Rocky (*scopulosum*) and to wish life (*vitam velle*). *Scopulosum* in the spiritual language signifies that he casts out of doors, and *vitam velle*, that it is afar off. When they retain these expressions in the natural state, they do not understand them, nor any expression in the natural state when they come into the spiritual state. When they write *scopulosum*, they write — —, and when they write *vitam velle*, they write — —, and they suppose that they have written it fully. They write the sense of the words by alphabetic letters, each one of which signifies a thing —. They write also by many signs, so that the greater the angelic wisdom is, the more things of wisdom they understand in the writing; the Word is thus written.

325. From these things it may be concluded that there is no ratio given by continuity between the natural and the spiritual; and that spirits and angels who are with men do not know that they are with them, nor an angel or a spirit that he is with a man. These wonderful things were disclosed to me before those in the spiritual world who were with me to-day, because they could be with me in my natural state and not before.

326. It is altogether similar between the thought, speech and writing of the angels of the Lord's celestial kingdom and of the angels of the spiritual kingdom, as there is between those who are in the spiritual kingdom in relation to those who are in the natural kingdom. This also has been confirmed by experience.*

---

* Following n. 326 in Tafel's Latin text is a paragraph "On the Spiritual Sense;" this and numbers following 339, 347, and 355 properly belong to *The Word of the Lord from Experience*, where they will be found in this volume, Nos. xxi., xxii., xxiii., xxiv. and xxvi. We make our numbering of paragraphs consecutive.

THE ENGLISH.

327. The garments of the English are not like their garments in the world, neither those of the virgins nor of the women. They are adapted altogether to their general affection. When viewed in the spiritual state they appear graceful and beautiful, because they are altogether in agreement with their genius. But when the same are seen in their natural state, they do not appear so beautiful. The reason is that garments signify truths, and therefore all are clothed according to the reception of truth.

328.* In London there are ten moderators of similar authority.

---

329. *The understanding teaches the will and does not lead it,* or faith teaches, but does not produce good works. For man can discern and see what is good and evil, but still act contrary thereto, and then he either shuns it, or holds it in hatred, the will in the understanding is then opposite, yea in time dissipates it. Truth seen is what one acknowledges, but this is not the truth of life. But what once becomes of the will is either evil or good, this is stirred up by the sight and by the understanding, or the thought, and then the will is stirred up, and thence it exists in the thought. It is thus effected in all things reborn. It then appears as if the will was aroused by the thought; but it is not so. It is as if the sight should teach the feet to walk cautiously, and the hands to do the work. It appears as if that leads, but it does not lead, but shows and teaches. It is altogether like the heart and the lungs. The lungs do not respire unless the heart also acts, nor can there be given a reciprocal conjunction from the lungs but from the heart. See more below.

330. *It is to be observed,* that there may be anything either spiritual, moral or civil whose effect man has produced and thence has loved; the man (1) hears it from another, or he reads it in a book. (2) Thence it becomes his thought. (3) In the thought there is raised up a perception of it, because this

---

* See note following n. 326.

was the first of that thing. (4) His affection is in the perception, thus the affection of truth. (5) This affection which is called the affection of truth is from the affection of good, which is of the will, thus from the will in the affection of truth there is effected the conjunction of good and truth, in which conjunction the will and the understanding or good and truth act as one. (6) Thus one is concealed in the other, within, and all are aroused from the ultimate, even through the hearing and sight, that is, the rousing up, namely because the will is concealed inmostly in the hearing, and thence in the thought, and it goes forth not otherwise than the spiritual sense and the celestial sense from the natural sense into the hearing, and thence sight is simultaneous. But it does not produce; production is effected by the will or the affection of good into the affection of truth, thence into the perception and from this into the thought; but not *vice versa*. From these things it is evident whence are appearances.

331. Thought is also given from hearing, and within the thought is perception, and within the perception is the affection of truth, and not at the same time the affection of the good of that truth. The affection of its good can be given with the love of self, of reputation, honor, and gain, but this is not marriage, but adultery. The reason is that this good which is merely natural, can be opposite to the good of truth itself, which is spiritual in various ways and respects. Examples may teach this.

332. When man is in his natural good, which in itself is evil, he then either does not know that [spiritual good], or denies it. He does so when he is in his proprium.

333. There is given the affection of knowing and understanding truth on account of glory, gain and remuneration. The love of knowing and understanding is the love of natural light; the love of knowing and understanding truths is the love of spiritual light, which love is especially given with those who are in the love of good, but it is also given with those who are in the love of glory. From experience it has been given me to know that the love of light on account of glory as also of use is given with those who are in the love of evil; but with them the love of evil is then hidden or is lulled to sleep. It touches only the surface, as beauty from various colors, and the more it is hidden or lulled to sleep, the more it can feel delight. The love of knowing and understanding truths is from the external, which can be given provided the internal is hidden or is lulled to sleep; but it is a spurious love; it is like some filthy object covered over with a beautiful color, yea, with gold, underneath which surface there is evil. Therefore when good is in evil, one cannot know and understand those things, yea, he holds them in hatred, for he then confirms himself against truths. Thus the internal dissipates the external. Yea, there is given a holy external and a profane internal, the internal is lulled to sleep, but not the external; the external is not asleep.

IN THE TREATISE ON THE TEN COMMANDMENTS.

334. It must treat of faith and of the understanding of truth.

335. (1) What faith is. (2) That there is conjunction with good works, and there is so much of faith as there is of life. (3) That life is the soul of faith. (4) That faith separate is not faith, it is inanimate. (5) It is the dragon; it is the he-goat; it is Philistia; it is Cain; it is Reuben. (6) What is faith? It is truth. (7) At this day how sterile [is faith separate], and religion is nothing.

336. (1) In heaven they altogether reject the dogma that the understanding is to be held under obedience to faith. (2) All things of theology can be comprehended by the understanding. (3) Not only by the spiritual understanding by the angels, but by the rational understanding by men. (4) Otherwise from theological authority they could say whatever they wished.

FOODS.

337. There were some in the lowest heaven, to whom the atmosphere above appeared like water. I spoke with them and they said that they have choice foods, and they take them from the table and keep them until evening, and eat therefrom at will; but it is not allowed them to hide them until morning. This is what is meant in the Lord's prayer, "Give us daily bread." Concerning the manna it is said that it bred worms when it was kept. Then they were to burn up what was left of the paschal lamb; neither should they let anything from the sacrifices remain over; also that the bread of faces should be replaced anew every day. Thence it is evident why everyone is provided with spiritual daily bread by the Lord, and that it is not given as their own, and thus there should be no care concerning to-morrow, what they should eat and drink. Thus and not otherwise are good spirits in their works, and in their life and faith. Nothing is given to the evil, but only to him who is in work. Thus also all are held in bonds, thus every use is remunerated.

338. Some are nourished at the tables of others, but those who are evil and hateful sit at the table and do not see the food.

MARRIAGE AND ADULTERY.

339. (1) Adultery is hell itself, thus it is the Devil himself and Satan. It has been shown by many things as also by experience, that all in hell are adulterers, that they rage like furies when they perceive conjugial love; which is a sign that they are from hell; that they desire to violate chaste marriages, and many other things; then that they are in the marriage of evil and falsity. (2) Marriage is heaven itself because all there are in conjugial love, everyone in his own degree. That love is the fundamental love of all the loves of heaven, because an angel by it becomes love in form, because they who are in marriage are in good and truth; and therefore heaven coöperates in marriages and nuptials and hell in adulteries and whoredoms. (3) Thence it follows that as far as a man detests adulteries as a diabolic sin, and looks to the Lord, so far he is in a like degree in heaven.

340. Marriage and adultery must be treated of especially, because he who is in marriage is in the conjunction of good and truth; but he who is in adultery is in evil and falsity. And because adultery is all sin against the Decalogue, for he who is in that is in all the evil of the Decalogue and *vice versa;* and because these are involved and as it were contained in marriage and adultery in summaries, therefore they must be treated of especially. (2) At this day in the Christian world adulteries are more prevalent than in any other religion, because they separate good from truth or charity from faith; and when these are separated, then from influx it cannot be otherwise. Therefore they confirm adulteries and not marriages; and therefore it is not known what conjugial love is, it must be shown how the faith of the present day separates and thus falsifies the Word, then how it perverts man's rational, thence adulteries are delightful, but not so marriages.

341. Adulteries are the worst of all abominations, because the seed of man is his life which is conjoined with the life of the wife, so that they are not two but one flesh; but when the lives of many men are immitted into one woman, there becomes such foulness that on account of the abomination it cannot be described, it becomes such before the angels.*

TO DO GOODS AND NOT TO FIGHT AGAINST EVILS IS TO DO GOODS FROM SELF AND NOT FROM THE LORD.

342. It is believed by many that they will be saved because they have done goods, as that they have given to the poor, benefited their neighbor, acted sincerely and justly in their duty and work, and yet have never fought against the evils opposed to their goods; believing that thus evils are removed. It appears to them, moreover, as if goods removed evils; saying in heart, "If I do good then I shall avoid evil." Nevertheless the case is as follows: that such a one does good from obedience to the precepts of the Lord, yet not from the Lord but from himself, thus not from any spiritual law except only apparently, but from a moral and civil law actually. In this case his evils

---

*See note following n. 326.

nevertheless remain; for although he does not do them, yet he is not averse to them. Consequently when the love of evil with its delight returns, he does not resist the evil, but either excuses it and does it, or omits doing it on account of himself and the world; moreover, he does not then know that it is evil. The case is otherwise when he fights against evil from the spiritual law; for, in so far as he does this, he censures evil, and he then loves good and its truth; and in proportion as he does good from the Lord and not from himself, in the same proportion the Lord, by the good and truth in the man, removes his evils.

343. I have heard spirits saying, that they know no otherwise than that to do good is to shun evil. But they receive for reply, that in this case they no otherwise shun evil than that they do not do it; but that nevertheless they do not hold evil in hatred, and reject[1] it as sin, unless as far as they have fought against it. By fighting against it evil is removed, and then good succeeds, that is, by combat the devil is removed and the Lord enters. To do good, and not to fight against evil, is to do good only in externals and not in internals; but to fight against evil and thus to do good, is to do good in internals. Man is not made spiritual except by combat. Some of those who have been sincere, just, chaste, and have not fought against what is insincere, unjust, and unchaste, are after death let into combats, and then it clearly appears how much they have done good from themselves, or on account of themselves, or from the Lord; and by combats they are reformed.

344. Before this they do not come into the affection of truth; nor their hearts into the perception and knowledge of it; nor are they taught what evil is and what good is. Their former state is thus one of ignorance.

345. Man does good from obedience, and he does good also from affection. He does good from obedience before he has fought against evil. This is the first state of man, and it may be a state of reformation; and he who is in this state and does not do evils is regenerated in the other life by combats against them or by temptations. To do good from affection takes place only when man has fought against evils; this is the state of man's regeneration and this state is the inverse of the former.

346. To do good from obedience is not from freedom, because not from affection; in it there is the thought of reward, and consequently afterwards of merit.

347. No one can do good from himself; it is the Lord with man who does the good, and no one comes to the Lord but he who removes evils from himself by combats against them. Hence it is that in proportion as any one thus removes evils, in the same proportion he does good from the Lord; and this good appears in like manner as if it were done by the man, but nevertheless the man always thinks of the Lord, and the angels have a perception that is from the Lord.

348. *In proportion as man shuns evils as sins, in the same proportion he does good not from himself but from the Lord.*

349. *In proportion as man shuns evil, in the same proportion his works become works of charity.*

THE DELIGHT FROM THE GLORY OF BEING WISE, AND THE DELIGHT OF COMMANDING.

350. I have sometimes seen that when they were in the delight of the love of ruling they acted like foolish persons, believing then that they were wiser than others. But when they were turned about they were led back into their understanding. They then saw that they had been foolish. But because they more greatly loved that former delight which was foolish, and turned themselves continually to that foolishness, they then seemed to be in that wisdom, thus by turns, and still their understanding could not lead them back, but the will led. Concerning this many may be named from experience, as Charles XII., Benz,[1] and others. This is a manifest sign that the will acts into the understanding, and not the understanding into the will. Nor is it so that they are converted by the Lord in the understanding by an influx of light into the voluntary, and that they are converted by hell to the delight of the will.

THE TEN COMMANDMENTS.

351. As far as man fights against evils as sins, and shuns evils as sins, so far the works which he does are goods, and so far they are charity.

As far as a man shuns evils as sins so far his spiritual mind is opened.

—So far his life becomes spiritual moral.

—So far he is in heaven, thus in the Lord, and the Lord is in him.

—So far he comes into the light of heaven, thus into the affection of truth on account of the truth.

—So far he is being regenerated, and is regenerated.

—So far the order is inverted and he acts from the will of good, and as if from the understanding.

—So far he is purified by truths.

—So far hereditary evil is removed.

—So far he increases in intelligence and wisdom.

—Many similar things from the heavenly doctrine where it treats of what is meant by *truths*.

—This is done successively, and afterward to eternity.

—So far he has faith.

THE LAST JUDGMENT.

352. (1) What the Last Judgment is.

(2) The Last Judgment has been effected three times.

(3) The Last Judgment was effected and is effected by the Lord from firsts by ultimates.

(4) The Last Judgment could not have been effected the second time, unless He Himself had come into the world, and by that as (in firsts) be also in ultimates.

(5) Without the Last Judgment effected by Him, thus without His Coming into the world, no one of mortals could have been saved.

(6) Unless the Lord had glorified His Human, even to its ultimates, no Last Judgment could be effected at this day.
—Thus hereafter no one could be saved.

(7) After the Last Judgment a new church is always to be established and is established, and before [the Last Judgment] it could not be nor can it be.

(8) Therefore it is predicted in the *Apocalypse*, that the New Jerusalem will descend from heaven after the Last Judgment, by which is meant the New Church.

(9) No one is received in that church thus in heaven after this except he who acknowledges God, one in Person and Essence, in whom is the Trinity, thus the Lord; and unless by some combats he has removed and shunned evils as sins against the Divine laws.

THE ENGLISH.

353. The English have a double theology, one for the learned and one for the unlearned.

The preachers compose their discourses so that the learned understand their theology and the unlearned theirs, and this is done from a certain fear on account of reputation and favor on both sides.

354. To the question whether they believe that the theology for the unlearned is true, they reply that they do not know otherwise when they utter that prayer in their temples, but not so when they compose their discourses.

355. It is then said to them, that the reason they do not know otherwise at that time is from influx out of heaven; and that it is not so when they compose their discourses, is from influx from their proprium; because they then think concerning themselves, their own learning, and fame and favor therefrom.

THE TEN COMMANDMENTS.

356. (1) Ten articles, what is effected with man when he fights against evils as sins, as before.

(2) Then the commandments of the Decalogue, where the evils are [named] which are sins, against which one must fight.

—Then of the spiritual which is then given to him, and in which he also comes; there is the spiritual there in every precept.

(3) What charity is, it is to do uses, everyone in his own function.

(4) What faith out of charity is, and what faith from charity is.

(5) Something concerning faith separated from charity, what its quality is when man is in it both as to life and doctrine.

OBSERVATIONS CONCERNING FAITH.

357. In a particular small work faith will be treated of, thus concerning faith separated from charity, after the work on the *Last Judgment*, in which all things will be described by articles, which are:

(1) What charity and faith are.

(2) One cannot be separated from the other. There is no charity where there is no faith, and there is no faith where there is no charity.

(3) As far as there is one, so far there is the other, in equal degree and in equal quality.

(4) Faith is truth.

(5) Faith does not produce charity, but charity faith.

—Before there is charity, those things which are supposed to be of faith, are only knowledges without life.

(6) Faith without charity is not possible.
—Faith without charity is no religion.
—Faith without charity falsifies the Word.
—Faith without charity blinds all the understanding of truth.
—It is the end of the church when there is not the faith of charity.
—Every church ends in Babylon, and in faith separate.
—Faith separate from charity is predicted in the *Apocalypse*, and is meant by the dragon and his two beasts.
—Faith without charity is meant by the he-goat in *Daniel* and in *Matthew*.
—Faith without charity is meant by Philistea.
—Faith without charity is meant by Cain.
—Faith without charity is meant by Reuben.
—Faith from charity, also faith without charity is meant by Peter.
—Charity is meant by James, and the works of charity by John. (See n 358–364 concerning faith.)

The quality of the faith of the present day is to be presented, such as it is, and the degrees of justification such as they are, they are to be described briefly, and that it is the whole of theology at the present day, also that if it is confirmed there arise many falsities, but not if it is not confirmed.

(1) The will is double, spiritual and natural. (2) Knowledges are the storehouse of faith. (3) All things of faith can be seen. (4) Falsities of faith are not faith. (5) Faith is truth.

FAITH.

358.* The Lord from eternity, who is Jehovah, came into the world that He might effect the Last Judgment and at the same time glorify His Human, and without this no mortal could have been saved; and they are saved who believe in Him and do good from Him. *This is the faith of the New Jerusalem.*

359. As far as faith is separated from the goods of charity it differs from that faith. Let him explore it who is able. Faith separate supposes: (1) That God the Father and God the Son are two, both from eternity. (2) It supposes that God the Son came into the world from the will of God the Father that He might make satisfaction for the human race, otherwise from the Divine justice, which they also call vindictive, it would have perished in eternal death. (3) It supposes that satisfaction was made by the Lord's fulfilling the law and by the passion of the cross. (4) It supposes that the mercy of God the Father was on account of those things of the Son. (5) It supposes imputation, the ascription of His merit to them who are in that faith, and who from it pray to the Father to have mercy for the Son's sake. (6) It supposes the justification of those who thus pray from trust and confidence. (7) It supposes the operation of the Holy Spirit with them. (8) It supposes the remission of all sins with them and thus salvation. (9) It supposes that then they will have an endeavor to do good, which deeply hidden operates, but not manifestly, and moves the will of man. Others, whom they believe to be less learned, suppose a manifest operation. (10) But most of those who confirm themselves in that faith, suppose that no one can do good from himself which is good, unless it is meritorious, thence that no good work saves, but faith alone, they say nothing about evil and about good of life, nor do they think of it. Some suppose that the influx of faith is instantaneous, and also that it is given in the last hour of death, and that their salvation is by faith alone howsoever they have lived.

---

* See note following n. 326.

360. They suppose there is something of temptation, and that liberation is by that faith.

361. In a summary, that God the Father sent the Son to make satisfaction for the human race, and that they who believe in Him are saved from His merit.

362. They divide into parties concerning instantaneous salvation by faith and vindictive justice.

363. Their books are full of these things, but they write confirmations of these subjects only.

364. Faith places the understanding under obedience to this faith, and he does not understand what the truth of faith is.

THE MORAVIANS.

365. I spoke with them of their brotherhood, whether it is of love or charity, they said no, but only of friendship, because they are of one opinion; they do not admit the expression love and charity in religion.

ARGUMENT CONCERNING THE JUDGMENT.

(1) By the judgments which have preceded, preparation has been made for the universal judgment [n. 134].
Concerning the new heavens which they made for themselves [n. 134].
(2) Concerning the going forth of some before the Last Judgment, who were in faith separate [n. 135].
And that they were first visited and separated [n. 135].
(3) Who they were that made for themselves heavens [n. 136].
It was seen that they acted there as in Sodom [n. 136].
(4) There were seen rocks carried away like a cloud [n. 137].
(5) Those who were in faith alone betook themselves upon rocks [n. 138].
How they dwelt there [n. 138].
Earthquakes preceded [n. 138].
(6) The wicked spirits in the plain were cast out [n. 139].
And the good reserved by the Lord were taken up in their place, and this is to open the sepulchres [n. 139].
(7) The destructions which preceded the Last Judgment [n. 140].
How the Divine sphere enters into them and thence opens up their interiors [n. 140].
(8) The quality of those upon whom the Last Judgment was effected [n. 141].
(9) The arrangement of the Reformed before the judgment, also where and how they were arranged [n. 142].
(10, 11) How they were first led forth [n. 143].
(12) The casting down of those in faith alone [n. 145].
And then exploration [n. 145].
(13) Likewise others [n. 146].
(14) Likewise others [n. 147].

- (15) Likewise others [n. 148].
- (16) How they were then seen [n. 149].
- (17) Their dispersion [n. 149, 150].
- (18) The angels wondered at such faith [n. 151].
- (18½) They have no conscience [n. 151].
- (19) The purifying of the middle lasts a long time [n. 152].
- (20) Some were seen at a table, clothed as with wedding garments, but within they were robbers [n. 153].
  They were cast down [n. 153].
- (21) They appeared as if sincere, yet they are wolves within [n. 153].
  Their lot [n. 154].
- (22) The exploration of the Reformed as to their quality, and their distinction into classes [n. 155].
- (23) Their ideas of the Lord [n. 156].
- (24) Of those who were in piety and external worship [n. 157].
  Their lot [n. 157].
- (25) Hypocrites, their lot [n. 158].
- (26) Priests who read the Word only that they may preach it [n. 159].
  Their lot [n. 159].
- (27) They are separated according to the internals of life which are affections [n. 160].
- (28) Dragons how they are explored [n. 161].
  Who those are who are in confirmation and in pride [n. 161–162].
  What they are [n. 161–162].
- (29) What is draconic [n. 161–162].
- (30) Anyone can know what charity is, that it is not to steal, etc. [n. 164].
- (31) The good who were left were allotted their habitations [n. 165].
- (32) Those who have understood and known many things, and with whom there was no will of good [n. 166].
  Their lot [n. 166].
- (33) Those who have not acknowledged the Lord, and have no good of charity; their rebellion and conjunction with the papists and Mohammedans [n. 167].
  Their lot [n 167].

- (34) Something said of the combat of the dragon with Michael [n. 168].
  The Lord seen in a cloud [n. 168].
  A representation of a tail [n. 168].
- (35) Those who are in faith alone and in the love of commanding look downward, their quality [n. 170.]
  Their quality [n. 170].
- (36) How they are distinguished according to their idea of God [n. 170].
- (37) Five classes [n. 171].
- (38) They persecuted me by inspirations and at the same time respirations and pulse; experience thence [n. 173].
- (39) The thought of those who are in faith alone described [n. 174].
  Their quality was such although they had not thought wickedly [n. 174].
- (40) Such were let out of the hells, they believing that they would then act well, but in vain, they were in anguish [n. 175].
- (41) The arrangement into societies [n. 176].
  The purification of societies [n. 176].
- (42) The arrangement takes place according to the affections of the life [n. 177].
  Not according to the affections of the understanding [n. 177].
  The nature of their ways afterwards [n. 177].
- (43) The most perfect arrangement is that of the Reformed [n. 178].
  The reason is that they have the Word and they go to the Lord [n. 178].
- (44) How they are taken up into heaven [n. 179].
  The Word of the Lord, they who have faith as a seed of mustard [n. 178].
- (45) The goats and their combats [n. 180].
- (46) In like manner [n. 181].
- (47) The dragon [n. 182].
- (48) Why it treats of them in the *Apocalypse* [n. 183].
- (49–52) Draconic spirits [n. 184–190].

- (53) The power of truth in the spiritual world [n. 191–193]. Experience [n. 193].
- (54) Those who have little of life, how life is inspired into them [n. 193].
- (55) The religion of those who are in faith alone, it is only knowledge [n. 194].
- (56) They who combat against evils receive the law as if inscribed on themselves [n. 195].
- (56½) Conducted into a mansion of heaven [n. 196].
  What is the opinion in the third heaven concerning those in faith alone; it is only knowledge [n. 196].
  According as they lived in the world so is their heaven [n. 196].
- (57) The quality of those who are in faith alone, and its quality as it interiorly appears [n. 197].
- (58) How the *Epistle of James* appears to them [n. 198].
- (59) They are received who believe in charity, provided they have lived the life of charity [199].
  One was turned about but he turned back afterwards [n. 199].
- (60) The arrangement of those who are in the faith of charity [n. 200].
- (61) In their factitious heavens there was a wintry light [n. 201].
- (62) The hells where they continually wrangle about their faith [n. 202].
  Their quality [n. 202].
- (63) By experience those who believed that they had faith, it was given them to know that they had no faith [n. 203].
- (64) Their interiors were closed [n. 204].
  They had a religion of the memory [n. 204].
  They were sensual [n. 204].
- (65) Faith alone of the church is not given, from experience [n. 205].
- (66) Those who are in no affection of truth, and yet reason much about truths, experience [n. 206].
- (67) Those who are in faith alone have no conscience [n. 207].

- (68) Those who believe in charity and do not live the life of charity, are not much unlike [those in faith alone] [n. 208].
- (69) How faith separate leads to evil of life [n. 209].
- (70) I spoke with Melancthon about faith alone, how false it is [n. 210].
- (71) Those who are in faith alone cannot be saved, what their quality is [n. 211].
- (72) Because all the societies of heaven are arranged according to the differences of love [n. 212].
- (73) An Englishman who wished to conjoin charity with faith, but it was not recognized [n. 213].
- (74) I read before the English their prayer before the Eucharist, and my discourse with them [n. 214].
- (75) English presbyters who made an idol of their faith [n. 215].
- (76) Discourse with the English concerning faith alone [n. 215-217].
- (77) The nature of their arguments for faith alone [n. 217].
- (78) Those were explored who confessed faith in the last hour of death, their quality [n. 218].
- (79) After the judgment many of those from faith alone were collected and rejected [n. 219].
- (80) Afterwards many wished to receive charity, but in vain, the reason [n. 220].

  The endeavor after justification [n. 220].
- (81) Free will with them [n. 221].
- (82) It is not allowed them to preach,—the hearers go out [n. 222].
- (83) The deserts where those are who are in faith alone [n. 224].
- (84) They were explored whether they know anything true, and it was found that they do not [n. 225].
- (85) Conversation with angels concerning the progression of truth to good [n. 226].
- (86) How the English write their discourses [n. 227].
- (87) That faith saves no one, a few things [n. 228].
- (88) It is like a dark chamber [n. 229].

- (89, 90) Their miserable state who have regarded evils as allowable, and their internal [n. 230].
- (91) All the states of love return after death, thus the states of faith if it enters the love [n. 230–232].
- (92) At this day they crucify the Lord [n. 232].
- (93) The ideas at this day concerning God, heaven, love, faith [n. 233].
- (94) The first state of man after death [n. 234].
- (95) Love produces the knowledge (*cognitionem*) of every good in the thought [n. 235].
- (96) They who are in the love of self cannot be admitted into heaven [n. 236].
- (97) They who are in the love of self can equally speak of the Divine, but yet after death they are against the Divine [n. 237].
- (98) They are enemies of the Lord, experience [n. 238].
- (99) Two opposite dominions of love [n. 239].
- (100) Their interiors and quality [n. 240].
- (101) Examples from those in the equestrian order [n. 241].
- (102) Love corresponds to flame, faith to light [n. 242].
- (103) The quality of those who worship the Lord from spiritual love [n. 243].
- (104) Affection makes the man, from changes induced and correspondences [n. 244].
- (105) The delight of the love of commanding exceeds every other delight [n. 245].
- (106) The delight of the love of commanding, into what it is turned after death [n. 246].
- (107) Everyone after death comes into his own love [n. 247].
- (108) Fr. Gyll, his mode of praying [n. 248].
- (109) The quality after death of him who is in the delight of commanding [n. 249].
- (110) Dreadful example [of hatred] against the Lord with those who think nothing from religion in their life [n. 250].

FIVE MEMORABLE RELATIONS.

I.

The Quality of the Merely Natural Man.

1. Once, from the desire of knowing the quality of the mind of the merely natural man, I looked up into heaven, and besought this knowledge from the Lord. The reason was that I had heard a most distinguished natural man, saying that he could see, understand and perceive many things just as rationally as they who are called spiritual, and thence angels of heaven; and he added to what he had said: "Has not each one a like rationality? What makes the difference except a frivolous opinion?" Suddenly then a certain satan ascended from the hells. Satans are all merely natural and can ratiocinate skilfully, but from the fallacies of the senses; wherefore they see falsities as truths; for all falsities derive their origin from those fallacies. When he came in sight he appeared at first with a bright and living face, afterwards with face deathly pale, finally with an infernal black face. I asked why his face underwent those changes. I received answer from heaven, that such are the successive states of the minds (*mens*) of those who are merely natural, for faces are types of minds (*animus*). The inmost of their minds (*mens*), because they are infernal, are represented by blackness in the face; the intermediates of their minds by the pallor of death, because they have falsified truths; but the outmosts, by a living whiteness, because while they are in externals, which is while they are in company, they can think, confirm, understand and teach truths. They have this ability, because rationality is human nature itself, for by it man is man, and is distinguished from beasts. But the rationality with satans is in externals alone; they have none, however, in internals; because in internals reigns the cupidity of adulterating the goods, and of falsifying the truths of the

church; and this cupidity inflows into their rationality and overshadows its light, and covers it with thick darkness, so that they do not see anything but falsities in place of verities.

2. After I had looked at his face, I looked into his eyes, and behold their pupils sparkled as from rays of light; afterwards they became opaque, and the irises became quite green, and finally, they appeared as if covered by a film, from which the whole crystalline lens in the pupil appeared like a cataract. Having seen these things I asked him whether he could see anything, and he said: "I see clearly and more than before." And I asked, "How can you see when your eyes have amaurosis? Perhaps you see something from fatuous light within." He responded, "What is fatuous light?" In order therefore that he might know what fatuous light is, I asked, "What do you think from your light?" He said, "I think in clear vision that beasts think just as rationally as man." Afterwards he said that God is nature, and nature is God; and then also that religion is vanity; and further, that nothing is good or evil but that which is delightful or undelightful and other like things.

3. When these things had been said, I proffered some genuine truths, which, before while he was in externals, he had seen and confirmed; and immediately when he heard them, he turned his eyes inward, acknowledged, and turned his eyes back again, and with a kind of border of the film which covered the pupil, he absorbed those truths, and injected them into his own fatuous light, and then he called them falsities; but because this appeared offensive before my sight, and as it were deadly, since in such a manner he slaughtered truths, from which, nevertheless, a man is a man and an angel is an angel, I abominated his presence; wherefore I turned my face from him; and when I looked back, behold I saw him sinking through a kind of gulf into hell; and because the place where he had stood stank from him, I went hastily home; for the Divine truth falsified by satans, in the spiritual world, stinks like the filth of the streets.

II.
The First State of Man After Death.

4. When any man after death comes into the spiritual world, which for the most part takes place the third day after he has expired, he appears to himself in a life similar to that in which he had been in the world, and in a similar house, chamber and bed-chamber, in a similar coat and clothing, and in a similar companionship within the house. If he was a king or a prince he appears in a similar palace, if a peasant in a similar cottage; rustic things surround the latter, splendid things the former. This happens to every one after death, to the end that death may not appear as death, but as a continuation of life, and that the last of natural life may become the first of spiritual life, and that from this a man may progress to his goal, which will be either in heaven or in hell.

5. That such a similarity of all things appears to the recently deceased is because their mind remains the same as it was in the world; and, because the mind is not only in the head, but also in the whole body, therefore a man has a similar body; for the body is the organ of the mind, and is continued from the head; wherefore the mind is the man himself, but then no longer a material man, but a spiritual man; and, because he is the same man after death, there are given to him things similar to those which he had possessed at home in the world, according to the ideas of his mind; but this lasts only some days. That the mind is in the whole body, and is the very man who lives after death, appears manifestly from the speech of the mouth and the action of the body being instantaneous with the will and thought of the mind; for the mouth speaks in an instant what the mind thinks, and the body executes in an instant what the mind wills. The erroneous belief that man lives after death a soul or mind, and this not under the appearance of a man, but under the appearance of a breath, as it were, of respiration, or as a bubble as it were, of air, is because men do not know that the mind makes the interior form of the whole body.

6. When newcomers into the spiritual world are in this first state, angels come to them for the sake of wishing them an auspicious arrival, and at the first they are greatly delighted from conversation with them, since they know that they do not think otherwise than that they still live in the former world; wherefore the angels ask them what they think of the life after death, to which the newcomers respond in conformity with their previous ideas: some that they do not know; some that they are breaths or ethereal appearances; some that they are airy transparent bodies; some that they are flitting spectres, some of them in ether and air, others in water, and others in the middle of the earth; and some say that they are souls like angels in the stars. Some of the newcomers deny that any man lives after death.

7. When they have heard these things the angels say, "Welcome, we will show something new, that you have not known, nor have you believed before, namely this, that every man lives a man after death, in a body altogether as he lived before." To these things the novitiate spirits reply, "This is not possible. Whence has he a body? Does it not lie with all things of it dead in the grave?" To these things the angels respond merrily, "We will demonstrate it to your sight." And they say, "Are you not men in perfect form? Look at yourselves and touch yourselves; and yet you have departed from the natural world. That you have not known this before now is because the first state of life after death is altogether like the last state of life before death." On hearing these things the new guests are astonished and exclaim from joy of heart, "Thanks be to God that we are alive, and that death has not extirpated us!" I have often heard novitiates instructed in this manner concerning their life after death, and have seen them gladdened on account of their resurrection.

III.

The Consummation of the Age, the Destruction of the World, and the End of the Church.

8. I have often heard the conversation of angels with new spirits, and once about the consummation of the age and the destruction of the world. And because those new spirits had hitherto known nothing of heaven and of hell nor of the life of man after death, nor of any other sense of the Word than the literal, they gave responses void of reason and full of paradoxes. They said that by the consummation of the age they understood the destruction of the world; by the coming of the Lord then, His appearing with the angels in a cloud; by the Last Judgment, sentences decreeing salvation and damnation upon all the dead after their resurrection from the grave. When the angels had heard these things they asked with smiling countenance, two or three times, whether the spirits said these things from faith of heart which is believed to be the truth; or from historical faith, which in itself is tradition from others; or from the indulgence of the imagination. To these questions the new guests replied with indignation, "What have we said from the indulgence of the imagination, or from mere tradition? Are not these things truths revealed in the Word? They must be of faith of heart." When these things were said the angels courteously answered, "It does no harm for you to believe thus, but that it is not so, you shall hereafter be instructed."

9. Immediately after this was said little flames appearing like tongues flowed down from heaven upon the heads of the newcomers, by which they were inspired with the affection of knowing from reason how they had faith; and they exclaimed, "What is faith but truth? Where is truth in its own light except in the understanding? If the understanding be in thick darkness, what then is faith but a somnambulist? And if to this faith be added confirmation from natural light separate from spiritual light, it becomes a bat." Among the newcomers was a certain priest, who, when he heard these things from his associates, said with an inflamed voice, "What has faith to do with the understanding?" The angels replied, "What is faith without the understanding, but a blind faith?" Suddenly then the little flame fell down from the top of the priest's head upon his shoe and shone there a little while.

10. After this the angels asked the novitiates what further they had thought from their faith, concerning the consummation of the age, and what they still thought. They replied, "We had thought of the destruction of the universe, both heaven and earth; since we read that heaven and earth should be destroyed, and it was said that they should pass away in smoke." The angels then inquired, "What heaven and what earth; the heaven and earth of the natural world or of the spiritual world? There are also heavens and earths here, heavens where the angels are, and lands upon which they dwell." At this the novitiates responded, "What is this? Perhaps you are joking? Are not angels spirits? What is a spirit but a breath of wind? And where is this breath? Does it not fly about in the atmospheric heaven, and go even to the stars?" The angels then replied, "You are now in the spiritual world, and as yet you know no otherwise than that you are in the natural world. Here heaven, where the angels are, is above your head, and hell, where the devils and satans are, is under your feet. Is not the soil, upon which you and we stand, earth? Stamp it with your feet and know." But at this, because it was foreign to previously conceived ideas, they wondered greatly; yet, because they were in enlightenment, from the little flames upon their heads, they listened willingly to the discourse of the angels, and comprehended the truths they uttered.

11. The angels asked further, "In what manner did you believe that the destruction of your world would take place?" They said, "By fire, about which we have believed and prophesied many things: some of us, that flames from heaven would be cast down everywhere upon the earth, as they were upon the sons of Aaron, and upon the burnt offering of Elijah; some, that the fire of the sun would be let loose, would break forth, and set the universe on fire; some, that the central fire of the earth would break the crust round about it, and hurl itself forth everywhere, as it does from the fire-vomiting mountains, Ætna, Vesuvius and Hecla; some, that a great comet would invade the atmosphere of the earth, and would set it on fire with the flame of its tail; some have said that the universe would not perish by fire, but would go to ruin, and fall to pieces, as does a house from age; and others have believed otherwise." When the angels had heard these things they said to one another, "O what simplicity! arising only from utter ignorance of the spiritual world and of the angels, and of their heavens and earths, and also from utter ignorance of the internal or spiritual sense of the Word! Thence all things of eternal life have become mere things of the memory, and not

of the reason; and if there be anything of reason, it is not above the memory but below it, where confirmations from fallacies counterfeit the light of reason. This was represented by what we lately saw, that the little flame fell down from the priest's head upon his shoe, and shone there; and this appears to us as if one were to take his hat from his head, and wrap it round the soles of his feet and thus walk."

12. The angels then said, "We have been chosen from heaven to instruct newcomers from the countries of the natural world, since all who arrive here from there, are in a foolish belief about heaven, yea, even about salvation; wherefore unless those follies are dissipated, which is effected by instruction, their rational, which is above the memory, and grows wise from the reception of celestial light, would be closed, and this being closed, from being men they would become animals, with this sole difference, that they would still be able to think from the external senses, and speak from this thought alone.

13. "Since this office of instruction is enjoined upon us, we will teach you what is meant in the Word by the consummation of the age." And they said, "The consummation of the church is meant, which consummation is also called desolation and devastation, and this is when there are no longer truths of faith and goods of charity in any essence of their own, and thus all the ways to heaven are obstructed." They also said, "This consummation appears scarcely anywhere in the world, because those things which are of faith are not truths but falsities, and those things which are of charity are not goods but only deeds of their own love, which, when they go forth in the breath of the mouth, do not elevate themselves to heaven, but as soon as they rise up they are turned aside and fall down to the earth, just as does the water of a bath when cast upon the shoulders, or as rotten fruit falls from trees in the time of winter.

14. "In this consummation or end of the church, it will be proclaimed from all pulpits, and the people will vociferate in all sanctuaries, 'Here is the dwelling-place of God! Here is the temple of God! Here is the church of God! Here is salvation! Here is the light of the Gospel!' And they do not at all know that they are in mere darkness, and that they dream the dream of the age. This is because they believe that falsi-

ties are truths, and truths falsities, as also that evils are goods, and goods evils. This night and this dream the Lord predicted in *Matthew* (xxiv. 37–39), and in *Luke* (xvii. 26 to the end).

15. "You shall be confirmed that the consummation of the age is the end of the church, not only from reason but also from sight. Know then that the end of the church will not be at all recognized on earth, though fully recognized in the heavens. Heaven and the church are like a single containing house. The church is the foundation and substructure, and heaven is its superstructure and roof; and the inhabitants are consociated like members of a family with domestics. When therefore the church, by evils and falsities slips from under, that house does not hold together except as to its walls, and within, communication with the angels of heaven is intercepted, and the stairway, by which there is ascent and descent, is taken away. Lest the house should then fall into utter ruin the Lord returns into the world and establishes a new church, and by it restores the house, and supports heaven. But this will appear more evidently before your sight, if we pray to the Lord, and go away from here and walk about."

IV.

The Sun of the Spiritual World and the Coming of the Lord in a Cloud.

16. While walking they first turned their faces to the east, where they saw the sun shining in its strength, and when they were under its direct rays, the novitiates asked the angels about that sun, whether it was the sun which they had seen in the former world, since its altitude above us and also its magnitude equals that; it grows red also and burns from fire in a similar manner, and also heat and light proceed from it in a like manner; and if it be the same sun are we not in nature? Whence is nature except from its own sun? But the angels said, "This sun is not the sun of the natural world, but the sun of the spiritual world. From this sun is our universe; from its light and heat angels live and spirits live; from its light both we and they have understanding and wisdom; from its heat both we and they have will and love. The essence of this sun is pure love, and the Lord Jesus Christ, who is the God of heaven and earth, and is one with God the Father, is in the midst of it.

17. "The Divine love proximately proceeding from Him, and encompassing Him, appears as a sun; wherefore by the light and heat thence proceeding, He has Omnipresence, Omniscience and Omnipotence, from end to end of both worlds. But the sun from which nature came into existence is pure fire; in the light and heat of which there is nothing of wisdom and love, wherefore nothing of life, but still it serves life, that is, wisdom and love, for a swathing and garment, in order that the forms of those lives may endure, and that they may have as it were times and spaces; but yet they do not have times and spaces; but love and wisdom only affect those who are in times and spaces, which takes place according to reception, and reception is according to the affection of being wise, and according to a life conformable to wisdom." When the novitiates heard these things, they exulted with joy, and said, "We perceive that our hearts exult with joy as never before." "You have this," replied the angels, "from the celestial and spiritual love and its delight which proceed from our sun."

18. When these things had been said, suddenly there was driven below the sun a bright cloud, which did not dull, but transmitted the light; and in that bright cloud appeared angels as with trumpets, and round about them were altars and tables, upon which in heaps lay half-open books; and above the cloud the Lord appeared, speaking out of the sun with the angels. Then from the cloud there fell as it were dew, which, being scattered about, was condensed into manna, some of which the angels took up and gave to their companions, who ate it. After a quarter of an hour, there was seen from the cloud a rain, which the angels called the morning rain, which flowed down, and dissolved the manna into its original dew. This was collected into drops of a sweet taste. The manna was soon fully melted and flowed into the ground and penetrated it. And then from the dwellers under that ground were heard voices of gladness. "Hey! Come forth! Be ready! Drops of the blessed water are falling from heaven! We are sprinkled!" For it was the melted manna which was dropping down.

19. After this the angels instructed the new guests about what they had heard and seen, saying, "The things, which you have seen, exhibit in a summary the Coming of the Lord, and the things which will then happen. God, who appeared out of the sun above the cloud, was the Lord our Saviour. The bright cloud under Him was the angelic heaven, where the Divine truth was in its own light. The speech of the Lord with the angels there, was inspiration. The trumpets seen in the hands and at the mouths of the angels, were not trumpets, but representations of their speech with one another from inspiration. The dew falling from the cloud upon the earth, and condensing into manna, represented the heavenly affections of the thoughts in their speech. The rain dissolving the manna, that heavenly food, into its original dew, which, absorbed by the earth, distilled through to the dwellers beneath, represented the influx of Divine truth from the Word with the men of the world who go forth and receive it in spirit and heart. The tables and the heaps of books upon them, were not tables nor books, but they were representations of the intentions of the mind, and thence of deeds, according to which the faithful and the unfaithful will be judged. That bright cloud, in which the angels were seen, represented the Divine truths of the Lord with them; for the spheres of thoughts from truths, and of affections from goods, proceeding from the angels, appear everywhere as clouds."

20. At this the new spirits inquired, "Why do you say that those things that were seen represent, and do not say that they are?" The angels answered, "Because each and all things which appear to the sight in this world are correspondences and representations, which contain in themselves truths, and thence signify them. Thus spiritual things are here presented under forms similar to natural things.

"The spiritual things which are proper to our world, as they here appear, are also described in the Word. For the Word was written by correspondences, in order that it may be at the same time for angels and for men. These things are first offered to your sight, and are seen, that you may know how the Coming of the Lord is to be understood."

V.

The Abomination of Desolation.

21. After this the angels prayed to the Lord. They then led the novitiates from the east to the south, and thence to the west, and they said, "Here you shall see the *abomination of desolation* predicted by the Lord through Daniel (*Matt.* xxiv. 15)." They then showed them a black cloud extending from the boundary of the east to the end of the west, and pouring thick darkness into the south and into the north at the sides. At the sight of the cloud the novitiates became terrified, and they asked, "What is that great black cloud and thick darkness and whence is it?" The angels replied, "They are satanic spirits, who have collected themselves into crowds, and by magical arts, by abuses of correspondences, and by phantasies, have formed for themselves as it were heavens, by seizing the hills, and building upon them high places and towers, as was done in the valley of the land of Shinar (*Gen.* xi. 1, *seq.*) in order that they may contrive for themselves ascents into the heavens where the angels are, for the purpose of thrusting them down; and because they are on high above this land they appear as though they were in the expanse of the sky, and the expanse appears as a cloud." And the angels said, "Lift up your eyes and stretch your sight." And behold they saw a multitude of spirits, and they heard heinous expressions from them, intermixed with the filthy things of lasciviousness, and sounds as of drunken revelers in brothels. And the angels said, "These are they who are meant by the dragon and his two beasts in the *Apocalypse* (Chap. xii. and xiii.). These are they who are meant by the harlot sitting upon many waters, and upon the scarlet beast (Chap. xvii.). They are all from the Christian world."

22. And the novitiates asked, "How can these things be called the abomination of desolation?" The angels replied, "They are all in falsities as to faith, and in evils as to life. The interiors of their minds are infernal, and the exteriors from feigned morality, are, as it were, heavenly; for they are sycophants and hypocrites, and because they are in the midst between the heavens where the angels are, and the earths where men are, no Divine truth from the Lord can pass through the heavens to the men of the earth, but it is first received by them, and being received is inverted and falsified, not otherwise than is the case with light falling upon an opaque cloud, and the heat of the sun falling into a swamp."

23. Then suddenly the eyes of the novitiates were opened, and they saw flowing down from that cloud hail mixed with fire, and they saw upon the earth as a result of that rain something sticky, and in that sticky substance worms. And farther towards the north they saw descending from the cloud, as it were, bruchi* and locusts, which consumed the grass of the earth. And eagles appeared flying out of a desert, and also birds of the evening, which devoured the worms and licked up that sticky substance as though it were water. Amazed by these things, the novitiates besought the angels to tell what they signified. They said, "The abomination of desolation upon the earth. The hail signifies falsified truths; the fire mingled with it, evils of life; the sticky substance upon the earth, coherence; the worms, life from those things; the bruchi and locusts, the falsities of faith; the birds signify men of the earth who eat no other food flowing down from the spiritual world; and the eagles signify ratiocinations and confirmations.

24. "Know therefore, that by 'the former heaven and the former earth' which John saw had passed away (*Apoc.* xxi. 1), nothing else is meant but those black expanses where the draconians and Babylonians have fixed their dwelling-places and called them heavens. So long as those expanses remain, the communication of men with the angelic heavens, thus also in a measure with the Lord, is intercepted; and when that communication is intercepted, then every truth and good of the Word is falsified and adulterated. Thus appears the abomination of desolation with us; but with the inhabitants of the earth it does not appear by any signs, wherefore they induce a belief in falsities, and by confirmations from the natural man they encircle that belief with a fatuous light, from which falsities are believed to be truths."

---

* A species of locust.

CONVERSATIONS WITH ANGELS.

1. One evil contains in itself innumerable lusts, interior and exterior, of which man knows nothing.
   All these are removed by the Lord, while man looks to the Lord, and shuns evil as of himself.
   Illustration by various examples with man, as of the stomach, the kidneys, the members devoted to generation.
   There is no need for man to know of these.
   Evil appears to man as one, and nevertheless they are in all lusts, interior and exterior, thus in successive order, but they are in the evil in simultaneous order. This also must be illustrated.
   Man is not purified by shunning evils solely on account of civil and moral causes; because by this he is purified only as to externals, but not as to internals.
   Thus no one is purified by the faith of the present day, which promotes only civil, moral and political works.
2. Those who, from confirmation within themselves, make the Human of the Lord like the human of another man, divide the Lord into two.
   They are in heart Socinians and Arians; with whom there is no church.
   Faith alone effects this.
3. He who is in faith alone cannot do otherwise than make God three.
   On the other hand, he who makes God three, loves faith alone.
4. The Lord and man are together in love towards the neighbor.
   Conjunction is effected by that love.
   Those who are in that love, love the Lord.
5. He who makes any evil allowable in his mind, continually does it.

There is then the endeavor to do it whenever it is possible. The endeavor resides not only in the mind, but also in the body.

That endeavor is the will, which is only restrained by external causes.

6. The internal man is not merely to understand, to think and to know.

But it is to will what he understands, thinks and knows.

Hence it can be seen what the internal man is when separated from the external, and what it is when not separated.

All the spiritual is in thought from will, and thought without will is external like a court.

7. There are three things which follow in order and make one: charity, faith and works,—like will, understanding and deeds.

If one is lacking, the remaining two fall or vanish.

8. Man is to act and think in spiritual things as of himself. Otherwise man would not be man. This is the image of God in man. This is given continually by the Lord.

It is given as the reciprocal of love, and thence is conjunction.

Otherwise the Word would be of no use.

Otherwise there would be no religion.

9. All things inflow with man, so that man is only a recipient organ.

He is an organ recipient of all things of heaven as to his mind, and recipient of the world as to his body.

As the eye is a recipient of light, the ears recipients of sound, and the remaining things of the body, so the understanding is a recipient of the light of heaven or of wisdom, and the will is a recipient of the heat of heaven, thus of love.

There is nothing in man but the faculty of receiving. It may be illustrated by the organs what the faculty is.

Natural objects are felt in the organs of the body as if they were in them, and spiritual objects in like manner are felt as if in the mind, although they are not there.

These are fallacies of sensation.

10. Fallacies arise from inverted ideas.
   As concerning God from Person and not from essence; concerning the neighbor from person or from the human form, and not from his quality; concerning heaven from place and not from love and wisdom; concerning the church from external worship, and not from charity and faith therefrom, which are its internals; yea, concerning various things from delights, and not from the loves from which they are.
11. The state of man as to the will or love is not changed after death. The reason is because it is his life.
   So also as to charity.
   The state of man as to the understanding is changed, and it is changed according to the love of the will.
   A man in the world may think that he is in heaven on account of the understanding, when yet he is not.
   Therefore the truths and goods in his understanding are taken away, because they do not agree with the love of the will.
12. Absurdities about instantaneous faith, and thus instantaneous salvation. Likewise about immediate mercy, because this makes one with instantaneous faith.
   Although indeed man is reformed and regenerated successively even to the end of life, and then to eternity.
   And he can never be perfectly regenerated, only as to the most general things, and some general things under them.
13. The understanding in spiritual things is destroyed with those of the clergy who have confirmed with themselves the falsities of the faith of the present day.
   It is not destroyed with the laity, because they have not confirmed it.
   How a clergyman closes his understanding in spiritual things with himself, and also with the laity. Confirmation closes it, why? Many kinds of confirmation. Confirmation by life is the worst.
14. How the sense of the letter of the Word is abolished when it passes into heaven and becomes spiritual.
   There is a putting off, and a revelation of the interiors of truth.

Experiments, that when truth lies hidden within with a man, the sense of the letter is open in heaven, and on the other hand it is dissipated, and sometimes with a noise; and if the confirmation of the love of evil lies hidden within, there appear as it were sparks of fire, and an explosion.

All things of the sense of the letter of the Word communicate with all things of the heavens.

Thus the Word is the conjunction of heaven and the church.

This cannot be comprehended without a knowledge of correspondences.

15. A false principle in spiritual things falsifies all things.

Thus it falsifies all things of the Word.

It falsifies while he is reading the Word even though man does not know it.

Falsities still insinuate themselves in each thing of the Word, from the side or in the middle.

This falsity is not manifested, unless while it is in the middle it is placed in direct view of the thought.

16. Truths do not falsify the Word wherever it is read, because they are continuously present in the series.

The good of life does not falsify the Word, because this is within in each and everything of the Word.

Thus the sense of the letter of the Word can be turned hither and thither, by the man who is in truths of doctrine and in the good of life.

17. With those who are in faith alone all good works become meritorious, even repentance.

They falsify the whole Word who confirm falsities within themselves, and they do not know this. Luther.

That all things are from God may be illustrated by all the correspondences with man; from the spheres around the angels.

Charity and faith make one like affection and thought, so that there is not given anything of one more than of the other.

Faith is described such as it is with the ancients, it is vivified by charity, the faith which is historical, in other respects denotes knowledge.

JUSTIFICATION AND GOOD WORKS.

WITH THE ROMAN CATHOLICS FROM THE COUNCIL OF TRENT.

I.

1. That the sin of Adam has been transfused into the whole human race, whereby his state, and from this the state of all men, became perverted and alienated from God, and men have thus become enemies and children of wrath. That therefore God the Father graciously sent His Son that He might reconcile, expiate, atone, make satisfaction, and thus redeem, and this by being made righteousness. That Christ did this by offering Himself up a sacrifice to God the Father, upon the wood of the cross, thus by His passion and blood.

II.

2. That the Lord Jesus Christ alone has merited. That this His merit is imputed, attributed and applied to man and transferred into him by God the Father through the Holy Spirit; and that thus the sin of Adam is removed from man, lust still remaining as a fomenter to sin. That this is effected, first by baptism, and afterward by the sacrament of repentance.

III.

3. That justification is effected by faith, hope and charity. That there is then effected a renovation of the interior man, whereby man from being an enemy becomes a friend, and from being a child of wrath becomes a child of God. That this is graciously effected by God the Father through the merit of His Son with the operation of the Holy Spirit. And that it is a union with Christ, because the man becomes a living member of His body, and, as it were, a branch in the vine.

IV.

4. Because these things are effected from grace and are given freely, and thus are gifts, and because Christ Jesus alone has merited, therefore no one can attribute anything of merit to himself.

V.

5. That because the reception of justification renovates man, and as this is effected by the transference of the merit of Christ into him, it follows that works are meritorious, and that the man who is justified and sanctified is not only reputed just and holy, but becomes just and holy.

VI.

6. That faith is from hearing when a man believes those things to be true which are Divinely revealed. That it is the commencement of justification, but that it operates by charity, because faith without works is dead.

VII.

7. That free-will is not destroyed, and that man ought to coöperate; and that he has the power to approach and recede, otherwise nothing could be given to him, and he would be like an inanimate body.

VIII.

8. That man makes satisfaction by satisfactory penances imposed on him by the minister; and that this derogates nothing from the satisfaction made by Christ, since we ought to suffer with Him.

IX.

9. Something about Predestination.

I.

CONFIRMATION OF THESE THINGS FROM THE COUNCIL OF TRENT.

10. That Adam, by the offense of his transgression, experienced an entire change and depravation of nature, both in body and soul; and that the ill effects of Adam's transgression were not confined to himself, but also extended to his posterity; and that it not only transmitted death and corporal sufferings upon all mankind, but likewise sin, which is the death of the soul. (Sess. v. 1546, June 17.)

11. That this sin of Adam, which originally was a single transgression, and has been transmitted by propagation, and not by imitation, is so implanted in the proprium of every man, and cannot be taken away by any other means than by the merit of the only Mediator, our Lord Jesus Christ, who has reconciled us to God by His blood, being made unto us justice, sanctification, and redemption. (Sess. v. 3, 1546, June 17.)

12. Everyone acknowledges and confesses, that by the transgression of Adam, all men became unclean, sons of wrath, under the power of the devil and of death. (Sess. vi. 1547, Jan. 13.)

13. That our heavenly Father, the Father of mercies, and God of all consolation, sent Christ Jesus His Son to men, in the blessed fullness of time, that He might redeem both the Jews who were under the law, and the Gentiles who followed not justice, that they might all lay hold of justice, and all receive the adoption of sons. Him God offered to be a propitiation through faith in His blood, not only for our sins, but likewise for the sins of the whole world. (Sess. vi., Chap. 2, Jan. 13.)

14. That God and our Lord offered Himself to God the Father on the altar of the cross, interceding by death, that He might work that eternal redemption; that the sacrifice of the mass was that propitiatory for the living and the dead. (Sess. xxii. 1, 2, Sept. 17, 1562.) Concerning the institution of the mass (pages 146, 148).

II.

Merit Is Not From Man.

15. That the sin of Adam which is in the proprium of everyone, cannot be taken away by the powers of human nature, nor by any other remedy than the merit of the one Mediator our Lord Jesus Christ. (Sess. v. 3, June 17, 1546.)

16. The meritorious cause of Justification is the dearly beloved the Only begotten of God, who when we were enemies, on account of the exceeding charity wherewith He loved us, merited justification for us, by His most holy passion on the wood of the cross, and made satisfaction for us unto God the Father. (Sess. vi. 7: 2; Jan. 13, 1547.)

17. Man is justified freely, because none of those things which precede justification, whether of faith or works, merit the grace of justification itself; for if it be grace, it is not by works, otherwise grace would not be grace. (Sess. vi. 8.)

18. There is a continual influx of virtue from Jesus Christ Himself, as from the head into the members, and from a vine into the branches; which virtue always precedes, accompanies and follows their works, and without which they could not by any means be acceptable and meritorious in the sight of God. That which is termed our justice, is the justice of God, because it is infused into us by God through the merit of Christ. Far be it, therefore, from any Christian man either to trust or glory in himself, and not in the Lord, whose goodness towards men is so great, that He wishes that the things which are His gifts may be their merits. (Sess. vi. 18.)

19. If anyone saith, that man may be justified in the sight of God by his own works, which are done either through the teaching of human nature, or through the teaching of the law, without Divine grace through Jesus Christ, let Him be accursed. (Can. 1, concerning Justification.)

20. If anyone saith, that without the preventing inspiration of the Holy Spirit, and without His help, man can believe, hope, love or be penitent as he ought, so that the grace of justification may be bestowed upon him, let him be accursed. (Canon 3, on Justification.)

21. If anyone saith, that men are just without the justice of Christ, whereby He merited for us to be justified, let him be accursed. (Canon 10, on Justification.)

22. For we, who can do nothing of ourselves, as of ourselves, can do all things, He coöperating, who strengthens us. Thus man has not wherein to glory, but all our glory is in Christ; in whom we live; in whom we merit; in whom we satisfy; bringing forth fruit worthy of repentance, which from Him have efficacy, by Him are offered to the Father, and through Him are accepted by the Father. [Sess. xiv.] (Chap. 8, concerning Satisfaction, p. 125.)

III.

They Do Them Through the Sacrament of Baptism and the Sacrament of Repentance.

23. The merit of Jesus Christ is applied both to adults and to infants, by the sacrament of baptism rightly administered; for there is no other name under heaven given to men, whereby we must be saved. Whence that voice, Behold the Lamb of God, who taketh away the sins of the world; and that other, As many as have been baptized, have put on Christ. (Sess. v., 1546, June 17, p. 5.)

24. If any one denies, that, by the grace of our Lord Jesus Christ, which is conferred in Baptism, the guilt of original sin is remitted, or asserts that the whole of that which has the true and proper nature of sin is not taken away; but says that it is only erased, or not imputed; let him be accursed. But that in the baptized there remains concupiscence or an incentive [to sin] the Synod confesses and is sensible of, and that this concupiscence is not sin, but is from sin, and inclines to sin. (Sess. v., 1546, June 17, p. 5.)

25. That from the merit of Christ they are justified by repentance, when they purpose to receive baptism, to begin a new life, and to keep the Divine commandments. (Sess. vi., Chap. 6.)

26. That by the sacrament of repentance, by the merit of Christ, the grace lost can be recovered. (Sess. vi., Chap. 14.)

27. Although Christ died for all, yet all do not receive the benefit of His death, but those only unto whom the merit of His passion is communicated. So, if they were not born in Christ, they never would be justified; seeing that, in that new birth, there is bestowed upon them, through the merit of His passion, the grace whereby they are made just. (Sess. vi., 1547, Jan. 13, Chap. 3.)

28. That the justification of the impious is a transference from that state wherein man is born a child of the first Adam, to the state of grace, and of the adoption of the sons of God through the second Adam, Jesus Christ, our Saviour. And this transference is effected by the laver of regeneration or baptism, and its vow. (*Ibid.*, Chap. 4.)

29. Justification is not only remission of sins, but also is sanctification and renovation of the interior man by the voluntary reception of grace and gifts, whence man from unjust becomes just, and from an enemy a friend, and an heir according to the hope of eternal life. (*Ibid.*, Chap. 7.)

30. Although no one can be just, but he to whom the merits of the passion of our Lord Jesus Christ are communicated, yet this is done in this justification of the impious, when by the merit of that same most holy passion, the charity of God is poured forth by the Holy Spirit, in the hearts of those who are justified, and is inherent therein; whence, man, through Jesus Christ, in whom he is ingrafted, receives, in the said justification, together with the remission of sins, all these [gifts] infused at once, faith, hope and charity. For faith, unless hope and charity be added thereto, neither unites man perfectly with Christ, nor makes him a living member of His body. (Chap. 7, sec. 3.)

31. For which reason it is said that faith without works is dead and profitless; faith worketh by charity; whence also they immediately hear the Word of Christ; "if thou wilt enter into life, keep the commandments;" thus receiving true and Christian justice, they are bidden immediately on being born again, to preserve it pure and spotless, as the first robe given them through Jesus Christ in lieu of that which Adam, by his disobedience, lost for himself and for us, that so they may bear it before the judgment seat of our Lord Jesus Christ, and may have eternal life. (*Ibid.*, Chap. 7, sec. 4.)

32. That man is justified by works, and not by faith only. (*Ibid.*, Chap. 10.)

33. That through Jesus Christ, they have access to grace. (*Ibid.*, Chap. 11.)

34. If anyone saith, that the just ought not, for their good works done in God, to expect and hope for an eternal recompense from God, through His mercy and the merit of Jesus Christ, if they persevere even to the end in well doing and in keeping the Divine commandments; let him be accursed. (*Ibid.*, Canon 26.)

35. If anyone saith, that by the said sacraments of the New Law grace is not conferred through the act performed, but that faith alone in the Divine promise suffices for the obtaining of grace; let him be accursed. (Sess. vii., Canon 8, concerning the Sacraments.)

IV.

36. These things are confirmed by all the things which precede, especially in I. and also in this.

37. That in adults, the beginning of justification is from the preventing grace of God, through Jesus Christ, that is, from His calling. They are disposed to convert themselves to their own justification, by freely assenting to and coöperating with that said grace; that man can reject grace; yet he is not able without the grace of God to move himself, etc. Whence it is said, "Turn ye to Me, and I will turn to you," we are admonished of our liberty. (Sess. vi., 1547, Jan. 13, Chap. 5.)

V.

38. Because justification is the renovation of the spirit of the mind; and because Christ dwells in those who are justified, or the justified are as branches in the vine, as is read in what was adduced before, therefore this follows.

39. That we are not only reputed, but are truly called, and are just, receiving justice within us, each one according to his own measure, which the Holy Spirit distributes to everyone as He wills, and according to each one's proper disposition and coöperation. (Sess. vi., 1547, Jan 13, Chap. 7, sec. 2.)

40. If anyone saith, that the good works of one that is justified are thus the gifts of God, that they are not also the good merits of him that is justified; or that the said justified, by the good works which he performs through the grace of God and the merit of Jesus Christ, whose living member he is, does not truly merit; let him be accursed. (Can. 32, p. 76.)

VI.

41. They are disposed by justice, when excited and assisted by Divine grace, conceiving faith by hearing, they are freely moved towards God, believing those things to be true which God has revealed and promised, and this especially, that God justifies the impious by grace, through the redemption which is in Christ Jesus. (Sess. vi., Jan. 13, Chap. 6.)

42. Man is justified by faith freely, because faith is the beginning of human salvation, the foundation and the root of all justification, without which it is impossible to please God, and to come to the fellowship of His sons. We are said to be justified freely, because none of those things which precede justification, whether faith or works, merit the grace itself of justification. For if it be grace, it is not now from works, otherwise grace would not be grace. (*Ibid.*, Chap. 7, sec. 4.)

43. The merit of Christ is ingrafted by faith, hope and charity; for faith, unless hope and charity be added thereto, neither unites man with Christ, nor makes him a living member of His body. (*Ibid.*, Chap. 7, sec. 3.)

44. For which reason it is said, that faith without works is dead and profitless; faith worketh by charity, whence also they immediately hear the Word of the Lord, "If you will enter into life, keep the commandments." (*Ibid.*, Chap. 7, sec. 4.)

45. That man is justified by works, not by faith alone. (*Ibid.*, Chap. 10.) That they have access by Jesus Christ. (*Ibid.*, Chap. 11.)

46. If anyone saith, that by faith alone the impious is justified, so as to mean that nothing else is required to coöperate in order to the obtaining the grace of justification, and that it is not in any way necessary that he be prepared and disposed by the movement of his own will, let him be accursed. (Canon 9.)

47. If any one saith that men are justified, either by the sole imputation of the justice of Christ, or by the sole remission of sins, to the exclusion of the grace and the charity which is poured forth in their hearts by the Holy Spirit, and is inherent in them, or says that the grace is only the favor of God, let him be accursed. (Canon 11.)

48. If anyone saith, that justifying faith is nothing else than confidence in the Divine mercy which remits sins through Jesus Christ, or that this confidence alone is that whereby we are justified, [let him be accursed]. (Canon 12, and more, Canon 13, 14, 19, 20, 21, 24, 29.)

VII.

49. If anyone saith, that free will moved and excited by God, by assenting to God exciting and calling, nowise coöperates towards disposing and preparing itself for obtaining the grace of justification, that it cannot refuse its consent, if it would, but that, as something inanimate, it does nothing whatever and is merely passive; let him be accursed. (Canon 4.)

50. If anyone saith, that by faith alone the impious is justified, so as to mean that nothing else is required to coöperate in order to the obtaining the grace of justification, and that it is not in any way necessary, that he be prepared and disposed by the movement of his own will; let him be accursed. (Canon 9.)

51. If any one saith, that the justified sins when he performs good works with a view to an eternal recompense; let him be accursed. (Canon 31.)

52. That by the sin of Adam, although free will, attenuated as it was in its powers, and bent down, was by no means extinguished. (Sess. vi., 1547, Jan. 13, Chap. 1.)

53. That man from free will can convert himself, by freely asserting and coöperating with that grace. (*Ibid.*, Chap. 5.)

VIII.

54. Concerning satisfaction; that man makes satisfaction by the punishments of satisfaction imposed upon him by the priest, and that this derogates nothing from the satisfaction of Christ. [Sess. xiv.]   (Chap. 9, p. 134, n. 32, 33.)

IX.

55. That no one, except from special revelation, can know whom God elects for himself. (Sess. vi., 1547, Jan. 13, Chap. xii., and more concerning predestination, Canons 15, 16, 17.)

A CONVERSATION WITH CALVIN

AND

FIFTY OF HIS FOLLOWERS

CONCERNING

THE ATHANASIAN CREED.

(PAGES 2, 3, 4.)

I.

CONCERNING THE PERSON OF CHRIST.

1. I read the *Athanasian Creed* before Calvin, and in it the following words: "The right faith is, that we believe and confess that our Lord Jesus Christ, the son of God, is both God and man; God from the substance of the Father, begotten before the ages, and Man from the substance of [the mother], born in the ages. . . . Who, although He be God and Man, is yet not two but one Christ. One, not by conversion of the Divinity into flesh, but by the assumption of humanity into God: One altogether; not by confusion of substance, but by unity of Person. For as the rational soul and the flesh is one man, so God and Man is one Christ."

2. (1) After I had read these words before Calvin, and, at the same time, before fifty priests his followers, I asked Calvin whether he had receded from these teachings in the Creed, which yet is acknowledged and received by the whole Christian world. Calvin said that he saw he had fully receded. (2) I asked why he had done so. He answered, that he had paid no attention to those words, and that now when he did pay attention, he saw that he had receded from them and had written according to his own thought. (3) I asked what he thought now. He answered, that if the Creed is true, and if it is universally acknowledged as the true doctrine concerning the

Trinity, and concerning the Divinity of Christ, he had clearly erred. (4) I asked whether he wished to acknowledge that the Divine and the Human, or God and Man, in Christ, is one Person, as soul and flesh are one man, according to the words in the Creed. He answered, that he wished to do so, but that he could not, because he had confirmed himself differently. (5) I asked whether he believed Christ to be one Person or two. He answered, one, if hypostatic union makes one, but that he had believed that the Son of God was another, and was with the Father; and Jesus Christ was separated from Him, because He was in heaven. (6) I asked whether there were thus two Christs. He answered, that there were, and that therein he had receded from the Creed. (7) I asked about the hypostatic union, from whom it was. He answered, that it was from God the Father, and that this was the idea he had had. (8) I asked about the soul of Christ, what it was, whether it was not the Divine itself, since it is said in *Luke*, that it was from the Holy Spirit and the Power of the Most High. He answered that he had seen this in *Luke*, but that he had tacitly believed within himself that it was from Joseph. (9) I asked whether Christ as to His Human is not the Son of God, as is openly said in *Luke* i. [35], and also when He was baptized, *Matt.* [iii. 17]; moreover, also by John [*John* i. 34], and also when He was transfigured [*Matt.* xvii. 5; *Mark* ix. 7; *Luke* ix. 35], and in many passages elsewhere. He answered that when he had mentioned and thought of[1] the *Son of God*, he had not meant Christ Jesus as to His Human. When I said that he understood what is contrary to Scripture, he answered that he sees that it is so, but that he had not thought that it was contrary to Scripture. I wished him to renounce it, but he was conscious of his thought while in the world, and he said, that, on that account he could not. (10) At last he confessed that he had thought Christ was the son of Joseph, but that he had not dared to write this.

3. Priests, his followers, were present to the number of fifty, and they heard Calvin give these answers to the questions; and I asked them whether they did not see, that, as to the Person of Christ, they had not fully receded from the *Athanasian Creed*. They answered that they had often read that

Creed but had paid no attention to those words there; and they were surprised that they saw them now for the first time with attention. They confessed that Calvin had openly dissented; and also confessed that as often as they had named Christ or heard Him named, they had not understood the Son of God but a pure man who was made Justice for the human race, and that when they had named God only, they had meant God the Father.

II.

CONCERNING THE TRINITY OF PERSONS FROM THE ATHANASIAN CREED READ BEFORE CALVIN.

4. I read, before Calvin and some priests his followers, these words from the *Athanasian Creed*: "There is one Person of the Father, another of the Son, and another of the Holy Spirit;" and also these: "Like as we are compelled by Christian verity to confess each Person by Himself as God and Lord, so are we forbidden by the Catholic religion, to say three Gods or three Lords."

5. (1) I asked Calvin whether, from these words, he had confessed or thought of three Gods, although with his lips he had said, and still says, there is one God. He answered that he had thought of three unanimous Gods. (2) I asked how he could reconcile and make his thought and speech to be one, when it is allowed to confess each Person to be a God by Himself. He answered that he could not. (3) I asked how three could be one; whether it was by unanimous consent, or in some other way. He answered that it was by influx. (4) I asked, how could one person continually think the same as another? must not each one think something by himself? He answered that he had not thought of this before, and that now when he did think of it, he perceived that each Person must also think something by Himself. (5) I asked how then were they one indivisible essence? did not the essence thus become divided? He answered, that sometimes it becomes divided, but that they finally accommodate themselves. (6) I asked him whether the essence is divided when the Son, as Mediator and

Intercessor, speaks to the Father. He answered, that it is then divided, but only at that moment. (7) I asked him whether there were not thus three Creators of the universe. He answered that there were, but that one did the work of creation through the other,—the Father through the Son, and the Son through the Holy Spirit. (8) I asked him what idea he had of the birth of the Lord from eternity. He answered that he had a vague idea.

III.

CONCERNING THE PERSONALITY OF CALVIN. HIS QUALITY.

6. Afterwards I asked Calvin how he could ascend into heaven with an idea of three gods, and with an idea of the Lord as being two. He answered that he had been admitted into a certain inferior society of heaven, and that he had dwelt there among the hindermost, who are not much explored; but that, when he had been explored, he had descended, because he could not subsist there; and that he had then betaken himself to Luther in the world of spirits, with whom he had dwelt for a certain period, and this because Luther acknowledged the Human of the Lord as Divine, and he did not seem to himself to be safe anywhere else. With regard to Calvin, the priests said that he was an upright man, but simple; and that he had written according to his own simple thought, not considering whether what he wrote was or was not in agreement with Sacred Scripture, as he had not reflected whether it was in agreement with the *Athanasian Creed*.

IV.

WITH PRIESTS OF THE REFORMED CONCERNING JUSTIFICATION.

7. Afterwards I spoke with those priests on the article concerning justification by faith alone. (1) They were asked what they meant by good works, whether merely such things as were enjoined by the Roman Catholics, or also the works of the second table of the Decalogue. They answered that they meant both. (2) They were asked whether the works of that table of the Decalogue contribute anything to salvation. They answered that they contribute nothing, but that they must still be done, because they are commanded. (3) They were asked whether, if a man does them, it is pleasing to God. They answered that it is, if men do not place merit in them. (4) They were asked how they understand these things in the Word: That he who does His commandments loves God and is loved by God; also, the passages about good fruits, and about the works according to which man shall be judged; besides many others. They answered, that works follow from faith. (5) They were asked how they follow from faith; thus, whether man shall do them, or whether we must believe that God does them through man. They answered that man must do them of his own strength, because they are civil works, and that God has no part in them. (6) They were asked whether these are the good works which follow faith. They answered that they are. (7) They were asked how they can follow faith, when there is nothing of God in them, but only what is of man, and when, therefore, there is no bond between faith and works. They answered that they follow faith because by the imputation of faith man's sins are remitted, and then whatever a man does is good in the eyes of God, thus also these works. (8) They were asked whether it is necessary for anyone to repent, since, by faith, all sins are remitted. They answered that one can if he wishes to, but that it contributes nothing to eternal life, but only to secular life. (9) They were asked, how then do good works follow faith? They answered, like fruits from a good tree. (10) They were asked whether faith produces good works in a similar manner as a tree produces fruit. They answered that by fruits from a good tree they mean all the works that a man does after he has received faith, because in the eyes of God they are good. (11) They were asked whether good works cohere with faith as fruit with a tree. They answered that they are not like that. (12) They were asked whether there is thus any bond between good works and faith. They answered that there is none. From these things the conclusion was reached that the phrase "Good works follow faith as fruit a tree," is only an expression, and nothing more.

GOD THE SAVIOUR, JESUS CHRIST.

1. The theology of the whole Christian world is founded on the worship of three Gods.
2. God is one in essence and Person.
3. In Him is a Trinity, and this must not be distinguished into Persons.
4. The Divine attributes constitute His essence.
5. These are many, and also succeeding.
6. The succeeding Divine attributes are creation and preservation, redemption and salvation, reformation and regeneration.
7. These are Divine, but that they are not as God is in Himself.
8. The one God willed to become a natural Man, and thus a full Man, for many reasons, the primary of which was the redemption of angels and men.
9. Passages from Scripture showing that there is one God.
10. He is the Redeemer and Saviour.
11. He came into the world.
12. As to His Human, He called Himself Jesus Christ.
13. Jehovah Himself came into the world and became the Saviour and Redeemer.
14. The one God is not only the Creator, but also the Redeemer and Regenerator.
15. As to the Divine truth, He descended and took upon Himself the Human, is confirmed in *John*, Chap. I.; also, that He was from eternity, also from His nativity, *Luke* i.
16. Passages from the Sacred Scripture showing that He is the Truth and the Light; also, that He is the Word and that He fulfilled the whole of it.
17. All things were made by Him.
18. In the spiritual sense, Divine truth is called the Son of God.
19. Divine truth is meant by Messiah, Christ, King, the Anointed, and David.

20. Divine truth is meant by angel and by one sent.

21. Divine truth is meant by glory.

22. In no other way could all things in the heavens and in the hells have been reduced into order.

23. In no other way could He destroy the old church and institute a new church.

24. In no other way could He admit temptations into Himself, and suffer.

25. In no other way could He be in the state of exinanition and pray to God the Father as though absent.

26. In no other way could He become Redemption and Justice from His own power.

27. Thus, in no other way could He unite the Human to the Divine and the reverse, and thus add the Human in time to the Divine from eternity.

28. In no other way could He be and become one with the Father.

29. All things which are in the Divine are together in the Human.

30. The Lord glorified His Human in the order in which He makes man spiritual, or an angel. Concerning the two states of man's regeneration.

31. Thus He made His Human Divine.

32. Thus He became the First and the Last, thus the all in all.

33. The Divine operation is from firsts through lasts, and because, in the church, lasts had failed, therefore, He made Himself the Last.

34. Man cannot be conjoined with God except by means of a visible and accessible Human.

35. Every male is born, as to his spiritual origin, from truth as a seed.

36. The reason why men have not hitherto perceived this, and why consequently there have been so many opinions about the human nature of Christ, is because men have had no distinct understanding concerning the nature of good and truth and of their marriage, nor concerning the nature of the will and the understanding, nor of the soul and the body.

37. The virgin also, of whom He was born, signifies the church as to the affection of truth.

38. It was necessary for Him to be born of a virgin in legitimate marriage with Joseph.

39. Christ alone is Man from eternity and natural Man in time.

40. In Him everything is Divine from the Divine in itself.

41. He alone is to be approached, that there may be salvation.

42. He must be approached immediately, and if He is approached immediately, communication is intercepted.

43. Here may be adduced those passages, which treat of the "great affliction," and the things which follow.

44. To worship three Gods is to worship none.

45. No one comes to God or is conjoined to Him, unless the Human be approached; otherwise God is not accessible.

46. Because God the Father is the Redeemer as to the Human.

47. In order that there may be conjunction, there must be a visible God, thus one accessible and fixed; this is not so apparent to Christians, but it is to all others.

48. The Divine truth suffered.

SPECIMEN AND SKETCH

OF THE

DOCTRINE OF THE NEW CHURCH

IN

A SUMMARY.

---

1. The churches in Germany, Hungary, Poland, Denmark, England, and Holland, which, by the Reformation, were separated from the Roman Catholic Church, differ from each other in various things; but they all agree in the articles concerning a Trinity of persons in the Divinity, the origin of sin from Adam, the imputation of the merit of Christ, and justification by faith alone. [*Brief Exposition*, n. 17.]

2. The Roman Catholics, before the Reformation, held entirely similar teachings respecting these four articles; similar respecting a Trinity of Persons in the Divinity, similar respecting the origin of sin from Adam, similar respecting the imputation of the merit of Christ, and similar respecting justification by faith, with the sole difference, that this faith they conjoined with good works. [*B. E.*, n. 19.]

3. The leading Reformers, Luther, Melancthon, and Calvin, retained all the dogmas concerning a Trinity of Persons in the Divinity, the origin of sin from Adam, the imputation of the merit of Christ, and justification by faith alone, as they had been held by the Roman Catholics; but in order that they might be totally severed from the Roman Catholics as to the very essentials of the church, which are faith and charity, they separated good works from faith, and declared that they were not at the same time saving. [*B. E.*, n. 21.]

4. Nevertheless, those leading Reformers adjoined good works to their faith, so that no one can see from reason, whether they are conjoined or separated. [*B. E.*, n. 24.]

5. But those leading Reformers adjoined good works to that faith in order that the doctrine may agree with the Sacred Scripture; then there is a conformity and not a discrepancy, unless the quality of the works tends to make it. [cf. *B. E.*, n. 27.]

6. The dogmas concerning the imputation of the merit of Christ and justification thereby have come from the idea of a Trinity of Persons, and hence of three gods. [*B. E.*, n. 30.]

7. All those dogmas appear as erroneous, and also become so, when the idea of a Trinity of Persons and hence of three gods is rejected, and the idea of one God, in Whom is the Divine Trinity is received. [*B. E.*, n. 39.]

8. Then the faith of the church of to-day concerning the reconciliation of the Father, satisfaction, mediation, imputation, and, from this, the remission of sins, and hence justification, regeneration, and sanctification, falls to the ground together with all else that depends on it.

9. In its place, faith truly saving, which is faith in one God, united with good works, is acknowledged and received. It is not imputative faith. [*B. E.*, n. 41.]

10. And this faith is faith in God the Saviour Jesus Christ, and in its simple form, is as follows: (1) There is one God, in Whom is the Divine Trinity, and He is the Lord Jesus Christ. (2) Saving faith is to believe in Him. (3) Evils must be shunned because they are of the devil and from the devil. (4) Goods must be done because they are of God and from God. (5) And these must be done by man as of himself, but he must believe that they are from the Lord in him and through him. [*B. E.*, n. 43.]

11. This faith can by no means be given together with the former faith, nor the former with it; and if they are together, such a collision and conflict takes place that everything of the church with man perishes. [*B. E.*, n. 102.]

12. The faith of the church of to-day has separated religion from the church, which consists solely in goods of life according to the truths of faith. [*B. E.*, n. 45.] Truths constitute the way to heaven. In hell —— ——* the Father, but in heaven the true God.

---

*The MS. here contains a word which Dr. Im. Tafel, the editor of the Latin edition, was unable to decipher.—Tr.

13. The faith of the church of to-day has falsified the Word, since this teaches nothing but the goods of life and the truths of faith, and salvation by their union.

14. The faith of the church of to-day has so far destroyed the church, that, at this day, there remains not any truth of the Word that has not been falsified, nor any good of religion that has not been adulterated.

15. This last state of the church of to-day induced by that faith is what is meant in the Word by the "consummation of the age," and by the "abomination of desolation." [*B. E.*, n. 70.]

16. This last state of the church of to-day is what is meant by the "great affliction such as was not from the beginning of the world to this time, nor ever shall be." (*Matt.* xxiv. 21.) [*B. E.*, n. 74.]

17. This state of the church, induced by that faith, is what is meant by these words: "After the affliction of those days the sun shall be darkened and the moon shall not give her light, and the stars shall fall from heaven, and the powers of the heavens shall be shaken." (*Matt.* xxiv. 29; *Apoc.* viii. 12.) [*B. E.*, n. 77.]

18. They who have been and are in the faith of the church to-day are meant by the he-goats in *Daniel* and in *Matthew*. [*B. E.*, n. 82.]

19. They who have been and are in the faith of the church of to-day are meant in the *Apocalypse* by "the dragon," his "two beasts," and the "false prophet," also by the "locusts." [*B. E.*, n. 87.]

20. They who have been and are in the faith of the church of to-day are meant, in the Old Testament, by the "Philistines;" and the faith itself by their idol. The rejection of the dogmas of the faith of the church of to-day and the revelation of the dogmas of the faith of the New Church is meant by these words in the *Apocalypse:* "He that sat upon the throne said, Behold I make all things new; and He said unto Me, Write, for these words are true and faithful." (Chap. xxi. 5.) [*B. E.*, n. 95.]

21. Further, that from the faith of the church of to-day, not a single good work can ever come forth which is not meritorious or hypocritical; consequently, that the good fruits of that faith are empty words. For it is a faith of imputation that is meant. [*cf. B. E.*, n. 47.]

23. *From the faith of the church of to-day a worship has abounded which is of the mouth alone and without life; when yet the worship of the mouth is acceptable to the Lord and efficacious according to the worship of the life, and not the reverse. [*B. E.*, n. 51.]

24. The former faith is a bundle of paradoxes which cohere and do not cohere, and therefore, its dogmas only enter into the memory and not into any understanding above the memory, but only into confirmations below it. For instance, the tenet concerning Free will. [*B. E.*, n. 53.]

25. The dogmas of the former faith cannot be learned and retained except with great difficulty, nor be preached and taught except very sparingly and with great caution lest the nakedness of the faith appear; and this, because true reason perceives and receives nothing of them. As concerning Free will. [*B. E.*, n. 58.]

26. The faith of the church of to-day takes away from God His Divine attributes, and ascribes to Him merely human attributes; as, that He regarded men from anger; that He willed to be reconciled; that He is reconciled by His love for the Son, and by intercession; that He willed to be appeased by the passion, and at sight of the misery of the Son; and thus to return to mercy and to impute and apply the merit of the Son to him who supplicates from faith alone; besides many other things. [*B. E.*, n. 60.]

27. From the faith of the church of to-day monstrous offspring have been born, and still may be born; such as salvation from immediate mercy; the doctrine of necessity, and the absence of liberty in spiritual things; that man, in respect to conversion, is like a stock and a stone; that there is no bond between faith and charity; that there is predestination; and, with some at this day, that God pays no attention to the deeds of man but to faith alone; besides others; also in respect to the sacraments, Baptism and the Eucharist; and, moreover, in re-

---

* In the Latin number 22 is omitted.

spect to the person of Christ; all of which have been drawn, in accordance with the principles of reason, from justification by faith alone. Heresies, from the first centuries to the present day, have sprung up from no other source than from this faith. [*B. E.*, n. 64.]

28. Unless the New Church be raised up by the Lord no one can be saved; and this is meant by these words, "Except those days be shortened there shall no flesh be saved." (*Matt.* xxiv. 2.) [*B. E.*, n. 91.] The reason is, because the old church is founded upon justification by faith alone, and this, upon the idea of three gods. Hence is all blindness and stupidity, unconcern, and the destruction of religion, so that scarcely anyone thinks about salvation. They who are skilled in these matters think nothing of the salvation of their own souls, or of the souls of their hearers.

The Reformed understand works of the intellect and not of the will, thus passive and not active works.

29. This church is the New Jerusalem, mentioned in *Apocalypse* xxi., which is there called the bride and wife of the Lamb. [*B. E.*, n. 99.]

30. The faith of the old church has shut heaven, and the faith of the New Church opens it.

31. The Roman Catholics at this day know nothing of the imputation of the merit of Christ, and of justification by faith therein, because they approach the pope as the vicar of Christ and worship saints, and only by monks are they taught about good works. [*B. E.*, n. 105.]

32. Therefore, if they recede from the vicarship and from the invocation of saints, and take the Holy Supper in both kinds, and approach the Lord, they can be initiated and introduced into the New Church more easily than the Reformed. [*B. E.*, n. 105.]

33. The faith of the New Church can in no wise be together with the faith of the former church, and if they are together such a collision and conflict takes place that everything of the church perishes with man. [*B. E.*, n. 102.]

Analysis: It must not be assumed that the imputation of the merit of Christ is retained, for thus a man, getting out of a pit falls into the pit again; because imputation is impossible, and faith therein has the same effect as before [so that] to escape Scylla he falls into Charybdis. [*cf. B. E.*, n. 104.]

Let the Sketch end with *Jeremiah* vii. 2, 3, 4, 9, 10, 11. [*B. E.*, n. 115, "conclusion."]

He who escapes the leopard falls on a bear and is torn to pieces. [*cf. B. E.*, n. 104.]

He who rescues himself from five of the dragon's heads falls into the other five. [*cf. B. E.*, n. 104.]

The Lord conjoins Himself to man according to reception, and reception is according to life.

Nothing added by man can be conjoined with the merit of Christ, either from its worthiness in comparison with that merit, or from its agreement with it.

Corollary.

Coronal Appendix.

INDEX OF WORDS.

Figures Refer to Numbers, Unless Otherwise Noted.

ABOMINATION.
  Of desolation, Five Mem. Rel., n. 21-24, p. 531, 532.

ABRAHAM.
  n. 253.

ADAM.
  n. 221.

ADULTERY.
  n. 339-341.

AFRICANS.
  115-124.

AGNES.
  n. 63.

ANGELS.
  Conversation with, p. 533.

ANTHONY OF PADUA.
  n. 65.

APES.
  n. 130.

APOSTOLIC CHURCH.
  n. 294-302.

ARGUMENT.
  Concerning the Judgment, p. 515-520.

ARRANGEMENT.
  Of the Reformed, n. 178.

BABEL.
  Or Babylon, n. 108.

BENEDICT XIV.
  n. 103.

BULL UNIGENITUS.
  n. 103-104.

CALVIN.
  n. 24, 25, Conv. with, p. 547-551.

CATHOLICS.
  Societies of, n. 112, 113.

CHARITY.
  n. 164, 208. (*See* FAITH.)

CHARLES XII.
  n. 237.

CHINESE.
  n. 133.

CHRIST.
  Person of, p. 547-554.

CHRISTIANS.
  In centre, n. 126.

COLORS.
  n. 267.

COMING OF LORD.
  Five Mem. Rel., n. 16-20, p. 528-530.

COMMANDMENTS.
  n. 334-336, 351, 356.

CONSUMMATION.
  Of Age, Five Mem. Rel., n. 8-15, p. 524-528.

CONSUMMATION OF AGE.
  Five Mem. Rel., n. 8-15, p. 524-528.

CONVENT.
  n. 9.

COUNCIL.
  Of Trent, Extracts from, p. 537-546.

DEGREES.
  n. 303-321.

DESOLATION.
  Abomination of, Five Mem. Rel., n. 21-24, p. 531-532.

INDEX OF WORDS

DEVIL WORSHIPERS.
n. 113.

DIPPEL.
n. 40.

DIVINE.
Idea of, n. 171-173.

DRAGON.
Dragonists, n. 161-168, 183-190.

DRINK.
n. 269.

DUTCH.
n. 13-23, 281.

EARTHQUAKES.
n. 138.

END OF WORLD.
(See CONSUMMATION OF AGE.)

ENGLISH.
n. 1-12, 213-216, 227, 268-276, 327-328, 353.

EXTERNAL BONDS.
n. 153-154.

FAITH.
n. 170, 191-229, 357-364.

FALSITIES.
n. 209.

FIGHT AGAINST EVILS.
n. 342-349.

FOOD.
n. 269, 337-338.

GARMENT.
n. 202.

GENEVIEVE.
n. 61-62.

GENTILES.
n. 125-133.

GNASHING OF TEETH.
n. 202.

GOD.
Idea of, n. 155-6, 171.

GOD THE SAVIOUR.
p. 552-554.

GOOD.
n. 342-349.

HEAVENS.
n. 135-179.

HEBREW.
n. 261.

HE-GOAT.
n. 180-182.

HELLS.
n. 175-177.

HYPOCRITES.
n. 158.

IDOLS.
n. 114.

IGNATIUS.
n. 67.

ISAAC.
n. 257.

JACOB.
n. 253, 257.

JAMES.
n. 198.

JERUSALEM.
n. 258.

JESUITS.
n. 106.

JEWS.
n. 251-261, 282-284, 292-293.

JUDAS.
n. 227.

JUDGMENT, LAST.
n. 134-179.

JUDGMENT.
Argument concerning, p. 515-520

JUSTIFICATION.
n. 220-222.

JUSTIFICATION AND GOOD WORKS.
p. 537-546.

LANGUAGE.
n. 324.

LEIBNITZ.
n. 262-264.

INDEX OF WORDS 563

LIFE AFTER DEATH.
n. 230-250, Five Mem. Rel., 4-7, p. 523-524.

LOCUSTS.
Five Mem. Rel., n. 23, 24, p. 532.

LONDON.
n. 12, 268-276, 282.

LORD.
n. 129. (*See* JESUS CHRIST.)

LOUIS XIV.
n. 104.

LOVE.
n. 233-250.

LOVE OF KNOWING.
n. 283-291.

LOVE OF RULING.
n. 139, 236-240, 245-249.

LUTHER.
n. 31-36, 198.

MANNA.
Five Mem. Rel., n. 18, 19, p. 529-530.

MANSIONS.
n. 196.

MARRIAGE.
n. 339-341.

MARY, VIRGIN.
n. 68.

MELANCTHON.
n. 26-30, 210.

MERIT.
p. 540.

MESSIAH.
n. 251-2, 259, p. 552.

MICHAEL.
n. 168.

MOHAMMED, MOHAMMEDANS.
n. 69-101, 126-129, 167.

MONKS.
n. 251, 252.

MORALITY.
n. 160, 201.

MORAVIANS.
n. 37-57, 278-284, 294-302, 365.

MOSES.
n. 251, 252.

NATURAL MAN.
Five Mem. Rel., n. 1-3, p. 521-522.

NEWTON.
n. 265-267, 273.

NOBILITY.
n. 241.

PAPISTS.
n. 59-68, 102-114, 142, 143.

PARISIANS.
n. 61.

PENN.
n. 58.

PIETY.
n. 157.

POPE.
n. 60, 102, 103.

PREACHERS.
n. 159, 187, 214, 272, 275, 277, 283, p. 547,

PRECIOUS STONES.
n. 254, 255.

PRESBYTERS.
n. 276.

PRIESTS. (*See* PREACHERS.)

PROTESTANTS OR REFORMED.
n. 134-179, 184.

PSALMS.
n. 133.

QUAKERS.
n. 48, 58.

REFORMED. (*See* PROTESTANTS.)

ROMAN CATHOLICS.
n. 128. (*See* PAPISTS, SAINTS.)

SAINTS.
n. 59-66.

SALVATION.
n. 197.

SAVIOUR.
God the, p. 552–554.

SENSUAL.
n. 204.

SERPENT.
n. 197, 224.

SHEEP.
n. 180, 181.

SOCIETIES.
n. 176, 177, 195.

SPECIMEN AND SKETCH.
Of the Doctrine of the New Church, p. 555–560.

SPIRITS.
n. 192–3.

SUN.
Five Mem. Rel., n. 16–21, p. 528–530.

TARTARY.
n. 133.

TRINITY.
p. 547–554.

UNDERSTANDING.
n. 329–333.

VACUUM.
n. 265, 266.

VERSAILLES.
n. 104.

VIRGIN MARY.
n. 129.

WEST INDIES.
n. 131.

WILL.
n. 329–333.

WISE.
n. 350.

WOLFF.
n. 262–264.

WORD.
n. 260–1.

WORKS.
n. 199.

XAVIER.
n. 66.

ZINZENDORF AND MORAVIANS.
n. 37–57, 298.

Theological Extracts

FROM

Swedenborg's Correspondence

THEOLOGICAL EXTRACTS

FROM

SWEDENBORG'S CORRESPONDENCE

FROM THE LATIN OF

EMANUEL SWEDENBORG

THEOLOGICAL EXTRACTS

FROM

SWEDENBORG'S CORRESPONDENCE.

ANSWER TO THREE QUESTIONS.

I.

FROM THE SIXTH LETTER OF EMANUEL SWEDENBORG TO DR. BEYER.*

MEMORANDUM.

"Several questions have been propounded to me by your friend, to which you will please to receive the following as an answer:

"I. My opinion concerning the writings of Bohme and L. . . . I have never read either; I was forbidden to read writers on dogmatic and systematic theology, before heaven was opened to me; because unfounded opinions and inventions might thereby have easily insinuated themselves, which afterwards could only have been removed with difficulty; wherefore, when heaven was opened to me, I had first to learn the Hebrew language, as well as the correspondences according to which the whole Bible is composed, which led me to read the Word of God over many times; and as God's Word is the source whence all theology must be derived, I was enabled thereby to receive instruction from the Lord, who is the Word.

"II. Query: *How soon a New Church may be expected?* Answer: The Lord is preparing at this time a New Heaven of those who believe in Him, acknowledge Him as the true God of

---

*Documents Concerning Swedenborg, Vol. II, pp. 260–261.

heaven and earth, and look to Him in their lives, which means to shun evil and do good; for from that heaven the New Jerusalem is to come down (see *Rev.* xxi. 2). I daily see spirits and angels, from ten to twenty thousand, descending and ascending, and being set in order. By degrees, as that heaven is being formed, the New Church likewise begins and increases. The universities in Christendom are now first being instructed, whence will come new ministers; for the new heaven has no influence over the old [clergy] who deem themselves too learned in the doctrine of justification by faith alone.

"III. *About the promised treatise on infinity, omnipotence and omnipresence.** Answer: There are many things on these subjects interspersed throughout the *Angelic Wisdom concerning the Divine Providence* (n. 46–54 and 157); also in the *Angelic Wisdom concerning the Divine Love and the Divine Wisdom*, (n. 4, 17, 19, 21, 44, 69, 72, 76, 106, 156, 318), and in the *Apocalypse Revealed* (n. 961); these subjects will be further treated of in the arcana of *Angelic Wisdom concerning Conjugial Love*: for to write a separate treatise on these Divine attributes, without the assistance of something to support them, would cause too great an elevation of the thoughts; wherefore these subjects have been treated in a series with other things which fall within the understanding." (Dated STOCKHOLM, February, 1767.)

II.

FROM THE SECOND LETTER OF EMANUEL SWEDENBORG TO F. C. OETINGER.†

"I. Query: Is a sign required to show that I have been sent by the Lord to do what I am doing? Answer: Signs and wonders do not take place at the present day, because they compel externally, and internally do not convince.

"What effect did the miracles in Egypt and Jehovah's descent on Mount Sinai have upon the Israelitish people, who,

---

*This work was promised by Swedenborg, in 1763, in the preface to the *Doctrine Concerning the Lord.*
†*Documents Concerning Swedenborg,* Vol. II., pp. 255–257.

notwithstanding, after the lapse of a month made for themselves a golden calf, and worshiped it in place of Jehovah? And what effect did the Lord's miracles have upon the Jewish nation, by whom He was notwithstanding crucified? The same would be the case now, should the Lord appear in the clouds with the angels and trumpets; as described in (*Luke* xiv. 16, 29-31). The sign, given at this day, will be enlightenment, and thence an acknowledgment and a reception of the truths of the New Church; with some also there will be an enlightenment which speaks (*illustratio loquens*), which is more than a sign. But some sign will perhaps still be given.

"II. Query: Whether I have conversed with the apostles? Answer: I have conversed with Paul for an entire year, and also on the subject of what he wrote in his *Epistle to the Romans* (iii. 28). Three times I spoke with John, once with Moses, a hundred times with Luther, who confessed to me that, contrary to an admonition received from an angel, he accepted the doctrine of faith alone solely for the purpose of separating from the Papists. With the angels, however, I have now conversed for twenty-two years, and I am still conversing with them daily; these the Lord has associated with me.

"There was no use in my mentioning this in my writings; for who would have believed it? and who would not have said, 'Show me a sign that I may believe'? And this every one would say who did not see it.

"III. Query: Why from being a philosopher I have been chosen? Answer: The cause of this has been, that the spiritual things which are being revealed at the present day may be taught and understood naturally and rationally: for spiritual truths have a correspondence with natural truths, because in these they terminate, and upon these they rest. That there is a correspondence of all spiritual things with all things of man, as well as with all things of the earth, may be seen in the work on *Heaven and Hell* (n. 87-102, and n. 103-115). For this reason I was introduced by the Lord first into the natural sciences, and thus prepared; and, indeed, from the year 1710 to 1744, when heaven was opened to me. Every one also is led by means of natural things to spiritual things; for man is born natural; by education he is made moral, and afterwards by regeneration from the Lord he becomes spiritual. The Lord has granted to me besides to love truths in a spiritual manner, *i. e.*, to love them, not for the sake of honor, nor for the sake of gain, but for the sake of the truths themselves; for he who loves truths for the sake of the truth, sees them from the Lord, because the Lord is the Way and the Truth (*John* xiv. 6); but he who loves them for the sake of honor or gain, sees them from himself; and seeing from oneself is equivalent to seeing falsities. Falsities that have been confirmed close the church, wherefore truths rationally understood have to open it. How else can spiritual things which transcend the understanding, be understood, acknowledged, and received? The dogma which has been handed down by the Papists, and accepted by the Protestants, namely, that the understanding is to be held in bondage under obedience to faith, has a second time closed the church, and what else is to open it again, except an understanding enlightened by the Lord; but on this subject see the *Apocalypse Revealed* (n. 914).

"IV. I am very sorry that you should have had to suffer for the translation of the book on *Heaven and Hell;* but what suffers more at the present day than the truth itself? How few there are who see it, yea, who are willing to see it! Do not allow yourself to be discouraged thereby, but be a defender of the truth.

"I remain your most obedient,

"EM. SWEDENBORG.

"STOCKHOLM, November 11, 1766."

THE NATURAL AND SPIRITUAL SENSE OF THE WORD.*

APPENDED TO THE

THIRD LETTER OF EMANUEL SWEDENBORG TO F. C. OETINGER.

" That in the Word there is an internal or spiritual sense, in its external or natural sense, as a precious stone in its matrix, or as a beautiful infant in its swaddling clothes, is a truth which has heretofore been altogether unknown in the Christian world, and hence also it is altogether unknown what is meant by the consummation of the age, the Coming of the Lord, the Last Judgment, and the New Jerusalem, on which subjects many things are spoken and predicted in the Word of each Testament, both Old and New. Without the unfolding and opening out of the literal sense of the Word by its spiritual sense, how can any one know intellectually what is signified by the things which the Lord predicted (in *Matthew* xxiv.), and also in the *Book of Revelation*, and in like manner in *Daniel*, and in the Prophets, in many passages? Make the experiment yourself, if you be so disposed, and read those passages of the prophetic Word which treat sometimes of wild beasts and cattle, sometimes of pools and swamps, sometimes of forests and brakes, sometimes of valleys and mountains, sometimes of screech-owls, of ochim, tziim, satyrs, etc., etc.; try whether you can perceive anything Divine therein, unless you believe it to lie concealed interiorly, on account of its being inspired by God, just as a precious stone lies concealed in its matrix, as was said above. That the precious stones, or treasures, which lie concealed within are those things which the internal sense contains, is fully demonstrated in the *Doctrine of the New*

---

* *Documents Concerning Swedenborg*, Vol. II., pp. 269-271. Dated Amsterdam, November 8, 1768.

Jerusalem concerning the Sacred Scripture (n. 5 to 26); and in the same Doctrine it is further proved that the literal sense is the basis, containant, and firmament of its spiritual sense (n. 27 to 36); also that Divine Truth in the literal sense of the Word is in its fullness, in its sanctity, and in its power (n. 37 to 40); and likewise, that the doctrine of the church is to be drawn from the literal sense of the Word, and to be confirmed thereby (n. 50 to 61); and, finally, that by the literal sense, through the medium of the spiritual sense, there is effected conjunction with the Lord, and consociation with the angels (n. 62 to 69).

"To the above I will add something new from the spiritual world : The rulers of the church who flock into that world after death, are first taught concerning the Sacred Scripture, that it contains a spiritual sense, which in the world was unknown to them; and they are also told, that the angels of heaven are in that sense, whilst man is in the sense of the letter; and further, that a translation or change of the latter sense into the former is effected with man, while he reads the Word in a state of holiness; that there is then a kind of unfolding or unswathing, like the breaking of the shell enclosing an almond, whereupon the shell is dispersed and the naked almond passes into heaven, and is received by the angels; and that it is also like the casting of a seed into the ground, where it is stripped of its coverings, and the germ is put forth. The seed in this case is the Word in the sense of the letter, and the germ which is put forth thence is the spiritual sense; the latter passes to the angels, and the former remains with man. The seed, nevertheless, remains with man in his mind as in its soil, and in time produces its germ and fructifies it, provided man by the seeds of life which are the truths of faith and the goods of charity, is conjoined to the Lord, and consociated with the angels. The above rulers are further admonished to receive thoroughly this belief, that the Word in its bosom is spiritual, because Divine; and that unless they receive this belief, they may be seduced by satans, so that they even deny the sanctity of the Word; in which case the church with them is dissipated. This further argument is also urged upon them, that if they do not believe the internal sense of the Word, the Word may finally appear to them as some unpolished and unconnected writing, or even as a book of all heresies, because from the literal sense, as from a kind of lake, heresies of every sort may be drawn forth and confirmed. Those who believe the internal sense of the Word, are afterwards received into companies of angelic spirits, who in process of time are elevated into heaven and become angels; but those who do not believe, are removed into companies of spirits, who in course of time are cast into hell, and become satans. Those are called satans there, who in the world had falsified every truth of the Word, and who in consequence thereof had imbibed falsities, so that at last they could no longer see anything of truth."

THE SON OF GOD.

I.

POSTSCRIPT TO THE NINTH LETTER OF EMANUEL SWEDENBORG TO DR. BEYER.*

"P. S. In the short treatise [*Brief Exposition*], which I have sent you, as well as in all my former writings, I do not mean a Son of God born from eternity, but the Son of God conceived and born in the world, in whom is the Divine Trinity. In the *Apostles' Creed*, which was the confession of faith of the Apostolic church, no other Son of God is mentioned, nor is any other meant in the Gospels (*Luke* i. 32, 35; *Matt.* iii. 17; xvii. 5; *John* xx. 31; 1 *John* v. 20, 21). The reason, however, why the Nicene Council afterwards adopted a Son of God from eternity, and added still another Divine person, was this, that it could not discover any other expedient for expelling the erroneous doctrine of Arius; and for this reason, especially, the present church insists that reason shall be bound, and placed under obedience to a blind faith. But, that this does not transcend man's faculty of comprehension, and that he is able to see and thus to believe, may be seen in (n. 117), and afterwards in (n. 44)."

II.

FROM THE THIRTEENTH LETTER OF EMANUEL SWEDENBORG TO DR. BEYER.†

"The small treatise entitled *A Brief Exposition of the Doctrines of the New Church*, I have sent only to Bishop Benzelstjerna, with strict injunctions not to lend it to anyone; for there are few in Sweden who penetrate with their understandings

---

* *Documents Concerning Swedenborg*, Vol. II., p 276. Dated Amsterdam, April 23, 1769.
    The same statement is made in Swedenborg's letter to Count Höpken, *Documents Concerning Swedenborg*, Vol. II., p. 281.
† *Documents Concerning Swedenborg*, Vol. II., pp. 307, 308.

into any matter belonging to theology, and unless they do so, they cannot receive any enlightenment from God's Word. For instance, they cannot understand that in *Romans* iii. 28, and in *Galatians* ii. 16, an imputative faith in the merit of Christ is not meant, but the faith of Jesus, which is a faith from Jesus in Jesus; and, likewise, that the works of the law of the Decalogue are not there meant, but the works of the Mosaic law, which were simply for the Jews; and further, that in *Romans* iv. is not meant the imputation of the faith of the present church. Nor are they willing to be enlightened in such texts of the Scriptures as concern God's Son, that by the Son of God is not meant a Son of God from eternity, but the Son of God conceived in time from Jehovah God, and born of the Virgin Mary, according to the distinct words of *Luke* i. 32, 35; *Matthew* iii. 17; *John* xx. 31; 1 *John* v. 20, 21, and other places. This is likewise agreeable to the *Apostles' Creed*, where no other Son of God is mentioned, whence it follows that the primitive church knew of no other. A Son of God from eternity was adopted in the *Nicene* and *Athanasian Creeds*, because they could find no other way by which to refute and expel the errors of Arius (compare the *Apostles' Creed*). I therefore adhere to the Apostolic church.

"To worship God the Saviour cannot be prohibited throughout Christendom, and still less among the Lutherans (see the *Augsburg Confession*, p. 19, and also the *Apology*, p. 226); nor can it be denied that in Christ Man is God and God is Man, with many other things which I mentioned in a former letter. The *Formula Concordiæ* explains also a Divine trinity in those who are reborn by faith (p. 695, *Apology*, p. 130); how much more then is a Divine trinity in God the Saviour, etc., etc. (*Col.* ii. 9). All this however and much more will be demonstrated in a work which will be published two years hence.* *The Brief Exposition* is a forerunner of it, and is to prepare the way for its reception. This little preliminary treatise has been spread throughout the whole of Christendom, Sweden excepted, because theology is now in its wintry state, and here in the north

---

* *True Christian Religion.*

the night lasts longer than in southern parts; wherefore they in their darkness may be supposed to kick against everything in the New Church which belongs to the understanding or to reason. Still there are those in the ecclesiastical order who are exceptions to this rule; I apply also to myself what the Lord has said to His disciples in *Matt.* x. 16." [I send you forth as sheep in the midst of wolves.]

["STOCKHOLM, October 30, 1769."]

APPROACHING THE SAVIOUR IMMEDIATELY.

I.

FIFTEENTH LETTER OF EMANUEL SWEDENBORG TO DR. BEYER.*

"Reverend Doctor and Lector:

"Only two days ago I received your favor of the 21st of last March, and on reading it through I was surprised at the reports which are said to have reached Gottenburg from Stockholm to the effect that you and Dr. Rosen are to be deposed, deprived of office, and banished from the country, a report to which certainly I can give no credence; for it contradicts my reason in the highest degree to believe that a person may be deprived of office and banished from the country, on the mere allegation of his being heretical, without the principal point of accusation against him being investigated. In the printed Minutes I cannot find that they have taken a single step in regard to the question itself, but that they have simply busied themselves in making attacks in abusive and unseemly language, when yet the real point of issue is this, whether it is allowable to approach immediately our Redeemer and Saviour Jesus Christ, or whether we must go a circuitous way, namely, to God the Father, that He may impute to us the merit and righteousness of His Son, and send the Holy Spirit. But that we may go to the other, which is the direct way, namely, to our Saviour Jesus Christ, is in accordance both with the *Augsburg Confession*, and the *Formula Concordiæ*, and also with our own prayers and hymns; and it entirely agrees with God's Word.

---

* *Documents Concerning Swedenborg*, Vol. II., pp. 352-356.

"In the *Augsburg Confession* are the following words: 'For [the Scripture] sets before us Christ alone as the Mediator, the Propitiator, the High Priest, and the Intercessor; He is to be invoked, or addressed; and He has promised that He will hear our prayers; and the Sacred Scripture very greatly approves of this worship, viz., that He should be invoked in all afflictions.' (1 *John* ii. 1.)

"In the *Formula Concordiæ* are these words: 'We have a command that we should call upon Christ according to this saying, "Come unto me all ye that labor,"' etc., which is certainly addressed to us; and Isaiah says (Chap. xi.), 'In that day there shall be a root of Jesse, which shall stand for an ensign of the people. On him shall nations call.' And in (*Psalm* xlv.), 'The rich among the people shall entreat Thy countenance.' And in (*Psalm* lxxii.), 'And all kings of the earth shall fall down before Him.' And in another verse, 'They shall pray before Him continually.' And in (*John* v. 23), Christ says, 'All shall honor the Son, even as they honor the Father.' See also Paul in (1 *Thess.* ii.). These are the identical words quoted from the work.

"In our Hymn-book are prayers and hymns addressed to Jesus Christ alone; as Hymn 266, of which I will quote only what follows:—

"'Lo! Jesus is my might;
He is my heart's delight.
O Jesus, hear my voice.

"'If I of Christ make sure,
I'll ever feel secure,
And freed from all my sins.

"'As Jesus is my shield,
I'll ne'er to Satan yield
Tho' he against me rage.

"'My cares and all my woe
On Him alone I'll throw,
Who is my strength and guard.

"'By day and night I rest
Safely on Jesus' breast,
In whom alone I trust.' (Verses 1, 3, 8.)

"Besides all this, two of my letters, which have been inserted and printed in the Gottenburg 'Minutes,' contain numerous proofs, adduced from the whole of the *Formula Concordiæ,* that our Saviour, even as to His Human, is God, which Luther and the *'Formula Concordiæ'* corroborate with all their power, and which is also in agreement with the entire Word of God. In proof of this I refer you only to (*Col.* ii. 9; 1 *John* v. 20. 21). More to the same purport has also been adduced from one of my works, an extract from which may be found in the printed 'Minutes' of the Gottenburg Consistory [Document 245, C. p. 291 *et seq.*]. This doctrine they there call *Swedenborgianism;* but for my part I call it *Genuine Christianity.*

"This is the question now at issue, which the members of the Consistory have, on their part, not touched upon at all, but respecting which they have simply burst forth into abusive language, which affects not simply my person and honor, but our Redeemer and His holiness. How they will answer for this after death, I will not here consider.

"As to the Son of God from eternity, which is likewise a controverted point, I have proved, that in the *Apostles' Creed,* which is received throughout the whole of Christendom, and which contains the doctrine of the Apostles themselves, no other Son of God is mentioned than the Son of God born in time, who is our Redeemer Himself, to whom every man can address himself, and to whom, by virtue of what is stated in the '*Augsburg Confession*' and the '*Formula Concordiæ,*' he must address himself, that he may obtain salvation. And if our freedom be interfered with in this respect, I would rather live in Tartary than among Christians. If any other be willing to go further—to a Son of God from eternity, he is at liberty to do so.

"Your letter, and your fear of harsh treatment, have induced me to develop and explain the point of issue in this manner, since theological subjects are of such a nature, that a person may easily wander about in darkness in respect to them, particularly if accusers, with a pretense of learning, try to blacken them by such coarse expressions, and seek to kill the 'man-child' with murderous words. However, I presume, and

I believe it as a certainty, that His Royal Majesty with the enlightened members of the Council will judge of this matter in its true light, and not according to the glosses of the Dean and others. For if you should be removed from office and exiled, what could the present as well as the future generations say, but that this had happened to you for no other reason than that you had approached immediately our Lord and Saviour, and that you had, notwithstanding, not denied the Trinity. What astonishment and indignation must not this cause in every one!

"This subject, in its whole extent, will soon be placed before the whole of Christendom,* and the judgment passed upon it. I will hereafter submit to the King, and to the Honorable Houses of the Realm in general: for during a session of the Diet, the House of the Clergy is not at liberty to submit to His Royal Majesty its own separate or independent opinion, which shall afterwards have the force of law. Theological matters belong to the other Houses also.

"With respect to your journey here, I do not think that your presence in Stockholm would greatly benefit your cause. I will only ask you to be kind enough to copy this letter, and send a copy to His Excellency Senator Stockenström, and another to His Excellency Senator R. Hermanson, informing them that it is done at my request. I intend to send a copy myself to the Chancellor of Justice, and one to His Excellency Count Ekeblad.

"Your obedient servant,

"EM. SWEDENBORG.

"STOCKHOLM, April 12, 1770."

---

*In the *True Christian Religion*, published in 1770.

II.

SIXTEENTH LETTER OF EMANUEL SWEDENBORG TO DR. BEYER.*

"REVEREND DOCTOR:

"I received your letter dated March 18, together with a copy of the one which you submitted to His Royal Majesty [Document 245, O]. You mention also that information had reached Gottenburg of a resolution which had been projected in the Privy Council; the subject, however, was reconsidered, after a copy of the letter which I had written to you (Document 245, R) was sent to Senator Ekeblad and the Chancellor of Justice, and the final result is contained in the letter addressed by the Chancellor to the Consistory of Gottenburg (Document 245, T), of which you will kindly let me have a copy. Had they retained the first project, according to which Swedenborgianism was not to be talked of or mentioned in conversation, when yet it signifies the worship of the Lord, what would have been the result, but a fear in the Clergy to speak about Christ and His care of humanity; for by so doing they would in this case have run the risk of a public admonition, for supporting 'Swedenborgianism,' and in consequence thereof Christianity would have declined in Sweden, and the country would have lapsed into Socinianism, and finally into heathenism, as may be concluded from (*Matt.* xii. 30, and *Mark* ix. 40). Such an offspring would have been born from the first project. For this reason also, when certain clergymen of this town, who are animated by a genuine zeal, first heard of this report, they were astonished, thinking that thus Christianity would die out in our country. I have heard that the bishop and many members of the venerable House of the Clergy expressed themselves handsomely at the Diet upon the doctrines, discussed there.

"Nothing of what the Consistory submitted against my writings has been communicated to me, so that I am totally ignorant of what passed in the Privy Council.

---

* *Documents Concerning Swedenborg*, Vol. II., pp. 369-370.

"Next June I will travel to Amsterdam, where I intend to publish the 'Universal Theology of the New Church.' The worship of the Lord is the foundation therein, and if upon that foundation the true house or temple be not built, others will erect upon it *lupanaria* or brothels.

"With respect to the dragonist spirits, they are all removed far away to the south, where certain places are assigned to the learned, to each his own cell, where they may confirm themselves in justification by faith alone, and those who confirm themselves therein by the Word of God, depart thence into a desert, and so on farther; and the rest, after making their escape, receive no homes; whither they direct their way, I do not yet know: in heaven there is no place for them. Their fate will be, as described in the *Apocalypse Revealed* (n. 421). But the abyss which is described there is now removed farther towards the south, as has been observed.

"I remain with all friendship and trust,
"Your most obedient servant,
"EM. SWEDENBORG.

"STOCKHOLM, April 30, 1770."

THE WORSHIP OF THE LORD AND THE ESTABLISHMENT OF THE NEW CHURCH.

I.

EMANUEL SWEDENBORG TO AUGUSTUS ALSTRÖMER.*

"WELL-BORN SIR,

"As I shall leave next week for Amsterdam, and as I understand that the religious trial of Drs. Beyer and Rosen has been settled by the Privy Council in an unexpected manner [cfr. Document 245, T], and as this will probably be talked about for a long time in Gottenburg, I have the honor to communicate to you what I submitted on this subject to His Majesty, so as to break the force of the malicious comments, which will no doubt issue from the mouths of certain persons, originating in their interior stupidity and perversity.

"Two gentlemen of the Supreme Court of Appeals (*Justitiae Revisionen*) told me that the Privy Council was the *pontifex maximus* in religious matters. At the time I did not make any reply; if, however, they should repeat this statement to me, I should say that, far from being the *pontifex maximus*, they are simply the *vicarius vicarii pontificis maximi*, since Christ, our Saviour is alone *pontifex maximus*; that the Houses of the Diet are His *vicarius*, and therefore are responsible to Him; and that the Privy Council is the *vicarius* of the Houses of the Diet, and only as such has plenipotentiary power; and, consequently, it is the *vicarius vicarii pontificis maximi*. Nor am I able to see in what their pontifical power consists, as they have simply assented to the opinion expressed by the Consistory of Gottenburg; and, without examining any of the religious sub-

---

* *Documents Concerning Swedenborg*, Vol. II., pp. 378–379.

jects in my books, have nevertheless prohibited them. The Roman Pope's styling himself *pontifex maximus* is due to arrogance; for he claims and takes upon himself all the power of Christ, our Saviour, making the people believe that he is Christ upon earth.

"I have not yet received any answer from the Privy Council; and when the subject was before them last week, it was resolved that it should be postponed, until those members who had gone into the country returned. I am well aware that they strike me upon my right cheek, but how they will be able to wipe off what the other cheek is anointed with, I cannot tell.

"Please give my kindest regards to Doctors Beyer and Rosen, and to all the rest who believe in our Saviour. I remain, with all respect and affection,

"Your most obedient servant,
"EM. SWEDENBORG.
"STOCKHOLM, July 19, 1770."

"The same sentiments, only in a rather more extended form, Swedenborg communicated to the Chancellor of Justice and the three Swedish Universities of Upsal, Lund, and Abo in a letter wherein was enclosed a copy of that which he had addressed to the King. A copy of this letter, which constitutes Document 245, AA, he also enclosed to Dr. Beyer."

II.

EIGHTEENTH LETTER OF EMANUEL SWEDENBORG TO DR. BEYER.*

"REVEREND DOCTOR:

"I received yesterday your last letter together with one from Dr. Rosen. Previously I had received one from Assessor Queckfelt, from which I was led to infer, that the case would take a new turn, if I presented myself before the Privy Council as a *tertius interveniens*, yet to do so would do no good, as

---

Documents Concerning Swedenborg, Vol. II., pp. 382-383.

I distinctly did so a short time before my departure [see close of Document 245, x., p. 376], and supported with weighty arguments the cause itself, as well as your case. I wonder that they keep stirring up this affair at Gottenburg; I will complain of them at the next Diet, when I send over my *Universa Theologia Novi Cœli et Novæ Ecclesiæ*,* which will leave the press towards the close of June. I will send two copies of this work to each House, and request them to appoint for its consideration a general committee from all the Houses, in order to put an end to the affair in this way. I am certain of this, that after the appearance of the book referred to, the Lord our Saviour will operate both mediately and immediately towards the establishment throughout the whole of Christendom of a New Church based upon this 'Theology.' The New Heaven, out of which the New Jerusalem will descend, will very soon be completed (*Rev.* xxi. 1–3). When our adversaries enter the other life, they will have their places assigned to them. I pity them. With my kindest remembrance to Doctor Rosen, I remain, with all affection,

"Your most obedient servant and friend,
"EM. SWEDENBORG.
"AMSTERDAM, April 30, 1771."

---

* *The True Christian Religion.*

SWEDENBORG, HIS MISSION, AND DANGER OF INTERCOURSE WITH SPIRITS.

I.

FROM A LETTER OF SWEDENBORG TO COUNT GUSTAVIUS BONDE.*

"You will express to him (Baron Hatzel) also my pleasure at his having derived satisfaction and light from the perusal of these writings, which is a sign of his having been in a state of enlightenment from heaven; for the matters which are there treated of cannot be comprehended without enlightenment, since they do not belong to the external but to the internal understanding. With respect to some verses in the books of Moses, which possess the property and power of introducing man to intercourse with spirits or enabling him to speak with them; I do not know of any verses in Scripture which have this property more than others; I only know that the Word of God is everywhere written in such a style, that when man reads it with affection and attention, spirits and angels have a part in it, and adjoin themselves to him; for the Word of God is so written that it forms a bond of union between heaven and earth (see what is written on this subject in the work on *Heaven and Hell*, n. 303 to 310). The Lord, nevertheless, so disposes it, that spirits and men are seldom brought together so closely as to converse with one another†; for by intercourse with spirits men are brought into such a condition as to their souls, that they are speedily in danger of their life‡; wherefore I would

---

* *Documents Concerning Swedenborg*, Vol. II., pp. 232-233.
† In the original draft the following words are added here: "for this is more dangerous than men suppose."
‡ The following words are added in the original draft: "Unless the Lord Himself bring them into this condition, and take them under His care, and protect them specially, as is the case with me."

dissuade all from cherishing such desires. The Lord Himself has been pleased to introduce me into converse and intercourse with spirits and angels for the reasons which have been explained in my writings; wherefore I am protected by the Lord Himself from the many desperate attempts and attacks of evil spirits. The way in which spirits and men are kept apart is this; spirits are kept in spiritual and men in natural thought and speech; whereby they are separated so as to make one only by correspondences; the nature of which has likewise been treated of. As long therefore as spirits are in a spiritual, and men in a natural state, they are not brought together so as to converse with one another, although they are together in affection; but when spirits converse with men they are out of their spiritual state, and in a natural state like men, and then they may bring them into danger of soul and life, as has been stated above. For this reason they have to be kept apart, so that the spirits do not know anything of man, nor man of them, although they are always together; for man cannot live unless he be associated with spirits, through whom he is connected with heaven and hell, and thereby receives his life.

["STOCKHOLM, August 11, 1760."]

II.

FROM A LETTER OF SWEDENBORG TO BEYER.*

"What you relate respecting your wife in her dying hours, was caused especially by the impression of two clergymen, who associated her in her thoughts with those spirits, from whom she then spoke; it happens sometimes with some in the hour of death that they are in the state of the spirit. Those spirits that first spoke through her belonged to the followers of the dragon, which was cast down from heaven (see *Rev.* xii.), and who became then so filled with hatred against the Saviour, and

---

Documents Concerning Swedenborg, Vol. II., pp. 308-309.

consequently against God's Word, and against everything belonging to the New Church, that they cannot bear to hear Christ mentioned. When the sphere of our Lord descends upon them out of heaven, they become like raving maniacs, and seek to hide themselves in holes and caverns, and thus save themselves, according to *Rev.* vi. 16. Your deceased wife was yesterday with me, and informed me on many things which she had thought, and spoken to you, her husband, and with those who led her astray. Were I at this time near you, I might relate to you many things on this subject, but I am not permitted to write about them.

"I have no time at present to express myself about the boy concerning whom you write.

"STOCKHOLM, October 30, 1769."

III.

FROM A LETTER OF SWEDENBORG TO THE LANDGRAVE OF HESSE-DARMSTADT.*

"In your gracious letter you ask how I came to have intercourse with angels and spirits, and whether this state could be imparted by one to another. Deign to receive favorably the following reply:

"The Lord our Saviour foretold that He would come again into the world, and institute a New Church; He predicted this (in *Rev.* xxi. and xxii.), and also in several places in the *Gospels.* But as He cannot come again into the world in Person, it was necessary that He should do it by means of a man, who should not only receive the doctrine of that church by his understanding, but also publish it by means of the press; and as the Lord had prepared me for this from my childhood, He manifested Himself in Person before me, His servant, and sent me to do this work. This took place in the year 1743; and afterwards He opened the sight of my spirit, and thus introduced me into the spiritual world, granting me to see the

---

Documents Concerning Swedenborg, Vol. II., pp. 387-388.

heavens and many of the wonderful things there, and also the hells, and to speak with angels and spirits, and this continually for twenty-seven years. I declare in truth, that this is so. This took place with me on account of the Church, which I mention above, the doctrine of which is contained in my books. The gift of conversing with spirits and angels cannot be transferred from one person to another, unless the Lord Himself, as has been the case with me, opens the sight of the spirit of that person. It is sometimes granted to a spirit to enter and to communicate some truth to a man; but still leave is not given to the man to speak with him mouth to mouth. This is also most dangerous, because the spirit enters into the affection of man's own love, which does not agree with the affection of heavenly love.

"With respect to the man who is infested by spirits, I have heard from heaven, that this was caused by a state of meditation in which he indulged; but that no danger is to be apprehended from them, because he is protected by the Lord. The only means by which he can be cured, is conversion, and supplication to the Lord our Saviour Jesus Christ. I remain with profound respect, most serene Duke and Landgrave,

"Your most humble servant,
"E. S.

["AMSTERDAM, 1771."]

IV.

SECOND LETTER FROM SWEDENBORG TO THE LANDGRAVE OF HESSE-DARMSTADT.*

"MOST SERENE DUKE,

"I have received and read with pleasure the letter which you addressed to me. I hope that the work which has just been printed under the title of *The True Christian Religion*, has reached you during the last few days. If you see fit, I should like you to instruct the learned among the clergy in your duchy

---

* *Documents Concerning Swedenborg*, Vol. II., pp. 388-389.

to report concerning it; but I pray that such among the learned of your clergy be selected as love the truth and are delighted with it. If they are not in the way of truth, they will not see light in that work, but only shade. What is related of the daughter of the Prince Margrave has no foundation, but has been invented by some gossiping newsmonger; I never heard of it before; but what is reported concerning the brother of the Queen of Sweden is true; yet it should not be regarded as a miracle, but only as a memorable occurrence of the kind related in the above work concerning Luther, Melancthon, and Calvin. For all these are simple testimonies, that I have been introduced by the Lord as to my spirit into the spiritual world, and that I converse with angels and spirits. It is further true that I conversed with the person whose name is mentioned in the journal in question, and six months ago with Stanislaus, King of Poland, which took place in a certain congregation or company in which he was, where no one knew who he was. The delight of his life consisted in desiring to be present incognito in assemblies of spirits and angels, as if he were one of them, and to converse familiarly with them

"Afterwards I saw him transferred into the northern quarter, and I heard that he was placed over some section of Roman Catholicism, whose chief moderator he is. He has also conversed frequently with the Pope who died lately, with whom he dwelt after his death, and to whom he succeeded; he descended also to a congregation or company consisting of Jesuits, over whom he ruled for a month; and afterwards I saw him ascending from them, when it was granted me to speak with him several times. But about the course and state of his life I am not allowed to divulge anything. Concerning the Pope who reigned some thirty or forty years ago, you may see what has been written in my latest work.

"I pray you to favor all those things which belong to the honor of God, and I remain, with a mind full of veneration,

"Yours, &c.

["Em. Swedenborg."]

["Amsterdam], July 13, 1771."

V.

EMANUEL SWEDENBORG'S LETTER TO VENATOR.*

"I hope that the work, entitled *The True Christian Religion*, which has recently left the press, is now in your hands, and also that the two copies which I sent at the same time to his Serene Highness the Duke and Landgrave have reached him; for I greatly desire to have your opinion concerning the things contained therein, knowing as I do that by enlightenment from the Lord you will more than others see in light the truths which are manifested there from the Word. To-day I send also my reply to the letter which his Serene Highness the Duke wrote to me lately; and in compliance with his orders I speak to him of several conversations I had with, among others, the Queen of Sweden and her brother. But these must by no means be regarded as miracles; for they are simply testimonies that I have been introduced by the Lord into the spiritual world, and have intercourse and converse there with angels and spirits; in order that the church, which has hitherto remained in ignorance concerning that world, may know that heaven and hell really exist, and that man lives after death a man, as before; and that thus no more doubts may flow into his mind in respect to his immortality. Please, deign to satisfy the Duke, your prince, on this score, that these things are not miracles, but merely testimonies that I converse with angels and spirits. The fact and the reason that there are no miracles at the present day, may be seen in the above mentioned work. The Lord says .... Wherefore those who do not believe unless they see miracles, are very easily led into fanaticism. I have seen two volumes full of miracles wrought by a certain Paris, which are nevertheless nothing but pure falsehoods, being in part fantastical and in part magical doings. The same is the case with the other miracles among the Roman Catholics. Examine also, if you please, those things that have been related by me on this subject in the above work. At this day faith will be established

---

* *Documents Concerning Swedenborg*, Vol. II., pp. 390–391.

and confirmed in the New Church only by the Word itself, and the truths which are derived thence; if these shine in a certain light before the eyes of those who read my last work, it is a sign that the Lord is present and enlightens; because He is the Word itself, and also the truths that are derived thence. Farewell in the Lord.

["Em. Swedenborg.]

["Amsterdam, July 13, 1771."]

VI.

EMANUEL SWEDENBORG TO THE KING OF SWEDEN.*

"Most Powerful and Most Gracious King:

"I feel compelled at this juncture to have recourse to Your Majesty's protection; for I have been treated as no one has ever been treated before in Sweden since the introduction of Christianity, and still less since the establishment of freedom here. I will first give you a brief account of things as they have happened. Upon my return from abroad the last time, I was informed that Bishop Filenius had confiscated my work entitled *De Amore Conjugiali*, which had appeared in Holland and had been sent to Norrköping. I therefore immediately enquired of some bishops whether this had been authorized by the House of the Clergy; they answered that they were aware of the confiscation, but that no general action had been taken, and that not a word about it had been entered upon the Minutes. Immediately afterwards the clergy from Gottenburg made a noise in their House about my books, and pushed matters so far, that the House appointed a committee *de Swedenborgianismo* [on Swedenborgianism], which consisted of bishops and professors. This committee sat for several months, and at last reported handsomely and reasonably on that subject, and thereby suppressed completely the disturbance which had been

---

* *Documents Concerning Swedenborg*, Vol. II., pp. 373-377.

made; but to put an end to it still more effectually, it was resolved that a humble memorial should be addressed to Your Royal Majesty, requesting that the Chancellor of Justice should inquire about the disturbances which had arisen in Gottenburg. When the Bishop and the Dean of that place, who are the torch and trumpet (*fax et tuba*) in this affair, discovered that they made no progress in the reverend House of the Clergy, they, to stir up and kindle the flame anew, commenced a publication of twenty sheets or more about 'Swedenborgianism,' which is filled with invectives; and after this had been sent to Stockholm, the matter was taken up and settled by Your Majesty in the Privy Council, in consequence of which the Chancellor of Justice dispatched to the Consistory of Gottenburg an official letter, wherein, I have reason to think, he assented to the opinion expressed by the Consistory.

"I received no more intimation than a child in the cradle of all that took place, of the committee in the reverend House of the Clergy, of the memorial they submitted to Your Royal Majesty, of the publication in Gottenburg on 'Swedenborgianism,' of the resolution which was passed by Your Royal Majesty in the Privy Council, and of the letter embodying it which was dispatched to the Consistory in Gottenburg. Of all this, from beginning to end, I received not the least intimation: all was done without my receiving a hearing; when yet the whole matter was about 'Swedenborgianism,' and the papers printed in Gottenburg are filled with coarse and reprehensible language without touching materially on the subject of 'Swedenborgianism,' which is the worship of the Lord our Saviour. Of these printed papers I had no other knowledge than what I received from a general commissary of war at Elsinore, and afterwards from a friend here in Stockholm who lent them to me for a day. Wherefore I still insist that everything that has taken place since my return home, has from beginning to end, been done without giving me a hearing.

"From a rumor which has spread here in town I have learned that from the office of the Chancellor of Justice a communication has been made to the Consistory of Gottenburg, to the effect that my books have been entirely forbidden to be imported into this country, and, further, that the same office has stigmatized my revelations as untrue and false. In reply to this I humbly beg to make the following statement: That our Saviour visibly revealed Himself before me, and commanded me to do what I have done, and what I have still to do; and that thereupon He permitted me to have intercourse with angels and spirits, I have declared before the whole of Christendom, as well in England, Holland, Germany, and Denmark, as in France and Spain, and also on various occasions in this country before their Royal Majesties, and especially when I enjoyed the grace to eat at their table, in the presence of the whole royal family, and also of five senators and others; at which time my mission constituted the sole topic of conversation. Subsequently, also, I have revealed this before many senators; and among these Count Tessin, Count Bonde, and Count Höpken have found it in truth to be so, and Count Höpken, a gentleman of enlightened understanding, still continues to believe so; without mentioning many others, as well at home as abroad, among whom are both kings and princes. All this, however, the office of the Chancellor of Justice, if the rumor is correctly stated, declares to be false; when yet it is the truth. Should they reply that the thing is inconceivable to them, I have nothing to gainsay, since I am unable to put the state of my sight and speech into their heads, in order to convince them; nor am I able to cause angels and spirits to converse with them; nor do miracles happen now; but their very reason will enable them to see this, when they thoughtfully read my writings, wherein much may be found which has never before been discovered, and which cannot be discovered except by real vision, and intercourse with those who are in the spiritual world. In order that reason may see and acknowledge this, I beg that one of your Excellencies may peruse what has been said on this subject in my book, '*De Amore Conjugiali*', in a memorable relation on pages 314 to 316; his Excellency Count Ekeblad and his Excellency Count Bjelke possess the book. If any doubt should still remain, I am ready to testify with the most solemn oath that may be prescribed to me, that this is the whole truth and a reality, without the least fallacy. That our Saviour permits me to experience this, is not on my own account, but for the sake of a sublime interest which concerns the eternal welfare of all Christians. Since such is the real state of things, it is wrong to declare it to be untruth and falsity; although it may be pronounced to be something that cannot be comprehended.

"If now the rumor which has been spread is correct, namely, that such things are contained in the letter which was sent from the office of the Chancellor of Justice to the Consistory of Gottenburg, it follows hence that my books are declared to be heretical, and that I am declared to speak untruths and falsehoods in matters of revelation, and further, that from beginning to end, all this has been determined upon without giving me a hearing. What else results from this, but that in agreement with the resolution any severe treatment may be brought forward by the Consistory of Gottenburg and Bishop Filenius, and my sentence may be pronounced upon me, without my being heard in the affair at all; for of what use is a declaration or a defence after the sentence has been pronounced?

"This is the reason why, as I said above, 'I am compelled to have recourse to Your Majesty, since I have been treated as no one has ever been treated before in Sweden since the introduction of Christianity, and still less since the establishment of freedom;' by being treated as I have been, without a hearing being granted me.

"As this, however, concerns not only my writings, but as a natural consequence my person also, I make a humble request, that the memorial should be communicated to me which was addressed to Your Royal Majesty in this matter by the House of the Clergy, likewise the minutes of the Privy Council, and the letter which was dispatched from the office of the Chancellor of Justice to the Consistory of Gottenburg, in order that I may at once be heard, and may show forth the whole of my treatment before the public at large.

"In respect to Doctors Beyer and Rosen of Gottenburg, I have given them no other advice than that they should approach our Saviour, *Jesus Christ, to whom all power has been given in heaven and on earth* (*Matt.* xxviii. 18), and should strive after their salvation; and as far as I have been able to learn, they have affirmed and insisted on this one point, which is also in conformity with the *Augsburg Confession*, the *Formula Con-*

cordiæ, and the whole Word of God; nevertheless for this acknowledgment alone they have become to a certain extent martyrs, at least so far as regards the cruel persecutions of the Bishop and the Dean of that town. The same expression also I apply to my books, which I regard as my own self, when, nevertheless, all that the Dean of Gottenburg has poured out against them, consists of sheer invectives, which do not contain a particle of truth.

"Your Royal Majesty's most humble and most dutiful servant and subject,

"EMANUEL SWEDENBORG.

["STOCKHOLM, May 10, 1770.]

"I enclose two letters I have addressed to Dr. Beyer; the first of these concerns the worship of the Lord which is shown to be in agreement with the *Augsburg Confession*, the *Formula Concordiæ*, and the whole Word of God."

THE PONTIFEX MAXIMUS IN RELIGIOUS MATTERS.*

EMANUEL SWEDENBORG TO THE UNIVERSITIES OF UPSAL, LUND, AND ABO.

"In a few days I shall depart for Amsterdam in order to publish there the *Universal Theology of the New Church*, the foundation of which is the worship of the Lord, our Saviour; on which foundation if no temple be now built, *lupanaria* (brothels) will be erected. And now, as I understand that the religious trial of Drs. Beyer and Rosen has been taken up by the Privy Council and settled in an unexpected manner, and as this will probably be talked about here and there during my absence, therefore, in order to break the force of the malicious comments, which will probably issue from the mouths of certain persons, prompted by their stupidity and interior perverseness, it becomes my duty in the interest of this matter to make known to you what I have in the enclosed document [Swedenborg's letter to the King, see X., p. 373] submitted to his Royal Majesty.

"Two gentlemen of the Supreme Court of Appeals (*Justiciæ Revisionen*) told me that the Privy Council was the *pontifex maximus* in religious matters. At the time I did not make any reply; if, however, they should repeat this statement to me, I should say that far from being the *pontifex maximus*, they are simply the *vicarius vicarii pontificis maximi*, since Christ, our Saviour, is alone *pontifex maximus*; that the Houses of the Diet are His *vicarius*, and therefore are responsible to Him, and that the Privy Council is the *vicarius* of the Houses of the Diet, and only as such has plenipotentiary power; and consequently it is the *vicarius vicarii pontificis maximi*. The Roman Pope's styling himself *pontifex maximus* is due to arro-

---

*Documents Concerning Swedenborg, Vol. II., pp. 380–381. See also pp. 378–389.

gance; for he claims and takes upon himself all the power of Christ our Saviour, making the people believe that he is Christ on earth.

"Every lesser *pontifex* or every *vicarius pontificis maximi* ought to have his consistory. The Houses of the Diet have theirs in the reverend House of the Clergy: the Privy Council has its especially in the universities: but in the settlement of the present matter it has made the Consistory of Gottenburg its consistory, to whose opinions it is said to have adhered *verbatim:* without being aware of the fact that this trial has been the most important and the most solemn that has been before any council during the last 1700 years, since it concerns the New Church which is predicted by the Lord in *Daniel* and in the *Apocalypse*, and agrees with what the Lord says in (*Matt.* xxiv. 22).

"I have not yet received any answer from the Privy Council; this matter has been before it once, when it was resolved to postpone it until those members of the council, who had previously examined it, should return.

"EM. SWEDENBORG.

"STOCKHOLM, July 23, 1770."

DISEASES AND THEIR CURE.

FROM THE TENTH LETTER OF EMANUEL SWEDENBORG TO DR. BEYER.*

"REVEREND DOCTOR AND DEAR FRIEND,
"Shortness of time would not permit me in my last letter to answer the point about the boy from Skara. If the account about him is true, it proves the communication of spirits with man. A genteel and rich family here in Stockholm are desirous of taking the boy into their house, and of educating him in whatever branch he may wish to learn. Should this arrangement be acceptable to the boy, and an opportunity present itself of his being brought here in company with a person travelling this way, the family would be pleased; in that case thirty dalers in silver might be furnished him to cover his travelling expenses, and if on his arrival he address himself to me, he will be taken to the family.

"I pass by his vision of white serpents, as this took place in his tender infancy; for which reason I do not enter into its explanation; besides, it may be explained either negatively or affirmatively. But his knowing the use of herbs and [the cure of] certain diseases, if really the case, is not on account of such diseases and cures existing in the other life among spirits and angels. There are, however, spiritual diseases [and cures] corresponding to natural diseases and cures in this world; wherefore when such effects takes place, they are due to correspondences. As there are no natural diseases among spirits in the spiritual world, neither are there any hospitals; but instead of these there are spiritual madhouses, in which are those who theoretically denied God, and in others such as denied Him practically. Those who in the world were idiots, on their arrival in the other world are likewise foolish and idiotic; but when their externals are removed and their internals opened, as is the case with all, then they are endowed with an understanding in accordance with their genius and their previous life; for real madness and insanity reside in the external or natural, and not in the internal or spiritual man.

["STOCKHOLM, November 14, 1769."]

---
*Documents Concerning Swedenborg, Vol. II., pp. 278-279.

SIGNIFICATION OF A MANGER

AND THE

USE OF JOHN'S BAPTISM.

FROM THE SIXTH LETTER OF EMANUEL SWEDENBORG TO DR. BEYER.*

"I have with pleasure perused your 'New Essays on the Gospels' (*Nya Försök öfwer Evangelierne*); fine interpretations are given in respect to the First Coming of the Lord. I wish to give here the signification of a manger, of the baptism of John, and of Elias. A 'manger' signifies instruction from the Word, because mules and horses signify the understanding of the Word (see *Apocalypse Revealed*, n. 298); and a manger contains their food; there being no room in the inn, signifies that there was no place of instruction in Jerusalem; wherefore it is said to the shepherds, who signify the church to come, 'This shall be the sign unto you; ye shall find the babe lying in a manger' (*Luke* ii. 12). The baptism of John prepared the heavens, so that the Jewish people might subsist, when God Himself should come down among them. John signified all the prophecies in the Old Testament respecting the Lord and His advent; likewise Elias, because he was the chief of the prophets.

"As here [in Stockholm] they now begin to think more of charity than before, asserting that faith and charity cannot be separated, therefore faith alone begins also to be called Moravain faith.

["EM. SWEDENBORG.]

"STOCKHOLM, February, 1767."

---

*Documents Concerning Swedenborg, Vol. II., pp. 260-261.

INFLUX.*

"When such as believe in nature see how these animals or insects are generated in the ground or on the leaves of plants, and when they examine the wonderful things in their organisms, and things made by their means, they think that nature produces them, not knowing that their formation and vivification is from the spiritual world, and their reception and clothing from the natural world; further, that the heat of the sun at the time of spring and summer dissolves and adapts the particles of purer nature for the reception of influx, and for the process of clothing. Wherefore the same argument and the same confirmation, which the believers of nature derive hence, are to me an argument for, and a confirmation of, a continual influx from the spiritual into the natural world. Written in the year 1750.

"The changes of caterpillars into butterflies, the government of bees, and many other things which are described in this book, are manifest signs of such influx." [See *Heaven and Hell*, n. 567, also n. 39, 108, 109.]

---

*On the fly-leaf of Swedenborg's copy of Swammerdam's *Biblia Naturæ*, which he presented to Count Höpkin, and which is now in the possession of Dr. Lovén of the "Carolinska Institut" in Stockholm, is written by his own hand the above remarks. See *Documents Concerning Swedenborg*, Vol. II., p. 750.

GAD AND ASHER.*

Angels also are distinguished into heavens, according to the variety of intellectual faith, thus which govern the interior human thoughts, for man has within himself a certain interior heaven; also a more interior one, and an inmost.

By the Divine mercy of God Messiah, it was permitted several times, to communicate thoughts to the life, with those who are in that intellectual heaven, or by thoughts to have intercourse with them, and by other means to speak with them. Yea, it was given to purify my thoughts to that degree, that they came immediately into contact with those who were in the heaven of intellectual faith. Then it was observed that they were those, who in the more interior sense, are meant by Gad; for although they know, and thus are able to believe that God Messiah, by the Holy Spirit, alone governs them, and that they have power only when immediately excited, still when they were removed, they at first willed to excite some disturbances, but after some contention with me they acquiesced.

Moreover also to-day, by the Divine Mercy of God Messiah, it was permitted to have lively experience, that spirits, although evil, namely, who are in perverted order, are nevertheless capable of giving delights to anyone; whilst they are in that exterior state, these are meant by Asher; for they were in the state of making themselves pleasant to their company, in preferring complaisance to the interior heaven, or to the interior man.

These are things which are arcana, and concerning which many things might be said—1747, 8th day of February—on which day it was permitted to annotate in the margin,† something concerning the blessings of the sons of Jacob (*Gen.* Chap. xlix.).

---

*In a copy of the original edition of *Heaven and Hell*, Latin, found in the library of the Bath (England) Society, is a sheet of paper containing a fragment of manuscript in Swedenborg's handwriting. Hyde in his *Bibliography of Swedenborg's Works*, n. 498, concludes that this fragment is a portion of the lost part of the *Spiritual Diary* of Swedenborg; belonging probably about n. 28 and 29. The fragment has been phototyped and published, together with an English translation, by Wm. Harbutt, A. R. C. A., The Grange, Bathampton, Bath. The translation is said to have been made by Dr. R. L. Tafel, but it is not in his handwriting. We have made some emendations after comparison with the Phototype copy.—Tr.

†See annotations in Swedenborg's Bible at *Gen.* xlix. 19. See also *Adversaria*, Vol. III., n. 7634.

END OF VOL. I.